# *Sparse Optimization Theory and Methods*

T0300478

**Yun-Bin Zhao**

School of Mathematics
University of Birmingham, Edgbaston, UK

**CRC Press**
Taylor & Francis Group
Boca Raton London New York

CRC Press is an imprint of the
Taylor & Francis Group, an **informa** business
A SCIENCE PUBLISHERS BOOK

CRC Press
Taylor & Francis Group
6000 Broken Sound Parkway NW, Suite 300
Boca Raton, FL 33487-2742

First issued in paperback 2020

© 2018 by Taylor & Francis Group, LLC
CRC Press is an imprint of Taylor & Francis Group, an Informa business

No claim to original U.S. Government works

ISBN-13: 978-1-138-08094-2 (hbk)
ISBN-13: 978-0-367-78110-1 (pbk)

**Visit the Taylor & Francis Web site at**
**http://www.taylorandfrancis.com**

**and the CRC Press Web site at**
**http://www.crcpress.com**

*To my daughter Jessie and my wife Lily for their constant support, and to the memory of my mother Suzhi Liu*

# Preface

The theory and algorithms for many practical problems, ranging from signal and image processing, compressed sensing, statistical regression and computer vision to machine learning, have witnessed significant new developments under the following hypothesis: The unknown data to process is sparse or can be sparsely approximated. Under this fundamental hypothesis, many problems can be formulated as the *sparse optimization problem* which seeks the sparse solution of an underdetermined linear system or the sparse point in a convex set.

Sparsity has long been exploited in signal and image processing as well as in statistics and learning communities. However, the rapid development in these fields by exploiting sparsity started only around 2004. Nowadays seeking sparsity has become a common request in many scientific areas. Lying at the crossroads between applied mathematics, operations research, electrical engineering, computer science and information science, sparse optimization has attracted considerable cross-disciplinary attention and has stimulated a plethora of new applications of sparsity in numerous fields, such as geophysical data analysis, medical imaging processing, communications, sensor network, and computational biology, to name a few.

The aim of this book is to introduce the theory and algorithms for typical sparse optimization problems arising in compressed sensing and Big Data processing. Sparse optimization is a fast-moving area and a much researched topic. It is almost impossible for a single monograph to cover every aspect and every piece of work in this rapid growing area. This book is an introduction to the sparse signal recovery from a mathematical optimization perspective. Although compressed sensing was developed with a number of mathematical tools, including linear algebra, optimization, approximation, random matrix, probability, functional analysis, harmonic analysis and graph theory, the only prior knowledge required for this book is basic linear algebra, convex analysis and optimization. The reader could be a researcher, graduate or postgraduate student in the areas of operations research, applied mathematics, numerical analysis, computer science, data science, signal and image processing, and machine learning.

This book contains eight chapters, and each chapter covers a relatively independent topic. However, the classic optimality conditions, including duality and complementary slackness property of convex optimization, are used as the common tool in this book to carry out both theoretical and algorithmic developments for sparse optimization problems.

**Yun-Bin Zhao**
Birmingham, United Kingdom

# Contents

# Symbol Description

$\mathbb{R}^n$    $n$-dimensional Euclidean space

$\mathbb{R}^n_+$    the set of $n$-dimensional non-negative vectors

$\mathbb{R}^n_{++}$    the set of $n$-dimensional positive vectors

$\mathbb{R}^{m \times n}$    the set of $m \times n$ matrices

$\|\cdot\|_p$    $\|x\|_p = (\Sigma^n_{i=1} |x_i|^p)^{1/p}$; $\ell_p$-norm when $p \geq 1$; $\ell_1$-norm when $p = 1$; $\ell_2$-norm when $p = 2$; $\ell_\infty$-norm when $p = \infty$; $\ell_p$-quasinorm when $0 < p < 1$; $\ell_0$-norm when $p = 0$

$\mathfrak{B}$    the $\ell_2$-ball $\mathfrak{B} = \{x : \|x\|_2 \leq 1\}$

$\mathfrak{B}^\phi$    the unit ball defined by the norm $\phi(\cdot)$, i.e., $\mathfrak{B}^\phi = \{x : \phi(x) \leq 1\}$

$|J|$    cardinality of the set $J$

$x$    column vector

$x^T$    vector transpose, row vector

$S_+(x)$    index set of positive entries of $x$, i.e., $S_+(x) = \{i : x_i > 0\}$

$S_-(x)$    index set of negative entries of $x$, i.e., $S_-(x) = \{i : x_i < 0\}$

$S_0(x)$    index set of null entries of $x$, i.e., $S_0(x) = \{i : x_i = 0\}$

$|x|$    absolute of $x \in \mathbb{R}^n$, i.e., $|x| = (|x_1|,...,|x_n|) \in \mathbb{R}^n_+$

$\mathcal{SD}(\cdot)$    sorting the entries of $|x|$ in descending order

$\sigma_k(\cdot)_1$    the best $k$-term approximation

supp    the support of a vector, i.e., $\mathrm{supp}(x) = \{i : x_i \neq 0\}$

$x_J$    subvector of $x \in \mathbb{R}^n$ pointed to by $J \subseteq \{1,...,n\}$

$I$    identify matrix

$\mathbf{e}^{(i)}$    $i$th coordinate vector ($i$th column vector of an identify matrix)

$\mathbf{e}$    vector of ones

$\partial$    subdifferential of a convex function

$\nabla$    gradient operator

$\nabla^2$    Hessian operator

$d^\mathcal{H}$    Hausdorff metric

$A$    matrix

$A^T$    matrix transpose

$A_J$    submatrix of $A$, columns pointed to by $J$ (i.e., $A_J$ is extracted from $A$ by deleting the columns not in $J$)

$\mathcal{N}(A)$    the null space of $A$, i.e., $\mathcal{N}(A) = \{u : Au = 0\}$

$\mathcal{R}(A)$    the range space of $A$, i.e., $\mathcal{R}(A) = \{u : u = Ax, x \in \mathbb{R}^n\}$

$\Pi_\Omega(\cdot)$    orthogonal projection into the convex set $\Omega$

spark    spark of matrix

rank    rank of matrix

$\mu(A)$    mutual coherence of matrix $A$

$\mu_1(k)$    Babel function

RIP    restricted isometry property

NSP    null space property

RSP    range space property

ERC    exact recovery condition

# Chapter 1

# Uniqueness of the Sparsest Solution of Linear Systems

## 1.1 Introduction

Let $x \in \mathbb{R}^n$ be an unknown vector which cannot be measured directly. To recover (reconstruct) such a vector, an obvious step is to take linear measurements of the form $y := Ax$, where $A$ is a given measurement matrix. Then, solve such a system of linear equations to obtain a solution $\hat{x}$. When the number of measurements is large enough, the reconstructed solution $\hat{x}$ would be equal to $x$, leading to the success of recovery of $x$. Compressed sensing is using a small number of measurements (as small as possible) to recover a wide range of signals. To expect the number of measurements being lower than the signal length, the measurement matrix $A \in \mathbb{R}^{m \times n}$ (also called sensing matrix) should have less rows than columns, i.e., $m < n$. This renders the linear system $y = Az$ underdetermined in the sense that it has infinitely many solutions. In this case, $x$ is not a unique vector complying with the same measurement vector $y$, and hence it is generally impossible to recover the vector $x$ from the linear measurements $y := Ax$ unless further information on $x$ is available.

Practical signals are usually structured, and the most useful signal structure is sparsity. Thus, a fundamental hypothesis in compressed sensing is that the unknown signal to recover is sparse or can be sparsely compressible. A vector is said to be sparse if it has a small number of non-zero entries, and a vector is said to be sparsely compressible if it can be approximated by a sparse vector. Under the sparsity hypothesis, compressed sensing problems and many other problems can be formulated as the so-called sparse optimization problem which seeks the sparsest solution of an underdetermined linear system or, in more general, the sparsest point in a convex set.

Consider the underdetermined linear system $Ax = b$, where $A$ is a given $m \times n$ matrix with $m < n$, and $b \in \mathbb{R}^m$ is a given vector. In terms of $\|x\|_0$, the number of non-zero components of the vector $x$, the problem of seeking the sparsest solution of an underdetermined linear system amounts exactly to the following sparse optimization problem:

$$\min\{\|x\|_0 : Ax = b\}, \tag{1.1}$$

which is referred to as the *standard $\ell_0$-minimization problem*. As a central mathematical model in compressed sensing, the theory and algorithms for the problem (1.1) have experienced an exciting and significant new development since around 2004. It is well known that being the unique solution to (1.1) is an essential requirement for a sparse signal to be exactly recovered by an algorithm. Therefore, a fundamental question is when the problem (1.1) admits a unique solution.

Although many exact recovery conditions for sparse signals (see Chapter 3 for details) imply the uniqueness of the sparsest solution of a linear system, these conditions are not developed directly to address the uniqueness issue regarding the solution of the $\ell_0$-minimization problem (1.1). In this chapter, we introduce some sufficient conditions which were developed to directly address the uniqueness issue of the sparsest solutions of linear systems. These uniqueness criteria are based on such algebraic notions as spark, mutual coherence, sub-mutual coherence, scaled mutual coherence, coherence rank, and sub-coherence rank. We also discuss the Babel-function-based uniqueness criterion as well as its improved version via the so-called sub-Babel function.

## 1.2   Spark

Let us begin with the spark, a crucial tool for the study of uniqueness of the sparsest solutions to underdetermined systems of linear equations.

**Definition 1.2.1** *The spark of $A \in \mathbb{R}^{m \times n}$, denoted by* spark$(A)$, *is the smallest number $k$ such that there is a set of $k$ columns in $A$ which are linearly dependent.*

The spark was first introduced by Donoho and Elad [83]. Clearly,

$$2 \leq \text{spark}(A) \leq m + 1 \tag{1.2}$$

for any matrix $A \in \mathbb{R}^{m \times n}$ with non-zero columns and $m < n$. Throughout this book, we use supp$(x)$ to denote the support of the vector $x \in \mathbb{R}^n$, i.e.,

$$\text{supp}(x) = \{i : x_i \neq 0\},$$

where $x_i, i = 1, \ldots, n$, are the components (entries) of $x$. Thus, $\|x\|_0$ coincides with the cardinality of the support of $x$, i.e., $\|x\|_0 = |\mathrm{supp}(x)|$. A vector $x \in \mathbb{R}^n$ is said to be $k$-sparse if it contains at most $k$ non-zero entries, i.e., $\|x\|_0 \leq k$.

Any solution of the linear system $Ax = b$ provides a representation of the data $b$ via the column vectors in $A$. In some situations, some columns in $A$ are so crucial that they must be used to express $b$. Such vital columns may reflect certain important factors that appear as some structures or prior information of $b$. In this case, the supports of solutions of a linear system may overlap. This motivates the following definition.

**Definition 1.2.2** *The support overlap $\Delta$ of solutions to the system $Az = b$ is the index set*

$$\Delta = \bigcap_{z \in \mathcal{L}} \mathrm{supp}(z),$$

*where $\mathcal{L} = \{z : Az = b\}$ is the solution set of the linear system.*

Of course, $\Delta = \emptyset$ when the supports of solutions of a linear system do not overlap. The first uniqueness criterion can be developed by the spark and support overlap.

**Theorem 1.2.3** *Let $\Delta$ be the support overlap of solutions to the system $Az = b$. If $x$ is a solution to this linear system satisfying*

$$\|x\|_0 < \frac{1}{2}(|\Delta| + \mathrm{spark}(A)), \tag{1.3}$$

*then $x$ is the unique sparsest solution to the linear system $Az = b$.*

*Proof.* Let $x$ be a solution to the system $Az = b$, satisfying (1.3). We prove the result by contradiction. Assume that $z \neq x$, with $\|z\|_0 \leq \|x\|_0$, is also a solution to the linear system. Since both $x$ and $z$ are the solutions to the linear system, we have $A(z - x) = 0$, which implies that the column vectors $\{a_i : i \in \mathrm{supp}(z - x)\}$ of $A$ are linearly dependent. By the definition of spark $(A)$, we have

$$\mathrm{spark}(A) \leq |\{a_i : i \in \mathrm{supp}(z - x)\}| = |\mathrm{supp}(z - x)| = \|z - x\|_0. \tag{1.4}$$

Note that for any vectors $u, v \in \mathbb{R}^n$, $\|Uv\|_0$, where $U = \mathrm{diag}(u)$, counts the number of non-zero entries of the vector $Uv$. Thus by the definition of the support overlap $\Delta$, the following inequality holds:

$$|\Delta| \leq \|Uv\|_0 \text{ for any } u, v \in \mathcal{L}, \tag{1.5}$$

where, $\mathcal{L} = \{w : Aw = b\}$. Also, we have the following inequality:

$$\|u - v\|_0 \leq \|u\|_0 + \|v\|_0 - \|Uv\|_0,$$

which holds for any $u, v \in \mathbb{R}^n$. Therefore, by setting $Z = \mathrm{diag}(z)$, we have

$$\|z - x\|_0 \leq \|z\|_0 + \|x\|_0 - \|Zx\|_0 \leq 2\|x\|_0 - \|Zx\|_0 \leq 2\|x\|_0 - |\Delta|, \tag{1.6}$$

where the second inequality follows from the assumption $\|z\|_0 \leq \|x\|_0$, and the last inequality follows from (1.5). Merging (1.4) and (1.6) leads to

$$\text{spark}(A) + |\Delta| \leq 2\|x\|_0,$$

which contradicts (1.3). Thus under (1.3), $x$ must be the unique sparsest solution to the linear system $Az = b$. □

Since $\|x\|_0 < \text{spark}(A)/2$ implies (1.3), the following classic result shown by Donoho and Elad [83] follows immediately from Theorem 1.2.3.

**Corollary 1.2.4** (Donoho and Elad [83]) *If the linear system $Az = b$ has a solution $x$ satisfying*

$$\|x\|_0 < \text{spark}(A)/2, \tag{1.7}$$

*then $x$ is the unique sparsest solution to the linear system.*

It is worth pointing out that for a single linear system with given $(A,b)$, the classic condition (1.7) is, generally, not a necessary condition for the sparsest solution of the linear system to be unique. In fact, the sparsity level of the unique sparsest solution of a linear system might be equal to or higher than $\text{spark}(A)/2$. As indicated by Theorem 1.2.3, for a given pair $(A,b)$ and when $|\Delta| \neq 0$, the solution $x$ of the system $Az = b$ satisfying

$$\text{spark}(A)/2 \leq \|x\|_0 < (|\Delta| + \text{spark}(A))/2$$

is the unique sparsest solution to the linear system. When $|\Delta| \neq 0$, the classic bound in (1.7) can be improved by at least $|\Delta|/2$, according to (1.3). Such an improvement can be useful, as shown with the following example.

**Example 1.2.5** Consider the linear system $Az = b$, where

$$A = \begin{bmatrix} 1 & 0 & 4 & 3 & 6 \\ 0 & 1 & 1 & 2 & 4 \\ 0 & 0 & 1 & 0 & 0 \end{bmatrix}, \quad b = \begin{bmatrix} 2 \\ 1/2 \\ 1/2 \end{bmatrix}.$$

It is evident that $\text{spark}(A) = 2$ for this example, as the last two columns of $A$ are linearly dependent. Clearly, $x^* = (0,0,1/2,0,0)$ is the sparsest solution to the linear system $Az = b$. However, the criterion (1.7) fails to confirm the uniqueness of this sparsest solution. Note that the third column of $A$ must be used to express $b$. So the third component $x_3$ of any solution to the linear system is non-zero, implying that $|\Delta| \geq 1$. We see that

$$\|x^*\|_0 = 1 < 1.5 \leq (|\Delta| + \text{spark}(A))/2.$$

Thus, by Theorem 1.2.3, $x^*$ is the unique sparsest solution of the linear system.

Given a matrix $A$, however, if we expect that *for any vector b* the linear system $Az = b$ admits at most one $k$-sparse solution (i.e., the $k$-sparse solution is unique if exists), then the condition (1.7) becomes necessary, as shown by the next theorem which was first shown in [83].

**Theorem 1.2.6** *Let $A \in \mathbb{R}^{m \times n}$ ($m < n$) be a given matrix containing at least $2k$ columns (i.e., $2k \leq n$). If for any vector $b \in \mathbb{R}^m$ the linear system $Az = b$ has at most one $k$-sparse solution, then $k < \text{spark}(A)/2$.*

*Proof.* Suppose that $2k \geq \text{spark}(A) = k_0$. By the definition of spark $(A)$, there is a set of $k_0$ columns in $A$ which are linearly dependent. Since $n \geq 2k \geq k_0$, there are $2k$ columns of $A$ which are linearly dependent. Thus there is a non-zero vector $u \in \mathbb{R}^n$ with $\|u\|_0 \leq 2k$ such that $Au = 0$. Split $u$ into $u = u' - u''$ such that $\|u'\|_0 \leq k$ and $\|u''\|_0 \leq k$, i.e., both $u'$ and $u''$ are $k$-sparse. By assumption (i.e., the system $Az = b$ has at most one $k$-sparse solution for any vector $b$), it follows from $Au' = Au''$ that $u' = u''$, and hence $u = 0$, leading to a contradiction. $\square$

The spark serves a useful purpose, but it is hard to compute, as shown by Tillmann and Pfetsch [208]. In order to obtain checkable sufficient conditions for uniqueness of the sparsest solutions, we may identify a computable lower bound of $\text{spark}(A)$, i.e., $0 < \xi(A) \leq \text{spark}(A)$. Clearly, any such lower bound $\xi(A)$ yields the following uniqueness criterion for the sparsest solutions: $\|x\|_0 \leq \xi(A)/2$. So in the next section, we discuss how to achieve a bound for $\text{spark}(A)$ from below. A popular tool is the mutual coherence.

## 1.3 Uniqueness via Mutual Coherence

Let $a_i, i = 1, \ldots, n$, denote the columns of $A$. The mutual coherence was introduced by Donoho and Hu in [85] .

**Definition 1.3.1** [85] *The mutual coherence of A is defined as*

$$\mu(A) := \max_{1 \leq i < j \leq n} \frac{|a_i^T a_j|}{\|a_i\|_2 \cdot \|a_j\|_2}$$

Thus, $\mu(A)$ is the maximal absolute value of the inner product between the normalized columns of $A$. By the definition, $\mu(A) \leq 1$ for any matrix. It is not very difficult to show that the mutual coherence of a matrix $A \in \mathbb{R}^{m \times n}$ ($m < n$) with $\ell_2$-normalized columns satisfies

$$\mu(A) \geq \sqrt{\frac{n-m}{m(n-1)}}$$

which is known as the Welch bound [222]. This lower bound can be achieved if the columns of a matrix form an equiangular tight frame (see Definitions 5.5 and 5.6, and Theorem 5.7 in [108]).

In order to obtain a good lower bound of spark$(A)$, let us first define the so-called scaled mutual coherence. We note that the spark$(A)$ is invariant under any nonsingular transformation of $A$ in the sense that

$$\text{spark}(A) = \text{spark}(WA)$$

for any nonsingular matrix $W \in \mathbb{R}^{m \times m}$. The mutual coherence, however, is not invariant under a nonsingular transformation. Namely, $\mu(A) \neq \mu(WA)$ in general. In order to obtain a certain tighter lower bound of spark$(A)$, it makes sense to consider the weighted inner product between the columns of $A$. Thus we define,

$$\mu_W(A) = \mu(WA) = \max_{1 \leq i < j \leq n} \frac{|(Wa_i)^T Wa_j|}{\|Wa_i\|_2 \cdot \|Wa_j\|_2},$$

which is referred to as the scaled (weighted) mutual coherence. This naturally leads to the next definition.

**Definition 1.3.2** *The optimal scaled mutual coherence (OSMC) of $A \in \mathbb{R}^{m \times n}$ is the constant given as*

$$\mu_*(A) := \inf_W \left\{ \mu_W(A) : W \in \mathbb{R}^{m \times m} \text{ is nonsingular} \right\}.$$

For any matrix $A \in \mathbb{R}^{m \times n}$ with $m < n$ and non-zero columns, $\mu_*(A)$ is always a positive number. In fact, the Welch bound remains valid for $\mu_*(A)$,

$$\mu_W(A) = \mu(WA) \geq \sqrt{\frac{n-m}{m(n-1)}},$$

no matter what nonsingular $W \in \mathbb{R}^{m \times m}$ is. To find a lower bound of spark$(A)$ via OSMC, we employ the following classic result.

**Theorem 1.3.3** (Gerschgorin's Theorem [112]) *If $\lambda$ is an eigenvalue of a square matrix $M = (m_{ij}) \in \mathbb{R}^{n \times n}$, then there exists a positive integer $i$ with $1 \leq i \leq n$ such that*

$$|\lambda - m_{ii}| \leq \sum_{1 \leq j \leq n, j \neq i} |m_{ij}|. \tag{1.8}$$

This result is very easy to verify. In fact, suppose that $x \neq 0$ is an eigenvector such that $Mx = \lambda x$. Let $|x_i| = \max_{1 \leq j \leq n} |x_j|$ be the largest absolute entries. Note that

$$\lambda x_i = (Mx)_i = \sum_{j=1}^{n} m_{ij} x_j,$$

which implies

$$(\lambda - m_{ii})x_i = \sum_{1 \le j \le n, j \ne i} m_{ij}x_j,$$

and hence,

$$|\lambda - m_{ii}| \cdot |x_i| \le \sum_{1 \le j \le n, j \ne i} |m_{ij}| \cdot |x_j|.$$

Note that $|x_j|/|x_i| \le 1$ for all $j \ne i$. The desired result (1.8) follows immediately from the inequality above.

From Definition 1.3.2, we have $\mu_*(A) \le \mu_W(A)$ for any $A \in \mathbb{R}^{m \times n}$ and any nonsingular $W \in \mathbb{R}^{m \times m}$. In particular, $\mu_*(A) \le \mu(A)$ for any matrix $A$. The OSMC provides the best theoretical lower bound for spark$(A)$ among all possible scaled mutual coherence, as claimed by the following result.

**Theorem 1.3.4** *Let* $A \in \mathbb{R}^{m \times n}(m < n)$ *be any given matrix with non-zero columns. Then*

$$\mu_*(A) \ge \max \left\{ \frac{1}{\text{spark}(A) - 1}, \sqrt{\frac{n - m}{m(n - 1)}} \right\}, \tag{1.9}$$

*and for any nonsingular* $W \in \mathbb{R}^{m \times m}$,

$$1 + \frac{1}{\mu_W(A)} \le 1 + \frac{1}{\mu_*(A)} \le \text{spark}(A). \tag{1.10}$$

*Moreover, if the system* $Az = b$ *has a solution* $x$ *satisfying*

$$\|x\|_0 < \left( |\Delta| + 1 + \frac{1}{\mu_*(A)} \right) / 2, \tag{1.11}$$

*where* $\Delta$ *is the support overlap (see Definition 1.2.2), then* $x$ *must be the unique sparsest solution of the linear system.*

*Proof.* Consider the scaled matrix $WA$, where $W$ is an arbitrary nonsingular matrix. Let $D$ be a diagonal matrix defined as

$$D = \text{diag}(1/\|Wa_1\|_2, \ldots, 1/\|Wa_n\|_2),$$

where $a_i, i = 1, \ldots, n$, are the columns of $A$. Then $WAD$ is $\ell_2$-normalized. Denote by $p = \text{spark}(A)$. We note that the nonsingular scaling and $\ell_2$-normalization do not affect the spark of the matrix, i.e.,

$$\text{spark}(WAD) = \text{spark}(WA) = \text{spark}(A) = p.$$

By the definition of spark, there are $p$ columns of $WAD$ that are linearly dependent. Let $(WAD)_S$ be the submatrix of $WAD$, consisting of such $p$ columns. Then the $p \times p$ Gram matrix

$$\overline{G}_{p \times p} := (WAD)_S^T (WAD)_S$$

is a singular positive semidefinite matrix due to the linear dependence of the columns of $(WAD)_S$. Since the columns of $(WAD)_S$ are $\ell_2$-normalized, all diagonal entries of $\overline{G}_{p \times p}$ are equal to 1, and off-diagonal entries are less than or equal to $\mu(WAD)$. By the singularity, $\lambda = 0$ is an eigenvalue of $\overline{G}_{p \times p}$. Thus, by Lemma 1.3.3 (Geršchgorin's theorem), there exists a row of the matrix, say the $i$th row, such that

$$1 = |0 - (\overline{G}_{p \times p})_{ii}| \leq \sum_{j \neq i} |(\overline{G}_{p \times p})_{ij}| \leq (p-1)\mu(WAD) = (p-1)\mu(WA),$$

where the last equality follows from the fact $\mu(WAD) = \mu(WA)$ (which is obvious from the definition of mutual coherence). Therefore,

$$\mu_W(A) = \mu(WA) \geq 1/(p-1) > 0.$$

This together with Welch bound leads to

$$\mu_W(A) \geq \max \left\{ \frac{1}{\text{spark}(A) - 1}, \sqrt{\frac{n-m}{m(n-1)}} \right\}.$$

Note that the inequality above holds for any nonsingular matrix $W \in \mathbb{R}^{m \times m}$. Taking the infimum of the left-hand sides of the above two inequalities yields

$$\mu_*(A) \geq 1/(p-1) > 0 \tag{1.12}$$

and the bound given in (1.9). Therefore,

$$\text{spark}(A) = p \geq 1 + \frac{1}{\mu_*(A)} \geq 1 + \frac{1}{\mu_W(A)},$$

where the first inequality follows from (1.12), and the second follows from the fact $\mu_*(A) \leq \mu_W(A)$ for any nonsingular matrix $W \in \mathbb{R}^{m \times m}$. Thus the bound (1.10) holds. The uniqueness condition (1.11) follows immediately from Theorem 1.2.3 and the above lower bound of spark via $\mu_*(A)$. □

From Theorem 1.3.4, we immediately obtain the next corollary.

**Corollary 1.3.5** *Suppose that the linear system $Az = b$ has a solution $x$ obeying one of the following conditions:*

(i)

$$\|x\|_0 < \left(1 + \frac{1}{\mu(A)}\right)/2; \tag{1.13}$$

(ii) *There is a nonsingular matrix $W$ such that*

$$\|x\|_0 < \left(1 + \frac{1}{\mu_W(A)}\right)/2; \tag{1.14}$$

(iii)

$$\|x\|_0 < \left(1 + \frac{1}{\mu_*(A)}\right)/2.$$

*Then x is the unique sparsest solution to the linear system.*

It is evident that (i) ⇒ (ii) ⇒ (iii). Condition (1.13) was shown by Donoho and Hu [85], and Elad and Bruckstein [96]. The OSMC provides a theoretical avenue to identify a tighter lower bound of spark$(A)$. To compute $\mu_*(A)$, however, it needs to solve a nonlinear minimization over nonsingular matrices, which is a difficult problem. To sacrifice a bit of tightness of the lower bound for spark$(A)$ with OSMC, we may use the checkable condition (1.14) provided that a suitable $W$ can be chosen such that $\mu_W(A) < \mu(A)$. This can be realized as follows: Perform a few steps of minimizing $\mu(WA)$ in the interior of the set of nonsingular matrices (this search can be confined to a smaller region such as the positive-definite cone), provided that a matrix $W$ is found such that $\mu(WA) < \mu(A)$. Any descent algorithm such as (sub)gradient-based nonlinear optimization algorithms can be used.

So far, plenty of effort has been made to improve the mutual coherence criterion (1.13), especially for matrices with certain structures. For instance, when $A = [\Phi \; \Psi]$ is a concatenation of two orthogonal matrices, Elad and Bruckstein [96] have shown that (1.13) can be improved to the following condition:

$$\|x\|_0 < 1/\mu(A).$$

When $A$ consists of $J$ concatenated orthogonal bases, Gribonval and Nielsen [122] have shown that the uniqueness condition for the sparsest solution of the system can be stated as follows:

$$\|x\|_0 < \frac{1}{2}\left(1 + \frac{1}{J-1}\right)/\mu(A).$$

However, these matrices with such structures limit their applications to rather special situations. Note that Theorems 1.2.3 and 1.3.4 are valid for general matrices. From both practical and mathematical points of view, it is interesting to improve the computable bound in (1.13) so that it can be applied to wider situations. The scaled-mutual-coherence condition (1.14) provides such an idea which, however, needs extra work to find an appropriate scaling matrix.

In the next section, we discuss another idea which can be used to improve the classic mutual coherence criteria. This improvement is based on the so-called sub-mutual coherence and coherence rank which turn out to be useful notions regarding uniqueness of the sparsest solutions to linear systems. One of the results in the next section claims that when the coherence rank of $A$ is smaller than $1/\mu(A)$, the lower bound $1 + 1/\mu(A)$ of spark(A), and thus (1.13), can be improved.

## 1.4 Improved Uniqueness Criteria via Coherence Rank

### 1.4.1 Sub-Mutual Coherence and Coherence Rank

Given a matrix $A = [a_1, \ldots, a_n] \in \mathbb{R}^{m \times n}$. Sort different values of the inner products $|a_i^T a_j| / (\|a_i\|_2 \|a_j\|_2)$ $(i \neq j)$ into descending order, and denote these different values by

$$\mu^{(1)}(A) > \mu^{(2)}(A) > \cdots > \mu^{(k)}(A).$$

Clearly, $\mu^{(1)}(A) = \mu(A)$. This motivates the following definition.

**Definition 1.4.1** *The value* $\mu^{(2)}(A)$ *is called the sub-mutual coherence of* $A \in \mathbb{R}^{m \times n}$, *which is the second largest absolute inner product between two normalized columns of* $A$ :

$$\mu^{(2)}(A) = \max_{1 \leq i < j \leq n} \left\{ \frac{|a_i^T a_j|}{\|a_i\|_2 \cdot \|a_j\|_2} : \frac{|a_i^T a_j|}{\|a_i\|_2 \cdot \|a_j\|_2} < \mu(A) \right\}.$$

Define the index set

$$\xi_A^{(i)} := \left\{ j : \frac{|a_i^T a_j|}{\|a_i\|_2 \cdot \|a_j\|_2} = \mu(A), \ j \neq i, j = 1, \ldots, n, \right\}, \ i = 1, \ldots, n.$$

Without loss of generality, we assume that the columns of $A$ are $\ell_2$-normalized. It is easy to see that $\xi_A^{(i)}$ is the index set of absolute entries equal to $\mu(A)$ in the $i$th row of the Gram matrix $G = A^T A$. Clearly, $\xi_A^{(i)}$ might be empty for some $i$ (when all entries in the $i$th row of $G$ are strictly smaller than $\mu(A)$), but at least one of these sets is nonempty, since the largest absolute entry of $G$ is equal to $\mu(A)$. Denote the cardinality of $\xi_A^{(i)}$ by $\alpha_A^{(i)}$, i.e.,

$$\alpha_A^{(i)} = |\xi_A^{(i)}|.$$

$\alpha_A^{(i)}$ denotes the number of entries equal to $\mu(A)$ in the $i$th row of $G$. Clearly, $0 \leq \alpha_A^{(i)} \leq n - 1$. Let,

$$\alpha(A) = \max_{1 \leq i \leq n} \alpha_A^{(i)}, \tag{1.15}$$

and let $i_0 \in \{1, \ldots, n\}$ be an index such that

$$\alpha(A) = \alpha_A^{(i_0)}.$$

Then we may define $\beta(A)$ as the largest one in the remaining $\alpha_A^{(i)}$ :

$$\beta(A) = \max_{1 \leq i \leq n, \ i \neq i_0} \alpha_A^{(i)}, \tag{1.16}$$

If there are more than one $\alpha_A^{(i)}$ equal to $\alpha(A)$, then $\beta(A) = \alpha(A)$. Otherwise, if $i_0$ is the only index such that $\alpha_A^{(i_0)} = \alpha(A)$, then $\beta(A) < \alpha(A)$, in which case $\beta(A)$ is the second largest one among $\alpha_A^{(i)}, i = 1, \ldots, n$.

**Definition 1.4.2** $\alpha(A)$, *given by (1.15), is called the coherence rank of $A$, and* $\beta(A)$, *given by (1.16), is called sub-coherence rank of $A$.*

By the definition of $\mu(A)$, there exists at least one off-diagonal absolute entry of the Gram matrix $G = A^T A$, say $|G_{ij}|$ (in the $i$th row), which is equal to $\mu(A)$. By the symmetry of $G$, we also have $|G_{ji}| = \mu(A)$ (in the $j$th row of $G$). Thus the symmetry of $G$ implies that $\beta(A) \geq 1$. So,

$$1 \leq \beta(A) \leq \alpha(A) \text{ for any } A \in \mathbb{R}^{m \times n}.$$

From the definition, the coherence rank of $A$ with normalized columns is the maximal number of the absolute entries equal to $\mu(A)$ in a row of its Gram matrix. In other words, $\alpha(A)$ is the maximal number of columns in $A$ that have the same largest angle with respect to a column, say the $i_0$-column, of $A$. Clearly, unless the columns of matrix are carefully selected, the coherence rank of a matrix (especially, a random matrix) would be very low, typically, equal to 1. An extreme case for the highest coherence rank is when all columns of $A$ are generated by a single vector. In this special case, we have $\mu(A) = 1$ and $\alpha(A) = \beta(A) = n - 1$. In general, $A$ has at least two independent columns, and hence $\alpha(A) < n - 1$. For the concatenation of two orthogonal bases $A = [\Psi \ \Phi] \in \mathbb{R}^{m \times 2m}$, where $\Psi, \Phi$ are $m \times m$ orthogonal matrices, we see that $\alpha(A) \leq m$. Clearly, for a random matrix $A$, its coherence rank is equal to 1 with high probability.

All $\mu(A), \mu^{(2)}(A), \alpha(A)$ and $\beta(A)$ can be obtained immediately from the Gram matrix of $A$ with $\ell_2$-normalized columns. For example, if $A$ is given as

$$A = \begin{bmatrix} 1/\sqrt{3} & 1 & 0 & 2\sqrt{2}/3 & 2\sqrt{2}/3 & 1\sqrt{5} \\ 1/\sqrt{3} & 0 & 1/\sqrt{3} & 1/3 & 0 & -2/\sqrt{5} \\ 1/\sqrt{3} & 0 & \sqrt{2}/\sqrt{3} & 0 & -1/3 & 0 \end{bmatrix},$$

then the Gram matrix of $A$ is

$$G = \begin{bmatrix} 1.0000 & 0.5774 & 0.8047 & 0.7368 & 0.3519 & -0.2582 \\ 0.5774 & 1.0000 & 0.0000 & 0.9428 & 0.9428 & 0.4472 \\ 0.8047 & 0.0000 & 1.0000 & 0.1925 & -0.2722 & -0.5164 \\ 0.7368 & 0.9428 & 0.1925 & 1.0000 & 0.8889 & 0.1235 \\ 0.3519 & 0.9428 & -0.2722 & 0.8889 & 1.0000 & 0.4216 \\ -0.2582 & 0.4472 & -0.5164 & 0.1235 & 0.4216 & 1.0000 \end{bmatrix}.$$

Clearly, for this example, $\mu(A) = 0.9428$, $\mu^{(2)}(A) = 0.8889$, $\alpha(A) = 2$ and $\beta(A) = 1$. In the next section, we show that when the coherence rank of a matrix is low, the condition (1.13) can be improved.

## 1.4.2 *Improved Lower Bounds of Spark(A)*

Let us first recall the Brauer's Theorem [35] (see also Theorem 2.3 in [217]) concerning the estimate of eigenvalues of a matrix. The Brauer's Theorem can be viewed as an extension of Geršchgorin's Theorem. Let $M \in \mathbb{R}^{n \times n}$ and

$$\sigma(M) = \{\lambda : \lambda \text{ is an eigenvalue of } M\}$$

be the spectrum of $M$. Let $\lambda$ be an eigenvalue of $M$ and $x \neq 0$ be an eigenvector associated with $\lambda$. Denote by $x_p$ and $x_k$ the components of $x$ with the largest and the second largest absolute values, respectively. From $Mx = \lambda x$, we have,

$$(\lambda - m_{pp})x_p = \sum_{1 \leq j \leq n, j \neq p} m_{pj}x_j,$$

$$(\lambda - m_{kk})x_k = \sum_{1 \leq j \leq n, j \neq k} m_{kj}x_j.$$

Therefore,

$$|(\lambda - m_{pp})x_p| \leq \sum_{1 \leq j \leq n, j \neq p} |m_{pj}| \cdot |x_j| \leq \sum_{1 \leq j \leq n, j \neq p} |m_{pj}| \cdot |x_k|,$$

$$|(\lambda - m_{kk})x_k| \leq \sum_{1 \leq j \leq n, j \neq k} |m_{kj}| \cdot |x_j| \leq \sum_{1 \leq j \leq n, j \neq k} |m_{kj}| \cdot |x_p|$$

If $x_k = 0$, then the first inequality implies that $\lambda - m_{pp} = 0$; otherwise, if $x_k \neq 0$, it follows from the above two inequalities that

$$|(\lambda - m_{pp})(\lambda - m_{kk})(x_k x_p)| \leq \left[ \sum_{1 \leq j \leq n, j \neq p} |m_{pj}| \right] \left[ \sum_{1 \leq j \leq n, j \neq k} |m_{kj}| \right] |x_k x_p|,$$

in which the term $|x_k x_p| \neq 0$ can be removed. This leads to the following result.

**Theorem 1.4.3** (Brauer [35]) *Let $M = (m_{ij})$ be an $n \times n$ matrix with $n \geq 2$. If $\lambda$ is an eigenvalue of $M$, then there is a pair $(p,q)$ of positive integers with $p \neq q$ $(1 \leq p, q \leq n)$ such that*

$$|\lambda - m_{pp}| \cdot |\lambda - m_{qq}| \leq \Delta_p \Delta_q,$$

*where*

$$\Delta_i := \sum_{1 \leq j \leq n, j \neq i} |m_{ij}|, \quad i = 1, \ldots, n.$$

*Denote by $K_{ij}(M) = \{z : |z - m_{ii}| \cdot |z - m_{jj}| \leq \Delta_i \Delta_j\}$ for $i \neq j$. Then,*

$$\sigma(M) \subseteq \bigcup_{i \neq j}^{n} K_{ij}(M).$$

This theorem is the key to obtain a computable lower bound of $\text{spark}(A)$ in terms of $\mu(A), \mu^{(2)}(A), \alpha(A)$ and $\beta(A)$. The normalized version of $A$ can be written as $AD$, where $D = \text{diag}(1/\|a_1\|_2, \ldots, 1/\|a_n\|_2)$. It is worth noting that all these constants and $\text{spark}(A)$ are invariant under the column normalization of $A$. That is,

$$\text{spark}(AD) = \text{spark}(A), \ \mu(AD) = \mu(A), \ \mu^{(2)}(AD) = \mu^{(2)}(A),$$

$$\alpha(AD) = \alpha(A), \ \beta(AD) = \beta(A).$$

We now prove the following lower bound for spark.

**Theorem 1.4.4** *Let $A \in \mathbb{R}^{m \times n}$ be a matrix with $m < n$. If $\alpha(A) \leq 1/\mu(A)$ and $\beta(A) < 1/\mu(A)$. Then $\mu^{(2)}(A) > 0$ and*

$$\text{spark}(A) \geq 1 + \frac{2\left[1 - \alpha(A)\beta(A)(\tilde{\mu}(A))^2\right]}{\mu^{(2)}(A)\left\{\tilde{\mu}(A)(\alpha(A) + \beta(A)) + \sqrt{[\tilde{\mu}(A)(\alpha(A) - \beta(A))]^2 + 4}\right\}},$$

(1.17)

*where $\tilde{\mu}(A) := \mu(A) - \mu^{(2)}(A)$.*

*Proof.* Without loss of generality, we assume that $A$ is a matrix with $\ell_2$-normalized columns. By the definition of $\text{spark}(A)$, there exist $p = \text{spark}(A)$ columns in $A$ which are linearly dependent. Let $A_S$ denote the submatrix consisting of such $p$ columns. We assume $A_S = [a_1, a_2, \ldots, a_p]$ without lost of generality. Since the columns of $A_S$ are linearly dependent, $A_S^T A_S$ is a $p \times p$ singular matrix. Since $A$ is $\ell_2$-normalized, diagonal entries of $A_S^T A_S$ are equal to 1, and absolute values of off-diagonal entries are less than or equal to $\mu(A)$. By the assumption, $\alpha(A) \leq 1/\mu(A)$, which together with (1.13) implies

$$1 + \alpha(A) \leq 1 + \frac{1}{\mu(A)} \leq \text{spark}(A).$$

Thus

$$\alpha(A) \leq \text{spark}(A) - 1 = p - 1.$$

Note that the entries of $A_S^T A_S$ are determined by $(A_S^T A_S)_{ij} = a_i^T a_j$, $i, j = 1, \ldots, p$. By singularity, $\lambda = 0$ is an eigenvalue of $A_S^T A_S$. Applying Theorem 1.4.3 to $A_S^T A_S$ and $\lambda = 0$, there exist two rows, $i \neq j$, such that

$$|0 - (A_S^T A_S)_{ii}| \cdot |0 - (A_S^T A_S)_{jj}| \leq \Delta_i \Delta_j = \left[\sum_{1 \leq k \leq p, k \neq i} |a_i^T a_k|\right]\left[\sum_{1 \leq k \leq p, k \neq j} |a_j^T a_k|\right],$$

(1.18)

where $(A_S^T A_S)_{ii} = (A_S^T A_S)_{jj} = 1$. So the left-hand side of (1.18) is equal to 1. By the definition of $\alpha(A)$ and $\beta(A)$ and noting that $A_S^T A_S$ is a submatrix of $A^T A$, for any pair of rows of the Gram matrix $A_S^T A_S$, we see that one of the rows has at most $\alpha(A)$ entries equal to $\mu(A)$ and the other row has at most $\beta(A)$ entries equal to $\mu(A)$, and the remaining entries on these rows must be smaller than or equal to $\mu^{(2)}(A)$). Thus the following inequality holds:

$$\left[ \sum_{1 \le k \le p, k \ne i} |a_i^T a_k| \right] \left[ \sum_{1 \le k \le p, k \ne j} |a_j^T a_k| \right]$$
$$\le \left[ \alpha(A)\mu(A) + (p - 1 - \alpha(A))\mu^{(2)}(A) \right] \left[ \beta(A)\mu(A) + (p - 1 - \beta(A))\mu^{(2)}(A) \right].$$
$$(1.19)$$

Denote by $\tilde{\mu}(A) := \mu(A) - \mu^{(2)}(A)$. Combining (1.18), (1.19) and noting that the left-hand side of (1.18) is 1 yields

$$1 \le \left[ \alpha(A)\tilde{\mu}(A) + (p - 1)\mu^{(2)}(A) \right] \left[ \beta(A)\tilde{\mu}(A) + (p - 1)\mu^{(2)}(A) \right], \quad (1.20)$$

which can be written as follows:

$$\left[ (p - 1)\mu^{(2)}(A) \right]^2 + \left[ (p - 1)\mu^{(2)}(A) \right] (\alpha(A) + \beta(A))\tilde{\mu}(A)$$
$$+ \alpha(A)\beta(A)(\tilde{\mu}(A))^2 - 1 \ge 0. \quad (1.21)$$

We now show that $\mu^{(2)}(A) \ne 0$. The assumptions $\alpha(A) \le 1/\mu(A)$ and $\beta(A) < 1/\mu(A)$ imply that

$$\alpha(A)\beta(A)(\mu(A))^2 < 1.$$

This, together with (1.21), implies that $\mu^{(2)}(A) \ne 0$. Consider the following quadratic equation in $t$:

$$t^2 + t(\alpha(A) + \beta(A))\tilde{\mu}(A) + \alpha(A)\beta(A)(\tilde{\mu}(A))^2 - 1 = 0.$$

It is evident that this equation has only one positive root. Inequality (1.21) implies that the quantity $(p-1)\mu^{(2)}(A)$ is larger or equal to the positive root of the above quadratic equation. That is,

$$(p - 1)\mu^{(2)}(A) \ge \frac{1}{2} \{ \sqrt{[\tilde{\mu}(A)(\alpha(A) + \beta(A))]^2 - 4(\alpha(A)\beta(A)(\tilde{\mu}(A))^2 - 1)}$$
$$- (\alpha(A) + \beta(A))\tilde{\mu}(A) \}$$
$$= \frac{1}{2} \{ \sqrt{[(\alpha(A) - \beta(A))\tilde{\mu}(A)]^2 + 4} - (\alpha(A) + \beta(A))\tilde{\mu}(A) \}$$
$$= \frac{2 \left[ 1 - \alpha(A)\beta(A)(\tilde{\mu}(A))^2 \right]}{(\alpha(A) + \beta(A))\tilde{\mu}(A) + \sqrt{[(\alpha(A) - \beta(A))\tilde{\mu}(A)]^2 + 4}},$$

which yields the bound in (1.17). □

Clearly, when $\mu(A) = \mu^{(2)}(A)$, the lower bound in (1.17) is reduced to $1 + 1/\mu(A)$. Let $T(A)$ denote the right-hand side of (1.17). Note that $\sqrt{t_1^2 + t_2^2} \leq t_1 + t_2$ for any real numbers $t_1, t_2 \geq 0$. We see that

$$T(A) = 1 + \frac{2\left(1 - \alpha(A)\beta(A)(\widetilde{\mu}(A))^2\right)}{\mu^{(2)}(A)\left\{\widetilde{\mu}(A)(\alpha(A) + \beta(A)) + \sqrt{[\widetilde{\mu}(A)(\alpha(A) - \beta(A))]^2 + 4}\right\}}$$

$$\geq 1 + \frac{2\left(1 - \alpha(A)\beta(A)(\widetilde{\mu}(A))^2\right)}{\mu^{(2)}(A)\left\{\widetilde{\mu}(A)(\alpha(A) + \beta(A)) + [\widetilde{\mu}(A)(\alpha(A) - \beta(A))] + 2\right\}}$$

$$= 1 + \frac{1 - \alpha(A)\beta(A)(\widetilde{\mu}(A))^2}{\mu^{(2)}(A)(1 + \alpha(A)\widetilde{\mu}(A))}. \tag{1.22}$$

The next result claims that when $\alpha \leq 1/\mu(A)$ and $\beta < 1/\mu(A)$, the lower bound in (1.17) is tighter than (1.13).

**Proposition 1.4.5** *If* $\alpha(A) \leq 1/\mu(A)$ *and* $\beta(A) < 1/\mu(A)$, *then* $T(A) > 1 + 1/\mu(A)$. *In particular, the following hold:*

(i) *If* $\alpha(A) < 1/\mu(A)$, *then*

$$T(A) \geq 1 + \frac{1}{\mu(A)} + \left[\frac{1}{\mu^{(2)}(A)} - \frac{1}{\mu(A)}\right](1 - \alpha(A)\mu(A)).$$

(ii) *If* $\alpha(A) \leq 1/\mu(A)$ *and* $\beta(A) < \alpha(A)$, *then*

$$T(A) \geq 1 + \frac{1}{\mu(A)} + \frac{\widetilde{\mu}(A)((1 - \alpha(A)\mu(A))}{\mu^{(2)}(A)\mu(A)} + \frac{\alpha(A)(\widetilde{\mu}(A))^2}{\mu^{(2)}(A)(1 + \alpha(A)\widetilde{\mu}(A))},$$

*where* $\widetilde{\mu}(A) = \mu(A) - \mu^{(2)}(A)$.

*Proof.* Under the conditions $\alpha(A) \leq 1/\mu(A)$ and $\beta(A) < 1/\mu(A)$, we have $\alpha(A)\beta(A) < 1/(\mu(A))^2$. By the definition, $\widetilde{\mu}(A) > 0$ since $\mu^{(2)}(A) < \mu(A)$. It follows from (1.22) that

$$T(A) > 1 + \frac{1 - (\widetilde{\mu}(A)/\mu(A))^2}{\mu^{(2)}(A)(1 + \alpha(A)\widetilde{\mu}(A))} \geq 1 + \frac{1 - (\widetilde{\mu}(A)/\mu(A))^2}{\mu^{(2)}(A)(1 + \widetilde{\mu}(A)/\mu(A))}$$

$$= 1 + \frac{1 - \widetilde{\mu}(A)/\mu(A)}{\mu^{(2)}(A)} = 1 + \frac{1}{\mu(A)},$$

where the second inequality follows from $\alpha(A) \leq 1/\mu(A)$, and the last equality follows from $\tilde{\mu}(A) = \mu(A) - \mu^{(2)}(A)$. In particular, if $\alpha(A) < 1/\mu(A)$, by noting that $\beta(A) \leq \alpha(A)$, it follows from (1.22) that

$$
\begin{aligned}
T(A) &\geq 1 + \frac{1 - (\alpha(A)\tilde{\mu}(A))^2}{\mu^{(2)}(A)(1 + \alpha(A)\tilde{\mu}(A))} = 1 + \frac{1 - \alpha(A)\tilde{\mu}(A)}{\mu^{(2)}(A)} \\
&= 1 + \frac{1}{\mu(A)} + \left[ \frac{1}{\mu^{(2)}(A)} - \frac{1}{\mu(A)} \right](1 - \alpha(A)\mu(A)).
\end{aligned}
$$

Finally, let us assume that $\alpha(A) \leq 1/\mu(A)$ and $\beta(A) < \alpha(A)$, in which case $\beta(A) \leq \alpha(A) - 1$. We see again from (1.22) that

$$
\begin{aligned}
T(A) &\geq 1 + \frac{1 - \alpha(A)(\alpha(A) - 1)(\tilde{\mu}(A))^2}{\mu^{(2)}(A)(1 + \alpha(A)\tilde{\mu}(A))} \\
&= 1 + \frac{1 - \alpha(A)\tilde{\mu}(A)}{\mu^{(2)}(A)} + \frac{\alpha(A)(\tilde{\mu}(A))^2}{\mu^{(2)}(A)(1 + \alpha(A)\tilde{\mu}(A))} \\
&= 1 + \frac{1}{\mu(A)} + \frac{\tilde{\mu}(A)((1 - \alpha(A)\mu(A))}{\mu^{(2)}(A)\mu(A)} + \frac{\alpha(A)(\tilde{\mu}(A))^2}{\mu^{(2)}(A)(1 + \alpha(A)\tilde{\mu}(A))},
\end{aligned}
$$

as desired. □

Therefore, the lower bound of $\text{spark}(A)$ given in (1.17) improves the bound in (1.13) when the coherence rank $\alpha(A)$ is small. Proposition 1.4.5 also indicates how much improvement might be made in this case. If the Gram matrix $G$ of the $\ell_2$-normalized $A$ has two rows containing $\alpha(A)$ entries with absolute values equal to $\mu(A)$, then $\alpha(A) = \beta(A)$, in which case the lower bound in (1.17) can be simplified to

$$
T(A) = \left( 1 + \frac{1}{\mu(A)} \right) + \left( \frac{1}{\mu^{(2)}(A)} - \frac{1}{\mu(A)} \right)(1 - \alpha(A)\mu(A)).
$$

Note that $G$ has at most one absolute entry equal to $\mu(A)$ in its every row if and only if $\alpha(A) = \beta(A) = 1$. In this special case, the condition $\alpha(A) < 1/\mu(A)$ holds trivially when $\mu(A) < 1$. Thus, the next corollary follows immediately from Theorem 1.4.4.

**Corollary 1.4.6** *Let $A \in \mathbb{R}^{m \times n}$ be a matrix with $m < n$. If $\mu(A) < 1$ and $\alpha(A) = 1$, then $\mu^{(2)}(A) > 0$, and*

$$
\text{spark}(A) \geq 1 + \frac{1}{\mu(A)} + \left( \frac{1}{\mu^{(2)}(A)} - \frac{1}{\mu(A)} \right)(1 - \mu(A)).
$$

Although Corollary 1.4.6 deals with a special case, matrices do usually satisfy the condition $\alpha(A) = 1$ and $\mu(A) < 1$. In fact, the case $\alpha(A) \geq 2$ arises only when $A$ has at least two columns, each has the same angle to a column of the matrix, and such an angle is the largest one between pairs of the columns in $A$. This phenomenon indicates that the coherence rank of a matrix (especially, a random matrix) is usually low, typically $\alpha(A) = 1$.

### 1.4.3 Improved Coherence Conditions

Consider the class of matrices

$$\mathcal{M} = \left\{ A \in \mathbb{R}^{m \times n} : \alpha(A) \leq 1/\mu(A), \ \beta(A) < 1/\mu(A) \right\} \quad (1.23)$$

and its subclasses

$$\mathcal{M}^* = \left\{ A \in \mathbb{R}^{m \times n} : \alpha(A) < 1/\mu(A) \right\}, \quad (1.24)$$

$$\mathcal{M}^{**} = \left\{ A \in \mathbb{R}^{m \times n} : \beta(A) < \alpha(A) \leq 1/\mu(A) \right\}. \quad (1.25)$$

The next result follows instantly from Theorem 1.4.4 and Corollary 1.2.4.

**Theorem 1.4.7** *Let $A \in \mathcal{M}$, where $\mathcal{M}$ is defined in (1.23). If the system $Az = b$ has a solution x obeying*

$$2\|x\|_0 < 1 + \frac{2\left(1 - \alpha(A)\beta(A)(\widetilde{\mu}(A))^2\right)}{\mu^{(2)}(A)\left\{ \widetilde{\mu}(A)(\alpha(A) + \beta(A)) + \sqrt{[\widetilde{\mu}(A)(\alpha(A) - \beta(A))]^2 + 4} \right\}}, \quad (1.26)$$

*where $\widetilde{\mu}(A) = \mu(A) - \mu^{(2)}(A)$, then x is the unique sparsest solution to the linear system.*

By Proposition 1.4.5, the bound given in (1.26) improves the one in (1.13) when $A$ is in class $\mathcal{M}$. This improvement is achieved by integrating more matrix information, such as sub-mutual coherence, coherence rank, and sub-coherence rank, instead of $\mu(A)$ only. Since $(\alpha(A), \beta(A), \mu(A), \mu^{(2)}(A))$ can be obtained straightforwardly from $G = A^T A$, the bound in (1.26) can be easily computed. The next result follows from Theorem 1.4.4 and Proposition 1.4.5 immediately.

**Theorem 1.4.8** (i) *Let $A \in \mathcal{M}^*$, where $\mathcal{M}^*$ is given in (1.24). If the system $Az = b$ has a solution x obeying*

$$\|x\|_0 < \frac{1}{2}\left[ 1 + \frac{1}{\mu(A)} + \left( \frac{1}{\mu^{(2)}(A)} - \frac{1}{\mu(A)} \right)(1 - \alpha(A)\mu(A)) \right], \quad (1.27)$$

*then x is the unique sparsest solution to the linear system.*

(ii) *Let $\widetilde{\mu}(A) = \mu(A) - \mu^{(2)}(A)$ and $A \in \mathcal{M}^{**}$, where $\mathcal{M}^{**}$ is defined in (1.25). If the system $Az = b$ has a solution x obeying*

$$\|x\|_0 < \frac{1}{2}\left[ 1 + \frac{1}{\mu(A)} + \frac{\widetilde{\mu}(A)((1 - \alpha(A)\mu(A))}{\mu^{(2)}(A)\mu(A)} + \frac{\alpha(A)(\widetilde{\mu}(A))^2}{\mu^{(2)}(A)(1 + \alpha(A)\widetilde{\mu}(A))} \right],$$

*then x is the unique sparsest solution to the linear system.*

(iii) *Suppose $\mu(A) < 1$ and $\alpha(A) = 1$. If the system $Az = b$ has a solution x satisfying*

$$\|x\|_0 < \frac{1}{2}\left[ 1 + \frac{1}{\mu(A)} + \left( \frac{1}{\mu^{(2)}(A)} - \frac{1}{\mu(A)} \right)(1 - \mu(A)) \right], \quad (1.28)$$

*then x is the unique sparsest solution to the linear system.*

Result (iii) above shows that for coherence-rank-1 matrices, the uniqueness criterion (1.13) can be improved to (1.28). As we have pointed out, matrices (especially random ones) are very likely to be coherence-rank-1, unless the matrix is particularly designed. The above uniqueness criteria can be further improved when a lower bound of the cardinality of $\Delta$, the support overlap of solutions of the linear system, is available. Taking Theorem 1.4.8 (iii) as an example, the following corollary is implied from Theorem 1.2.3 and the fact that the right-hand side of (1.28) is bounded by spark$(A)$.

**Corollary 1.4.9** *Let $A \in \mathbb{R}^{m \times n}$, where $m < n$, be a matrix with $\mu(A) < 1$ and $\alpha(A) = 1$. Suppose $|\Delta| \geq \gamma^*$ where $\gamma^*$ is known. If the linear system $Az = b$ has a solution $x$ satisfying*

$$\|x\|_0 < \frac{1}{2}\left[\gamma^* + \left(1 + \frac{1}{\mu(A)}\right) + \left(\frac{1}{\mu^{(2)}(A)} - \frac{1}{\mu(A)}\right)(1 - \mu(A))\right],$$

*then $x$ is the unique sparsest solution to the linear system.*

## 1.5 Babel Function and Sub-Babel Function

Let $A = [a_1, \dots, a_n] \in \mathbb{R}^{m \times n}$ be a matrix with $\ell_2$-normalized columns. $\Lambda$ denotes a subset of $\{1, \dots, n\}$. The so-called Babel-function was introduced by Tropp in [210], and it is defined as

$$\mu_1(p) = \max_{\Lambda \subseteq \{1,\dots,n\}, |\Lambda| = p} \max_{j \notin \Lambda} \sum_{i \in \Lambda} |a_i^T a_j|, \quad 1 \leq p \leq n - 1. \tag{1.29}$$

When, $p = 1$, we see that $\mu_1(1) = \mu(A)$. Clearly, $\mu_1(p)$ is monotonically nondecreasing in $p$, i.e., $\mu_1(p^1) \leq \mu_1(p^2)$ for any $p^1 \leq p^2$. By this function, the following lower bound for spark is obtained in [210]:

$$\text{spark}(A) \geq \widehat{q} := \min_{2 \leq q \leq n} \{q : \mu_1(q - 1) \geq 1\}. \tag{1.30}$$

This relation is easy to understand. It is easy to show that *if $\mu_1(q - 1) < 1$, then any $q$ columns of $A$ are linearly independent*. In fact, if there are $q$ columns of $A$ are linearly dependent, say $a_1, \dots, a_q$, then $\lambda = 0$ is an eigenvalue of the Gram matrix of $A_S = [a_1, \dots, a_q]$. By Lemma 1.3.3, there exists $j \in \{1, \dots, q\}$ such that,

$$1 = |0 - (A_S^T A_S)_{jj}| \leq \sum_{1 \leq k \leq q, k \neq j} |a_j^T a_k| \leq \mu_1(q - 1),$$

where the second inequality follows from (1.29). Thus by the definition of spark$(A)$, $p = \text{spark}(A)$ implies that $\mu_1(p - 1) \geq 1$. In other words,

$$\text{spark} = p \in \{q : \mu_1(q - 1) \geq 1\},$$

which immediately implies (1.30).

The Babel function can be equivalently defined/computed in terms of the Gram matrix $G = A^T A$. In fact, sorting every row of abs$(G)$ in descending order yields the matrix $\widehat{G} = (\widehat{G}_{ij})$ with the first column equal to the vector of ones, consisting of the diagonal entries of $G$. Therefore, as pointed out in [95], for $1 \le p \le n-1$, the Babel function can be written as follows:

$$\mu_1(p) = \max_{1 \le k \le n} \sum_{j=2}^{p+1} |\widehat{G}_{kj}| = \sum_{j=2}^{p+1} |\widehat{G}_{k_0 j}|, \tag{1.31}$$

where $k_0$ denotes an index such that the above maximum is achieved. Clearly $k_0$ depends on $p$. From (1.31), by setting $p = q - 1$ which by the range of $p$ implies that $2 \le q \le n$, and noting that any entry $|\widehat{G}_{ij}| \le \mu(A)$, it is easy to see that

$$\mu_1(q-1) = \sum_{j=2}^{q} |\widehat{G}_{k_0 j}| \le (q-1)\mu(A).$$

This together with (1.30) implies that $1 \le (\widehat{q}-1)\mu(A)$, and hence

$$\text{spark}(A) \ge \widehat{q} \ge 1 + \frac{1}{\mu(A)}.$$

This means that the lower bound of spark$(A)$ in (1.30) is never worse than the bound in (1.13). Also, the following Babel-function-based uniqueness condition is obtained.

**Theorem 1.5.1** [210] *If a linear system $Az = b$ has a solution $x$ obeying*

$$2\|x\|_0 < \min_{2 \le q \le n} \{q : \mu_1(q-1) \ge 1\}, \tag{1.32}$$

*then $x$ is the unique sparsest solution to this linear system.*

Some immediate questions arise: *Can we compare the lower bounds in (1.30) and (1.17)? Can the lower bounds in (1.30) and (1.17) be improved?* We first show that the Babel-function-based lower bound of spark$(A)$ in (1.30) can be improved by using the so-called sub-Babel function.

**Definition 1.5.2** *The sub-Babel function, denoted by $\mu_1^{(2)}(p)$ where $1 \le p \le n - 1$, is defined as follows:*

$$\mu_1^{(2)}(p) = \max_{1 \le k \le n, k \ne k_0} \sum_{j=2}^{p+1} |\widehat{G}_{kj}|, \tag{1.33}$$

*where $k_0$ is determined in (1.31).*

Clearly, $\mu_1^{(2)}(p) \leq \mu_1(p)$ for any $1 \leq p \leq n-1$. We have the following improved version of (1.30). Again, Brauer's Theorem plays a key role in establishing such an enhanced result.

**Theorem 1.5.3** *For any $A \in \mathbb{R}^{m \times n}$ with $m < n$ and $\ell_2$-normalized columns, the following holds:*

$$\text{spark}(A) \geq q^* := \min_{2 \leq q \leq n} \left\{ q : \mu_1(q-1) \cdot \mu_1^{(2)}(q-1) \geq 1 \right\}. \tag{1.34}$$

*Proof.* Let $p = \text{spark}(A)$. By the definition of spark, $p \geq 2$ and there are $p$ columns of $A$ that are linearly dependent. Without loss of generality, we assume that $A_S = [a_1, a_2, \ldots, a_p]$ is the submatrix consisting of such $p$ columns. The Gram matrix $A_S^T A_S \in \mathbb{R}^{p \times p}$ is singular, and all of its diagonal entries are equal to 1. By Theorem 1.4.3 (Brauer's Theorem), for any eigenvalue $\lambda$ of $A_S^T A_S$, there are two different rows, say $i$th and $j$th rows $(i \neq j)$, such that

$$|\lambda - (A_S^T A_S)_{ii}| \cdot |\lambda - (A_S^T A_S)_{jj}| \leq \Delta_i \Delta_j = \left[ \sum_{1 \leq k \leq p, k \neq i} |a_i^T a_k| \right] \left[ \sum_{1 \leq k \leq p, k \neq j} |a_j^T a_k| \right],$$
$$\tag{1.35}$$

where $(A_S^T A_S)_{ii} = (A_S^T A_S)_{jj} = 1$. By the definition of Babel and sub-Babel functions, we have

$$\max\{\Delta_i, \Delta_j\} \leq \mu_1(p-1),$$
$$\min\{\Delta_i, \Delta_j\} \leq \mu_1^{(2)}(p-1).$$

It follows from (1.35) that

$$(\lambda - 1)^2 \leq \Delta_i \Delta_j = \max\{\Delta_i, \Delta_j\} \cdot \min\{\Delta_i, \Delta_j\} \leq \mu_1(p-1) \cdot \mu_1^{(2)}(p-1).$$

In particular, since $\lambda = 0$ is an eigenvalue of $A_S^T A_S$, we have

$$\mu_1(p-1) \cdot \mu_1^{(2)}(p-1) \geq 1. \tag{1.36}$$

So $p = \text{spark}(A)$ implies that $p$ must satisfy (1.36), i.e.,

$$p \in \left\{ q \geq 2 : \mu_1(q-1) \cdot \mu_1^{(2)}(q-1) \geq 1 \right\}.$$

Therefore,

$$\text{spark}(A) = p \geq \min_{2 \leq q \leq n} \left\{ q : \mu_1(q-1) \cdot \mu_1^{(2)}(q-1) \geq 1 \right\} =: q^*,$$

which is exactly the lower bound of $\text{spark}(A)$ given in (1.34). □.

We now point out that (1.34) is an improved version of (1.30).

**Proposition 1.5.4** *Let $\widehat{q}$ and $q^*$ be defined in (1.30) and (1.34), respectively. Then $q^* \geq \widehat{q}$. In particular, if $\mu_1^{(2)}(q^* - 1) < 1/\mu_1(\widehat{q} - 1)$, then $q^* > \widehat{q}$.*

*Proof.* Note that $\mu_1^{(2)}(p) \leq \mu_1(p)$ for any $1 \leq p \leq n - 1$. In particular, $\mu_1^{(2)}(q^* - 1) \leq \mu_1(q^* - 1)$. Thus the inequality

$$\mu_1(q^* - 1) \cdot \mu_1^{(2)}(q^* - 1) \geq 1 \tag{1.37}$$

implies that $\mu_1(q^* - 1) \geq 1$. Thus $q^* \in \{q \geq 2: \mu_1(q - 1) \geq 1\}$, which indicates that

$$q^* \geq \min_{2 \leq q \leq n} \{q: \mu_1(q - 1) \geq 1\} = \widehat{q}.$$

We now prove that the above inequality holds strictly when the value of the sub-Babel function at $q^* - 1$ is relatively small in the sense that $\mu_1^{(2)}(q^* - 1) < 1/\mu_1(\widehat{q} - 1)$, that is,

$$\mu_1(\widehat{q} - 1) \cdot \mu_1^{(2)}(q^* - 1) < 1.$$

Combining this inequality and (1.37) leads to

$$\mu_1(q^* - 1) \cdot \mu_1^{(2)}(q^* - 1) > \mu_1(\widehat{q} - 1) \cdot \mu_1^{(2)}(q^* - 1).$$

That is,

$$\mu_1(q^* - 1) > \mu_1(\widehat{q} - 1).$$

Since $\mu_1(q - 1)$ is a non-decreasing function in $q$, the inequality above implies that $q^* > \widehat{q}$. □.

From Proposition 1.5.4, we immediately obtain the following result, which is an enhanced version of Theorem 1.5.1.

**Corollary 1.5.5** *If the linear system $Az = b$ has a solution $x$ obeying*

$$2\|x\|_0 < \min_{2 \leq q \leq n} \left\{q: \ \mu_1(q - 1) \cdot \mu_1^{(2)}(q - 1) \geq 1\right\},$$

*then $x$ is the unique sparsest solution to this linear system.*

When the coherence rank of $A$ is relatively small, the bound in (1.34) is also an improved version of the one in (1.17), as shown in the next result.

**Proposition 1.5.6** *Let $A \in \mathbb{R}^{m \times n}$ be a given matrix with $m < n$ and $\ell_2$-normalized columns. Let $q^*$ be given in (1.34). If $\alpha(A) < 1/\mu(A)$ and $\alpha(A) \leq q^* - 1$, then*

$$q^* \geq 1 + \frac{2\left[1 - \alpha(A)\beta(A)(\widetilde{\mu}(A))^2\right]}{\mu^{(2)}(A)\left\{\widetilde{\mu}(A)(\alpha(A) + \beta(A)) + \sqrt{[\widetilde{\mu}(A)(\alpha(A) - \beta(A))]^2 + 4}\right\}},$$

*where $\widetilde{\mu}(A) = \mu(A) - \mu^{(2)}(A)$.*

*Proof.* From (1.31) and (1.33), we see that there is a number $k_1$, $k_1 \neq k_0$, such that

$$\mu_1(q^* - 1) = \sum_{j=2}^{q^*} |\widehat{G}_{k_0 j}|, \quad \mu_1^{(2)}(q^* - 1) = \sum_{j=2}^{q^*} |\widehat{G}_{k_1 j}|.$$

By the assumption $\alpha(A) \leq q^* - 1$ and the definitions of $\alpha(A)$, $\beta(A)$ and $q^*$, we have

$$1 \leq \mu_1(q^* - 1) \cdot \mu_1^{(2)}(q^* - 1) = \left[\sum_{j=2}^{q^*} |\widehat{G}_{k_0 j}|\right]\left[\sum_{j=2}^{q^*} |\widehat{G}_{k_1 j}|\right]$$

$$\leq \left[\alpha(A)\mu(A) + (q^* - 1 - \alpha(A))\mu^{(2)}(A)\right]$$
$$\cdot \left[\beta(A)\mu(A) + (q^* - 1 - \beta(A))\mu^{(2)}(A)\right]$$

$$= \left[\alpha(A)\widetilde{\mu}(A) + (q^* - 1)\mu^{(2)}(A)\right]\left[\beta(A)\widetilde{\mu}(A) + (q^* - 1)\mu^{(2)}(A)\right],$$

which is the same inequality as (1.20) with $p$ being replaced by $q^*$. Repeating the same proof following (1.20), we obtain

$$q^* \geq 1 + \frac{2\left[1 - \alpha(A)\beta(A)(\widetilde{\mu}(A))^2\right]}{\mu^{(2)}(A)\left\{\widetilde{\mu}(A)(\alpha(A) + \beta(A)) + \sqrt{[\widetilde{\mu}(A)(\alpha(A) - \beta(A))]^2 + 4}\right\}},$$

where $\widetilde{\mu}(A) = \mu(A) - \mu^{(2)}(A)$. □

Let us briefly compare the Babel-function-based bound (1.30) and those developed in Section 1.4. It seems any one of these bounds cannot definitely dominate the other in general. For instance, if $\alpha(A) \leq \widehat{q} - 1$ and $\alpha(A) < 1/\mu(A)$ where $\widehat{q}$ is given in (1.30), then

$$1 \leq \mu_1(\widehat{q} - 1) = \max_{1 \leq k \leq n} \sum_{j=2}^{\widehat{q}} |\widehat{G}_{kj}| \leq \alpha(A)\mu(A) + (\widehat{q} - 1 - \alpha(A))\mu^{(2)}(A).$$

Therefore, we have

$$\widehat{q} \geq 1 + \frac{1 - \alpha(A)\widetilde{\mu}(A)}{\mu^{(2)}(A)} = 1 + \frac{1}{\mu(A)} + \left(\frac{1}{\mu^{(2)}(A)} - \frac{1}{\mu(A)}\right)(1 - \alpha(A)\mu(A)).$$

In this case (i.e., $\alpha(A) < 1/\mu(A)$ and $\alpha(A) \leq \widehat{q} - 1$), the Babel-function-based bound (1.30) is at least as tight as the bound in (1.27). However, when $\widehat{q} - 1 < \alpha(A)$, the bound (1.27) and the one in Theorem 1.4.7 cannot be worse than (1.30). Indeed, let us assume that $\alpha(A) < 1/\mu(A)$ and $\widehat{q} - 1 < \alpha(A) \leq p - 1$, where $p = \text{spark}(A)$. Then (1.27) indicates that

$$p = \left\lceil 1 + \frac{1}{\mu(A)} + \left(\frac{1}{\mu^{(2)}(A)} - \frac{1}{\mu(A)}\right)(1 - \alpha(A)\mu(A))\right\rceil + t^*$$

for some integer $t^* \geq 0$. This can be written as

$$\widehat{q} = \left[ 1 + \frac{1}{\mu(A)} + \left( \frac{1}{\mu^{(2)}(A)} - \frac{1}{\mu(A)} \right) (1 - \alpha(A)\mu(A)) \right] + t^* - (p - \widehat{q}).$$

If $t^* < p - \widehat{q}$, then the above equality implies that

$$\widehat{q} \leq 1 + \frac{1}{\mu(A)} + \left( \frac{1}{\mu^{(2)}(A)} - \frac{1}{\mu(A)} \right) (1 - \alpha(A)\mu(A)).$$

By Proposition 1.4.5, the right-hand side of the above is dominated by $T(A)$. Thus, as a lower bound of spark, (1.17) is not worse than (1.30) in such a case.

## 1.6 Notes

The spark was introduced by Donoho and Elad in [83]. This quantity is closely related to the Kruskal's rank of a matrix $A$, denoted by $\mathrm{krank}(A)$, which is the maximal number $k$ such that any subset of $k$ columns of $A$ are linearly independent. The Kruskal's rank was originally introduced in [148]. Clearly, $\mathrm{rank}(A) \geq \mathrm{krank}(A)$, and $\mathrm{spark}(A) = \mathrm{krank}(A) + 1$. In [117], Gorodnitsky and Rao studied the uniqueness issue of sparse solutions of linear systems under the so-called *unique representation property (URP)* which is related to a class of $m \times n$ matrices with Kruskal's rank equal to $m$. The spark provides a guaranteed uniqueness condition for the sparse solutions of systems of linear equations, as shown in Corollary 1.2.4. This result can follow instantly from Theorem 1.2.3 in this chapter which involves the support overlap of solutions of a system of linear equations. The spark is known in linear matroid theory as the girth of the vector matroid associated with the columns of a matrix (see Cho, Chen and Ding [64]), and it also appears in graph and coding theory (see Vardy [216] and Diestel [79]). Determining the girth of a binary matroid is NP-hard [216, 64], so is determining the spark of a general matrix, as shown in [208] by Tillmann and Pfetsch.

The spark is difficult to compute. This motivates one to identify certain computable lower bounds of the spark. The mutual coherence is one of those tools used to develop a computable sufficient condition for uniqueness of the sparse solutions of linear systems. The mutual coherence was first introduced by Dohono and Hu in [85], and it was later used in more general framework by many researchers (see Elad and Bruckstein [96], Gribonval and Nielsen [122], Donoho and Elad [83], Feuer and Nemirovski [100], Bruckstein, Donoho and Elad [37], Elad [95], and Foucart and Rauhut [108]). The mutual coherence is also a crucial tool for the performance and stability analysis of various compressed sensing algorithms, such as $\ell_1$-minimization [83, 100, 84, 107, 103, 174, 108], orthogonal matching pursuit [210, 211, 84, 68, 89, 228, 130], and thresholding algorithms [25, 26, 22, 104, 108, 228].

However, the mutual coherence criteria are restrictive in many situations. It is worth considering how such criteria can be enhanced. Remarkable improvements were made to some special matrices, especially to the union of orthogonal matrices. For instance, when $A$ is the union of Fourier and canonical bases, Donoho and Hu [85] showed that the solution of a linear system satisfying $\|x\|_0 < 1/\mu(A)$ must be the unique sparsest solution to the linear system. This result was extended to the union of generic orthogonal pairs of bases by Elad and Bruckstein [96]. When $A$ consists of $J$ concatenated orthogonal bases, Gribonval and Nielsen [122] proved that the uniqueness condition can be stated as $\|x\|_0 < \frac{1}{2}\left(1 + \frac{1}{J-1}\right)/\mu(A)$. For a general matrix $A$, it remains important from a mathematical point of view to improve the mutual-coherence-based uniqueness criteria, so that they can be applied to wider situations. One avenue is to consider the scaled mutual coherence discussed in Section 1.3, which enables us to obtain a tighter lower bound for the spark if a suitable scaling matrix is used. The notions of coherence rank and sub-mutual coherence were introduce by Zhao in [240]. The classic Brauder's Theorem was also first used in [240] to establish the enhanced results, such as Theorems 1.4.3, 1.4.7 and 1.5.3. From the discussion in this chapter, when the coherence rank of a matrix is low, the classic lower bound (1.13) for spark can be improved.

The spark and coherence are not the only tools that can be used to develop the uniqueness criteria for the sparse solutions of linear systems. Other sufficient criteria that serve different purposes in compressed sensing can also imply the uniqueness of the sparse solutions of linear systems, such as restricted isometry property (Candès and Tao [51]), null space property (NSP) (Cohen, Dahmen, and DeVore [65], and Zhang [237]), exact recovery condition (Tropp [210, 211]), range space property (RSP) of $A^T$ (Zhao [241, 242]), and verifiable conditions (Juditsky, Karzan, and Nemirovski [140]).

A common feature of mutual-coherence-based bounds for the spark is that all these bounds include $1/\mu(A)$ as a factor. This implies that the mutual coherence of the matrix should be made as low as possible. In fact, a sensing matrix with small mutual coherence is highly desirable in compressed sensing. This stimulates the sensing-matrix optimization which aims to choose or design a sensing matrix by minimizing mutual coherence in a certain way. Elad [94] adopted an averaged mutual coherence, instead of the standard mutual coherence, to deal with the optimal design of sensing matrices. Following Elad's work, various design approaches for sensing matrix have been proposed in the literature, including Duarte-Carvajalino and Sapiro [91], Zelnik-Manor et al. [232], Abolghasemi et al. [1], Bai et al. [14, 15], Sadeghi and Babaie-Zadeh [198], and Obermeier and Martinez-Lorenzo [182]. A common purpose of these approaches is to design the matrix such that its Gram matrix is as close as possible to a target Gram matrix in order to achieve the low mutual coherence of the matrix.

# Chapter 2

# Uniqueness of Solutions to $\ell_1$-Minimization Problems

Consider the standard $\ell_1$-minimization problem

$$\min_z\{\|z\|_1 : Az = b\}, \tag{2.1}$$

and the $\ell_1$-minimization problem with non-negative constraints

$$\min_z\{\|z\|_1 : Az = b, z \geq 0\}, \tag{2.2}$$

where $A \in \mathbb{R}^{m \times n}(m < n)$ and $b \in \mathbb{R}^m$ are given. We also consider the more general problem

$$\min_z\{\|z\|_1 : z \in P\}, \tag{2.3}$$

where $P \subseteq \mathbb{R}^n$ is a given polyhedral set. The solution of (2.1) is called *the least $\ell_1$-norm solution* of the linear system $Az = b$. The solution of (2.2) is called *the least $\ell_1$-norm non-negative solution* of the system $Az = b$, and the solution of (2.3) is referred to as *the least $\ell_1$-norm point* in polyhedron $P$. Uniqueness of solutions to these problems plays a vital role in many aspects of sparse optimization problems. For instance, the uniqueness of the solution to $\ell_1$-minimization is essential for the exact recovery of a sparse signal via $\ell_1$-minimization.

This chapter is devoted to the uniqueness characterization of the solutions to the problems (2.1)–(2.3). Since each of these problems is of independent interest and has their own broad applications in sparse signal and image recovery, we provide a detailed analysis for each of these problems. In the next two chapters, we will discuss how the uniqueness characterization made in this chapter can be used to deeply interpret the relationship of $\ell_0$- and $\ell_1$-minimization problems and to develop a theory for sparse signal recoveries.

We employ the classic strict complementary slackness property (SCSP) of linear programs to derive a necessary and sufficient condition for the uniqueness of solutions to the problems (2.1)–(2.3). Other applications of SCSP in sparse optimization will be found in later chapters.

## 2.1 Strict Complementary Slackness Property (SCSP)

The SCSP is a crucial tool for developing theory and algorithms for sparse optimization problems. Let us first recall the SCSP of linear programming (LP) problems. Consider the LP problem

$$\min_{x}\{c^T x: \ Qx = d, \ x \geq 0\}, \tag{2.4}$$

and its dual problem

$$\max_{y,s}\{d^T y: \ Q^T y + s = c, \ s \geq 0\}, \tag{2.5}$$

where $Q$ is a given $m' \times n$ matrix, and $d \in \mathbb{R}^{m'}$ and $c \in \mathbb{R}^n$ are two given vectors. Suppose that the problems (2.4) and (2.5) are feasible (i.e., their feasible sets are nonempty). Under this assumption, both problems admit finite optimal objective values. The solution of an LP can be completely characterized by the Karush-Kuhn-Tucker (KKT) optimality condition (see Karush [143], and Kuhn and Tucker [149]). That is, $x^*$ is a solution of (2.4) if and only if $x^*$ is feasible to (2.4), and there are vectors $y^* \in \mathbb{R}^{m'}$ and $s^* \in \mathbb{R}^n$ such that the following conditions hold:

$$Q^T y^* + s^* = c, \ s^* \geq 0, \ c^T x^* = d^T y^*.$$

The vector $(y^*, s^*)$, satisfying the condition above, is a solution to the problem (2.5). The condition $c^T x^* = d^T y^*$ indicates that there is no duality gap between the optimal values of the objectives of (2.4) and (2.5). This is called the strong duality property.

**Lemma 2.1.1** (Strong Duality) [114, 69] *$x^*$ and $(y^*, s^*)$ are the solutions to the problems (2.4) and (2.5), respectively, if and only if they satisfy the following conditions:*

$$Qx^* = d, \ x^* \geq 0, \ Q^T y^* + s^* = c, \ s^* \geq 0, \ c^T x^* = d^T y^*.$$

These conditions imply that

$$0 = c^T x^* - d^T y^* = (Q^T y^* + s^*)^T x^* - (Qx^*)^T y^* = (x^*)^T s^*.$$

Thus by the nonnegativity of $(x^*, s^*)$, the condition $c^T x^* = d^T y^*$ in Lemma 2.1.1 can be written as $(x^*)^T s^* = 0$, i.e.,

$$x_i^* s_i^* = 0, \ i = 1, \ldots, n,$$

which is called the *complementary slackness property*. Moreover, Goldman and Tucker [114] proved that when (2.4) and (2.5) are feasible, there always exists a solution pair $(x^*, (y^*, s^*))$ satisfying

$$x^* \geq 0, \ s^* \geq 0, \ (x^*)^T s^* = 0, \ x^* + s^* > 0.$$

This means that $x^*$ and $s^*$ are strictly complementary, in the sense that for each pair of components $(x_i^*, s_i^*)$, one and only one of them is equal to zero. This is called the *strict complementary slackness property* (SCSP). For any linear program, the strictly complementary solution always exists provided that the set of solutions of the LP problem is nonempty (equivalently, both (2.4) and (2.5) are feasible). We now summarize this classic result as follows. As this result will be frequently used in this and later chapters, a detailed proof of this result is also included here for completeness.

**Lemma 2.1.2** (Goldman and Tucker [114]) *If (2.4) and (2.5) are feasible, then there is a pair of strictly complementary solutions to (2.4) and (2.5).*

*Proof.* Under the assumption, the LP problems (2.4) and (2.5) have solutions with finite optimal objcctive value $\gamma^*$. The solution set of (2.5) can be written as:

$$\text{SOL} := \{(y,s): \ Q^T y + s = c, \ s \geq 0, \ d^T y \geq \gamma^*\}.$$

It suffices to prove the following statement: For each $1 \leq i \leq n$, there exists a solution pair, denoted by $(x^{(i)}, (y^{(i)}, s^{(i)}))$, satisfying that either the $i$th component of $x^{(i)}$ (denoted by $x_i^{(i)}$) is positive or the $i$th component of $s^{(i)}$ (denoted by $s_i^{(i)}$) is positive. Since the solution set of the LP problem is convex, $\bar{x}$ and $(\bar{y}, \bar{s})$ defined by

$$\bar{x} = \frac{1}{n} \sum_{i=1}^{n} x^{(i)}, \ (\bar{y}, \bar{s}) = \left( \frac{1}{n} \sum_{i=1}^{n} y^{(i)}, \frac{1}{n} \sum_{i=1}^{n} s^{(i)} \right)$$

are the solutions to the LP problems (2.4) and (2.5), respectively. If the above statement is true, then $\bar{x}$ and $\bar{s}$ are strictly complementary. We now prove the above statement. For each $1 \leq i \leq n$, we consider the following LP problem:

$$\min_{y,s}\{-s_i: \ -Q^T y - s = -c, \ s \geq 0, \ d^T y \geq \gamma^*\}, \tag{2.6}$$

where the feasible set of (2.6) is exactly the SOL, i.e., the solution set of (2.5).

*Case 1.* The problem (2.6) is unbounded (i.e., its objective has no finite lower bound in the feasible set) or the optimal objective value of (2.6) is negative. In this case, the problem (2.5) has a solution, denoted by $(y^{(i)}, s^{(i)})$, such that $s_i^{(i)} > 0$.

*Case 2.* Suppose that the optimal value of (2.6) is equal to zero. Consider the following Lagrangian dual of (2.6):

$$\max_{x,\tau}\{-c^T x + \gamma^* \tau : Qx - \tau d = 0, \ x \geq \mathbf{e}^{(i)}, \ \tau \geq 0\}.$$

By the strong duality, the solution $(x, \tau)$ of this problem satisfies the conditions

$$-c^T x + \gamma^* \tau = 0, \ Qx - \tau d = 0, \ x \geq \mathbf{e}^{(i)}, \ \tau \geq 0. \tag{2.7}$$

*Subcase (i):* $\tau > 0$. Then the above condition can be written as

$$c^T (x/\tau) = \gamma^*, \ Q(x/\tau) = d, \ (x/\tau) \geq \mathbf{e}^{(i)}/\tau \geq 0,$$

which shows that $x/\tau$ is a solution to the problem (2.4) and its $i$th component is positive.

*Subcase (ii):* $\tau = 0$. Then the system (2.7) is reduced to $c^T x = 0$, $Qx = 0$ and $x \geq \mathbf{e}^{(i)}$. Let $x^*$ be any solution of (2.4). Then $x^* + x$ is also a solution of (2.4) with $i$th component $x_i^* + x_i \geq 1$. $\square$

## 2.2 Least $\ell_1$-Norm Solution

Throughout this section, we assume that $x$ is a solution to the underdetermined linear system:

$$Az = b.$$

A necessary and sufficient condition for $x$ to be the unique least $\ell_1$-norm solution of this system can be developed via the SCSP.

### 2.2.1 Preliminary

Note that for any solution $z$ to the system $Az = b$. we have $A(z - x) = 0$. So $z$ can be represented as $z = x + u$, where $u \in \mathcal{N}(A) = \{u : Au = 0\}$, the null space of $A$. Thus we consider the following set:

$$C = \{u : \|u + x\|_1 \leq \|x\|_1, \ Au = 0\}.$$

Clearly, $x$ is the unique least $\ell_1$-norm solution to the system $Az = b$ if and only if $C = \{0\}$. By introducing variable $t \in \mathbb{R}_+^n$, the conditions in $C$ can be written as

$$|u + x| \leq t, \ \mathbf{e}^T t \leq \|x\|_1, \ Au = 0. \tag{2.8}$$

By introducing the non-negative variables $\alpha, \beta \in \mathbb{R}_+^n$ and $r \in \mathbb{R}_+$, the system in (2.8) can be written as

$$u + x + \alpha = t, \ u + x - \beta = -t, \ \mathbf{e}^T t + r = \|x\|_1, \ Au = 0, \tag{2.9}$$

where the variables $(t, \alpha, \beta, r)$ are non-negative, except $u$. Note that any $u$, satisfying (2.8), is bounded. In fact, for every $1 \le i \le n$, we have

$$-2\|x\|_1 \le -x_i - t_i \le u_i \le t_i - x_i \le 2\|x\|_1.$$

Define $\rho := 2\|x\|_1 + 1$. Then $v = \rho \mathbf{e} - u$ is non-negative for any $u$ satisfying (2.8). By the substitution $u = \rho \mathbf{e} - v$, we can write the system (2.9) as the one with all variables non-negative. That is,

$$\begin{cases} (\rho \mathbf{e} - v) + x + \alpha = t, \ (\rho \mathbf{e} - v) + x - \beta = -t, \ \mathbf{e}^T t + r = \|x\|_1, \\ A(\rho \mathbf{e} - v) = 0, \end{cases} \tag{2.10}$$

where the variables $(v, t, \alpha, \beta, r)$ are non-negative. Note that the set $\{z: A'z = b', z \ge 0\}$ with given $(A', b')$ is exactly the solution set of the following linear program with zero objective:

$$\min\{0^T z: A'z = b', z \ge 0\}.$$

Thus, the study of the solution of a linear system can be transformed into the study of the solution of an LP problem. We use this simple idea to characterize the uniqueness of the least $\ell_1$-norm solution of a system of linear equations. Therefore, we introduce the objective function $0^T t$ into (2.10), leading to the following LP problem:

$$\begin{aligned} \min_{(v,t,\alpha,\beta,r)} \quad & 0^T t \\ \text{s.t.} \quad & -v - t + \alpha = -x - \rho \mathbf{e}, \\ & v - t + \beta = x + \rho \mathbf{e}, \\ & -Av = -\rho A\mathbf{e}, \\ & \mathbf{e}^T t + r = \|x\|_1, \\ & v, \ t, \ \alpha, \ \beta \in \mathbb{R}_+^n, \ r \in \mathbb{R}_+, \end{aligned} \tag{2.11}$$

where the linear constraints can be written as

$$\begin{bmatrix} -I & -I & I & 0 & 0 \\ I & -I & 0 & I & 0 \\ -A & 0 & 0 & 0 & 0 \\ 0 & \mathbf{e}^T & 0 & 0 & 1 \end{bmatrix} \begin{bmatrix} v \\ t \\ \alpha \\ \beta \\ r \end{bmatrix} = \begin{bmatrix} -x - \rho \mathbf{e} \\ x + \rho \mathbf{e} \\ -\rho A\mathbf{e} \\ \|x\|_1 \end{bmatrix}.$$

The LP problem (2.11) is in the form of (2.4). The following observation is useful for later analysis in this section.

**Lemma 2.2.1** *$x$ is the unique least $\ell_1$-norm solution of the system $Az = b$ if and only if*

$$(v^*, t^*, \alpha^*, \beta^*, r^*) = (\rho \mathbf{e}, \ |x|, \ |x| - x, \ |x| + x, \ 0) \tag{2.12}$$

*is the unique solution to the LP problem (2.11).*

*Proof.* (i) Assume that $x$ is the unique least $\ell_1$-norm solution to the linear system $Az = b$. We prove that (2.12) is the unique solution to the problem (2.11). Let $(v,t,\alpha,\beta,r)$ be an arbitrary solution of (2.11), then it satisfies the following conditions:

$$
\begin{cases}
(\rho\mathbf{e}-v)-t+\alpha=-x \\
-(\rho\mathbf{e}-v)-t+\beta=x \\
A(\rho\mathbf{e}-v)=0 \\
\mathbf{e}^T t+r=\|x\|_1 \\
v,\,t,\,\alpha,\,\beta\in\mathbb{R}^n_+ \\
r\in\mathbb{R}_+.
\end{cases}
\tag{2.13}
$$

By setting $\tilde{v}=\rho\mathbf{e}-v$ and eliminating $\alpha,\beta$ and $r$ from the above conditions, we have

$$|\tilde{v}+x|\le t,\; A\tilde{v}=0,\; \mathbf{e}^T t\le\|x\|_1. \tag{2.14}$$

By further eliminating $t$ from the above conditions, we obtain

$$\|\tilde{v}+x\|_1\le\|x\|_1,\; A\tilde{v}=0,$$

which implies that $\tilde{x}=\tilde{v}+x$ is also the least $\ell_1$-norm solution to the linear system $Az=b$. Since $x$ is the unique least $\ell_1$-norm solution of the linear system (by assumption), we must have $\tilde{v}=0$. This in turn implies from (2.14) that $t=|x|$. Substituting $\rho\mathbf{e}-v=\tilde{v}=0$ and $t=|x|$ into (2.13), we can immediately obtain

$$\alpha=|x|-x,\; \beta=|x|+x,\; r=0.$$

Therefore, if $x$ is the unique solution to the system $Az=b$, then (2.12) is the only solution to the problem (2.11).

(ii) To prove the converse is also true, it is sufficient to show that if $x$ is not the unique least $\ell_1$-norm solution of the system $Az=b$, Then the solution of (2.11) is also not unique. Assume $\tilde{x}\ne x$ is also the least $\ell_1$-norm solution to the system $Az=b$ (and thus $\|\tilde{x}\|_1=\|x\|_1$). Note that $(v^*,t^*,\alpha^*,\beta^*,r^*)$ given in (2.12) is always a solution to the problem (2.11). We now construct another solution for the problem (2.11). By setting $\tilde{v}=\tilde{x}-x$, we have

$$A\tilde{v}=0,\; \|x\|_1=\|\tilde{x}\|_1=\|\tilde{v}+x\|_1.$$

By the definition of $\rho$ and $\tilde{v}$, we have

$$\|\tilde{v}\|_1=\|\tilde{x}-x\|_1\le\|x\|_1+\|\tilde{x}\|_1=2\|x\|_1\le\rho,$$

which indicates that $\rho\mathbf{e}-\tilde{v}\ge 0$. Therefore, it is easy to verify that the vector

$$
\begin{aligned}
(v,t,\alpha,\beta,r) &:= (\rho\mathbf{e}-\tilde{v},\; |x+\tilde{v}|,\; |x+\tilde{v}|-(x+\tilde{v}),\; |x+\tilde{v}|+(x+\tilde{v}),\; 0) \\
&= (\rho\mathbf{e}-\tilde{v},\; |\tilde{x}|,\; |\tilde{x}|-\tilde{x},\; |\tilde{x}|+\tilde{x},\; 0)
\end{aligned}
$$

satisfies the constraints in (2.11), and hence the above vector is a solution to the problem (2.11). Since $\tilde{v} \neq 0$, this solution is different from the one given in (2.12). □

The Lagrangian dual of (2.11) is given as follows:

$$\max_{(y,\bar{y},\hat{y},\omega)} \quad -(x+\rho e)^T(y-\bar{y}) - \rho e^T A^T \hat{y} + \omega \|x\|_1$$

s.t.

$$\begin{bmatrix} -I & I & -A^T & 0 \\ -I & -I & 0 & e \\ I & 0 & 0 & 0 \\ 0 & I & 0 & 0 \\ 0 & 0 & 0 & 1 \end{bmatrix} \begin{pmatrix} y \\ \bar{y} \\ \hat{y} \\ w \end{pmatrix} \leq \begin{bmatrix} 0 \\ 0 \\ 0 \\ 0 \\ 0 \end{bmatrix}.$$

That is,

$$\text{(DLP)} \quad \max_{(y,\bar{y},\hat{y},\omega)} \quad -(x+\rho e)^T(y-\bar{y}) - \rho e^T A^T \hat{y} + \omega \|x\|_1$$

$$\text{s.t.} \quad -(y-\bar{y}) - A^T \hat{y} \leq 0 \tag{2.15}$$
$$-(y+\bar{y}) + \omega e \leq 0 \tag{2.16}$$
$$y \leq 0 \tag{2.17}$$
$$\bar{y} \leq 0 \tag{2.18}$$
$$\omega \leq 0, \tag{2.19}$$

where $y,\bar{y} \in \mathbb{R}^n, \hat{y} \in \mathbb{R}^m$ and $\omega \in \mathbb{R}$ are the dual variables. Let $s^{(1)}$, $s^{(2)}$, $s^{(3)}$, $s^{(4)} \in \mathbb{R}^n_+$ and $s \in \mathbb{R}_+$ be the dual slack variables associated with the constraints (2.15) through (2.19), respectively, i.e.,

$$s^{(1)} = (y-\bar{y}) + A^T\hat{y}, \ s^{(2)} = (y+\bar{y}) - \omega e, \ s^{(3)} = -y, \ s^{(4)} = -\bar{y}, \ s = -\omega. \tag{2.20}$$

### 2.2.2 Necessary Condition (I): Range Space Property of $A^T$

We now show that if $x$ is the unique least $\ell_1$-norm solution to the system $Az = b$, then $\mathcal{R}(A^T)$, the range space of $A^T$, must satisfy certain properties. Throughout this chapter, we use the following notation:

$$S_+(x) = \{i : x_i > 0\}, \ S_-(x) = \{i : x_i < 0\}, \ S_0(x) = \{i : x_i = 0\}.$$

**Lemma 2.2.2** *If $x$ is the unique least $\ell_1$-norm solution to the system $Az = b$, then there exist $y,\bar{y} \in \mathbb{R}^n$ and a number $\omega < 0$ satisfying $y - \bar{y} \in \mathcal{R}(A^T)$ and*

$$\begin{cases} \omega < y_i + \bar{y}_i, \ y_i < 0 \text{ and } \bar{y}_i < 0 & \text{for all } i \in S_0(x), \\ y_i = 0 \text{ and } \bar{y}_i = \omega & \text{for all } i \in S_-(x), \\ y_i = \omega \text{ and } \bar{y}_i = 0 & \text{for all } i \in S_+(x). \end{cases} \tag{2.21}$$

*Proof.* Assume that $x$ is the unique least $\ell_1$-norm solution to the system $Az = b$. By Lemma 2.2.1, the problem (2.11) has a unique solution given as

$$(v^*, t^*, \alpha^*, \beta^*, r^*) = (\rho \mathbf{e}, |x|, |x| - x, |x| + x, 0). \quad (2.22)$$

Since both (2.11) and its dual problem (DLP) are feasible, by Lemma 2.1.2, there exists a solution $(y, \bar{y}, \hat{y}, \omega)$ of (DLP) such that $(v^*, t^*, \alpha^*, \beta^*, r^*)$ and $(y, \bar{y}, \hat{y}, \omega)$ form a pair of strictly complementary solutions of linear programs (2.11) and (DLP). As defined in (2.20), $s^{(1)}, s^{(2)}, s^{(3)}, s^{(4)} \in \mathbb{R}^n_+$ and $s \in \mathbb{R}_+$ are the slack variables of (DLP). By the SCSP, we have

$$(v^*)^T s^{(1)} = 0, \ (t^*)^T s^{(2)} = 0, \ (\alpha^*)^T s^{(3)} = 0, \ (\beta^*)^T s^{(4)} = 0, \ r^* s = 0, \quad (2.23)$$

and

$$v^* + s^{(1)} > 0, \ t^* + s^{(2)} > 0, \ \alpha^* + s^{(3)} > 0, \ \beta^* + s^{(4)} > 0, \ r^* + s > 0. \quad (2.24)$$

First, since $v^* = \rho \mathbf{e} > 0$, we must have $s^{(1)} = 0$, i.e.,

$$A^T \hat{y} = -(y - \bar{y}), \quad (2.25)$$

which implies that $y - \bar{y} \in \mathcal{R}(A^T)$. From (2.22), we see that $r^* = 0$ and

$$\begin{cases} t_i^* = x_i > 0, \ \alpha_i^* = 0 \ \text{and} \ \beta_i^* = 2x_i > 0 & \text{for all } i \in S_+(x), \\ t_i^* = |x_i| > 0, \ \alpha_i^* = 2|x_i| > 0 \ \text{and} \ \beta_i^* = 0 & \text{for all } i \in S_-(x), \\ t_i^* = 0, \ \alpha_i^* = 0 \ \text{and} \ \beta_i^* = 0 & \text{for all } i \in S_0(x). \end{cases}$$

Thus from (2.23) and (2.24), we conclude that $s > 0$ and

$$\begin{cases} s_i^{(2)} = 0, \ s_i^{(3)} > 0 \ \text{and} \ s_i^{(4)} = 0 & \text{for all } i \in S_+(x), \\ s_i^{(2)} = 0, \ s_i^{(3)} = 0 \ \text{and} \ s_i^{(4)} > 0 & \text{for all } i \in S_-(x), \\ s_i^{(2)} > 0, \ s_i^{(3)} > 0 \ \text{and} \ s_i^{(4)} > 0 & \text{for all } i \in S_0(x). \end{cases}$$

By the definition of these slack variables, the solution vector $(y, \bar{y}, \hat{y}, \omega)$ of (DLP) satisfies (2.25), $\omega = -s < 0$ and

$$\begin{cases} \omega - (y_i + \bar{y}_i) = 0, \ y_i < 0 \ \text{and} \ \bar{y}_i = 0 & \text{for all } i \in S_+(x), \\ \omega - (y_i + \bar{y}_i) = 0, \ y_i = 0 \ \text{and} \ \bar{y}_i < 0 & \text{for all } i \in S_-(x), \\ \omega - (y_i + \bar{y}_i) < 0, \ y_i < 0 \ \text{and} \ \bar{y}_i < 0 & \text{for all } i \in S_0(x). \end{cases}$$

These are the conditions given in (2.21). □

Lemma 2.2.2 provides a necessary condition for $x$ to be the unique least $\ell_1$-norm solution to the system $Az = b$. This condition arises naturally from the SCSP, and can be restated more concisely.

**Lemma 2.2.3** *Let $x \in \mathbb{R}^n$ be given. The following two statements are equivalent:*

(i) *There are vectors $y, \bar{y} \in \mathbb{R}^n$ and $\omega \in \mathbb{R}$ satisfying (2.21) and $\omega < 0$ and $y - \bar{y} \in \mathcal{R}(A^T)$.*

(ii) *There is a vector $\eta \in \mathcal{R}(A^T)$ such that $\eta_i = 1$ for all $i \in S_+(x)$, $\eta_i = -1$ for all $i \in S_-(x)$, and $|\eta_i| < 1$ for all $i \in S_0(x)$.*

*Proof.* (i) $\Rightarrow$ (ii). Assume that $(y, \bar{y}, \omega)$, where $\omega < 0$ and $y - \bar{y} \in \mathcal{R}(A^T)$, satisfies (2.21). Set $\eta = (y - \bar{y})/\omega$. We immediately see that $\eta \in \mathcal{R}(A^T)$, and $\eta_i = (y_i - \bar{y}_i)/\omega = 1$ for every $x_i > 0$ (since $y_i = \omega$ and $\bar{y}_i = 0$ for this case). Similarly, we have $\eta_i = -1$ for every $i$ with $x_i < 0$. For $x_i = 0$, since $\omega < y_i + \bar{y}_i$, $y_i < 0$ and $\bar{y}_i < 0$, we have $|y_i + \bar{y}_i| < |\omega|$. Thus,

$$|\eta_i| = |y_i - \bar{y}_i|/|\omega| \le |y_i + \bar{y}_i|/|\omega| < 1.$$

(ii) $\Rightarrow$ (i). Assume that there is a vector $\eta \in \mathcal{R}(A^T)$ such that $\eta_i = 1$ for all $i \in S_+(x)$, $\eta_i = -1$ for all $i \in S_-(x)$, and $|\eta_i| < 1$ for all $i \in S_0(x)$. We now construct a vector $(y, \bar{y}, \omega)$ satisfying (2.21) and $\omega < 0$ and $y - \bar{y} \in \mathcal{R}(A^T)$. Indeed, we first set $\omega = -1$, and then set $y_i = 0$ and $\bar{y}_i = -1$ for $i \in S_-(x)$, and $y_i = -1$ and $\bar{y}_i = 0$ for $i \in S_+(x)$. For those $i$ with $x_i = 0$, since $|\eta_i| < 1$, we choose the number $\varepsilon_i$ such that $0 < \varepsilon_i < (1 - |\eta_i|)/2$. Then we define $y_i$ and $\bar{y}_i$ as follows:

$$\begin{cases} y_i = -\varepsilon_i - \eta_i \text{ and } \bar{y}_i = -\varepsilon_i & \text{if } \eta_i > 0, \\ y_i = -\varepsilon_i \text{ and } y_i = \eta_i - \varepsilon_i & \text{otherwise.} \end{cases} \quad (2.26)$$

From the above construction, it is easy to see that $y - \bar{y} = -\eta \in \mathcal{R}(A^T)$. To verify that $(y, \bar{y}, \omega)$ satisfies (2.21), by the construction of $(y, \bar{y})$, it is sufficient to show that $\omega < y_i + \bar{y}_i$, $y_i < 0$, $\bar{y}_i < 0$ for all $x_i = 0$. Indeed, (2.26) implies that $y_i$ and $\bar{y}_i$ are negative and that

$$0 > y_i + \bar{y}_i = \begin{cases} -2\varepsilon_i - \eta_i & \text{if } \eta_i > 0 \\ -2\varepsilon_i + \eta_i & \text{otherwise} \end{cases} = -2\varepsilon_i - |\eta_i| > -1 = \omega,$$

where the last inequality follows from the choice of $\varepsilon_i$. Thus, the constructed vector $(y, \bar{y}, \omega)$ satisfies the conditions in (2.21). □

For the convenience of later discussions, we introduce the following notion.

**Definition 2.2.4** *The range space property (RSP) of $A^T$ at $x$ is satisfied if there is a vector $\eta \in \mathcal{R}(A^T)$ such that*

$$\begin{cases} \eta_i &= 1 & \text{for all} & i \in S_+(x), \\ \eta_i &= -1 & \text{for all} & i \in S_-(x), \\ |\eta_i| &< 1 & \text{for all} & i \in S_0(x). \end{cases} \quad (2.27)$$

The RSP of $A^T$ at $x$ is easy to verify by simply solving the LP problem

$$\min\{\tau: A_{S_+}^T y = \mathbf{e}_{S_+}, A_{S_-}^T y = -\mathbf{e}_{S_-}, A_{S_0}^T y = \eta_{S_0}, \|\eta_{S_0}\|_\infty \le \tau\}, \quad (2.28)$$

where, $S_+$, $S_-$ and $S_0$ are the short for $S_+(x)$, $S_-(x)$ and $S_0(x)$, respectively. We immediately have the following fact.

**Lemma 2.2.5** *The RSP of $A^T$ at $x$ is satisfied if and only if $\tau^* < 1$, where $\tau^*$ is the optimal value of the LP problem (2.28).*

Using the above notion and combining Lemmas 2.2.2 and 2.2.3 yields the following result.

**Theorem 2.2.6** *If $x$ is the unique least $\ell_1$-norm solution to the system $Az = b$, then the RSP of $A^T$ at $x$ is satisfied.*

## 2.2.3 Necessary Condition (II): Full-Column-Rank Property

In order to completely characterize the uniqueness of the least $\ell_1$-norm solution of the system $Az = b$, we need to establish another necessary condition. Still, let $x$ be a solution of this system. For simplicity, we also use $S_+, S_-$ and $S_0$ to denote $S_+(x), S_-(x)$ and $S_0(x)$, respectively. We first have the following observation.

**Lemma 2.2.7** *The matrix*

$$H = \begin{bmatrix} A_{S_+} & A_{S_-} \\ -\mathbf{e}_{S_+}^T & \mathbf{e}_{S_-}^T \end{bmatrix} \quad (2.29)$$

*has full column rank if and only if the matrix below has full column rank*

$$E = \begin{bmatrix} -I_{|S_+|} & 0 & -I_{|S_+|} & 0 \\ 0 & I_{|S_-|} & 0 & -I_{|S_-|} \\ A_{S_+} & A_{S_-} & 0 & 0 \\ 0 & 0 & \mathbf{e}_{S_+}^T & \mathbf{e}_{S_-}^T \end{bmatrix}, \quad (2.30)$$

*where $I_{|J|}$ denotes the $|J| \times |J|$ identity matrix and 0's denote zero matrices with suitable sizes.*

*Proof.* Adding the first $|S_+| + |S_-|$ rows of $E$ into its last row yields the matrix

$$E' := \begin{bmatrix} -I_{|S_+|} & 0 & -I_{|S_+|} & 0 \\ 0 & I_{|S_-|} & 0 & -I_{|S_-|} \\ A_{S_+} & A_{S_-} & 0 & 0 \\ -\mathbf{e}_{S_+}^T & \mathbf{e}_{S_-}^T & 0 & 0 \end{bmatrix} = \begin{bmatrix} E_1 & E_2 \\ H & 0 \end{bmatrix},$$

where $E_1 = \begin{bmatrix} -I_{|S_+|} & 0 \\ 0 & I_{|S_-|} \end{bmatrix}$ and $E_2 = \begin{bmatrix} -I_{|S_+|} & 0 \\ 0 & -I_{|S_-|} \end{bmatrix}$. Note that $E_2$ is a nonsingular square matrix, and the lower-left block of $E'$ is $H$. Any elementary row operations do not change the (column) rank of a matrix. Thus, $H$ has full column rank if and only if $E$ has full column rank. □

We now prove the next necessary condition for the uniqueness of the least $\ell_1$-norm solution.

**Theorem 2.2.8** *If $x$ is the unique least $\ell_1$-norm solution to the system $Az = b$, then the matrix $H$, given by (2.29), has full column rank.*

*Proof.* We show this result by contradiction. Assume that the columns of $H$ are linearly dependent. Then by Lemma 2.2.7, the columns of the matrix $E$ in (2.30) are also linearly dependent. Hence, there exists a non-zero vector $d = (d_1, d_2, d_3, d_4)$ with $d_1, d_3 \in \mathbb{R}^{|S_+|}$ and $d_2, d_4 \in \mathbb{R}^{|S_-|}$ such that

$$Ed = \begin{bmatrix} -I_{|S_+|} & 0 & -I_{|S_+|} & 0 \\ 0 & I_{|S_-|} & 0 & -I_{|S_-|} \\ A_{S_+} & A_{S_-} & 0 & 0 \\ 0 & 0 & e_{S_+}^T & e_{S_-}^T \end{bmatrix} \begin{pmatrix} d_1 \\ d_2 \\ d_3 \\ d_4 \end{pmatrix} = 0. \tag{2.31}$$

Since $d \neq 0$, the above system implies that $(d_1, d_2) \neq 0$. Let $z = (z_1, z_2, z_3, z_4)$, where

$$z_1 = \rho e_{S_+} > 0, \ z_2 = \rho e_{S_-} > 0, \ z_3 = x_{S_+} > 0, \ z_4 = -x_{S_-} > 0. \tag{2.32}$$

Then $z$ satisfies

$$\begin{bmatrix} -I_{|S_+|} & 0 & -I_{|S_+|} & 0 \\ 0 & I_{|S_-|} & 0 & -I_{|S_-|} \\ A_{S_+} & A_{S_-} & 0 & 0 \\ 0 & 0 & e_{S_+}^T & e_{S_-}^T \end{bmatrix} \begin{bmatrix} z_1 \\ z_2 \\ z_3 \\ z_4 \end{bmatrix} = \begin{bmatrix} -x_{S_+} - \rho e_{S_+} \\ x_{S_-} + \rho e_{S_-} \\ \rho(A_{S_+} e_{S_+} + A_{S_-} e_{S_-}) \\ \|x_{S_+}\|_1 + \|x_{S_-}\|_1 \end{bmatrix}. \tag{2.33}$$

Note that $z > 0$ and $d \neq 0$. There is a small number $\lambda \neq 0$ such that

$$\tilde{z} = (\tilde{z}_1, \tilde{z}_2, \tilde{z}_3, \tilde{z}_4) = z + \lambda d = (z_1 + \lambda d_1, \ldots, z_4 + \lambda d_4) \geq 0 \tag{2.34}$$

is also a non-negative solution to the system (2.33). Clearly, $\tilde{z} \neq z$ since $\lambda \neq 0$ and $d \neq 0$. We now prove that the solution of the problem (2.11) is not unique. As we have pointed out in previous section, the vector

$$(v, t, \alpha, \beta, r) = (\rho e, \ |x|, \ |x| - x, \ |x| + x, \ r = 0)$$

is always a solution to the problem (2.11). We now construct another solution to this problem. Let $\tilde{r} = 0$ and let $\tilde{v}, \tilde{t}, \tilde{\alpha}, \tilde{\beta} \in \mathbb{R}^n_+$ be defined as follows:

$$\begin{bmatrix} \tilde{v}_{S_+} \\ \tilde{v}_{S_-} \\ \tilde{v}_{S_0} \end{bmatrix} = \begin{bmatrix} \tilde{z}_1 \\ \tilde{z}_2 \\ \rho e_{S_0} \end{bmatrix} \in \mathbb{R}^n_+, \quad \begin{bmatrix} \tilde{t}_{S_+} \\ \tilde{t}_{S_-} \\ \tilde{t}_{S_0} \end{bmatrix} = \begin{bmatrix} \tilde{z}_3 \\ \tilde{z}_4 \\ 0 \end{bmatrix} \in \mathbb{R}^n_+,$$

$$
\begin{bmatrix} \tilde{\alpha}_{S_+} \\ \tilde{\alpha}_{S_-} \\ \tilde{\alpha}_{S_0} \end{bmatrix} = \begin{bmatrix} 0 \\ 2\tilde{z}_4 \\ 0 \end{bmatrix} \in \mathbb{R}^n_+, \quad \begin{bmatrix} \tilde{\beta}_{S_+} \\ \tilde{\beta}_{S_-} \\ \tilde{\beta}_{S_0} \end{bmatrix} = \begin{bmatrix} 2\tilde{z}_3 \\ 0 \\ 0 \end{bmatrix} \in \mathbb{R}^n_+.
$$

The nonnegativity of $(\tilde{v}, \tilde{t}, \tilde{\alpha}, \tilde{\beta}, \tilde{r})$ follows from (2.34). We now show that these vectors satisfy the constraints of (2.11). This can be verified straightaway. By (2.31), (2.33) and the above definition of $(\tilde{v}, \tilde{t}, \tilde{\alpha}, \tilde{\beta}, \tilde{r})$, we see that

$$
\rho \begin{bmatrix} \mathbf{e}_{S_+} \\ \mathbf{e}_{S_-} \\ \mathbf{e}_{S_0} \end{bmatrix} - \begin{bmatrix} \tilde{v}_{S_+} \\ \tilde{v}_{S_-} \\ \tilde{v}_{S_0} \end{bmatrix} - \begin{bmatrix} \tilde{t}_{S_+} \\ \tilde{t}_{S_-} \\ \tilde{t}_{S_0} \end{bmatrix} + \begin{bmatrix} \tilde{\alpha}_{S_+} \\ \tilde{\alpha}_{S_-} \\ \tilde{\alpha}_{S_0} \end{bmatrix}
$$
$$
= \begin{bmatrix} \rho \mathbf{e}_{S_+} - z_1 - z_3 - \lambda(d_1 + d_3) \\ \rho \mathbf{e}_{S_-} - z_2 + z_4 - \lambda(d_2 - d_4) \\ 0 \end{bmatrix} = - \begin{bmatrix} x_{S_+} \\ x_{S_-} \\ 0 \end{bmatrix},
$$

where the last equality follows from (2.32) and $d_1 + d_3 = 0$ and $d_2 - d_4 = 0$ which follows from (2.31). Thus $(\rho \mathbf{e} - \tilde{v}) - \tilde{t} + \tilde{\alpha} = -x$. So the vectors satisfy the first constraint in (2.11). Similarly, other constraints in (2.11) can be verified by using (2.31) and (2.33) and the above choice of $(\tilde{v}, \tilde{t}, \tilde{\alpha}, \tilde{\beta}, \tilde{r})$. Thus $(\tilde{v}, \tilde{t}, \tilde{\alpha}, \tilde{\beta}, \tilde{r})$ is also a solution to the problem (2.11). Note that $(d_1, d_2) \neq 0$ and

$$
\begin{bmatrix} \tilde{v}_{S_+} \\ \tilde{v}_{S_-} \\ \tilde{v}_{S_0} \end{bmatrix} = \begin{bmatrix} \tilde{z}_1 \\ \tilde{z}_2 \\ \rho \mathbf{e}_{S_0} \end{bmatrix} = \begin{bmatrix} z_1 \\ z_2 \\ \rho \mathbf{e}_{S_0} \end{bmatrix} + \lambda \begin{bmatrix} d_1 \\ d_2 \\ 0 \end{bmatrix} = \rho \mathbf{e} + \lambda \begin{bmatrix} d_1 \\ d_2 \\ 0 \end{bmatrix}.
$$

The last equality follows from (2.32). It implies that $\tilde{v} \neq v$. Therefore, the problem (2.11) has two different solutions: $(v, t, \alpha, \beta, r) \neq (\tilde{v}, \tilde{t}, \tilde{\alpha}, \tilde{\beta}, \tilde{r})$. By the assumption of the theorem, $x$ is the unique least $\ell_1$-norm solution to the linear system. By Lemma 2.2.1, this implies that (2.11) has a unique solution, leading to a contradiction. As a result, the matrix $H$ in (2.29) must have full column rank. □

Merging Theorems 2.2.6 and 2.2.8 immediately yields the next result.

**Theorem 2.2.9** *If $x$ is the unique least $\ell_1$-norm solution to the system $Ax = b$, then the matrix*

$$
H = \begin{bmatrix} A_{S_+} & A_{S_-} \\ -\mathbf{e}_{S_+}^T & \mathbf{e}_{S_-}^T \end{bmatrix}
$$

*has full column rank and the RSP of $A^T$ at $x$ is satisfied.*

## 2.2.4 Sufficient Condition

We now prove that the necessary condition in Theorem 2.2.9 is also sufficient to ensure that $x$ is the unique least $\ell_1$-norm solution to the system of linear equations. We first prove the following property of (DLP).

**Lemma 2.2.10** *Let $x \in \mathbb{R}^n$ be a given vector. If $y, \bar{y} \in \mathbb{R}^n$ with $y - \bar{y} \in \mathcal{R}(A^T)$ and a scalar $\omega < 0$ satisfy the conditions in (2.21), then $(y, \bar{y}, \omega)$ together with a vector*

$$\hat{y} \in \{u : y - \bar{y} = -A^T u\}$$

*is a solution of (DLP).*

*Proof.* Let $(y, \bar{y}, \omega)$ satisfy the assumption of this lemma. Let $\hat{y}$ be a vector in the set $\{u : y - \bar{y} = -A^T u\}$. Then $(y, \bar{y}, \hat{y}, \omega)$ satisfies the following system:

$$
\begin{cases}
-(y - \bar{y}) = A^T \hat{y}, & \\
-(y_i + \bar{y}_i) + \omega = 0, \ y_i < 0 \text{ and } \bar{y}_i = 0 & \text{if } i \in S_+(x), \\
-(y_i + \bar{y}_i) + \omega = 0, \ y_i = 0 \text{ and } \bar{y}_i < 0 & \text{if } i \in S_-(x), \qquad (2.35) \\
-(y_i + \bar{y}_i) + \omega < 0, \ y_i < 0 \text{ and } \bar{y}_i < 0 & \text{if } i \in S_0(x), \\
\omega < 0. &
\end{cases}
$$

Clearly, the conditions in (2.35) imply that $(y, \bar{y}, \hat{y}, \omega)$ satisfies the constraints (2.15)–(2.19), so it is a feasible point of (DLP). Notice that the optimal value of the objective of (2.11) is zero. By Lemma 2.1.1 , the maximum value of the objective of (DLP) is also zero. To prove the optimality of $(y, \bar{y}, \hat{y}, \omega)$, it is sufficient to verify that at this point the objective of (DLP) attains the maximum value. Indeed,

$$
\begin{aligned}
-(x + \rho \mathbf{e})^T (y - \bar{y}) - \rho \mathbf{e}^T A^T \hat{y} + \omega \|x\|_1 &= -x^T (y - \bar{y}) + \omega \|x\|_1 \\
&= \sum_{i \in S_+(x)} -x_i(y_i - \bar{y}_i) + \sum_{i \in S_-(x)} -x_i(y_i - \bar{y}_i) + \omega \|x\|_1 \\
&= \sum_{i \in S_+(x)} -x_i(\omega - 0) + \sum_{i \in S_-(x)} -x_i(0 - \omega) + \omega \|x\|_1 \\
&= (-\omega) \left( \sum_{i \in S_+(x)} x_i + \sum_{i \in S_-(x)} -x_i \right) + \omega \|x\|_1 \\
&= 0,
\end{aligned}
$$

where the first equality follows from the first condition in (2.35), and the third equality follows from the second and third conditions in (2.35). Thus $(y, \bar{y}, \hat{y}, \omega)$ is a solution of (DLP). □

We are now ready to prove the sufficiency of the condition in Theorem 2.2.9.

**Theorem 2.2.11** *Let $x$ be a solution to the linear system $Az = b$. If the RSP of $A^T$ at $x$ is satisfied and the matrix (2.29) has full column rank, then $x$ is the unique least $\ell_1$-norm solution to the linear system.*

*Proof.* By the assumption, the RSP of $A^T$ at $x$ is satisfied. Then by Lemma 2.2.3, there is a vector $(y, \bar{y}, \omega)$ with $\omega < 0$ and $y - \bar{y} \in \mathcal{R}(A^T)$ such that (2.21) is satisfied. By Lemma 2.2.10, the vector $(y, \bar{y}, \omega)$ with a vector $\hat{y} \in \{u : y - \bar{y} = -A^T u\}$ is a solution of (DLP). Since $(y, \bar{y}, \omega)$ satisfies (2.21), we have that

$$
\begin{cases}
y_i = \omega < 0 & \text{for all } i \in S_+(x), \\
\bar{y}_i = \omega < 0 & \text{for all } i \in S_-(x), \\
\omega < y_i + \bar{y}_i, \; y_i < 0 \text{ and } \bar{y}_i < 0 & \text{for all } i \in S_0(x).
\end{cases}
\tag{2.36}
$$

As defined in (2.20), $(s^{(1)}, s^{(2)}, s^{(3)}, s^{(4)}, s) \in \mathbb{R}^{4n+1}_+$ denote the slack variables associated with the constraints (2.15)–(2.19) of (DLP), respectively. From (2.36), we see that the following components of these slack variables are positive:

$$
\begin{cases}
s_i^{(2)} = y_i + \bar{y}_i - \omega > 0, \; s_i^{(3)} = -y_i > 0 \text{ and } s_i^{(4)} = -\bar{y}_i > 0 & \text{for } i \in S_0(x), \\
s_i^{(3)} = -y_i = -\omega > 0 & \text{for } i \in S_+(x), \\
s_i^{(4)} = -\bar{y}_i = -\omega > 0 & \text{for } i \in S_-(x), \\
s = -\omega > 0.
\end{cases}
$$

We now prove that under the assumption of the theorem, the problem (2.11) has a unique solution. To this goal, let $(v, t, \alpha, \beta, r)$ be an arbitrary solution of (2.11). By the complementary slackness condition, the positiveness of the above components of the dual slack variables implies that the corresponding components of $(v, t, \alpha, \beta, r)$ must be zero. Therefore,

$$
t_i = 0, \; \alpha_i = 0 \text{ and } \beta_i = 0 \quad \text{for all } i \in S_0(x), \tag{2.37}
$$
$$
\alpha_i = 0 \quad \text{for all } i \in S_+(x), \tag{2.38}
$$
$$
\beta_i = 0 \quad \text{for all } i \in S_-(x), \tag{2.39}
$$
$$
r = 0. \tag{2.40}
$$

By (2.37), it follows from the first constraint in (2.11) that $\rho - v_i = t_i - \alpha_i - x_i = 0$ for every $i \in S_0(x)$, i.e., $v_i = \rho$ for all $i \in S_0(x)$. Since $(v, t, \alpha, \beta, r)$ satisfies the constraints in (2.11), by substituting these known components of $(v, t, \alpha, \beta, r)$ into the constraints in (2.11), we see that the remaining components $(v_{S_+}, v_{S_-}, t_{S_+}, t_{S_-}, \alpha_{S_-}, \beta_{S_+})$ of the solution $(v, t, \alpha, \beta, r)$ satisfy the following conditions:

$$
-v_{S_+} - t_{S_+} = -x_{S_+} - \rho e_{S_+}, \tag{2.41}
$$
$$
-v_{S_-} - t_{S_-} + \alpha_{S_-} = -x_{S_-} - \rho e_{S_-}, \tag{2.42}
$$
$$
v_{S_+} - t_{S_+} + \beta_{S_+} = x_{S_+} + \rho e_{S_+}, \tag{2.43}
$$
$$
v_{S_-} - t_{S_-} = x_{S_-} + \rho e_{S_-}, \tag{2.44}
$$
$$
A_{S_+} v_{S_+} + A_{S_-} v_{S_-} = \rho (A_{S_+} e_{S_+} + A_{S_-} e_{S_-}),
$$
$$
e_{S_+}^T t_{S_+} + e_{S_-}^T t_{S_-} = \|x\|_1,
$$
$$
(v_{S_+}, v_{S_-}, t_{S_+}, t_{S_-}, \alpha_{S_-}, \beta_{S_+}) \geq 0.
$$

By combining (2.41) and (2.43) and combining (2.42) and (2.44), we immediately see that $\alpha_{S_-}$ and $\beta_{S_+}$ are uniquely determined by $t_{S_-}$ and $t_{S_+}$, i.e.,

$$\alpha_{S_-} = 2t_{S_-}, \ \beta_{S_+} = 2t_{S_+}. \tag{2.45}$$

Thus substituting (2.45) into (2.42) and (2.43) leads to the reduced system

$$\begin{aligned}
-v_{S_+} - t_{S_+} &= -x_{S_+} - \rho e_{S_+}, \\
v_{S_-} - t_{S_-} &= x_{S_-} + \rho e_{S_-}, \\
A_{S_+} v_{S_+} + A_{S_-} v_{S_-} &= \rho(A_{S_+} e_{S_+} + A_{S_-} e_{S_-}), \\
e_{S_+}^T t_{S_+} + e_{S_-}^T t_{S_-} &= \|x\|_1, \\
(v_{S_+}, v_{S_-}, t_{S_+}, t_{S_-}) &\geq 0,
\end{aligned} \tag{2.46}$$

where the coefficient matrix of the system of linear equations is given by (2.30). By Lemma 2.2.7, this coefficient matrix has full column rank since the matrix (2.29) has full column rank. Note that

$$v_{S_+} = \rho e_{S_+}, \ v_{S_-} = \rho e_{S_-}, \ t_{S_+} = x_{S_+}, \ t_{S_-} = -x_{S_-} \tag{2.47}$$

is a solution to the system (2.46). Therefore, it is the unique solution to this system since the coefficient matrix has full column rank. In summary, under the assumption of the theorem, the solution $(v, t, \alpha, \beta, r)$ of (2.11) is uniquely determined by (2.37)–(2.40), (2.45) and (2.47). It is easy to see that this solution is exactly the one given by

$$(v, t, \alpha, \beta, r) = (\rho e, |x|, |x| - x, |x| + x, 0).$$

Thus, the problem (2.11) has a unique solution. By Lemma 2.2.1, $x$ must be the unique least $\ell_1$-norm solution to the system $Ax = b$. □

Clearly, if $(A_{S_+}, A_{S_-})$ (equally, $A_{\text{supp}(x)}$) has full column rank, so is the matrix $H$ defined in (2.29). Thus, an immediate consequence of Theorem 2.2.11 is the following result due to Fuchs [111].

**Corollary 2.2.12** (Fuchs [111]) *If the system $Az = b$ has a solution $x$ satisfying (2.27) and the columns of $A$ corresponding to the support of $x$ are linearly independent, then $x$ is the unique least $\ell_1$-norm solution to the system $Az = b$.*

This sufficient condition was first obtained by Fuchs [111] through the tool of convex quadratic optimization, instead of the SCSP of an LP problem. As we have shown above, a unique feature of the SCSP-based analysis is that the SCSP yields both the sufficiency of derived uniqueness conditions and the necessity of these conditions, leading to a complete characterization for the uniqueness of the least $\ell_1$-norm solution of a linear system (see the discussion in the next section for details).

It is also worth mentioning that although the linear independence of the columns of $A_{\mathrm{supp}(x)}$ implies that the columns of $H$ in (2.29) are linearly independent, the converse is not true in general. In fact, when $H$ has full column rank, the columns of $A_{\mathrm{supp}(x)}$ can be linearly dependent. For instance, let

$$
A_{S_+} = \begin{bmatrix} -1 & 1 \\ 1 & -1 \\ 0 & 0 \end{bmatrix}, \; A_{S_-} = \begin{bmatrix} 0 \\ 0 \\ 1 \end{bmatrix}, \; H = \begin{bmatrix} A_{S_+} & A_{S_-} \\ -\mathbf{e}_{S_+}^T & \mathbf{e}_{S_-}^T \end{bmatrix} = \begin{bmatrix} -1 & 1 & 0 \\ 1 & -1 & 0 \\ 0 & 0 & 1 \\ -1 & -1 & 1 \end{bmatrix}.
$$

For this example, $H$ has full column rank, but $(A_{S_+}, A_{S_-})$ does not. Thus, the full-rank properties of $H$ and $(A_{S_+}, A_{S_-})$ are not equivalent in general. However, as pointed out below, the two properties are equivalent if the RSP of $A^T$ at $x$ is also satisfied.

### 2.2.5 Uniqueness Characterization

The conditions derived in previous sections capture a full picture of the uniqueness of the least $\ell_1$-norm solutions of linear systems. Combining Theorems 2.2.9 and 2.2.11 immediately yields the following theorem.

**Theorem 2.2.13** *$x$ is the unique least $\ell_1$-norm solution to the system $Az = b$ if and only if the matrix $H = \begin{bmatrix} A_{S_+} & A_{S_-} \\ -\mathbf{e}_{S_+}^T & \mathbf{e}_{S_-}^T \end{bmatrix}$ has full column rank and the RSP of $A^T$ at $x$ is satisfied.*

We now point out that the matrix $H$ in Theorem 2.2.13 can be further simplified to $(A_{S_+}, A_{S_-})$ due to the RSP of $A^T$ at $x$. In fact, if the RSP of $A^T$ at $x$ is satisfied, there is a vector $u$ such that

$$
\begin{bmatrix} \mathbf{e}_{S_+} \\ -\mathbf{e}_{S_-} \end{bmatrix} = \begin{bmatrix} A_{S_+}^T \\ A_{S_-}^T \end{bmatrix} u,
$$

which means the last row of $H$ can be represented by its other rows. Thus, when the RSP of $A^T$ at $x$ is satisfied, we have

$$
\mathrm{rank} \begin{bmatrix} A_{S_+} & A_{S_-} \\ -\mathbf{e}_{S_+}^T & \mathbf{e}_{S_-}^T \end{bmatrix} = \mathrm{rank}(A_{S_+} \; A_{S_-}) = \mathrm{rank}(A_{\mathrm{supp}(x)}).
$$

Therefore, in Theorem 2.2.13, $H$ can be replaced by $A_{\mathrm{supp}(x)}$, leading to the following theorem.

**Theorem 2.2.14** *$x$ is the unique least $\ell_1$-norm solution to the system $Az = b$ if and only if the RSP of $A^T$ at $x$ is satisfied and $A_{\mathrm{supp}(x)}$ has full column rank.*

Each of Theorems 2.2.9 and 2.2.11 alone can only give a half picture of the uniqueness of the least $\ell_1$-norm solution of a linear system, which altogether yields the complete uniqueness characterization. The necessary and sufficient condition in Theorem 2.2.14 (or equally, Theorem 2.2.13) provides a good basis to understand the relationship of $\ell_0$- and $\ell_1$-minimization, the internal mechanism of $\ell_1$-minimization, and the theoretical performance of $\ell_1$-minimization and other sparse-signal-recovery methods (see Chapters 3–6 for details). We now close this section by giving a simple example to demonstrate that the criterion in Theorem 2.2.14 can be used to check the uniqueness of the least $\ell_1$-norm solution of a linear system.

**Example 2.2.15** Consider the linear system $Az = b$ with

$$
A = \begin{bmatrix} 1 & 0 & 1 & -1 \\ 0 & -1 & 1 & 4 \\ 0 & 0 & 1 & 1 \end{bmatrix}, \quad b = \begin{bmatrix} 1/2 \\ 1/2 \\ 0 \end{bmatrix},
$$

to which $x = (1/2, -1/2, 0, 0)^T$ is a solution with $\mathrm{supp}(x) = \{1, 2\}$, $S_+(x) = \{1\}$ and $S_-(x) = \{2\}$. Clearly, $A_{\mathrm{supp}(x)}$, consisting of the first two columns of $A$, has full column rank. By taking $y = (1, 1, -5/2)^T$, we have $\eta = A^T y = (1, -1, -1/2, 1/2)^T \in \mathcal{R}(A^T)$, which clearly satisfies (2.27). Thus, the RSP of $A^T$ at $x$ is satisfied. By Theorem 2.2.14, $x$ is the unique least $\ell_1$-norm solution to the system $Az = b$.

## 2.3 Least $\ell_1$-Norm Non-negative Solution

Real-world signals are usually structured. A practical signal recovery model would involve more constraints than an underdetermined system of linear equations, such as non-negative constraints, linear inequalities or certain regularization terms. In this section, we focus on the uniqueness characterization of the solution to the problem (2.2), i.e., the following $\ell_1$-minimization problem with non-negative constraints:

$$
\min_{z} \{ \|z\|_1 : Az = b, z \geq 0 \}.
$$

It is evident that $x$ is the unique solution to this problem if and only if there is no non-negative solution $w \neq x$ satisfying $\|w\|_1 \leq \|x\|_1$, i.e.,

$$
\{w : Aw = b, w \geq 0, \|w\|_1 \leq \|x\|_1\} = \{x\}.
$$

Note that $\|u\|_1 = e^T u$ for any non-negative vector $u \geq 0$. The above uniqueness condition can be written as follows:

$$
\{w : Aw = Ax, e^T w \leq e^T x, w \geq 0\} = \{x\}.
$$

We consider the following LP problem with variables $w \in \mathbb{R}^n$ :

$$\min_{w}\{0^T w : Aw = Ax, \ e^T w \leq e^T x, \ w \geq 0\}, \tag{2.48}$$

which is always feasible (since $w = x$ is a feasible point). By introducing a slack variable $t$, the problem (2.48) becomes

$$\min_{w,t}\{0^T w : Aw = Ax, \ e^T w + t = e^T x, \ (w,t) \geq 0\}. \tag{2.49}$$

From the above observation, we immediately have the following lemma.

**Lemma 2.3.1** $x \geq 0$ *is the unique least $\ell_1$-norm non-negative solution to the system $Az = b$ if and only if $w = x$ is the unique solution to the problem (2.48), i.e., $(w,t) = (x,0)$ is the unique solution to the problem (2.49).*

We begin to derive the necessary conditions for $x \geq 0$ to be the least $\ell_1$-norm non-negative solution of a system of linear equations.

**Lemma 2.3.2** *If $x$ is the unique least $\ell_1$-norm non-negative solution to the system $Az = b$, then the matrix*

$$\widehat{H} := \begin{bmatrix} A_{S_+} \\ e_{S_+}^T \end{bmatrix} \tag{2.50}$$

*has full column rank, where $S_+$ is the short for $S_+(x)$.*

*Proof.* Suppose that the columns of $\widehat{H}$, defined in (2.50), are linearly dependent. Then there is a vector $u \in \mathbb{R}^{|S_+|}$ such that

$$\widehat{H}u = \begin{bmatrix} A_{S_+} \\ e_{S_+}^T \end{bmatrix} u = 0, \ u \neq 0. \tag{2.51}$$

Note that $w = x$ is a solution of (2.49). We now construct another solution for this problem. Define $(\widetilde{w}, \widetilde{t})$ as follows:

$$\widetilde{w}_{S_+} = x_{S_+} + \lambda u, \ \widetilde{w}_{S_0} = 0, \ \widetilde{t} = 0.$$

Since $x_{S_+} > 0$, there exists a small scalar $\lambda \neq 0$ such that

$$\widetilde{w}_{S_+} = x_{S_+} + \lambda u \geq 0.$$

It follows from (2.51) that $(\widetilde{w}, \widetilde{t})$ given as above satisfies the constraints of (2.49). Thus $(\widetilde{w}, \widetilde{t})$ is also a solution to the problem (2.49). Note that $\widetilde{w}_{S_+} \neq x_{S_+}$ (since $\lambda u \neq 0$) which implies that the solution of (2.49) is not unique. By Lemma 2.3.1, $x \geq 0$ is not the unique least $\ell_1$-norm non-negative solution to the system $Az = b$, leading to a contradiction. This shows that $\widehat{H}$ must have full column rank. $\quad\square$

The Lagrangian dual problem of (2.49) is given as

$$\max_{y,\tau}\{(Ax)^T y \mid (e^T x)\tau : A^T y + \tau e \leq 0, \ \tau \leq 0\}. \tag{2.52}$$

In what follows, we use $s \in \mathbb{R}_+^n$ and $r \in \mathbb{R}_+$ to denote the slack variables of the problem (2.52), i.e.,

$$s = -(A^T y + \tau \mathbf{e}) \geq 0, \quad r = -\tau \geq 0.$$

**Lemma 2.3.3** *If $x \geq 0$ is the unique least $\ell_1$-norm non-negative solution to the system $Az = b$, then there is a vector $\eta \in \mathcal{R}(A^T)$ satisfying*

$$\eta_i = 1 \text{ for } i \in S_+(x), \text{ and } \eta_i < 1 \text{ for } i \notin S_+(x).$$

*Proof.* Note that the problems (2.49) and (2.52) are feasible. Therefore, by Lemma 2.3.1, there is a solution $(w^*, t^*)$ of (2.49) and a solution $(y^*, \tau^*)$ of (2.52) which are strictly complementary. Let $(s^*, r^*) = (-A^T y^* - \tau^* \mathbf{e}, -\tau^*)$ be the value of the associated slack variables of (2.52). Then by the strict complementarity, we have

$$t^* r^* = 0, \ (w^*)^T s^* = 0, \ t^* + r^* > 0, \ w^* + s^* > 0. \tag{2.53}$$

Since $x \geq 0$ is the unique least $\ell_1$-norm non-negative solution to the system $Az = b$, by Lemma 2.3.1, $(x, 0)$ is the unique solution of (2.49). Thus,

$$(w^*, t^*) = (x, 0), \tag{2.54}$$

which implies that $w_i^* > 0$ for all $i \in S_+(x)$, and $w_i^* = 0$ for all $i \notin S_+(x)$. From (2.53) and (2.54), we see that $r^* > 0$, $s_i^* = 0$ for all $i \in S_+(x)$, and $s_i^* > 0$ for all $i \notin S_+(x)$. That is, $\tau^* < 0$ and

$$(A^T y^* + \tau^* \mathbf{e})_i = 0 \text{ for all } i \in S_+(x),$$

$$(A^T y^* + \tau^* \mathbf{e})_i < 0 \text{ for all } i \notin S_+(x),$$

which are equivalent to

$$\left[ A^T \left( \frac{y^*}{-\tau^*} \right) - \mathbf{e} \right]_i = 0 \text{ for all } i \in S_+(x),$$

$$\left[ A^T \left( \frac{y^*}{-\tau^*} \right) - \mathbf{e} \right]_i < 0 \text{ for all } i \notin S_+(x).$$

Setting $\eta = A^T y^* / (-\tau^*)$, we have $\eta \in \mathcal{R}(A^T)$ and $\eta_i = 1$ for all $i \in S_+(x)$, and $\eta_i < 1$ for all $i \notin S_+(x)$. $\square$

**Definition 2.3.4** (RSP$^+$ of $A^T$ at $x$) *We say that the range space property plus (RSP$^+$) of $A^T$ at $x \geq 0$ is satisfied if there is a vector $\eta \in \mathcal{R}(A^T)$ satisfying*

$$\eta_i = 1 \text{ for all } i \in S_+(x), \text{ and } \eta_i < 1 \text{ for all } i \notin S_+(x). \tag{2.55}$$

As shown in Lemma 2.3.3, the $RSP^+$ of $A^T$ at $x$ turns out to be a necessary condition for $x$ to be the unique least $\ell_1$-norm non-negative solution of the linear system. The next result shows that the combined necessary conditions in Lemmas 2.3.3 and 2.3.2 become sufficient for $x$ to be the unique least $\ell_1$-norm non-negative solution of a linear system.

**Lemma 2.3.5** *Let $x \geq 0$ be a solution to the system $Az = b$. If the $RSP^+$ of $A^T$ at $x$ is satisfied and the matrix $\widehat{H}$ given in (2.50) has full column rank, then $x \geq 0$ is the unique least $\ell_1$-norm non-negative solution to the system $Az = b$.*

*Proof.* By Lemma 2.3.1, to prove that $x$ is the unique least $\ell_1$-norm non-negative solution to the system $Az = b$, it is sufficient to prove that (2.49) has a unique solution $(x, 0)$. First, the $RSP^+$ of $A^T$ at $x \geq 0$ implies that there exist $\eta$ and $y$ such that

$$A^T y = \eta, \ \eta_i = 1 \text{ for all } i \in S_+(x), \text{ and } \eta_i < 1 \text{ for all } i \notin S_+(x).$$

By setting $\tau = -1$, the relation above can be written as

$$(A^T y)_i + \tau = 0 \ \text{ for } i \in S_+(x), \ (A^T y)_i + \tau < 0 \text{ for all } i \notin S_+(x), \qquad (2.56)$$

which indicates that $(y, \tau)$ is a feasible point to the problem (2.52). We now verify that $(y, \tau)$ is a solution of the problem (2.52). By (2.56), the objective value of (2.52) at $(y, \tau)$ is

$$
\begin{aligned}
(Ax)^T y + (e^T x)\tau &= x^T(A^T y) + (e^T x)\tau = \sum_{i \in S_+} x_i(A^T y)_i + \tau \sum_{i \in S_+} x_i \\
&= -\tau \sum_{i \in S_+} x_i + \tau \sum_{i \in S_+} x_i = 0. \qquad (2.57)
\end{aligned}
$$

Since the optimal value of (2.49) is zero, by the LP duality theory, the optimal value of the dual problem is also zero. Thus it follows from (2.57) that the point $(y, \tau)$ satisfying (2.56) is a solution to the problem (2.52).

We now prove that the solution of (2.49) is uniquely determined under the assumption of the theorem. Assume that $(w^*, t^*)$ is an arbitrary solution of (2.49). Then,

$$Aw^* = Ax, \ e^T w^* + t^* = e^T x, \ (w^*, t^*) \geq 0. \qquad (2.58)$$

Note that $(y, \tau)$, satisfying (2.56), is a solution of (2.52). Thus, $(w^*, t^*)$ and $(y, \tau), s)$ are a solution pair to the LP problems (2.49) and (2.52). From (2.56), we see that $r = -\tau = 1 > 0$ and

$$s_i = -((A^T y)_i + \tau) > 0 \text{ for all } i \notin S_+(x).$$

By complementary slackness property, this implies that $t^* = 0$ and $w_i^* = 0$ for all $i \notin S_+(x)$. Substituting these components into (2.58), the remaining components of $(w^*, t^*)$ satisfy that

$$A_{S_+} w_{S_+}^* = A_{S_+} x_{S_+}, \quad \mathbf{e}_{S_+}^T w_{S_+}^* = \mathbf{e}_{S_+}^T x_{S_+}, \quad w_{S_+}^* \geq 0.$$

By the assumption, $\widehat{H} = \begin{bmatrix} A_{S_+} \\ \mathbf{e}_{S_+}^T \end{bmatrix}$ has full column rank, so $w_{S_+}^* = x_{S_+}$ must be the unique solution to the above system. Therefore, $(w^*, t^*) = (x, 0)$ is the only solution to the problem (2.49). By Lemma 2.3.1, $x$ is the unique least $\ell_1$-norm non-negative solution to the system $Az = b$. $\square$

Merging Lemmas 2.3.2, 2.3.3 and 2.3.5, we obtain the following result.

**Theorem 2.3.6** $x \geq 0$ *is the unique least $\ell_1$-norm non-negative solution to the system $Az = b$ if and only if the $\mathrm{RSP}^+$ of $A^T$ at $x$ holds and $A_{S_+}$ has full column rank, where $S_+ = S_+(x)$.*

*Proof.* By combining Lemmas 2.3.2, 2.3.3 and 2.3.5, we immediately obtain the following fact: $x \geq 0$ is the unique least $\ell_1$-norm non-negative solution to the system $Az = b$ if and only if the following two properties are satisfied:

(i) The $\mathrm{RSP}^+$ of $A^T$ at $x$ is satisfied.

(ii) $\widehat{H} = \begin{bmatrix} A_{S_+(x)} \\ \mathbf{e}_{S_+(x)}^T \end{bmatrix}$ has full column rank.

It is obvious that when the $\mathrm{RSP}^+$ of $A^T$ at $x$ is satisfied, we have $\mathbf{e}_{S_+} = A_{S_+}^T u$ for some $u \in \mathbb{R}^m$, which implies that $A_{S_+}$ has full column rank if and only if $\begin{bmatrix} A_{S_+} \\ \mathbf{e}_{S_+}^T \end{bmatrix}$ has full column rank. Thus, $\widehat{H}$ can be simplified to $A_{S_+(x)}$ when the $\mathrm{RSP}^+$ of $A^T$ at $x$ is satisfied. Therefore, the desired result follows. $\square$

It is very easy to use the necessary and sufficient condition in Theorem 2.3.6 to check the uniqueness of the least $\ell_1$-norm non-negative solution of a linear system.

**Example 2.3.7** Consider the linear system $Az = b$ with

$$A = \begin{bmatrix} -1 & -1 & 0 & -1 \\ 0 & -1 & 1 & -6 \\ 0 & -1 & 0 & 1 \end{bmatrix}, \quad b = \begin{bmatrix} -1 \\ 1 \\ 0 \end{bmatrix},$$

to which $x = (1, 0, 1, 0)^T$ is a non-negative solution with $S_+(x) = \{1, 3\}$. The submatrix $A_{S_+(x)}$ has full column rank. By choosing $y = (-1, 1, 0)^T$, we obtain $\eta = A^T y = (1, 0, 1, -5)^T \in \mathcal{R}(A^T)$, which clearly satisfies (2.55). Thus, the $\mathrm{RSP}^+$ of $A^T$ at $x$ is satisfied. By Theorem 2.3.6, $x$ is the unique least $\ell_1$-norm non-negative solution to the linear system.

**Example 2.3.8** Consider the linear system $Az = b$ with

$$A = \begin{bmatrix} 1 & 0 & -0.1 & -0.2 \\ 0 & -1 & 0 & 1 \\ 1 & -1 & 0 & 1 \end{bmatrix}, \quad b = \begin{bmatrix} -1 \\ 0 \\ 1 \end{bmatrix}.$$

For this example, it is easy to verify that $x = (1, 20/3, 20/3, 20/3)^T$ with $S_+(x) = \{1, 2, 3, 4\}$ is a least $\ell_1$-norm non-negative solution of the system $Az = b$. By taking $y = (-10, -12, 11)^T$, we get $\eta = A^T y = (1, 1, 1, 1)^T \in \mathcal{R}(A^T)$. Thus, the RSP$^+$ of $A^T$ at $x$ is satisfied. However, the matrix $A_{S_+} = A$ does not have full column rank. According to Theorem 2.3.6, $x$ is definitely NOT the unique least $\ell_1$-norm non-negative solution to the system $Az = b$. As a matter of fact, the vector $\widetilde{x} = (1, 0, 20, 0)^T$ with $S_+(\widetilde{x}) = \{1, 3\}$ is another least $\ell_1$-norm non-negative solution, for which the associated matrix $A_{S_+(\widetilde{x})}$ has full column rank. However, it is easy to verify that there is no vector $y$ such that $A^T y = (1, \eta_2, 1, \eta_4)^T$ with $\eta_2, \eta_4 < 1$. Thus, the RSP$^+$ of $A^T$ at $\widetilde{x}$ does not hold.

## 2.4 Least $\ell_1$-Norm Points in Polyhedra

We now extend the results developed in Sections 2.2 and 2.3 for the standard linear system $Az = b$ to a more complicated system with linear inequalities. In many practical scenarios, the sparse optimization model needs to include more complicated constraints or regularization terms in the objective in order to capture the structure of the target signals, to incorporate certain prior information of the signal, or to recover the sparse signal from certain nonlinear measurements. This motivates one to analyze the uniqueness of the least $\ell_1$-norm point in a polyhedron. An important application of the result developed in this section will be given in Chapter 4.

Let $B \in \mathbb{R}^{m_1 \times n}, C \in \mathbb{R}^{m_2 \times n}$ and $D \in \mathbb{R}^{m_3 \times n}$ be three given matrices with $m_1 + m_2 + m_3 < n$. We consider the following $\ell_1$-minimization problem with general linear constraints:

$$\min_x \{\|x\|_1 : Bx \geq b^{(1)}, Cx \leq b^{(2)}, Dx = b^{(3)}\}, \tag{2.59}$$

where $b^{(1)} \in \mathbb{R}^{m_1}, b^{(2)} \in \mathbb{R}^{m_2}$ and $b^{(3)} \in \mathbb{R}^{m_3}$ are given vectors. Denoted by

$$P = \{x \in \mathbb{R}^n : Bx \geq b^{(1)}, Cx \leq b^{(2)}, Dx = b^{(3)}\}. \tag{2.60}$$

$P$ is a polyhedron, and any polyhedron can be represented this way. Therefore, the solution of (2.59) is referred to as the least $\ell_1$-norm point in $P$.

The following notation is frequently used in this chapter: Given a matrix $M \in \mathbb{R}^{m \times n}$ and index sets $J_1 \subseteq \{1, \ldots, m\}$ and $J_2 \subseteq \{1, \ldots, n\}$, $M_{J_1, J_2}$ denotes the submatrix of $M$, consisting of the entries $m_{ij}$ with $i \in J_1$ and $j \in J_2$. In other words, $M_{J_1, J_2}$ is obtained by deleting the rows in $M$ with $i \notin J_1$ and deleting the columns in $M$ with $j \notin J_2$.

## 2.4.1 Restricted Range Space Property of $A^T$

Let $x^*$ be a solution of the problem (2.59). At $x^*$, some inequalities among $Bx \geq b^{(1)}$ and $Cx \leq b^{(2)}$ might be binding. The later analysis demonstrates that the uniqueness characterization of $x^*$ is closely related to those binding constraints at this point. To facilitate the later analysis, let us use the index sets $\mathcal{A}_1(x^*)$ and $\overline{\mathcal{A}_1}(x^*)$, respectively, to record the binding and non-binding constraints in the first group of the inequalities $Bx \geq b^{(1)}$, i.e.,

$$\mathcal{A}_1(x^*) = \{i: (Bx^*)_i = b_i^{(1)}\}, \ \overline{\mathcal{A}_1}(x^*) = \{i: (Bx^*)_i > b_i^{(1)}\}.$$

Similarly, we define the index sets for the second group of the inequalities $Cx \leq b^{(2)}$ as follows:

$$\mathcal{A}_2(x^*) = \{i: (Cx^*)_i = b_i^{(2)}\}, \ \overline{\mathcal{A}_2}(x^*) = \{i: (Cx^*)_i < b_i^{(2)}\}.$$

By introducing $\alpha \in \mathbb{R}_+^{m_1}$ and $\beta \in \mathbb{R}_+^{m_2}$, the problem (2.59) can be written as

$$\min_x \{\|x\|_1: Bx - \alpha = b^{(1)}, Cx + \beta = b^{(2)}, Dx = b^{(3)}, \alpha \geq 0, \beta \geq 0\}. \quad (2.61)$$

We can immediately see the following observation.

**Lemma 2.4.1** (i) *For any solution $(x^*, \alpha^*, \beta^*)$ to the problem (2.61), we have*

$$\begin{cases} \alpha_i^* = 0 & \text{for all } i \in \mathcal{A}_1(x^*), \\ \alpha_i^* = (Bx^*)_i - b_i^{(1)} > 0 & \text{for all } i \in \overline{\mathcal{A}_1}(x^*), \\ \beta_i^* = 0 & \text{for all } i \in \mathcal{A}_2(x^*), \\ \beta_i^* = b_i^{(2)} - (Cx^*)_i > 0 & \text{for all } i \in \overline{\mathcal{A}_2}(x^*). \end{cases} \quad (2.62)$$

(ii) *$x^*$ is the unique solution to the problem (2.59) if and only if $(x^*, \alpha^*, \beta^*)$, where $\alpha^*$ and $\beta^*$ are determined by (2.62), is the unique solution to (2.61).*

Denote by $\Phi = \begin{bmatrix} B \\ C \\ D \end{bmatrix}$, which is an $(m_1 + m_2 + m_3) \times n$ matrix. The following notion is an extension of the ones in previous sections.

**Definition 2.4.2 (RRSP of $\Phi^T$ at $x^*$)** *Let $x^* \in P$, where $P$ is defined as (2.60). We say that $\Phi^T$ satisfies the restricted range space property (RRSP) at $x^*$ if there are vectors $\eta \in \mathcal{R}(\Phi^T)$ and $g = \begin{bmatrix} g^{(1)} \\ g^{(2)} \\ g^{(3)} \end{bmatrix}$ such that $\eta = \Phi^T g$, where $\eta$ and $g$ satisfy the following properties:*

$$\eta_i = 1 \text{ for } i \in S_+(x^*), \ \eta_i = -1 \text{ for } i \in S_-(x^*), \ |\eta_i| < 1 \text{ for } i \in S_0(x^*),$$

*and $(g^{(1)}, g^{(2)}, g^{(3)}) \in \mathcal{F}(x^*)$, where*

$$\mathcal{F}(x^*) := \{(g^{(1)}, g^{(2)}, g^{(3)}) \in \mathbb{R}^{m_1} \times \mathbb{R}^{m_2} \times \mathbb{R}^{m_3} : g_i^{(1)} > 0 \text{ for all } i \in \mathcal{A}_1(x^*),$$
$$g_i^{(1)} = 0 \text{ for all } i \in \overline{\mathcal{A}_1}(x^*), \ g_i^{(2)} < 0 \text{ for all } i \in \mathcal{A}_2(x^*),$$
$$g_i^{(2)} = 0 \text{ for all } i \in \overline{\mathcal{A}_2}(x^*)\}. \tag{2.63}$$

When the problem does not include any inequality constraint, the definition above is reduced to the standard RSP notion defined in Section 2.2. The RRSP of $\Phi^T$ at $x^*$ is a natural condition for the uniqueness of the least $\ell_1$-norm point in polyhedron $P$, as shown by the following theorem.

**Theorem 2.4.3 (Uniqueness characterization)** *$x^*$ is the unique solution to the $\ell_1$-minimization problem (2.59) if and only if the RRSP of $\Phi^T$ at $x^*$ is satisfied, and the matrix*

$$\widetilde{H}(x^*) = \begin{bmatrix} B_{\mathcal{A}_1, S_+} & B_{\mathcal{A}_1, S_-} \\ C_{\mathcal{A}_2, S_+} & C_{\mathcal{A}_2, S_-} \\ D_{S_+} & D_{S_-} \end{bmatrix} \tag{2.64}$$

*has full column rank, where $\mathcal{A}_1 = \mathcal{A}_1(x^*)$, $\mathcal{A}_2 = \mathcal{A}_2(x^*)$, $S_+ = S_+(x^*)$ and $S_- = S_-(x^*)$.*

Theorem 2.4.3 provides a complete characterization for the uniqueness of the least $\ell_1$-norm point in $P$. An important application of this theorem will be given in Chapter 4. The remainder of this section is devoted to the proof of Theorem 2.4.3.

### 2.4.2 Proof of Necessity

By introducing $u, v, t \in \mathbb{R}^n_+$, where $t$ satisfies $|x| \leq t$, the problem (2.61) can be written as the linear program

$$\min_{(x,t,u,v,\alpha,\beta)} \quad e^T t$$
$$\text{s.t.} \quad x + u - t = 0, \ -x + v - t = 0, \tag{2.65}$$
$$Bx - \alpha = b^{(1)}, \ Cx + \beta = b^{(2)}, \ Dx = b^{(3)},$$
$$(t, u, v, \alpha, \beta) \geq 0.$$

The key variable of this problem is $x$, and the remaining variables $(t, u, v, \alpha, \beta)$ are determined by $x$. The following statement is obvious.

**Lemma 2.4.4** (i) *For any solution $(x^*, t^*, u^*, v^*, \alpha^*, \beta^*)$ of the problem (2.65), we have*

$$t^* = |x^*|, \ u^* = |x^*| - x^*, \ v^* = |x^*| + x^*$$

*and $(\alpha^*, \beta^*)$ is given by (2.62).*

(ii) $x^*$ *is the unique solution to the problem (2.59) if and only if*

$$(x, t, u, v, \alpha, \beta) = (x^*, |x^*|, |x^*| - x^*, |x^*| + x^*, \alpha^*, \beta^*)$$

*is the unique solution to the problem (2.65), where $(\alpha^*, \beta^*)$ is given by (2.62).*

It is very easy to verify that the Lagrangian dual of (2.65) in terms of the variables $h^{(1)}, \ldots, h^{(5)}$ is given as follows:

(DP) $\qquad \max_{(h^{(1)},\ldots,h^{(5)})} \quad (b^{(1)})^T h^3 + (b^{(2)})^T h^4 + (b^{(3)})^T h_5$

$\qquad\qquad$ s.t. $\qquad h^{(1)} - h^{(2)} + B^T h^{(3)} + C^T h^{(4)} + D^T h^{(5)} = 0,$

$$-h^{(1)} - h^{(2)} \leq \mathbf{e}, \qquad\qquad\qquad (2.66)$$

$$h^{(1)} \leq 0, \qquad\qquad\qquad\qquad (2.67)$$

$$h^{(2)} \leq 0, \qquad\qquad\qquad\qquad (2.68)$$

$$-h^{(3)} \leq 0, \qquad\qquad\qquad\qquad (2.69)$$

$$h^{(4)} \leq 0. \qquad\qquad\qquad\qquad (2.70)$$

(DP) is always feasible since

$$(h^{(1)}, \ldots, h^{(5)}) = (0, \ldots, 0)$$

satisfies its constraints. Let $s^{(1)}, \ldots, s^{(5)}$ be the non-negative slack variables associated with the constraints (2.66) through (2.70), respectively. Then (DP) can be written as

$\qquad \max_{(h^{(i)}, s^{(i)}, i=1,\ldots,5)} \quad (b^{(1)})^T h^{(3)} + (b^{(2)})^T h^{(4)} + (b^{(3)})^T h^{(5)}$

$\qquad\qquad$ s.t. $\qquad h^{(1)} - h^{(2)} + B^T h^{(3)} + C^T h^{(4)} + D^T h^{(5)} = 0, \qquad (2.71)$

$$s^{(1)} - h^{(1)} - h^{(2)} = \mathbf{e}, \qquad\qquad\qquad (2.72)$$

$$s^{(2)} + h^{(1)} = 0, \qquad\qquad\qquad\qquad (2.73)$$

$$s^{(3)} + h^{(2)} = 0, \qquad\qquad\qquad\qquad (2.74)$$

$$s^{(4)} - h^{(3)} = 0, \qquad\qquad\qquad\qquad (2.75)$$

$$s^{(5)} + h^{(4)} = 0, \qquad\qquad\qquad\qquad (2.76)$$

$$s^{(1)}, \ldots, s^{(5)} \geq 0.$$

It can be shown that if $x^*$ is the unique solution to the problem (2.59), then the RRSP of $\Phi^T$ at $x^*$ must be satisfied.

**Lemma 2.4.5** *If $x^*$ is the unique solution to the problem (2.59), then there are vectors $h^{(1)}, h^{(2)} \in \mathbb{R}^n$ and*

$$(g^{(1)}, g^{(2)}, g^{(3)}) \in \mathbb{R}^{m_1} \times \mathbb{R}^{m_2} \times \mathbb{R}^{m_2}$$

*satisfying*

$$h^{(2)} - h^{(1)} = \Phi^T \begin{bmatrix} g^{(1)} \\ g^{(2)} \\ g^{(3)} \end{bmatrix} \tag{2.77}$$

*and*

$$
\begin{cases}
h_i^{(1)} = -1 \text{ and } h_i^{(2)} = 0 & \text{for all } i \in S_+(x^*), \\
h_i^{(1)} = 0 \text{ and } h_i^{(2)} = -1 & \text{for all } i \in S_-(x^*), \\
h_i^{(1)} < 0, h_i^{(2)} < 0 \text{ and } h_i^{(1)} + h_i^{(2)} > -1 & \text{for all } i \in S_0(x^*), \\
g_i^{(1)} > 0 & \text{for all } i \in \mathcal{A}_1(x^*), \\
g_i^{(1)} = 0 & \text{for all } i \in \overline{\mathcal{A}_1}(x^*), \\
g_i^{(2)} < 0 & \text{for all } i \in \mathcal{A}_2(x^*), \\
g_i^{(2)} = 0 & \text{for all } i \in \overline{\mathcal{A}_2}(x^*).
\end{cases} \tag{2.78}
$$

*Proof.* Assume that $x^*$ is the unique solution to the problem (2.59). By Lemma 2.4.4, the vector

$$(x, t, u, v, \alpha, \beta) = (x^*, |x^*|, |x^*| - x^*, |x^*| + x^*, \alpha^*, \beta^*) \tag{2.79}$$

is the unique solution of (2.65), where $(\alpha^*, \beta^*)$ is given by (2.62). By the SCSP of linear programs (see Lemma 2.1.2), there exists a solution $(h^{(1)}, \ldots, h^{(5)})$ to the problem (DP) such that the associated vector $(s^{(1)}, \ldots, s^{(5)})$, determined by (2.72)–(2.76), and the vectors $(t, u, v, \alpha, \beta)$, given by (2.79), are strictly complementary, i.e.,

$$t^T s^{(1)} = u^T s^{(2)} = v^T s^{(3)} = \alpha^T s^{(4)} = \beta^T s^{(5)} = 0 \tag{2.80}$$

and

$$t + s^{(1)} > 0, \ u + s^{(2)} > 0, \ v + s^{(3)} > 0, \ \alpha + s^{(4)} > 0, \ \beta + s^{(5)} > 0. \tag{2.81}$$

For the above-mentioned solution $(h^{(1)}, \ldots, h^{(5)})$ of (DP), let

$$g^{(1)} = h^{(3)}, \ g^{(2)} = h^{(4)}, \ g^{(3)} = h^{(5)}.$$

Then it follows from (2.71) that

$$h^{(2)} - h^{(1)} = B^T h^{(3)} + C^T h^{(4)} + D^T h^{(5)} = \Phi^T \begin{bmatrix} g^{(1)} \\ g^{(2)} \\ g^{(3)} \end{bmatrix}. \tag{2.82}$$

From (2.79), we see that the solution of (2.65) satisfies the following properties:

$$\begin{cases} t_i = x_i^* > 0, \; u_i = 0 \text{ and } v_i = 2x_i^* > 0 & \text{for all } i \in S_+(x^*), \\ t_i = |x_i^*| > 0, \; u_i = 2|x_i^*| > 0 \text{ and } v_i = 0 & \text{for all } i \in S_-(x^*), \\ t_i = 0, \; u_i = 0 \text{ and } v_i = 0 & \text{for all } i \in S_0(x^*). \end{cases}$$

Thus, from (2.80) and (2.81), it follows that

$$\begin{cases} s_i^{(1)} = 0, \; s_i^{(2)} > 0 \text{ and } s_i^{(3)} = 0 & \text{for all } i \in S_+(x^*), \\ s_i^{(1)} = 0, \; s_i^{(2)} = 0 \text{ and } s_i^{(3)} > 0 & \text{for all } i \in S_-(x^*), \\ s_i^{(1)} > 0, \; s_i^{(2)} > 0 \text{ and } s_i^{(3)} > 0 & \text{for all } i \in S_0(x^*). \end{cases}$$

From (2.72), (2.73) and (2.74), the above relations imply that

$$\begin{cases} h_i^{(1)} + h_i^{(2)} = -1, \; h_i^{(1)} < 0 \text{ and } h_i^{(2)} = 0 & \text{for all } i \in S_+(x^*), \\ h_i^{(1)} + h_i^{(2)} = -1, \; h_i^{(1)} = 0 \text{ and } h_i^{(2)} < 0 & \text{for all } i \in S_-(x^*), \\ h_i^{(1)} + h_i^{(2)} > -1, \; h_i^{(1)} < 0 \text{ and } h_i^{(2)} < 0 & \text{for all } i \in S_0(x^*). \end{cases}$$

From (2.75) and (2.76), we see that

$$s^{(4)} = h^{(3)} \geq 0, \; s^{(5)} = -h^{(4)} \geq 0.$$

It follows from (2.62), (2.80) and (2.81) that

$$h_i^{(3)} = s_i^{(4)} > 0 \text{ for } i \in \mathcal{A}_1(x^*), \; h_i^{(3)} = s_i^{(4)} = 0 \text{ for } i \in \overline{\mathcal{A}_1}(x^*),$$

$$-h_i^{(4)} = s_i^{(5)} > 0 \text{ for } i \in \mathcal{A}_2(x^*), \; -h_i^{(4)} = s_i^{(5)} = 0 \text{ for } i \in \overline{\mathcal{A}_2}(x^*).$$

Note that $g^{(1)} = h^{(3)}$, $g^{(2)} = h^{(4)}$ and $g^{(3)} = h^{(5)}$. The above conditions imply that

$$g_i^{(1)} = h_i^{(3)} > 0 \text{ for } i \in \mathcal{A}_1(x^*), \; g_i^{(1)} = h_i^{(3)} = 0 \text{ for } i \in \overline{\mathcal{A}_1}(x^*),$$

$$g_i^{(2)} = h_i^{(4)} < 0 \text{ for } i \in \mathcal{A}_2(x^*), \; g_i^{(2)} = h_i^{(4)} = 0 \text{ for } i \in \overline{\mathcal{A}_2}(x^*).$$

Thus, $h^{(1)}, h^{(2)}, g^{(1)}, g^{(2)}$ and $g^{(3)}$ satisfy (2.82) and the following conditions:

$$\begin{cases} h_i^{(1)} = -1 \text{ and } h_i^{(2)} = 0 & \text{for all } i \in S_+(x^*), \\ h_i^{(1)} = 0 \text{ and } h_i^{(2)} = -1 & \text{for all } i \in S_-(x^*), \\ h_i^{(1)} < 0, \; h_i^{(2)} < 0 \text{ and } h_i^{(1)} + h_i^{(2)} > -1 & \text{for all } i \in S_0(x^*), \\ g_i^{(1)} > 0 & \text{for all } i \in \mathcal{A}_1(x^*), \\ g_i^{(1)} = 0 & \text{for all } i \in \overline{\mathcal{A}_1}(x^*), \\ g_i^{(2)} < 0 & \text{for all } i \in \mathcal{A}_2(x^*), \\ g_i^{(2)} = 0 & \text{for all } i \in \overline{\mathcal{A}_2}(x^*). \end{cases}$$

Therefore, (2.78) is a necessary condition for $x^*$ to be the unique solution of (2.59). □

The following result can be immediately obtained from Lemma 2.4.5.

**Corollary 2.4.6** *If $x^*$ is the unique solution to the problem (2.59), then the RRSP of $\Phi^T$ at $x^*$ is satisfied.*

*Proof.* It is sufficient to show that the necessary conditions in Lemma 2.4.5 is equivalent to the RRSP of $\Phi^T$ at $x^*$. Assume that $h^{(1)}, h^{(2)} \in \mathbb{R}^n$ and $g = (g^{(1)}, g^{(2)}, g^{(3)}) \in \mathbb{R}^{m_1} \times \mathbb{R}^{m_2} \times \mathbb{R}^{m_3}$ satisfy the systems (2.77) and (2.78). By setting $\eta = h^{(2)} - h^{(1)}$, we see from (2.78) that $\eta_i = 1$ for $x_i^* > 0$, and $\eta_i = -1$ for $x_i^* < 0$. Note that for $x_i^* = 0$, we have $|\eta_i| = |h_i^{(2)} - h_i^{(1)}| < |h_i^{(2)} + h_i^{(1)}| < 1$, which follows from the fact $h_i^{(1)} < 0$, $h_i^{(2)} < 0$ and $h_i^{(2)} + h_i^{(1)} > -1$. Therefore, $\eta$ satisfies that $\eta \in \mathcal{R}(\Phi^T)$ and

$$\eta_i = 1 \text{ for } i \in S_+(x^*), \ \eta_i = -1 \text{ for } i \in S_-(x^*), \ |\eta_i| < 1 \text{ for } i \in S_0(x^*).$$

We also see from (2.78) that $g = (g^{(1)}, g^{(2)}, g^{(3)}) \in \mathcal{F}(x^*)$ which is the set given in (2.63). Thus, the RRSP of $A^T$ at $x^*$ is satisfied.

Conversely, suppose that RRSP of $A^T$ holds at $x^*$. Then there exist $\eta$ and $g = (g^{(1)}, g^{(2)}, g^{(3)})$ satisfying the conditions in Definition 2.4.2. We now prove that there exist $h^{(1)}$ and $h^{(2)}$ such that $h^{(1)}, h^{(2)}$ and $g$ satisfy the conditions (2.77) and (2.78). In fact, let $h_i^{(1)} = -1$ and $h_i^{(2)} = 0$ for all $i \in S_+(x^*)$, and $h_i^{(1)} = 0$ and $h_i^{(2)} = -1$ for all $i \in S_-(x^*)$. For $i \in S_0(x^*)$, by noting that $|\eta_i| < 1$, we define the components of $h_i^{(1)}$ and $h_i^{(2)}$ as follows:

$$\begin{cases} h_i^{(1)} = -\varepsilon_i - \eta_i \text{ and } h_i^{(2)} = -\varepsilon_i & \text{if } \eta_i > 0, \\ h_i^{(1)} = -\varepsilon_i \text{ and } h_i^{(2)} = \eta_i - \varepsilon_i & \text{otherwise,} \end{cases}$$

where $0 < \varepsilon_i < (1 - |\eta_i|)/2$ is a positive number. By the above choice, we immediately have $h^{(2)} - h^{(1)} = \eta \in \mathcal{R}(A^T)$ and it is easy to see that $(h^{(1)}, h^{(2)})$ and $(g^{(1)}, g^{(2)}, g^{(3)})$ satisfy the condition (2.78). □

The RRSP of $\Phi^T$ at $x^*$ is a necessary condition for the uniqueness of the solution to the problem (2.59). This condition alone is not enough to ensure that the solution of (2.59) is unique. Another necessary condition is also required to ensure that $x^*$ is the unique least $\ell_1$-norm point in $P$.

**Lemma 2.4.7** *If $x^*$ is the unique solution to the problem (2.59), then $\widetilde{H}(x^*)$, defined by (2.64), has full column rank.*

*Proof.* Let $x^*$ be the unique solution of (2.59). Assume the contrary that $\widetilde{H}(x^*)$ has linearly dependent columns. Then there is a vector $d = \begin{bmatrix} u \\ v \end{bmatrix} \neq 0$, where $u \in \mathbb{R}^{|S_+|}$ and $v \in \mathbb{R}^{|S_-|}$, such that $\widetilde{H}(x^*)d = 0$. Note that $x^*$ satisfies

$$Bx^* \geq b^{(1)}, \ Cx^* \leq b^{(2)}, \ Dx^* = b^{(3)}.$$

Eliminating the zero components of $x^*$ from the above system yields

$$
\begin{cases}
B_{\mathcal{A}_1, S_+} x^*_{S_+} + B_{\mathcal{A}_1, S_-} x^*_{S_-} = (b^{(1)})_{\mathcal{A}_1}, \\
C_{\mathcal{A}_2, S_+} x^*_{S_+} + C_{\mathcal{A}_2, S_-} x^*_{S_-} = (b^{(2)})_{\mathcal{A}_2}, \\
D_{S_+} x^*_{S_+} + D_{S_-} x^*_{S_-} = b^{(3)}, \\
B_{\overline{\mathcal{A}_1}, S_+} x^*_{S_+} + B_{\overline{\mathcal{A}_1}, S_-} x^*_{S_-} > (b^{(1)})_{\overline{\mathcal{A}_1}}, \\
C_{\overline{\mathcal{A}_2}, S_+} x^*_{S_+} + C_{\overline{\mathcal{A}_2}, S_-} x^*_{S_-} < (b^{(2)})_{\overline{\mathcal{A}_2}},
\end{cases}
$$

where, $\mathcal{A}_i = \mathcal{A}_i(x^*), \overline{\mathcal{A}_i} = \overline{\mathcal{A}_i}(x^*)$ for $i = 1, 2$, and $S_+ = S_+(x^*)$ and $S_- = S_-(x^*)$. We define $x(\lambda) \in \mathbb{R}^n$ as $x(\lambda)_{S_+} = x^*_{S_+} + \lambda u$, and $x(\lambda)_{S_-} = x^*_{S_-} + \lambda v$, and $x(\lambda)_i = 0$ for all $i \notin S_+ \cup S_-$. From the above system and the definition of $x(\lambda)$, we see that for any sufficiently small $|\lambda| \neq 0$, the vector $(x(\lambda)_{S_+}, x(\lambda)_{S_-})$ satisfies the following system:

$$
\widetilde{H}(x^*) \begin{bmatrix} x(\lambda)_{S_+} \\ x(\lambda)_{S_-} \end{bmatrix} = \begin{bmatrix} (b^{(1)})_{\mathcal{A}_1} \\ (b^{(2)})_{\mathcal{A}_2} \\ b^{(3)} \end{bmatrix},
$$

$$
\left[ B_{\overline{\mathcal{A}_1}, S_+}, B_{\overline{\mathcal{A}_1}, S_-} \right] \begin{bmatrix} x(\lambda)_{S_+} \\ x(\lambda)_{S_-} \end{bmatrix} > (b^{(1)})_{\overline{\mathcal{A}_1}},
$$

$$
\left[ C_{\overline{\mathcal{A}_2}, S_+}, C_{\overline{\mathcal{A}_2}, S_-} \right] \begin{bmatrix} x(\lambda)_{S_+} \\ x(\lambda)_{S_-} \end{bmatrix} < (b^{(2)})_{\overline{\mathcal{A}_2}}.
$$

In other words, there exists a small number $\delta > 0$ such that for any $\lambda \neq 0$ with $|\lambda| \in (0, \delta)$, the vector $x(\lambda)$ is feasible to the problem (2.59). In particular, choose $\lambda^* \neq 0$ such that $|\lambda^*| \in (0, \delta)$, $x^*_{S_+} + \lambda^* u > 0$, $x^*_{S_-} + \lambda^* v < 0$ and

$$
\lambda^* (e^T_{S_+} u - e^T_{S_-} v) \leq 0. \tag{2.83}
$$

Then, we see that $x(\lambda^*) \neq x^*$ since $\lambda^* \neq 0$ and $(u, v) \neq 0$. Moreover, we have

$$
\begin{aligned}
\|x(\lambda^*)\|_1 &= e^T_{S_+}(x^*_{S_+} + \lambda^* u) - e^T_{S_-}(x^*_{S_-} + \lambda^* v), \\
&= e^T_{S_+} x^*_{S_+} - e^T_{S_-} x^*_{S_-} + \lambda^*(e^T_{S_+} u - e^T_{S_-} v) \\
&\leq e^T_{S_+} x^*_{S_+} - e^T_{S_-} x^*_{S_-} = \|x^*\|_1,
\end{aligned}
$$

where the inequality follows from (2.83). As $\|x^*\|_1$ is the least objective value of (2.59), it implies that $x(\lambda^*)$ is also a solution to this problem, contradicting to the uniqueness of $x^*$. Hence, $\widetilde{H}(x^*)$ must have full column rank. □

Combining Corollary 2.4.6 and Lemma 2.4.7 yields the desired necessary conditions.

**Theorem 2.4.8** *If $x^*$ is the unique solution to the problem (2.59), then the RRSP of $\Phi^T$ at $x^*$ holds and $\widetilde{H}(x^*)$, given in (2.64), has full column rank.*

## 2.4.3 Proof of Sufficiency

We now prove that the converse of Theorem 2.4.8 is also valid, i.e., the RRSP of $\Phi^T$ at $x^*$ combined with the full-column-rank property of $\widetilde{H}(x^*)$ is a sufficient condition for the uniqueness of $x^*$. We start with a property of (DP).

**Lemma 2.4.9** *Let $x^*$ satisfy the constraints of the problem (2.59). If there exist $h^{(1)}, h^{(2)} \in \mathbb{R}^n$ and*

$$g = (g^{(1)}, g^{(2)}, g^{(3)}) \in \mathbb{R}^{m_1} \times \mathbb{R}^{m_2} \times \mathbb{R}^{m_3}$$

*such that*

$$h^{(2)} - h^{(1)} = \Phi^T g \tag{2.84}$$

*and*

$$
\begin{cases}
h_i^{(1)} = -1 \text{ and } h_i^{(2)} = 0 & \text{for all } i \in S_+(x^*), \\
h_i^{(1)} = 0 \text{ and } h_i^{(2)} = -1 & \text{for all } i \in S_-(x^*), \\
h_i^{(1)} < 0, \ h_i^{(2)} < 0 \text{ and } h_i^{(1)} + h_i^{(2)} > -1 & \text{for all } i \in S_0(x^*), \\
g_i^{(1)} = 0 \text{ for all } i \in \overline{\mathcal{A}_1}(x^*), \\
g_i^{(2)} = 0 \text{ for all } i \in \overline{\mathcal{A}_2}(x^*), \\
g^{(1)} \geq 0, \\
g^{(2)} \leq 0,
\end{cases}
\tag{2.85}
$$

*then the vector $(h^{(1)}, h^{(2)}, h^{(3)}, h^{(4)}, h^{(5)})$, with $h^{(3)} = g^{(1)}, h^{(4)} = g^{(2)}$ and $h^{(5)} = g^{(3)}$, is a solution to (DP) and $x^*$ is a solution to (2.59).*

*Proof.* This lemma follows directly from the optimality condition of linear programs by verifying that the objective value of (DP) at $(h^{(1)}, h^{(2)}, h^{(3)}, h^{(4)}, h^{(5)})$ is equal to $\|x^*\|_1$. Let $(h^{(1)}, \ldots, h^{(5)})$ be the vector satisfying the condition of the lemma. It is evident that $(h^{(1)}, \ldots, h^{(5)})$ satisfies the constraints of (DP). We now further prove that $(h^{(1)}, \ldots, h^{(5)})$ is a solution to (DP). Since $\Phi^T g = h^{(2)} - h^{(1)}$, we have

$$(\Phi^T g)^T x^* = (h^{(2)} - h^{(1)})^T x^* = \|x^*\|_1,$$

where the second equality follows from the choice of $h^{(1)}$ and $h^{(2)}$. Thus,

$$
\begin{aligned}
\|x^*\|_1 &= g^T \Phi x^* \\
&= g_1^T B x^* + g_2^T C x^* + g_3^T D x^* \\
&= (h^{(3)})^T B x^* + (h^{(4)})^T C x^* + (h^{(5)})^T D x^* \\
&= (h^{(3)})^T B x^* + (h^{(4)})^T C x^* + (h^{(5)})^T b^{(3)}.
\end{aligned}
\tag{2.86}
$$

where the last equality follows from $D x^* = b^{(3)}$. Note that

$$(B x^*)_i = b_i^{(1)} \text{ for } i \in \mathcal{A}_1(x^*), \text{ and } (C x^*)_i = b_i^{(2)} \text{ for } i \in \mathcal{A}_2(x^*). \tag{2.87}$$

We also note that $h^{(3)} = g^{(1)}$, $h^{(4)} = g^{(2)}$, $g_i^{(1)} = 0$ for all $i \in \overline{\mathcal{A}_1}(x^*)$, and $g_i^{(2)} = 0$ for all $i \in \overline{\mathcal{A}_2}(x^*)$. This implies that

$$h_i^{(3)} = 0 \text{ for all } i \in \overline{\mathcal{A}_1}(x^*), \text{ and } h_i^{(4)} = 0 \text{ for all } i \in \overline{\mathcal{A}_2}(x^*). \tag{2.88}$$

By (2.87) and (2.88), we see that

$$(h^{(3)})^T B x^* + (h^{(4)})^T C x^* = (h^{(3)})^T b^{(1)} + (h^{(4)})^T b^{(2)},$$

which together with (2.86) implies that

$$(b^{(1)})^T h^{(3)} + (b^{(2)})^T h^{(4)} + (b^{(3)})^T h^{(5)} = \|x^*\|_1.$$

Thus, the objective value of (DP) at $(h^{(1)}, \dots, h^{(5)})$ coincides with the objective value of (2.59) at $x^*$. By the strong duality, $(h^{(1)}, \dots, h^{(5)})$ is a solution of (DP), and $x^*$ is a solution to the problem (2.59). □

We now prove the desired sufficient condition for the uniqueness of solutions of the problem (2.59).

**Theorem 2.4.10** *Let $x^*$ satisfy the constraints of the problem (2.59). If the RRSP of $\Phi^T$ at $x^*$ holds and $\widetilde{H}(x^*)$, defined by (2.64), has full column rank, then $x^*$ is the unique solution to the problem (2.59).*

*Proof.* By the assumption of the theorem, the RRSP of $\Phi^T$ at $x^*$ holds. Then from the proof of Corollary 2.4.6, the RSP of $\Phi^T$ at $x^*$ is equivalent to that there exist vectors $h^{(1)}, h^{(2)} \in \mathbb{R}^n$ and $g = (g^{(1)}, g^{(2)}, g^{(3)}) \in \mathbb{R}^{m_1} \times \mathbb{R}^{m_2} \times \mathbb{R}^{m_3}$ satisfying (2.77) and (2.78), which imply the conditions in (2.84) and (2.85). As $x^*$ is a feasible point to the problem (2.59), by Lemma 2.4.9, the vector $(h^{(1)}, h^{(2)}, h^{(3)}, h^{(4)}, h^{(5)})$ with $h^{(3)} = g^{(1)}, h^{(4)} = g^{(2)}$ and $h^{(5)} = g^{(3)}$ is a solution to (DP). At this solution, let the slack vectors $s^{(1)}, \dots, s^{(5)}$ be given as (2.72)–(2.76). Also, from Lemma 2.4.9, $x^*$ is a solution to (2.59). Thus, by Lemma 2.4.4, $(x, t, u, v, \alpha, \beta) = (x^*, |x^*|, |x^*| - x^*, |x^*| + x^*, \alpha^*, \beta^*)$, where $(\alpha^*, \beta^*)$ is given by (2.62), is a solution to (2.65).

We now further show that $x^*$ is the unique solution to (2.59). Note that

$$B x^* \geq b^{(1)}, \ C x^* \leq b^{(2)}, \ D x^* = b^{(3)}.$$

As shown in the proof of Lemma 2.4.7, removing zero components of $x^*$ from the system above yields

$$\widetilde{H}(x^*) \begin{bmatrix} x_{S_+}^* \\ x_{S_+}^* \\ x_{S_-}^* \end{bmatrix} = \begin{bmatrix} (b^{(1)})_{\mathcal{A}_1} \\ (b^{(2)})_{\mathcal{A}_2} \\ b^{(3)} \end{bmatrix}, \tag{2.89}$$

where $\mathcal{A}_1 = \mathcal{A}_1(x^*)$ and $\mathcal{A}_1 = \mathcal{A}_1(x^*)$. Let $(\widetilde{x}, \widetilde{t}, \widetilde{u}, \widetilde{v}, \widetilde{\alpha}, \widetilde{\beta})$ be an arbitrary solution of (2.65). By Lemma 2.4.4, it must hold that

$$\widetilde{t} = |\widetilde{x}|, \ \widetilde{u} = |\widetilde{x}| - \widetilde{x}, \ \widetilde{v} = |\widetilde{x}| + \widetilde{x}.$$

By the complementary slackness property, the non-negative vectors $(\widetilde{t}, \widetilde{u}, \widetilde{v}, \widetilde{\alpha}, \widetilde{\beta})$ and $(s^{(1)}, \dots, s^{(5)})$ are complementary, i.e.,

$$\widetilde{t}^T s^{(1)} = \widetilde{u}^T s^{(2)} = \widetilde{v}^T s^{(3)} = \widetilde{\alpha}^T s^{(4)} = \widetilde{\beta}^T s^{(5)} = 0. \tag{2.90}$$

As $(h^{(1)}, h^{(2)}, g)$ satisfies (2.78), we see that $h_i^{(1)} + h_i^{(2)} > -1$, $h_i^{(1)} < 0$ and $h_i^{(2)} < 0$ for $x_i^* = 0$, and that $g_i^{(1)} > 0$ for all $i \in \mathcal{A}_1(x^*)$ and $g_i^{(2)} < 0$ for all $i \in \mathcal{A}_2(x^*)$. By the definition of $(s^{(1)}, \dots, s^{(5)})$, the following components of these slack variables are positive:

$$
\begin{aligned}
s_i^{(1)} &= 1 + h_i^{(1)} + h_i^{(2)} > 0 & \text{for all } i \in S_0(x^*), \\
s_i^{(4)} &= h_i^{(3)} = g_i^{(1)} > 0 & \text{for all } i \in \mathcal{A}_1(x^*), \\
s_i^{(5)} &= -h_i^{(4)} = -g_i^{(2)} > 0 & \text{for all } i \in \mathcal{A}_2(x^*).
\end{aligned}
$$

These conditions, together with (2.90), imply that

$$\widetilde{t}_i = 0 \text{ for } i \in S_0(x^*), \ \widetilde{\alpha}_i = 0 \text{ for } i \in \mathcal{A}_1(x^*), \ \widetilde{\beta}_i = 0 \text{ for } i \in \mathcal{A}_2(x^*). \tag{2.91}$$

Since $\widetilde{t} = |\widetilde{x}|$, the first relation in (2.91) implies that $\widetilde{x}_i = 0$ for all $i \notin S_+(x^*) \cup S_-(x^*)$. Note that

$$B\widetilde{x} - \widetilde{\alpha} = b^{(1)}, \ C\widetilde{x} + \widetilde{\beta} = b^{(2)}, \ D\widetilde{x} = b^{(3)}.$$

Removing $\widetilde{x}_i = 0$ for $i \notin S_+ \cup S_-$ from the above system and using (2.91), we obtain

$$\widetilde{H}(x^*) \begin{bmatrix} \widetilde{x}_{S_+} \\ \widetilde{x}_{S_-} \end{bmatrix} = \begin{bmatrix} (b^{(1)})_{\mathcal{A}_1} \\ (b^{(2)})_{\mathcal{A}_2} \\ b^{(3)} \end{bmatrix}. \tag{2.92}$$

By the assumption of the theorem, the matrix $\widetilde{H}(x^*)$ has full column rank. Thus it follows from (2.89) and (2.92) that $\widetilde{x}_{S_+} = x_{S_+}^*$ and $\widetilde{x}_{S_-} = x_{S_-}^*$ which, together with the fact $\widetilde{x}_i = 0$ for all $i \notin S_+ \cup S_-$, imply that $\widetilde{x} = x^*$. By assumption, $(\widetilde{x}, \widetilde{t}, \widetilde{u}, \widetilde{v}, \widetilde{\alpha}, \widetilde{\beta})$ is an arbitrary solution of (2.65). Thus,

$$(x, t, u, v, \alpha, \beta) = (x^*, |x^*|, |x^*| - x^*, |x^*| + x^*, \alpha^*, \beta^*)$$

is the unique solution to the problem (2.65), and hence (by Lemma 2.4.4) $x^*$ is the unique solution to the problem (2.59). □

Combining Theorems 2.4.8 and 2.4.10 yields Theorem 2.4.3.

## 2.5 Notes

The $\ell_1$-minimization problem is a long-lasting research topic in the fields of numerical analysis and optimization [20, 34, 33, 167, 61]. It had a great impact when it was introduced by Chen, Donoho and Saunders [62] in 1998 to tackle the NP-hard $\ell_0$-minimization problems arising from signal and imaging processing. $\ell_1$-minimization itself can be also viewed as a sparse optimization problem thanks to its capability of locating sparse solutions of linear systems. The uniqueness of the solution to $\ell_1$-minimization is desirable in many situations when $\ell_1$-minimization is used as a tractable method for $\ell_0$-minimization problems or when it is used as a decoding method in compressed sensing. A good feature of $\ell_1$-minimization is that the uniqueness condition for the solution of this problem can be completely characterized, as shown in this chapter. The solution of the standard $\ell_1$-minimization can be characterized by the classic KKT optimality conditions which claim that $x^*$ *is a solution to the standard $\ell_1$-minimization problem if and only if there exists a vector $\eta \in \mathcal{R}(A^T)$ obeying that $\eta_i = 1$ for $x_i^* > 0$, $\eta_i = -1$ for $x_i^* < 0$, and $|\eta_i| \leq 1$ for $x_i^* = 0$.* The KKT conditions cannot, however, guarantee that the solution of the problem is unique. Fuchs [111] discovered that by strengthening the condition "$|\eta_i| \leq 1$ for $x_i^* = 0$" in the above KKT condition to "$|\eta_i| < 1$ for $x_i^* = 0$" and by requiring that $A_{\text{supp}(x^*)}$ have full column rank, then the solution $x^*$ is unique. In complex cases, Candès et al. [49] pointed out that the Fuch's condition is necessary for partial Fourier matrices. Plumbley [189] showed that Fuch's condition is necessary for real matrices. This sufficient and necessary condition for the uniqueness of solutions to $\ell_1$-minimization were also found in several independent work (see, e.g., Grasmair et al. [119], Zhao [241], Foucart and Rauhut [108], Zhang et al. [234], and Gilbert [113]). The notion of RSP of $A^T$ at $x$ was coined in [241, 242].

The non-negative constraints are quite common in mathematical optimization and numerical analysis (see Chen and Plemmons [61]). The $\ell_1$-minimization with non-negative constraints has found numerous applications in signal and image processing [87, 19, 38, 218, 144, 88, 221, 106, 137], machine learning [167, 34, 33, 167, 129], and pattern recognition and computer vision [218, 205]. The necessary and sufficient condition stated in Theorem 2.3.6 was developed by Zhao [242]. Theorem 2.4.3 regarding the $\ell_1$-minimization problems with inequality constraints was actually shown by Zhao and Xu [249]. Various analytic methods have been used for the study of the uniqueness of solutions of $\ell_1$-minimization. The discussion in this chapter demonstrates that the strict complementary slackness property (SCSP) of linear programming problems provides a unified tool to characterize the uniqueness of solutions of any linear $\ell_1$-minimization problem.

Some sufficient criteria for the uniqueness of solutions to the $\ell_1$-minimization problems can be also obtained from exact recovery conditions for sparse signals when $\ell_1$-minimization is used as a decoding method. For instance, each of the following conditions implies that the standard $\ell_1$-minimization admits a unique solution: The mutual coherence condition (1.2.4) [96, 83], exact recovery condition (ERC) [111, 210], restricted isometric property (RIP) [51, 48, 45], null space property (NSP) [235, 65, 144, 108], range space property (RSP) of order $k$ of $A^T$ [241, 242], outwardly $k$-neighborliness property [87], and the verifiable conditions in [141, 140]. However, these sufficient conditions may not be the necessary conditions for the solution of $\ell_1$-minimization to be unique. They serve other purposes instead of only ensuring the uniqueness of solutions to the $\ell_1$-minimization problems.

# Chapter 3

# Equivalence of $\ell_0$- and $\ell_1$-Minimization

The $\ell_1$-minimization method cannot always solve an $\ell_0$-minimization problem. In this chapter, we first discuss the condition under which the $\ell_0$- and $\ell_1$-minimization problems are equivalent. This condition indicates that the uniqueness of the solution to an $\ell_0$-minimization problem cannot guarantee that the problem can be solved by $\ell_1$-minimization, and the multiplicity of the solutions to an $\ell_0$-minimization problem cannot also prevent the problem from being solved by $\ell_1$-minimization. It is the RSP of $A^T$ at a solution of the $\ell_0$-minimization problem that determines whether the $\ell_0$-minimization problem can be solved by $\ell_1$-minimization. We also discuss the equivalence of $\ell_0$-minimization and weighted $\ell_1$-minimization, and we prove that there exists a weight such that the solution of weighted $\ell_1$-minimization coincides with that of $\ell_0$-minimization. More importantly, we introduce the RSP-based uniform and non-uniform recovery theories for sparse vectors. The so-called *RSP of order k of $A^T$* turns out to be a necessary and sufficient condition for every $k$-sparse vector to be exactly recovered by $\ell_1$-minimization. As a result, this condition ensures strong equivalence between $\ell_0$- and $\ell_1$-minimization problems.

## 3.1    Equivalence and Strong Equivalence

Many practical problems can be formulated as the $\ell_0$-minimization problem

$$\min_{x}\{\|x\|_0 : x \in P\}, \tag{3.1}$$

where

$$P = \{x \in \mathbb{R}^n : Ax = b, \ Bx \leq d\}$$

is a polyhedral set, determined by matrices $A \in \mathbb{R}^{m \times n} (m < n)$ and $B \in \mathbb{R}^{l \times n} (l \leq n)$. The problem (3.1) seeks the sparsest point in a polyhedral set. In particular, when $(B,d) = (0,0)$ and $(B,d) = (-I,0)$, respectively, the problem (3.1) is reduced to the following cases:

$$\min_{x} \{\|x\|_0 : Ax = b\}, \tag{3.2}$$

and

$$\min_{x} \{\|x\|_0 : Ax = b, \ x \geq 0\}. \tag{3.3}$$

The $\ell_0$-minimization problem is known to be NP-hard [177, 6]. Various methods have been proposed to solve this problem. See [62, 53, 126, 230, 37, 214, 246, 245, 248]. From a computational point of view, it is natural to consider the $\ell_1$-minimization problem

$$\min_{x} \{\|x\|_1 : x \in P\}, \tag{3.4}$$

for which there are efficient algorithms, such as the interior-point method. Extensive study has been made to address the question: When does $\ell_1$-minimization solve the $\ell_0$-minimization problem? This motivates one to address the issue of equivalence between $\ell_0$- and $\ell_1$-minimization problems. In this chapter, we take (3.2) and (3.3) as examples to demonstrate that the range space property (RSP) of $A^T$ at a vector yields a broad understanding of the relationship of $\ell_0$- and $\ell_1$-minimization. A strengthened version of RSP of $A^T$ at a vector is a crucial tool to develop a theory for the uniform and non-uniform recovery of sparse vectors with $\ell_1$-minimization. Let us first clarify the notions of equivalence and strong equivalence of $\ell_0$- and $\ell_1$-minimization.

**Definition 3.1.1** *Problems (3.1) and (3.4) are said to be equivalent if the $\ell_0$-problem (3.1) has a solution that coincides with the unique solution of the $\ell_1$-problem (3.4). The problems (3.1) and (3.4) are said to be strongly equivalent if the unique solution of (3.1) coincides with the unique solution of (3.4).*

Clearly, if two problems are strongly equivalent, they must be equivalent, but the converse is not true in general. Equivalence does not require that the $\ell_0$-minimization problem have a unique solution. An $\ell_0$-minimization problem with multiple solutions might still be equivalent to the $\ell_1$-minimization problem provided that one of the solutions of $\ell_0$-minimization problem is the unique solution to the $\ell_1$-minimization problem. Both equivalence and strong equivalence are defined under the requirement that the $\ell_1$-minimization problem possess a unique solution. The uniqueness theorem for an $\ell_1$-minimization problem has been characterized in Chapter 2. It will be used in this chapter to interpret the efficiency and limitations of $\ell_1$-minimization for solving $\ell_0$-minimization problems.

While the discussions in this chapter are mainly made to (3.2) and (3.3), it is not difficult to generalize the analysis for these cases to the problems with more complicated linear constraints.

## 3.2 Standard $\ell_0$- and $\ell_1$-Minimization Problems

It is well known that many practical problems across disciplines can be formulated as (3.2) which seeks the sparsest solution of an underdetermined system of linear equations. Associated with (3.2) is the following $\ell_1$ heuristic counterpart:

$$\min_{x}\{\|x\|_1 : Ax = b\}. \tag{3.5}$$

The $\ell_1$-minimization method was introduced by Chen, Donoho and Saunders [62] in 1998 to tackle $\ell_0$-minimization problems arising from signal and image processing, and by Mangasarian [167] in 1996 to deal with the sparse solution of certain optimization problems arising from machine learning. The term 'exact recovery' and 'guaranteed recovery' have been widely used in the literature. To avoid possible ambiguity, let us first clarify these terms with the following definition.

**Definition 3.2.1** *A vector $x \in P \subseteq \mathbb{R}^n$ is said to be exactly recovered or have a guaranteed recovery by $\ell_1$-minimization if $x$ is the unique solution to the $\ell_1$-minimization problem (3.4).*

It was shown in Theorem 2.2.14 that if $x$ is the unique solution to the problem (3.5), then $A_{\text{supp}(x)}$ has full column rank. Note that when $A_{\text{supp}(x)}$ has full column rank, the number of its columns, i.e., $|\text{supp}(x)| = \|x\|_0$, is less than or equal to the number of its rows. Thus, the following corollary follows instantly from Theorem 2.2.14, which claims that when an $\ell_1$-minimization problem has a unique solution, such a solution contains at most $m$ non-zero entries.

**Corollary 3.2.2** *For any matrix $A \in \mathbb{R}^{m \times n}$ with $m < n$, if $x$ is the unique solution to the $\ell_1$-minimization problem in (3.5), then $\|x\|_0 \leq m$.*

Thus, any $x \in \mathbb{R}^n$ that can be exactly recovered by $\ell_1$-minimization must be a $m$-sparse vector. This partially justifies the role of $\ell_1$-minimization as a sparsity-seeking method. Corollary 3.2.2 implies that any $x$ with sparsity level $\|x\|_0 > m$ is definitely not the unique solution of $\ell_1$-minimization, and hence there is no guaranteed recovery for such a vector via $\ell_1$-minimization. Note that Gaussian elimination or other linear algebraic methods can also find a solution with $\|x\|_0 \leq m$. But these methods cannot guarantee that the found solution is the sparsest one, or the one which is sufficiently sparse. In contrast, a large amount of empirical results [62, 51, 53, 37, 107, 95, 246] have shown that the $\ell_1$-minimization method often produces a truly sparse solution which is either the sparsest one or the one with $\|x\|_0$ significantly lower than $m$ if such a sparse solution exists. Therefore, it is natural to ask the question: When does $\ell_1$-minimization find the sparsest solution of an underdetermined system of linear equations? In other words, it is important to understand the conditions for equivalence and strong equivalence between $\ell_0$- and $\ell_1$-minimization problems. Let us recall the notion of the individual RSP of $A^T$ at $x$ (see Definition 3.6.5): *A matrix $A^T$ is said to satisfy the RSP at $x \in \mathbb{R}^n$ if there exists a vector $\eta \in \mathcal{R}(A^T)$ such that*

$$\begin{cases} \eta_i &= 1 & \text{for all} & x_i > 0 \\ \eta_i &= -1 & \text{for all} & x_i < 0 \\ |\eta_i| &< 1 & \text{for all} & x_i = 0. \end{cases}$$

This property, defined at $x$, can be referred to as the *individual RSP of $A^T$ at $x$*. The RSP of $A^T$ is the key to understanding the relationship of $\ell_0$- and $\ell_1$-minimization. The next fact follows instantly from Theorem 2.2.14.

**Theorem 3.2.3** *The $\ell_0$- and $\ell_1$-problems, (3.2) and (3.5), are equivalent (in the sense of Definition 3.1.1) if and only if the RSP of $A^T$ holds at a solution of the $\ell_0$-minimization problem (3.2).*

*Proof.* If (3.2) and (3.5) are equivalent, by Definition 3.1.1, the problem (3.2) must have a solution which is the unique solution to the problem (3.5). By Theorem 2.2.14, $A^T$ satisfies the individual RSP at this solution.

Conversely, suppose that the RSP of $A^T$ at a solution $x$ of the $\ell_0$-minimization problem (3.2) is satisfied. We now prove that $x$ is the unique solution to the $\ell_1$-problem (3.5). Note that at any sparsest solution $x$ of the underdetermined system $Az = b$, the column vectors of $A_{\text{supp}(x)}$ must be linearly independent, i.e., $A_{\text{supp}(x)}$ has full column rank. In fact, suppose that one of the columns of $A_{\text{supp}(x)}$, say $a_i$, can be represented by other columns of $A_{\text{supp}(x)}$, i.e.,

$$a_i = \sum_{j \in \text{supp}(x), j \neq i} \lambda_j a_j.$$

Then,

$$b = Ax = \sum_{j \in \text{supp}(x)} x_j a_j = \sum_{j \in \text{supp}(x), j \neq i} (x_j + \lambda_j x_i) a_j = \sum_{j \in \text{supp}(x), j \neq i} \tilde{x}_j a_j,$$

where $\tilde{x}_j = x_j + \lambda_j x_i$ for all $j \in \text{supp}(x)$ and $j \neq i$. Thus a solution sparser than $x$ can be found, leading to a contradiction. Thus $A_{\text{supp}(x)}$ always has full column rank at any sparsest solution of an underdetermined system of linear equations. Since the RSP of $A^T$ at $x$ is satisfied, by Theorem 2.2.14 again, $x$ is the unique solution to the problem (3.5). So (3.2) and (3.5) are equivalent. □

It is worth mentioning that Donoho [81] characterized the equivalence of $\ell_0$- and $\ell_1$-minimization from a geometric point of view, and Dossal [90] had shown that Donoho's geometric result can be understood/obtained by extending Fuchs' analysis in [111], which may yield the same result as above. Theorem 3.2.3 can be used to deeply interpret the relationship of $\ell_0$- and $\ell_1$-minimization. Let us decompose the family of systems of linear systems into three groups as follows:

$G'$: Both (3.2) and (3.5) have unique solutions.

$G''$: The problem (3.5) has a unique solution and (3.2) has multiple solutions.

$G'''$: The problem (3.2) has multiple solutions.

Clearly, every underdetermined system of linear equations falls into one and only one of these groups. By Theorem 2.2.14, the linear systems in $G'''$ do not satisfy either the RSP of $A^T$ or the full-column-rank property at any of their solutions. This means the guaranteed recovery by $\ell_1$-minimization can only possibly happen for the sparse solutions of the linear systems in $G' \cup G''$. Theorem 3.2.3 shows that any conditions ensuring the equivalence between $\ell_0$- and $\ell_1$-minimization must imply that the individual RSP of $A^T$ at a solution of the $\ell_0$-minimization problem is satisfied.

**Example 3.2.4** (Equivalence) Consider the system $Az = b$ with

$$A = \begin{bmatrix} 2 & 0 & -4 & 10 & -1 \\ 0 & 1 & 4 & -9 & 2 \\ 2 & 0 & -4 & 10 & 3 \end{bmatrix}, \text{ and } b = \begin{bmatrix} 2 \\ -1 \\ 2 \end{bmatrix}.$$

It is straightforward to verify that the following six solutions are the sparsest solutions to the above linear system:

$$\begin{bmatrix} 0 \\ 1 \\ -1/2 \\ 0 \\ 0 \end{bmatrix}, \begin{bmatrix} 1 \\ -1 \\ 0 \\ 0 \\ 0 \end{bmatrix}, \begin{bmatrix} 0 \\ 4/5 \\ 0 \\ 1/5 \\ 0 \end{bmatrix}, \begin{bmatrix} 1/2 \\ 0 \\ -1/4 \\ 0 \\ 0 \end{bmatrix}, \begin{bmatrix} 0 \\ 0 \\ 2 \\ 1 \\ 0 \end{bmatrix}, \begin{bmatrix} 4/9 \\ 0 \\ 0 \\ 1/9 \\ 0 \end{bmatrix}.$$

We now verify that $A^T$ satisfies the RSP at $x^* = (4/9, 0, 0, 1/9, 0)^T$. It is sufficient to find a vector $\eta = (1, \eta_2, \eta_3, 1, \eta_5)^T$ in the range space of $A^T$ with $|\eta_2| < 1$, $|\eta_3| < 1$ and $|\eta_5| < 1$. Indeed, by taking $u = (1/2, 4/9, 0)^T$, we have that $\eta = A^T u = (1, 4/9, -2/9, 1, 7/18)^T$. Therefore, the RSP of $A^T$ at $x^*$ is satisfied. By Theorem 3.2.3, $x^*$ has a guaranteed recovery via $\ell_1$-minimization. Thus, for this example, $\ell_0$- and $\ell_1$-minimization problems are equivalent.

It is easy to verify that among the six sparsest solutions in Example 3.2.4, $x^* = (4/9, 0, 0, 1/9, 0)^T$ is the only one at which the RSP of $A^T$ holds. In fact, by Theorem 3.2.3, if the RSP of $A^T$ holds at a solution of an $\ell_0$-minimization problem, this solution is the unique solution to the $\ell_1$-minimization problem. We immediately have the following corollary.

**Corollary 3.2.5** *For any given underdetermined system of linear equations, there exists at most one solution of the problem (3.2), at which the RSP of $A^T$ is satisfied.*

**Example 3.2.6** (Strong equivalence) Consider the system $Az = b$ with

$$A = \begin{bmatrix} 1 & 0 & 1 & -\sqrt{3} & 1 & 0 \\ 1 & 1 & 1 & -\sqrt{2} & 0 & -1 \\ 0 & 1 & 1 & 1 & -1 & -1 \end{bmatrix}, \text{ and } b = \begin{bmatrix} -1 \\ -1 \\ -1 \end{bmatrix}.$$

Clearly, $x^* = (0,0,-1,0,0,0)^T$ is the unique solution to the $\ell_0$-minimization problem. It is easy to find a vector $\eta = (\eta_1, \eta_2, -1, \eta_4, \eta_5, \eta_6)$ in $\mathcal{R}(A^T)$ with $\eta_3 = -1$ and $|\eta_i| < 1$ for all $i \neq 3$. In fact, by taking $y = (-1/3, -1/3, -1/3)^T$, we have

$$\eta = A^T y = \left( -\frac{2}{3}, -\frac{2}{3}, -1, \frac{\sqrt{3}+\sqrt{2}-1}{3}, 0, \frac{2}{3} \right).$$

Thus the individual RSP of $A^T$ at $x^*$ is satisfied. By Theorem 3.2.3, $\ell_0$- and $\ell_1$-minimization are strongly equivalent, and thus $x^*$ has a guaranteed recovery by $\ell_1$-minimization.

From the above discussion, the equivalence between $\ell_0$- and $\ell_1$-minimization can be achieved not only for a subclass of the problems in $G'$, but also for a subclass of the problems in $G''$. Many traditional sufficient conditions developed in compressed sensing scenarios, such as the mutual conditions, RIP, NSP or similar conditions (see Section 3.6 for details) imply the strong equivalence of $\ell_0$- and $\ell_1$-minimization. These conditions, however, cannot apply to the linear systems in $G''$, and hence cannot explain the success of $\ell_1$-minimization in solving the $\ell_0$-minimization problems with multiple sparsest solutions. The simulation shows that the success frequency of $\ell_1$-minimization is higher than what has predicted by uniform recovery conditions which imply the strong equivalence of $\ell_0$- and $\ell_1$-minimization. Therefore, the actual performance of $\ell_1$-minimization can be better interpreted via the RSP-based analysis. This analysis indicates that the uniqueness of the solutions to an $\ell_0$-minimization problem is not necessary for the $\ell_0$-minimization problem to be solved via $\ell_1$-minimization, and the multiplicity of the solutions of an $\ell_0$-minimization problem does also not prohibit the problem from being solved by $\ell_1$-minimization. Thus the actual success frequency of $\ell_1$-minimization is certainly higher than what has indicated by the strong-equivalence-based theory.

## 3.3 Problems with Non-negative Constraints

Non-negative constraints appear in many practical problems. In this case, the problem (3.3) seeks the sparsest non-negative solution to an underdetermined system of linear equations. Associated with (3.3) is the following $\ell_1$-minimization with non-negative constraints:

$$\min_{x}\{\|x\|_1 : Ax = b, \, x \geq 0\}. \tag{3.6}$$

Clearly, the sparsest non-negative solution of the system $Ax = b$ may not be the sparsest solution of this system. In other words, the solutions of (3.2) and (3.3) are usually different. The problems with non-negative constraints have their own unique features. In this section, we discuss the condition under which (3.3) and (3.6) are equivalent. First, we have the following observation for the sparsest non-negative solutions.

**Lemma 3.3.1** *If $x \geq 0$ is the sparsest non-negative solution to the problem (3.3), then $A_{S_+(x)} = A_{\mathrm{supp}(x)}$ has full column rank, where $S_+(x) = \{i : x_i > 0\}$.*

*Proof.* Let $x$ be a solution to the problem (3.3), which is the sparsest non-negative solution of the system of linear equations. Assume that the columns of $A_{S_+(x)}$ are linearly dependent. Under this assumption, there exists a vector $v$ such that $A_{S_+(x)}v = 0$ and $v \neq 0$. Consider the vector $x_{S_+(x)} + \lambda v$ where $\lambda \in \mathbb{R}$. Note that $b = A_{S_+(x)}x_{S_+(x)}$ and $x_{S_+(x)} > 0$. By the definition of $v$, we see that

$$A_{S_+(x)}\left(x_{S_+(x)} + \lambda v\right) = b \text{ for any } \lambda \in \mathbb{R}.$$

Since $x_{S_+(x)} > 0$ and $v \neq 0$, there exists a number $\lambda^*$ such that $x_{S_+(x)} + \lambda^* v \geq 0$ and at least one of the components of $x_{S_+(x)} + \lambda^* v$ is equal to zero. Define $\tilde{x} \in \mathbb{R}^n_+$ as follows:

$$\tilde{x}_{S_+(x)} = x_{S_+(x)} + \lambda^* v \geq 0, \, \tilde{x}_i = 0 \text{ for all } i \notin S_+(x).$$

Clearly, $\tilde{x}$ is a feasible point of the problem (3.3) and $\|\tilde{x}\|_0 \leq \|x\|_0 - 1$. So $\tilde{x}$ is sparser than $x$, leading to a contradiction. Thus, when $x$ is a solution of (3.3), $A_{S_+(x)}$ must have full column rank. $\square$

Different from the individual RSP property as given in Definition 2.2.4, we define a similar notion for nonnegativity situations.

**Definition 3.3.2** (RSP$^+$ of $A^T$ at $x \geq 0$) *The matrix $A^T$ is said to satisfy the range space property plus (RSP$^+$) at a non-negative point $x \in \mathbb{R}^n_+$ if there exists a vector $\eta \in \mathcal{R}(A^T)$ such that*

$$\eta_i = 1 \text{ for all } x_i > 0, \quad \eta_i < 1 \text{ for all } x_i = 0. \tag{3.7}$$

To distinguish from the RSP of $A^T$ at $x \in \mathbb{R}^n$, the matrix property described in Definition 3.3.2 is referred to as the "RSP$^+$ of $A^T$ at $x \in \mathbb{R}^n_+$". A big difference between the RSP and the RSP$^+$ above is in that the components $\eta_i$ corresponding to $x_i = 0$ in RSP$^+$ can be any number smaller than 1, instead of $|\eta_i| < 1$ in the standard RSP notion. Thus RSP$^+$ of $A^T$ at $x \geq 0$ is generally not the RSP of $A^T$ at $x \geq 0$. By Theorem 2.3.6 and Lemma 3.3.1, we immediately have the following result.

**Theorem 3.3.3** *Problems (3.3) and (3.6) are equivalent (in the sense of Defini-tion 3.1.1) if and only if $A^T$ satisfies the RSP$^+$ at a solution of (3.3).*

*Proof.* Assume that (3.3) and (3.6) are equivalent. By Definition 3.1.1, the prob-lem (3.3) has a solution $x \geq 0$ which is the unique solution of (3.6). Thus, by Theorem 2.3.6, the RSP$^+$ of $A^T$ at $x$ must hold. We now assume that the RSP$^+$ holds at $x$ which is a solution of (3.3). By Lemma 3.3.1, the matrix $A_{S_+}$ has full column rank. Thus by Theorem 2.3.6 again, $x$ must be the unique solution to the problem (3.6), and hence (3.3) and (3.6) are equivalent. □

The above result indicates that the RSP$^+$ of $A^T$ at a solution of the problem (3.3) is necessary and sufficient for the problems (3.3) and (3.6) to be equivalent. This property is implicitly given, since the solution of $\ell_0$-minimization is not readily available before we actually solve it. However, this necessary and suffi-cient condition can efficiently interpret the success and failure of $\ell_1$-minimization when solving the $\ell_0$-minimization problems with non-negative constraints. As indicated by Theorem 3.3.3, any sufficient conditions for strong equivalence or equivalence of (3.3) and (3.6) must imply the RSP$^+$ of $A^T$ at a solution of (3.3).

**Example 3.3.4** Consider the linear system $Az = b$, where

$$A = \begin{bmatrix} 0 & -1 & -1 & 0 & 1 & -1 \\ 0 & 0 & -1 & 1 & 0 & -2 \\ 1 & 0 & 1 & 0 & 1 & -1 \end{bmatrix}, \text{ and } b = \begin{bmatrix} 1 \\ 1 \\ 0 \end{bmatrix}.$$

For this example, the system $Az = b$ does not have a solution $x$ with $\|x\|_0 = 1$. So, $x^* = (1,0,1,0,0,0)^T$ is the sparsest non-negative solution to the linear system. Let us check the RSP$^+$ of $A^T$ at $x^*$. By taking $u = (-1/2, 1/2, 1)^T$, we have

$$\eta = A^T u = (1, -1/2, 1, 1/2, 1/2, -3/2)^T \in \mathcal{R}(A^T),$$

where the first and third components of $\eta$ (corresponding to $S_+(x^*) = \{1,3\}$) are equal to 1, and other components of $\eta$ are less than 1. Thus, the RSP$^+$ of $A^T$ at $x^*$ is satisfied. By Theorem 3.3.3, $\ell_0$- and $\ell_1$-minimization are equivalent.

To further understand the efficiency and limitations of $\ell_1$-minimization, let us decompose the set of linear systems with non-negative solutions into the follow-ing three subsets:

$G'_+$ : Both the problems (3.6) and (3.3) have unique solutions

$G''_+$ : The problem (3.6) has a unique solution, but (3.3) has multiple solutions

$G'''_+$ : The problem (3.6) has multiple solutions.

Clearly, every linear system with non-negative solutions falls into one and only one of the above categories. Note that there is no guaranteed success for $\ell_1$-minimization when solving $\ell_0$-minimization problems with the linear systems in group $G'''_+$, due to the multiplicity of $\ell_1$-minimizers in this case.

**Example 3.3.5** Consider the system $Az = b$ with

$$A = \begin{bmatrix} 2 & 0 & -3 & -1 & 5 & -4 \\ -2 & 0 & -3 & 1 & -5 & 0 \\ 0 & -2 & 5 & -2 & 9 & 2 \end{bmatrix}, \text{ and } b = \begin{bmatrix} 1 \\ -1 \\ 1 \end{bmatrix}.$$

For this example, it is easy to verify that $Az = b$ has multiple sparsest non-negative solutions:

$$x^{(1)} = \left(0, \frac{2}{5}, 0, 0, \frac{1}{5}, 0\right)^T, \ x^{(2)} = (0,0,0,4,1,0)^T, \ x^{(3)} = \left(\frac{2}{9}, 0, 0, 0, \frac{1}{9}, 0\right)^T.$$

Since $\|x^{(1)}\|_1 > \|x^{(3)}\|_1$ and $\|x^{(2)}\|_1 > \|x^{(3)}\|_1$, by Theorem 3.3.3, the RSP$^+$ of $A^T$ is impossible to hold at $x^{(1)}$ and $x^{(2)}$, since otherwise they must be the unique least $\ell_1$-norm non-negative solution of the linear system. Therefore, we only need to check the RSP$^+$ of $A^T$ at $x^{(3)}$. Taking $u = (1/2, 0, -1/6)^T$ yields

$$\eta = A^T u = (1, 1/3, -7/3, -1/6, 1, -7/3)^T \in \mathcal{R}(A^T),$$

where the first and fifth components are 1, and the others are strictly less than 1. Thus, the RSP$^+$ of $A^T$ at $x^{(3)}$ is satisfied. By Theorem 3.3.3, $x^{(3)}$ is the unique least $\ell_1$-norm non-negative solution to the linear system, i.e., $x^{(3)}$ is the solution of (3.6). So the $\ell_1$-minimization method can solve the $\ell_0$-minimization problem, although this $\ell_0$-minimization problem has multiple solutions.

As shown in Example 3.3.5, $\ell_0$- and $\ell_1$-minimization can be equivalent, provided that the RSP$^+$ of $A^T$ is satisfied at a solution of the $\ell_0$-minimization problem, irrespective of the multiplicity of the solutions to the $\ell_0$-minimization problem. The following corollary is an immediate consequence of Theorem 3.3.3.

**Corollary 3.3.6** *For any $\ell_0$-minimization problem (3.3), there exists at most one solution of (3.3) at which $A^T$ satisfies the RSP$^+$.*

It is well known that many conditions for exact recoveries of sparse vectors in the field of compressed sensing actually guarantee the strong equivalence of $\ell_0$- and $\ell_1$-minimization (please refer to Section 3.6 for details of some exact recovery criteria). The analysis based on RSP$^+$ of $A^T$ goes far beyond the scope of linear systems in $G'_+$. It can explain not only the strong equivalence but also the performance of the $\ell_1$-minimization method when the solution of an $\ell_0$-minimization problem is not unique. So the RSP$^+$-based analysis actually identifies a broader class of $\ell_0$-minimization problems in $G'_+ \cup G''_+$ that can be solved by $\ell_1$-minimization. This analysis also sheds light on the boundary of efficiency of $\ell_1$-minimization. Failing to satisfy the RSP$^+$ of $A^T$ at a solution of (3.3), such a solution is impossible to be located with $\ell_1$-minimization.

## 3.4 Application to Linear Programming

The RSP$^+$-based analysis can be also applied to the sparsest solution of the following LP problem:

$$\min_{x}\{c^T x : Ax = b, \ x \geq 0\}, \tag{3.8}$$

where $A \in \mathbb{R}^{m \times n}$ with $m < n - 1$. In many situations, reducing the number of activities is vital to achieve the efficient planning, management and resource allocations. The sparsest solution of (3.8) is meaningful. For instance, in production planning scenarios, the decision variables $x_i \geq 0$, $i = 1, \ldots, n$, indicate which production activities/events should take place and how much resources should be allocated to them in order to achieve the optimal objective value. The sparsest solution of a linear program provides the smallest number of activities to achieve the optimal objective value. We denote by $\rho^*$ the optimal value of the LP problem in (3.8), which can be obtained by solving the problem by an interior point method or the simplex method. We assume that (3.8) is feasible and has a finite optimal value $\rho^*$. Thus the solution set of (3.8) is given by

$$\{x : Ax = b, \ x \geq 0, \ c^T x = \rho^*\}.$$

So the sparsest solution to this problem is a solution to the following $\ell_0$-problem:

$$\min_{x}\left\{ \|x\|_0 : \begin{bmatrix} A \\ c^T \end{bmatrix} x = \begin{bmatrix} b \\ \rho^* \end{bmatrix}, \ x \geq 0 \right\}. \tag{3.9}$$

Therefore, the discussion regarding the equivalence of $\ell_0$- and $\ell_1$-minimization problems in Section 3.3 can directly apply to (3.9) and the following $\ell_1$-minimization problem:

$$\min_{x}\left\{ \|x\|_1 : \begin{bmatrix} A \\ c^T \end{bmatrix} x = \begin{bmatrix} b \\ \rho^* \end{bmatrix}, \ x \geq 0 \right\}. \tag{3.10}$$

For instance, combining Theorems 2.3.6 and 3.3.3, yields Theorem 3.4.1.

**Theorem 3.4.1** $x^*$ *is the unique least $\ell_1$-norm element in the solution set of the LP problem in (3.8) if and only if $H = \begin{bmatrix} A \\ c^T \end{bmatrix}_{S_+(x^*)}$ has full column rank, and there exists a vector $\eta \in \mathbb{R}^n$ obeying*

$$\eta \in \mathcal{R}([A^T, c]), \ \eta_i = 1 \text{ for } i \in S_+(x^*), \text{ and } \eta_i < 1 \text{ for } i \notin S_+(x^*), \tag{3.11}$$

*where $S_+(x^*) = \{i : x_i^* > 0\}$. Moreover, the sparsest solution $x^*$ of the problem (3.8) is the unique solution to the problem (3.10) if and only if the conditions in (3.11) at this solution are satisfied.*

Note that the degenerated solutions of LP problems have been studied since 1950s (see [120, 121] and the references therein). Any degenerated solution of (3.8) has a sparsity level lower than $m$, i.e., $\|x\|_0 < m$. Thus a degenerated solution is actually a sparse solution of the LP problem, although it may not be the sparsest one. From this perspective, the sparse solution of an LP problem has already been studied for a long time under the name of degenerated solutions. Clearly, the most degenerated solution is the sparsest solution of the LP problem. It is well known that finding a degenerated solution requires extra effort than non-degenerated ones, and finding the most degenerated solution (i.e., the sparsest one) becomes even harder. By applying the RSP$^+$-based theory to the problems (3.9) and (3.10), we obtain a further understanding of the most degenerated solution of the LP problem. As indicated by Theorem 3.4.1, whether such a solution can be easily found or not is closely related to the range space property of the matrix $[A^T, c]$. If the RSP$^+$ (or RSP) property of such a matrix holds at the sparsest solution of the LP problem (3.8), Theorem 3.4.1 claims that this sparsest solution (i.e., the most degenerated solution) of (3.8) can be found by solving the $\ell_1$-minimization problem (3.10) which is equivalent to an LP problem.

## 3.5  Equivalence of $\ell_0$-Problem and Weighted $\ell_1$-Problem

From the discussions in Sections 3.2 and 3.3, we see that the standard $\ell_1$-minimization method may fail to find a solution of an $\ell_0$-minimization problem, unless $A^T$ satisfies the individual RSP at a sparsest solution of the $\ell_0$-problem.

**Example 3.5.1** Consider the system $Az = b$ with

$$A = \begin{bmatrix} 1 & 4 & 0 & -2 & 0 \\ 2 & 0 & 2 & -3 & 4 \\ 3 & 4 & 2 & -2 & 4 \end{bmatrix}, \text{ and } b = \begin{bmatrix} 2 \\ 4 \\ 6 \end{bmatrix}.$$

Clearly, $x^* = (2,0,0,0,0)$ is the only sparsest solution of the underlying $\ell_0$-minimization problem. Consider the vector $\hat{x} = (0,1/2,0,0,1)^T$ which is also a solution to the linear system. By using Theorem 2.2.14, it is very easy to verify that $A_{S_+(\hat{x})}$ has full column rank and the RSP of $A^T$ at $\hat{x}$ also holds. So $\hat{x}$ is the only solution to the underlying $\ell_1$-minimization problem. The RSP of $A^T$ at $\hat{x}$ is easy to verify, for instance, by taking $u = (0,0,1/4)^T$, the vector $\eta = A^T u = (3/4,1,1/2,-1/2,1)^T$ satisfies the RSP condition. Note that $\|x^*\|_1 > \|\hat{x}\|_1$. This implies that the $\ell_1$-minimization method is impossible to find $x^*$. So for this example $\ell_1$- and $\ell_0$-minimization are not equivalent. It is straightforward to verify that the RSP of $A^T$ fails to hold at $x^* = (2,0,0,0,0)$, i.e., there exists no vector $u \in \mathbb{R}^3$ such that $\eta = A^T u$ with $\eta_1 = 1$ and $|\eta_i| < 1$ for $i = 2, \ldots, 5$.

The $\ell_1$-minimization problem (3.4) is a special case of the weighted $\ell_1$-minimization problem

$$\min_x \{\|Wx\|_1 : x \in P\},$$

where $P \subseteq \mathbb{R}^n$ is a certain polyhedral set, and the matrix $W \in \mathbb{R}^{n \times n}$ is called a weight. Once a weight $W$ is fixed, similar to standard $\ell_1$-minimization, the weighted $\ell_1$-minimization can only solve a subclass of $\ell_0$-minimization problems. So it does not admit any advantage over the standard $\ell_1$-minimization in terms of the their overall capability of solving $\ell_0$-minimization problems. It is very easy to give examples of $\ell_0$-minimization problems which can be solved by $\ell_1$-minimization, but not by weighted $\ell_1$-minimization with a prescribed weight, and vice versa. However, given an $\ell_0$-minimization problem, weighted $\ell_1$-minimization may succeed to solve the $\ell_0$-minimization problem if an appropriate weight is selected. Since the weight in the objective may set priority of (or impose preference on) the components of the feasible vectors of the problem, the solution of a weighted $\ell_1$-minimization problem depends on the choice of weight. It turns out that through weight selection, the weighted $\ell_1$-minimization method may find, in theory, any solution of the $\ell_0$-minimization problem. This useful property of weighted $\ell_1$-minimization provides a theoretical basis for the development of certain algorithms for $\ell_0$-minimization problems. The interested readers may refer to Chapters 7 and 8 for more details. In what follows, we still denote by

$$S_+(x) = \{i : x_i > 0\}, \ S_-(x) = \{i : x_i < 0\}, \ S_0(x) = \{i : x_i = 0\}.$$

As indicated by Theorem 2.2.14, $x$ is the unique solution to the standard $\ell_1$-minimization if and only if the following two conditions hold simultaneously:

(i) $A_{\text{supp}(x)}$ has full column rank;

(ii) There exists a vector $\eta \in \mathcal{R}(A^T)$ such that $\eta_i = 1$ for $i \in S_+(x)$, $\eta_i = -1$ for $i \in S_-(x)$ and $|\eta_i| < 1$ for $i \in S_0(x)$.

The condition (ii) above can be written as follows: There is a vector $\eta \in \mathcal{R}(A^T)$ such that

$$\eta_{S_+(x)} = e_{S_+(x)}, \ \eta_{S_-(x)} = -e_{S_-(x)}, \ \|\eta_{S_0(x)}\|_\infty < 1.$$

Using Theorem 2.2.14, we can characterize the uniqueness of the solution of a weighted $\ell_1$-minimization problem. For simplicity, we only focus on the weight $W$ which is a diagonal matrix. That is, $W = \text{diag}(w)$ for some vector $w$.

**Theorem 3.5.2** *Let $W = \text{diag}(w)$, where $w \in \mathbb{R}^n_{++}$ is a given positive vector. Then $x$ is the unique solution to the weighted $\ell_1$-minimization problem*

$$\min_z \{\|Wz\|_1 : Az = b\} \tag{3.12}$$

*if and only if the following conditions hold:* (i) $A_{\text{supp}(x)}$ *has full column rank, and* (ii) *there is a vector* $\xi \in \mathcal{R}(A^T)$ *satisfying*

$$
\begin{cases}
\xi_i & = & w_i & \text{for all } i \in S_+(x), \\
\xi_i & = & -w_i & \text{for all } i \in S_-(x), \\
|\xi_i| & < & w_i & \text{for all } i \in S_0(x),
\end{cases}
$$

*that is,*

$$\xi_{S_+(x)} = w_{S_+(x)}, \ \xi_{S_-(x)} = -w_{S_-(x)}, \ |\xi_{S_0(x)}| < w_{S_0(x)}.$$

*Proof.* By the nonsingular linear transformation $u = Wx$, the problem (3.12) can be written as the following standard $\ell_1$-minimization problem:

$$\min_u \{\|u\|_1 : (AW^{-1})u = b\}. \tag{3.13}$$

As $W$ is a diagonal matrix with positive diagonal entries, the vectors $u$ and $x$ satisfying $u = Wx$ share the same support sets. Specifically,

$$S_+(u) = S_+(x), \ S_-(u) = S_-(x). \tag{3.14}$$

Clearly, $x$ is the unique solution to the problem (3.12) if and only if $u$ is the unique solution to the problem (3.13). By Theorem 2.2.14, $u = Wx$ is the unique solution of (3.13) if and only if the following two conditions hold:

- $(AW^{-1})_{\text{supp}(u)}$ has full column rank;

- There exists a vector $\eta \in \mathcal{R}(W^{-1}A^T)$ such that:

$$\eta_{S_+(u)} = \mathbf{e}_{S_+(u)}, \ \eta_{S_-(u)} = -\mathbf{e}_{S_-(u)}, \ \|\eta_{S_0(u)}\|_\infty < 1. \tag{3.15}$$

Note that $W^{-1}$ is a diagonal nonsingular matrix. $(AW^{-1})_{\text{supp}(u)}$ has full column rank if and only if $A_{\text{supp}(u)}$ has full column rank. Thus it follows from (3.14) that $A_{\text{supp}(x)}$ has full column rank. Note that $\eta \in \mathcal{R}(W^{-1}A^T)$ is equivalent to $\xi := W\eta \in \mathcal{R}(A^T)$. Thus the conditions in (3.15) are equivalent to

$$
\begin{aligned}
\xi_{S_+(x)} & = & (W\eta)_{S_+(x)} = w_{S_+(x)}, \\
\xi_{S_-(x)} & = & (W\eta)_{S_-(x)} = -w_{S_-(x)}, \\
|\xi_{S_0(x)}| & = & |(W\eta)_{S_0(x)}| < w_{S_0(x)},
\end{aligned}
$$

as desired. □

For any $x^*$ satisfying $Ax^* = b$, if $A_{\text{supp}(x^*)}$ has full column rank, we can prove that there exists a weight $w$ such that $x^*$ is the unique solution to the weighted $\ell_1$-minimization problem (3.12). In other words, such a vector can be exactly recovered, in theory, via the weighted $\ell_1$-minimization method.

**Lemma 3.5.3** *Let $x^*$ be a solution to the system $Az = b$ with $A_{\text{supp}(x^*)}$ having full column rank. Let $W = \text{diag}(w)$, where $w \in \mathbb{R}^n_+$ satisfies one of the following conditions:*

(i) $w \in \mathbb{R}^n_{++}$ *and* $w_{S_0(x^*)} > v^*$, *where $v^*$ is a solution to the linear program*

$$\min_{(y,v)} \quad \mathbf{e}^T v$$
$$\text{s.t.} \quad A_{S_+(x^*)}^T y = w_{S_+(x^*)}, \ A_{S_-(x^*)}^T y = -w_{S_-(x^*)}, \tag{3.16}$$
$$|A_{S_0(x^*)}^T y| \leq v.$$

(ii) $w \in \mathbb{R}^n_+$ *and*

$$w_{S_0(x^*)} > \left| A_{S_0(x^*)}^T A_{\text{supp}(x^*)} (A_{\text{supp}(x^*)}^T A_{\text{supp}(x^*)})^{-1} \right| w_{\text{supp}(x^*)}. \tag{3.17}$$

*Then $x^*$ is the unique solution to the weighted $\ell_1$-minimization problem in (3.12), where $W = \text{diag}(w)$.*

*Proof.* (i) When $A_{\text{supp}(x^*)}$ has full column rank, the range space of $A_{\text{supp}(x^*)}^T$ is a full space, i.e., $\mathcal{R}(A_{\text{supp}(x^*)}^T) = \mathbb{R}^{|\text{supp}(x^*)|}$. Thus for any vector $(u, v)$ where $u \in \mathbb{R}^{|S_+(x^*)|}$ and $v \in \mathbb{R}^{|S_-(x^*)|}$, there is a vector $y \in \mathbb{R}^m$ such that $A_{S_+(x^*)}^T y = u$ and $A_{S_-(x^*)}^T y = -v$. This implies that the problem (3.16) is always feasible for any given $w_{S_+(x^*)} > 0$ and $w_{S_-(x^*)} > 0$. Due to the nonnegativity of the objective, the problem (3.16) has a solution. Let $(y^*, v^*)$ be a solution to this problem. Clearly, we must have that $v^* = |A_{S_0(x^*)}^T y^*|$ at the solution. Note that $w_{S_0(x^*)} > v^*$. By setting $\xi = A^T y^*$, from the problem (3.16), we see that

$$\begin{aligned} \xi_{S_+(x^*)} &= (A^T y)_{S_+(x^*)} = A_{S_+(x^*)}^T y = w_{S_+(x^*)}, \\ \xi_{S_-(x^*)} &= (A^T y)_{S_-(x^*)} = A_{S_-(x^*)}^T y = -w_{S_-(x^*)}, \\ |\xi_{S_0(x^*)}| &= |A_{S_0(x^*)}^T y^*| = v^* < w_{S_0(x^*)}. \end{aligned}$$

Thus, by Theorem 3.5.2, $x^*$ is the unique solution to the weighted $\ell_1$-minimization problem in (3.12).

(ii) Let $x^*$ be a solution to the linear system $Az = b$, and let $A_{\text{supp}(x^*)}$ have full column rank. Denote by $S = \text{supp}(x^*)$ and $S_0 = S_0(x^*)$ for simplicity. Assume that $x \neq x^*$ is an arbitrary solution to the problem (3.12). Note that $A_S x_S^* = b$ and $A_S x_S + A_{S_0} x_{S_0} = b$. We have $A_S(x_S - x_S^*) + A_{S_0} x_{S_0} = 0$. Thus,

$$x_S^* = x_S + (A_S^T A_S)^{-1} A_S^T A_{S_0} x_{S_0}, \tag{3.18}$$

which implies that

$$|x_S^*| \leq |x_S| + |(A_S^T A_S)^{-1} A_S^T A_{S_0}| \cdot |x_{S_0}|.$$

Therefore,

$$
\begin{aligned}
\|Wx^*\|_1 - \|Wx\|_1 &= w^T|x^*| - w^T|x| \\
&= w_S^T|x_S^*| - w_S^T|x_S| - w_{S_0}^T|x_{S_0}| \\
&\leq w_S^T|(A_S^T A_S)^{-1}A_S^T A_{S_0}| \cdot |x_{S_0}| - w_{S_0}^T|x_{S_0}| \\
&= \left(|A_{S_0}^T A_S(A_S^T A_S)^{-1}|w_S - w_{S_0}\right)^T |x_{S_0}|.
\end{aligned}
$$

Since $x \neq x^*$, it follows from (3.18) that $x_{S_0} \neq 0$. Combining (3.17) and the inequality above yields $\|Wx^*\|_1 < \|Wx\|_1$, which holds for any solution $x \neq x^*$ of the linear system. Thus $x^*$ is the unique solution to the weighted $\ell_1$-minimization problem in (3.12). □

An $\ell_0$-minimization problem is not always equivalent to an $\ell_1$-minimization problem, unless the RSP of $A^T$ is satisfied at a solution of the former. However, if $x$ is a solution to an $\ell_0$-minimization problem, then there exists a weight $w \in \mathbb{R}_+^n$ accordingly such that $x$ is the unique solution to the weighted $\ell_1$-problem (3.19), as indicated by the next result. Note that at any sparsest solution $x^*$ of the system $Az = b$, the associated matrix $A_{\text{supp}(x^*)}$ always has full column rank. Thus the following theorem is an immediate consequence of Lemmas 3.5.3.

**Theorem 3.5.4** *Let* $x^*$ *be a solution for the* $\ell_0$-*minimization problem (3.2). Let* $W = diag(w)$, *where* $w$ *satisfies one of the following conditions:*

(i) $w \in \mathbb{R}_+^n$ *and* $w_{S_0(x^*)} > \left| A_{S_0(x^*)}^T A_{\text{supp}(x^*)} \left( A_{\text{supp}(x^*)}^T A_{\text{supp}(x^*)} \right)^{-1} \right| w_{\text{supp}(x^*)}.$

(ii) $w \in \mathbb{R}_{++}^n$ *and* $w_{S_0(x^*)} > v^*$, *where* $v^* \in \mathbb{R}^{|S_0(x^*)|}$ *is a solution of (3.16).*

*Then* $x^*$ *is the unique solution to the weighted* $\ell_1$-*minimization problem in (3.12), and thus the two problems (3.2) and (3.12) are equivalent.*

In the rest of this section, we consider the equivalence of the problem (3.3) and the following weighted $\ell_1$-problem with non-negative constraints:

$$
\min_x \{\|Wx\|_1 : Ax = b, \ x \geq 0\}, \tag{3.19}
$$

where $W = diag(w)$ and $w \in \mathbb{R}_{++}^n$. By the nonsingular transformation, $u = Wx$, the problem above can be written as

$$
\min_u \{\|u\|_1 : (AW^{-1})u = b, \ u \geq 0\}. \tag{3.20}
$$

Clearly, $x$ is the unique solution to (3.19) if and only if $u = Wx$ is the unique solution to (3.20). Thus any weighted $\ell_1$-minimization problem with $W = diag(w)$, where $w$ is a positive vector in $\mathbb{R}^n$, is nothing but a standard $\ell_1$-minimization problem with a scaled matrix $AW^{-1}$. Lemma 3.3.1 claims that at any solution of (3.3), the associated matrix $A_{S_+(x)}$ has full column rank. Note that

$\text{supp}(x) = S_+(x)$ for any non-negative vector. Applying Theorem 2.3.6 to the $\ell_1$-minimization problem (3.20), we conclude that $u$ is the unique solution of (3.20) if and only if (i) $(AW^{-1})_{S_+(u)}$ has full column rank, and (ii) there exists a vector $\zeta \in \mathcal{R}(W^{-1}A^T)$ such that $\zeta_i = 1$ for $u_i > 0$ and $\zeta_i < 1$ for $u_i = 0$. By the nonsingularity of $W^{-1}$ and the fact that $u$ and $x$ share the same support and sign, the above item (i) is equivalent to saying that $A_{S_+(x)}$ has full column rank. By the one-to-one correspondence between solutions of (3.19) and (3.20), and by transforming back to the weighted $\ell_1$-minimization problem using $u = Wx$ and $\eta = W\zeta$, we reach the following statement.

**Corollary 3.5.5** $x^*$ *is the unique solution to the weighted $\ell_1$-minimization problem (3.19) if and only if (i) $A_{S_+}$ has full column rank, where $S_+ = \{i : x_i^* > 0\}$, and (ii) there is an $\eta \in \mathcal{R}(A^T)$ such that $\eta_i = w_i$ for all $x_i^* > 0$, and $\eta_i < w_i$ for all $x_i^* = 0$.*

We may call the property (ii) above the *weighted RSP$^+$ of $A^T$ at $x^*$*. The discussion in Sections 3.2 and 3.3 can be made easily to the weighted $\ell_1$-minimization method. For instance, the counterpart of Theorem 3.3.3 for the equivalence between $\ell_0$- and weighted $\ell_1$-minimization can be stated by using the above notion of weighted RSP$^+$. Similar to Theorem 3.5.4, we can prove the following theorem for non-negative cases.

**Theorem 3.5.6** *Let $x^*$ be a solution to the $\ell_0$-minimization problem (3.3). If the weight $w \in \mathbb{R}_+^n$ is chosen such that*

$$w_{S_0(x^*)} > A_{S_0(x^*)}^T A_{S_+(x^*)} \left( A_{S_+(x^*)}^T A_{S_+(x^*)} \right)^{-1} w_{S_+(x^*)}, \qquad (3.21)$$

*then $x^*$ is the unique solution to the weighted $\ell_1$-minimization problem (3.19).*

*Proof.* Suppose that $x^*$ is a solution of (3.3). By Lemma 3.3.1, $A_{S_+(x^*)}$ has full column rank. Let $\tilde{x} \neq x^*$ be an arbitrary solution of (3.3). It is sufficient to show that $\|Wx^*\|_1 < \|W\tilde{x}\|_1$, where $W$ satisfies (3.21). By assumption, $A\tilde{x} = b$ and $\tilde{x} \geq 0$, which can be written as

$$A_{S_+(x^*)}\tilde{x}_{S_+(x^*)} + A_{S_0(x^*)}\tilde{x}_{S_0(x^*)} = b, \ \tilde{x}_{S_+(x^*)} \geq 0, \ \tilde{x}_{S_0(x^*)} \geq 0.$$

The first condition above, combined with $A_{S_+(x^*)}x_{S_+(x^*)} = b$, implies that

$$A_{S_+(x^*)}(\tilde{x}_{S_+(x^*)} - x_{S_+(x^*)}) + A_{S_0(x^*)}\tilde{x}_{S_0(x^*)} = 0.$$

From the above equality, we see that

$$\tilde{x}_{S_+(x^*)} = x_{S_+(x^*)} - \left[ A_{S_+(x^*)}^T A_{S_+(x^*)} \right]^{-1} A_{S_+(x^*)}^T A_{S_0(x^*)}\tilde{x}_{S_0(x^*)}. \qquad (3.22)$$

Note that $\tilde{x} \neq x^*$. The above relation implies that $\tilde{x}_{S_0(x^*)} \neq 0$, since otherwise $\tilde{x}_{S_+(x^*)} = x^*_{S_+(x^*)}$ and hence $\tilde{x} = x^*$, leading to a contradiction. By (3.22) and noting that $\tilde{x}$ and $x^*$ are non-negative vectors, we have

$$\|Wx\|_1 - \|W\tilde{x}\|_1 = w^T x - w^T \tilde{x}$$

$$= w^T_{S_+(x^*)} x_{S_+(x^*)} - \left( w^T_{S_+(x^*)} \tilde{x}_{S_+(x^*)} + w^T_{S_0(x^*)} \tilde{x}_{S_0(x^*)} \right)$$

$$= \left[ w^T_{S_+(x^*)} \left[ A^T_{S_+(x^*)} A_{S_+(x^*)} \right]^{-1} A^T_{S_+(x^*)} A_{S_0(x^*)} - w^T_{S_0(x^*)} \right] \tilde{x}_{S_0(x^*)}$$

$$= \left[ A^T_{S_0(x^*)} A_{S_+(x^*)} \left[ A^T_{S_+(x^*)} A_{S_+(x^*)} \right]^{-1} w_{S_+(x^*)} - w_{S_0(x^*)} \right]^T \tilde{x}_{S_0(x^*)}.$$

By (3.21) and the fact $\tilde{x}_{S_0(x^*)} \neq 0$ and $\tilde{x}_{S_0(x^*)} \geq 0$, the right-hand side of the above equality is negative, i.e., $\|Wx^*\|_1 < \|W\tilde{x}\|_1$. Therefore, $x^*$ is the unique solution to (3.19). □

The result above shows that for any $\ell_0$-minimization problem, there is a weight such that the weighted $\ell_1$-minimization problem is equivalent to the $\ell_0$-minimization problem. Although such a weight is not available beforehand, this theoretical result remains useful in developing an efficient computational method for $\ell_0$-minimization problems. See Chapter 8 for further discussions.

## 3.6 Sparse Vector Recovery

Many signals and images are sparse or can be sparsely approximated. Via suitable linear and non-adaptive measurements of such signals, one may reconstruct the signal by solving a system of linear equations. The standard compressed sensing theory indicates that if the signal is sparse enough, it can be reconstructed by various (decoding) methods when the number of measurements is far lower than the signal length (see [48, 82]).

Suppose that we would like to recover a sparse vector $x^* \in \mathbb{R}^n$. To serve this purpose, a sensing matrix $A \in \mathbb{R}^{m \times n}$ with $m \ll n$ is designed, and the measurements $y := Ax^*$ are acquired. As shown by Theorem 1.2.3, $x^*$ is the unique sparsest solution to the system $Az = y$ when $x^*$ is sufficiently sparse. Particularly, if $\|x^*\|_0 < \text{spark}(A)/2$, then $x^*$ is the unique solution to the following $\ell_0$-minimization problem:

$$\min_x \{\|x\|_0 : Ax = y := Ax^*\}. \tag{3.23}$$

In this case, solving the problem (3.23) can recover the sparse signal $x^*$. Due to the NP-hardness of this problem, various heuristic approaches were developed for the $\ell_0$-minimization problems. These approaches are usually referred to as the decoding methods or compressed sensing algorithms. The theoretical performance of various decoding methods have been intensively studied since around

2004, including $\ell_1$-minimization (or weighted $\ell_1$-minimization), thresholding methods, orthogonal matching pursuits, and their variants. A large body of numerical experiments and practical applications indicate that the $\ell_1$-minimization method

$$\min_{x}\{\|x\|_1 : Ax = y := Ax^*\} \tag{3.24}$$

is one of the most plausible sparse optimization approaches for solving $\ell_0$-minimization problems. Denote by $\widehat{x}$ the solution of the $\ell_1$-minimization problem in (3.24). One of the fundamental questions in sparse vector recovery is: What class of sensing matrices can guarantee the exact recovery of $x^*$, i.e., $\widehat{x} = x^*$? To ensure the exact recovery of $x^*$ via $\ell_1$-minimization, the following three conditions are often required in compressed sensing theory:

(C1)  $x^*$ is the unique sparsest solution to the linear system $Ax = y$;

(C2)  $\widehat{x}$ is the unique least $\ell_1$-norm solution to the same system $Ax = y$;

(C3)  $\widehat{x}$ coincides with $x^*$.

Clearly, satisfying (C1)–(C3) requires that (3.23) and (3.24) are strongly equivalent in the sense of Definition 3.1.1. Many existing recovery theories comply with this framework. The exact recovery of every $k$-sparse vector $x^*$ with a single sensing matrix $A$ and precise measurements $y$, i.e., $y = Ax^*$, is called the *uniform recovery* of $k$-sparse vectors. The uniform recovery aims to achieve exact recovery of every $k$-sparse vector with the same sensing matrix. Let us first recall a few traditional conditions for uniform recoveries of $k$-sparse vectors, which have been widely exploited in the literature. The mutual coherence condition [83, 122, 96, 100]

$$\|x^*\|_0 \le (1 + \frac{1}{\mu(A)})/2 \tag{3.25}$$

can be seen as the first type of conditions for exact recovery of $k$-sparse vectors via $\ell_1$-minimization. As shown in [83, 122], any vector $x^*$ satisfying (3.25) must be the unique solution to both (3.23) and (3.24), and hence two problems are strongly equivalent. In other words, the uniform recovery of $k$-sparse vectors with sparsity level $k$ lower than $(1 + 1/\mu(A))/2$ can be achieved via $\ell_1$-minimization.

Other coherence criteria for uniform recoveries have also been developed, such as the one based on the Babel function $\mu_1(k)$ (see Definition 1.29). Let $A \in \mathbb{R}^{m \times n}(m < n)$ be a matrix with $\ell_2$-normalized columns $a_i, i = 1, \dots, n$. It was shown in [210, 83] that if

$$\mu_1(k) + \mu_1(k-1) < 1, \tag{3.26}$$

then every $k$-sparse vector can be exactly recovered by $\ell_1$-minimization. However, mutual-coherence-type criteria are usually restrictive, rendering such criteria inapplicable in many practical situations. Candès and Tao [51, 52] introduced the notion of restricted isometry property (RIP) with constant $\delta_k$, where $k$ is a certain integer number.

**Definition 3.6.1** (RIP of order $k$) [51] *The matrix A is said to satisfy the restricted isometry property (RIP) of order k with constant $\delta_k \in (0,1)$ if*

$$(1 - \delta_k)\|x\|_2^2 \leq \|Ax\|_2^2 \leq (1 + \delta_k)\|x\|_2^2$$

*holds for all k-sparse vector $x \in \mathbb{R}^n$.*

Candès and Tao [51] proved that if $\delta_{2k} + \delta_{3k} < 1$, every $k$-sparse vector can be exactly reconstructed via $\ell_1$-minimization. This result was improved to $\delta_{2k} < \sqrt{2} - 1$ by Candès in [45], and was further improved in [107, 41, 174, 108, 7, 44]. Finally, Cai and Zhang [44] improved this bound to $\delta_{2k} < 1/\sqrt{2}$. The RIP-based recovery condition is more relaxed than the mutual-coherence-type criteria. It is known that the mutual coherence condition (3.25) implies the RIP (see, e.g., Theorem 5.1 in [97]), and so does the condition (3.26) (see Theorem 5.3 in [108]). However, the RIP remains not a necessary condition for the uniform recovery. The next concept is more relaxed than the RIP.

**Definition 3.6.2** (NSP of order $k$) [65, 237, 108] *The matrix $A \in \mathbb{R}^{m \times n} (m < n)$ is said to satisfy the null space property (NSP) of order k if*

$$\|v_S\|_1 < \|v_{\overline{S}}\|_1$$

*holds for any nonzero vector $v \in \mathcal{N}(A)$ and any $S \subseteq \{1,\dots,n\}$ with $|S| \leq k$, where $\overline{S} = \{1,\dots,n\}\backslash S$.*

The following slightly strengthened versions of the NSP of order $k$ are particularly useful in the study of stability of some compressed sensing algorithms.

**Definition 3.6.3** (i) (Stable NSP of order $k$) [65, 108] *The matrix $A \in \mathbb{R}^{m \times n} (m < n)$ is said to satisfy the stable null space property of order k with constant $\rho \in (0,1)$ if*

$$\|v_S\|_1 \leq \rho \|v_{\overline{S}}\|_1$$

*holds for any $v \in \mathcal{N}(A)$ and any $S \subseteq \{1,\dots,n\}$ with $|S| \leq k$.*

(ii) (Robust NSP of order $k$) [65, 108] *The matrix $A \in \mathbb{R}^{m \times n} (m < n)$ is said to satisfy the robust null space property of order k with constants $\rho' \in (0,1)$ and $\rho'' > 0$ if*

$$\|v_S\|_1 \leq \rho'\|v_{\overline{S}}\|_1 + \rho''\|Av\|$$

*holds for any vector $v \in \mathbb{R}^n$ and any $S \subseteq \{1,\dots,n\}$ with $|S| \leq k$.*

The NSP property appeared in [85, 83, 122, 235] and was formally called the null space property by Cohen et al. [65]. The NSP is strictly weaker than the RIP (see [40]). The Babel-function condition (3.26) implies the NSP of order

$k$ (see Theorem 5.15 in [108]). In fact, the NSP of order $k$ is a necessary and sufficient condition for every $k$-sparse vector to be exactly reconstructed with $\ell_1$-minimization [65, 202, 97, 108, 40]. As a result, any sufficient condition for the uniform recovery of $k$-sparse vectors necessarily implies the NSP.

It is also worth introducing the so-called exact recovery condition (ERC) proposed by Tropp in [210].

**Definition 3.6.4** (ERC of order $k$) [210] *The matrix $A \in \mathbb{R}^{m \times n} (m < n)$ is said to satisfy the exact recovery condition (ERC) of order $k$ if for any support $S \subseteq \{1,\ldots,n\}$ with $|S| \le k$, the following holds*

$$\max_{i \notin S} \|A_S^+ a_i\|_1 < 1,$$

*where $A_S^+ = (A_S^T A_S)^{-1} A_S^T$ is the Moore-Penrose pseudo-inverse of $A_S$.*

Under this condition, the uniform recovery of every $k$-sparse vector via $\ell_1$-minimization can be also achieved. It is known that a matrix $A$ satisfying the mutual coherence condition $\mu(A) < 1/(2k-1)$ must satisfy the ERC of order $k$ (see [210, 95] for details). Some other conditions for exact recoveries can also be found in the literature, such as the so-called verifiable condition in [141]. Listing all such conditions goes beyond the scope of this section. From the above discussion, we see the following relations:

$$\left.\begin{array}{r} \text{RIP of order } 2k \text{ with } \delta_{2k} < 1/\sqrt{2} \Rightarrow \\ \text{Stable NSP of order } k \Rightarrow \\ \text{Robust NSP of order } k \Rightarrow \\ \mu_1(k) + \mu_1(k-1) < 1 \Rightarrow \\ \mu(A) < 1/(2k-1) \Rightarrow \\ \text{ERC of order } k \Rightarrow \end{array}\right\} \text{NSP of order } k.$$

The NSP of order $k$ is a necessary and sufficient condition for uniform recoveries, and thus every condition listed above implies the NSP of order $k$. The NSP notion is particularly convenient for the analysis of noiseless sparse recoveries where only underdetermined systems of linear equations are involved. However, the NSP-based analysis is not convenient for those sparse optimization problems with inequalities or more complicated constraints. In the next section, we introduce the notion of "*RSP of order $k$ of $A^T$*" which is a strengthened version of the individual RSP of $A^T$ at a vector discussed in Section 2.2. It turns out that this matrix property is also a necessary and sufficient condition for the uniform recovery of every $k$-sparse vector. Thus it is equivalent to the NSP of order $k$. The RSP concept is originated from the fundamental optimality conditions of convex optimization problems. It captures deep and intrinsic properties of the $\ell_1$-minimization problem. It reflects the desired property of a sensing matrix for uniform recoveries. The RSP of order $k$ of $A^T$ enables us not only to achieve the uniform recovery of every $k$-sparse vector via $\ell_1$-minimization, but also to develop certain non-uniform recovery criteria for sparse vectors with certain structures, such as nonnegativity and other restrictions (see Section 3.7 and Chapter 4 for details).

## 3.6.1 Uniform Recovery: RSP-Based Analysis

The sparsity recovery theory can be developed under different assumptions and in terms of different decoding (recovery) approaches, such as $\ell_1$-minimization methods, orthogonal matching pursuits and thresholding methods. In what follows, we focus on the $\ell_1$-minimization method and discuss how a recovery theory can be developed based on the range space property (RSP) of a transposed sensing matrix. It turns out that the uniform recovery can be fully characterized by the following notion which was first introduced in [241].

**Definition 3.6.5** [241] (RSP of order $k$ of $A^T$) *Let $A \in \mathbb{R}^{m \times n}$ with $m < n$. The matrix $A^T$ is said to satisfy the range space property (RSP) of order $k$ if for any disjoint subsets $S_1, S_2$ of $\{1, \ldots, n\}$ with $|S_1| + |S_2| \leq k$, the range space $\mathcal{R}(A^T)$ contains a vector $\eta$ satisfying that $\eta_i = 1$ for all $i \in S_1$, $\eta_i = -1$ for all $i \in S_2$, and $|\eta_i| < 1$ for all other components.*

The notion above is motivated from the uniqueness analysis of the solution to the standard $\ell_1$-minimization problem. As shown in Chapter 2, a vector $\hat{x}$ is the unique solution to the problem $\min\{\|z\|_1 : Az = A\hat{x}\}$ if and only if $A_{\text{supp}(\hat{x})}$ has full column rank and the following individual RSP of $A^T$ at $\hat{x}$ is satisfied: There is a vector $\eta \in \mathcal{R}(A^T)$ such that $\eta_i = 1$ for $\hat{x}_i > 0$, $\eta_i = -1$ for $\hat{x}_i < 0$, and $|\eta_i| < 1$ for $\hat{x}_i = 0$. The individual RSP of $A^T$ at $\hat{x}$ guarantees that $\hat{x}$ can be exactly recovered by $\ell_1$-minimization. From this fact, in order to exactly reconstruct every $k$-sparse vector with $\ell_1$-minimization, the individual RSP of $A^T$ should be satisfied at every $k$-sparse vector, leading to the matrix property described in Definition 3.6.5, which is independent of any specific $k$-sparse vector. The RSP of order $k$ of $A^T$ is rooted in and originated from the fundamental optimality conditions of $\ell_1$-minimization problems. It is a naturally strengthened uniqueness condition of the solution to the $\ell_1$-minimization problem.

We now show that the RSP of order $k$ of $A^T$ is a necessary and sufficient condition for the uniform recovery of $k$-sparse vectors. We begin with the following lemma.

**Lemma 3.6.6** *If $A^T$ has the RSP of order $k$, then any $k$ columns of $A$ are linearly independent.*

*Proof.* Let $S \subseteq \{1, \ldots, n\}$ be any subset with $|S| = k$. We denote the elements in $S$ by $\{q_1, \ldots, q_k\}$. We prove that the columns of $A_S$ are linearly independent under the assumption of the lemma. It is sufficient to show that $u = 0$ is the only solution to the system $A_S u = 0$. In fact, assume that $A_S u = 0$. Then the vector $z \in \mathbb{R}^n$ with components $z_S = u$ and $z_{\overline{S}} = 0$ is in the null space of $A$. Thus $\|z\|_0 = \|u\|_0 \leq |S| \leq k$, i.e., $z$ is a $k$-sparse vector. Consider the disjoint sets $S_1 = S$, and $S_2 = \emptyset$. By the RSP of order $k$, there exists a vector $\eta \in \mathcal{R}(A^T)$ with $\eta_i = 1$ for all $i \in S_1 = S$. By the orthogonality of $\mathcal{N}(A)$ and $\mathcal{R}(A^T)$, we have

$$0 = z^T \eta = z_S^T \eta_S + z_{\overline{S}}^T \eta_{\overline{S}} = z_S^T \eta_S = u^T \eta_S.$$

Note that $\eta_i = 1$ for all $i \in S = S_1$, the above relation implies that

$$\sum_{j=1}^{k} u_j = 0. \tag{3.27}$$

Now we consider any $k'$ with $1 \leq k' \leq k$, and the pair of disjoint sets

$$S_1 = \{q_1, q_2, \ldots, q_{k'}\}, \quad S_2 = \{q_{k'+1}, \ldots, q_k\}.$$

By the RSP of order $k$, there exist a vector $\widetilde{\eta} \in \mathcal{R}(A^T)$ with $\widetilde{\eta}_{q_i} = 1$ for every $i = 1, \ldots, k'$ and $\widetilde{\eta}_{q_i} = -1$ for every $i = k' + 1, \ldots, k$. By the orthogonality of $\mathcal{N}(A)$ and $\mathcal{R}(A^T)$ again, we have

$$0 = z^T \widetilde{\eta} = z_S \widetilde{\eta}_S + z_{\overline{S}} \widetilde{\eta}_{\overline{S}} = u^T \widetilde{\eta}_S.$$

That is,

$$(u_1 + \cdots + u_{k'}) - (u_{k'+1} + \cdots + u_k) = 0,$$

which holds for every $k'$ with $1 \leq k' \leq k$. Specifically, let $k' = k-1, k-2, \ldots, 1$ respectively, we obtain the following relations:

$$(u_1 + \cdots + u_{k-1}) - u_k = 0,$$
$$(u_1 + \cdots + u_{k-2}) - (u_{k-1} + u_k) = 0,$$
$$\vdots$$
$$u_1 - (u_2 + \cdots + u_k) = 0.$$

It follows from these relations and (3.27) that all components of $u$ are equal to zero. This implies that any $k$ columns of $A$ are linearly independent. □

As shown by the next result, the RSP concept can be used to characterize the uniform recovery of every $k$-sparse vector.

**Theorem 3.6.7** *Every $k$-sparse vector $x^*$ with given measurements $y := Ax^*$ can be exactly recovered by the $\ell_1$-minimization (3.24) if and only if $A^T$ has the RSP of order $k$.*

*Proof.* First we assume that $A^T$ satisfies the RSP of order $k$. Let $x^*$ be an arbitrary vector with $\|x^*\|_0 \leq k$. Let $S_1 = S_+(x) = \{i: x_i^* > 0\}$ and $S_2 = S_-(x^*) = \{i: x_i^* < 0\}$. Clearly, $S_1$ and $S_2$ are disjoint, satisfying $|S_1| + |S_2| \leq k$. By the RSP of order $k$, there is a vector $\eta \in \mathcal{R}(A^T)$ such that $\eta_i = 1$ for all $i \in S_1$, $\eta_i = -1$ for all $i \in S_2$, and $|\eta_i| < 1$ for other components. This implies that the individual RSP of $A^T$ holds at $x^*$. Also, it follows from Lemma 3.6.6 that any $k$ columns of $A$ are linearly independent. Since $|S_1| + |S_2| = \|x^*\|_0 \leq k$, the matrix $A_{S_1 \cup S_2} = A_{\mathrm{supp}(x^*)}$ has full column rank. By Theorem 3.2.3, $x^*$ is the unique solution to the problem (3.24). So $x^*$ can be exactly recovered by $\ell_1$-minimization.

Conversely, assume that any $k$-sparse vector can be exactly recovered by $\ell_1$-minimization. We prove that $A^T$ satisfies the RSP of order $k$. Indeed, let $x^*$ be an arbitrary $k$-sparse vector, and let $y$ be the given measurements, i.e., $y := Ax^*$. Under the assumption, $x^*$ can be exactly recovered by $\ell_1$-minimization, so $x^*$ is the unique solution to the problem (3.24). By Theorem 2.2.14, the individual RSP of $A^T$ at $x^*$ is satisfied. This implies that there is a vector $\eta \in \mathcal{R}(A^T)$ such that $\eta_i = 1$ for $i \in S_1$, $\eta_i = -1$ for $i \in S_2$, and $|\eta_i| < 1$ for $i \notin S_1 \cup S_2$, where $S_1 = S_+(x^*) = \{i: x_i^* > 0\}$ and $S_2 = S_-(x^*) = \{i: x_i^* < 0\}$. Since $x^*$ can be any $k$-sparse vector, the above property holds for any disjoint subsets $S_1, S_2 \subseteq \{1, \ldots, n\}$ with $|S_1| + |S_2| \leq k$. Thus $A^T$ satisfies the RSP of order $k$. $\square$

This theorem shows that the RSP of order $k$ of $A^T$ completely characterizes the uniform recovery of $k$-sparse vectors by $\ell_1$-minimization, and hence it is equivalent to the NSP of order $k$. It is worth mentioning that Donoho [81] characterized the exact recovery condition from a geometric perspective. His condition is called '$k$-neighborly' property. Zhang [237] characterized the uniform recovery by using null space property of $A$ (see also [108]), and Juditsky and Nemirovski [141] proposed a verifiable condition for the uniform recovery. As shown in Section 3.2, the RSP of $A^T$ at an individual solution of an $\ell_0$-minimization problem does not imply the uniqueness of the sparsest solution of the $\ell_0$-minimization problem (as shown in Section 3.2). The RSP of order $k$ of $A^T$ is stronger than the individual RSP of $A^T$ at a specific point. It requires that the individual RSP of $A^T$ be satisfied at every $k$-sparse vector, so it is a global property instead of a local property. As indicated by the next corollary, the RSP of order $k$ of $A^T$ complies with the conditions (C1)–(C3). In other words, it implies that $\ell_0$- and $\ell_1$-minimization problems are strongly equivalent in the sense of Definition 3.1.1.

**Corollary 3.6.8** *Let $A \in \mathbb{R}^{m \times n}$ with $m < n$. If $A^T$ satisfies the RSP of order $k$, then any $k$-sparse vector $x^* \in \mathbb{R}^n$ with measurements $y := Ax^*$ is the unique solution to both the $\ell_0$-minimization problem (3.23) and the $\ell_1$-minimization problem (3.24).*

*Proof.* Suppose that $A^T$ satisfies the RSP of order $k$. Then, by Theorem 3.6.7, any $x^*$ with $\|x^*\|_0 \leq k$ can be exactly recovered by $\ell_1$-minimization. Thus, $x^*$ is the unique solution to the $\ell_1$-minimization problem (3.24). We now prove that $x^*$

is the unique solution to the problem (3.23). Assume that there exists a solution $x'$ to the problem (3.23). Then $Ax' = Ax^*$ with $\|x'\|_0 \leq \|x^*\|_0 \leq k$. Let $S_1 = S_+(x') = \{i : x_i' > 0\}$ and $S_2 = S_-(x') = \{i : x_i' < 0\}$. Since $A^T$ satisfies the RSP of order $k$, the individual RSP of $A^T$ at $x'$ is satisfied. Since any $k$ columns of $A$ are linearly independent (by Theorem 3.6.7), so are the columns of $A_{\text{supp}(x')}$ with $|\text{supp}(x')| = \|x'\|_0 \leq k$. Thus, by Theorem 2.2.14, $x'$ is also the unique solution to the $\ell_1$-minimization problem (3.24). Therefore, $x' = x^*$, which shows that $x^*$ is the unique solution to the $\ell_0$-minimization problem (3.23). □

Thus, the RSP of order $k$ of $A^T$ is a sufficient condition for the strong equivalence of $\ell_0$- and $\ell_1$-minimization.

**Corollary 3.6.9** *Let $A \in \mathbb{R}^{m \times n}$ with $m < n$. If $A^T$ satisfies the RSP of order $k$, then the two problems $\min\{\|x\|_0 : Ax = b\}$ and $\min\{\|x\|_1 : Ax = b\}$ are strongly equivalent in the sense of Definition 3.1.1, provided that the linear system $Az = y$ admits a $k$-sparse solution.*

Any sufficient condition for uniform recoveries of $k$-sparse vectors necessarily implies that $A^T$ satisfies the RSP of order $k$.

**Lemma 3.6.10** *Let $A$ be an $m \times n$ matrix, where $m < n$. Suppose that one of the following conditions holds:*

(i) $\mu(A) < 1/(2k - 1)$.

(ii) $\mu_1(k) + \mu_1(k - 1) < 1$.

(iii) *The matrix $A$ has the RIP of order $2k$ with constant $\delta_{2k} < 1/\sqrt{2}$.*

(iv) *The matrix $A$ has the NSP of order $k$ (or even the stronger ones: stable NSP or robust stable NSP of order $k$).*

(v) *The matrix $A$ has the ERC of order $k$.*

*Then $A^T$ satisfies the RSP of order $k$.*

*Proof.* As we have pointed out at the beginning of this section, each of the conditions listed above implies that every $k$-sparse vector can be exactly recovered by $\ell_1$-minimization (i.e., the uniform recovery is achieved). By Theorem 3.6.7, this in turn implies that $A^T$ satisfies the RSP of order $k$. □

Finally, we point out that although checking the individual RSP at a point $x$ is easy, checking the RIP, NSP, and RSP of order $k$ for a matrix is generally difficult (see [208]).

### 3.6.2  Beyond Uniform Recovery

The purpose of uniform recoveries is to exactly recover every $k$-sparse vector with a single sensing matrix. So certain strong assumptions are required on the matrix. These assumptions imply that the target sparse vector is the unique solution to both $\ell_0$- and $\ell_1$-minimization problems (i.e., two problems are strongly equivalent). Through the notion of RSP of order $k$ of $A^T$, we provide a complete characterization for the uniform recovery in Section 3.6.1. Interestingly, this notion can be conveniently generalized to deal with sparse vector reconstructions in more complicated environments. It can be customized to the situation where the standard uniform recovery does not apply. Such an extension is important not only from a mathematical point of view, but from the viewpoint of many practical applications as well.

By Lemma 3.6.6 and Theorem 3.6.7, to achieve the uniform recovery of $k$-sparse vectors with $\ell_1$-minimization, it must hold that $k < \text{spark}(A)$. This means through $\ell_1$-minimization it is impossible to achieve the uniform recovery of $k$-sparse vectors with the sparsity level $k$ higher than or equal to $\text{spark}(A)$. Recall the three conditions (C1)–(C3) which are assumed in traditional compressed sensing theory. According to Theorem 2.2.14, (C1) is not a necessary condition for a vector to be exactly recovered by $\ell_1$-minimization. In order to recover a vector with a relatively high sparsity level by $\ell_1$-minimization, one possible way is to relax the condition (C1). Let us first relax this condition by dropping the uniqueness requirement of the sparsest solution to the system $Ax = y$, where $y$ denotes the measurement vector. Then we immediately have the following observation.

**Proposition 3.6.11**  *Let $A \in \mathbb{R}^{m \times n}$ ($m < n$) be a given matrix. Suppose that any $k$-sparse vector $x^*$ with measurements $y := Ax^*$ is a sparsest solution (but not necessarily the unique sparsest solution) to the system $Ax = y$. Then $k < \text{spark}(A)$.*

*Proof.* Note that for any sparsest solution $x$ to the system $Ax = y := Ax^*$, the corresponding columns of $A_{\text{supp}(x)}$ are linearly independent (since otherwise, a sparser solution than $x$ can be found). Thus under the assumption of this proposition, the matrix $A_{\text{supp}(x^*)}$ has full column rank for any $k$-sparse vector $x^*$. This means any $k$ columns of $A$ are linearly independent. So $k < \text{spark}(A)$.  □

This proposition indicates that even if we relax the condition (C1) by only requiring that $x^*$ be a sparsest solution (not necessarily the unique sparsest solution) to the system $Ax = y := Ax^*$, $k = \text{spark}(A)$ is still an unattainable upper bound for the sparsity level of vectors if we expect to recover these $k$-sparse vectors with the same matrix. Thus, from a mathematical point of view, the sparse vector $x$ with a higher sparsity level such as

$$\text{spark}(A) \le \|x\|_0 < m$$

can be possibly recovered only in a non-uniform-recovery manner. This is also motivated by some practical applications, where an unknown signal might not be sparse enough and its sparsity level is higher than the uniform recovery bound. Theorem 2.2.14 makes it possible to handle such a situation by abandoning the traditional hypothesis (C1). So Theorem 2.2.14 provides a theoretical basis to develop some non-uniform recovery criteria for some sparse vectors, going beyond the scope of uniform recoveries. Towards this goal, we introduce the following matrix property.

**Definition 3.6.12** (Relaxed RSP of order $q$ of $A^T$) *Let $A \in \mathbb{R}^{m \times n}$ with $m < n$. $A^T$ is said to satisfy the relaxed range space property of order $q$ if the following two properties hold:*

(i) *There exists a pair of disjoint subsets $S_1, S_2 \subseteq \{1, \ldots, n\}$ such that $|S_1| + |S_2| = q$ and $A_{S_1 \cup S_2}$ has full column rank.*

(ii) *For any disjoint $S_1, S_2 \subseteq \{1, \ldots, n\}$ satisfying that $|S_1| + |S_2| \leq q$ and $A_{S_1 \cup S_2}$ has full column rank, the space $\mathcal{R}(A^T)$ contains a vector $\eta$ such that $\eta_i = 1$ for $i \in S_1$, $\eta_i = -1$ for $i \in S_2$, and $|\eta_i| < 1$ otherwise.*

The essential difference between this notion and the standard RSP of order $k$ is obvious. The RSP of order $k$ requires that the individual RSP holds for any disjoint subsets $S_1, S_2$ of $\{1, \ldots, n\}$ with $|S_1| + |S_2| \leq k$, but the relaxed RSP of order $q$ requires that the individual RSP holds only for those disjoint subsets $S_1, S_2$ such that $|S_1| + |S_2| \leq q$ and $A_{S_1 \cup S_2}$ has full column rank. Based on this concept, we have the next result induced from Theorem 2.2.14 immediately.

**Theorem 3.6.13** (i) *If $A^T$ has the relaxed RSP of order $q$, then $q \leq m$. (ii) Assume that the measurements of the form $y = Ax$ are taken. Then any $x$ with $\|x\|_0 \leq q$ and $A_{\text{supp}(x)}$ having full column rank can be exactly recovered by $\ell_1$-minimization if and only if $A^T$ has the relaxed RSP of order $q$.*

The bound $q \leq m$ above follows directly from the condition (i) in Definition 3.6.12. It is not difficult to see the remarkable difference between Theorems 3.6.13 and 3.6.7. Theorem 3.6.7 claims that every vector with sparsity $\|x\|_0 \leq k$ can be exactly recovered with a sensing matrix satisfying the RSP of order $k$ of $A^T$, where $k < \text{spark}(A)$ is an unattainable upper bound for uniform recoveries. Different from this result, Theorem 3.6.13 makes it possible to use a matrix satisfying the relaxed RSP of order $q$ of $A^T$, where $\text{spark}(A) \leq q < m$, to exactly recover part (not all) of sparse vectors with sparsity level in the range $\text{spark}(A) \leq \|x\|_0 < q$, to which the standard uniform recovery theory is difficult to apply.

The relaxed RSP-based non-uniform recovery theory has abandoned the traditional recovery hypothesis (C1) in uniform recovery. In such cases, of course, only some vectors (signals) with sparsity levels higher than spark$(A)$ can be exactly recovered, i.e., those vectors at which the individual RSP of $A^T$ and full column rank property are satisfied. Theorems 3.6.7 and 3.6.13 also shed light on the limitations of $\ell_1$-minimization in sparse vector recovery.

## 3.7 Sparse Non-negative Vector Recovery

It is well known that the non-negative constraints are quite common in optimization, numerical analysis, and in various applications, such as non-negative signal and image processing [87, 19, 38, 218, 88, 221, 144, 242], machine learning [167, 34, 33, 165, 129], pattern recognition and computer vision [218, 205]. Due to the importance of non-negative signals in practical applications, it is worth extending the RSP-based recovery theory to sparse non-negative vectors.

### 3.7.1 Uniform Recovery: RSP$^+$-Based Analysis

Let us first introduce the following definition, which is a strengthened version of the individual RSP$^+$ of $A^T$ at a point, as discussed in Section 3.2.

**Definition 3.7.1** (RSP$^+$ of order $k$ of $A^T$) *Let $A$ be an $m \times n$ matrix ($m < n$). $A^T$ is said to satisfy the range space property plus (RSP$^+$) of order $k$ if for any subset $S \subseteq \{1,\dots,n\}$ with $|S| \leq k$, $\mathcal{R}(A^T)$ contains a vector $\eta$ such that $\eta_i = 1$ for all $i \in S$, and $\eta_i < 1$ for all $i \notin S$.*

Similar to Lemma 3.6.6, we can show that if $A^T$ satisfies the RSP$^+$ of order $k$, then $k$ must be bounded by spark$(A)$.

**Lemma 3.7.2** *If $A^T$ satisfies the RSP$^+$ of order $k$, then any $k$ columns of $A$ are linearly independent, so $k <$ spark$(A)$.*

*Proof.* Let $S \subseteq \{1,\dots,n\}$ be an arbitrary subset with cardinality $|S| = k$. Denote the elements in $S$ by $q_i, i = 1,\dots,k$, i.e., $S = \{q_1,\dots,q_k\}$. Suppose that $A^T$ has the RSP$^+$ of order $k$. We now prove that $A_S$ has full column rank. It is sufficient to show that $\mathcal{N}(A_S) = \{0\}$. That is, $v = 0$ is the only solution to $A_S v = 0$. Indeed, suppose that $A_S v = 0$. Then $z \in \mathbb{R}^n$ with $z_S = v$ and $z_{\overline{S}} = 0$ is in the null space of $A$. By the RSP$^+$ of order $k$, there exists a vector $\eta \in \mathcal{R}(A^T)$ such that every component of $\eta_S$ is 1, i.e., $\eta_{q_i} = 1$ for $i = 1,\dots,k$. By the orthogonality of the null space of $A$ and the range space of $A^T$, we have

$$z_{q_1} + z_{q_2} + \cdots + z_{q_k} = z_S^T \eta_S = z^T \eta = 0. \tag{3.28}$$

Now let $k'$ be an arbitrary number with $1 \leq k' < k$, and $S_{k'} = \{q_1, q_2, \dots, q_{k'}\} \subseteq S$. Since $|S_{k'}| \leq |S| = k$, it follows from the definition of RSP$^+$ of order $k$, there is a vector $\widetilde{\eta} \in \mathcal{R}(A^T)$ with $\widetilde{\eta}_{q_i} = 1$ for every $i = 1,\dots,k'$ and $\widetilde{\eta}_j < 1$ for every $j \in$

$S \backslash S_{k'}$. By the orthogonality of $\mathcal{N}(A)$ and $\mathcal{R}(A^T)$ again, it follows from $z^T \widetilde{\eta} = 0$ that

$$(z_{q_1} + \cdots + z_{q_{k'}}) + (\widetilde{\eta}_{q_{k'+1}} z_{q_{k'+1}} + \cdots + \widetilde{\eta}_{q_k} z_{s_k}) = 0,$$

which is equivalent to

$$(z_{q_1} + \cdots + z_{q_{k'}}) + (z_{q_{k'+1}} + \cdots + z_{q_k}) + z_{q_{k'+1}}(\widetilde{\eta}_{q_{k'+1}} - 1) + \cdots + z_{q_k}(\widetilde{\eta}_{q_k} - 1) = 0.$$

This, together with (3.28), implies that

$$(\widetilde{\eta}_{q_{k'+1}} - 1)z_{q_{k'+1}} + \cdots + (\widetilde{\eta}_{q_k} - 1)z_{q_k} = 0,$$

where $\widetilde{\eta}_{q_i} < 1$ for $i = k'+1, \ldots, k$. Since such relations hold for every $k' = 1, \ldots, k-1$. In particular, when $k' = k-1$, the relation above is reduced to $(\widetilde{\eta}_{q_k} - 1)z_{q_k} = 0$ which implies that $z_{q_k} = 0$. When $k' = k-2$, the relation above becomes

$$(\widetilde{\eta}_{q_{k-1}} - 1)z_{q_{k-1}} + (\widetilde{\eta}_{q_k} - 1)z_{q_k} = 0.$$

This together with $z_{q_k} = 0$ and $\widetilde{\eta}_{q_{k-1}} < 1$ implies that $z_{q_{k-1}} = 0$. Continuing by considering $k' = k-3, \ldots, 1$, we deduce that all components of $z_S = v$ are zero. Thus the columns of $A_S$ are linearly independent. By the definition of spark$(A)$, we must have $k = |S| < \text{spark}(A)$. □

The RSP$^+$ of order $k$ of $A^T$ can completely characterize the uniform recovery of $k$-sparse non-negative vectors by $\ell_1$-minimization, as shown by the next result.

**Theorem 3.7.3** *Any $k$-sparse non-negative vector $x^* \geq 0$ with given measurements in the form $y := Ax^*$ can be exactly recovered by the $\ell_1$-method*

$$\min_z \{\|z\|_1 : Az = y := Ax^*, z \geq 0\} \tag{3.29}$$

*if and only if $A^T$ has the RSP$^+$ of order $k$.*

*Proof.* Assume that $A^T$ satisfies the RSP$^+$ of order $k$. Let $x^* \geq 0$ be an arbitrary $k$-sparse vector with given measurements $y = Ax^*$. Let $S = \{i : x_i^* > 0\}$. Since $|S| = \|x^*\|_0 \leq k$, by the RSP$^+$ of order $k$, there is a vector $\eta \in \mathcal{R}(A^T)$ such that $\eta_i = 1$ for all $i \in S$, and $\eta_i < 1$ for all $i \notin S$. So the individual RSP$^+$ of $A^T$ holds at $x^* \geq 0$. Moreover, it follows from Lemma 3.7.2 that $A_S$ has full column rank. Hence, by Theorem 2.3.6, $x^*$ is the unique solution to the $\ell_1$-minimization problem (3.29). So $x^*$ can be exactly recovered by $\ell_1$-minimization.

Conversely, assume that any $k$-sparse non-negative vector $x^* \geq 0$ with given measurements of the form $y := Ax^*$ can be exactly recovered by (3.29). We now prove that $A^T$ satisfies the RSP$^+$ of order $k$. Let $S = S_+(x^*) = \{i : x_i^* > 0\}$. Under the assumption, $x^*$ is the unique solution to the problem (3.29). By Theorem 2.3.6, the RSP$^+$ of $A^T$ at $x^*$ is satisfied, i.e., there is a vector $\eta \in \mathcal{R}(A^T)$ such that

$$\eta_i = 1 \text{ for all } i \in S, \ \eta_i < 1 \text{ otherwise.} \tag{3.30}$$

Since $x^*$ can be any $k$-sparse non-negative vectors, this implies that $S = S_+(x^*)$ can be any subset of $\{1,\ldots,n\}$ with $|S| \le k$, and for every such subset there exists accordingly a vector $\eta \in \mathcal{R}(A^T)$ satisfying (3.30). By Definition 3.7.1, $A^T$ satisfies the $\text{RSP}^+$ of order $k$. □

The above theory shows that the $\text{RSP}^+$ of $A^T$ is a sufficient and necessary condition for the uniform recovery of non-negative $k$-sparse vectors. There are several equivalent conditions in the literature. Denote by $a_j$, $1 \le j \le n$, the columns of $A$ and let $a_0 = 0$. Let $P = conv(a_0, a_1, \ldots, a_n)$ be the convex hull of $a_j$, $0 \le j \le n$. The polytope $P$ is said to be *outwardly k-neighborly* if every subset of $k$ vertices not including $a_0 = 0$ spans a face of this polytope. This concept was introduced by Donoho and Tanner [87]. They proved that the polytope $P$ is *outwardly k-neighborly* if and only if any non-negative $k$-sparse solution $x^*$ of the system $Az = b$ is the unique solution to the $\ell_1$-minimization problem. In other words, the outwardly $k$-neighborly property is a geometric characterization of the uniform recovery of $k$-sparse non-negative vectors. Khajehnejad et al. [144] characterized the uniform recovery by using the property of null space of $A$. They have shown that every non-negative $k$-sparse vector can be exactly recovered if and only if for every vector $v \ne 0$ in $\mathcal{N}(A)$, and every index set $S \subseteq \{1,\ldots,n\}$ with $|S| = k$ such that $v_{\overline{S}} \ge 0$, it holds that $\mathbf{e}^T v > 0$. Some other equivalent properties, such as the strictly half $k$-balanced and the strictly half $k$-thick, were also introduced by Zhang [235]. Clearly, these properties are different from the $\text{RSP}^+$ of order $k$ which is derived from the optimality conditions as well as the strict complementary slackness property of linear programs. The $\text{RSP}^+$ of order $k$ of $A^T$ provides an alternative characterization of the uniform recovery from the perspective of the range space of $A^T$. Although from different perspectives, all the above-mentioned properties (outwardly $k$-neighborly, strictly half $k$-balanced, null space property of $A$, and $\text{RSP}^+$ of $A^T$) are equivalent since each of these properties is a necessary and sufficient condition for the uniform recovery of $k$-sparse non-negative vectors. In particular, each of these properties implies the strong equivalence between $\ell_0$- and $\ell_1$-minimization problems with non-negative constraints.

The $\text{RSP}^+$ of order $k$ of $A^T$ is stronger than the individual $\text{RSP}^+$ of $A^T$ at a specific vector. The former requires that the individual $\text{RSP}^+$ of $A^T$ holds at every $k$-sparse non-negative vector. By contrast, the individual $\text{RSP}^+$ of $A^T$ holds at a $k$-sparse vector does not imply that the underlying linear system has a unique sparsest non-negative solution, as shown by the example in Section 3.3. However, $\text{RSP}^+$ of order $k$ of $A^T$ implies that the linear system possesses unique $k$-sparse non-negative solution if such a solution exists.

**Corollary 3.7.4** *If $A^T$ has the RSP$^+$ of order $k$, then any $k$-sparse non-negative vector $\widehat{x} \geq 0$ with measurements $y = A\widehat{x}$ is the unique solution to the $\ell_0$-minimization problem*

$$\min_{x}\{\|x\|_0 : Ax = y, \, x \geq 0\} \tag{3.31}$$

*and the $\ell_1$-minimization problem*

$$\min_{x}\{\|x\|_1 : Ax = y, \, x \geq 0\}. \tag{3.32}$$

*Proof.* By Theorem 3.7.3, under the RSP$^+$ of order $k$, any $k$-sparse non-negative vector $\widehat{x} \geq 0$ can be exactly recovered by $\ell_1$-minimization, i.e, $\widehat{x}$ is the unique solution to the problem (3.32). We now prove that $\widehat{x}$ is also the unique solution to the $\ell_0$-minimization problem (3.31). Let $z$ be any given solution of (3.31). Note that any solution $z$ of (3.31) must satisfy that $\|z\|_0 \leq \|\widehat{x}\|_0 \leq k$, i.e., $z$ is $k$-sparse. Let $S = \{i : z_i > 0\}$. Since $|S| = \|z\|_0 \leq k$, by the RSP$^+$ of order $k$, there is a vector $\eta \in \mathcal{R}(A^T)$ such that $\eta_i = 1$ for all $i \in S$, and $\eta_i < 1$ for all $i \notin S$. Thus the individual RSP$^+$ of $A^T$ at $z$ is satisfied. By Lemma 3.7.2, any $k$ columns of $A$ are linearly independent. Since the number of the columns of $A_S$, where $S = \{i : z_i > 0\}$, is less than $k$, this implies that $A_S$ has full column rank. By Theorem 2.3.6, $z$ is also the unique solution to the $\ell_1$-minimization problem, and hence $z = \widehat{x}$. This means $\widehat{x}$ is the unique solution to the $\ell_0$-minimization problem. $\Box$

From the aforementioned discussion and the corollary above, we immediately have the following statement.

**Corollary 3.7.5** *Let $A \in \mathbb{R}^{m \times n}$ ($m < n$) with columns $a_i, i = 1, \ldots, n$. Suppose one of the following properties is satisfied:*

■ *$A^T$ satisfies the RSP$^+$ of order $k$.*

■ *The polytope $P = conv(0, a_1, \ldots, a_n)$ is outwardly $k$-neighborly.*

■ *For every vector $v \neq 0$ in $\mathcal{N}(A)$ and every $S \subseteq \{1, \ldots, n\}$ with $|S| = k$ such that $v_{\overline{S}} \geq 0$, it holds that $e^T v > 0$.*

*Then the problems (3.31) and (3.32) are strongly equivalent, provided that the linear system $Az = y$ admits a $k$-sparse non-negative solution.*

### 3.7.2 Non-uniform Recovery of Non-negative Vectors

From a geometric perspective, Donoho and Tanner [87] introduced the so-called weak neighborliness conditions for non-uniform recoveries via $\ell_1$-minimization. They have shown that under such a condition most non-negative $k$-sparse vectors can be exactly recovered via $\ell_1$-minimization. Ayaz and Rauhut [12] focused on the non-uniform recovery of signals with given sparsity and signal length by $\ell_1$-minimization. Different from their methods, we introduce the so-called relaxed RSP$^+$ of order $q$ in what follows, which is a range space property of $A^T$ that can guarantee the exact recovery of some vectors which may have higher sparsity level, going beyond the scope of uniform recoveries.

Given a sensing matrix $A$, Theorem 2.3.6 claims that a non-negative vector $x^*$ can be exactly recovered by $\ell_1$-minimization provided that the RSP$^+$ of $A^T$ at $x^*$ is satisfied and that the matrix $A_{S_+(x^*)}$, where $S_+(x^*) = \{i : x_i^* > 0\}$, has full column rank. Such a vector is not necessarily the unique sparsest non-negative solution to the linear system, as shown by Example 3.3.5, and it may not even be the sparsest non-negative solution as well. For instance, let

$$
A = \begin{bmatrix} 6 & 4 & 1.5 & 4 & -1 \\ 6 & 4 & -0.5 & 4 & 0 \\ 0 & -2 & 31.5 & -1 & -1.5 \end{bmatrix}, \quad y = \begin{bmatrix} 4 \\ 4 \\ -1 \end{bmatrix} = Ax^*,
$$

where $x^* = (1/3, 1/2, 0, 0, 0)^T$. It is easy to see that $\tilde{x} = (0, 0, 0, 1, 0)^T$ is the unique sparsest non-negative solution to the system $Ax = y$, while $x^*$ is the unique least $\ell_1$-norm non-negative solution to the system $Ax = y$. Although $x^*$ is not the sparsest non-negative solution, it can be exactly recovered by the $\ell_1$-minimization method. So it is interesting to develop a recovery condition without requiring that the targeted vector be a sparsest solution to the underlying linear system. The concept of RSP$^+$ of order $k$ of $A^T$ can be easily adapted to handle these cases. So we introduce the following definition.

**Definition 3.7.6** (*Relaxed RSP$^+$ of order $q$ of $A^T$*) *Let $A$ be an $m \times n$ matrix ($m < n$). $A^T$ is said to satisfy the relaxed range space property plus (RSP$^+$) of order $q$ if the following two properties are satisfied:*

(i) *There exists a subset $S \subseteq \{1,\ldots,n\}$ such that $|S| = q$ and $A_S$ has full column rank;*

(ii) *For any subset $S \subseteq \{1,\ldots,n\}$ such that $|S| \leq q$ and $A_S$ has full column rank, the space $\mathcal{R}(A^T)$ contains a vector $\eta$ such that $\eta_i = 1$ for $i \in S$, and $\eta_i < 1$ otherwise.*

The relaxed RSP$^+$ of order $q$ only requires that the individual RSP$^+$ of $A^T$ holds for those subsets $S \subseteq \{1,\ldots,n\}$ such that $|S| \leq q$ and $A_S$ has full column rank, while the RSP$^+$ of order $k$ of $A^T$ requires that the individual RSP$^+$ holds for any subset $S \subseteq \{1,\ldots,n\}$ with $|S| \leq k$. So the relaxed RSP$^+$ of order $q$ is less restrictive than the RSP$^+$ of order $k$. We have the following result.

**Theorem 3.7.7** *Suppose that there exists a subset $S \subseteq \{1,\ldots,n\}$ such that $|S| = q$ and $A_S$ has full column rank. Then $A^T$ has the relaxed RSP$^+$ of order $q$ if and* *only if any q-sparse vector $x^* \geq 0$, at which $A_{S_+(x^*)}$ has full column rank, can be exactly recovered by the $\ell_1$-minimization*

$$\min_z \{\|z\|_1 : Az = y := Ax^*, \ z \geq 0\}.$$

*Proof.* Assume that $A^T$ has the relaxed RSP$^+$ of order $q$. Let $x^*$ be an arbitrary non-negative vector such that $\|x^*\|_0 \leq q$ and $A_{\text{supp}(x^*)}$ has full column rank. Denote by $S = \text{supp}(x^*) = S_+(x^*) = \{i : x_i^* > 0\}$. Since $A^T$ has the relaxed RSP$^+$ of order $q$, there is an $\eta \in \mathcal{R}(A^T)$ such that $\eta_i = 1$ for $i \in S$, and $\eta_i < 1$ otherwise. This implies that the RSP$^+$ of $A^T$ at $x^*$ is satisfied. Since $A_{\text{supp}(x^*)}$ has full column rank, by Theorem 2.3.6, $x^*$ must be the unique least $\ell_1$-norm non-negative solution to the linear system $Az = y := Ax^*$. In other words, $x^*$ can be exactly recovered by the $\ell_1$-minimization method. Conversely, we assume that any $q$-sparse $x^* \geq 0$, at which $A_{\text{supp}(x^*)}$ has full column rank, can be exactly recovered by $\ell_1$-minimization. We now prove that $A^T$ must have the relaxed RSP$^+$ of order $q$. Denote by $S = S_+(x^*) = \{i : x_i^* > 0\}$. Since $x^*$ can be exactly recovered by the $\ell_1$-minimization method, it follows from Theorem 2.3.6 that the RSP$^+$ of $A^T$ at $x^*$ is satisfied. Since $x^*$ can be any vector such that $\|x^*\|_0 \leq q$ and $A_{\text{supp}(x^*)}$ has full column rank, this implies that the condition (ii) in Definition 3.7.6 holds. By the assumption, there is a subset $S \subseteq \{1, \ldots, n\}$ satisfying the condition (i) in Definition 3.7.6 as well. Therefore, $A^T$ satisfies the relaxed RSP$^+$ of order $q$. □

We may further relax the notion of RSP$^+$ and relaxed RSP$^+$, especially when the partial information is available for the target vector. For instance, when the sparsity level $\|x\|_0 = k$ is known, we may introduce the next definition.

**Definition 3.7.8** (PRSP$^+$ of order $q$ of $A^T$). *We say that $A^T$ has the partial range space property plus (PRSP$^+$) of order $q$ if for any subset $S$ of $\{1, \ldots, n\}$ with $|S| = q$ and $A_S$ having full column rank, the range space $\mathcal{R}(A^T)$ contains a vector $\eta$ such that $\eta_i = 1$ for all $i \in S$, and $\eta_i < 1$ otherwise.*

Different from the RSP$^+$ of order $k$, the PRSP$^+$ of order $q$ only requires that the individual RSP$^+$ holds for those subset $S$ with cardinality $|S| = q$ and $A_S$ having full column rank. Based on such a definition, we have the next result which follows from Theorem 2.3.6 straightaway.

**Theorem 3.7.9** *$A^T$ has the partial range space property plus (PRSP$^+$) of order $q$ if and only if any non-negative vector $x^* \geq 0$, with $\|x^*\|_0 = q$ and $A_{\text{supp}(x^*)}$ having full column rank, can be exactly recovered by the $\ell_1$-minimization problem*

$$\min_z \{\|z\|_1 : Az = y := Ax^*, \ z \geq 0\}.$$

## 3.8 Notes

The $\ell_0$-minimization problem is NP-hard (Natarajan [177], and Amaldi and Kann [6]). It is natural to investigate when $\ell_1$-minimization, as a heuristic method, can guarantee to find the solution of an $\ell_0$-minimization problem. This amounts to identifying the conditions under which the two problems are equivalent or strongly equivalent in the sense of Definition 3.1.1. The RSP-based analysis has indicated that $\ell_0$- and $\ell_1$-minimization problems are equivalent if and only if the RSP of $A^T$ holds at a solution of the $\ell_0$-minimization problem.

The first type of conditions for uniform recoveries might be the one using mutual coherence [85, 96, 83, 100, 122]. It is well known that if the solution $x$ to the system $Az = b$ satisfying $\|x\|_0 < (1 + 1/\mu(A))/2$, then this vector can be exactly recovered by $\ell_1$-minimization. The same result holds under the condition $\mu_1(k) + \mu_1(k-1) < 1$, where $\mu_1(k)$ is the Babel function [210, 83]. These mutual-coherence-type conditions are very conservative in many situations. Several other uniform recovery conditions have been developed since 2004. Candès and Tao [51] introduced the restricted isometry property (RIP) and proved that if the RIP condition $\delta_{2k} + \delta_{3k} < 1$ is satisfied, then the uniform recovery of every $k$-sparse signal can be achieved by $\ell_1$-minimization. This result was improved to $\delta_{2k} < \sqrt{2} - 1$ by Candès [45], and was improved several times later by other researchers (see Foucart and Lai [107], Cai, Wang and Xu [41], Mo and Li [174], Cai and Zhang [43], Foucart and Rauhut [108], Zhou, Kong and Xiu [250], Andersson and Strömberg [7], and Cai and Zhang [44]). The best-known bound $\delta_{2k} < 1/\sqrt{2}$ was shown by Cai and Zhang [44]. The null space property appeared in the work of Donoho and Hu [85], Donoho and Elad [83], and Gribonval and Nielsen [122]. The formal study of exact recovery of sparse vectors via the null space property was carried out by Cohen, Dahmen and DeVore [65] and Zhang [235, 236]. The work in [236] was published later in [237]. The term 'null space property' was coined in [65]. The ERC condition was introduced by Tropp [210] and can be found also in the work of Fuch [111]. The so-called verifiable condition for uniform recoveries was introduced by Juditski and Nemirovski [141]. Theorem 3.6.7 was shown and the term 'range space property of order $k$ of $A^T$' was coined by Zhao [241].

For non-negative signals, several conditions for uniform recoveries have been developed. Donoho and Tanner [87] introduced the outwardly $k$-neighborly property of a polytope formed by the origin and columns of the sensing matrix, and they proved that this geometric property is a necessary and sufficient condition for the uniform recovery of $k$-sparse non-negative vectors via $\ell_1$-minimization. Zhang [235, 236] introduced the property called strictly half $k$-balanced and the strictly half $k$-thick and used them to characterize the exact recovery of $k$-sparse non-negative vectors with $\ell_1$-minimization. Khajehnejad et al. [144] characterized the uniform recovery of $k$-sparse non-negative vectors from a null space property perspective. Zhao [242] characterized the uniform recovery of non-negative sparse vectors from the perspective of range space property of order $k$ of $A^T$. Theorem 3.7.3 was first shown in [242]. When certain prior information, such as the sign restriction, is available, Juditsky, Karzan, and Nemirovski [140] developed some exact recovery criteria via $\ell_1$-minimization based on the notion of $s$-semigoodness. When the sparsity level or other structures of a non-negative signal is available, the relaxed or partial RSP$^+$ of $A^T$, discussed in Section 3.7.2, provides the non-uniform recovery conditions for such vectors.

While the discussion in this chapter was focused on $\ell_1$-minimization (as a decoding method), there are other important decoding approaches based on which the sparse-signal-recovery theory can be established, such as (orthogonal) matching pursuits (Mallat and Zhang [166], and Davis, Mallat and Zhang [76]) and thresholding family of methods (see Blumensath and Davies [26], Beck and Teboulle [22], Foucart [104], and Blumensath [24]). The efficiency of orthogonal matching pursuits (OMP) for the sparse vector recovery was analyzed by Tropp [210, 211]. The further analysis of OMP has been extensively performed in the literature (see Tropp and Gilbert [212], Davenport and Wakin [74], Wang and Shim [220], Chang and Wu [56], Cohen, Dahmen and DeVore [66], and Wen et al. [223]). Some variants of (orthogonal) matching pursuits have also been proposed, including the so-called regularized OMP in [181], compressive sampling matching pursuit (CoSaMP) in [180], subspace pursuit in [68], and simultaneous OMP [213, 77].

The theoretical equivalence between $\ell_0$-minimization and weighted $\ell_1$-minimization problems presented in Section 3.5 was first discussed by Zhao and Kocvara [245] and Zhao and Luo [248]. Such a relationship between the two problems provides a useful basis to develop the reweighted $\ell_1$-algorithm for $\ell_0$-minimization problems. See Chapters 7 and 8 for details.

Although the RIP and NSP recovery conditions are widely assumed in compressed sensing scenarios, Bandeira et al. [16] and Tillmann and Pfetsch [208] have shown that it is NP-hard to compute the RIP and NSP constants of a given matrix. Note that the NSP characterizes the uniform recovery from the perspective of the null space of a sensing matrix, while the RSP characterizes the uniform recovery from its orthogonal space, i.e., the range space of a transposed sensing matrix. Similar to the NSP, it is generally difficult to certify the RSP of order $k$ for a given matrix.

# *Chapter 4*

# 1-Bit Compressed Sensing

1-bit compressed sensing (CS) is an important class of sparse optimization problems, which has been studied since 2008. In this chapter, we focus on the case where the amplitude information of a sparse signal is lost and only sign measurements of the signal are available. Some relaxation models were proposed for 1-bit CS in the literature. However, the solution of these models might not be consistent with the sign measurements of the target signal. In order to develop a model which satisfies the consistency requirement, we show that the 1-bit CS with sign measurements can be reformulated equivalently as an $\ell_0$-minimization problem with linear constraints. This reformulation promotes a natural LP-based decoding method for 1-bit CS, referred to as the 1-bit basis pursuit. Different from traditional models, the solution of 1-bit basis pursuit always meets the consistency requirement. The uniqueness condition for the solution of $\ell_1$-minimization over a polyhedral set developed in Chapter 2 provides a useful basis to develop a sign-recovery theory for sparse signals through sign measurements. It turns out that if the sign of a sparse signal can be exactly recovered from sign measurements via 1-bit basis pursuit, then the transposed sensing matrix must admit a certain restricted range space property (RRSP). Conversely, if the transposed sensing matrix satisfies a slightly enhanced RRSP, then the sign of a sparse signal can be exactly recovered from sign measurements with 1-bit basis pursuit.

## 4.1 Introduction

Compressed sensing (CS) has experienced a significant development in the field of signal and image processing. One of the main issues that has been addressed is how a sparse signal can be reconstructed from limited number of measurements via a decoding algorithm. As pointed out in Chapter 3, an extreme case of CS can be cast as the problem of seeking the sparsest solution of an underdetermined linear system, i.e.,

$$\min_x \{\|x\|_0 : Ax = b\},$$

where $A \in \mathbb{R}^{m \times n}$ ($m < n$) is a sensing (or measurement) matrix, and $b \in \mathbb{R}^m$ stands for the vector of non-adaptive measurements. It is known that the reconstruction of a sufficiently sparse signal from a reduced number of measurements can be achieved if $A$ satisfies certain properties, such as the RIP, NPS, RSP and ERC (see Chapter 3 for details). Note that measurements must be quantized. Fine quantization provides more information on a signal, making the signal more likely to be reconstructed from measurements. However, fine quantization imposes a huge burden on measurement systems, and causes slower sampling rates and increased costs for hardware systems [219, 156, 29]. In some applications, only partial information, such as the sign or support of a signal, is actually needed. To recover such incomplete information, the fine quantization of measurements is not necessary. Also, fine quantization introduces error to measurements. This motivates one to consider sparse signal recovery through lower bits of measurements. An extreme quantization is only one bit per measurement. As demonstrated in [30, 28, 29], it is possible to recover certain useful features/structure of the signal from 1-bit measurements. This stimulates the development of 1-bit compressed sensing (1-bit CS) [30, 28, 125, 152, 154, 153, 187]. A widely studied 1-bit CS model is the following $\ell_0$-minimization with sign constraints:

$$\min_x \{\|x\|_0 : \text{sign}(Ax) = y\}, \tag{4.1}$$

where $A \in \mathbb{R}^{m \times n}$ is a sensing matrix and $y \in \mathbb{R}^m$ is the vector of sign measurements. Throughout the chapter, we assume that $m < n$. The sign function in (4.1) is applied element-wise.

In general, only the acquired 1-bit information is insufficient to exactly reconstruct a sparse signal. For instance, if $\text{sign}(Ax^*) = y$, where $y \in \{1, -1\}^m$, then any sufficiently small perturbation $x^* + u$ also satisfies this equation, making the exact recovery of $x^*$ impossible by whatever decoding algorithms. Although the sign measurements may not be enough for reconstructing a signal, they might be adequate to recover part of the information (e.g., support or sign) of the target signal. Thus 1-bit CS still has some applications in signal and imaging processing (see [28, 29, 31, 125, 152, 32, 72]).

In this chapter, we focus on the 1-bit CS problem (4.1) and develop some conditions under which the sign or support of a sparse signal can be exactly recovered from sign measurements via the so-called 1-bit basis pursuit. Throughout the chapter, we assume that the sign measurements $y \in \mathbb{R}^m$ are given, and we denote them by

$$J_+(y) = \{i : y_i = 1\}, \ J_-(y) = \{i : y_i = -1\}, \ J_0(y) = \{i : y_i = 0\}.$$

Clearly, $(J_+(y), J_-(y), J_0(y))$ is a partition of the set $\{1,2,\ldots,m\}$. We use $A_{i,\bullet}$ to denote the $i$th row of the matrix $A \in \mathbb{R}^{m\times n}$, and we use $A^+$ to denote the submatrix of $A$ formed by deleting the rows of $A$ which are not indexed by $J_+(y)$, i.e., $A^+$ consists of the rows $A_{i,\bullet}$ for $i \in J_+(y)$. Similarly, $A^-$ and $A^0$ denote the submatrices by deleting those rows in $A$ not indexed by $J_-(y)$ and $J_0(y)$, respectively. Still, $\mathbf{e}$ with a suitable dimension is the vector of ones, i.e., $\mathbf{e} = (1,\ldots,1)^T$.

## 4.2  Sign Measurements and Recovery Criteria

The *standard sign function* is defined as

$$\text{sign}(t) = \begin{cases} 1 & \text{if } t > 0 \\ 0 & \text{if } t = 0 \\ -1 & \text{if } t < 0 \end{cases}. \tag{4.2}$$

Many studies in 1-bit CS have been carried out with the following *nonstandard sign function*:

$$\text{sign}(t) = \begin{cases} 1 & \text{if } t \geq 0 \\ -1 & \text{if } t < 0 \end{cases}. \tag{4.3}$$

The function (4.3) maps both zero and positive numbers to 1, yielding the 1-bit measurement vector $y \in \{1,-1\}^m$. The 1-bit CS problem with a nonstandard sign function may not cause any inconvenience or difficulty when the magnitude of all components of $|Ax^*|$ is relatively large, in which case the sign measurements $y := \text{sign}(Ax^*)$ are stable in the sense that any small perturbation of $Ax^*$ does not affect its sign. However, failing to differentiate zero from positive values may yield ambiguity of measurements when a sensing vector is nearly orthogonal to the signal, i.e., when $|A_{i,\bullet}x^*|$ is small. Such ambiguity might prevent correct sign measurements from being acquired, due to signal noise or computation/quantization error.

The reliability of the measurement vector $y$ is vital since the signal $x^*$ is reconstructed or estimated based on this vector. When the magnitude of $|A_{i,\bullet}x^*|$ is very small, the errors or noises do affect the reliability of measurements. For instance, let us consider a sensing matrix $A \in \mathbb{R}^{m\times n}$ whose rows are drawn uniformly from the surface of the $n$-dimensional ball, i.e., $\{u \in \mathbb{R}^n : \|u\|_2 = 1\}$. Given a small number $\varepsilon > 0$, it is quite clear that a drawn vector lies in the following region of the unit surface with a positive probability:

$$\{u \in \mathbb{R}^n : \|u\|_2 = 1,\ |u^T x^*| \leq \varepsilon\}.$$

The sensing row vector $A_{i,\bullet}$ drawn in this region yields a small value $|A_{i,\bullet}x^*| \approx 0$. Thus in the above region $\text{sign}(A_{i,\bullet}x^*)$ is sensitive or uncertain in the sense that any small error might totally flip the sign of the vector $A_{i,\bullet}x^*$, leading to an incorrect sign measurement. In this situation, not only the acquired information $y_i$ is unreliable, but also the value $y_i = 1$ or $-1$ does not reflect the fact $A_{i,\bullet}x^* \approx 0$.

However, the information $A_{i,\bullet}x^* \approx 0$ (showing that $x^*$ is nearly orthogonal to the sensing vector $A_{i,\bullet}$) is particularly useful to help locate the position of the vector $x^*$ in space. Using nonstandard sign function, the information $A_{i,\bullet}x^* \approx 0$ is overlooked in 1-bit CS models. Thus the nonstandard sign function may introduce certain ambiguity into the 1-bit CS model since $Ax^* > 0$, $Ax^* = 0$ and $0 \neq Ax^* \geq 0$ yield the same measurements $y = (1, 1, \ldots, 1)^T$. Once $y$ is acquired, the information concerning which of the above cases yields the vector $y$ in 1-bit CS problems is completely lost. This may cause difficulty to recover the correct information of the target signal no matter which algorithms are used.

By using the standard sign function to distinguish the cases $Ax^* > 0$, $Ax^* = 0$, and $0 \neq Ax^* \geq 0$, the measurements $y$ would carry more relevant information of the signal and increase the chance for the information (such as support or sign) of a signal to be correctly recovered. Thus in this chapter we focus on the 1-bit CS problem with standard sign function. It is worth mentioning that although we focus on the standard sign function, it is straightforward to generalize the analysis in this chapter to the following more practical sign function:

$$\text{sign}_\varepsilon(t) = \begin{cases} 1 & \text{if } t > \varepsilon \\ 0 & \text{if } -\varepsilon \leq t \leq \varepsilon \\ -1 & \text{if } t < -\varepsilon \end{cases},$$

where $\varepsilon \geq 0$ is a given parameter.

In traditional compressed sensing, the exact recovery of $x^*$ is possible since the magnitude information of signals are also acquired in measurements. So the error bound $\|\tilde{x} - x^*\|$ can be used as a recovery criterion, where $\|\cdot\|$ can be any norm and $\tilde{x}$ denotes the reconstructed vector by a decoding method. In 1-bit CS, however, only the sign measurements $y = \text{sign}(Ax^*)$ are available, a small perturbation of $x^*$ might also be consistent with $y$. As we pointed out before, when $y \in \{1, -1\}^m$, any small perturbation $x^* + u$ is consistent with $y$. When $y \in \{1, -1, 0\}^m$ with $J_0 = \{i : y_i = 0\} \neq \emptyset$, it is also evident that any small perturbation $x^* + u$ with $u \in \mathcal{N}(A^0)$ is also consistent with $y$. Thus a 1-bit CS problem may have infinitely many solutions and the sparsest solution of the sign equation $y = \text{sign}(Ax)$ is usually not unique. In this situation, we may use the sign recovery, support recovery or other criteria. The sign recovery of $x^*$ means that the constructed vector $\tilde{x}$ satisfies

$$\text{sign}(\tilde{x}) = \text{sign}(x^*). \tag{4.4}$$

The support recovery $\text{supp}(\tilde{x}) = \text{supp}(x^*)$ can be viewed as a relaxed version of the sign recovery. The following criterion:

$$\|(x/\|x\|_2) - (x^*/\|x^*\|_2)\| \leq \varepsilon$$

was also used in the 1-bit CS literature, where $\varepsilon > 0$ is a small tolerance. In this chapter, we use (4.4) as the major recovery criterion. One of the major fact shown in this chapter is that the sign of a sparse signal can be recovered from sign measurements by an LP decoding method if the transposed sensing matrix satisfies a certain range space property.

## 4.3  Relaxation Models

The 1-bit CS problem (4.1) is difficult to solve precisely due to the NP-hardness of the problem. It makes sense to consider certain relaxations of the problem. Using the standard sign function, we see that

$$
\begin{aligned}
(Ax)_i > 0, \ y_i = \text{sign}((Ax)_i) = 1 \quad &\Rightarrow \quad y_i(Ax)_i > 0, \\
(Ax)_i = 0, \ y_i = \text{sign}((Ax)_i) = 0 \quad &\Rightarrow \quad y_i(Ax)_i = 0, \\
(Ax)_i < 0, \ y_i = \text{sign}((Ax)_i) = -1 \quad &\Rightarrow \quad y_i(Ax)_i > 0.
\end{aligned}
$$

Using the nonstandard sign function, there are only two cases:

$$
\begin{aligned}
(Ax)_i \geq 0, \ y_i = \text{sign}((Ax)_i) = 1 \quad &\Rightarrow \quad y_i(Ax)_i \geq 0, \\
(Ax)_i < 0, \ y_i = \text{sign}((Ax)_i) = -1 \quad &\Rightarrow \quad y_i(Ax)_i > 0.
\end{aligned}
$$

Thus no matter the standard or nonstandard sign function is used, the condition $y = \text{sign}(Ax)$ implies that

$$
YAx \geq 0, \tag{4.5}
$$

where $Y = \text{diag}(y)$. Thus the following fact is obvious.

**Lemma 4.3.1** *For any given $A \in \mathbb{R}^{m \times n}$ and any given $y \in \{1, -1\}^m$ or $y \in \{1, 0, -1\}^m$, the following holds:*

$$
\{x: \ \text{sign}(Ax) = y\} \subseteq \{x: \ YAx \geq 0\}. \tag{4.6}
$$

The target signal $x^*$ is assumed to be nontrivial, i.e., $x^* \notin \mathcal{N}(A)$, since otherwise it is almost impossible to recover the (support, sign or other) information of the target signal no matter which decoding methods are used. However, the system (4.5) includes trivial solutions, such as $x = 0$ and $0 \neq x \in \mathcal{N}(A)$. To exclude these trivial solutions, an extra constraint, such as $\|x\|_2 = 1$ or $\|Ax\|_1 = m$ should be introduced to the problem, resulting in the following relaxation models for the 1-bit CS problem (4.1):

$$
\min_x \{\|x\|_0 : \ YAx \geq 0, \ \|x\|_2 = 1\}, \tag{4.7}
$$

$$
\min_x \{\|x\|_0 : \ YAx \geq 0, \ \|Ax\|_1 = m\}. \tag{4.8}
$$

These sparse optimization problems remain difficult to solve directly. To achieve more tractable models, we consider the following $\ell_1$-minimization problems:

$$
\min_x \{\|x\|_1 : \ YAx \geq 0, \ \|x\|_2 = 1\}, \tag{4.9}
$$

$$\min_x\{\|x\|_1 : YAx \geq 0, \|Ax\|_1 = m\}. \tag{4.10}$$

These along with other similar problems have been studied over the past few years. The right-hand-side numbers, 1 and $m$, in (4.9) and (4.10) are not essential and can be replaced with any positive numbers. The problem (4.9) is a nonconvex optimization problem, while (4.10) can be a convex problem when $y \in \{1, -1\}^m$. In fact, under the condition $YAx \geq 0$ with $y \in \{1, -1\}^m$, we have $y_i(Ax)_i = |(Ax)_i|$ for every $i = 1, \ldots, m$, and hence,

$$\|Ax\|_1 = \sum_{i=1}^{m}|(Ax)_i| = \sum_{i=1}^{m}y_i(Ax)_i = \mathbf{e}^T(YAx).$$

Thus when $y \in \{1, -1\}^m$, the problem (4.10) can be written as

$$\min_x\{\|x\|_1 : YAx \geq 0, \mathbf{e}^T(YAx) = m\}. \tag{4.11}$$

Many developments for 1-bit CS problems were based on this observation.

## 4.4 Consistency Condition

The basic requirement for the relaxation problem of 1-bit CS is that the solution $x$ generated by the relaxation problem should be consistent with the acquired measurements in the sense that

$$\text{sign}(Ax) = y := \text{sign}(Ax^*), \tag{4.12}$$

where $x^*$ is the target signal. That is, the solution of the relaxation problem should satisfy the constraint of the 1-bit CS problem, although the solution may not be the same as the target signal. We may show that the traditional models based on (4.5) do not always satisfy the consistency condition unless certain assumptions are imposed on the sensing matrix $A$.

The solution $x$ of (4.9) and (4.10) might not satisfy the constraint $y = \text{sign}(Ax)$, since the feasible sets of these problems are not equivalent to that of (4.1). It is easy to see that the opposite of (4.6) does not hold in general, i.e.,

$$\{x : YAx \geq 0\} \not\subseteq \{x : \text{sign}(Ax) = y\}.$$

For instance, let $y \in \{1, -1\}^m$ with $J_-(y) = \{i : y_i = -1\} \neq \emptyset$. Clearly, any vector $0 \neq \tilde{x} \in \mathcal{N}(A)$ satisfies $YA\tilde{x} \geq 0$. For such a vector, however, $\text{sign}(A\tilde{x}) = \text{sign}(0) \neq y$ no matter $\text{sign}(\cdot)$ is standard or nonstandard, and hence $\tilde{x} \notin \{x : \text{sign}(Ax) = y\}$. In that follows, we further demonstrate that even if some trivial-solution excluders, such as $\|x\|_2 = 1$ and $\|Ax\|_1 = m$, are included into a relaxation model, there is still no guarantee for the consistency being met.

### 4.4.1 Nonstandard Sign Function

Let us first consider the nonstandard sign function. In this case, when $J_-(y) = \{i : y_i = -1\} \neq \emptyset$, it is evident that $x = 0$ and $0 \neq x \in \mathcal{N}(A)$ are not contained in the set $\{x : \mathrm{sign}(Ax) = y\}$. It follows from Lemma 4.3.1 that if $J_-(y) \neq \emptyset$, the following relations holds:

$$\{x : \mathrm{sign}(Ax) = y\} \subseteq \{x : YAx \geq 0, \ x \neq 0\}, \tag{4.13}$$

$$\{x : \mathrm{sign}(Ax) = y\} \subseteq \{x : YAx \geq 0, \ Ax \neq 0\}. \tag{4.14}$$

This means that the feasible sets of (4.9) and (4.10) are relaxation of that of (4.1). But the opposite directions of above relations do not hold in general, that is,

$$\{x : YAx \geq 0, \ x \neq 0\} \nsubseteq \{x : \mathrm{sign}(Ax) = y\},$$

and

$$\{x : YAx \geq 0, \ Ax \neq 0\} \nsubseteq \{x : \mathrm{sign}(Ax) = y\},$$

unless certain assumptions are imposed on $A$. To see this, let $y \in \{1, -1\}^m$ with $J_-(y) \neq \emptyset$. We note that any non-zero vector

$$\tilde{x} \in \{x : A^- x = 0, \ 0 \neq A^+ x \geq 0\}$$

satisfies $YA\tilde{x} \geq 0$. For such a vector, however, $\mathrm{sign}(A\tilde{x}) = \mathbf{e} \neq y$. In this case, $\{x : YAx \geq 0, \ x \neq 0\}$ and $\{x : YAx \geq 0, \ Ax \neq 0\}$ are not the subsets of $\{x : \mathrm{sign}(Ax) = y\}$. The trivial-solution excluder $\|x\|_2 = 1$ cannot exclude the vector $\tilde{x}$ from the set $\{x : YAx \geq 0, \ x \neq 0\}$, and the excluder $\|Ax\|_1 = m$ cannot exclude such a vector from the set $\{x : YAx \geq 0, \ Ax \neq 0\}$ as well. For example,

$$A = \begin{bmatrix} -1 & 2 & 0 & 1 \\ 1 & -1 & 1 & 0 \end{bmatrix}, \text{ and } y = \begin{bmatrix} 1 \\ -1 \end{bmatrix}. \tag{4.15}$$

Consider the vector $x(\alpha) = (\alpha, \alpha, 0, 0)^T$. Clearly, for any positive number $\alpha > 0$,

$$x(\alpha) \in \{x : YAx \geq 0, \ x \neq 0\},$$

and

$$x(\alpha) \in \{x : YAx \geq 0, \ Ax \neq 0\}.$$

However, $\mathrm{sign}(Ax(\alpha)) = (1, 1)^T \neq y$. This implies that when $J_-(y) \neq \emptyset$, the feasible sets of (4.9) and (4.10) are not the same as that of (4.1), and thus the solutions of (4.9) and (4.10) might not satisfy the consistency condition.

To meet the consistency requirement, some conditions are required, as shown by the following lemma.

**Lemma 4.4.1** *Let $A \in \mathbb{R}^{m \times n}$ and $y \in \{1, -1\}^m$ with $J_-(y) = \{i : y_i = -1\} \neq \emptyset$. Let* sign *$(\cdot)$ be the non-standard sign function in (4.3). Then the following two statements hold:*

(i)
$$\{x : YAx \geq 0, \; x \neq 0\} \subseteq \{x : sign(Ax) = y\} \qquad (4.16)$$

*if and only if*

$$\mathcal{N}(A_{i,\bullet}) \cap \{d : A^+ d \geq 0, \; A^- d \leq 0\} = \{0\} \; \text{for all} \; i \in J_-(y). \qquad (4.17)$$

(ii)
$$\{x : YAx \geq 0, \; Ax \neq 0\} \subseteq \{x : sign(Ax) = y\}$$

*if and only if*

$$\mathcal{N}(A_{i,\bullet}) \cap \{d : A^+ d \geq 0, \; A^- d \leq 0, \; Ad \neq 0\} = \emptyset \; \text{for all} \; i \in J_-(y). \qquad (4.18)$$

*Proof.* We first prove that (4.17) implies (4.16). Let $z$ be an arbitrary vector in the set $\{x : YAx \geq 0, \; x \neq 0\}$. Since $y \in \{1, -1\}^m$, it is evident that $YAz \geq 0$ and $z \neq 0$ is equivalent to

$$A^+ z \geq 0, \; A^- z \leq 0, \; z \neq 0, \qquad (4.19)$$

which together with (4.17) implies

$$z \notin \mathcal{N}(A_{i,\bullet}) \; \text{for all} \; i \in J_-(y),$$

i.e., $A_{i,\bullet} z \neq 0$ for all $i \in J_-(y)$. This together with $A^- z \leq 0$ implies that $A^- z < 0$. Thus under the condition (4.17), the system (4.19) becomes

$$A^+ z \geq 0, \; A^- z < 0, \; z \neq 0,$$

which implies that $sign(Az) = y$. Thus (4.16) holds.

We now prove that (4.16) implies (4.17). Assume that (4.17) does not hold. Then there is a vector $d^* \neq 0$ and an element $i^* \in J_-(y)$ such that:

$$A_{i^*,\bullet} d^* = 0, \; A^+ d^* \geq 0, \; A^- d^* \leq 0.$$

This implies that $d^* \in \{x : YAx \geq 0, \; x \neq 0\}$. Since $sign(\cdot)$ is nonstandard, we see that $sign(A_{i^*,\bullet} d^*) = 1 \neq y_{i^*} = -1$. So $d^* \notin \{x : sign(Ax) = y\}$, and hence (4.16) does not hold. Therefore, (4.16) implies (4.17). The item (ii) Can be easily shown by a proof similar to Item (i). □

Based on the above analysis, we immediately have the following statement.

**Theorem 4.4.2** *Let* sign *$(\cdot)$ be the nonstandard sign function, and let $A \in \mathbb{R}^{m \times n}$ and $y \in \{1, -1\}^m$ be given.*

(i) *If $J_-(y) = \emptyset$ (i.e., $y = \mathbf{e}$), then $\{x : sign(Ax) = y\} = \{x : YAx \geq 0\}$.*

(ii) *If $J_-(y) \neq \emptyset$, then $\{x: \text{sign}(Ax) = y\} = \{x: YAx \geq 0, x \neq 0\}$ if and only if (4.17) is satisfied.*

(iii) *If $J_-(y) \neq \emptyset$, then $\{x: \text{sign}(Ax) = y\} = \{x: YAx \geq 0, Ax \neq 0\}$ if and only if (4.18) is satisfied.*

Item (i) is obvious by noting that $y = \mathbf{e}$. Items (ii) and (iii) immediately follow from (4.13), (4.14) and Lemma 4.4.1. It is easy to verify that the example (4.15) does not satisfy (4.17) and (4.18).

## 4.4.2 Standard Sign Function

We now consider the standard sign function. Suppose that $A$ is a non-zero matrix. It is easy to see the following observation.

**Proposition 4.4.3** *Let $\text{sign}(\cdot)$ be the standard sign function in (4.2). Then $\{x: YAx \geq 0\} \neq \{x: \text{sign}(Ax) = y\}$ for any non-zero matrix $A \in \mathbb{R}^{m \times n} (m < n)$.*

*Proof.* If $y = 0$, then $\{x: YAx \geq 0\} = \mathbb{R}^n$ and

$$\{x: 0 = \text{sign}(Ax)\} = \{x: Ax = 0\} = \mathcal{N}(A) \neq \mathbb{R}^n.$$

If $y \neq 0$, we see that $\mathcal{N}(A) \subseteq \{x: YAx \geq 0\}$, but any vector in $\mathcal{N}(A)$ fails to satisfy the equation $\text{sign}(Ax) = y$. □

In general, the set $\{x: YAx \geq 0\}$ can be remarkably larger than the set $\{x: \text{sign}(Ax) = y\}$. In what follows, we focus on the case $0 \neq y \in \{1, -1, 0\}^m$. In this case, if $J_0(y) = \{i: y_i = 0\} \neq \emptyset$, both the vectors in $\mathcal{N}(A)$ and the vectors $x$ satisfying $A^0 x \neq 0$ do not satisfy the constraint $\text{sign}(Ax) = y$. So these vectors must be excluded from the set $\{x: YAx \geq 0\}$ in order to get a tighter relaxation for the set $\{x: \text{sign}(Ax) = y\}$. This means that only vectors satisfying $Ax \neq 0$ and $A^0 x = 0$ (i.e., $x \in \mathcal{N}(A^0) \backslash \mathcal{N}(A)$) should be considered. Thus we have the next result.

**Theorem 4.4.4** *Let $0 \neq y \in \{1, 0, -1\}^m$ and $A \in \mathbb{R}^{m \times n}$ be given. Let $\text{sign}(\cdot)$ be the standard sign function in (4.2). Then the following two statements hold:*

(i) $\{x: \text{sign}(A\,x) = y\} \subseteq \{x: YAx \geq 0, A^0 x = 0, Ax \neq 0\}$.

(ii) $\{x: YAx \geq 0, A^0 x = 0, Ax \neq 0\} \subseteq \{x: \text{sign}(Ax) = y\}$        (4.20)

*if and only if for all $i \in J_+(y) \cup J_-(y)$, the following holds:*

$$\mathcal{N}(A_{i,\bullet}) \cap \{d: A^+ d \geq 0, A^- d \leq 0, A^0 d = 0, Ad \neq 0\} = \emptyset. \quad (4.21)$$

*Proof.* Item (i) follows from Lemma 4.3.1 and the discussion before this theorem. We now prove Item (ii). We first prove that the condition (4.21) holding for all $i \in$

$J_+(y) \cup J_-(y)$ implies (4.20). Assume that (4.21) holds for all $i \in J_+(y) \cup J_-(y)$, and let $\hat{x}$ be an arbitrary vector in the set $\{x: YAx \geq 0, A^0x = 0, Ax \neq 0\}$. Thus

$$A^+\hat{x} \geq 0, \ A^-\hat{x} \leq 0, \ A^0\hat{x} = 0, \ A\hat{x} \neq 0. \tag{4.22}$$

As $y \neq 0$, the set $J_+(y) \cup J_-(y) \neq \emptyset$. It follows from (4.21) and (4.22) that

$$\hat{x} \notin \mathcal{N}(A_{i,\bullet}) \ \text{ for all } \ i \in J_+(y) \cup J_-(y),$$

which implies that the inequalities $A^+\hat{x} \geq 0$ and $A^-\hat{x} \leq 0$ in (4.22) must hold strictly. Thus,

$$A^+\hat{x} > 0, \ A^-\hat{x} < 0, \ A^0\hat{x} = 0, \ A\hat{x} \neq 0,$$

which implies that $\text{sign}(A\hat{x}) = y$. So (4.20) holds.

We now further prove that (4.20) implies that (4.21) holds for all $i \in J_+(y) \cup J_-(y)$. It is sufficient to show that if there is $i \in J_+(y) \cup J_-(y)$ such that (4.21) does not hold, then (4.20) does not hold. Indeed, assume that (4.21) is not satisfied for some $i^* \in J_+(y) \cup J_-(y)$. Then there exists a vector $\hat{d}$ satisfying

$$A^+\hat{d} \geq 0, \ A^-\hat{d} \leq 0, \ A^0\hat{d} = 0, \ A\hat{d} \neq 0, \ A_{i^*,\bullet}\hat{d} = 0.$$

This implies that

$$\hat{d} \in \{x: YAx \geq 0, A^0x = 0, Ax \neq 0\}.$$

However, $\text{sign}(A_{i^*,\bullet}\hat{d}) = 0 \neq y_{i^*}$ where $y_{i^*} = 1$ or $-1$, since $i^* \in J_+(y) \cup J_-(y)$. This means $\hat{d} \notin \{x: \text{sign}(Ax) = y\}$. Thus (4.20) does not hold. □

**Corollary 4.4.5** *Under the conditions of Theorem 4.4.4, the set $\{x: \text{sign}(Ax) = y\}$ coincides with $\{x: YAx \geq 0, A^0x = 0, Ax \neq 0\}$ if and only if the condition (4.21) holds for all $i \in J_+(y) \cup J_-(y)$.*

To guarantee that (4.7) and (4.8) are equivalent to (4.1), and that (4.9) and (4.10) are equivalent to the problem

$$\min_x \{\|x\|_1: \text{sign}(Ax) = y\}, \tag{4.23}$$

the conditions (4.17), (4.18) or (4.21), depending on the definition of the sign function, must be imposed on the matrix. Without these conditions, the feasible set of sparse optimization problems (4.7)–(4.10) are strictly larger than that of (4.1) and (4.23), and thus their solutions might not satisfy the consistency requirement.

## 4.5    Reformulation of 1-Bit Compressed Sensing

The analysis in Section 4.4 indicates that $y = \text{sign}(Ax)$ is generally not equivalent to the system (4.5) even if a trivial-solution excluder such as $\|x\|_2 = 1$ or $\|Ax\|_1 = m$ is included, unless the sensing matrix $A$ satisfies certain conditions. The 1-bit CS method based on (4.5) may generate a solution inconsistent with sign measurements. This motivates us to reformulate the 1-bit CS problem as an equivalent $\ell_0$-minimization problem without involving a sign function. Such a reformulation yields an LP decoding method which always generates a solution consistent with sign measurements.

We focus on the 1-bit CS problem with standard sign function. (The results for nonstandard sign function follows from the derived results by setting $J_0(y) = \emptyset$.) Given sign measurements $y \in \{-1, 1, 0\}^m$, we still use the following notations:

$$J_+(y) = \{i : y_i = 1\}, \ J_-(y) = \{i : y_i = -1\}, \ J_0(y) = \{i : y_i = 0\}. \quad (4.24)$$

Recalling that $A^+, A^-, A^0$ are submatrices of $A$, their rows are indexed by $J_+(y)$, $J_-(y)$ and $J_0(y)$, respectively. When there is no ambiguity arising, we simply use $J_+$ and $J_-$ to denote $J_+(y)$ and $J_-(y)$, respectively. By using (4.24), the constraint $\text{sign}(Ax) = y$ can be written as

$$\text{sign}(A^+x) = \mathbf{e}_{J_+}, \ \text{sign}(A^-x) = -\mathbf{e}_{J_-}, \ A^0x = 0. \quad (4.25)$$

Rearranging the order of the components of $y$ and the order of the associated rows of $A$ if necessary, we may assume without loss of generality that

$$A = \begin{pmatrix} A^+ \\ A^- \\ A^0 \end{pmatrix}, \ y = \begin{pmatrix} \mathbf{e}_{J_+} \\ -\mathbf{e}_{J_-} \\ 0 \end{pmatrix}.$$

Then the problem (4.1) with $y \in \{1, -1, 0\}^m$ can be restated equivalently to

$$\begin{aligned} \min \quad & \|x\|_0 \\ \text{s.t.} \quad & \text{sign}(A^+x) = \mathbf{e}_{J_+}, \\ & \text{sign}(A^-x) = -\mathbf{e}_{J_-}, \\ & A^0x = 0. \end{aligned} \quad (4.26)$$

Consider the system in $u \in \mathbb{R}^n$

$$A^+u \geq \mathbf{e}_{J_+}, \ A^-u \leq -\mathbf{e}_{J_-}, \ A^0u = 0. \quad (4.27)$$

Clearly, if $x$ satisfies the system (4.25), i.e., $x$ is a feasible vector to the problem (4.26), then there exists a number $\tau > 0$ such that $u = \tau x$ satisfies the system (4.27); conversely, if $u$ satisfies the system (4.27), then $x = u$ satisfies the system

(4.25). Note that $\|x\|_0 = \|\tau x\|_0$ for any $\tau \neq 0$. Thus (4.26) can be reformulated as the following $\ell_0$-minimization problem with linear constraints:

$$\begin{aligned}\min \quad & \|x\|_0 \\ \text{s.t.} \quad & A^+x \geq \mathbf{e}_{J_+}, \ A^-x \leq -\mathbf{e}_{J_-}, \ A^0x = 0.\end{aligned} \tag{4.28}$$

Since the feasible set of the problem (4.28) is a polyhedral set, the solution of this problem is the sparsest point in a polyhedral set. The following observation is made immediately from the relation of (4.25) and (4.27).

**Lemma 4.5.1** *If $x^*$ is a solution to the problem (4.26), then there exists a positive number $\tau > 0$ such that $\tau x^*$ is a solution to the $\ell_0$-minimization problem (4.28); conversely, if $x^*$ is a solution to the $\ell_0$-minimization problem (4.28), then $x^*$ is also a solution to the problem (4.26).*

As a result, to study the 1-bit CS problem (4.26), it is sufficient to investigate the sparse optimization problem (4.28), which seeks for the sparsest point in a polyhedral set. This makes it possible to use the analytical tool for traditional compressed sensing to study the 1-bit CS problem (4.26). Motivated by (4.28), we consider its $\ell_1$-minimization counterpart

$$\begin{aligned}\min \quad & \|x\|_1 \\ \text{s.t.} \quad & A^+x \geq \mathbf{e}_{J_+}, \ A^-x \leq -\mathbf{e}_{J_-}, \ A^0x = 0,\end{aligned} \tag{4.29}$$

which can be seen as a natural decoding method for the 1-bit CS problem (4.26). The problem (4.29) is referred to as the *1-bit basis pursuit*. It is worth stressing that the solution of (4.29) is always consistent with $y$ as indicated by Lemma 4.5.1. The later analysis in this chapter indicates that the 1-bit basis pursuit enables us to develop a sign-recovery theory for sparse signals from sigh measurements. For the convenience of analysis, we define the index sets $\mathcal{A}_1(\cdot)$, $\overline{\mathcal{A}_1}(\cdot)$, $\mathcal{A}_2(\cdot)$, and $\overline{\mathcal{A}_2}(\cdot)$ which are used frequently in the remainder of this chapter. Let $x^* \in \mathbb{R}^n$ satisfy the constraints of (4.29). Define

$$\mathcal{A}_1(x^*) = \{i: \ (A^+x^*)_i = 1\}, \ \overline{\mathcal{A}_1}(x^*) = \{i: \ (A^+x^*)_i > 1\},$$

$$\mathcal{A}_2(x^*) = \{i: \ (A^-x^*)_i = -1\}, \ \overline{\mathcal{A}_2}(x^*) = \{i: \ (A^-x^*)_i < -1\}.$$

Clearly, $\mathcal{A}_1(x^*)$ and $\mathcal{A}_2(x^*)$ are the index sets for active constraints among the inequalities $A^+x^* \geq \mathbf{e}_{J_+}$ and $A^-x^* \leq -\mathbf{e}_{J_-}$, respectively. $\overline{\mathcal{A}_1}(x^*)$ is the index set for inactive constraints in the first group of inequalities in (4.29) (i.e., $A^+x^* \geq \mathbf{e}_{J_+}$), and $\overline{\mathcal{A}_2}(x^*)$ is the index set for inactive constraints in the second group of inequalities in (4.29) (i.e., $A^-x^* \leq -\mathbf{e}_{J_-}$).

In the remaining chapter, we describe some necessary and sufficient conditions for the exact recovery of the sign of sparse signals from sigh measurements. In classic CS, it has been shown in Chapter 3 that *any k-sparse signal can be exactly recovered with $\ell_1$-minimization if and only if the transposed sensing matrix* *admits the range space property (RSP) of order k.* The reformulation of the 1-bit CS problem described in this section allows us to develop an analogous recovery theory for the sign of sparse signals with 1-bit basis pursuit. This development naturally yields the notion of restricted range space property which gives rise to some necessary and sufficient conditions for non-uniform and uniform sign recovery for sparse signals.

## 4.6 Non-uniform Sign Recovery

Let $x^*$ denote the vector to recover. We assume that the sign measurements $y = \text{sign}(Ax^*)$ are available. From this information, we use the 1-bit basis pursuit (4.29) to recover the sign of $x^*$. The recovery of the sign of an individual sparse vector is referred to as the *non-uniform sign recovery*. We develop certain necessary and sufficient conditions for such recoveries.

Let the sign measurements $y \in \{1, -1, 0\}^m$ be given, and let $J_+(y)$, $J_-(y)$ and $J_0(y)$ be specified in (4.24). We now consider the matrix $A = \begin{bmatrix} A^+ \\ A^- \\ A^0 \end{bmatrix}$, recall the notion of RRSP of $A^T$ in Chapter 2, and define the notation below.

**Definition 4.6.1** (RRSP of $A^T$ at $x^*$) *Let $x^* \in \mathbb{R}^n$ satisfy $y = \text{sign}(Ax^*)$. We say that $A^T$ satisfies the restricted range space property (RRSP) at $x^*$ if there are vectors $\eta \in \mathcal{R}(A^T)$ and $w = (w^+, w^-, w^0) \in \mathcal{F}(x^*)$ such that $\eta = A^T w$ and*

$$\eta_i = 1 \text{ for all } x_i^* > 0, \ \eta_i = -1 \text{ for all } x_i^* < 0, \ |\eta_i| < 1 \text{ for all } x_i^* = 0,$$

*where $\mathcal{F}(x^*)$ is the set defined as*

$$\mathcal{F}(x^*) = \{w = (w^+, w^-, w^0) \in \mathbb{R}^{|J_+|} \times \mathbb{R}^{|J_-|} \times \mathbb{R}^{|J_0|} : w_i^+ > 0 \text{ for } i \in \mathcal{A}_1(x^*),$$
$$w_i^+ = 0 \text{ for } i \in \overline{\mathcal{A}_1}(x^*), \ w_i^- < 0 \text{ for } i \in \mathcal{A}_2(x^*),$$
$$w_i^- = 0 \text{ for } i \in \overline{\mathcal{A}_2}(x^*)\}. \tag{4.30}$$

The RRSP of $A^T$ at $x^*$ is a natural condition for the uniqueness of the solution to the 1-bit basis pursuit (4.29), as shown in the following theorem, which follows immediately from Theorem 2.4.3. In fact, by setting $B = A^+$, $C = A^-$ and $D = A^0$, by Theorem 2.4.3, we immediately obtain the following uniqueness characterization of the solution of the 1-bit basis pursuit (4.29).

**Theorem 4.6.2** (Necessary and sufficient condition) *$x^*$ is the unique solution to the 1-bit basis pursuit (4.29) if and only if the RRSP of $A^T$ at $x^*$ holds and the matrix*

$$H(x^*) = \begin{bmatrix} (A^+)_{\mathcal{A}_1(x^*),S_+} & (A^+)_{\mathcal{A}_1(x^*),S_-} \\ (A^-)_{\mathcal{A}_2(x^*),S_+} & (A^-)_{\mathcal{A}_2(x^*),S_-} \\ (A^0)_{S_+} & (A^0)_{S_-} \end{bmatrix} \tag{4.31}$$

*has full column rank, where* $S_+ = \{i: x_i^* > 0\}$ *and* $S_- = \{i: x_i^* < 0\}$.

Recalling that for the standard $\ell_1$-minimization $\min\{\|z\|_1 : Az = b\}$, Theorem 2.2.14 claims that $\tilde{x}$ is the unique solution to this problem if and only if $A_{\mathrm{supp}(\tilde{x})}$ has full column rank and there exists a vector $\eta = A^T w$ for some $w \in \mathbb{R}^m$ satisfying the following conditions: $\eta_i = 1$ for $\tilde{x}_i > 0$, $\eta_i = -1$ for $\tilde{x}_i < 0$, and $|\eta_i| < 1$ for $\tilde{x}_i = 0$. In this situation, there is no other restriction on $w \in \mathbb{R}^n$, even when this result has been generalized to the $\ell_1$-minimization with non-negative constraints (see Theorem 2.3.6 in Chapter 2). However, the problem (4.29) with equality and inequality constraints is more complex than the standard $\ell_1$-minimization problem. The uniqueness condition for the solution of (4.29) has a restricted choice of $w$, which is confined to the set (4.30). The uniqueness of solutions to (4.29) is an important property needed in sign reconstruction of sparse vectors. Theorem 4.6.2, together with certain strengthened RRSP of $A^T$, provides a fundamental basis to develop a sign-recovery theory for sparse signals from sign measurements. Let us begin with the following lemma.

**Lemma 4.6.3** *Let* $x^*$ *be a sparsest solution of the $\ell_0$-minimization problem in (4.28) and denoted by* $S_+ = \{i: x_i^* > 0\}$ *and* $S_- = \{i: x_i^* < 0\}$. *Then* $A_{S_+ \cup S_-}$ *has full column rank, and therefore,*

$$\widetilde{H}(x^*) = \begin{bmatrix} (A^+)_{\mathcal{A}_1(x^*),S_+} & (A^+)_{\mathcal{A}_1(x^*),S_-} \\ (A^-)_{\mathcal{A}_2(x^*),S_+} & (A^-)_{\mathcal{A}_2(x^*),S_-} \\ (A^0)_{S_+} & (A^0)_{S_-} \\ (A^+)_{\overline{\mathcal{A}_1}(x^*),S_+} & (A^+)_{\overline{\mathcal{A}_1}(x^*),S_-} \\ (A^-)_{\overline{\mathcal{A}_2}(x^*),S_+} & (A^-)_{\overline{\mathcal{A}_2}(x^*),S_-} \end{bmatrix} \tag{4.32}$$

*has full column rank. Furthermore, if*

$$|\mathcal{A}_1(x^*) \cup \mathcal{A}_2(x^*)| = \max\{|\mathcal{A}_1(x) \cup \mathcal{A}_2(x)| : x \in F^*\}, \tag{4.33}$$

*where* $F^*$ *is the solution set of the problem (4.28), then* $H(x^*)$ *given in (4.31) has full column rank.*

*Proof.* We use $J_+$ and $J_-$ to denote $J_+(y)$ and $J_-(y)$, respectively. Note that $x^*$ is the sparsest solution to the system

$$A^+ x^* \geq e_{J_+}, \ A^- x^* \leq -e_{J_-}, \ A^0 x^* = 0. \tag{4.34}$$

Eliminating the zero components of $x^*$ from (4.34) leads to

$$\begin{cases} (A^+)_{S_+} x_{S_+}^* + (A^+)_{S_-} x_{S_-}^* \geq e_{J_+} \\ (A^-)_{S_+} x_{S_+}^* + (A^-)_{S_-} x_{S_-}^* \leq -e_{J_-} \\ (A^0)_{S_+} x_{S_+}^* + (A^0)_{S_-} x_{S_-}^* = 0. \end{cases} \tag{4.35}$$

Since $x^*$ is a sparsest solution of the above system, it is not very difficult to see that the coefficient matrix of (4.35), i.e.,

$$\widehat{H} = A_{S_+ \cup S_-} = \begin{bmatrix} (A^+)_{S_+} & (A^+)_{S_-} \\ (A^-)_{S_+} & (A^-)_{S_-} \\ (A^0)_{S_+} & (A^0)_{S_-} \end{bmatrix},$$

has full column rank. In fact, if there is a column of $\widehat{H}$ which can be linearly represented by other columns of $\widehat{H}$, then this column can be eliminated from the system (4.35) so that a solution sparser than $x^*$ can be found for the system (4.35) (which is also a solution to (4.34)), leading to a contradiction. Note that

$$J_+ = A_1(x^*) \cup \overline{A_1}(x^*), \quad J_- = A_2(x^*) \cup \overline{A_2}(x^*). \tag{4.36}$$

Performing row permutations on $\widehat{H}$, if necessary, yields $\widetilde{H}(x^*)$ given in (4.32). Note that row permutations do not affect the column rank of a matrix. Since $\widehat{H}$ has full column rank, the matrix $\widetilde{H}(x^*)$ must have full column rank.

We now show that $H(x^*)$ given in (4.31) (which is a submatrix of $\widetilde{H}(x^*)$) has full column rank if the set $A_1(x^*) \cup A_2(x^*)$ admits the maximum cardinality amongst the sparsest solutions of the problem in the sense that

$$|A_1(x^*) \cup A_2(x^*)| = \max\{|A_1(x) \cup A_2(x)| : x \in F^*\},$$

where $F^*$ is the solution set of (4.28). We prove this by contradiction. Assume that the columns of $H(x^*)$ are linearly dependent, then there is a non-zero vector $d = (u, v) \in \mathbb{R}^{|S_+|} \times \mathbb{R}^{|S_-|}$ such that

$$H(x^*)d = H(x^*) \begin{bmatrix} u \\ v \end{bmatrix} = 0.$$

Since $d \neq 0$ and $\widetilde{H}(x^*)$ in (4.32) has full column rank, it follows that

$$\begin{bmatrix} (A^+)_{\overline{A_1}(x^*), S_+} & (A^+)_{\overline{A_1}(x^*), S_-} \\ (A^-)_{\overline{A_2}(x^*), S_+} & (A^-)_{\overline{A_2}(x^*), S_-} \end{bmatrix} \begin{bmatrix} u \\ v \end{bmatrix} \neq 0. \tag{4.37}$$

Define the vector $x(\lambda)$ as follows:

$$x(\lambda)_{S_+} = x^*_{S_+} + \lambda u, \ x(\lambda)_{S_-} = x^*_{S_-} + \lambda v, \ x(\lambda)_i = 0 \ \text{ for all } \ i \notin S_+ \cup S_-,$$

where $\lambda \in \mathbb{R}$. Clearly, we have

$$\text{supp}(x(\lambda)) \subseteq \text{supp}(x^*) \ \text{ for any } \lambda \in \mathbb{R}.$$

By the definition of $A_1(x^*), A_2(x^*), \overline{A_1}(x^*)$ and $\overline{A_2}(x^*)$, the system (4.35) can be further written as follows:

$$\begin{cases} (A^+)_{A_1(x^*), S_+} x^*_{S_+} + (A^+)_{A_1(x^*), S_-} x^*_{S_-} = e_{A_1(x^*)}, \\ (A^-)_{A_2(x^*), S_+} x^*_{S_+} + (A^-)_{A_2(x^*), S_-} x^*_{S_-} = -e_{A_2(x^*)}, \\ (A^0)_{S_+} x^*_{S_+} + (A^0)_{S_-} x^*_{S_-} = 0, \\ (A^+)_{\overline{A_1}(x^*), S_+} x^*_{S_+} + (A^+)_{\overline{A_1}(x^*), S_-} x^*_{S_-} > e_{\overline{A_1}(x^*)}, \\ (A^-)_{\overline{A_2}(x^*), S_+} x^*_{S_+} + (A^-)_{\overline{A_2}(x^*), S_-} x^*_{S_-} < -e_{\overline{A_2}(x^*)}, \end{cases}$$

From the above system and the definition of $x(\lambda)$, we see that for any sufficiently small $|\lambda| \neq 0$, the vector $(x(\lambda)_{S_+}, x(\lambda)_{S_-})$ satisfies the system

$$H(x^*) \begin{bmatrix} x(\lambda)_{S_+} \\ x(\lambda)_{S_-} \end{bmatrix} = \begin{bmatrix} \mathbf{e}_{\mathcal{A}_1(x^*)} \\ -\mathbf{e}_{\mathcal{A}_2(x^*)} \\ 0 \end{bmatrix}, \tag{4.38}$$

$$\left[ (A^+)_{\overline{\mathcal{A}_1(x^*)}, S_+}, \ (A^+)_{\overline{\mathcal{A}_1(x^*)}, S_-} \right] \begin{bmatrix} x(\lambda)_{S_+} \\ x(\lambda)_{S_-} \end{bmatrix} > \mathbf{e}_{\overline{\mathcal{A}_1(x^*)}}, \tag{4.39}$$

$$\left[ (A^-)_{\overline{\mathcal{A}_2(x^*)}, S_+}, \ (A^-)_{\overline{\mathcal{A}_2(x^*)}, S_-} \right] \begin{bmatrix} x(\lambda)_{S_+} \\ x(\lambda)_{S_-} \end{bmatrix} < -\mathbf{e}_{\overline{\mathcal{A}_2(x^*)}}. \tag{4.40}$$

Equality (4.38) holds for any $\lambda \in \mathbb{R}^n$. Starting at $\lambda = 0$, we continuously increase the value of $|\lambda|$. In this process, if one of the components of the vector $(x(\lambda)_{S_+}, x(\lambda)_{S_-})$ becomes zero and this vector still satisfies (4.38)–(4.40), then a solution of (4.34), which is sparser than $x^*$, is found. This is a contradiction. Thus without loss of generality, we assume that $\text{supp}(x(\lambda)) = \text{supp}(x^*)$ is maintained when $|\lambda|$ is continuously increased. It follows from (4.37) that there is a number $\lambda^* \neq 0$ such that $(x(\lambda^*)_{S_+}, x(\lambda^*)_{S_-})$ satisfies (4.38)–(4.40) (and hence it is a solution to (4.34)) and one of the inactive constraints in (4.39) and (4.40) becomes active. Therefore, $|\mathcal{A}_1(x(\lambda^*)) \cup \mathcal{A}_2(x(\lambda^*))| > |\mathcal{A}_1(x^*) \cup \mathcal{A}_2(x^*)|$. This contradicts the assumption (4.33). Thus, $H(x^*)$ must have full column rank. □

From Lemma 4.6.3, the full-rank property of (4.31) can be guaranteed if $x^*$ is the sparsest solution consistent with sign measurements and $|\mathcal{A}_1(x^*) \cup \mathcal{A}_2(x^*)|$ is maximal in the sense of (4.33). Thus by Theorem 4.6.2, the RRSP described in Definition 4.6.1 is a key criterion for $x^*$ to be the unique solution of (4.29). So from Lemma 4.6.3 and Theorem 4.6.2, we obtain the following connection between 1-bit CS problem and 1-bit basis pursuit.

**Corollary 4.6.4** *Suppose that $x^*$ is a solution to the $\ell_0$-minimization problem (4.28) with $|\mathcal{A}_1(x^*) \cup \mathcal{A}_2(x^*)|$ being maximal among all solutions of (4.28). Then $x^*$ is the unique solution to (4.29) if and only if the RRSP of $A^T$ at $x^*$ holds.*

The RRSP of $A^T$ at $x^*$ is a key condition for the sign recovery of $x^*$. However, this property is defined at $x^*$, which is unknown in advance. In order to develop some recovery conditions which are independent of the unknown vector, we need to further strengthen the notion of RRSP of $A^T$ at an individual vector. Thus we introduce the so-called *necessary RRSP and sufficient RRSP of order $k$ with respect to sign measurements*. These matrix properties provide deep insights into the non-uniform sign recovery for sparse vectors from sign measurements via 1-bit basis pursuit. For given measurements $y \in \{1, -1, 0\}^m$, let

$$\mathcal{P}(y) = \{ (S_+(x), S_-(x)) : \ y = \text{sign}(Ax) \}, \tag{4.41}$$

where $S_+(x) = \{i : x_i > 0\}$ and $S_-(x) = \{i : x_i < 0\}$. $\mathcal{P}(y)$ is the set of all possible partitions of the support of signals which are consistent with $y$. Recall that $J_+$ and $J_-$ are shorts for $J_+(y)$ and $J_-(y)$, respectively. The necessary RRSP property is defined as follows.

**Definition 4.6.5** (NRRSP of order $k$ with respect to $y$) $A^T = \begin{bmatrix} A^+ \\ A^- \\ A^0 \end{bmatrix}^T$ *is said*

*to satisfy the necessary restricted range space property (NRRSP) of order $k$ with respect to $y$ if there are a pair $(S_+, S_-) \in \mathcal{P}(y)$ with $|S_+ \cup S_-| \le k$ and a pair $(T_1, T_2)$ with $T_1 \subseteq J_+, T_2 \subseteq J_-$ and $T_1 \cup T_2 \ne J_+ \cup J_-$ such that matrix*

$$\begin{bmatrix} (A^+)_{J_+ \setminus T_1, S_+} & (A^+)_{J_+ \setminus T_1, S_-} \\ (A^-)_{J_- \setminus T_2, S_+} & (A^-)_{J_- \setminus T_2, S_-} \\ (A^0)_{S_+} & (A^0)_{S_-} \end{bmatrix}$$

*has full column rank, and that there is a vector $\eta \in \mathcal{R}(A^T)$ satisfying the following two conditions:*

*(i)* $\eta_i = 1$ *for* $i \in S_+$, $\eta_i = -1$ *for* $i \in S_-$, $|\eta_i| < 1$ *otherwise;*

*(ii)* $\eta = A^T w$ *for some* $w = (w^+, w_-, w_0) \in \mathcal{F}(T_1, T_2)$, *where*

$$\mathcal{F}(T_1, T_2) := \{w = (w^+, w^-, w^0) \in \mathbb{R}^{|J_+|} \times \mathbb{R}^{|J_-|} \times \mathbb{R}^{|J_0|} : (w^+)_{J_+ \setminus T_1} > 0,$$
$$(w^-)_{J_- \setminus T_2} < 0, (w^+)_{T_1} = 0, (w^-)_{T_2} = 0\}. \tag{4.42}$$

This matrix property is a necessary condition for the non-uniform recovery of the sign of a $k$-sparse vector, as shown by the following theorem.

**Theorem 4.6.6** *Assume that the measurements $y = \mathrm{sign}(Ax^*)$ are given, where $x^*$ is an unknown $k$-sparse signal. If the 1-bit basis pursuit (4.29) has a unique solution $\tilde{x}$ satisfying*

$$\mathrm{sign}(\tilde{x}) = \mathrm{sign}(x^*),$$

*then $A^T$ must satisfy the NRRSP of order $k$ with respect to $y$.*

*Proof.* Let $x^*$ be an unknown $k$-sparse signal. Suppose that the measurements $y = \mathrm{sign}(Ax^*)$ are given. Clearly, $(S_+(x^*), S_-(x^*)) \in \mathcal{P}(y)$. Assume that $\tilde{x}$ is the unique solution of (4.29) satisfying $\mathrm{sign}(\tilde{x}) = \mathrm{sign}(x^*)$. Then,

$$(S_+(\tilde{x}), S_-(\tilde{x})) = (S_+(x^*), S_-(x^*)).$$

From Theorem 4.6.2, the uniqueness of $\tilde{x}$ implies that the RRSP of $A^T$ at $\tilde{x}$ is satisfied and

$$H(\tilde{x}) = \begin{bmatrix} (A^+)_{A_1(\tilde{x}), S_+(\tilde{x})} & (A^+)_{A_1(\tilde{x}), S_-(\tilde{x})} \\ (A^-)_{A_2(\tilde{x}), S_+(\tilde{x})} & (A^-)_{A_2(\tilde{x}), S_-(\tilde{x})} \\ (A^0)_{S_+(\tilde{x})} & (A^0)_{S_-(\tilde{x})} \end{bmatrix}$$

has full column rank. Define the set

$$T_1 = \overline{\mathcal{A}_1(\tilde{x})} = J_+ \setminus \mathcal{A}_1(\tilde{x}), \quad T_2 = \overline{\mathcal{A}_2(\tilde{x})} = J_- \setminus \mathcal{A}_2(\tilde{x}). \tag{4.43}$$

It is evident that at any solution of (4.29), at least one of the inequalities of (4.29) must be active. Thus $\mathcal{A}_1(\tilde{x}) \cup \mathcal{A}_2(\tilde{x}) \neq \emptyset$, which implies that $T_1 \cup T_2 \neq J_+ \cup J_-$. By (4.43), we see that

$$J_+ \setminus T_1 = \mathcal{A}_1(\tilde{x}), \quad J_- \setminus T_2 = \mathcal{A}_2(\tilde{x}).$$

Hence, the matrix

$$\begin{bmatrix} (A^+)_{J_+ \setminus T_1, S_+(\tilde{x})} & (A^+)_{J_+ \setminus T_1, S_-(\tilde{x})} \\ (A^-)_{J_- \setminus T_2, S_+(\tilde{x})} & (A^-)_{J_- \setminus T_2, S_-(\tilde{x})} \\ (A^0)_{S_+(\tilde{x})} & (A^0)_{S_-(\tilde{x})} \end{bmatrix} = H(\tilde{x})$$

has full column rank. The RRSP of $A^T$ at $\tilde{x}$ implies that (i) and (ii) in Definition 4.6.5 are satisfied with $(T_1, T_2)$ given as (4.43) and

$$(S_+, \ S_-) := (S_+(\tilde{x}), \ S_-(\tilde{x})) = (S_+(x^*), \ S_-(x^*)).$$

This implies that $A^T$ satisfies the NRRSP of order $k$ with respect to $y$.   □

An interesting question is whether this necessary condition is also sufficient for the non-uniform sign recovery. The answer to this question is still not clear at the moment. However, a slight enhancement of the NRRSP property by varying the choices of $(S_+, \ S_-)$ and $(T_1, \ T_2)$ leads to the next matrix property which turns out to be a sufficient condition for the sign recovery of a $k$-sparse vector.

**Definition 4.6.7** (SRRSP of order $k$ with respect to $y$) $A^T = \begin{bmatrix} A^+ \\ A^- \\ A^0 \end{bmatrix}^T$ *is said to satisfy the sufficient restricted range space property (SRRSP) of order $k$ with respect to $y$ if for any $(S_+, \ S_-) \in \mathcal{P}(y)$ with $|S_+ \cup S_-| \leq k$, there is a pair $(T_1, T_2)$ such that $T_1 \subseteq J_+, \ T_2 \subseteq J_-, \ T_1 \cup T_2 \neq J_+ \cup J_-$ and the matrix*

$$\begin{bmatrix} (A^+)_{J_+ \setminus T_1, S_+} & (A^+)_{J_+ \setminus T_1, S_-} \\ (A^-)_{J_- \setminus T_2, S_+} & (A^-)_{J_- \setminus T_2, S_-} \\ (A^0)_{S_+} & (A^0)_{S_-} \end{bmatrix} \tag{4.44}$$

*have full column rank, and for any such pair $(T_1, T_2)$, there is a vector $\eta$ satisfying the following conditions:*

*(i) $\eta_i = 1$ for $i \in S_+$, $\eta_i = -1$ for $i \in S_-$, $|\eta_i| < 1$ otherwise;*

*(ii) $\eta = A^T w$ for some $w \in \mathcal{F}(T_1, T_2)$ which is defined by (4.42).*

Note that when the matrix (4.44) has full column rank, so does $A_{S_+ \cup S_-}$. Thus we immediately have the next lemma.

**Lemma 4.6.8** *Let $A^T$ satisfy the SRRSP of order k with respect to y. Then for any $(S_+, S_-) \in \mathcal{P}(y)$ with $|S_+ \cup S_-| \le k$, $A_{S_+ \cup S_-}$ must have full column rank.*

The next theorem claims that if $x^*$ is a sparsest solution to the system $y = \text{sign}(Ax)$, then $\text{sign}(x^*)$ can be exactly recovered by (4.29) provided that $A^T$ satisfies the SRRSP of order $k$ with respect to $y$.

**Theorem 4.6.9** *Let the measurements $y = \text{sign}(Ax^*)$ be given, where $x^*$ is a k-sparse vector. Assume that $A^T = \begin{bmatrix} A^+ \\ A^- \\ A^0 \end{bmatrix}^T$ satisfies the SRRSP of order k with respect to y. Then the 1-bit basis pursuit (4.29) has a unique solution, denoted by $x'$, which satisfies*

$$\text{supp}(x') \subseteq \text{supp}(x^*).$$

*Furthermore, if $x^*$ is a sparsest solution to $y = \text{sign}(Ax)$, then*

$$\text{sign}(x') = \text{sign}(x^*).$$

*Proof.* Let $x^*$ be a $k$-sparse vector consistent with $y$, i.e., $\text{sign}(Ax^*) = y$. This implies that

$$(Ax^*)_i > 0 \text{ for } i \in J_+, \ (Ax^*)_i < 0 \text{ for } i \in J_-, \text{ and } (Ax^*)_i = 0 \text{ for } i \in J_0.$$

Thus, there is a scalar $\tau > 0$ such that $\tau(Ax^*)_i \ge 1$ for all $i \in J_+$ and $\tau(Ax^*)_i \le -1$ for all $i \in J_-$. Therefore, $\tau x^*$ is a feasible vector to the problem (4.29), i.e.,

$$A^+(\tau x^*) \ge \mathbf{e}_{J_+}, \tag{4.45}$$
$$A^-(\tau x^*) \le -\mathbf{e}_{J_-}, \tag{4.46}$$
$$A^0(\tau x^*) = 0.$$

The first two conditions, (4.45) and (4.46), imply that

$$\tau \ge \frac{1}{(Ax^*)_i} \text{ for all } i \in J_+, \ \tau \ge \frac{1}{-(Ax^*)_i} \text{ for all } i \in J_-.$$

Let $\tau^*$ be the smallest $\tau$ satisfying the above inequalities. Then,

$$\tau^* = \max \left\{ \max_{i \in J_+} \frac{1}{(Ax^*)_i}, \ \max_{i \in J_-} \frac{1}{-(Ax^*)_i} \right\} = \max_{i \in J_+ \cup J_-} \frac{1}{|(Ax^*)_i|}.$$

By this choice of $\tau^*$, one of the inequalities in (4.45) and (4.46) becomes equality at $\tau^* x^*$. Let $T_0'$ and $T_0''$ be the sets of indices for active constraints in (4.45) and (4.46), i.e.,

$$T_0' = \left\{ i \in J_+ : [A^+(\tau^* x^*)]_i = 1 \right\}, \ T_0'' = \left\{ i \in J_- : [A^-(\tau^* x^*)]_i = -1 \right\}.$$

By the choice of $\tau^*$, we see that $T_0' \cup T_0'' \neq \emptyset$. In what follows, we denote by $S_+ = \{i : x_i^* > 0\}$ and $S_- = \{i : x_i^* < 0\}$. Note that $x^*$ is $k$-sparse and consistent with $y$. By the definition of $\mathcal{P}(y)$, we see that $(S_+, S_-) \in \mathcal{P}(y)$ and $|S_+ \cup S_-| \leq k$.

If the null space

$$
\mathcal{N}\left(\begin{bmatrix} (A^+)_{T_0',S_+} & (A^+)_{T_0',S_-} \\ (A^-)_{T_0'',S_+} & (A^-)_{T_0'',S_-} \\ (A^0)_{S_+} & (A^0)_{S_-} \end{bmatrix}\right) \neq \{0\},
$$

then let $d = \begin{bmatrix} u \\ v \end{bmatrix} \neq 0$ be a vector in this null space. It follows from Lemma 4.6.8 that $A_{S_+ \cup S_-}$ has full column rank. Thus $A_{S_+ \cup S_-} d \neq 0$. This implies that

$$
\begin{bmatrix} (A^+)_{J_+ \setminus T_0',S_+} & (A^+)_{J_+ \setminus T_0',S_-} \\ (A^-)_{J_- \setminus T_0'',S_+} & (A^-)_{J_- \setminus T_0'',S_-} \end{bmatrix} \begin{bmatrix} u \\ v \end{bmatrix} \neq 0. \tag{4.47}
$$

Consider the vector $x(\lambda)$ with components

$$
x(\lambda)_{S_+} = \tau^* x_{S_+}^* + \lambda u, \ x(\lambda)_{S_-} = \tau^* x_{S_-}^* + \lambda v, \ x(\lambda)_i = 0 \text{ for all } i \notin S_+ \cup S_-,
$$

where $\lambda \in \mathbb{R}$. Thus $\text{supp}(x(\lambda)) \subseteq \text{supp}(x^*)$ for any $\lambda \in \mathbb{R}$. By (4.47), if $|\lambda|$ continuously increases starting from zero, it is not difficult to see that there exists a critical value $\lambda^* \neq 0$ satisfying the following two properties:

- For any $\lambda$ with $0 < |\lambda| < |\lambda^*|$, $x(\lambda)$ remains feasible to (4.29), and the active constraints at $\tau^* x^*$ in (4.45) and (4.46) are still active at $x(\lambda)$, and the inactive constraints at $\tau^* x^*$ are still inactive at $x(\lambda)$.

- $x(\lambda^*)$ is a feasible vector to (4.29), the active constraints at $\tau^* x^*$ in (4.45) and (4.46) are still active at $x(\lambda^*)$, but one of the inactive constraints at $\tau^* x^*$ becomes active at $x(\lambda^*)$.

Denote by $x' = x(\lambda^*)$ and

$$
T_1' = \{i \in J_+ : (A^+ x')_i = 1\}, \ T_1'' = \{i \in J_- : (A^- x')_i = -1\}.
$$

The construction of $x'$ implies that

$$
T_0' \subseteq T_1', \ T_0'' \subseteq T_1''.
$$

So the index set for active constraints is augmented at $x'$. Now replace the role of $\tau^* x^*$ with $x'$ and repeat the same analysis above. If the null space

$$
\mathcal{N}\left(\begin{bmatrix} (A^+)_{T_1',S_+} & (A^+)_{T_1',S_-} \\ (A^-)_{T_1'',S_+} & (A^-)_{T_1'',S_-} \\ (A^0)_{S_+} & (A^0)_{S_-} \end{bmatrix}\right) \neq \{0\},
$$

then pick a vector $d' = \begin{bmatrix} u' \\ v' \end{bmatrix} \neq 0$ from this null space. Since $A_{S_+ \cup S_-}$ has full column rank, we must have that

$$\begin{bmatrix} (A^+)_{J_+ \setminus T_1', S_+} & (A^+)_{J_+ \setminus T_1', S_-} \\ (A^-)_{J_- \setminus T_1'', S_+} & (A^-)_{J_- \setminus T_1'', S_-} \end{bmatrix} \begin{bmatrix} u' \\ v' \end{bmatrix} \neq 0.$$

Therefore, we can continue to update $x'$ by considering $x'(\lambda)$ with components

$$x'(\lambda)_{S_+} = x'_{S_+} + \lambda u', \ x'(\lambda)_{S_-} = x'_{S_-} + \lambda v', \ x'(\lambda)_i = 0 \text{ for all } i \notin S_+ \cup S_-,$$

where $\lambda \in \mathbb{R}$. Similar to the above analysis, there exists a critical value $\lambda'$ such that $x'(\lambda')$ remains feasible to the problem (4.29) and one of the inactive constraints at $x'$ becomes active at $x'(\lambda')$. Let $x'' = x'(\lambda')$ and define

$$T_2' = \{i \in J_+ : (A^+ x'')_i = 1\}, \ T_2'' = \{i \in J_- : (A^- x'')_i = -1\}.$$

These index sets for active constraints are further augmented in the sense that

$$T_0' \subseteq T_1' \subseteq T_2', \ T_0'' \subseteq T_1'' \subseteq T_2''.$$

Since $A_{S_+ \cup S_-}$ has full column rank, after repeating the above process a finite number of times (at most $|J_+| + |J_-|$ times), we must stop at a vector, denoted by $\hat{x}$, such that

$$\widehat{T}' = \{i \in J_+ : (A^+ \hat{x})_i = 1\}, \ \widehat{T}'' = \{i \subset J_- : (A^- \hat{x})_i = -1\},$$

and

$$\mathcal{N}\left( \begin{bmatrix} (A^+)_{\widehat{T}', S_+} & (A^+)_{\widehat{T}', S_-} \\ (A^-)_{\widehat{T}'', S_+} & (A^-)_{\widehat{T}'', S_-} \\ (A^0)_{S_+} & (A^0)_{S_-} \end{bmatrix} \right) = \{0\}. \tag{4.48}$$

Thus the matrix above has full column rank. From the above analysis, we have

$$\text{supp}(\hat{x}) \subseteq \text{supp}(x^*).$$

Define

$$T_1 := \overline{\mathcal{A}_1(\hat{x})} \subseteq J_+, \ T_2 := \overline{\mathcal{A}_2(\hat{x})} \subseteq J_-. \tag{4.49}$$

So $T_1$ and $T_2$ are the index sets for inactive constraints at $\hat{x}$. By the construction of $\hat{x}$, we see that $\mathcal{A}_1(\hat{x}) \cup \mathcal{A}_2(\hat{x}) \neq \emptyset$, which implies that $(T_1, T_2)$, defined by (4.49), satisfies that $T_1 \cup T_2 \neq J_+ \cup J_-$.

We now further prove that $\hat{x}$ is the unique solution to (4.29). By Theorem 4.6.2, it is sufficient to prove that $A^T$ has the RRSP at $\hat{x}$ and the matrix

$$H(\hat{x}) = \begin{bmatrix} (A^+)_{\mathcal{A}_1(\hat{x}), \hat{S}_+} & (A^+)_{\mathcal{A}_1(\hat{x}), \hat{S}_-} \\ (A^-)_{\mathcal{A}_2(\hat{x}), \hat{S}_+} & (A^-)_{\mathcal{A}_2(\hat{x}), \hat{S}_-} \\ (A^0)_{\hat{S}_+} & (A^0)_{\hat{S}_-} \end{bmatrix}$$

has full column rank, where $\widehat{S}_+ = \{i: \widehat{x}_i > 0\}$ and $\widehat{S}_- = \{i: \widehat{x}_i < 0\}$. Note that $\widehat{x}$ is consistent with $y$ and satisfies that $\mathrm{supp}(\widehat{x}) \subseteq \mathrm{supp}(x^*)$. Thus $(\widehat{S}_+, \widehat{S}_-) \in \mathcal{P}(y)$ and $\widehat{S}_+ \cup \widehat{S}_- \subseteq S_+ \cup S_-$. It follows from (4.48) that

$$
\begin{bmatrix}
(A^+)_{\widehat{T}',S_+} & (A^+)_{\widehat{T}',S_-} \\
(A^-)_{\widehat{T}'',S_+} & (A^-)_{\widehat{T}'',S_-} \\
(A^0)_{S_+} & (A^0)_{S_-}
\end{bmatrix}
$$

has full column rank. Note that $\widehat{S}_+ \cup \widehat{S}_- \subseteq S_+ \cup S_-$. The matrix

$$
Q := \begin{bmatrix}
(A^+)_{\widehat{T}',\widehat{S}_+} & (A^+)_{\widehat{T}',\widehat{S}_-} \\
(A^-)_{\widehat{T}'',\widehat{S}_+} & (A^-)_{\widehat{T}'',\widehat{S}_-} \\
(A^0)_{\widehat{S}_+} & (A^0)_{\widehat{S}_-}
\end{bmatrix}
$$

must have full column rank. Note that

$$
\widehat{T}' = J_+ \setminus T_1 = \mathcal{A}_1(\widehat{x}), \quad \widehat{T}'' = J_- \setminus T_2 = \mathcal{A}_2(\widehat{x}). \tag{4.50}
$$

Thus,

$$
H(\widehat{x}) = \begin{bmatrix}
(A^+)_{J_+ \setminus T_1,\widehat{S}_+} & (A^+)_{J_+ \setminus T_1,\widehat{S}_-} \\
(A^-)_{J_- \setminus T_2,\widehat{S}_+} & (A^-)_{J_- \setminus T_2,\widehat{S}_-} \\
(A^0)_{\widehat{S}_+} & (A^0)_{\widehat{S}_-}
\end{bmatrix} = Q
$$

has full column rank.

Since $A^T$ has the SRRSP of order $k$ with respect to $y$, there is a vector $\eta \in \mathcal{R}(A^T)$ and $w = (w^+, w^-, w^0) \in \mathcal{F}(T_1, T_2)$ satisfying that $\eta = A^T w$, where $\eta_i = 1$ for $i \in \widehat{S}_+$, $\eta_i = -1$ for $i \in \widehat{S}_-$, and $|\eta_i| < 1$ otherwise. The set $\mathcal{F}(T_1, T_2)$ is defined in (4.42). From (4.49), we see that the conditions $(w^+)_{T_1} = 0$ and $(w^-)_{T_2} = 0$ in (4.42) coincides with the condition $(w^+)_i = 0$ for $i \in \overline{\mathcal{A}_1(\widehat{x})}$ and $(w^-)_i = 0$ for $i \in \overline{\mathcal{A}_2(\widehat{x})}$. This, together with (4.50), implies that $\mathcal{F}(T_1, T_2)$ coincides with the set $\mathcal{F}(\widehat{x})$ defined in (4.30). Thus the RRSP of $A^T$ holds at $\widehat{x}$ (see Definition 4.6.1). Since $H(\widehat{x})$ has full column rank, $\widehat{x}$ must be the unique solution to the problem (4.29).

Furthermore, suppose that the $k$-sparse vector $x^*$ is a sparsest vector consistent with $y$. From the above analysis, $\widehat{x}$ is also consistent with $y$. From the construction process of $\widehat{x}$, we see that

$$
\mathrm{supp}(\widehat{x}) \subseteq \cdots \subseteq \mathrm{supp}(x'') \subseteq \mathrm{supp}(x') \subseteq \mathrm{supp}(\tau^* x^*) = \mathrm{supp}(x^*).
$$

Since $x^*$ is a sparsest vector consistent with $y$, we deduce that

$$
\mathrm{supp}(\widehat{x}) = \mathrm{supp}(x^*),
$$

therefore $\widehat{x}$ is also a sparsest vector consistent with $y$. When $x^*$ is a sparsest solution, it is not difficult to see that the sign of non-zero components of the vectors, from $\tau^* x^*$ to $x'$, and to $x''$, and finally to $\hat{x}$, does not change throughout the construction process for these vectors. For instance, suppose the current vector is $x'$. Note that the next point $x''$ is defined as $x'' = x' + \lambda' d'$ where $d_i' = 0$ for all $i \notin S_+ \cup S_-$ and $d_{S_+ \cup S_-}'$ is a vector in the null space (4.48). By the choice of the critical value $\lambda'$, which is the smallest one yielding a new active constraints, we conclude that

$$x_i'' = (x' + \lambda' d')_i > 0 \text{ for all } i \in S_+' = \{i : x_i' > 0\},$$
$$x_i'' = (x' + \lambda' d')_i < 0 \text{ for all } i \in S_-' = \{i : x_i' < 0\},$$

i.e.,

$$\text{sign}(x'') = \text{sign}(x' + \lambda' d') = \text{sign}(x').$$

In fact, if there is a non-zero component of $x' + \lambda' d'$, say the $i$th component, holds a different sign from the corresponding non-zero component of $x_i'$, then by continuity and by the convexity of the feasible set of (4.29), there is a $\bar{\lambda}$ lying between zero and $\lambda'$ such that the $i$th component of $x' + \bar{\lambda} d'$ is equal to zero. Thus $x' + \bar{\lambda} d'$ is sparser than $x^*$. Since $x' + \bar{\lambda} d'$ is also a feasible vector to (4.29), it is consistent with $y$. This is a contradiction, as $x^*$ is a sparsest vector consistent with $y$. Therefore, we must have

$$\text{sign}(x^*) = \text{sign}(\tau^* x^*) = \text{sign}(x') = \text{sign}(x'') = \cdots = \text{sign}(\hat{x}).$$

The proof is complete. □

In summary, we have the following statements for non-uniform recoveries:

■ If the 1-bit basis pursuit exactly recovers the sign of a $k$-sparse signal consistent with sign measurements $y$, then the sensing matrix $A$ must admit the NRRSP of order $k$ with respect to $y$.

■ If $A$ admits the SRRSP of order $k$ with respect to $y$ (see Definition 4.6.7), then from sign measurements, the 1-bit basis pursuit exactly recovers the sign of $k$-sparse signals which are the sparsest vectors consistent with $y$.

## 4.7 Uniform Sign Recovery

In Theorems 4.6.6 and 4.6.9, we discussed the conditions for non-uniform recovery of the sign of an individual $k$-sparse vector. Since only a single vector is considered, the sign measurement vector $y$ is fixed in non-uniform recovery scenarios. In this section, we further strengthen the notions and conditions in last section in order to develop certain necessary and sufficient conditions for the uniform sign recovery of every $k$-sparse signal through a single sensing matrix. Note that the sign measurements $y$ depend on $k$-sparse vectors. To discuss the uniform sign recovery, let us first define the set of sign measurements:

$$Y^k = \{y : y = \text{sign}(Ax), \|x\|_0 \leq k\}.$$

For any disjoint subsets $S_+$, $S_- \subseteq \{1,\dots,n\}$ satisfying $|S_+ \cup S_-| \le k$, there is a $k$-sparse vector $x$ such that $\{i : x_i > 0\} = S_+$ and $\{i : x_i < 0\} = S_-$. Thus any such disjoint subsets $(S_+, S_-)$ must be in the set $\mathcal{P}(y)$ for some $y \in Y^k$, where $\mathcal{P}(y)$ is defined in (4.41). We now introduce the NRRSP of order $k$ which is independent of the specific sign vector $y$. It is a strengthened version of Definition 4.6.5 ,

**Definition 4.7.1** (NRRSP of order $k$ of $A^T$) *The matrix $A^T$ is said to satisfy the necessary restricted range space property (NRRSP) of order $k$ if for any disjoint subsets $S_+$, $S_-$ of $\{1,\dots,n\}$ with $|S_+ \cup S_-| \le k$, there exist $y \in Y^k$ and $(T_1, T_2)$ such that $(S_+, S_-) \in \mathcal{P}(y)$, $T_1 \subseteq J_+(y)$, $T_2 \subseteq J_-(y)$, $T_1 \cup T_2 \ne J_+(y) \cup J_-(y)$ and*

$$
\begin{bmatrix}
A_{J_+(y)\setminus T_1,S_+} & A_{J_+(y)\setminus T_1,S_-} \\
A_{J_-(y)\setminus T_2,S_+} & A_{J_-(y)\setminus T_2,S_-} \\
A_{J_0(y),S_+} & A_{J_0(y),S_-}
\end{bmatrix}
$$

*has full column rank, and there is a vector $\eta \in \mathcal{R}(A^T)$ satisfying the following properties:*

(i) $\eta_i = 1$ *for* $i \in S_+$, $\eta_i = -1$ *for* $i \in S_-$, $|\eta_i| < 1$ *otherwise;*

(ii) $\eta = A^T w$ *for some* $w \in \mathcal{F}(T_1, T_2)$, *which is defined by (4.42)*

The NRRSP of order $k$ of $A^T$ is a necessary condition for the uniform sign recovery for every $k$-sparse signal from sign measurements via 1-bit basis pursuit.

**Theorem 4.7.2** *Let $A \in \mathbb{R}^{m \times n}$ be a given matrix and assume that for any $k$-sparse vector $x^*$, the sign measurements $y := \mathrm{sign}(Ax^*)$ can be acquired. If the sign of any $k$-sparse vector $x^*$ can be exactly recovered via the 1-bit basis pursuit (4.29) in the sense that (4.29) has a unique solution $\tilde{x}$ such that*

$$\mathrm{sign}(\tilde{x}) = \mathrm{sign}(x^*),$$

*then $A^T$ must satisfy the NRRSP of order $k$.*

*Proof.* Let $x^*$ be an arbitrary $k$-sparse signal with $S_+ = \{i : x_i^* > 0\}$ and $S_- = \{i : x_i^* < 0\}$. Clearly, $|S_+ \cup S_-| \le k$. Let $y = \mathrm{sign}(Ax^*)$ be the acquired sign measurements. We still use $A^+, A^-, A^0$ to denote the partition of the matrix $A$ according to the indices $J_+(y), J_-(y)$ and $J_0(y)$. Then we see that $y \in Y^k$ and $(S_+, S_-) \in \mathcal{P}(y)$. Assume that $\tilde{x}$ is the unique solution of (4.29) satisfying $\mathrm{sign}(\tilde{x}) = \mathrm{sign}(x^*)$, which implies that

$$(S_+(\tilde{x}),\ S_-(\tilde{x})) = (S_+,\ S_-). \tag{4.51}$$

It follows from Theorem 4.6.2 that the uniqueness of $\tilde{x}$ implies that the matrix

$$
H(\tilde{x}) =
\begin{bmatrix}
(A^+)_{\mathcal{A}_1(\tilde{x}),S_+} & (A^+)_{\mathcal{A}_1(\tilde{x}),S_-} \\
(A^-)_{\mathcal{A}_2(\tilde{x}),S_+} & (A^-)_{\mathcal{A}_2(\tilde{x}),S_-} \\
(A^0)_{S_+} & (A^0)_{S_-}
\end{bmatrix}
$$

has full column rank and there is a vector $\eta \in \mathcal{R}(A^T)$ such that

(i) $\eta_i = 1$ for $i \in S_+(\tilde{x})$, $\eta_i = -1$ for $i \in S_-(\tilde{x})$, and $|\eta_i| < 1$ otherwise;

(ii) $\eta = A^T w$ for some $w \in \mathcal{F}(\tilde{x})$ given as

$$\mathcal{F}(\tilde{x}) = \{w = (w^+, w^-, w^0) \in \mathbb{R}^{|J_+(y)|} \times \mathbb{R}^{|J_-(y)|} \times \mathbb{R}^{|J_0(y)|} :$$
$$(w^+)_i > 0 \text{ for } i \in \mathcal{A}_1(\tilde{x}), \ (w^-)_i < 0 \text{ for } i \in \mathcal{A}_2(\tilde{x}),$$
$$(w^+)_i = 0 \text{ for } i \in \overline{\mathcal{A}_1}(\tilde{x}), \ (w^-)_i = 0 \text{ for } \overline{\mathcal{A}_2}(\tilde{x})\}.$$

Let $T_1 = \overline{\mathcal{A}_1}(\tilde{x}) \subseteq J_+(y)$ and $T_2 = \overline{\mathcal{A}_2}(\tilde{x}) \subseteq J_-(y)$. It is easy to see that at any solution of the 1-bit basis pursuit, at least one of its inequality constraints must be active. In fact, if this is not true, i.e., at the current solution $x$, all inequality constraints are inactive, then there exists a scalar $\tau \in (0,1)$ such that $\tau x$ satisfies all constraints and $\|\tau x\|_1 < \|x\|_1$, leading to a contradiction. Thus when $\tilde{x}$ is a solution to (4.29), we must have that $\mathcal{A}_1 \cup \mathcal{A}_2 \neq \emptyset$, which implies that $T_1 \cup T_2 \neq J_+(y) \cup J_-(y)$. Clearly,

$$\mathcal{A}_1(\tilde{x}) = J_+(y) \backslash T_1, \quad \mathcal{A}_1(\tilde{x}) = J_-(y) \backslash T_2. \tag{4.52}$$

Therefore, the full-column-rank property of $H(\tilde{x})$ implies that

$$\begin{bmatrix} A_{J_+(y) \backslash T_1, S_+} & A_{J_+(y) \backslash T_1, S_-} \\ A_{J_-(y) \backslash T_2, S_+} & A_{J_-(y) \backslash T_2, S_-} \\ A_{J_0(y), S_+} & A_{J_0(y), S_-} \end{bmatrix}$$

has full column rank. By (4.51) and (4.52), the aforementioned properties (i) and (ii) coincide with (i) and (ii) in Definition 4.7.1. Since $x^*$ is an arbitrary $k$-sparse vector, these properties hold for any disjoint subsets $(S_+, S_-)$ of $\{1, \ldots, n\}$ described in Definition 4.7.1. Thus $A^T$ satisfies the NRRSP of order $k$. □

The 1-bit basis pursuit is equivalent to an LP problem. The nonuniqueness of solutions to an LP problem appears only when the optimal facit of its feasible set is parallel to its objective hyperplane. For randomly generated LP problems, however, the probability for this event is zero. This indicates that the uniqueness assumption for the solution of (4.29) is very mild. Therefore when $A$ is randomly generated according to some probability distribution, with high probability the RRSP of $A^T$ holds at the solution $\tilde{x}$ of (4.29) and in the meantime the matrix $H(\tilde{x})$ admits full column rank. Based on such a mild assumption, as shown in Theorem 4.7.2, the NRRSP of order $k$ is a necessary requirement for the uniform recovery of the sign of every $k$-sparse vector from sign measurements via (4.29).

At the moment, however, it is not clear whether the NRRSP of order $k$ is also a sufficient criterion for uniform sign recoveries. In what follows, we show that a sufficient condition for uniform sign recoveries can be developed by slightly enhancing such necessary matrix property, i.e., by considering all possible sign measurements $y \in Y^k$ as well as the pairs $(T_1, T_2)$ described in Definition 4.7.1. This naturally leads to the next definition.

**Definition 4.7.3** (SRRSP of order $k$ of $A^T$) *The matrix $A^T$ is said to satisfy the sufficient restricted range space property (SRRSP) of order $k$ if for any disjoint subsets $(S_+, S_-)$ of $\{1,\ldots,n\}$ with $|S_+ \cup S_-| \leq k$, and for any $y \in Y^k$ such that $(S_+, S_-) \in \mathcal{P}(y)$, there are $T_1$ and $T_2$ such that $T_1 \subseteq J_+(y)$, $T_2 \subseteq J_-(y)$, $T_1 \cup T_2 \neq J_+(y) \cup J_-(y)$ and*

$$\begin{bmatrix} A_{J_+(y)\backslash T_1, S_+} & A_{J_+(y)\backslash T_1, S_-} \\ A_{J_-(y)\backslash T_2, S_+} & A_{J_-(y)\backslash T_2, S_-} \\ A_{J_0(y), S_+} & A_{J_0(y), S_-} \end{bmatrix}$$

*has full column rank, and for any such a pair $(T_1, T_2)$, there is a vector $\eta \in \mathcal{R}(A^T)$ satisfying the following properties:*

(i) $\eta_i = 1$ *for* $i \in S_+$, $\eta_i = -1$ *for* $i \in S_-$, $|\eta_i| < 1$ *otherwise;*

(ii) $\eta = A^T w$ *for some* $w \in \mathcal{F}(T_1, T_2)$ *which is defined by (4.42).*

This notion, taking into account all possible sign measurement vectors $y$, is stronger than Definition 4.6.7. Clearly, when a matrix has the SRRSP of order $k$, it must satisfy the SRRSP of order $k$ with respect to $y \in Y^k$. The SRRSP of order $k$ is a sufficient condition for the recovery of the sign of every $k$-sparse signal from sign measurements via (4.29), provided that these vectors are the sparsest ones consistent with sign measurements, as shown in the next theorem.

**Theorem 4.7.4** *Suppose that $A^T$ satisfies the SRRSP of order $k$ and the sign measurements $y := \text{sign}(Ax^*)$ can be acquired for any $k$-sparse signal $x^*$. Then the 1-bit basis pursuit (4.29) has a unique solution $\widetilde{x}$ satisfying*

$$\text{supp}(\widetilde{x}) \subseteq \text{supp}(x^*). \tag{4.53}$$

*Furthermore, for any $k$-sparse vector $x^*$ which is the sparsest vector satisfying $y := \text{sign}(Ax^*)$, i.e., $x^*$ is a sparsest point in the set*

$$\{x: \ \text{sign}(Ax) = \text{sign}(Ax^*)\}, \tag{4.54}$$

*the sign of $x^*$ can be exactly recovered by (4.29), i.e., the unique solution $\widetilde{x}$ of (4.29) satisfies*

$$\text{sign}(\widetilde{x}) = \text{sign}(x^*).$$

*Proof.* Let $x^*$ be an arbitrary $k$-sparse vector, and let measurements $y := \text{sign}(Ax^*)$ be taken. Since $A^T$ has the SRRSP of order $k$, $A^T$ must have the SRRSP of order $k$ with respect to this individual vector $y$. By Theorem 4.6.9, the problem (4.29) has a unique solution, denoted by $\widetilde{x}$, which satisfies that $\text{supp}(\widetilde{x}) \subseteq \text{supp}(x^*)$. Furthermore, if $x^*$ is the sparsest vector satisfying (4.54), then by Theorem 4.6.9 again, we must have that $\text{sign}(\widetilde{x}) = \text{sign}(x^*)$. Therefore the sign of $x^*$ can be exactly recovered. □

The above theorem indicates that, in general, the SRRSP of order $k$ guarantees that at least part of the support of $x^*$ can be exactly recovered by (4.29) in the sense of (4.53). When $x^*$ is a sparsest vector in the set (4.54), a stronger result can be obtained, that is, the sign (and thus the full support) of $x^*$ can be exactly recovered by (4.29).

In summary, we have the following statements for uniform sign recoveries:

■ If the 1-bit basis pursuit exactly recovers the sign of a $k$-sparse signal from sign measurements, then $A^T$ must admit the so-called NRRSP of order $k$.

■ If the matrix $A^T$ satisfies the SRRSP of order $k$, then from sign measurements, the 1-bit basis pursuit exactly recovers the sign of a $k$-sparse signal which is a sparsest vector consistent with sign measurements.

## 4.8  Notes

1-bit quantization, known as signum-coding or four-level phase coding, has appeared in synthetic aperture radar (SAR) literature (see Alberti et al. [5], Franceschetti et al. [109], and Pascazio and Schirinzi [185]). 1-bit quantization is robust to noise and nonlinear distortion or saturation, and it may ease the burden on hardware measurement system and make real-time SAR image processing possible. The 1-bit compressed sensing (1-bit CS) was introduced by Boufounos and Baraniuk [30]. Due to low bit measurements and processing costs, 1-bit CS models received considerable attention in several areas including wireless sensor networks (Sakdejayont et al. [199], Shen, Fang and Li [201], Chen and Wu [60], and Zayyani, Haddadi and Korki [231]), radar image processing (Dong and Zhang [80]), optical image processing (Bourquard, Aguet and Unser [31]), and matrix completion (Davenport et al. [72]). Greedy, convex and nonconvex optimization algorithms have been proposed for 1-bit CS problems. It seems that the first greedy method is the matching sign pursuit (MSP) which was proposed by Boufounos [28]. Laska et al. [154] proposed the restricted step shrinkage (RSS) method. Jacques et al. [138] developed the binary iterative hard thresholding (BIHT) method. A modified version of the BIHT called the adaptive outlier pursuit (AOP) was considered by Yan, Yang and Osher [227]. Other discussions on greedy methods can be found in [125, 142, 115, 159]. The algorithms based on the relaxation (4.5) of the sign constraint can be convex or nonconvex, depending on the nature of trivial solution excluders. The relaxation (4.5) was first proposed by Boufounos and Baraniuk [30], and was used by many other researchers. See Boufounos [29], Laska et al. [154], Movahed, Panahi and Durisi [176], Plan and Vershynin [187, 188], Shen and Shuter [200], and Ai et al. [4].

Different from traditional relaxation methods which were largely based on the relaxation (4.5), the reformulations (4.28) and (4.29) make it possible to develop a sign-recovery theory for $k$-sparse signals from sign measurements by extending the RSP-based analytical methods to 1-bit CS problems. The 1-bit basis pursuit (4.1) is equivalent to a linear programming problem. Using linear programming as a decoding method will inevitably yield a certain range space property, such as the RRSP of the sensing matrix thanks to the fundamental optimality conditions of linear programs. Theorem 4.6.2 concerning the uniqueness of the solution to 1-bit basis pursuit (4.1) naturally leads to the restricted range space property (RRSP) of the sensing matrix, which provides a deep connection between sensing matrices and the sign (or support) recovery from sign measurements. The RRSP and analogous concepts were introduced by Zhao and Xu [249] and Xu [226]. Based on these notions, the conditions for non-uniform and uniform sign recoveries can be developed, as shown by Theorems 4.6.6, 4.6.9, 4.7.2 and 4.7.4 in this chapter.

Analogous to the standard compressed sensing, the number of measurements required to achieve the expected sparsity recovery is also an important issue in 1-bit CS settings. Some results on the number of sign measurements have been achieved according to specific recovery criteria. In terms of $\ell_2$-reconstruction error, Jacques et al. [138] proved that with high probability $k$-sparse signals can be estimated up to normalization from at least $O(k\ln(n/k))$ 1-bit measurements, where $n$ is the signal length. Baraniuk et al. [18] considered the minimization of the number of 1-bit measurements by optimizing the decay of the $\ell_2$-reconstruction error as a function of the over-sampling factor $m/(k\ln(n/k))$, where $m$ denotes the number of measurements. In terms of support recovery, Acharya et al. [2] pointed out that $O(k^2\ln n)$ is a nearly tight bound for the number of 1-bit measurements needed for support recovery.

The standard 1-bit CS theory is based on the assumption that sign measurements are error-free. However, due to the noise in signal acquisition/transmision and the error in computation, some sign measurements might be flipped to opposite ones. In this case, the sign measurements are in the form $y = \text{sign}(Ax + u)$, where $u$ is a noise vector. Several approaches have been proposed to address this recovery issue from noise sign measurements, by Yan, Yang and Osher [227], Movahed, Panahi and Durisi [176], Jacques et al. [138], Li et al. [158], Dai et al. [67], and Baraniuk et al. [18]. When $b$ is a fixed (known) vector instead of a noise vector, Knudson, Saab and Ward [146] show that from the quantized affine measurements $\text{sign}(Ax + b)$ with a given vector $b$, the norm of the sparse signal can be estimated under a suitable assumption. Other variants of 1-bit CS problems were studied in the literature. For example, Huang et al. [136] proposed a mixed 1-bit CS model by taking into account the situation where a measurement is saturated and falls outside the quantization measurable range.

# Chapter 5

# Stability of Linear Sparse Optimization Methods

The presence of noise in data is an unavoidable issue due to sensor imperfection, estimation inaccuracy, statistical or communication errors. For instance, signals might be contaminated by some form of random noise and the measurements of signals are subject to quantization error. Thus a huge effort is made in sparse data recovery, to ensure that the recovery method is stable in the sense that recovery errors stay under control when the measurements are slightly inaccurate and when the data is not exactly sparse [37, 95, 97, 108]. The stability of many recovery algorithms, including $\ell_1$-minimization, has been extensively studied under various assumptions such as the RIP, NSP and mutual coherence. In this chapter, we introduce a unified approach to establish a stability theory for linear $\ell_1$-minimization problems, including linear Dantzig Selector (DS), under a mild assumption called the *weak range space property* of a transposed sensing (or design) matrix. This matrix property is shown to be a necessary and sufficient condition for the standard $\ell_1$-minimization method to be stable in the sense of Definition 5.1.1 in this chapter. The classic Hoffman's Lemma concerning the error bound of linear systems is employed as a major tool in this chapter to the study of stability of linear $\ell_1$-minimization. This tool combined with the sparsity assumption provides some recovery error bounds measured by the so-called Robinson's constant for linear sparse optimization methods. A byproduct of this study is a unified stability result for linear $\ell_1$-minimization. This result holds under various matrix properties which are widely utilized in traditional compressed sensing theory, including the RSP of order $k$ of $A^T$ which was introduced to characterize the uniform recovery of $k$-sparse vectors via $\ell_1$-minimization (see Chapter 3).

## 5.1 Introduction

Some notations will be used throughout this and the following chapters. Let $\phi :$ $\mathbb{R}^q \to \mathbb{R}_+$ denote a general norm on $\mathbb{R}^q$ satisfying

$$\phi(\mathbf{e}^{(i)}) = 1 \text{ for all } i = 1, \ldots, q,$$

where $\mathbf{e}^{(i)} \in \mathbb{R}^q$, $i = 1, \ldots, q$, are the standard basis of $\mathbb{R}^q$, i.e., the column vectors of the $q \times q$ identity matrix. In particular, $\| \cdot \|_p$ denotes the $\ell_p$-norm, i.e.,

$$\|x\|_p = \left( \sum_{i=1}^{q} |x_i|^p \right)^{1/p},$$

where $x \in \mathbb{R}^q$ and $p \in [1, \infty]$. For any two norms $\phi' : \mathbb{R}^n \to \mathbb{R}_+$ and $\phi'' : \mathbb{R}^m \to \mathbb{R}_+$, the induced matrix norm $\|Q\|_{\phi' \to \phi''}$ of the matrix $Q \in \mathbb{R}^{m \times n}$ is defined as

$$\|Q\|_{\phi' \to \phi''} = \max_{\phi'(x) \leq 1} \phi''(Qx).$$

In particular, $\|Q\|_{p \to q} = \max_{\|x\|_p \leq 1} \|Qx\|_q$ where $p, q \geq 1$.

Let $A \in \mathbb{R}^{m \times n}$ and $M \in \mathbb{R}^{m \times q}$, where $m < n$ and $m \leq q$, be two full-row-rank matrices, i.e., $\text{rank}(A) = \text{rank}(M) = m$. Let $y \in \mathbb{R}^m$ be a given vector. Consider the following $\ell_1$-minimization problem:

$$\min_x \{\|x\|_1 : \phi(M^T(Ax - y)) \leq \varepsilon\}, \tag{5.1}$$

where $\varepsilon \geq 0$ is a given parameter. The given data $(M, A, y, \varepsilon)$ is referred to as the problem data of (5.1). In signal recovery scenarios, $A$ is referred to as a sensing or measurement matrix, and $y = A\hat{x} + \theta$ stands for the measurements acquired for the target signal $\hat{x}$. The measurements may not be accurate. So the vector $\theta \in \mathbb{R}^m$, bounded as $\phi(M^T \theta) \leq \varepsilon$, stands for noise or measurement error. Clearly, the problem (5.1) includes several important special cases.

■ When $\varepsilon = 0$, by noting that $M^T$ has full column rank, it follows from $\phi(M^T(Ax - y)) = 0$ that $Ax = y$. Thus when $\varepsilon = 0$, the problem (5.1) is reduced to the standard $\ell_1$-minimization

$$\min_x \{\|x\|_1 : Ax = y\}.$$

The use of $\ell_1$-norm for promoting sparsity in data processing has a long history [161, 206, 157, 86, 167, 62, 165], and a significant further development of the theory and algorithms for sparse data reconstruction via $\ell_1$-minimization was made in the framework of compressed sensing since around 2004 (see [83, 51, 50, 84, 45, 95, 97]).

∎ When $\varepsilon > 0$, $M = I$ and $\phi(\cdot) = \|\cdot\|_p$, the problem (5.1) becomes the well known $\ell_1$-minimization with $\ell_p$-norm constraint

$$\min_x \{\|x\|_1 : \|Ax - y\|_p \leq \varepsilon\}, \tag{5.2}$$

which has been extensively studied in compressed sensing. The problem

$$\min_x \{\|x\|_1 : \|Ax - y\|_2 \leq \varepsilon\}$$

is particularly popular and has numerous applications in the area of sparse signal recovery [62, 82, 95, 97, 108].

∎ When $M$ coincides with $A$, the problem (5.1) becomes

$$\min_x \{\|x\|_1 : \phi(A^T(Ax - y)) \leq \varepsilon\}. \tag{5.3}$$

Taking $\phi(\cdot) = \|\cdot\|_\infty$, this problem becomes the standard Dantzig Selector (DS) problem

$$\min_x \{\|x\|_1 : \|A^T(Ax - y)\|_\infty \leq \varepsilon\}, \tag{5.4}$$

which was introduced by Candès and Tao [47, 46] in 2007.

The problem (5.3) and the general version (5.1) can be also called the Dantzig Selector (DS) problems although they are more general than the standard DS problem (5.4). In this chapter, we focus on the linear recovery models. That is, the models can be equivalent to linear optimization problems. The stability issue of nonlinear recovery problems will be dealt with separately in the upcoming chapter.

In traditional compressed sensing, it is typically assumed that the target vector $x$ satisfies a certain inaccurate measurement condition leading to the recovery problem (5.2). It is interesting to know how close the solution of (5.2) is to the target vector $x$, in other words, how accurate the reconstructed vector $x^*$ is (via some algorithm) compared to the target signal $x$. The aim of stability analysis is to estimate the error $\|x - x^*\|$. The major stability results have been achieved by Donoho, Candès, Romberg, Tao, and others (e.g., [84, 51, 50, 45]). However, many stability results have been developed under some restrictive assumptions imposed on the sensing matrix, and the analytic methods for establishing such stability results vary depending on different assumptions. In this chapter, we aim to ease these assumptions and establish a unified stability theorem for linear-type recovery methods by taking into account settings where the sensing matrix may satisfy a property less restrictive than the ones used in the literature.

Let us first clarify the notion of stability of a recovery method. For a given vector $x \in \mathbb{R}^n$, the best $k$-term approximation of $x$ is defined as follows:

$$\sigma_k(x)_1 := \inf_u \{\|x - u\|_1 : \|u\|_0 \leq k\},$$

where $k$ is a given integer number. For example, $x = (\varepsilon_1, \varepsilon_2, \varepsilon_3, \varepsilon_4) \in \mathbb{R}^4$, where $|\varepsilon_1| \geq |\varepsilon_2| \geq |\varepsilon_3| \geq |\varepsilon_4|$. Then it is easy to verify that $\sigma_3(x)_1 = |\varepsilon_4|$, $\sigma_2(x)_1 = |\varepsilon_3| + |\varepsilon_4|$ and $\sigma_1(x)_1 = |\varepsilon_2| + |\varepsilon_3| + |\varepsilon_4|$. The stability of (5.1) is defined as follows.

**Definition 5.1.1** *Let $x$ be the original vector obeying the constraint of (5.1). The problem (5.1) is said to be stable in sparse vector recovery if there is a solution $x^*$ of (5.1) approximating $x$ with error*

$$\|x - x^*\|_2 \leq C' \sigma_k(x)_1 + C'' \varepsilon,$$

*where $C'$ and $C''$ are constants depending only on the problem data $(M, A, y, \varepsilon)$.*

In this chapter, we consider a more relaxed condition than the RSP of order $k$ of $A^T$ defined in Chapter 3. We show that the linear $\ell_1$-minimization method is stable under a mild matrix property which is less restrictive than the existing conditions in the stability literature. This matrix property is called *weak range space property of $A^T$* (see Definition 5.3.1 for details). It turns out that this property is a desired sufficient condition for many linear sparse minimization methods to be stable. This property is also necessary for standard $\ell_1$-minimization to be stable for any given measurement vector $y \in \{Ax : \|x\|_0 \leq k\}$. Let us first recall a classic Lemma due to Hoffman concerning the error bound of linear systems.

## 5.2 Hoffman's Error Bound for Linear Systems

Let $P \in \mathbb{R}^{n_1 \times q}$ and $Q \in \mathbb{R}^{n_2 \times q}$ be two real matrices. Defining a set $F \subseteq \mathbb{R}^{n_1 + n_2}$ by

$$F = \{(b, d) : \text{ for some } z \in \mathbb{R}^q \text{ such that } Pz \leq b \text{ and } Qz = d\}.$$

Let $\|\cdot\|_{\alpha_1}$ and $\|\cdot\|_{\alpha_2}$ be norms on $\mathbb{R}^q$ and $\mathbb{R}^{n_1 + n_2}$, respectively. Robinson [192] proved that the quantity

$$\mu_{\alpha_1, \alpha_2}(P, Q) := \max_{\|(b,d)\|_{\alpha_2} \leq 1, (b,d) \in F} \left( \min_{z \in \mathbb{R}^q} \{\|z\|_{\alpha_1} : Pz \leq b, \ Qz = d\} \right) \quad (5.5)$$

is a finite real number. It was shown in [192] that the extreme value in (5.5) is attained. In this chapter, we use $\alpha_1 = \infty$, in which case $\|x\|_\infty$ is a polyhedral norm in the sense that the closed unit ball $\{x : \|x\|_\infty \leq 1\}$ is a polyhedron. Define the optimal value of the internal minimization in (5.5) as

$$g(b, d) = \min_z \{\|z\|_{\alpha_1} : Pz \leq b, \ Qz = d\},$$

where $(b, d) \in F$. Then,

$$\mu_{\alpha_1, \alpha_2}(P, Q) = \max_{(b,d) \in \widetilde{\mathcal{B}} \cap F} g(b, d),$$

where $\widetilde{\mathcal{B}} = \{(b,d): \ \|(b,d)\|_{\alpha_2} \leq 1\}$ is the unit ball in $\mathbb{R}^{n_1 \times n_2}$. As pointed out in [192], $g(b,d)$ is convex over $F$ if $\|\cdot\|_{\alpha_1}$ is a polyhedral norm. In this case, $\mu_{\alpha_1,\alpha_2}(P,Q)$ is the maximum of a convex function over the bounded set $\widetilde{\mathcal{B}} \cap F$. From the definition of $\mu_{\alpha_1,\alpha_2}(P,Q)$, we obtain the following corollary.

**Corollary 5.2.1** *For any $(b,d) \in F$, there exists a point $x \in \{z: Pz \leq b, \ Qz = d\}$ such that*

$$\|x\|_{\alpha_1} \leq \mu_{\alpha_1,\alpha_2}(P,Q)\|(b,d)\|_{\alpha_2}.$$

Let $M' \in \mathbb{R}^{m \times q}$ and $M'' \in \mathbb{R}^{\ell \times q}$ be two given matrices. Consider the specific $(P,Q)$ of the form

$$P = \begin{bmatrix} I_N & 0 \\ -I & 0 \end{bmatrix} \in \mathbb{R}^{(|N|+m) \times (m+\ell)}, \ Q = \begin{bmatrix} M' \\ M'' \end{bmatrix}^T \in \mathbb{R}^{q \times (m+\ell)}, \tag{5.6}$$

where $N$ is a subset of $\{1,\ldots,m\}$ and $I_N$ is obtained from the $m \times m$ identity matrix $I$ by deleting the rows corresponding to indices not in $N$. Robinson [192] defined the following constant:

$$\sigma_{\alpha_1,\alpha_2}(M',M'') := \max_{N \subseteq \{1,\ldots,m\}} \mu_{\alpha_1,\alpha_2}\left(\begin{bmatrix} I_N & 0 \\ -I & 0 \end{bmatrix}, \begin{bmatrix} M' \\ M'' \end{bmatrix}^T\right).$$

The constant $\sigma_{\alpha_1,\alpha_2}(M',M'')$ defined above is referred to as the *Robinson's constant* determined by $(M',M'')$. As shown in [192], the Hoffman's Lemma [133] in terms of $\sigma_{\alpha_1,\alpha_2}(M',M'')$ with $(\alpha_1,\alpha_2) = (\infty,2)$ is stated as follows.

**Lemma 5.2.2** (Hoffman's Lemma) *Let $M' \in \mathbb{R}^{m \times q}$ and $M'' \in \mathbb{R}^{\ell \times q}$ be given matrices and*

$$\mathcal{F} = \{z \in \mathbb{R}^q: \ M'z \leq b, \ M''z = d\}.$$

*For any vector $x$ in $\mathbb{R}^q$, there is a point $x^* \in \mathcal{F}$ with*

$$\|x - x^*\|_2 \leq \sigma_{\infty,2}(M',M'') \left\| \begin{bmatrix} (M'x-b)^+ \\ M''x-d \end{bmatrix} \right\|_1.$$

Given the solution set $\mathcal{F}$ of a linear system, Hoffman's Lemma indicates that the distance from a point in space to $\mathcal{F}$ can be measured in terms of the Robinson's constant and the quantity of the linear system being violated at this point. For completeness, a detailed proof of Lemma 5.2.2 is given below. The idea of this proof is due to Robinson [192].

*Proof of Lemma 5.2.2.* Let $x$ be any given vector in $\mathbb{R}^n$. Let $x^*$ be the orthogonal projection of $x$ into the set

$$\mathcal{F} = \{z \in \mathbb{R}^q: \ M'z \leq b, \ M''z = d\},$$

i.e.,

$$x^* = \arg\min_z\{\|x-z\|_2 : z \in \mathcal{F}\}.$$

This means that $x^* \in \mathcal{F}$ is the closest point to $x$ in terms of $\ell_2$-norm distance. By the property of the orthogonal projection to a convex set, we have

$$(z-x^*)^T(x-x^*) \le 0 \text{ for any } z \in \mathcal{F}.$$

This is equivalent to saying that $x^*$ is a solution to the following linear program:

$$\min_z\{(x^*-x)^Tz : M'z \le b, M''z = d\}. \tag{5.7}$$

By the KKT optimality condition, there is a vector $(u^*,v^*) \in \mathbb{R}^m \times \mathbb{R}^\ell$ such that

$$\begin{bmatrix} M' \\ M'' \end{bmatrix}^T \begin{bmatrix} u^* \\ v^* \end{bmatrix} = x-x^*, \ (u^*)^T(M'x^*-b)=0, \ u^* \ge 0. \tag{5.8}$$

Conversely, any such vector $(u^*,v^*)$ satisfying the condition (5.8) implies that $x^*$ is a solution to the problem (5.7). Denoted by

$$N = \{i : (M'x^*-b)_i < 0, \ 1 \le i \le m\}.$$

From the complementary slackness condition

$$(u^*)^T(M'x^*-b)=0, \ u^* \ge 0, \ M'x^* \le b,$$

we see that $u_i^* = 0$ for $i \in N$, i.e., $u_N^* = 0$. By the definition of $I_N$, the condition $u_N^* = 0$ is equivalent to $I_N u^* \le 0$ and $u^* \ge 0$. Thus we see that the optimality conditions, described in (5.8), can be written as

$$\begin{bmatrix} M' \\ M'' \end{bmatrix}^T \begin{bmatrix} u^* \\ v^* \end{bmatrix} = x-x^*, \ \begin{bmatrix} I_N & 0 \\ -I & 0 \end{bmatrix} \begin{bmatrix} u^* \\ v^* \end{bmatrix} \le 0.$$

Let $(P,Q)$ be given by (5.6) and $(b,d) = (0, x-x^*)$. From Corollary 5.2.1, there is a pair of vectors $(u^*,v^*)$ satisfying the above system and the following bound:

$$\begin{aligned}
\left\| \begin{bmatrix} u^* \\ v^* \end{bmatrix} \right\|_\infty &\le \ \mu_{\infty,2}\left( \begin{bmatrix} I_N & 0 \\ -I & 0 \end{bmatrix}, \begin{bmatrix} M' \\ M'' \end{bmatrix}^T \right) \left\| \begin{bmatrix} 0 \\ x-x^* \end{bmatrix} \right\|_2 \\
&\le \ \max_{N \subseteq \{1,\dots,m\}} \mu_{\infty,2}\left( \begin{bmatrix} I_N & 0 \\ -I & 0 \end{bmatrix}, \begin{bmatrix} M' \\ M'' \end{bmatrix}^T \right) \|x-x^*\|_2 \\
&= \ \sigma_{\infty,2}(M',M'')\|x-x^*\|_2, \tag{5.9}
\end{aligned}$$

where the last equality follows from the definition of Robinson's constant. Thus,

$$\begin{aligned}
\|x-x^*\|_2^2 &= \ \begin{bmatrix} u^* \\ v^* \end{bmatrix}^T \begin{bmatrix} M' \\ M'' \end{bmatrix}(x-x^*) \\
&= \ (u^*)^T(M'x-b)+(v^*)^T(M''x-d)-(u^*)^T(M'x^*-b) \\
&\quad -(v^*)^T(M''x^*-d) \\
&= \ (u^*)^T(M'x-b)+(v^*)^T(M''x-d).
\end{aligned}$$

Since $u^* \geq 0$, we have

$$(u^*)^T(M'x - b) \leq (u^*)^T(M'x - b)^+.$$

Therefore,

$$
\begin{aligned}
\|x - x^*\|_2^2 &\leq (u^*)^T(M'x - b)^+ + (v^*)^T(M''x - d) \\
&\leq \left\| \begin{bmatrix} u^* \\ v^* \end{bmatrix} \right\|_\infty \cdot \left\| \begin{bmatrix} (M'x - b)^+ \\ M''x - d \end{bmatrix} \right\|_1 \\
&\leq \sigma_{\infty,2}(M', M'')\|x - x^*\|_2 \left\| \begin{bmatrix} (M'x - b)^+ \\ M''x - d \end{bmatrix} \right\|_1,
\end{aligned}
$$

where the second inequality follows from the Hölder inequality, and the last inequality follows from (5.9). The desired result follows immediately. □

## 5.3 Weak RSP of Order $k$ of $A^T$

It is well known that the optimality conditions completely characterize the solution of a convex $\ell_1$-minimization problem. Most theory and algorithms for convex optimization are based on the Karush-Kuhn-Tucker (KKT) optimality conditions, so is the stability theory for $\ell_1$-minimization problems. In fact, by the KKT optimality conditions, $\widehat{x}$ is a solution to the standard $\ell_1$-minimization

$$\min_x \{\|x\|_1 : Ax = y\}$$

if and only if there is a vector $\eta \in \mathcal{R}(A^T)$ satisfying

$$\eta_i = 1 \text{ for } \widehat{x}_i > 0, \ \eta_i = -1 \text{ for } \widehat{x}_i < 0, \ \text{and } |\eta_i| \leq 1 \text{ otherwise.} \tag{5.10}$$

Define the pair $(S_1, S_2)$ as $S_1 = \{i : \widehat{x}_i > 0\}$ and $S_2 = \{i : \widehat{x}_i < 0\}$. The condition (5.10) is written as

$$\eta_i = 1 \text{ for } i \in S_1, \ \eta_i = -1 \text{ for } i \in S_2, \ |\eta_i| \leq 1 \text{ for } i \notin S_1 \cup S_2. \tag{5.11}$$

The condition (5.10) or (5.11) is called the individual weak RSP of $A^T$ at $\widehat{x}$. If we expect that every $k$-sparse vector $\widehat{x}$ is a solution to the standard $\ell_1$-minimization problem with measurements $y = A\widehat{x}$, then the condition (5.11) must hold for any disjoint subsets $(S_1, S_2)$ with $|S_1 \cup S_2| \leq k$. This naturally leads to the matrix property described as follows.

**Definition 5.3.1** (Weak RSP of order $k$ of $A^T$) *The matrix $A^T$ is said to satisfy the weak range space property (weak RSP) of order $k$ if for any disjoint subsets $S_1, S_2$ of $\{1, \ldots, n\}$ with $|S_1| + |S_2| \leq k$, there is a vector $\eta \in \mathcal{R}(A^T)$ satisfying*

$$\eta_i = 1 \text{ for } i \in S_1, \ \eta_i = -1 \text{ for } i \in S_2, \ |\eta_i| \leq 1 \text{ for } i \notin S_1 \cup S_2.$$

Unlike the RSP of order $k$ of $A^T$ (in Definition 3.6.5), the inequality "$|\eta_i| \leq 1$ for $i \notin S_1 \cup S_2$" in Definition 5.3.1 is not required to hold strictly. Thus the RSP of order $k$ implies the weak RSP of order $k$ of $A^T$, but the converse clearly does not hold. The weak RSP of order $k$ of $A^T$ is directly tied to (and naturally originated from) the fundamental optimality conditions for the standard $\ell_1$-minimization problem. This property can be seen as a strengthened optimality condition for the individual standard $\ell_1$-minimization problem.

We will demonstrate that the weak RSP of order $k$ of $A^T$, together with Lemma 5.2.2, provides an efficient way to develop a stability theory for the linear $\ell_1$-minimization method. All traditional RIP, NSP, ERC, mutual coherence conditions and their variants imply the weak RSP of $A^T$, and we show that each of these traditional conditions can imply an identical recovery error bound in terms of the Robinson's constant. Moreover, the stability of $\ell_1$-minimization under the RSP of order $k$ of $A^T$ or NSP of order $k$ can be immediately obtained as a byproduct of the generic stability results discussed in this chapter.

## 5.4 Stability of Standard $\ell_1$-Minimization

In this section, we focus on the case where the non-adaptive measurements $y \in \mathbb{R}^m$ are accurate, i.e., $y = A\widehat{x}$, where $\widehat{x} \in \mathbb{R}^m$ is the sparse vector to reconstruct. The situation with inaccurate measurements will be discussed in the next section. To see how mild the weak RSP assumption is, let us first show that the weak RSP of order $k$ of $A^T$ is a necessary condition for the standard $\ell_1$-minimization problem with any given measurement vector $y \in \{Ax : \|x\|_0 \leq k\}$ to be stable in sparse vector reconstruction.

**Theorem 5.4.1** *Let $A \in \mathbb{R}^{m \times n}$ be a given matrix with $m < n$ and $rank(A) = m$. Suppose that for any given vector $y \in \{Ax : \|x\|_0 \leq k\}$, the following holds: For any $x \in \mathbb{R}^n$ satisfying $Ax = y$, there is a solution $x^*$ of the $\ell_1$-minimization problem*

$$\min_z \{\|z\|_1 : Az = y\} \tag{5.12}$$

*such that*

$$\|x - x^*\| \leq C\sigma_k(x)_1,$$

*where $\| \cdot \|$ is a norm and $C$ is a constant dependent only on the problem data $(A, y)$. Then $A^T$ must satisfy the weak RSP of order $k$.*

*Proof.* Let $(S_1, S_2)$ be any pair of disjoint subsets of $\{1, \ldots, n\}$ with $|S_1| + |S_2| \leq k$. To prove that $A^T$ satisfies the weak RSP of order $k$, it is sufficient to show that there exists a vector $\eta \in \mathcal{R}(A^T)$ satisfying (5.11). Indeed, let $\widehat{x}$ be a $k$-sparse vector in $\mathbb{R}^n$ such that:

$$\{i : \widehat{x}_i > 0\} = S_1, \ \{i : \widehat{x}_i < 0\} = S_2. \tag{5.13}$$

Consider the problem

$$\min_z \{\|z\|_1 : Az = y := A\hat{x}\}.$$

By assumption, there is a solution $x^*$ of the problem above such that

$$\|\hat{x} - x^*\| \leq C\sigma_k(\hat{x})_1,$$

where $C$ depends only on the problem data $(A, y)$. Since $\hat{x}$ is $k$-sparse, we see that $\sigma_k(\hat{x})_1 = 0$ and hence $\hat{x} = x^*$. This, together with (5.13), implies that

$$\{i : x_i^* > 0\} = S_1, \ \{i : x_i^* < 0\} = S_2, \ x_i^* = 0 \text{ for all } i \notin S_1 \cup S_2. \quad (5.14)$$

Note that $x^*$ is a solution of (5.12). $x^*$ must satisfy the KKT optimality condition, i.e., there exists a vector $u \in \mathbb{R}^m$ such that

$$A^T u \in \partial \|x^*\|_1,$$

where $\partial \|x^*\|_1$ is the subgradient of the $\ell_1$-norm at $x^*$, which is given as

$$\partial \|x^*\|_1 = \{v \in \mathbb{R}^n : v_i = 1 \text{ for } x_i^* > 0, \ v_i = -1 \text{ for } x_i^* < 0, \ |v_i| \leq 1 \text{ otherwise}\}.$$

By setting $\eta = A^T u \in \partial \|x^*\|_1$, we immediately see that

$$\eta_i = 1 \text{ for } x_i^* > 0, \ \eta_i = -1 \text{ for } x_i^* < 0, \text{ and } |\eta_i| \leq 1 \text{ for } x_i^* = 0,$$

which together with (5.14) implies that the vector $\eta = A^T u$ satisfies (5.11). Note that $S_1$ and $S_2$ are arbitrary disjoint subsets of $\{1, \dots, n\}$ with $|S_1| + |S_2| \leq k$. We conclude that $A^T$ must satisfy the weak RSP of order $k$. □

We now further show that the weak RSP of order $k$ of $A^T$ is also a sufficient condition for the $\ell_1$-minimization problem to be stable. Note that the problem (5.12) can be written as

$$\min_{(x,t)} \{e^T t : \ -x + t \geq 0, \ x + t \geq 0, \ Ax = y, \ t \geq 0\}. \quad (5.15)$$

The dual problem of (5.15) is given as

$$\max_{(w,u,v)} \{y^T w : A^T w - u + v = 0, \ u + v \leq e, \ (u, v) \geq 0\}. \quad (5.16)$$

Note that any solution $(x^*, t^*)$ of (5.15) must satisfy that $t^* = |x^*|$. It is evident that $x^*$ is a solution of (5.12) if and only if $(x^*, t^*)$, where $t^* = |x^*|$, is a solution of (5.15). The following characterization of the solution of (5.12) follows immediately from the KKT optimality conditions of the problem (5.15).

**Lemma 5.4.2** *$x^*$ is a solution to the problem (5.12) if and only if there are vectors $t^*, u^*, v^* \in \mathbb{R}_+^n$ and $w^* \in \mathbb{R}^m$ such that $(x^*, t^*, u^*, v^*, w^*) \in T$, where*

$$T = \{(x, t, u, v, w) : \ Ax = y, \ x \leq t, \ -x \leq t, \ A^T w - u + v = 0,$$
$$u + v \leq e, \ y^T w = e^T t, \ (u, v, t) \geq 0\}. \quad (5.17)$$

*Moreover, any point $(x, t, u, v, w) \in T$ satisfies $t = |x|$.*

The set in (5.17) can be written as

$$T = \{z = (x,t,u,v,w) : M'z \le b, \; M''z = d\}, \tag{5.18}$$

where $b = (0,0,\mathbf{e},0,0,0)$ and $d = (y,0,0)$ and

$$M' = \begin{bmatrix} I & -I & 0 & 0 & 0 \\ -I & -I & 0 & 0 & 0 \\ 0 & 0 & I & I & 0 \\ 0 & 0 & -I & 0 & 0 \\ 0 & 0 & 0 & -I & 0 \\ 0 & -I & 0 & 0 & 0 \end{bmatrix}, \tag{5.19}$$

$$M'' = \begin{bmatrix} A & 0 & 0 & 0 & 0 \\ 0 & 0 & -I & I & A^T \\ 0 & -\mathbf{e}^T & 0 & 0 & y^T \end{bmatrix}. \tag{5.20}$$

We now prove that the RSP of order $k$ of $A^T$ is a sufficient condition for the standard $\ell_1$-minimization to be stable in sparse vector recovery.

**Theorem 5.4.3** *Let $A \in \mathbb{R}^{m \times n}$ be a given matrix with $m < n$ and $\mathrm{rank}(A) = m$, and let $y$ be any given vector in $\mathbb{R}^m$. If $A^T$ satisfies the weak RSP of order $k$, then for any $x \in \mathbb{R}^n$, there is a solution $x^*$ to the problem (5.12) such that*

$$\|x - x^*\|_2 \le \gamma\{2\sigma_k(x)_1 + (1+c)\|Ax - y\|_1\}, \tag{5.21}$$

*where*

$$c = \|(AA^T)^{-1}A\|_{\infty \to \infty},$$

*and $\gamma = \sigma_{\infty,2}(M',M'')$ is the Robinson's constant with $(M',M'')$ given in (5.19) and (5.20). Moreover, for any $x$ satisfying $Ax = y$, there is a solution $x^*$ to the problem (5.12) such that*

$$\|x - x^*\|_2 \le 2\gamma\sigma_k(x)_1. \tag{5.22}$$

*Proof.* Let $x \in \mathbb{R}^n$ be an arbitrary given vector and let $t = |x|$. We now construct a vector $(\tilde{u}, \tilde{v}, \tilde{w})$, which is a feasible point to the problem (5.16). Let $S$ be the support set of the $k$ largest components of $|x|$. Defined as

$$S_+ = \{i : x_i > 0, \; i \in S\}, \quad S_- = \{i : x_i < 0, \; i \in S\},$$

which are two disjoint sets. Clearly, we have $S = S_+ \cup S_-$ with cardinality $|S_+ \cup S_-| = |S| \le k$. Since $A^T$ has the weak RSP of order $k$, there exists a vector $\eta \in \mathcal{R}(A^T)$ such that $A^T\tilde{w} = \eta$ for some $\tilde{w} \in \mathbb{R}^m$ and $\eta$ satisfies the conditions

$$\eta_i = 1 \text{ for } i \in S_+, \; \eta_i = -1 \text{ for } i \in S_-, \; |\eta_i| \le 1 \text{ for } i \notin S = S_+ \cup S_-,$$

which implies that

$$(A^T \widetilde{w})_S = \eta_S = \text{sign}(x_S). \qquad (5.23)$$

We define $(\widetilde{u}, \widetilde{v})$ as follows:

$$\widetilde{u}_i = 1 \text{ and } \widetilde{v}_i = 0 \text{ for all } i \in S_+,$$

$$\widetilde{u}_i = 0 \text{ and } \widetilde{v}_i = 1 \text{ for all } i \in S_-,$$

$$\widetilde{u}_i = (|\eta_i| + \eta_i)/2 \text{ and } \widetilde{v}_i = (|\eta_i| - \eta_i)/2 \text{ for all } i \notin S.$$

From this definition, $(\widetilde{u}, \widetilde{v})$ satisfies that

$$(\widetilde{u}, \widetilde{v}) \geq 0, \ \widetilde{u} + \widetilde{v} \leq \mathbf{e}, \ \widetilde{u} - \widetilde{v} = \eta = A^T \widetilde{w}.$$

Thus $(\widetilde{u}, \widetilde{v}, \widetilde{w})$ is a feasible point to the problem (5.16). We now estimate the distance of $(x, t, \widetilde{u}, \widetilde{v}, \widetilde{w})$ to the set $T$ defined in (5.17) which can be written as (5.18). Applying Lemma 5.2.2 to (5.18), for the point $(x, t, \widetilde{u}, \widetilde{v}, \widetilde{w})$ with $t = |x|$, we can conclude that there exists a point $(x^*, t^*, u^*, v^*, w^*) \in T$ such that

$$\left\| \begin{bmatrix} x \\ t \\ \widetilde{u} \\ \widetilde{v} \\ \widetilde{w} \end{bmatrix} - \begin{bmatrix} x^* \\ t^* \\ u^* \\ v^* \\ w^* \end{bmatrix} \right\|_2 \leq \gamma \left\| \begin{bmatrix} (x-t)^+ \\ (-x-t)^+ \\ Ax - y \\ A^T \widetilde{w} - \widetilde{u} + \widetilde{v} \\ (\widetilde{u} + \widetilde{v} - \mathbf{e})^+ \\ \mathbf{e}^T t - y^T \widetilde{w} \\ (\vartheta)^- \end{bmatrix} \right\|_1, \qquad (5.24)$$

where $\gamma = \sigma_{\infty,2}(M', M'')$ is the Robinson's constant determined by $(M', M'')$ given in (5.19) and (5.20), and $(\vartheta)^-$ denotes the vector $((\widetilde{u})^-, (\widetilde{v})^-, (t)^-)$. By the aforementioned choice of $(\widetilde{u}, \widetilde{v}, \widetilde{w})$, we have

$$(\widetilde{u} + \widetilde{v} - \mathbf{e})^+ = 0, \ A^T \widetilde{w} - \widetilde{u} + \widetilde{v} = 0, \ (\vartheta)^- = 0.$$

Note that $t = |x|$, which implies that $(x-t)^+ = (-x-t)^+ = 0$. Thus the inequality (5.24) is reduced to

$$\|(x, t, \widetilde{u}, \widetilde{v}, \widetilde{w}) - (x^*, t^*, u^*, v^*, w^*)\|_2 \leq \gamma \left\| \begin{bmatrix} Ax - y \\ \mathbf{e}^T t - y^T \widetilde{w} \end{bmatrix} \right\|_1. \qquad (5.25)$$

Denoted by $h = Ax - y$. The choice of $(t, \widetilde{u}, \widetilde{v}, \widetilde{w})$ implies that

$$\mathbf{e}^T t - y^T \widetilde{w} = \mathbf{e}^T |x| - (Ax - h)^T \widetilde{w} = \|x\|_1 - x^T (A^T \widetilde{w}) + h^T \widetilde{w}.$$

Substituting this into (5.25) and noting that

$$\|x - x^*\|_2 \leq \|(x, t, \widetilde{u}, \widetilde{v}, \widetilde{w}) - (x^*, t^*, u^*, v^*, w^*)\|_2,$$

we obtain

$$\|x - x^*\|_2 \leq \gamma \{\|Ax - y\|_1 + |\|x\|_1 - x^T(A^T\widetilde{w}) + h^T\widetilde{w}|\}. \tag{5.26}$$

Since $\operatorname{rank}(A) = m$ and $\|\eta\|_\infty \leq 1$, it follows from $A^T\widetilde{w} = \eta$ that

$$\|\widetilde{w}\|_\infty = \|(AA^T)^{-1}A\eta\|_\infty \leq \|(AA^T)^{-1}A\|_{\infty\to\infty}\|\eta\|_\infty \leq c, \tag{5.27}$$

where the constant $c = \|(AA^T)^{-1}A\|_{\infty\to\infty}$. By (5.23), we have

$$(x_S)^T(A^T\widetilde{w})_S = (x_S)^T\eta_S = (x_S)^T\operatorname{sign}(x_S) = \|x_S\|_1,$$

and

$$\left|(x_{\overline{S}})^T(A^T\widetilde{w})_{\overline{S}}\right| \leq \|x_{\overline{S}}\|_1\|(A^T\widetilde{w})_{\overline{S}}\|_\infty = \|x_{\overline{S}}\|_1\|\eta_{\overline{S}}\|_\infty \leq \|x_{\overline{S}}\|_1 = \sigma_k(x)_1.$$

Thus we have

$$\begin{aligned}\|x\|_1 - x^T(A^T\widetilde{w}) + h^T\widetilde{w} &= \|x\|_1 - (x_S)^T(A^T\widetilde{w})_S - (x_{\overline{S}})^T(A^T\widetilde{w})_{\overline{S}} + h^T\widetilde{w}\\ &= \|x\|_1 - \|x_S\|_1 - (x_{\overline{S}})^T(A^T\widetilde{w})_{\overline{S}} + h^T\widetilde{w}\\ &= \sigma_k(x)_1 - (x_{\overline{S}})^T(A^T\widetilde{w})_{\overline{S}} + h^T\widetilde{w}.\end{aligned}$$

Therefore,

$$\begin{aligned}\left|\|x\|_1 - x^T(A^T\widetilde{w}) + h^T\widetilde{w}\right| &\leq \sigma_k(x)_1 + \left|(x_{\overline{S}})^T(A^T\widetilde{w})_{\overline{S}}\right| + |h^T\widetilde{w}|\\ &\leq 2\sigma_k(x)_1 + \|h\|_1 \cdot \|\widetilde{w}\|_\infty\\ &\leq 2\sigma_k(x)_1 + c\|Ax - y\|_1, \end{aligned} \tag{5.28}$$

where the last inequality follows from (5.27). Combining (5.28) and (5.26) yields (5.21). If $x$ is a solution to $Az = y$, then (5.21) is reduced to (5.22). □

Combining Theorems 5.4.1 and 5.4.3 yields the following statement.

**Corollary 5.4.4** *Let $A \in \mathbb{R}^{m\times n}$ be a matrix with $m < n$ and $\operatorname{rank}(A) = m$. Then $A^T$ satisfies the weak RSP of order $k$ if and only if the $\ell_1$-minimization problem*

$$\min_x\{\|x\|_1 : Ax = y\}$$

*is stable in sparse vector reconstruction for any given measurement vector $y \in \{Ax : \|x\|_0 \leq k\}$.*

*Proof.* Theorem 5.4.3 indicates that the weak RSP of order $k$ of $A^T$ is a sufficient condition for the standard $\ell_1$-minimization problem to be stable for any given measurements $y \in \mathbb{R}^m$. Note that under the assumption of Theorem 5.4.3, $\{Ax : x \in \mathbb{R}^n\} = \mathbb{R}^m$ (due to the fact $\operatorname{rank}(A) = m$). So the standard $\ell_1$-minimization method is stable for any given $y \in \{Ax : \|x\|_0 \leq k\} \subseteq \mathbb{R}^m$, that is, for any $x \in \mathbb{R}^n$

there is a solution $x^*$ of the standard $\ell_1$-minimization problem such that $\|x - x^*\|_2 \leq C\sigma_1(x)_1$, where the constant $C$ depends only on the problem data $(A, y)$. On the other hand, Theorem 5.4.1 claims that if the standard $\ell_1$-minimization problem is stable for any given $y \in \{Ax : \|x\|_0 \leq k\}$, then the matrix $A^T$ must satisfy the weak RSP of order $k$. □

Thus the weak RSP of $A^T$ is the mildest condition governing the stableness of the standard $\ell_1$-minimization problem with any given measurement vector $y \in \{Ax : \|x\|_0 \leq k\}$. Corollary 5.4.4 indicates that this condition cannot be relaxed without damaging the stability (in the sense of Definition 5.1.1) of the standard $\ell_1$-minimization problem. Many traditional stability assumptions imply the weak RSP of order $k$ of $A^T$. The following unified stability result follows immediately from Theorem 5.4.3.

**Corollary 5.4.5** *Let $(A, y)$ be given, where $y \in \mathbb{R}^m$ and $A \in \mathbb{R}^{m \times n}$ with $m < n$ and $rank(A) = m$. Suppose that one of the following properties hold:*

($c^1$)  *A is a matrix with $\ell_2$-normalized columns and $\mu_1(k) + \mu_1(k-1) < 1$.*

($c^2$)  *RIP of order 2k with constant $\delta_{2k} < 1/\sqrt{2}$.*

($c^3$)  *Stable NSP of order k with constant $0 < \rho < 1$.*

($c^4$)  *Robust NSP of order k with constant $0 < \rho' < 1$ and $\rho'' > 0$.*

($c^5$)  *NSP of order k.*

($c^6$)  *ERC of order k.*

($c^7$)  *RSP of order k of $A^T$.*

*Then for any $x \in \mathbb{R}^n$, the solution $x^*$ of (5.12) approximates x with error*

$$\|x - x^*\|_2 \leq 2\gamma\sigma_k(x)_1 + \gamma(1 + c)\|Ax - y\|_1,$$

*where $c = \|(AA^T)^{-1}A\|_{\infty \to \infty}$, and $\gamma = \sigma_{\infty,2}(M', M'')$ is the Robinson's constant determined by (5.19) and (5.20). In particular, for any x with $Ax = y$, the solution $x^*$ of the problem (5.12) approximates x with error*

$$\|x - x^*\|_2 \leq 2\gamma\sigma_k(x)_1.$$

All conditions ($c^1$)–($c^7$) listed above have been described in Chapter 3, and have been shown to be essential for the exact recovery of $k$-sparse vectors. The above corollary claims that these conditions are also essential to ensure that the linear $\ell_1$-minimization method is stable. As pointed out in Chapter 3, each of the conditions ($c^1$)–($c^6$) implies ($c^7$), and hence implies the weak RSP of order $k$ of $A^T$. Since each of these conditions ensures the uniform recovery of $k$-sparse vectors, each implies that the solution of the standard $\ell_1$-minimization is unique. This fact, together with Theorem 5.4.3, immediately implies Corollary 5.4.5, which is a unified stability result in the sense that every condition among ($c^1$)–($c^7$) implies the same recovery error bound in terms of Robinson's constants.

## 5.5   Linear Dantzig Selector

Consider the norm

$$\phi(\cdot) = \alpha \|\cdot\|_\infty + (1-\alpha)\|\cdot\|_1,$$

where $\alpha \in [0,1]$ is a fixed constant. The problem (5.1) with this norm is stated as:

$$\min_x \{\|x\|_1 : \ \alpha\|M^T(Ax-y)\|_\infty + (1-\alpha)\|M^T(Ax-y)\|_1 \le \varepsilon\}, \qquad (5.29)$$

where $M \in \mathbb{R}^{m\times q}$ and $A \in \mathbb{R}^{m\times n}$ are given matrices and $\varepsilon$ is a given parameter. By choosing $\alpha = 1$ and $\alpha = 0$ in (5.29), respectively, we obtain the following two important special cases:

$$\min_x \{\|x\|_1 : \ \|M^T(Ax-y)\|_\infty \le \varepsilon\}, \qquad (5.30)$$

$$\min_x \{\|x\|_1 : \ \|M^T(Ax-y)\|_1 \le \varepsilon\}. \qquad (5.31)$$

A common feature of (5.29)–(5.31) is that their constraints can be linearly represented, and hence these problems are equivalent to linear programming problems. Particularly, when $M = A$, the problem (5.30) is reduced to the standard Dantzig Selector (DS) problem proposed by Candès and Tao [47]. In this book, all the problems (5.29)–(5.31) are referred to as the linear DS problems. When $\varepsilon = 0$, all these problems are reduced to the standard $\ell_1$-minimization problem provided that $M$ has full row rank.

Let us first write (5.29) as an explicit linear programming problem. Introduction of two auxiliary variables $(\xi, v)$ into (5.29) leads to

$$\min_{(x,\xi,v)} \quad \|x\|_1$$

$$\text{s.t.} \quad \alpha\xi + (1-\alpha)e^T v \le \varepsilon,$$
$$\|M^T(Ax-y)\|_\infty \le \xi,$$
$$|M^T(Ax-y)| \le v,$$
$$\xi \in \mathbb{R}_+, \ v \in \mathbb{R}^q_+,$$

where $e$ is the vector of ones in $\mathbb{R}^q$. Furthermore, by introducing variables $t \in \mathbb{R}^n_+$ such that $|x| \le t$, the problem above is reformulated as the linear program below:

$$\min_{(x,t,\xi,v)} \quad \tilde{e}^T t$$

$$\text{s.t.} \quad x \le t, \ -x \le t, \ \alpha\xi + (1-\alpha)e^T v \le \varepsilon,$$
$$-\xi e \le M^T(Ax-y) \le \xi e,$$
$$-v \le M^T(Ax-y) \le v, \qquad (5.32)$$
$$t \in \mathbb{R}^n_+, \ \xi \in \mathbb{R}_+, \ v \in \mathbb{R}^q_+.$$

where $\widetilde{\mathbf{e}}$ is the vector of ones in $\mathbb{R}^n$. Clearly, any solution $(x,t,\xi,v)$ of the problem (5.32) must satisfy the following relations:

$$t = |x|, \quad \|M^T(Ax-y)\|_\infty \leq \xi, \quad |M^T(Ax-y)| \leq v.$$

To obtain the dual problem of (5.32), we may write (5.32) in the form $\min_z \{r^T z : Qz \geq h, \ z \geq 0\}$ with problem data $(Q,h,r)$, to which the Lagrangian dual is given as $\max_w \{h^T w : Q^T w \leq r, \ w \geq 0\}$. So it is straightforward to verify that the dual problem of (5.32) is given as follows:

$$
\begin{aligned}
\max_{w^{(i)},i=1,\dots,7} \quad & -\varepsilon w^{(3)} + y^T M(w^{(4)} - w^{(5)} - w^{(6)} + w^{(7)}) \\
\text{s.t.} \quad & w^{(1)} + w^{(2)} \leq \widetilde{\mathbf{e}}, \\
& -w^{(1)} + w^{(2)} + A^T M(w^{(4)} - w^{(5)} - w^{(6)} + w^{(7)}) = 0, \qquad (5.33) \\
& -\alpha w^{(3)} + \mathbf{e}^T w^{(4)} + \mathbf{e}^T w^{(5)} \leq 0, \\
& -(1-\alpha)w^{(3)}\mathbf{e} + w^{(6)} + w^{(7)} \leq 0, \\
& w^{(i)} \geq 0, \ i = 1,\dots,7,
\end{aligned}
$$

where $w^{(1)}$, $w^{(2)} \in \mathbb{R}^n_+$, $w^3 \in \mathbb{R}_+$ and $w^{(4)},\dots,w^{(7)} \in \mathbb{R}^q_+$. It is obvious that $x^*$ is a solution to the problem (5.29) if and only if $(x^*,t^*,\xi^*,v^*)$, where $t^* = |x^*|$, is a solution to the problem (5.32). By the KKT optimality conditions of (5.32), we immediately obtain the following characterization of the solution of (5.29).

**Lemma 5.5.1** *$x^*$ is a solution of the DS problem (5.29) if and only if there exist a vector $(t^*,\xi^*,v^*,w_*^{(1)},\dots,w_*^{(7)})$ such that $(x^*,t^*,\xi^*,v^*,w_*^{(1)},\dots,w_*^{(7)}) \in T^*$, where $T^*$ is the set of points $(x,t,\xi,v,w^{(1)},\dots,w^{(7)})$ satisfying the following systems:*

$$
\begin{cases}
x \leq t, \ -x \leq t, \ \alpha\xi + (1-\alpha)\mathbf{e}^T v \leq \varepsilon, \\
-\xi\mathbf{e} \leq M^T(Ax-y) \leq \xi\mathbf{e}, \ M^T(Ax-y) \leq v, \ -M^T(Ax-y) \leq v, \\
-w^{(1)} + w^{(2)} + A^T M(w^{(4)} - w^{(5)} - w^{(6)} + w^{(7)}) = 0, \\
w^{(1)} + w^{(2)} \leq \widetilde{\mathbf{e}}, \ -\alpha w^{(3)} + \mathbf{e}^T w^{(4)} + \mathbf{e}^T w^{(5)} \leq 0, \\
-(1-\alpha)w^{(3)}\mathbf{e} + w^{(6)} + w^{(7)} \leq 0, \\
-\varepsilon w^{(3)} + y^T M(w^{(4)} - w^{(5)} - w^{(6)} + w^{(7)}) = \widetilde{\mathbf{e}}^T t, \\
w^{(1)}, \ w^{(2)} \in \mathbb{R}^n_+, \ w^3 \in \mathbb{R}_+, \ w^{(4)},\dots,w^{(7)} \in \mathbb{R}^q_+, \\
t \in \mathbb{R}^n_+, \ \xi \in \mathbb{R}_+, \ v \in \mathbb{R}^q_+.
\end{cases} \qquad (5.34)
$$

*Moreover, any point $(x,t,\xi,v,w^{(1)},\dots,w^{(7)}) \in T^*$ satisfies that $t = |x|, \|M^T(Ax - y)\|_\infty \leq \xi$ and $|M^T(Ax-y)| \leq v$.*

Note that $t \in \mathbb{R}^n_+$, $\xi \in \mathbb{R}_+$ and $v \in \mathbb{R}^q_+$ are implied from other conditions in (5.34). Thus these conditions can be omitted from (5.34) without affecting the set $T^*$. It is easy to write $T^*$ in the form

$$T^* = \{z = (x,t,\xi,v,w^{(1)},\dots,w^{(7)}) : M^1 z \leq d^1, \ M^2 z = d^2\}, \qquad (5.35)$$

where

$$d^1 = \left(0,0,\varepsilon, y^T M, -y^T M, y^T M, -y^T M, \widetilde{e}^T, 0,0,0,0,0,0,0,0,0\right)^T, \quad d^2 = 0$$

and

$$M^2 = \begin{bmatrix} 0 & 0 & 0 & 0 & -I & I & 0 & A^T M & -A^T M & -A^T M & A^T M \\ 0 & \widetilde{e}^T & 0 & 0 & 0 & 0 & \varepsilon & -y^T M & y^T M & y^T M & -y^T M \end{bmatrix}, \tag{5.36}$$

$$M^1 = \begin{bmatrix} Q_1 & 0 \\ 0 & Q_2 \end{bmatrix} \tag{5.37}$$

with

$$Q_1 = \begin{bmatrix} I & -I & 0 & 0 \\ -I & -I & 0 & 0 \\ 0 & 0 & \alpha & (1-\alpha)e^T \\ M^T A & 0 & -\mathbf{e} & 0 \\ -M^T A & 0 & -\mathbf{e} & 0 \\ M^T A & 0 & 0 & -I \\ -M^T A & 0 & 0 & -I \end{bmatrix},$$

$$Q_2 = \begin{bmatrix} I & I & 0 & 0 & 0 & 0 & 0 \\ 0 & 0 & -\alpha & e^T & e^T & 0 & 0 \\ 0 & 0 & -(1-\alpha)\mathbf{e} & 0 & 0 & I & I \\ -I & 0 & 0 & 0 & 0 & 0 & 0 \\ 0 & -I & 0 & 0 & 0 & 0 & 0 \\ 0 & 0 & -1 & 0 & 0 & 0 & 0 \\ 0 & 0 & 0 & -I & 0 & 0 & 0 \\ 0 & 0 & 0 & 0 & -I & 0 & 0 \\ 0 & 0 & 0 & 0 & 0 & -I & 0 \\ 0 & 0 & 0 & 0 & 0 & 0 & -I \end{bmatrix},$$

where $0's$ are zero matrices and $I's$ are identity matrices with suitable sizes. We now prove that the DS problem (5.29) is stable if $A^T$ satisfies the weak RSP of order $k$.

**Theorem 5.5.2** *Let $A \in \mathbb{R}^{m \times n}$ and $M \in \mathbb{R}^{m \times q}$ be two given matrices with $m < n, m \leq q$ and $rank(A) = rank(M) = m$. Suppose that $A^T$ satisfies the weak RSP of order $k$. Then for any $x \in \mathbb{R}^n$, there is a solution $x^*$ of the DS problem (5.29) approximating $x$ with error*

$$\|x - x^*\|_2 \leq \gamma(\alpha \|\vartheta\|_\infty + (1-\alpha)\|\vartheta\|_1 - \varepsilon)^+$$
$$+ \gamma\{2\sigma_k(x)_1 + \widehat{c}(\varepsilon + \|\vartheta\|_\infty)\}, \tag{5.38}$$

*where $\vartheta = M^T(Ax - y)$ and $\gamma = \sigma_{\infty,2}(M^1, M^2)$ is the Robinson's constant with $(M^1, M^2)$ given in (5.36) and (5.37). The constant $\widehat{c}$ in (5.38) is given as*

$$\widehat{c} = \max_{G \subseteq \{1,...,q\}, |G|=m} \|M_G^{-1}(AA^T)^{-1}A\|_{\infty \to 1},$$

*where $M_G$ represents all possible $m \times m$ invertible submatrix of $M$. In particular, for any $x$ satisfying the constraints of (5.29), there is a solution $x^*$ of (5.29) approximating $x$ with error*

$$\|x - x^*\|_2 \leq \gamma \{2\sigma_k(x)_1 + \widehat{c}\varepsilon + \widehat{c}\|M^T(Ax - y)\|_\infty\} \leq 2\gamma\{\sigma_k(x)_1 + \widehat{c}\varepsilon\}. \quad (5.39)$$

*Proof.* Let $x \in \mathbb{R}^n$ be an arbitrarily given vector. Then we set $(t, \xi, v)$ as follows:

$$t = |x|, \ \xi = \|M^T(Ax - y)\|_\infty, \ v = |M^T(Ax - y)|. \quad (5.40)$$

Let $S$ be the support of the $k$ largest components of $|x|$. We decompose $S$ into $S'$ and $S''$, where

$$S' = \{j : j \in S, x_j > 0\}, \ S'' = \{j : j \in S, x_j < 0\},$$

which implies that $S'$ and $S''$ are disjoint and satisfy $|S' \cup S''| = |S| \leq k$. Note that $A^T$ satisfies the weak RSP of order $k$. There exists a vector $\zeta = A^T u^*$ for some $u^* \in \mathbb{R}^m$ satisfying the following properties:

$$\zeta_i = 1 \text{ for } i \in S', \ \zeta_i = -1 \text{ for } i \in S'', \text{ and } |\zeta_i| \leq 1 \text{ for } i \notin S' \cup S''.$$

We now construct a vector $(w^{(1)}, \dots, w^{(7)})$ such that it is a feasible point to the problem (5.33). First, $w^{(1)}$ and $w^{(2)}$ can be defined as follows:

$$w_i^{(1)} = 1 \text{ and } w_i^{(2)} = 0 \text{ for all } i \in S';$$

$$w_i^{(1)} = 0 \text{ and } w_i^{(2)} = 1 \text{ for all } i \in S'';$$

$$w_i^{(1)} = (1 + \zeta_i)/2 \text{ and } w_i^{(2)} = (1 - \zeta_i)/2 \text{ for all } i \notin S' \cup S''.$$

This choice of $(w^{(1)}, w^{(2)})$ satisfies that $w^{(1)} - w^{(2)} = \zeta$. Note that $M$ is a full-row-rank matrix. There exists an invertible $m \times m$ submatrix of $M$, denoted by $M_{\mathfrak{J}}$, where $\mathfrak{J} \subseteq \{1, \dots, q\}$ with $|\mathfrak{J}| = m$. Let $h \in \mathbb{R}^q$ be the vector given as $h_{\mathfrak{J}} = M_{\mathfrak{J}}^{-1} u^*$ and $h_{\overline{\mathfrak{J}}} = 0$ where $\overline{\mathfrak{J}} = \{1, \dots, q\} \backslash \mathfrak{J}$. Thus $Mh = u^*$. The non-negative vectors $w^{(3)}, \dots, w^{(7)}$ are defined as follows:

$$w^{(3)} = \|h\|_1, \ w^{(4)} = \alpha(h)^+, \ w^{(5)} = -\alpha(h)^-,$$

$$w^{(6)} = -(1 - \alpha)(h)^-, \ w^{(7)} = (1 - \alpha)(h)^+,$$

which implies that

$$e^T(w^{(4)} + w^{(5)}) = \alpha e^T|h| = \alpha\|h\|_1 = \alpha w^{(3)},$$

$$w^{(6)} + w^{(7)} = (1 - \alpha)|h| \leq (1 - \alpha)w^{(3)}e,$$

$$w^{(4)} - w^{(5)} - w^{(6)} + w^{(7)} = \alpha(h)^+ + \alpha(h)^- + (1 - \alpha)(h)^- + (1 - \alpha)(h)^+$$
$$= (h)^+ + (h)^- = h. \quad (5.41)$$

Therefore,

$$A^T M(w^{(4)} - w^{(5)} - w^{(6)} + w^{(7)}) = A^T(Mh) = A^T u^* = \zeta = w^{(1)} - w^{(2)}.$$

Thus the vector $(w^{(1)}, \ldots, w^{(7)})$ constructed above satisfies the constraints of (5.33). We now consider the set $T^*$ written as (5.35) and the vector $(x, t, \xi, v, w^{(1)}, \ldots, w^{(7)})$, where $(t, \xi, v)$ is chosen as (5.40) and $w^{(1)}, \ldots, w^{(7)}$ are chosen as above. Applying Lemma 5.2.2 to $(M^1, M^2)$ given in (5.36) and (5.37), we conclude that there exists a point $(x^*, t^*, \xi^*, v^*, w_*^{(1)}, \ldots, w_*^{(7)}) \in T^*$ such that

$$\left\| \begin{bmatrix} x \\ t \\ \xi \\ v \\ w^{(1)} \\ \vdots \\ w^{(7)} \end{bmatrix} - \begin{bmatrix} x^* \\ t^* \\ \xi^* \\ v^* \\ w_*^{(1)} \\ \vdots \\ w_*^{(7)} \end{bmatrix} \right\|_2 \leq \gamma \left\| \begin{bmatrix} (x-t)^+ \\ (-x-t)^+ \\ (\alpha\xi + (1-\alpha)e^T v - \varepsilon)^+ \\ (M^T(Ax-y) - \xi e)^+ \\ (-M^T(Ax-y) - \xi e)^+ \\ (M^T(Ax-y) - v)^+ \\ (-M^T(Ax-y) - v)^+ \\ (w^{(1)} + w^{(2)} - \widetilde{e})^+ \\ (-\alpha w^{(3)} + e^T w^{(4)} + e^T w^{(5)})^+ \\ (-(1-\alpha)w^{(3)}e + w^{(6)} + w^{(7)})^+ \\ A^T M(w^{(4)} - w^{(5)} - w^{(6)} + w^{(7)}) - w^{(1)} + w^{(2)} \\ \widetilde{e}^T t + \varepsilon w^{(3)} - y^T M(w^{(4)} - w^{(5)} - w^{(6)} + w^{(7)}) \\ (Y)^+ \end{bmatrix} \right\|_1,$$

(5.42)

where $\gamma = \sigma_{\infty,2}(M^1, M^2)$ is the Robinson's constant with $(M^1, M^2)$ given in (5.36) and (5.37) and

$$(Y)^+ = ((-t)^+, \ (-\xi)^+, \ (-v)^+, \ (-w^{(1)})^+, \ \ldots, \ (-w^{(7)})^+).$$

It follows from (5.40) that

$$(x-t)^+ = (-x-t)^+ = 0,$$
$$(M^T(Ax-y) - \xi e)^+ = 0,$$
$$(-M^T(Ax-y) - \xi e)^+ = 0,$$
$$(M^T(Ax-y) - v)^+ = 0,$$
$$(-M^T(Ax-y) - v)^+ = 0.$$

The nonnegativity of $(t, \xi, v, w^{(1)}, \ldots, w^{(7)})$ implies that $(Y)^+ = 0$. Since $(w^{(1)}, \ldots, w^{(7)})$ is a feasible point to the problem (5.33), we also see that

$$\left( w^{(1)} + w^{(2)} - \widetilde{e} \right)^+ = 0,$$

$$\left( -\alpha w^{(3)} + e^T w^{(4)} + e^T w^{(5)} \right)^+ = 0,$$

$$\left(-(1-\alpha)w^{(3)}\mathbf{e}+w^{(6)}+w^{(7)}\right)^+=0,$$

$$A^TM(w^{(4)}-w^{(5)}-w^{(6)}+w^{(7)})-w^{(1)}+w^{(2)}=0.$$

Note that

$$\left\|x-x^*\right\|_2\le\left\|(x,t,\xi,v,w^{(1)},\dots,w^{(7)})-(x^*,t^*,\xi^*,v^*,w_*^{(1)},\dots,w_*^{(7)})\right\|_2.$$

The inequality (5.42) is then reduced to

$$\|x-x^*\|_2\le\gamma\left\|\begin{bmatrix}(\alpha\xi+(1-\alpha)\mathbf{e}^Tv-\varepsilon)^+\\\tilde{\mathbf{e}}^Tt+\varepsilon w^{(3)}-y^TM(w^{(4)}-w^{(5)}-w^{(6)}+w^{(7)})\end{bmatrix}\right\|_1.$$

Denoted by $\vartheta=M^T(Ax-y)$, it implies that $y^TM=x^TA^TM-\vartheta^T$. From (5.40), (5.41) and $A^TMh=A^Tu^*=\zeta$, we immediately have

$$\left(\alpha\xi+(1-\alpha)\mathbf{e}^Tv-\varepsilon\right)^+=(\alpha\|\vartheta\|_\infty+(1-\alpha)\|\vartheta\|_1-\varepsilon)^+ \tag{5.43}$$

and

$$\begin{aligned}|\tilde{\mathbf{e}}^Tt+\varepsilon w^{(3)}-y^TM(w^{(4)}-w^{(5)}-w^{(6)}+w^{(7)})|\\=|\tilde{\mathbf{e}}^T|x|+\varepsilon w^{(3)}-(x^TA^TM-\vartheta^T)h|\\=|\tilde{\mathbf{e}}^T|x|+\varepsilon w^{(3)}-x^T\zeta+\vartheta^Th|\\\le 2\sigma_k(x)_1+\varepsilon\|h\|_1+\|\vartheta\|_\infty\|h\|_1,\end{aligned} \tag{5.44}$$

where the last inequality follows from the fact $|\vartheta^Th|\le\|\vartheta\|_\infty\|h\|_1$ and

$$\begin{aligned}|\tilde{\mathbf{e}}^T|x|-x^T\zeta|&=|\tilde{\mathbf{e}}^T|x|-x_S^T\zeta_S-x_{\overline{S}}^T\zeta_{\overline{S}}|\\&\le\|x\|_1-\|x_S\|_1+\|x_{\overline{S}}^T\|_1\|\zeta_{\overline{S}}\|_\infty\\&\le 2\|x_{\overline{S}}^T\|_1=2\sigma_k(x)_1.\end{aligned}$$

Consider all invertible $m\times m$ submatrices of $M$. Define the constant

$$\hat{c}=\max_{G\subseteq\{1,\dots,q\},|G|=m}\|M_G^{-1}(AA^T)^{-1}A\|_{\infty\to 1}.$$

Note that, $h_{\overline{\mathfrak{J}}}=0$ and $M_{\mathfrak{J}}h_{\mathfrak{J}}=u^*=(AA^T)^{-1}A\zeta$. We have

$$\begin{aligned}\|h\|_1&=\|h_{\mathfrak{J}}\|_1=\|M_{\mathfrak{J}}^{-1}(AA^T)^{-1}A\zeta\|_1\\&\le\|M_{\mathfrak{J}}^{-1}(AA^T)^{-1}A\|_{\infty\to 1}\|\zeta\|_\infty\le\hat{c}.\end{aligned} \tag{5.45}$$

Combining (5.43)–(5.45) yields

$$\|x-x^*\|_2\le\gamma\{2\sigma_k(x)_1+(\alpha\|\vartheta\|_\infty+(1-\alpha)\|\vartheta\|_1-\varepsilon)^++\hat{c}(\varepsilon+\|\vartheta\|_\infty)\},$$

which is the bound given in (5.38). In particular, if $x$ is a feasible point to the problem (5.29), then $(\alpha\|\vartheta\|_\infty + (1-\alpha)\|\vartheta\|_1 - \varepsilon)^+ = 0$, and hence

$$\|x - x^*\|_2 \leq \gamma\{2\sigma_k(x)_1 + \widehat{c}(\varepsilon + \|\vartheta\|_\infty)\}. \tag{5.46}$$

Note that

$$\|\vartheta\|_\infty \leq \alpha\|\vartheta\|_\infty + (1-\alpha)\|\vartheta\|_1 \leq \varepsilon.$$

The error bound given in (5.39) follows immediately from (5.46). □

As we have pointed out in Corollary 5.4.5, many traditional conditions in compressed sensing theory imply the weak RSP of order $k$ of $A^T$. From Theorem 5.5.2, the next corollary provides a unified stability result for the linear DS problems in the sense that various traditional stability conditions imply identical error bounds (5.38) and (5.39).

**Corollary 5.5.3** *Let A and M be given as in Theorem 5.5.2. Suppose that one of the conditions $(c^1)$–$(c^7)$ listed in Corollary 5.4.5 holds. Then the conclusions of Theorem 5.5.2 are valid for the problem (5.29).*

## 5.6  Special Cases

Theorem 5.5.2 can be seen as a unified stability result for a number of sparse recovery methods. The stability results for many special cases of (5.29) can be obtained instantly from this theorem. For instance, by setting $\alpha = 1$ and $\alpha = 0$, respectively, Theorem 5.5.2 claims that under the weak RSP of order $k$, both the DS problems (5.30) and (5.31) are stable in sparse vector recovery. Furthermore, by setting $M = I$ and $M = A$, respectively, the stability results for the standard DS and $\ell_1$-minimization with $\ell_\infty$-norm or $\ell_1$-norm constraint can be obtained immediately from Theorem 5.5.2.

### 5.6.1  Standard Dantzig Selector

As an example, let us first state the result for the standard DS, corresponding to the case $M = A$ and $\alpha = 1$ in (5.29). Combining Theorem 5.5.2 and Corollary 5.5.3 yields the following corollary.

**Corollary 5.6.1** *Let $A \in \mathbb{R}^{m \times n}$ with $m < n$ and $rank(A) = m$. Consider the standard DS problem (5.4), that is,*

$$\min_x\{\|x\|_1 :\ \|A^T(Ax - y)\|_\infty \leq \varepsilon\}.$$

*Then the following two statements hold true:*

(i) *If $A^T$ satisfies the weak RSP of order $k$, then for any $x \in \mathbb{R}^n$, there is a solution $x^*$ of (5.4) approximating $x$ with error*

$$\|x - x^*\|_2 \leq \gamma\{2\sigma_k(x)_1 + (\|A^T(Ax - y)\|_\infty - \varepsilon)^+ + c_A\varepsilon$$
$$+ c_A\|A^T(Ax - y)\|_\infty\},$$

*where $\gamma = \sigma_{\infty,2}(M^1, M^2)$ is the Robinson's constant determined by $(M^1, M^2)$ given in (5.36) and (5.37) with $M = A$ and $\alpha = 1$, and $c_A$ is a constant given as*

$$c_A = \max_{G \subseteq \{1,\dots,n\}, |G|=m} \|A_G^{-1}(AA^T)^{-1}A\|_{\infty \to 1},$$

*where $A_G$ stands for all possible $m \times m$ invertible submatrix of $A$. In particular, for any $x$ satisfying $\|A^T(Ax - y)\|_\infty \leq \varepsilon$, there is a solution $x^*$ of (5.4) approximating $x$ with error*

$$\|x - x^*\|_2 \leq \gamma\{2\sigma_k(x)_1 + c_A\varepsilon + c_A\|A^T(Ax - y)\|_\infty\}$$
$$\leq 2\gamma\{\sigma_k(x)_1 + c_A\varepsilon\}. \tag{5.47}$$

(ii) *Every matrix property listed in Corollary 5.5.3 are sufficient to ensure that the problem (5.4) is table, i.e., for any $x$ obeying $\|A^T(Ax - y)\|_\infty \leq \varepsilon$, there is a solution $x^*$ of (5.4) such that (5.47) holds.*

Item (i) above indicates that the weak RSP of $A^T$ is a sufficient condition for the standard DS to be stable in sparse signal recovery. In the next chapter, we prove that this condition is also a necessary condition for the standard DS to be stable. Item (ii) above indicates that the error bound (5.47) holds under any of the conditions named in Corollary 5.5.3. Letting $\alpha = 0$ and $M = A$, the stability theorem for (5.31), which is similar to Corollary 5.6.1, can be immediately obtained from Theorem 5.5.2 as well. Such a result is omitted here.

### 5.6.2 Weighted Dantzig Selector

When the matrix $A$ does not satisfy a desired matrix property, such as the RIP, NSP, RSP or REC, a scaled version of this matrix, i.e., $AU$, where $U$ is a non-singular matrix, might admit a desired property. This phenomenon has been observed through scaled mutual coherence in Chapter 1. This partially explains why a weighted $\ell_1$-minimization algorithm (e.g., [53, 246, 245]) often numerically outperforms the standard $\ell_1$-minimization in sparse signal recovery. The stability theorem in this chapter can be easily generalized to the weighted $\ell_1$-minimization problems. Take the following weighted DS as an example:

$$\min\{\|Wx\|_1 : \|A^T(Ax - y)\|_\infty \leq \varepsilon\}, \tag{5.48}$$

where $W$ is a nonsingular diagonal matrix. Is this problem stable in sparse data recovery? With transformation $u = Wx$, this problem can be written as

$$\min\{\|u\|_1 : \ \|A^T(AW^{-1}u - y)\|_\infty \leq \varepsilon\},$$

which is in the form

$$\min\{\|u\|_1 : \ \|M^T(\widetilde{A}u - y)\|_\infty \leq \varepsilon\}$$

with $\widetilde{A} = AW^{-1}$ and $M = A$. Thus it is straightforward to extend the stability results in this chapter to the weighted DS (5.48) under the weak RSP assumption on the scaled matrix $\widetilde{A} = AW^{-1}$.

### 5.6.3 $\ell_1$-Minimization with $\ell_\infty$-Norm Constraints

The standard $\ell_1$-minimization only applies to the case when the measurements of a signal are accurate. However, the practical measurements are usually inaccurate. Thus the measurements $y$ for the sparse data $\widehat{x} \in \mathbb{R}^n$ are given as $y = A\widehat{x} + u$, where $u$ denotes the noise or error satisfying $\phi(u) \leq \varepsilon$ for some norm $\phi(\cdot)$ and noise level $\varepsilon > 0$. Letting $\alpha = 1$ and $M = I$ in (5.1), we obtain the model

$$\min\{\|x\|_1 : \ \|Ax - y\|_\infty \leq \varepsilon\}. \tag{5.49}$$

This problem is referred to as the $\ell_1$-minimization problem with $\ell_\infty$-norm constraint. Since it is a special case of (5.1), the stability result for (5.49) follows directly from Theorem 5.5.2 by simply setting $M = I$ and $\alpha = 0$. Note that when $M = I$, the constant $\widehat{c}$ in Theorem 5.5.2 is reduced to

$$c^* = \|(AA^T)^{-1}A\|_{\infty \to 1}. \tag{5.50}$$

**Theorem 5.6.2** *Let A be an $m \times n$ matrix with $m < n$ and $rank(A) = m$. Suppose that $A^T$ satisfy the weak RSP of order k. Then for any $x \in \mathbb{R}^n$, there is a solution $x^*$ of the problem (5.49) such that*

$$\|x - x^*\|_2 \leq \gamma_1 \left\{ 2\sigma_k(x)_1 + (\|Ax - y\|_\infty - \varepsilon)^+ + c^*\varepsilon + c^*\|Ax - y\|_\infty \right\},$$

*where the constant $c^*$ is given by (5.50), and $\gamma_1 = \sigma_{\infty,2}(M^{(1)}, M^{(2)})$ is the Robinson's constant determined by a pair of matrices $(M^{(1)}, M^{(2)})$ which rely only on the problem data $(A, y, \varepsilon)$. In particular, for any $x$ with $\|Ax - y\|_\infty \leq \varepsilon$, there is a solution $x^*$ of (5.49) such that*

$$\|x - x^*\|_2 \leq 2\gamma_1 \{\sigma_k(x)_1 + c^*\varepsilon\}.$$

Although this theorem is obtained from Theorem 5.5.2 straightaway, the linear structure of (5.49) allows this theorem to be directly established as that of

Theorem 5.5.2. Let us roughly outline the key ingredients which can be used to prove this theorem directly. The problem (5.49) can be written as

$$\min_{(x,t)} \left\{ e^T t : \ -x+t \geq 0, \ x+t \geq 0, \ t \geq 0, \ -\varepsilon e \leq Ax - y \leq \varepsilon e \right\}, \qquad (5.51)$$

to which the dual problem is given as

$$\max_{(u,v,w,w')} \ (y - \varepsilon e)^T w - (y + \varepsilon e)^T w'$$

$$\text{s.t.} \quad u + v \leq e, \ A^T (w - w') = u - v,$$
$$(u, v, w, w') \geq 0.$$

Clearly, $x^*$ is a solution to the problem (5.49) if and only if $(x^*, t^*)$, where $t^* = |x^*|$, is a solution to the problem (5.51). By the optimality condition (5.51), we may characterize the solution set of (5.49) as follows.

**Lemma 5.6.3** $x^*$ *is a solution to the problem (5.49) if and only if there are vectors* $t^*, u^*, v^*$ *in* $\mathbb{R}^n_+$ *and* $w^*, w'^*$ *in* $\mathbb{R}^m_+$ *such that* $(x^*, t^*, u^*, v^*, w^*, w'^*) \in T^\infty$, *where* $T^\infty$ *is the set of points* $(x, t, u, v, w, w')$ *satisfying the following system:*

$$\begin{cases} -x+t \geq 0, \ x+t \geq 0, \ -\varepsilon e \leq Ax - y \leq \varepsilon e, \\ A^T (w - w') = u - v, \ u + v \leq e, \\ e^T t = (y - \varepsilon e)^T w - (y + \varepsilon e)^T w', \\ (t, u, v, w, w') \geq 0. \end{cases}$$

*For any point* $(x, t, u, v, w, w') \in T^\infty$, *it must hold that* $t = |x|$.

The set $T^\infty$ can be written in the form

$$T^\infty = \{ z = (x, t, u, v, w, w') : \ M^{(1)} z \leq b^{(1)}, \ M^{(2)} z = b^{(2)} \},$$

where $b^{(1)} = (0, 0, y + \varepsilon e, \varepsilon e - y, 0, e, 0, 0, 0)$, $b^{(2)} = 0$, and

$$M^{(1)} = \begin{bmatrix} I & -I & 0 & 0 & 0 & 0 \\ -I & -I & 0 & 0 & 0 & 0 \\ A & 0 & 0 & 0 & 0 & 0 \\ -A & 0 & 0 & 0 & 0 & 0 \\ 0 & -I & 0 & 0 & 0 & 0 \\ 0 & 0 & I & I & 0 & 0 \\ 0 & 0 & 0 & 0 & -I_m & 0 \\ 0 & 0 & 0 & 0 & 0 & -I_m \\ 0 & 0 & -I & 0 & 0 & 0 \\ 0 & 0 & & -I & 0 & 0 \end{bmatrix}, \qquad (5.52)$$

$$M^{(2)} = \begin{bmatrix} 0 & 0 & -I & I & A^T & -A^T \\ 0 & e^T & 0 & 0 & -(y - \varepsilon e)^T & (y + \varepsilon e)^T \end{bmatrix}, \qquad (5.53)$$

where $I$ and $I_m$ are $n$- and $m$-dimensional identity matrices, respectively. By using the Robinson's constant $\gamma_1 = \sigma_{\infty,2}(M^{(1)}, M^{(2)})$ where the matrices are given in (5.52) and (5.53), applying Lemma 5.2.2, and following a proof similar to that of Theorem 5.5.2, we can prove Theorem 5.6.2 directly. A detailed proof can be found in Zhao, Jiang and Luo [244].

### 5.6.4 $\ell_1$-Minimization with $\ell_1$-Norm Constraints

For the problem with $\ell_1$-norm constraint

$$\min_x \{\|x\|_1 : \|Ax - y\|_1 \leq \varepsilon\}, \tag{5.54}$$

we can immediately obtain the next result from Theorem 5.5.2.

**Theorem 5.6.4** *Let $A \in \mathbb{R}^{m \times n}$ with $m < n$ and rank$(A) = m$. Let $A^T$ satisfy the weak RSP of order $k$. Then for any $x \in \mathbb{R}^n$, there is a solution $x^*$ of (5.54) such that*

$$\|x - x^*\|_2 \leq \gamma_2 \left\{ 2\sigma_k(x)_1 + (\|Ax - y\|_1 - \varepsilon)^+ + c^*(\varepsilon + \|Ax - y\|_1) \right\},$$

*where $c^*$ is given by (5.50), and $\gamma_2 = \sigma_{\infty,2}(M^*, M^{**})$ is the Robinson's constant determined by a certain pair of $(M^*, M^{**})$ relying only on the problem data $(A, y, \varepsilon)$. In particular, for any $x$ with $\|Ax - y\|_1 \leq \varepsilon$, there is a solution $x^*$ of (5.54) such that*

$$\|x - x^*\|_2 \leq 2\gamma_2 \{\sigma_k(x)_1 + c^*\varepsilon\}.$$

This theorem follows from Theorem 5.5.2 straightaway. It can be also shown directly by using its own linear structure and a proof similar to that of Theorem 5.5.2. Note that the problem (5.54) is equivalent to

$$\min_{(x,r)} \left\{ \|x\|_1 : |Ax - y| \leq r, \; e^T r \leq \varepsilon, \; r \in \mathbb{R}^m_+ \right\}. \tag{5.55}$$

It is evident that $x^*$ is a solution of the problem (5.54) if and only if there is a vector $r^*$ such that $(x^*, r^*)$ is a solution to the problem (5.55), which can be written as the linear program

$$\min_{(x,t,r)} \quad e^T t$$

$$\text{s.t.} \quad x \leq t, \; -x \leq t, \; Ax - y \leq r, \; -Ax + y \leq r \tag{5.56}$$

$$e^T r \leq \varepsilon, \; t \geq 0, \; r \geq 0,$$

to which the dual problem is given as follows:

$$\max \quad -y^T(v_3 - v_4) - \varepsilon v_5$$

$$\text{s.t} \quad A^T(v_3 - v_4) + v_1 - v_2 = 0,$$

$$v_3 + v_4 \leq v_5 e,$$

$$v_1 + v_2 \leq e,$$

$$v_i \geq 0, \; i = 1, \ldots, 5,$$

where $v_1, v_2 \in \mathbb{R}^n_+, v_3, v_4 \in \mathbb{R}^m_+$, and $v_5 \in \mathbb{R}_+$. By the optimality condition of (5.56), the solution set of (5.54) can be characterized as follows.

**Lemma 5.6.5** *$x^*$ is a solution to the problem (5.54) if and only if there are vectors $t^*, v_1^*, v_2^* \in \mathbb{R}^n_+, v_3^*, v_4^*, r^* \in \mathbb{R}^m_+$ and $v_5^* \in \mathbb{R}_+$ such that $(x^*, t^*, r^*, v_1^*, \ldots, v_5^*) \in T^{(1)}$, where $T^{(1)}$ is the set of points $(x, t, r, v_1, \ldots, v_5)$ satisfying*

$$
\begin{cases}
x \le t, \ -x \le t, \ Ax - r \le y, \ -Ax - r \le -y, \\
\mathbf{e}^T r \le \varepsilon, \ A^T (v_3 - v_4) + v_1 - v_2 = 0, \\
v_3 + v_4 - v_5 \mathbf{e} \le 0, \ v_1 + v_2 \le \mathbf{e}, \\
\mathbf{e}^T t = -y^T (v_3 - v_4) - v_5 \varepsilon, \\
v_i \ge 0, \ i = 1, \ldots, 5, \\
(r, t) \ge 0.
\end{cases}
\tag{5.57}
$$

*Moreover, for any $(x, t, r, v_1, \ldots, v_5) \in T^{(1)}$, it must hold that $t = |x|$.*

The set $T^{(1)}$ can be represented as follows:

$$
T^{(1)} = \{ z = (x, t, r, v_1, \ldots, v_5) : \ M^* z \le b^*, \ M^{**} z = b^{**} \},
$$

where $b^{**} = 0$, $b^*$ is a vector consisting of $0, y, -y, \mathbf{e}$ and $\varepsilon$, The matrix $M^*$ captures all coefficients of the inequalities in (5.57), and $M^{**}$ is the matrix capturing all coefficients of the equalities in (5.57). $M^*$ and $M^{**}$ depend only on the problem data $(A, y, \varepsilon)$, and are omitted here. Theorem 5.6.4 can be shown directly by a proof similar to that of Theorem 5.5.2. The detailed and direct proof has been provided in [244]. We close this section by stating a unified result for the $\ell_1$-minimization problems with $\ell_\infty$- and $\ell_1$-norm constraints, respectively.

**Corollary 5.6.6** *Let the problem data $(A, y, \varepsilon)$ be given, where $A \in \mathbb{R}^{m \times n}$ with $m < n$ and $\text{rank}(A) = m$. Let $c^*$ be the constant given in (5.50), and let $\gamma_1$ and $\gamma_2$ be the Robinson's constants given in Theorems 5.6.2 and 5.6.4, respectively. Suppose that the solutions to (5.49) and (5.54) are unique. If $A$ satisfies one of the conditions $(c^1)$–$(c^7)$ in Corollary 5.4.5, then the following statements hold true:*

*(i) For any x satisfying $\|Ax - y\|_\infty \le \varepsilon$, the solution $x^*$ of (5.49) approximates x with error*

$$
\|x - x^*\|_2 \le 2\gamma_1 \{ \sigma_k(x)_1 + c^* \varepsilon \}.
$$

*(ii) For any x satisfying $\|Ax - y\|_1 \le \varepsilon$, the solution $x^\#$ of (5.54) approximates x with error*

$$
\|x - x^\#\|_2 \le 2\gamma_2 \{ \sigma_k(x)_1 + c^* \varepsilon \}.
$$

A difference between the stability results in this chapter and the traditional ones in the literature is that the recovery error bounds in this chapter are measured by Robinson's constants instead of the conventional RIP, NSP, ERC or other constants. Also, each of the matrix properties $(c^1)$–$(c^7)$ in Corollary 5.4.5 implies an identical stability result. From this point of view, the notion of weak RSP provides a unified means to the study of stability of linear sparse optimization problems, alleviating the effort of traditional analysis which was carried out differently from assumption to assumption and from problem to problem. The analysis made in this chapter indicates that Hoffman's Lemma with sparsity assumption provides an efficient way to interpret the sparse-signal-recovery behaviour of the $\ell_1$-minimization method. This analytic method can be also extended to nonlinear sparse optimization problems, including the LASSO [207, 128] and the nonlinear Dantzig Selector. This will be discussed in the upcoming chapter.

## 5.7 Notes

Lemma 5.2.2, known as Hoffman's Lemma, was first proved by Hoffman in [133]. Similar error bounds appeared in Rosenbloom [194]. Section 5.2 follows the idea of the paper [192] by Robinson. Hoffman's Lemma has found many applications in mathematical optimization (see Güler [123], Güler et al. [124], and Luo, Pang, and Ralph [163]). In this and next chapters, Hoffman's Lemma, combined with sparsity assumption, is used to establish the unified stability theorems for several linear and nonlinear sparse optimization methods.

The stability of sparse recovery methods has been widely investigated under various conditions, such as the mutual coherence, RIP, NSP, stable or the robust stable NSP. A good summary of stability results under these conditions can be found in Foucart and Rauhut [108, 105]. Different from these results, the stability theorems discussed in this chapter were developed under the *weak RSP of order k of $A^T$*, which was introduced by Zhao, Jiang and Luo in [244]. The classic KKT optimality conditions provide a fundamental tool for understanding the internal mechanism of the $\ell_1$-minimization method. The weak RSP of $A^T$ results from strengthening the KKT optimality conditions for $\ell_1$-minimization problems in order to achieve a stable recovery of sparse vectors. Clearly, no matter which (deterministic or random) matrices are used, the weak RSP of $A^T$ and its slightly stronger version, namely, the RSP of order $k$ of $A^T$, are the desired matrix properties regarding the success and stableness of $\ell_1$-minimization methods in sparse vector recovery. As shown by Corollary 5.5.3, the weak RSP of $A^T$ cannot be relaxed without damaging the stability of $\ell_1$-minimization, since this property is a necessary and sufficient condition for standard $\ell_1$-minimization to be stable for any given measurement vector $y \in \{Ax : \|x\|_0 \leq k\}$. Developing unified stability theorems for some sparse optimization methods by using Hoffman's Lemma and the notion of weak RSP of order $k$ of $A^T$ was carried out by Zhao et al. in [244, 248]. Theorems 5.4.1 and 5.4.3, including Corollaries 5.4.4 and 5.4.5, were taken from [244]. The stability of $\ell_1$-minimization methods under the ERC of order $k$, given in Corollary 5.4.5, was first pointed out in this chapter. The stable recovery via the standard DS was analyzed by Candès and Tao in [47, 46]. It was shown in [47, 46] that if $A$ satisfies the RIP of order $2k$ with $\delta_{2k} < \sqrt{2} - 1$, then the solution $x^*$ of the standard DS approximates the vector $x$ satisfying $y = Ax + u$ where $\|A^T u\|_\infty \le \varepsilon$ with error

$$\|x - x^*\|_2 \le \frac{C}{\sqrt{k}} \sigma_k(x)_1 + D\sqrt{k}\varepsilon.$$

where $C$ and $D$ are constants depending only on $\delta_{2k}$. The stable recovery under the weak RSP of $A^T$ given in Theorem 5.5.2 was shown in [247] by Zhao and Li. When the RSP of $A^T$ is defined locally at a vector $x^*$, it is called the individual RSP of $A^T$ at $x^*$. This local property is essential to achieve a non-uniform recovery of the vector $x^*$. See Fuchs [111], Plumbley [189], Zhao [241, 242], and Foucart and Rauhut [108]. A stability analysis for $\ell_1$-minimization at an individual sparse vector was also discussed in Zhang and Yin [233], under an assumption equivalent to the individual RSP of $A^T$.

The existence of $A^T$ that satisfies the weak RSP of order $k$ can follow directly from the analysis for the existence of a RIP matrix. The existence of a RIP matrix was implied from the results shown by Candès and Tao [52]. For partial random Fourier matrices, they obtained the bound

$$m \ge Ck \ln^5(n) \ln(\zeta^{-1})$$

for the number of required measurements to achieve the RIP of order $k$ with probability $1 - \zeta$, where $C$ is a universal constant. This result was improved by several authors. See Rudelson and Vershynin [195], Rauhut [190], and Cheraghchi at al. [63]. The existence of a RIP matrix is also implied from the analysis for (sub) Gaussian and Bernoulli sensing matrices. The RIP of Gaussian matrices was first proved by Candès and Tao [52], and the RIP for subgaussian matrices were shown by Mendelson et al. [173] and Baraniuk et al. [17]. A typical result they proved for Gaussian matrices can be summarized as follows: Let A be an $m \times n (m \ll n)$ Gaussian random matrix. Then there exists a universal constant $C > 0$ such that the RIP constant of $A/\sqrt{m}$ satisfies $\delta_{2k} \le \tau$ (where $0 < \tau < 1$) with probability at least $1 - \zeta$ provided

$$m \ge C\tau^{-2} \left( k(1 + \ln(n/k)) + \ln(2\zeta^{-1}) \right). \tag{5.58}$$

Cai et al. [44] have shown that the RIP of order $2k$ with constant $\delta_{2k} < 1/\sqrt{2}$ guarantees the uniform recovery of every $k$-parse vector via $\ell_1$-minimization. Thus the condition $\delta_{2k} < 1/\sqrt{2}$ implies that $A^T$ must satisfy the RSP of order $k$, and hence $A^T$ satisfies the weak RSP of order $k$. Combining these facts and taking $\tau = 1/\sqrt{2}$ in (5.58), we can immediately make the following observation:

■ Let A be an $m \times n$ $(m \ll n)$ Gaussian random matrix. Then there exists a universal constant $C > 0$ such that $A^T/\sqrt{m}$ satisfies the weak RSP of order $k$ with probability at least $1 - \zeta$ provided

$$m \ge 2C \left( k(1 + \ln(n/k)) + \ln(2\zeta^{-1}) \right). \tag{5.59}$$

Combining Theorem 5.5.2 and the above observation leads to the following result in terms of random matrices:

■ Let A be an $m \times n$ $(m \ll n)$ Gaussian random matrix with full row rank, and let $y$ be a given vector in $\mathbb{R}^m$. Then there exists a universal constant $C > 0$ such that with probability at least $1 - \zeta$ the standard $\ell_1$-minimization, with matrix $A/\sqrt{m}$, is stable provided that (5.59) is satisfied.

Bandeira et al. [16] and Tillmann and Pfetsch [208] proved that the RIP and NSP is hard to certify. Note that the RSP of order $k$ of $A^T$ is equivalent to the NSP of order $k$ of $A$ and that the weak RSP of $A^T$ is a slightly relaxed version of the RSP of $A^T$. Thus the RSP or weak RSP is also difficult to certify, due to the hardness of certifying the NSP [16, 208]. How to deterministically construct a matrix satisfying the weak RSP (including the matrices satisfying the RIP, NSP or RSP) remains an open question in this field.

# Chapter 6

# Stability of Nonlinear Sparse Optimization Methods

In Chapter 5, the stability issue of linear sparse optimization methods was addressed under the so-called weak range space property of order $k$ of transposed sensing matrices. Nonlinear sparse optimization methods have also attracted plenty of attention in statistical learning, sparse data recovery and mathematical optimization. In this chapter, we extend the results established for linear sparse optimization to nonlinear sparse optimization methods under the same hypothesis. We prove that the weak RSP assumption is still sufficient to ensure that some nonlinear sparse optimization methods are stable in sparse data recovery, including $\ell_1$-minimization with an $\ell_2$-norm constraint, nonlinear Dantzig Selector (DS) and LASSO. A by-product of this investigation is a unified stability theorem for these nonlinear sparse optimization methods under various matrix properties, including the RIP condition $\delta_{2k} < 1/\sqrt{2}$, standard NSP of order $k$ and RSP of order $k$. The recovery error bounds for DS and LASSO are established in terms of the Robinson's constant, instead of the conventional RIP and NSP constants. Different from the standard tool used in this area, the analysis in this chapter is carried out deterministically, and the key analytic tools used here include the error bound for linear systems due to Hoffman [133] and Robinson [192] and the polytope approximation of the unit balls due to Dudley [92] and Barvinok [21]. It turns out that the weak RSP of order $k$ of $A^T$ is a necessary and sufficient condition for the linear DS being stable in sparse vector recovery. As a result, the weak RSP assumption cannot be relaxed for the standard $\ell_1$-minimization and the standard DS in order to guarantee the stable recovery of sparse vectors via these methods.

## 6.1 Introduction

We still use $\phi : \mathbb{R}^q \to \mathbb{R}_+$ to denote a general norm on $\mathbb{R}^q$ satisfying

$$\phi(\mathbf{e}^{(i)}) = 1 \text{ for all } i = 1, \ldots, q,$$

where $\mathbf{e}^{(i)} \in \mathbb{R}^q, i = 1, \ldots, q$ are the standard basis of $\mathbb{R}^q$, i.e., the column vectors of the $q \times q$ identity matrix. We still consider the $\ell_1$-minimization problem in the form

$$\min_{x}\{\|x\|_1 : \phi(M^T(Ax - y)) \le \varepsilon\}, \tag{6.1}$$

where $\varepsilon \ge 0$ is a given parameter and $y \in \mathbb{R}^m$ is a given vector. In this chapter, we focus on the nonlinear problem of the form (6.1), i.e., the norm $\phi$ is a nonlinear function, which cannot be represented as a finite number of linear constraints. Applying only to linear systems, Lemma 5.2.2 cannot be used directly to develop the recovery error bounds for nonlinear sparse optimization problems.

In this chapter, we still consider the matrices $A \in \mathbb{R}^{m \times n}$ $(m < n)$ and $M \in \mathbb{R}^{m \times q}$ $(m \le q)$ with $\text{rank}(A) = \text{rank}(M) = m$. The problem (6.1) includes several special cases. When $\varepsilon > 0$, $M = I$ and $\phi(\cdot) = \|\cdot\|_2$, the problem (6.1) becomes

$$\min_{x}\{\|x\|_1 : \|Ax - y\|_2 \le \varepsilon\},$$

which is referred to as the $\ell_1$-minimization with an $\ell_2$-norm constraint. This method has been widely studied in the field of compressed sensing [62, 82, 95, 97, 108]. Taking $M = A$ in (6.1) leads to the problem

$$\min_{x}\{\|x\|_1 : \phi(A^T(Ax - y)) \le \varepsilon\}, \tag{6.2}$$

which is still called the Dantzig Selector (DS) although it is more general than the standard one. Here the constraint is nonlinear in the sense that it cannot be represented as the linear constraint, for instance, $\phi = \|\cdot\|_p$ with $p \in (1, \infty)$.

Closely related to (6.1) is the following minimization problem:

$$\min_{x}\{\phi(M^T(Ax - y)) : \|x\|_1 \le \mu\}, \tag{6.3}$$

where $\mu$ is a given parameter. This problem also includes several important special cases. When $M = I$ and $\phi(\cdot) = \|\cdot\|_2$, the problem (6.3) is the well known LASSO (least absolute shrinkage and selection operator) problem introduced by Tibshirani [207]:

$$\min_{x}\{\|Ax - y\|_2 : \|x\|_1 \le \mu\}. \tag{6.4}$$

In addition, setting $M = A$ in (6.3) yields the model

$$\min_{x}\{\phi(A^T(Ax - y)) : \|x\|_1 \le \mu\}, \tag{6.5}$$

which is closely related to the DS problem (6.2). In this chapter, the problem (6.3) is also called an LASSO problem despite the fact that it is more general than (6.4) and (6.5).

To recover the sparse vector $\widehat{x}$ satisfying $\phi(M^T(A\widehat{x}-y)) \leq \varepsilon$, the problem (6.1) seeks the $\ell_1$-minimizer $x$ that complies with the bound $\phi(M^T(Ax-y)) \leq \varepsilon$, while the problem (6.3) minimizes the error $\phi(M^T(Ax-y))$ by assuming that the recovered data $x$ and the original data $\widehat{x}$ obey the same $\ell_1$-norm bound. The purpose of the stability analysis for sparse optimization methods is to check whether the difference between the original data and the found solution of a recovery method can stay under control under some conditions.

A typical feature of the current stability theory for DS and LASSO is that the constants in error bounds are usually measured by the conventional RIP, REC or other individual matrix constants. In this traditional framework, different matrix assumptions require distinct analysis and yield different stability constants determined by the assumed matrix conditions, such as the RIP, NSP and REC constants. The purpose of this chapter is to develop certain unified stability results for the general problems (6.1) and (6.3) under a mild constant-free matrix condition. In fact, it turns out that this assumption is both necessary and sufficient for the standard DS to be stable in sparse data recovery, and thus it cannot be relaxed without affecting the stability of the DS method. This matrix condition was described in Definition 5.1.1.

For the LASSO-type problem (6.3), we introduce the following definition.

**Corollary 6.1.1** *Let $\widehat{x}$ be the original data obeying the constraint of (6.3). The problem (6.3) is said to be stable in sparse data recovery if there is a solution $x^*$ of (6.3) approximating $\widehat{x}$ with error*

$$\|\widehat{x}-x^*\|_2 \leq C_1\sigma_k(\widehat{x})_1 + C_2(\mu - \|\widehat{x}\|_1) + C_3\mu\phi(M^T(A\widehat{x}-y)),$$

*where $C_1, C_2$ and $C_3$ are three constants depending only on the problem data $(M,A,y,\mu)$.*

This chapter is organized as follows. In Section 6.2, we provide some useful properties of the orthogonal projection operator. In Section 6.3, we discuss the polytope approximation of the unit ball. In Section 6.4, we show that the weak RSP condition is necessary for many sparse optimization methods to be stable in sparse vector recovery. In Sections 6.5–6.7, we show that the weak RSP condition ensures the stableness of the $\ell_1$-minimization with an $\ell_2$-norm constraint, nonlinear DS, and LASSO. All discussions are carried out under the same assumption, i.e., the weak RSP of $A^T$.

## 6.2 Orthogonal Projection Operator

Let us first recall the Hausdorff matric. Given two sets $\Omega_1, \Omega_2 \subseteq \mathbb{R}^m$, we use $d^{\mathcal{H}}(\Omega_1, \Omega_2)$ to denote the Hausdorff distance of $(\Omega_1, \Omega_2)$, i.e.,

$$d^{\mathcal{H}}(\Omega_1, \Omega_2) = \max \left\{ \sup_{u \in \Omega_1} \inf_{z \in \Omega_2} \|u - z\|_2, \ \sup_{z \in \Omega_2} \inf_{u \in \Omega_1} \|u - z\|_2 \right\}. \quad (6.6)$$

Given a closed convex set $\Omega \subseteq \mathbb{R}^n$, let $\Pi_\Omega(x)$ denote the orthogonal projection of $x \in \mathbb{R}^n$ into $\Omega$, i.e.,

$$\Pi_\Omega(x) := \arg\min_u \{ \|x - u\|_2 : \ u \in \Omega \}.$$

$\Pi_\Omega(\cdot)$ is called the orthogonal projection operator. We now provide a few inequalities concerning the projection operator. These inequalities are of independent interest and will be used in our later analysis.

**Lemma 6.2.1** *Let $\Omega$ and $T$ be compact convex sets in $\mathbb{R}^n$. Then for any $x \in \mathbb{R}^n$,*

$$\|\Pi_\Omega(x) - \Pi_T(x)\|_2^2 \leq d^{\mathcal{H}}(\Omega, T)(\|x - \Pi_\Omega(x)\|_2 + \|x - \Pi_T(x)\|_2).$$

*Proof.* By the property of the projection operator, we have

$$(x - \Pi_\Omega(x))^T (v - \Pi_\Omega(x)) \leq 0 \text{ for all } v \in \Omega, \quad (6.7)$$

$$(x - \Pi_T(x))^T (u - \Pi_T(x)) \leq 0 \text{ for all } u \in T. \quad (6.8)$$

We project $\Pi_T(x) \in T$ into $\Omega$ to obtain the point $\widehat{v} = \Pi_\Omega(\Pi_T(x)) \in \Omega$ and $\Pi_\Omega(x) \in \Omega$ into $T$ to obtain the point $\widehat{u} = \Pi_T(\Pi_\Omega(x)) \in T$. By the definition of Hausdorff metric, we have

$$\|\widehat{v} - \Pi_T(x)\|_2 \leq d^{\mathcal{H}}(\Omega, T), \quad (6.9)$$

$$\|\widehat{u} - \Pi_\Omega(x)\|_2 \leq d^{\mathcal{H}}(\Omega, T). \quad (6.10)$$

Substituting $\widehat{v}$ into (6.7) and $\widehat{u}$ into (6.8), respectively, yields

$$(x - \Pi_\Omega(x))^T (\widehat{v} - \Pi_\Omega(x)) \leq 0, \quad (6.11)$$

$$(x - \Pi_T(x))^T (\widehat{u} - \Pi_T(x)) \leq 0. \quad (6.12)$$

Note that

$$
\begin{aligned}
&\|\Pi_\Omega(x) - \Pi_T(x)\|_2^2 \\
&= (\Pi_\Omega(x) - x + x - \Pi_T(x))^T (\Pi_\Omega(x) - \Pi_T(x)) \\
&= (\Pi_\Omega(x) - x)^T (\Pi_\Omega(x) - \Pi_T(x)) + (x - \Pi_T(x))^T (\Pi_\Omega(x) - \Pi_T(x))
\end{aligned}
$$

$$(6.13)$$

Thus, by (6.11) and (6.12), it follows from (6.13) that

$$\|\Pi_\Omega(x) - \Pi_T(x)\|_2^2$$
$$\leq (\Pi_\Omega(x) - x)^T (\hat{v} - \Pi_T(x)) + (x - \Pi_T(x))^T (\Pi_\Omega(x) - \hat{u})$$
$$\leq \|x - \Pi_\Omega(x)\|_2 \|\Pi_T(x) - \hat{v}\|_2 + \|x - \Pi_T(x)\|_2 \|\Pi_\Omega(x) - \hat{u}\|_2$$
$$\leq d^{\mathcal{H}}(\Omega, T)(\|x - \Pi_\Omega(x)\|_2 + \|x - \Pi_T(x)\|_2),$$

where the last inequality follows from (6.9) and (6.10). □

The next lemma plays an important role in the stability analysis of nonlinear sparse optimization methods.

**Lemma 6.2.2** (i) *Let $\Omega \subseteq T$ be two compact convex sets in $\mathbb{R}^n$. Then for any $x \in \mathbb{R}^n$,*

$$\|\Pi_\Omega(x) - \Pi_T(x)\|_2^2 \leq d^{\mathcal{H}}(\Omega, T)\|x - \Pi_\Omega(x)\|_2. \tag{6.14}$$

(ii) *Let $\Omega, U, T$ be three compact convex sets in $\mathbb{R}^n$ satisfying $\Omega \subseteq T$ and $U \subseteq T$. Then for any $x \in \mathbb{R}^n$ and any $u \in U$,*

$$\|x - \Pi_\Omega(x)\|_2 \leq d^{\mathcal{H}}(\Omega, T) + 2\|x - u\|_2, \tag{6.15}$$

*and for any $x \in \mathbb{R}^n$ and any $v \in \Omega$,*

$$\|x - \Pi_U(x)\|_2 \leq d^{\mathcal{H}}(U, T) + 2\|x - v\|_2. \tag{6.16}$$

*Proof.* By the definition of projection operator, the inequalities (6.7) and (6.8) hold trues. Since $\Pi_\Omega(x) \in \Omega \subseteq T$ and $\Pi_\Omega(\Pi_T(x)) \in \Omega$, substituting $u = \Pi_\Omega(x) \in T$ in (6.8), and letting $v = \Pi_\Omega(\Pi_T(x))$ in (6.7), we immediately have

$$(x - \Pi_T(x))^T (\Pi_\Omega(x) - \Pi_T(x)) \leq 0, \tag{6.17}$$

$$(x - \Pi_\Omega(x))^T (\Pi_\Omega(\Pi_T(x)) - \Pi_\Omega(x)) \leq 0. \tag{6.18}$$

Since $\Omega \subseteq T$ and $\Pi_T(x) \in T$, by the definition of Hausdorff metric, we have

$$d^{\mathcal{H}}(\Omega, T) = \sup_{w \in T} \inf_{z \in \Omega} \|w - z\|_2$$
$$\geq \inf_{z \in \Omega} \|\Pi_T(x) - z\|_2$$
$$= \|\Pi_T(x) - \Pi_\Omega(\Pi_T(x))\|_2. \tag{6.19}$$

By (6.17), (6.18) and (6.19), it follows from (6.13) that

$$\|\Pi_\Omega(x) - \Pi_T(x)\|_2^2$$
$$\leq (\Pi_\Omega(x) - x)^T (\Pi_\Omega(x) - \Pi_T(x))$$
$$= (\Pi_\Omega(x) - x)^T [\Pi_\Omega(x) - \Pi_\Omega(\Pi_T(x)) + \Pi_\Omega(\Pi_T(x)) - \Pi_T(x)]$$
$$\leq (\Pi_\Omega(x) - x)^T [\Pi_\Omega(\Pi_T(x)) - \Pi_T(x)]$$
$$\leq \|x - \Pi_\Omega(x)\|_2 \|\Pi_\Omega(\Pi_T(x)) - \Pi_T(x)\|_2$$
$$\leq d^{\mathcal{H}}(\Omega, T)\|x - \Pi_\Omega(x)\|_2.$$

Thus (6.14) holds. We now prove (6.15). For any $u \in U \subseteq T$, we clearly have

$$\|x - \Pi_T(x)\|_2 \leq \|x - u\|_2.$$

Thus by (6.14) and triangle inequality, we have

$$
\begin{aligned}
\|x - \Pi_\Omega(x)\|_2 &\leq \|x - \Pi_T(x)\|_2 + \|\Pi_T(x) - \Pi_\Omega(x)\|_2 \\
&\leq \|x - u\|_2 + \sqrt{d^{\mathcal{H}}(\Omega, T)\|x - \Pi_\Omega(x)\|_2} \quad (6.20)
\end{aligned}
$$

for any $x \in \mathbb{R}^n$ and $u \in U$. Note that the quadratic equation $t^2 - \beta t - \alpha = 0$ in $t$, where $\alpha \geq 0$ and $\beta \geq 0$, has a unique non-negative root

$$t^* = \frac{\beta + \sqrt{\beta^2 + 4\alpha}}{2}.$$

Thus for any $t \geq 0$ such that $t^2 - \beta t - \alpha \leq 0$, it must imply that

$$t \leq t^* = \frac{\beta + \sqrt{\beta^2 + 4\alpha}}{2}.$$

Therefore by setting

$$t = \sqrt{\|x - \Pi_\Omega(x)\|_2}, \ \alpha = \|x - u\|_2 \ \text{and} \ \beta = \sqrt{d^{\mathcal{H}}(\Omega, T)},$$

it immediately follows from (6.20) that

$$\sqrt{\|x - \Pi_\Omega(x)\|_2} \leq \frac{\sqrt{d^{\mathcal{H}}(\Omega, T)} + \sqrt{d^{\mathcal{H}}(\Omega, T) + 4\|x - u\|_2}}{2}.$$

Note that $(t_1 + t_2)^2 \leq 2(t_1^2 + t_2^2)$ for any real numbers $t_1$ and $t_2$. The above inequality implies that

$$
\begin{aligned}
\|x - \Pi_\Omega(x)\|_2 &\leq \left( \frac{\sqrt{d^{\mathcal{H}}(\Omega, T)} + \sqrt{d^{\mathcal{H}}(\Omega, T) + 4\|x - u\|_2}}{2} \right)^2 \\
&\leq \frac{2\{d^{\mathcal{H}}(\Omega, T) + (d^{\mathcal{H}}(\Omega, T) + 4\|x - u\|_2)\}}{4} \\
&= d^{\mathcal{H}}(\Omega, T) + 2\|x - u\|_2.
\end{aligned}
$$

Since (6.15) is symmetric in the sense that the roles of $U$ and $\Omega$ can be interchanged, the inequality (6.16) follows immediately. $\square$

In particular, letting $u = \Pi_U(x)$ in (6.15), we also obtain the inequalities

$$\|x - \Pi_\Omega(x)\|_2 \leq d^{\mathcal{H}}(\Omega, T) + 2\|x - \Pi_U(x)\|_2,$$

$$\|x - \Pi_U(x)\|_2 \leq d^{\mathcal{H}}(U, T) + 2\|x - \Pi_\Omega(x)\|_2$$

for any compact convex sets $\Omega, U \subseteq T$.

## 6.3   Polytope Approximation of Unit Balls

In this section, we introduce the classic Dudley's theorem concerning the approximation of the unit $\ell_2$-ball. We also introduce the Barvinok's Theorem concerning the polytope approximation of symmetric convex bodies, including the unit ball defined by a general norm.

### *6.3.1   $\ell_2$-Ball*

The unit $\ell_2$-ball in $\mathbb{R}^m$

$$\mathfrak{B} = \{z \in \mathbb{R}^m : \|z\|_2 \leq 1\}$$

is the intersection of the half spaces $\{z : a^T z \leq 1\}$ which are tangent to the surface of $\mathfrak{B}$, i.e.,

$$\mathfrak{B} = \bigcap_{\|a\|_2 = 1} \{z \in \mathbb{R}^m : a^T z \leq 1\}. \tag{6.21}$$

Any finite number of half spaces in (6.21) yields a polytope approximation of the unit ball $\mathfrak{B}$ in $\mathbb{R}^m$. Dudley [92] established the following result.

**Lemma 6.3.1** (Dudley [92]) *There exists a constant $\tau$ such that for every integer number $\kappa > m$ there is a polytope*

$$\mathcal{P}_\kappa = \bigcap_{\|a^i\|_2 = 1, 1 \leq i \leq \kappa} \{z \in \mathbb{R}^m : (a^i)^T z \leq 1\} \tag{6.22}$$

*containing $\mathfrak{B}$ in $\mathbb{R}^m$ and satisfying*

$$d^{\mathcal{H}}(\mathfrak{B}, \mathcal{P}_\kappa) \leq \frac{\tau}{\kappa^{2/(m-1)}}, \tag{6.23}$$

*where $d^{\mathcal{H}}(\cdot, \cdot)$ is the Hausdorff metric defined by (6.6).*

A detailed discussion on the Dudley's polytope approximation of $\mathfrak{B}$ can be found in Cheang and Barron [59] and Dudley's original paper [92]. The above lemma claims that the polytope $\mathcal{P}_\kappa$ can approximate $\mathfrak{B}$ to any level of accuracy provided that $\kappa$ is large enough. For $\mathcal{P}_\kappa$ given by (6.22), we use

$$\Gamma_{\mathcal{P}_\kappa} := [a^1, \ldots, a^\kappa]$$

to denote the $m \times \kappa$ matrix with $a^i \in \mathbb{R}^m$, $i = 1, \ldots, \kappa$ as its column vectors. We also use the symbol

$$\text{Col}(\Gamma_{\mathcal{P}_\kappa}) = \{a^1, a^2, \ldots, a^\kappa\}$$

to denote the set of column vectors of $\Gamma_{\mathcal{P}_\kappa}$. Thus in terms of $\Gamma_{\mathcal{P}_\kappa}$, the polytope $\mathcal{P}_\kappa$ can be written as follows:

$$\mathcal{P}_\kappa = \{z \in \mathbb{R}^m : (\Gamma_{\mathcal{P}_\kappa})^T z \leq \mathbf{e}\},$$

where $\mathbf{e}$ is the vector of ones in $\mathbb{R}^\kappa$. Let $\{\mathcal{P}_\kappa\}_{\kappa>m}$ be the polytopes given in (6.22) and satisfying (6.23). We may construct the sequence of polytopes $\{\widetilde{\mathcal{P}}_J\}_{J>m}$ as follows:

$$\widetilde{\mathcal{P}}_J = \bigcap_{m<\kappa\leq J} \mathcal{P}_\kappa. \tag{6.24}$$

Thus for every $J > m$, $\widetilde{\mathcal{P}}_J$ is still a polytope formed by a finite number of half spaces in the form $(a^i)^T z \leq 1$ where $\|a^i\|_2 = 1$. We still use $\Gamma_{\widetilde{\mathcal{P}}_J}$ to denote the matrix with these vectors $a^i$'s as its column vectors and $\mathrm{Col}(\Gamma_{\widetilde{\mathcal{P}}_J})$ to denote the collection of the column vectors of $\Gamma_{\widetilde{\mathcal{P}}_J}$. Thus,

$$\widetilde{\mathcal{P}}_J = \{z \in \mathbb{R}^m : (\Gamma_{\widetilde{\mathcal{P}}_J})^T z \leq \mathbf{e}\}, \tag{6.25}$$

where $\mathbf{e}$ is the vector of ones with dimension equal to the cardinality of $\mathrm{Col}(\Gamma_{\widetilde{\mathcal{P}}_J})$. The following property of this polytope is useful in later analysis.

**Lemma 6.3.2** *Let $\{\mathcal{P}_\kappa\}_{\kappa>m}$ be any sequence of the polytopes given in (6.22) and satisfying (6.23). For any $J > m$, let $\widetilde{\mathcal{P}}_J$ be given in (6.24). Then for any point $z \in \{z \in \mathbb{R}^m : \|z\|_2 = 1\}$, there exists a vector $a^i \in \mathrm{Col}(\Gamma_{\widetilde{\mathcal{P}}_J})$ such that*

$$\|z - a^i\|_2 \leq \sqrt{\frac{2\tau}{J^{2/(m-1)} + \tau}}. \tag{6.26}$$

*Proof.* Let $z$ be any point on the unit sphere $\{z \in \mathbb{R}^m : \|z\|_2 = 1\}$. Since $\mathcal{B} \subseteq \widetilde{\mathcal{P}}_J$, where $J > m$, the straight line passing through $z$ and the center of $\mathcal{B}$ crosses a point, denoted by $z'$, on the surface of polytope $\widetilde{\mathcal{P}}_J$. Clearly, $\|z'\|_2 \geq 1$ and $z = z'/\|z'\|_2$. Thus $z$ is the orthogonal projection of $z'$ onto $\mathcal{B}$. Note that $\mathcal{B} \subseteq \widetilde{\mathcal{P}}_J \subseteq \mathcal{P}_J$ for any $J > m$. By the definition of Hausdorff metric and Lemma 6.3.1, we obtain

$$\|z - z'\|_2 \leq d^{\mathcal{H}}(\mathcal{B}, \widetilde{\mathcal{P}}_J) \leq d^{\mathcal{H}}(\mathcal{B}, \mathcal{P}_J) \leq \frac{\tau}{J^{2/(m-1)}}. \tag{6.27}$$

Since $z'$ is on the surface of $\widetilde{\mathcal{P}}_J$, there is a vector $a^{i_0} \in \mathrm{Col}(\Gamma_{\widetilde{\mathcal{P}}_J})$ such that $(a^{i_0})^T z' = 1$. Note that

$$\|z' - z\|_2 = \|z' - \frac{z'}{\|z'\|_2}\|_2 = \|z'\|_2 - 1, \quad \|a^{i_0}\|_2 = \|z\|_2 = 1,$$

and $(a^{i_0})^T z' = 1$. We immediately have

$$\begin{aligned}
\|z - a^{i_0}\|_2^2 &= \|z\|_2^2 + \|a^{i_0}\|_2^2 - 2(a^{i_0})^T z \\
&= 2(1 - (a^{i_0})^T z) = 2(1 - \frac{(a^{i_0})^T z'}{\|z'\|_2}) \\
&= 2(1 - \frac{1}{\|z'\|_2}) = \frac{2\|z' - z\|_2}{\|z' - z\|_2 + 1} \\
&\leq \frac{2(\tau/J^{2/(m-1)})}{(\tau/J^{2/(m-1)}) + 1} = \frac{2\tau}{\tau + J^{2/(m-1)}},
\end{aligned}$$

where the inequality follows from (6.27) as well as the monotonicity of the function $2t/(t+1)$ over $[0,\infty)$. The above inequality implies that (6.26) holds true. $\square$

This lemma indicates that any vector on the surface of $\mathfrak{B}$ can be approximated by a vector in $\mathrm{Col}(\Gamma_{\widetilde{\mathcal{P}}_J})$ with error (6.23).

## 6.3.2 General Unit Ball

Let $\phi(\cdot)$ be a given norm on $\mathbb{R}^q$. Consider the following unit ball in $\mathbb{R}^q$ defined by the norm $\phi$ :

$$\mathfrak{B}^{\phi} = \{z \in \mathbb{R}^q : \phi(z) \leq 1\}. \tag{6.28}$$

Let $\phi^*(\cdot)$ be the dual norm of $\phi$, i.e.,

$$\phi^*(u) = \max_{\phi(z) \leq 1} u^T z.$$

By this definition,

$$z^T u \leq \phi(z) \phi^*(u) \text{ for any } z, u \in \mathbb{R}^q.$$

In particular, the dual norm of the $\ell_{\alpha_1}$-norm, $\alpha_1 \in [1,\infty]$, is the $\ell_{\alpha_2}$-norm with $\alpha_2 \in [1,\infty]$, where $\alpha_1$ and $\alpha_2$ satisfy that $1/\alpha_1 + 1/\alpha_2 = 1$. For instance, the $\ell_1$-norm and $\ell_\infty$-norm are dual to each other. In this chapter, we restrict our attention on the norm $\phi$ satisfying $\phi(e^{(i)}) = 1$ and $\phi^*(e^{(i)}) = 1$ for all $i = 1, \ldots, q$. Clearly, any $\ell_p$-norm, $p \in [1,\infty]$, satisfies this property. It is well known that the unit ball (6.28) can be represented as:

$$\mathfrak{B}^{\phi} = \bigcap_{\phi^*(a)=1} \{z \in \mathbb{R}^q : a^T z \leq 1\}.$$

In other words, $\mathfrak{B}^{\phi}$ is the intersection of all half spaces in the form $\{z \in \mathbb{R}^q : a^T z \leq 1\}$ where $a \in \mathbb{R}^q$ and $\phi^*(a) = 1$. Any finite number of the vectors $a^i \in \mathbb{R}^q$ with $\phi^*(a^i) = 1$, $i = 1, \ldots, k$ yield the following polytope approximation of $\mathfrak{B}^{\phi}$ :

$$\mathfrak{B}^{\phi} \subseteq \bigcap_{1 \leq i \leq k} \{z \in \mathbb{R}^q : (a^i)^T z \leq 1\}.$$

Note that

$$1 = \phi^*(a^i) = \sup_{\phi(u) \leq 1} (a^i)^T u = (a^i)^T u^*$$

for some $u^*$ with $\phi(u^*) = 1$. Thus every half space $\{z \in \mathbb{R}^q : (a^i)^T z \leq 1\}$ with $\phi^*(a^i) = 1$ must be a support half space of $\mathfrak{B}^{\phi}$ in the sense that it contains $\mathfrak{B}^{\phi}$, and the plane $\{z : (a^i)^T z = 1\}$ touches $\mathfrak{B}^{\phi}$ at a point on its boundary. Conversely, any support half space of $\mathfrak{B}^{\phi}$ can be represented this way, i.e., $\{z : (a^i)^T z \leq 1\}$ with some $a^i$ satisfying $\phi^*(a^i) = 1$. Note that $\mathfrak{B}^{\phi}$ is a symmetric convex body in the sense that if $z$ is in the set, so is $-z$. There is a symmetric polytope approximation of $\mathfrak{B}^{\phi}$, as claimed by the next theorem due to Barvinok [21].

**Theorem 6.3.3** (Barvinok [21]) *For any constant* $\chi > \frac{e}{4\sqrt{2}} \approx 0.48$, *there exists a* $\varepsilon_0 = \varepsilon_0(\chi)$ *such that for any* $0 < \varepsilon < \varepsilon_0$ *and for any symmetric convex body B in* $\mathbb{R}^q$, *there is a symmetric polytope in* $\mathbb{R}^q$, *denoted by* $P_\varepsilon$, *with N vertices such that* $N \leq \left(\frac{\chi}{\sqrt{\varepsilon}} \ln \frac{1}{\varepsilon}\right)^q$ *and* $P_\varepsilon \subseteq B \subseteq (1+\varepsilon)P_\varepsilon$.

Applied to the unit ball $\mathfrak{B}^\phi$ in $\mathbb{R}^q$, the Barvinok's theorem claims that for every sufficiently small $\varepsilon > 0$ there is a symmetric polytope $P_\varepsilon$ satisfying that

$$P_\varepsilon \subseteq \mathfrak{B}^\phi \subseteq (1+\varepsilon)P_\varepsilon.$$

Thus $(1+\varepsilon)P_\varepsilon$ is an outer approximation of $\mathfrak{B}^\phi$. To get a tighter approximation of $\mathfrak{B}^\phi$, we may compress the polytope $(1+\varepsilon)P_\varepsilon$ by shifting all affine planes, expanded by the faces of $(1+\varepsilon)P_\varepsilon$, toward $\mathfrak{B}^\phi$ until they touch $\mathfrak{B}^\phi$ on its boundary. By such compression of $(1+\varepsilon)P_\varepsilon$, the resulting polytope denoted by $\widehat{P}_\varepsilon$ is then formed by a finite number of support half spaces of $\mathfrak{B}^\phi$. Therefore, there exists a set of vectors $a^i \in \mathbb{R}^q$ for $i = 1, \ldots, J$ with $\phi^*(a^i) = 1$ such that

$$\widehat{P}_\varepsilon = \bigcap_{i=1}^{J} \{z \in \mathbb{R}^q : (a^i)^T z \leq 1\}.$$

We now further add the $2m$ half spaces $(\pm e^{(i)})^T z \leq 1$, $i = 1, \ldots, q$ to $\widehat{P}_\varepsilon$, where $e^{(i)}, i = 1, \ldots, q$ are the standard bases of $\mathbb{R}^q$. This yields the polytope

$$\overline{P}_\varepsilon := \widehat{P}_\varepsilon \cap \left\{z \in \mathbb{R}^q : (e^{(i)})^T z \leq 1, \ -(e^{(i)})^T z \leq 1, \ i = 1, \ldots, q\right\}.$$

Clearly, we have the relation

$$P_\varepsilon \subseteq \mathfrak{B}^\phi \subseteq \overline{P}_\varepsilon \subseteq \widehat{P}_\varepsilon \subseteq (1+\varepsilon)P_\varepsilon.$$

Throughout the paper, we let $\varepsilon_k \in (0, \varepsilon_0)$, where $\varepsilon_0$ is the constant specified in Theorem 6.3.3, be a positive and strictly decreasing sequence satisfying that $\varepsilon_k \to 0$ as $k \to \infty$. We consider the sequence of polytopes $\{\mathcal{Q}_{\varepsilon_j}\}_{j \geq 1}$, where

$$\mathcal{Q}_{\varepsilon_j} = \bigcap_{k=1}^{j} \overline{P}_{\varepsilon_k}. \qquad (6.29)$$

Then for every $\varepsilon_j$, the polytope $\mathcal{Q}_{\varepsilon_j}$ is an outer approximation of $\mathfrak{B}^\phi$, satisfying

$$P_{\varepsilon_j} \subseteq \mathfrak{B}^\phi \subseteq \mathcal{Q}_{\varepsilon_j} \subseteq \overline{P}_{\varepsilon_j} \subseteq (1+\varepsilon_j)P_{\varepsilon_j}. \qquad (6.30)$$

$\mathcal{Q}_{\varepsilon_j}$ is formed by a finite number (say, $\kappa$) of half spaces, denoted by $\{z \in \mathbb{R}^q : (a^i)^T z \leq 1\}$ where $\phi^*(a^i) = 1$ for $i = 1, \ldots, \kappa$. We use

$$\Gamma_{\mathcal{Q}_{\varepsilon_j}} :- \left[a^1, \ldots, a^\kappa\right]$$

to denote the $m \times \kappa$ matrix with the vectors $a^i$'s as its column vectors, and we use

$$\text{Col}(\Gamma_{\mathcal{Q}_{\varepsilon_j}}) = \{a^1, \ldots, a^\kappa\}$$

to denote the set of column vectors of $\Gamma_{\mathcal{Q}_{\varepsilon_j}}$. Then $\mathcal{Q}_{\varepsilon_j}$ can be represented as

$$\begin{aligned} \mathcal{Q}_{\varepsilon_j} &= \{z \in \mathbb{R}^q : (a^i)^T z \leq 1, \; i = 1, \ldots, \kappa\} \\ &= \{z \in \mathbb{R}^q : (\Gamma_{\mathcal{Q}_{\varepsilon_j}})^T z \leq \mathbf{e}\}, \end{aligned} \tag{6.31}$$

where $\mathbf{e}$ denotes the vector of ones in $\mathbb{R}^\kappa$. Similar to Lemma 6.3.2, we obtain the following lemma.

**Lemma 6.3.4** *For any $j \geq 1$, let $\mathcal{Q}_{\varepsilon_j}$ be constructed as (6.29). Then for any*

$$a^* \in \{z \in \mathbb{R}^q : \phi(z) = 1\},$$

*there is a vector $a^i \in \text{Col}(\Gamma_{\mathcal{Q}_{\varepsilon_j}})$ such that*

$$(a^*)^T a^i \geq \frac{1}{1+\varepsilon_j}.$$

*Proof.* Let $a^*$ be any point on the unit sphere $\{z \in \mathbb{R}^q : \phi(z) = 1\}$, i.e., $\phi(a^*) = 1$. Note that $\mathcal{Q}_{\varepsilon_j}$ satisfies (6.30). The straight line starting from the origin and passing through the point $a^*$ on the surface of $\mathcal{B}^\phi$ will shoot a point $z'$ on the boundary of $\mathcal{Q}_{\varepsilon_j}$ and a point $z''$ on the boundary of $(1+\varepsilon_j)P_{\varepsilon_j}$. From (6.30), we see that $z'' = (1+\varepsilon'')a^*$ for some number $\varepsilon'' \leq \varepsilon_j$. Note that $z'$ is situated between $a^*$ and $z''$. This implies that $z' = (1+\varepsilon')a^*$ for some $\varepsilon' \leq \varepsilon''$. Since $z'$ is on the boundary of $\mathcal{Q}_{\varepsilon_j}$, it must be on a face of this polytope and hence there exists a vector $a^i \in \text{Col}(\Gamma_{\mathcal{Q}_{\varepsilon_j}})$ such that $(a^i)^T z' = 1$. Note that $z' = (1+\varepsilon')a^*$ where $\varepsilon' \leq \varepsilon'' \leq \varepsilon_j$. Thus,

$$1 = (a^i)^T z' = (1+\varepsilon')(a^i)^T a^*$$

which implies that

$$(a^i)^T a^* = \frac{1}{1+\varepsilon'} \geq \frac{1}{1+\varepsilon_j},$$

as desired. □

## 6.4 A Necessary Condition for Stability

By the KKT optimality condition, the $k$-sparse vector $\widehat{x}$ is a solution to the standard $\ell_1$-minimization problem

$$\min_x \{\|x\|_1 : Ax = y = A\widehat{x}\}$$

if and only if there is a vector $\zeta \in \mathcal{R}(A^T)$ satisfying

$$\zeta_i = 1 \text{ for } \widehat{x}_i > 0, \ \zeta_i = -1 \text{ for } \widehat{x}_i < 0, \text{ and } |\zeta_i| \leq 1 \text{ for } \widehat{x}_i = 0.$$

This range space property of $A^T$ depends on the individual vector $\widehat{x}$. As we have pointed out in previous chapters, to expect that every $k$-sparse vector can be recovered by $\ell_1$-minimization, we need to strengthen such an individual property so that it is independent of any specific $k$-sparse vector. This naturally leads to the notion of weak RSP of order $k$ of $A^T$ described in Definition 5.3.1. Many existing sparse recovery conditions imply this matrix property. It was shown in Chapter 5 that the weak RSP of order $k$ of $A^T$ is a necessary and sufficient condition for the standard $\ell_1$-minimization problem with any measurement vector $y \in \{Ax : \|x\|_0 \leq k\}$ being stable in the sense of Definition 5.1.1. It is a mild condition to guarantee the stableness of many other linear sparse optimization methods as well. In this chapter, we continue to prove that the weak RSP of order $k$ of $A^T$ is also a mild condition governing the stableness of many nonlinear sparse optimization methods. First, let us generalize Theorem 5.4.1 to a class of nonlinear sparse optimization problems.

**Theorem 6.4.1** *Let $\varphi : \mathbb{R}^q \to \mathbb{R}_+$ be a convex function on $\mathbb{R}^q$ satisfying that $\varphi(0) = 0$ and $\varphi(u) > 0$ for $u \neq 0$. Let $A \in \mathbb{R}^{m \times n}$ and $M \in \mathbb{R}^{m \times q}$ be two matrices with $m < n$, $m \leq q$ and $rank(A) = rank(M) = m$. Suppose that for any given $\varepsilon \geq 0$ and for any given $y \in \mathbb{R}^m$, the vector $x \in \mathbb{R}^n$ satisfying $\varphi(M^T(Ax - y)) \leq \varepsilon$ can be approximated by a solution $x^*$ of the problem*

$$\min_z \{\|z\|_1 : \varphi(M^T(Az - y)) \leq \varepsilon\} \tag{6.32}$$

*with error*

$$\|x - x^*\|_2 \leq C' \sigma_k(x)_1 + C'' \gamma(\varepsilon), \tag{6.33}$$

*where $C'$ and $C''$ are constants depending on the problem data $(M, A, y, \varepsilon)$, and $\gamma(\cdot)$ is a certain continuous function satisfying $\gamma(0) = 0, \gamma(\varepsilon) > 0$ for $\varepsilon > 0$, and $C'' \gamma(\varepsilon) \to 0$ as $\varepsilon \to 0$. Then $A^T$ must satisfy the weak RSP of order $k$.*

*Proof.* Let $S_1, S_2 \subseteq \{1, \ldots, n\}$ be two arbitrarily given disjoint sets satisfying $|S_1| + |S_2| \leq k$. We prove that there is a vector $\zeta \in \mathcal{R}(A^T)$ such that

$$\zeta_i = 1 \text{ for } i \in S_1, \ \zeta_i = -1 \text{ for } i \in S_2, \text{ and } |\zeta_i| \leq 1 \text{ otherwise.} \tag{6.34}$$

In fact, let $\widehat{x}$ be a $k$-sparse vector in $\mathbb{R}^n$ with

$$\{i : \widehat{x}_i > 0\} = S_1 \text{ and } \{i : \widehat{x}_i < 0\} = S_2.$$

Let $\varepsilon \geq 0$ be a fixed small parameter such that

$$C'' \gamma(\varepsilon) < \min_{\widehat{x}_i \neq 0} |\widehat{x}_i|. \tag{6.35}$$

Let the measurement vector $y \approx A\widehat{x}$ be accurate enough such that $\varphi(M^T(A\widehat{x} - y)) \leq \varepsilon$. Consider the problem (6.32) with such a pair $(y, \varepsilon)$. By the assumption, any feasible point of (6.32) can be approximated by a solution $x^*$ of (6.32) with error (6.33). Since $\widehat{x}$ is $k$-sparse, we have $\sigma_k(\widehat{x})_1 = 0$. Thus (6.33) is the reduced to

$$\|\widehat{x} - x^*\|_2 \leq C'' \gamma(\varepsilon),$$

which, together with (6.35), implies that for $\widehat{x}_i > 0$, the corresponding $x_i^*$ must be positive and for $\widehat{x}_i < 0$ the corresponding component $x_i^*$ must be negative. Thus,

$$S_1 = \{i : \widehat{x}_i > 0\} \subseteq \{i : x_i^* > 0\}, \ S_2 = \{i : \widehat{x}_i < 0\} \subseteq \{i : x_i^* < 0\}. \quad (6.36)$$

Note that $x^*$ is a solution of (6.32), at which a constraint qualification is satisfied. In fact, if $\varepsilon = 0$, the constraint is reduced to the linear equation $Ax = y$, and if $\varepsilon > 0$, the Slater's constraint qualification is satisfied. In fact, since $A$ is a full row rank matrix, there is a vector $z$ such that $Az = y$, and hence $\varphi(M^T(Az - y)) < \varepsilon$. So $x^*$ satisfies the KKT optimality condition, i.e.,

$$0 \in \partial_x \left\{ \|x\|_1 + \lambda \left[ \varphi(M^T(Ax - y)) - \varepsilon \right] \right\} \Big|_{x = x^*},$$

where $\lambda$ is a Lagrangian multiplier and $\partial_x$ denotes the subgradient with respect to $x$. As the domains of the functions $\varphi(M^T(Ax - y))$ and $\|x\|_1$ are $\mathbb{R}^n$, by Theorem 23.8 in [193], the above optimality condition is equivalent to

$$0 \in \left\{ \partial \|x^*\|_1 + \lambda A^T M \partial \varphi(M^T(Ax^* - y)) \right\},$$

where $\partial \varphi(M^T(Ax^* - y))$ is the subgradient of $\varphi$ at $M^T(Ax^* - y)$, and $\partial \|x^*\|_1$ is the subgradient of the $\ell_1$-norm at $x^*$, i.e.,

$$\partial \|x^*\|_1 = \{\zeta \in \mathbb{R}^n : \zeta_i = 1 \text{ for } x_i^* > 0, \ \zeta_i = -1 \text{ for } x_i^* < 0, \ |\zeta_i| \leq 1 \text{ for } x_i^* = 0\}.$$

Thus there is a vector $v \in \partial \varphi(M^T(Ax^* - y))$ and a vector $\zeta \in \partial \|x^*\|_1$ such that

$$\zeta + \lambda A^T M v = 0.$$

Setting $u = -\lambda M v$ yields $\zeta = A^T u$. Since $\zeta \in \partial \|x^*\|_1$, we see that $\zeta_i = 1$ for $x_i^* > 0$, $\zeta_i = -1$ for $x_i^* < 0$, and $|\zeta_i| \leq 1$ for $x_i^* = 0$. This, together with (6.36), implies that the vector $\zeta$ satisfies (6.34). Note that $S_1$ and $S_2$ are arbitrary and disjoint subsets of $\{1, \dots, n\}$ with $|S_1| + |S_2| \leq k$. By Definition 5.3.1, $A^T$ must satisfy the weak RSP of order $k$. $\square$.

We now define the so-called strong stability of sparse optimization problems.

**Definition 6.4.2** *Let $\widehat{x}$ be the target vector obeying the constraint of (5.1). The $\ell_1$-minimization method (5.1) is said to be strongly stable in sparse data recovery if the solution $x^*$ of the problem (5.1) approximates $\widehat{x}$ with error*

$$\|\widehat{x} - x^*\|_2 \leq C' \sigma_k(\widehat{x})_1 + C'' \varepsilon,$$

*where $C'$ and $C''$ are constants depending only on the problem data $(M, A)$, i.e., $C'$ and $C''$ are independent of $(y, \varepsilon)$.*

For strong stability, the condition $C''\gamma(\varepsilon) = C''\varepsilon \to 0$ as $\varepsilon \to 0$ is satisfied. Thus according to Theorem 6.4.1, any condition that implies the strong stability of the $\ell_1$-optimization method must imply the weak RSP of $A^T$.

As shown by Theorem 6.4.1, the weak RSP of $A^T$ is a necessary condition for many sparse optimization methods to be stable. Thus the condition cannot be relaxed if we anticipate these methods being stable in sparse data recovery. In later sections, we show that the weak RSP of $A^T$ is also a sufficient condition for a wide range of nonlinear optimization methods to be stable, including $\ell_1$-minimization with an $\ell_2$-norm constraint, nonlinear DS, and LASSO. It is worth noting that the traditional error bounds for a recovery method is measured in terms of the conventional matrix constants, such as the RIP, stable NSP and robust NSP. Different from these assumptions, the weak RSP of $A^T$ is a constant-free condition, based on which a unified stability theorem can be developed for some nonlinear sparse optimization methods.

Before we start to analyze nonlinear sparse optimization methods, let us first characterize the conditions for the stableness of linear DS problems. In Chapter 5, we have shown that the weak RSP of $A^T$ is a sufficient condition for the linear DS problem to be stable in sparse data recovery. From Theorem 6.4.1, we deduce that this assumption is also necessary. So we have the following complete characterization of the stability of linear DS problems.

**Theorem 6.4.3** *Consider the standard DS problem (5.4), where $A \in \mathbb{R}^{m \times n}$ is a matrix with $m < n$ and $\mathrm{rank}(A) = m$. Then the following two statements are equivalent:*

(i) *For any $x$ satisfying $\|A^T(Ax - y)\|_\infty \leq \varepsilon$, there is a solution $x^*$ of the problem (5.4) approximating $x$ with error*

$$\|x - x^*\|_2 \leq \gamma\{2\sigma_k(x)_1 + c_A\varepsilon + c_A\|A^T(Ax - y)\|_\infty\}$$
$$\leq 2\gamma\{\sigma_k(x)_1 + c_A\varepsilon\},$$

*where $c_A$ and $\gamma = \sigma_{\infty,2}(M^1, M^2)$ are given in Corollary 5.6.1.*

(ii) *$A^T$ satisfies the weak RSP of order $k$.*

## 6.5 $\ell_1$-Minimization with $\ell_2$-Norm Constraints

We now consider the stability of the problem

$$\gamma^* := \min_x\{\|x\|_1 : \|Ax - y\|_2 \leq \varepsilon\}, \tag{6.37}$$

where $\varepsilon > 0$, and $\gamma^*$ denotes the optimal value of the problem. This problem is referred to as the $\ell_1$-minimization problem with an $\ell_2$-norm constraint. Let $S^*$ be the solution set of (6.37). Clearly, $S^*$ can be represented as

$$S^* = \{x \subset \mathbb{R}^n : \|x\|_1 \leq \gamma^*, \|Ax - y\|_2 \leq \varepsilon\}.$$

Then the problem (6.37) can be written as

$$\gamma^* = \min_x \{\|x\|_1 : u = (Ax - y)/\varepsilon, \ u \in \mathcal{B}\}, \tag{6.38}$$

where $\mathcal{B} = \{z \in \mathbb{R}^m : \|z\|_2 \leq 1\}$ is the unit $\ell_2$-ball. Since the constraint of (6.37) is nonlinear, the KKT optimality condition of (6.37) is not a linear system, and thus the solution set $S^*$ is not a polyhedron in general. This renders Lemma 5.2.2 inapplicable to this case. To overcome this, we may replace $\mathcal{B}$ in (6.38) with the polytope approximation $\widetilde{\mathcal{P}}_J$ defined in (6.24), which is represented as (6.25). Let us begin with several technical results before we actually establish the stability theorem for (6.37).

**Lemma 6.5.1** *Let $\{\mathcal{P}_\kappa\}_{\kappa > m}$ be given as (6.22) and $\widetilde{\mathcal{P}}_J$ be given as (6.24) which is written as (6.25). Let $S_{\widetilde{\mathcal{P}}_J}$ be the set*

$$S_{\widetilde{\mathcal{P}}_J} = \{x \in \mathbb{R}^n : \|x\|_1 \leq \gamma^*, \ u = (Ax - y)/\varepsilon, \ u \in \widetilde{\mathcal{P}}_J\}, \tag{6.39}$$

*where $\gamma^*$ is the optimal value of the problem (6.37). Then,*

$$d^{\mathcal{H}}(S^*, S_{\widetilde{\mathcal{P}}_J}) \to 0 \text{ as } J \to \infty.$$

*Proof.* Note that $\mathcal{B} \subseteq \widetilde{\mathcal{P}}_J \subseteq \mathcal{P}_J$ for every $J > m$. By the definition of Hausdorff metric and Lemma 6.3.1, we see that for any $J > m$,

$$d^{\mathcal{H}}(\mathcal{B}, \widetilde{\mathcal{P}}_J) \leq d^{\mathcal{H}}(\mathcal{B}, \mathcal{P}_J) \leq \frac{\tau}{J^{2/(m-1)}}. \tag{6.40}$$

By (6.25), the set $S_{\widetilde{\mathcal{P}}_J}$, given by (6.39), can be rewritten as

$$S_{\widetilde{\mathcal{P}}_J} = \{x \in \mathbb{R}^n : \|x\|_1 \leq \gamma^*, \ (\Gamma_{\widetilde{\mathcal{P}}_J})^T (Ax - y) \leq \varepsilon \mathbf{e}\},$$

where $\gamma^*$ is the optimal value of (6.37) and $\mathbf{e}$ is the vector of ones with dimension $|\text{Col}(\Gamma_{\widetilde{\mathcal{P}}_J})|$. Clearly, $S^* \subseteq S_{\widetilde{\mathcal{P}}_J}$ due to the fact $\mathcal{B} \subseteq \widetilde{\mathcal{P}}_J$. We now prove that $d^{\mathcal{H}}(S^*, S_{\widetilde{\mathcal{P}}_J}) \to 0$ as $J \to \infty$. Since $S^*$ is a subset of $S_{\widetilde{\mathcal{P}}_J}$, by the definition of Hausdorff metric, we see that

$$d^{\mathcal{H}}(S^*, S_{\widetilde{\mathcal{P}}_J}) = \sup_{w \in S_{\widetilde{\mathcal{P}}_J}} \inf_{z \in S^*} \|w - z\|_2 = \sup_{w \in S_{\widetilde{\mathcal{P}}_J}} \|w - \Pi_{S^*}(w)\|_2, \tag{6.41}$$

where $\Pi_{S^*}(w) \in S^*$ is the projection of $w$ into $S^*$. The operator $\Pi_{S^*}(w)$ is continuous in $w$ and $S_{\widetilde{\mathcal{P}}_J}$ is a compact convex set for any $\widetilde{\mathcal{P}}_J$. Thus for every polytope $\widetilde{\mathcal{P}}_J$, the superimum in (6.41) can be attained. That is, there exists a point, denoted by $w^*_{\widetilde{\mathcal{P}}_J} \in S_{\widetilde{\mathcal{P}}_J}$, such that

$$d^{\mathcal{H}}(S^*, S_{\widetilde{\mathcal{P}}_J}) = \left\| w^*_{\widetilde{\mathcal{P}}_J} - \Pi_{S^*}(w^*_{\widetilde{\mathcal{P}}_J}) \right\|_2. \tag{6.42}$$

We also note that $S^* \subseteq S_{\widetilde{\mathcal{P}}_{J+1}} \subseteq S_{\widetilde{\mathcal{P}}_J}$ for any $J > m$, which implies that $d^{\mathcal{H}}(S^*, S_{\widetilde{\mathcal{P}}_{J+1}}) \leq d^{\mathcal{H}}(S^*, S_{\widetilde{\mathcal{P}}_J})$. Thus there exists a number $\widehat{\delta} \geq 0$ such that

$$\lim_{J \to \infty} d^{\mathcal{H}}(S^*, S_{\widetilde{\mathcal{P}}_J}) = \widehat{\delta} \geq 0.$$

It is sufficient to prove that $\widehat{\delta} = 0$. Noting that $w^*_{\widetilde{\mathcal{P}}_J} \in S_{\widetilde{\mathcal{P}}_J}$ for any $J > m$, we have

$$\left\| w^*_{\widetilde{\mathcal{P}}_J} \right\|_1 \leq \gamma^* \text{ and } (\Gamma_{\widetilde{\mathcal{P}}_J})^T (Aw^*_{\widetilde{\mathcal{P}}_J} - y) \leq \varepsilon e \text{ for any } J > m.$$

Thus the sequence $\{w^*_{\widetilde{\mathcal{P}}_J}\}_{J>m}$ is bounded and

$$\sup_{a^i \in \mathrm{Col}(\Gamma_{\widetilde{\mathcal{P}}_J})} (a^i)^T (Aw^*_{\widetilde{\mathcal{P}}_J} - y) \leq \varepsilon \text{ for any } J > m.$$

Note that $\mathrm{Col}(\Gamma_{\widetilde{\mathcal{P}}_{J'}}) \subseteq \mathrm{Col}(\Gamma_{\widetilde{\mathcal{P}}_J})$ for any $m < J' \leq J$. Thus the inequality above implies that for any fixed integer number $J' > m$,

$$\sup_{a^i \in \mathrm{Col}(\Gamma_{\widetilde{\mathcal{P}}_{J'}})} (a^i)^T (Aw^*_{\widetilde{\mathcal{P}}_J} - y) \leq \sup_{a^i \in \mathrm{Col}(\Gamma_{\widetilde{\mathcal{P}}_J})} (a^i)^T (Aw^*_{\widetilde{\mathcal{P}}_J} - y) \leq \varepsilon$$

for any $J \geq J'$. As the sequence $\{w^*_{\widetilde{\mathcal{P}}_J}\}_{J \geq J'}$ is bounded, pasting through to a subsequence of $\{w^*_{\widetilde{\mathcal{P}}_J}\}_{J \geq J'}$ if necessary, we may assume that $w^*_{\widetilde{\mathcal{P}}_J} \to w^*$ as $J \to \infty$. Clearly, $\|w^*\|_1 \leq \gamma^*$. Thus it follows from the above inequality that

$$\sup_{a^i \in \mathrm{Col}(\Gamma_{\widetilde{\mathcal{P}}_{J'}})} (a^i)^T (Aw^* - y) \leq \varepsilon, \tag{6.43}$$

which holds for any given $J' > m$. It is not difficult to show that (6.43) implies

$$\|Aw^* - y\|_2 \leq \varepsilon.$$

We show this by contradiction. Assume that $\|Aw^* - y\|_2 > \varepsilon$, which implies that

$$\max_{\|a\|_2 = 1} a^T (Aw^* - y) = \|Aw^* - y\|_2 > \varepsilon,$$

where the maximum attains at $a^* = (Aw^* - y)/\|Aw^* - y\|_2$. By continuity, there exists a neighborhood of $a^*$, denoted by $U = a^* + \delta^* \mathcal{B}$, where $\delta^* > 0$ is a small number, such that any point

$$a \in U \cap \{z \in \mathbb{R}^m : \|z\|_2 = 1\}$$

satisfies the inequality

$$a^T (Aw^* - y) \geq \frac{1}{2} (\|Aw^* - y\|_2 + \varepsilon). \tag{6.44}$$

Note that the polytope $\widetilde{\mathcal{P}}_J$ achieves (6.40). Let $J'$ be an integer number such that

$$\sqrt{\frac{2\tau}{(J')^{2/(m-1)} + \tau}} \leq \delta^*.$$

Then applying Lemma 6.3.2 to $\widetilde{\mathcal{P}}_{J'}$, there is a vector $a^i \in \mathrm{Col}(\Gamma_{\widetilde{\mathcal{P}}_{J'}})$ such that

$$\|a^i - a^*\|_2 \leq \sqrt{\frac{2\tau}{(J')^{2/(m-1)} + \tau}} \leq \delta^*.$$

This implies that $a^i \in U \cap \{z \in \mathbb{R}^m : \|z\|_2 = 1\}$. By (6.44), we must have

$$(a^i)^T (Aw^* - y) \geq \frac{1}{2}(\|Aw^* - y\|_2 + \varepsilon) > \varepsilon.$$

This contradicts (6.43). Thus we must have $\|Aw^* - y\|_2 \leq \varepsilon$, which together with the fact $\|w^*\|_1 \leq \gamma^*$ implies that $w^* \in S^*$. Therefore, $\Pi_{S^*}(w^*) = w^*$. It follows from (6.42) and the continuity of $\Pi_{S^*}(\cdot)$ that

$$\hat{\delta} = \lim_{J \to \infty} d^{\mathcal{H}}(S^*, S_{\widetilde{\mathcal{P}}_J}) = \lim_{J \to \infty} \|w^*_{\widetilde{\mathcal{P}}_J} - \Pi_{S^*}(w^*_{\widetilde{\mathcal{P}}_J})\|_2 = \|w^* - \Pi_{S^*}(w^*)\|_2 = 0,$$

as desired. □

By Lemma 6.3.1, for each integer number $\kappa > 2m$, there is a polytope $\mathcal{P}_\kappa$ of the form (6.22) which approximates the $\ell_2$-ball with error (6.23), and $\mathcal{P}_\kappa$ can be represented as $\mathcal{P}_\kappa = \{z \in \mathbb{R}^m : (\Gamma_{\mathcal{P}_\kappa})^T z \leq \mathbf{e}\}$, where $\mathbf{e}$ is the vector of ones in $\mathbb{R}^\kappa$. We now construct a polytope by adding the following $2m$ half-spaces to $\mathcal{P}_\kappa$:

$$(\pm \mathbf{e}^{(i)})^T z \leq 1, \ i = 1, \ldots, m$$

where $\mathbf{e}^{(i)}, i = 1, \ldots, m$, denote the standard basis of $\mathbb{R}^m$. Let $\widehat{\kappa}$ denote the cardinality of the set $\mathrm{Col}(\Gamma_{\mathcal{P}_\kappa}) \cup \{\pm \mathbf{e}^{(i)} : i = 1, \ldots, m\}$. This yields the polytope

$$\mathcal{P}_{\widehat{\kappa}} := \mathcal{P}_\kappa \cap \{z \in \mathbb{R}^m : \ (\mathbf{e}^{(i)})^T z \leq 1, \ -(\mathbf{e}^{(i)})^T z \leq 1, \ i = 1, \ldots, m\}. \tag{6.45}$$

Therefore,

$$\mathrm{Col}(\Gamma_{\mathcal{P}_{\widehat{\kappa}}}) = \mathrm{Col}(\Gamma_{\mathcal{P}_\kappa}) \cup \{\pm \mathbf{e}_i : i = 1, \ldots, m\}$$

and $\widehat{\kappa} = |\mathrm{Col}(\Gamma_{\mathcal{P}_{\widehat{\kappa}}})|$. Clearly, $\kappa \leq \widehat{\kappa} \leq \kappa + 2m$ which together with $\kappa > 2m$ implies that $1 \leq \widehat{\kappa}/\kappa \leq 2$. Let $\tau$ be the constant in Lemma 6.3.1 and let $\tau' = 4^{1/(m-1)}\tau$. By the definition of Hausdorff metric and Lemma 6.3.1, we see that the polytope $\mathcal{P}_{\widehat{\kappa}}$ constructed as (6.45) satisfies

$$d^{\mathcal{H}}(\mathcal{B}, \mathcal{P}_{\widehat{\kappa}}) \leq d^{\mathcal{H}}(\mathcal{B}, \mathcal{P}_\kappa) \leq \frac{\tau}{\kappa^{2/(m-1)}} = \frac{\tau}{\widehat{\kappa}^{2/(m-1)}} \left(\frac{\widehat{\kappa}}{\kappa}\right)^{2/(m-1)} \leq \frac{\tau'}{\widehat{\kappa}^{2/(m-1)}}. \tag{6.46}$$

Using $\mathcal{P}_{\hat{\kappa}}$ in (6.45) which satisfies (6.46), we construct the sequence of polytopes $\{\tilde{\mathcal{P}}_J\}$ as follows:

$$\tilde{\mathcal{P}}_J = \bigcap_{m < \hat{\kappa} \leq J} \mathcal{P}_{\hat{\kappa}}. \tag{6.47}$$

Then Lemma 6.5.1 remains valid for the sequence of polytopes given in (6.47). Therefore,

$$d^{\mathcal{H}}(S^*, S_{\tilde{\mathcal{P}}_J}) \to 0 \text{ as } J \to \infty.$$

With this we immediately obtain the next corollary.

**Corollary 6.5.2** *Let $S_{\tilde{\mathcal{P}}_J}$ denote the set (6.39) with $\tilde{\mathcal{P}}_J$ being given in (6.47). Let $\varepsilon' > 0$ be any fixed small number. Then there is an integer $J_0 > 2m$ such that*

$$d^{\mathcal{H}}(S^*, S_{\tilde{\mathcal{P}}_{J_0}}) \leq \varepsilon'. \tag{6.48}$$

In what follows, we focus on the fixed polytope $\tilde{\mathcal{P}}_{J_0}$ constructed as above. This polytope is an outer approximation of $\mathcal{B}$ with error (6.48). We use

$$\hat{n} = |\text{Col}(\Gamma_{\tilde{\mathcal{P}}_{J_0}})|$$

to denote the number of columns of $\Gamma_{\tilde{\mathcal{P}}_{J_0}}$ and use $\hat{\mathbf{e}}$ to denote the vector of ones in $\mathbb{R}^{\hat{n}}$ to distinguish it from the vector of ones in other spaces. Replacing $\mathcal{B}$ in (6.38) by $\tilde{\mathcal{P}}_{J_0}$ leads to the following approximation of (6.37):

$$\begin{aligned} \gamma^*_{\tilde{\mathcal{P}}_{J_0}} &:= \min_x \{\|x\|_1 : u = (Ax - y)/\varepsilon, \ u \in \tilde{\mathcal{P}}_{J_0}\} \\ &= \min_x \{\|x\|_1 : (\Gamma_{\tilde{\mathcal{P}}_{J_0}})^T (Ax - y) \leq \varepsilon \hat{\mathbf{e}}\}, \end{aligned} \tag{6.49}$$

where $\gamma^*_{\tilde{\mathcal{P}}_{J_0}}$ is the optimal value of the above problem. Denote by

$$S^*_{\tilde{\mathcal{P}}_{J_0}} = \{x \in \mathbb{R}^n : \|x\|_1 \leq \gamma^*_{\tilde{\mathcal{P}}_{J_0}}, \ u = (Ax - y)/\varepsilon, \ u \in \tilde{\mathcal{P}}_{J_0}\}$$

the solution set of (6.49). Let $S_{\tilde{\mathcal{P}}_{J_0}}$ be the set defined by (6.39) with $\tilde{\mathcal{P}}_J$ replaced by $\tilde{\mathcal{P}}_{J_0}$. Clearly,

$$S^* \subseteq S_{\tilde{\mathcal{P}}_{J_0}}, \quad S^*_{\tilde{\mathcal{P}}_{J_0}} \subseteq S_{\tilde{\mathcal{P}}_{J_0}}.$$

The first relation is obvious, and the second follows from the fact $\gamma^*_{\tilde{\mathcal{P}}_{J_0}} \leq \gamma^*$ as $\mathcal{B} \subseteq \tilde{\mathcal{P}}_{J_0}$. The problem (6.49) can be written as

$$\min_{(x,t)} \tilde{\mathbf{e}}^T t$$

$$\text{s.t. } (\Gamma_{\tilde{\mathcal{P}}_{J_0}})^T (Ax - y) \leq \varepsilon \hat{\mathbf{e}}\}, \ x \leq t, \ -x \leq t, \ t \in \mathbb{R}^n_+,$$

where $\widetilde{\mathbf{e}}$ stands for the vector of ones in $\mathbb{R}^n$. The dual problem of this linear program is given as follows:

$$\max_{(v_1,v_2,v_3)} \quad -\left[\varepsilon\widehat{\mathbf{e}} + (\Gamma_{\widetilde{\mathcal{P}}_{J_0}})^T y\right]^T v_3$$

$$\text{s.t.} \quad A^T \Gamma_{\widetilde{\mathcal{P}}_{J_0}} v_3 + v_1 - v_2 = 0, \tag{6.50}$$

$$v_1 + v_2 \le \widetilde{\mathbf{e}},$$

$$(v_1, v_2, v_3) \ge 0.$$

The statement below follows immediately from the KKT optimality condition of the above linear program.

**Lemma 6.5.3** $x^* \in \mathbb{R}^n$ *is a solution of the problem* (6.49) *if and only if there are vectors* $t^*, v_1^*, v_2^* \in \mathbb{R}_+^n$ *and* $v_3^* \in \mathbb{R}_+^{\widehat{n}}$ *such that* $(x^*, t^*, v_1^*, v_2^*, v_3^*) \in \mathfrak{D}^*$ *where* $\mathfrak{D}^*$ *is the set of points* $(x, t, v_1, v_2, v_3)$ *satisfying the following system:*

$$\begin{cases} x \le t, \ -x \le t, \ (\Gamma_{\widetilde{\mathcal{P}}_{J_0}})^T (Ax - y) \le \varepsilon\widehat{\mathbf{e}}, \\ A^T \Gamma_{\widetilde{\mathcal{P}}_{J_0}} v_3 + v_1 - v_2 = 0, \ v_1 + v_2 \le \widetilde{\mathbf{e}}, \\ \widetilde{\mathbf{e}}^T t = -\left[\varepsilon\widehat{\mathbf{e}} + (\Gamma_{\widetilde{\mathcal{P}}_{J_0}})^T y\right]^T v_3, \\ (t, v_1, v_2, v_3) \ge 0. \end{cases} \tag{6.51}$$

*Moreover, for any point* $(x, t, v_1, v_2, v_3) \in \mathfrak{D}^*$, *it must hold that* $t = |x|$.

The set (6.51) is determined by a linear system, which can be written in the following form:

$$\mathfrak{D}^* = \{z = (x, t, v_1, v_2, v_3) : M^+ z \le b^+, \ M^{++} z = b^{++}\}, \tag{6.52}$$

where $b^{++} = 0$, and

$$M^+ = \begin{bmatrix} I & -I & 0 & 0 & 0 \\ -I & -I & 0 & 0 & 0 \\ (\Gamma_{\widetilde{\mathcal{P}}_{J_0}})^T A & 0 & 0 & 0 & 0 \\ 0 & 0 & I & I & 0 \\ 0 & -I & 0 & 0 & 0 \\ 0 & 0 & -I & 0 & 0 \\ 0 & 0 & 0 & -I & 0 \\ 0 & 0 & 0 & 0 & -I_{\widehat{n}} \end{bmatrix}, \ b^+ = \begin{bmatrix} 0 \\ 0 \\ (\Gamma_{\widetilde{\mathcal{P}}_{J_0}})^T y + \varepsilon\widehat{\mathbf{e}} \\ e \\ 0 \\ 0 \\ 0 \\ 0 \end{bmatrix}, \tag{6.53}$$

$$M^{++} = \begin{bmatrix} 0 & 0 & I & -I & A^T \Gamma_{\widetilde{\mathcal{P}}_{J_0}} \\ 0 & \widetilde{\mathbf{e}}^T & 0 & 0 & \varepsilon\widehat{\mathbf{e}}^T + y^T \Gamma_{\widetilde{\mathcal{P}}_{J_0}} \end{bmatrix}, \tag{6.54}$$

where $I$ and $I_{\widehat{n}}$ are the $n \times n$ and $\widehat{n} \times \widehat{n}$ identity matrices, respectively. We now state and prove the stability theorem for the $\ell_1$-minimization problem with an $\ell_2$-norm constraint.

**Theorem 6.5.4** *Let the problem data* $(A, y, \varepsilon)$ *of (6.37) be given, where* $\varepsilon > 0$, $y \in \mathbb{R}^m$ *and* $A \in \mathbb{R}^{m \times n}$ $(m < n)$ *and* $\text{rank}(A) = m$. *Let* $\varepsilon' > 0$ *be any prescribed small number and let the polytope* $\widetilde{\mathcal{P}}_{J_0}$ *be constructed as (6.47) and satisfy (6.48). Suppose that* $A^T$ *satisfies the weak RSP of order k. Then for any* $x \in \mathbb{R}^n$, *there is a solution* $x^*$ *of (6.37) such that*

$$\|x - x^*\|_2 \leq 2\gamma_3 \left\{ 2\sigma_k(x)_1 + \widehat{n}(\|Ax - y\|_2 - \varepsilon)^+ + c_1\varepsilon + c_1\|Ax - y\|_\infty \right\} + 2\varepsilon',$$
(6.55)

*where* $\widehat{n} = |\text{Col}(\Gamma_{\widetilde{\mathcal{P}}_{J_0}})|$, $c_1 = \|(AA^T)^{-1}A\|_{\infty \to 1}$, *and* $\gamma_3 = \sigma_{\infty,2}(M^+, M^{++})$ *is the Robinson's constant determined by* $(M^+, M^{++})$ *given in (6.53) and (6.54). In particular, for any x satisfying* $\|Ax - y\|_2 \leq \varepsilon$, *there is a solution* $x^*$ *of (6.37) such that*

$$\|x - x^*\|_2 \leq 4\gamma_3\sigma_k(x)_1 + 4c_1\gamma_3\varepsilon + 2\varepsilon'.$$

*Proof.* Let $x$ be any point in $\mathbb{R}^n$ and $t = |x|$. We use $S \subseteq \{1, \ldots, n\}$ to denote the support of the $k$ largest entries of $|x|$. That is, $S$ is the set of indices of non-zero entries among the $k$ largest absolute components of $x$. Clearly, the cardinality $|S| = |S_+ \cup S_-| \leq k$ where

$$S_+ = \{i \in S : x_i > 0\}, \quad S_- = \{i \in S : x_i < 0\}.$$

Since $A^T$ satisfies the weak RSP of order $k$, there exists a vector $\eta = A^T g$ for some $g \in \mathbb{R}^m$, satisfying that

$$\eta_i = 1 \text{ for } i \in S_+, \ \eta_i = -1 \text{ for } i \in S_-, \text{ and } |\eta_i| \leq 1 \text{ for } i \in \overline{S},$$

where $\overline{S} = \{1, \ldots, n\} \setminus S$. We now construct a vector $(\widetilde{v}_1, \widetilde{v}_2, \widetilde{v}_3)$ such that they are feasible to the problem (6.50). Set

$$(\widetilde{v}_1)_i = 1 \text{ and } (\widetilde{v}_2)_i = 0 \text{ for all } i \in S_+,$$

$$(\widetilde{v}_1)_i = 0 \text{ and } (\widetilde{v}_2)_i = 1 \text{ for all } i \in S_-,$$

$$(\widetilde{v}_1)_i = (|\eta_i| + \eta_i)/2 \text{ and } (\widetilde{v}_2)_i = (|\eta_i| - \eta_i)/2 \text{ for all } i \in \overline{S}.$$

This choice of $\widetilde{v}_1$ and $\widetilde{v}_2$ ensures that

$$(\widetilde{v}_1, \widetilde{v}_2) \geq 0, \ \widetilde{v}_1 + \widetilde{v}_2 \leq \widetilde{e} \text{ and } \widetilde{v}_1 - \widetilde{v}_2 = \eta.$$

We now construct the vector $\widetilde{v}_3$. By the construction of $\widetilde{\mathcal{P}}_{J_0}$, we see that

$$\{\pm e^{(i)} : i = 1, \ldots, m\} \subseteq \text{Col}(\Gamma_{\widetilde{\mathcal{P}}_{J_0}}).$$

It is not difficult to show that there exists a vector $\widetilde{v}_3 \in \mathbb{R}_+^{\widehat{n}}$ satisfying

$$\Gamma_{\widetilde{\mathcal{P}}_{J_0}} \widetilde{v}_3 = -g, \ \|\widetilde{v}_3\|_1 = \|g\|_1.$$

In fact, without loss of generality, we assume that $\{-\mathbf{e}^{(i)} : i = 1,\ldots,m\}$ are arranged as the first $m$ columns and $\{\mathbf{e}^{(i)} : i = 1,\ldots,m\}$ are arranged as the second $m$ columns in matrix $\Gamma_{\widetilde{\mathcal{P}}_{J_0}}$. We choose $\tilde{v}_3$ as follows: For every $i = 1,\ldots,m$, then let $(\tilde{v}_3)_i = g_i$ if $g_i \geq 0$; otherwise, let $(\tilde{v}_3)_{m+i} = -g_i$ if $g_i < 0$, and all other entries of $\tilde{v}_3 \in \mathbb{R}^{\widehat{N}}$ are set to be zero. This selection of $\tilde{v}_3$ guarantees that $\tilde{v}_3 \geq 0$, $\Gamma_{\widetilde{\mathcal{P}}_{J_0}} \tilde{v}_3 = -g$ and

$$\|\tilde{v}_3\|_1 = \|g\|_1 = \|(AA^T)^{-1}A\eta\|_1 \leq \|(AA^T)^{-1}A\|_{\infty\to 1}\|\eta\|_\infty \leq c_1, \qquad (6.56)$$

where the last inequality follows from the fact $c_1 = \|(AA^T)^{-1}A\|_{\infty\to 1}$ and $\|\eta\|_\infty \leq 1$.

Let $\mathfrak{D}^*$ be given as in Lemma 6.5.3. $\mathfrak{D}^*$ can be written as (6.52). For the vector $(x,t,\tilde{v}_1,\tilde{v}_2,\tilde{v}_3)$, applying Lemma 5.2.2 with $(M',M'') = (M^+,M^{++})$ where $M^+$ and $M^{++}$ are given as (6.53) and (6.54), there is a point in $\mathfrak{D}^*$, denoted by $(\hat{x},\hat{t},\hat{v}_1,\hat{v}_2,\hat{v}_3)$, such that

$$\left\|\begin{bmatrix} x \\ t \\ \tilde{v}_1 \\ \tilde{v}_2 \\ \tilde{v}_3 \end{bmatrix} - \begin{bmatrix} \hat{x} \\ \hat{t} \\ \hat{v}_1 \\ \hat{v}_2 \\ \hat{v}_3 \end{bmatrix}\right\|_2 \leq \gamma_3 \left\|\begin{bmatrix} \left((\Gamma_{\widetilde{\mathcal{P}}_{J_0}})^T(Ax-y) - \varepsilon\hat{\mathbf{e}}\right)^+ \\ (x-t)^+ \\ (-x-t)^+ \\ (-t)^+ \\ A^T\Gamma_{\widetilde{\mathcal{P}}_{J_0}}\tilde{v}_3 + \tilde{v}_1 - \tilde{v}_2 \\ (\tilde{v}_1 + \tilde{v}_2 - \hat{\mathbf{e}})^+ \\ \hat{\mathbf{e}}^T t + \left(\varepsilon\hat{\mathbf{e}} + (\Gamma_{\widetilde{\mathcal{P}}_{J_0}})^T y\right)^T \tilde{v}_3 \\ (\tilde{\vartheta})^+ \end{bmatrix}\right\|_1, \qquad (6.57)$$

where $(\tilde{\vartheta})^+$ denotes $((-\tilde{v}_1)^+,(-\tilde{v}_2)^+,(-\tilde{v}_3)^+)$, and $\gamma_3 = \sigma_{\infty,2}(M^+,M^{++})$ is the Robinson's constant determined by $(M^+,M^{++})$ in (6.53) and (6.54). Since $(\tilde{v}_1,\tilde{v}_2,\tilde{v}_3)$ is a feasible point to the problem (6.50), we have

$$(\tilde{\vartheta})^+ = 0, \quad (\tilde{v}_1 + \tilde{v}_2 - \hat{\mathbf{e}})^+ = 0, \quad A^T\Gamma_{\widetilde{\mathcal{P}}_{J_0}}\tilde{v}_3 + \tilde{v}_1 - \tilde{v}_2 = 0.$$

As $t = |x|$, we have,

$$(x-t)^+ = (-x-t)^+ = (-t)^+ = 0.$$

Thus (6.57) is reduced to

$$\|x - \hat{x}\|_2 \leq \gamma_3 \left\{\left\|\left[(\Gamma_{\widetilde{\mathcal{P}}_{J_0}})^T(Ax-y) - \varepsilon\hat{\mathbf{e}}\right]^+\right\|_1 + \left|\hat{\mathbf{e}}^T t + \left[\varepsilon\hat{\mathbf{e}} + (\Gamma_{\widetilde{\mathcal{P}}_{J_0}})^T y\right]^T \tilde{v}_3\right|\right\}. \tag{6.58}$$

Note that $\|a^i\|_2 = 1$ for every $a^i \in \mathrm{Col}(\Gamma_{\widetilde{\mathcal{P}}_{J_0}})$. Thus $(a^i)^T(Ax-y) \leq \|Ax-y\|_2$, which implies that

$$\left[(a^i)^T(Ax-y) - \varepsilon\right]^+ \leq (\|Ax-y\|_2 - \varepsilon)^+.$$

Therefore,

$$\left[ (\Gamma_{\widetilde{\mathcal{P}}_{J_0}})^T (Ax - y) - \varepsilon \widehat{e} \right]^+ \leq (\|Ax - y\|_2 - \varepsilon)^+ \widehat{e},$$

and hence

$$\left\| \left[ (\Gamma_{\widetilde{\mathcal{P}}_{J_0}})^T (Ax - y) - \varepsilon \widehat{e} \right]^+ \right\|_1 \leq \widehat{n} (\|Ax - y\|_2 - \varepsilon)^+. \tag{6.59}$$

By the definition of $\eta$, we see that

$$x^T A^T g = x^T \eta = \|x_S\|_1 + x_{\overline{S}}^T \eta_{\overline{S}},$$

and thus

$$\left| \widetilde{e}^T |x| - x^T A^T g \right| = \left| \|x\|_1 - \|x_S\|_1 - x_{\overline{S}}^T \eta_{\overline{S}} \right| \leq \|x_{\overline{S}}\|_1 + |x_{\overline{S}}^T \eta_{\overline{S}}| \leq 2\|x_{\overline{S}}\|_1 = 2\sigma_k(x)_1.$$

We also note that

$$\|g\|_1 = \|(AA^T)^{-1} A\eta\|_1 \leq \|(AA^T)^{-1} A\|_{\infty \to 1} \|\eta\|_\infty \leq c_1. \tag{6.60}$$

Denoting by $\phi = Ax - y$ and noting that $\Gamma_{\widetilde{\mathcal{P}}_{J_0}} \widetilde{v}_3 = -g$, we have

$$
\begin{aligned}
\left| \widetilde{e}^T t + \left[ \varepsilon \widehat{e} + (\Gamma_{\widetilde{\mathcal{P}}_{J_0}})^T y \right]^T \widetilde{v}_3 \right| &= \left| \widetilde{e}^T |x| + x^T A^T \Gamma_{\widetilde{\mathcal{P}}_{J_0}} \widetilde{v}_3 - \phi^T \Gamma_{\widetilde{\mathcal{P}}_{J_0}} \widetilde{v}_3 + \varepsilon \widehat{e}^T \widetilde{v}_3 \right| \\
&= \left| \widetilde{e}^T |x| - x^T A^T g + \phi^T g + \varepsilon \widehat{e}^T \widetilde{v}_3 \right| \\
&\leq 2\sigma_k(x)_1 + |\phi^T g| + |\varepsilon \widehat{e}^T \widetilde{v}_3| \\
&\leq 2\sigma_k(x)_1 + \|\phi\|_\infty \|g\|_1 + \varepsilon \|\widetilde{v}_3\|_1 \\
&\leq 2\sigma_k(x)_1 + c_1 \|Ax - y\|_\infty + \varepsilon c_1, \tag{6.61}
\end{aligned}
$$

where the last inequality follows from (6.56) and (6.60). Combining (6.58), (6.59) and (6.61) leads to

$$\|x - \widehat{x}\|_2 \leq \gamma_3 \left[ \widehat{n} (\|Ax - y\|_2 - \varepsilon)^+ + 2\sigma_k(x)_1 + c_1 \varepsilon + c_2 \|Ax - y\|_2 \right]. \tag{6.62}$$

Note that the set $S_{\widetilde{\mathcal{P}}_{J_0}}$ and $S^*$ are compact convex sets. Let $x^*$ and $\overline{x}$ denote the projection of $x$ onto $S^*$ and $S_{\widetilde{\mathcal{P}}_{J_0}}$, respectively, namely,

$$x^* = \Pi_{S^*}(x) \in S^*, \quad \overline{x} = \Pi_{S_{\widetilde{\mathcal{P}}_{J_0}}}(x) \in S_{\widetilde{\mathcal{P}}_{J_0}}.$$

Since $S^* \subseteq S_{\widetilde{\mathcal{P}}_{J_0}}$, we have $\|x - \overline{x}\|_2 \leq \|x - x^*\|_2$. By (6.48), $d^{\mathcal{H}}(S^*, S_{\widetilde{\mathcal{P}}_{J_0}}) \leq \varepsilon'$, which together with Lemma 6.2.2 implies that

$$
\begin{aligned}
\|x^* - \overline{x}\|_2^2 &\leq d^{\mathcal{H}}(S^*, S_{\widetilde{\mathcal{P}}_{J_0}})(\|x - x^*\|_2 + \|x - \overline{x}\|_2) \\
&\leq \varepsilon'(\|x - x^*\|_2 + \|x - \overline{x}\|_2). \tag{6.63}
\end{aligned}
$$

Note that $\hat{x} \in S^*_{\widetilde{\mathcal{P}}_{J_0}} \subseteq S_{\widetilde{\mathcal{P}}_{J_0}}$ and $\bar{x}$ is the projection of $x$ into the convex set $S_{\widetilde{\mathcal{P}}_{J_0}}$.
Thus $\|x - \bar{x}\|_2 \leq \|x - \hat{x}\|_2$. By triangle inequality and (6.63), we have

$$
\begin{aligned}
\|x - x^*\|_2 &\leq \|x - \bar{x}\|_2 + \|\bar{x} - x^*\|_2 \\
&\leq \|x - \hat{x}\|_2 + \|\bar{x} - x^*\|_2 \\
&\leq \|x - \hat{x}\|_2 + \sqrt{\varepsilon'(\|x - x^*\|_2 + \|x - \bar{x}\|_2)}. \quad (6.64)
\end{aligned}
$$

Since $\|x - \bar{x}\|_2 \leq \|x - x^*\|_2$, it follows from (6.64) that

$$
\|x - x^*\|_2 \leq \|x - \hat{x}\|_2 + \sqrt{2\varepsilon'\|x - x^*\|_2},
$$

which implies

$$
\|x - x^*\|_2 \leq \left( \frac{\sqrt{2\varepsilon'} + \sqrt{2\varepsilon' + 4\|x - \hat{x}\|_2}}{2} \right)^2 \leq 2\varepsilon' + 2\|x - \hat{x}\|_2,
$$

where the last inequality follows from the fact $(t_1 + t_2)^2 \leq 2(t_1^2 + t_2^2)$. Combining
the inequality above and (6.62) immediately yields (6.55), i.e.,

$$
\|x - x^*\|_2 \leq 2\varepsilon' + 2\gamma_3 \left\{ \hat{n}(\|Ax - y\|_2 - \varepsilon)^+ + 2\sigma_k(x)_1 + c_1\varepsilon + c_1\|Ax - y\|_\infty \right\}.
$$

In particularly, when $x$ satisfies $\|Ax - y\|_2 \leq \varepsilon$, the above inequality is reduced to

$$
\begin{aligned}
\|x - x^*\|_2 &\leq 2\varepsilon' + 2\gamma_3 \left\{ 2\sigma_k(x)_1 + 2\sigma_k(x)_1 + c_1\varepsilon + c_1\|Ax - y\|_\infty \right\} \\
&\leq 4\gamma_3 \sigma_k(x)_1 + 4c_1\gamma_3\varepsilon + 2\varepsilon',
\end{aligned}
$$

as desired. □

We immediately have the following corollary which provides an identical
recovery error bound under various traditional assumptions.

**Corollary 6.5.5** *Let the problem data $(A, y, \varepsilon)$ be given, where $\varepsilon > 0$, $y \in \mathbb{R}^m$
and $A \in \mathbb{R}^{m \times n} (m < n)$ with $\text{rank}(A) = m$. Let $\varepsilon'$ be any prescribed small number
and let the polytope $\widetilde{\mathcal{P}}_{J_0}$ achieve (6.48). Then under each of the listed conditions
in Corollary 5.4.5, for any $x \in \mathbb{R}^n$ with $\|Ax - y\|_2 \leq \varepsilon$ there is a solution $x^*$ of
(6.37) such that*

$$
\|x - x^*\|_2 \leq 4\gamma_3 \sigma_k(x)_1 + 4c_1\gamma_3\varepsilon + 2\varepsilon'.
$$

*where $c_1$ and $\gamma_3$ are the constants given in Theorem 6.5.4.*

## 6.6 Nonlinear Dantzig Selector

For linear standard DS problems, Theorem 6.4.3 claims that the DS method is
stable in the sense of Definition 5.1.1 if and only if $A^T$ satisfies the weak RSP of

order $k$. In this section, we deal with the nonlinear version of the problem (6.1) which is referred to as a nonlinear DS problem, where $\varepsilon > 0$ and the constraint $\phi(M^T(Ax - y)) \le \varepsilon$ cannot be represented equivalently as a finite number of linear constraints, for example, when $\phi = \|\cdot\|_p$ with $p \in (1, \infty)$. We show that such a nonlinear DS method remains stable in sparse vector recovery under the weak RSP assumption.

In this section, $\rho^*$ stands for the optimal value of (6.1) and $S^*$ the solution set of the problem (6.1), which clearly can be written as

$$S^* = \{x \in \mathbb{R}^n : \|x\|_1 \le \rho^*, \ \phi(M^T(Ax - y)) \le \varepsilon\}.$$

In terms of $\mathcal{B}^\phi$ in $\mathbb{R}^q$, the nonlinear problem (6.1) can be written as

$$\rho^* = \min_{(x,u)} \{\|x\|_1 : \ u = M^T(Ax - y)/\varepsilon, \ u \in \mathcal{B}^\phi\}. \tag{6.65}$$

Unlike the linear DS discussed in Chapter 5, the nonlinearity of the constraint prohibits from applying Lemma 5.2.2 directly to establish a stability result. A natural idea is to use a certain polytope approximation of the unit ball $\mathcal{B}^\phi$ in $\mathbb{R}^q$. As pointed out in Section 6.3, the polytope $\mathcal{Q}_{\varepsilon_j}$ that is defined by (6.29) and satisfies the relation (6.30) is an outer approximation of the unit ball $\mathcal{B}^\phi$. Similar to the analysis for $\ell_1$-minimization with an $\ell_2$-norm constraint, we need to show several technical results before we actually prove the main stability theorem for nonlinear DS methods. Let us first define a set which is a relaxation of the solution set $S^*$ of the problem (6.1). Note that

$$S^* = \{x \in \mathbb{R}^n : \|x\|_1 \le \rho^*, \ u = M^T(Ax - y)/\varepsilon, \ u \in \mathcal{B}^\phi\}.$$

Replacing $\mathcal{B}^\phi$ with polytope $\mathcal{Q}_{\varepsilon_j}$ yields the following relaxed set of $S^*$:

$$S_{\varepsilon_j} = \{x \in \mathbb{R}^n : \|x\|_1 \le \rho^*, \ u = M^T(Ax - y)/\varepsilon, \ u \in \mathcal{Q}_{\varepsilon_j}\}. \tag{6.66}$$

Clearly, $S^* \subseteq S_{\varepsilon_j}$ thanks to the fact $\mathcal{B}^\phi \subseteq \mathcal{Q}_{\varepsilon_j}$.

**Lemma 6.6.1** *Let $S_{\varepsilon_j}$ be the set defined in (6.66), where $\mathcal{Q}_{\varepsilon_j}$ is the polytope given in (6.29), as an outer approximation of $\mathcal{B}^\phi$. For every $j$, let $x_{\varepsilon_j}$ be an arbitrary point in $S_{\varepsilon_j}$. Then every accumulation point $\hat{x}$ of the sequence $\{x_{\varepsilon_j}\}_{j \ge 1}$ must satisfy that*

$$\phi(M^T(A\hat{x} - y)) \le \varepsilon.$$

*Proof.* Recall that

$$\mathcal{Q}_{\varepsilon_j} = \{u \in \mathbb{R}^q : \ (a^i)^T u \le 1 \text{ for all } a^i \in \text{Col}(\Gamma_{\mathcal{Q}_{\varepsilon_j}})\}.$$

As $x_{\varepsilon_j} \in S_{\varepsilon_j}$ for any $j \ge 1$. By (6.66), we see that for any $j \ge 1$,

$$\|x_{\varepsilon_j}\|_1 \le \rho^*, \text{ and } (a^i)^T[M^T(Ax_{\varepsilon_j} - y)] \le \varepsilon \text{ for all } a^i \in \text{Col}(\Gamma_{\mathcal{Q}_{\varepsilon_j}}). \tag{6.67}$$

So the sequence $\{x_{\varepsilon_j}\}_{j\geq 1}$ is bounded. Let $\widehat{x}$ be any accumulation point of this sequence. Passing through to a subsequence if necessary, we may assume that $x_{\varepsilon_j} \to \widehat{x}$ as $j \to \infty$. We prove the lemma by contradiction. Assume that $\phi(M^T(A\widehat{x}-y)) > \varepsilon$. Then we define

$$\widehat{\sigma} := \frac{\phi(M^T(A\widehat{x}-y)) - \varepsilon}{\varepsilon},$$

which is a positive constant. Since $\varepsilon_j \to 0$ as $j \to \infty$, there is an integer number $j_0$ such that $\varepsilon_j < \widehat{\sigma}$ for any $j \geq j_0$. By the definition of $\Gamma_{\mathcal{Q}_{\varepsilon_j}}$, we have

$$\mathrm{Col}(\Gamma_{\mathcal{Q}_{\varepsilon_{j'}}}) \subseteq \mathrm{Col}(\Gamma_{\mathcal{Q}_{\varepsilon_j}}) \text{ for any } j \geq j' \geq j_0. \tag{6.68}$$

Thus for any fixed integer number $j' \geq j_0$, the following holds for all $j \geq j'$ :

$$\sup_{a^i \in \mathrm{Col}(\Gamma_{\mathcal{Q}_{\varepsilon_{j'}}})} (a^i)^T [M^T(Ax_{\varepsilon_j} - y)] \leq \sup_{a^i \in \mathrm{Col}(\Gamma_{\mathcal{Q}_{\varepsilon_j}})} (a^i)^T [M^T(Ax_{\varepsilon_j} - y)] \leq \varepsilon,$$

where the first inequality follows from (6.68) and the last inequality follows from (6.67). For every fixed $j' \geq j_0$. Letting $x_{\varepsilon_j} \to \widehat{x}$ as $j \to \infty$, it follows from the above inequality that

$$\sup_{a^i \in \mathrm{Col}(\Gamma_{\mathcal{Q}_{\varepsilon_{j'}}})} (a^i)^T [M^T(A\widehat{x} - y)] \leq \varepsilon. \tag{6.69}$$

Consider the vector $\widehat{a} = M^T(A\widehat{x}-y)/\phi(M^T(A\widehat{x}-y))$ which is on the surface of the unit ball $\mathcal{B}^\phi$. Note that $\varepsilon_{j'} < \widehat{\sigma}$. Applying Lemma 6.3.4 to $\mathcal{Q}_{\varepsilon_{j'}}$, we conclude that for the vector $\widehat{a}$, there is a vector $a^i \in \mathrm{Col}(\Gamma_{\mathcal{Q}_{\varepsilon_{j'}}})$ such that

$$(a^i)^T \widehat{a} \geq \frac{1}{1+\varepsilon_{j'}} > \frac{1}{1+\widehat{\sigma}},$$

which implies

$$(a^i)^T [M^T(A\widehat{x} - y)] > \frac{\phi(M^T(A\widehat{x}-y))}{1+\widehat{\sigma}} = \varepsilon, \tag{6.70}$$

where the equality follows from the definition of $\widehat{\sigma}$. Since $a^i \in \mathrm{Col}(\Gamma_{\mathcal{Q}_{\varepsilon_{j'}}})$, the inequality (6.70) contradicts (6.69). Therefore, for any accumulation point $\widehat{x}$ of the sequence $\{x_{\varepsilon_j}\}_{j\geq 1}$, we must have that $\phi(M^T(A\widehat{x}-y)) \leq \varepsilon$. $\square$

Based on the above lemma, we may prove the next one.

**Lemma 6.6.2** *Let $S^*$ be the solution set of the problem (6.1) and let $S_{\varepsilon_j}$ be given in (6.66) as a relaxed set of $S^*$ . Then $d^{\mathcal{H}}(S^*, S_{\varepsilon_j}) \to 0$ as $j \to \infty$.*

*Proof.* As $S^* \subseteq S_{\varepsilon_j}$, by the definition of Hausdorff metric, we see that

$$d^{\mathcal{H}}(S^*, S_{\varepsilon_j}) = \sup_{x \in S_{\varepsilon_j}} \inf_{z \in S^*} \|x - z\|_2 = \sup_{x \in S_{\varepsilon_j}} \|x - \Pi_{S^*}(x)\|_2. \tag{6.71}$$

Note that $S^*$ and $S_{\varepsilon_j}$ are compact convex sets and the projection operator $\Pi_{S^*}(x)$ is continuous in $\mathbb{R}^n$. The superimum in (6.71) can be attained for every polytope $S_{\varepsilon_j}$. Thus there exists a point in $S_{\varepsilon_j}$, denoted by $x_{\varepsilon_j}$, such that

$$d^{\mathcal{H}}(S^*, S_{\varepsilon_j}) = \|x_{\varepsilon_j} - \Pi_{S^*}(x_{\varepsilon_j})\|_2.$$

Note that $S^* \subseteq S_{\varepsilon_{j+1}} \subseteq S_{\varepsilon_j}$ for any $j \geq 1$. The sequence $\{d^{\mathcal{H}}(S^*, S_{\varepsilon_j})\}_{j \geq 1}$ is non-increasing and non-negative, and hence the limit $\lim_{j \to \infty} d^{\mathcal{H}}(S^*, S_{\varepsilon_j})$ exists. Passing through to a subsequence if necessary, we may assume that the sequence $\{x_{\varepsilon_j}\}_{j \geq 1}$ tends to $\widehat{x}$. Note that $x_{\varepsilon_j} \in S_{\varepsilon_j}$ which indicates that $\|x_{\varepsilon_j}\|_1 \leq \rho^*$ and hence $\|\widehat{x}\|_1 \leq \rho^*$. By Lemma 6.6.1, $\widehat{x}$ must satisfy that $\phi(M^T(A\widehat{x} - y)) \leq \varepsilon$ which, together with the fact $\|\widehat{x}\|_1 \leq \rho^*$, implies that $\widehat{x} \in S^*$. Therefore, $\Pi_{S^*}(\widehat{x}) = \widehat{x}$ and hence

$$\lim_{j \to \infty} d^{\mathcal{H}}(S^*, S_{\varepsilon_j}) = \lim_{j \to \infty} \|x_{\varepsilon_j} - \Pi_{S^*}(x_{\varepsilon_j})\|_2 = \|\widehat{x} - \Pi_{S^*}(\widehat{x})\|_2 = 0,$$

as desired.  □

Throughout the remainder of this section, let $\varepsilon'$ be any fixed small constant (for instance, a small number in $(0, \varepsilon)$). By Lemma 6.6.2. there is an integer number $j_0$ such that $S_{\varepsilon_{j_0}}$, defined as (6.66), satisfies

$$d^{\mathcal{H}}(S^*, S_{\varepsilon_{j_0}}) \leq \varepsilon', \tag{6.72}$$

where $S_{\varepsilon_{j_0}}$ is determined by the fixed polytope $\mathcal{Q}_{\varepsilon_{j_0}}$, as an outer approximation of $\mathcal{B}^{\phi}$. We use $\widehat{n}$ to denote the number of the columns of $\Gamma_{\mathcal{Q}_{\varepsilon_{j_0}}}$ and use $\widehat{e}$ to denote the vector of ones in $\mathbb{R}^{\widehat{n}}$ to distinguish the vector of ones in other spaces. Replacing $\mathcal{B}^{\phi}$ in (6.65) with $\mathcal{Q}_{\varepsilon_{j_0}}$ leads to the following relaxation of (6.1):

$$\begin{aligned} \rho_{j_0}^* : &= \min_{(x,u)}\{\|x\|_1 : u = M^T(Ax - y)/\varepsilon, \ u \in \mathcal{Q}_{\varepsilon_{j_0}}\} \\ &= \min_{x}\{\|x\|_1 : (\Gamma_{\mathcal{Q}_{\varepsilon_{j_0}}})^T[M^T(Ax - y)] \leq \varepsilon \widehat{e}\}, \end{aligned} \tag{6.73}$$

where $\rho_{j_0}^*$ denotes the optimal value of the above minimization problem. Clearly, $\rho_{j_0}^* \leq \rho^*$ due to the fact $\mathcal{B}^{\phi} \subseteq \mathcal{Q}_{\varepsilon_{j_0}}$. Let $S_{\varepsilon_{j_0}}^*$ be the solution set of the problem (6.73), which can be represented as follows:

$$S_{\varepsilon_{j_0}}^* = \{x \in \mathbb{R}^n : \|x\|_1 \leq \rho_{j_0}^*, \ u = M^T(Ax - y)/\varepsilon, \ u \in \mathcal{Q}_{\varepsilon_{j_0}}\}.$$

By (6.66), we immediately see that $S_{\varepsilon_{j_0}}^* \subseteq S_{\varepsilon_{j_0}}$ since $\rho_{j_0}^* \leq \rho^*$. The problem (6.73) can be written as

$$\min_{(x,t)} \ \widetilde{\mathbf{e}}^T t$$

$$\text{s.t.} \quad (\Gamma_{\mathcal{Q}_{\varepsilon_{j_0}}})^T [M^T (Ax - y)] \leq \varepsilon \widehat{\mathbf{e}},$$

$$x \leq t, \ -x \leq t, \ t \in \mathbb{R}_+^n,$$

where $\widetilde{\mathbf{e}}$ is the vector of ones in $\mathbb{R}^n$. It is evident that $t = |x|$ holds at any solution of the problem. The Lagrangian dual of the above problem is given as

$$\max_{(w_1, w_2, w_3)} \quad -\left[ \varepsilon \widehat{\mathbf{e}} + (M\Gamma_{\mathcal{Q}_{\varepsilon_{j_0}}})^T y \right]^T w_3$$

$$\text{s.t.} \quad (A^T M \Gamma_{\mathcal{Q}_{\varepsilon_{j_0}}}) w_3 + w_1 - w_2 = 0, \tag{6.74}$$

$$w_1 + w_2 \leq \widetilde{\mathbf{e}},$$

$$w_1, \ w_2, \ w_3 \geq 0.$$

By the KKT optimality conditions, the solution set of the problem (6.73) can be characterized.

**Lemma 6.6.3** $x^* \in \mathbb{R}^n$ *is a solution of the problem (6.73) if and only if there are vectors* $t^*, w_1^*, w_2^* \in \mathbb{R}_+^n$ *and* $w_3^* \in \mathbb{R}_+^{\widehat{n}}$ *such that* $(x^*, t^*, w_1^*, w_2^*, w_3^*) \in \mathfrak{D}^{(1)}$, *where* $\mathfrak{D}^{(1)}$ *is the set of vectors* $(x, t, w_1, w_2, w_3)$ *satisfying the following system:*

$$
\begin{cases}
x \leq t, \ -x \leq t, \ (\Gamma_{\mathcal{Q}_{\varepsilon_{j_0}}})^T [M^T (Ax - y)] \leq \varepsilon \widehat{\mathbf{e}}, \\
w_1 + w_2 \leq \widetilde{\mathbf{e}}, \ A^T M \Gamma_{\mathcal{Q}_{\varepsilon_{j_0}}} w_3 + w_1 - w_2 = 0, \\
\widetilde{\mathbf{e}}^T t = -\left[ \varepsilon \widehat{\mathbf{e}} + (M\Gamma_{\mathcal{Q}_{\varepsilon_{j_0}}})^T y \right]^T w_3, \\
(t, \ w_1, \ w_2, \ w_3) \geq 0.
\end{cases}
\tag{6.75}
$$

By optimality, we see that $t = |x|$ for any point $(x, t, w_1, w_2, w_3) \in \mathfrak{D}^{(1)}$. The set $\mathfrak{D}^{(1)}$ defined by (6.75) can be reformulated as

$$\mathfrak{D}^{(1)} = \{ z = (x, t, w_1, w_2, w_3) : \overline{M}^1 z \leq \overline{b}^1, \ \overline{M}^2 z = \overline{b}^2 \},$$

where $\overline{b}^2 = 0, \overline{b}^1 = [0, 0, \widetilde{\mathbf{e}}^T, ((M\Gamma_{\mathcal{Q}_{\varepsilon_{j_0}}})^T y + \varepsilon \widehat{\mathbf{e}})^T, 0, 0, 0, 0]^T$ and

$$
\overline{M}^1 =
\begin{bmatrix}
I & -I & 0 & 0 & 0 \\
-I & -I & 0 & 0 & 0 \\
0 & 0 & I & I & 0 \\
(M\Gamma_{\mathcal{Q}_{\varepsilon_{j_0}}})^T A & 0 & 0 & 0 & 0 \\
0 & -I & 0 & 0 & 0 \\
0 & 0 & -I & 0 & 0 \\
0 & 0 & 0 & -I & 0 \\
0 & 0 & 0 & 0 & -\widehat{I}
\end{bmatrix},
\tag{6.76}
$$

$$\overline{M}^2 = \begin{bmatrix} 0 & 0 & I & -I & A^T M \Gamma_{\mathcal{Q}_{\varepsilon_{j_0}}} \\ 0 & \widetilde{e}^T & 0 & 0 & \varepsilon \widehat{e}^T + y^T M \Gamma_{\mathcal{Q}_{\varepsilon_{j_0}}} \end{bmatrix}, \tag{6.77}$$

where $I \in \mathbb{R}^{n \times n}$ and $\widehat{I} \in \mathbb{R}^{\widehat{n} \times \widehat{n}}$ are identity matrices and $0's$ are zero-matrices with suitable sizes. We now state and prove the main stability theorem for nonlinear DS problems.

**Theorem 6.6.4** *Given the problem data* $(A, M, y, \varepsilon)$, *where* $A \in \mathbb{R}^{m \times n}$ $(m < n)$ *and* $M \in \mathbb{R}^{m \times q}$ $(m \le q)$ *with* rank$(A) =$ rank$(M) = m$. *Let* $\varepsilon'$ *be a fixed small constant and let* $\mathcal{Q}_{\varepsilon_{j_0}}$ *be the fixed polytope such that (6.72) is achieved. Suppose that* $A^T$ *satisfies the weak RSP of order* $k$. *Then for any* $x \in \mathbb{R}^n$, *there is a solution* $x^*$ *of the problem (6.1) approximating* $x$ *with error*

$$\|x - x^*\|_2 \le 2\overline{\gamma}\{2\sigma_k(x)_1 + \widehat{n}\left(\phi(M^T(Ax - y)) - \varepsilon\right)^+ + \widehat{c}\varepsilon$$
$$+ \widehat{c}\phi(M^T(Ax - y))\} + \varepsilon', \tag{6.78}$$

*where* $\widehat{c}$ *is the constant given in Theorem 5.5.2, and* $\overline{\gamma} = \sigma_{\infty,2}(\overline{M}^1, \overline{M}^2)$ *is the Robinson constant determined by* $(\overline{M}^1, \overline{M}^2)$ *in (6.76) and (6.77). Moreover, for any* $x$ *satisfying the constraint of (6.1), there is a solution* $x^*$ *of (6.1) approximating* $x$ *with error*

$$\|x - x^*\|_2 \le 2\overline{\gamma}\{2\sigma_k(x)_1 + c\varepsilon + c\phi(M^T(Ax - y))\} + \varepsilon'$$
$$\le 4\overline{\gamma}\{\sigma_k(x)_1 + c\varepsilon\} + \varepsilon'. \tag{6.79}$$

*Proof.* Let $x$ be any given vector in $\mathbb{R}^n$. Let $S$ be the support set of the $k$ largest entries of $|x|$. Let $S' = \{i \in S : x_i > 0\}$ and $S'' = \{i \in S : x_i < 0\}$. Clearly, $|S'| + |S''| \le |S| \le k$, and $S'$ and $S''$ are disjointed. Since $A^T$ satisfies the weak RSP of order $k$, there exists a vector $\zeta = A^T u^*$ for some $u^* \in \mathbb{R}^m$ satisfying $\zeta_i = 1$ for $i \in S'$, $\zeta_i = -1$ for $i \in S''$, and $|\zeta_i| \le 1$ for $i \notin S' \cup S''$. For the fixed small constant $\varepsilon'$, there exists an integer number $j_0$ such that the polytope $\mathcal{Q}_{\varepsilon_{j_0}}$, represented as (6.31), ensures that the set $S_{\varepsilon_{j_0}}$, defined by (6.66), achieves the bound (6.72).

We now construct a feasible solution $(\widetilde{w}_1, \widetilde{w}_2, \widetilde{w}_3)$ to the problem (6.74). Set

$$(\widetilde{w}_1)_i = 1 \text{ and } (\widetilde{w}_2)_i = 0 \text{ for all } i \in S',$$

$$(\widetilde{w}_1)_i = 0 \text{ and } (\widetilde{w}_2)_i = 1 \text{ for all } i \in S'',$$

$$(\widetilde{w}_1)_i = (|\zeta_i| + \zeta_i)/2 \text{ and } (\widetilde{w}_2)_i = (|\zeta_i| - \zeta_i)/2 \text{ for all } i \notin S' \cup S''.$$

This choice ensures that

$$(\widetilde{w}_1, \widetilde{w}_2) \ge 0, \ \widetilde{w}_1 + \widetilde{w}_2 \le \widetilde{e} \text{ and } \widetilde{w}_1 - \widetilde{w}_2 = \zeta.$$

We now construct the vector $\widetilde{w}_3$. By the definition of $\mathcal{Q}_{\varepsilon_{j_0}}$, we see that $\{\pm e^{(i)} : i = 1,\ldots,q\} \subseteq \mathrm{Col}(\Gamma_{\mathcal{Q}_{\varepsilon_{j_0}}})$, the set of column vectors of $\Gamma_{\mathcal{Q}_{\varepsilon_{j_0}}}$ with cardinality $|\mathrm{Col}(\Gamma_{\mathcal{Q}_{\varepsilon_{j_0}}})| = \widehat{n}$. It is not difficult to show that there exists a vector $\widetilde{w}_3 \in \mathbb{R}_+^{\widehat{n}}$ satisfying $M\Gamma_{\mathcal{Q}_{\varepsilon_{j_0}}}\widetilde{w}_3 = -u^*$. First, since $M$ is a full row rank matrix, there is an $m \times m$ invertible submatrix $M_{\mathfrak{J}}$ with $|\mathfrak{J}| = m$ consisting of $m$ independent columns in $M$. Then by choosing $\widetilde{h} \in \mathbb{R}^q$ such that $\widetilde{h}_i = 0$ for all $i \notin \mathfrak{J}$ and $\widetilde{h}_{\mathfrak{J}} = -M_{\mathfrak{J}}^{-1}u^*$ which implies that $M\widetilde{h} = -u^*$. We now find $\widetilde{w}_3$ such that $\Gamma_{\mathcal{Q}_{\varepsilon_{j_0}}}\widetilde{w}_3 = \widetilde{h}$. In fact, without loss of generality, we assume that $\{-e^{(i)} : i = 1,\ldots,q\}$ are arranged as the first $q$ columns of $\Gamma_{\mathcal{Q}_{\varepsilon_{j_0}}}$ and $\{e^{(i)} : i = 1,\ldots,q\}$ are arranged as the second $q$ columns of $\Gamma_{\mathcal{Q}_{\varepsilon_{j_0}}}$. For every $i = 1,\ldots,q$, set $(\widetilde{w}_3)_i = \widetilde{h}_i$ if $\widetilde{h}_i \geq 0$; otherwise, set $(\widetilde{w}_3)_{q+i} = -\widetilde{h}_i$ if $\widetilde{h}_i < 0$. The remaining entries of $\widetilde{w}_3 \in \mathbb{R}^{\widehat{n}}$ are set to be zero. By this choice of $\widetilde{w}_3$, we see that $\widetilde{w}_3 \geq 0$ satisfying that $\Gamma_{\mathcal{Q}_{\varepsilon_{j_0}}}\widetilde{w}_3 = -\widetilde{h}$ and

$$
\begin{aligned}
\|\widetilde{w}_3\|_1 &= \|\widetilde{h}\|_1 = \|\widetilde{h}_{\mathfrak{J}}\|_1 = \|M_{\mathfrak{J}}^{-1}u^*\|_1 = \|M_{\mathfrak{J}}^{-1}(AA^T)^{-1}A\zeta\|_1 \\
&\leq \|M_{\mathfrak{J}}^{-1}(AA^T)^{-1}A\|_{\infty \to 1}\|\zeta\|_\infty \leq \widehat{c},
\end{aligned}
\tag{6.80}
$$

where $\widehat{c}$ is the constant given in Theorem 5.5.2. By the triangle inequality and the fact $\phi^*(e^{(i)}) = 1$, $i = 1,\ldots,q$, we have

$$
\phi^*(\widetilde{h}) = \phi^*\left(\sum_{j \in \mathfrak{J}}\widetilde{h}_j e^{(j)}\right) \leq \sum_{j \in \mathfrak{J}}\phi^*(\widetilde{h}_j e^{(j)}) = \sum_{j \in \mathfrak{J}}|\widetilde{h}_j|\phi^*(e^{(j)}) = \sum_{j \in \mathfrak{J}}|\widetilde{h}_j| = \|\widetilde{h}\|_1 \leq \widehat{c},
$$

$$
\tag{6.81}
$$

where the last inequality follows from (6.80).

For the vector $(x, t, \widetilde{w}_1, \widetilde{w}_2, \widetilde{w}_3)$ with $t = |x|$, applying Lemma 5.2.2 with $(M^1, M^2) = (\overline{M}^1, \overline{M}^2)$, where $\overline{M}^1$ and $\overline{M}^2$ are given in (6.76) and (6.77), there is a point in $\mathfrak{D}^{(1)}$, denoted by $(\widehat{x}, \widehat{t}, \widehat{w}_1, \widehat{w}_2, \widehat{w}_3)$, such that

$$
\left\|\begin{bmatrix} x \\ t \\ \widetilde{w}_1 \\ \widetilde{w}_2 \\ \widetilde{w}_3 \end{bmatrix} - \begin{bmatrix} \widehat{x} \\ \widehat{t} \\ \widehat{w}_1 \\ \widehat{w}_2 \\ \widehat{w}_3 \end{bmatrix}\right\|_2 \leq \overline{\gamma}\left\|\begin{bmatrix} (x-t)^+ \\ (-x-t)^+ \\ ((-t)^+\left((\Gamma_{\mathcal{Q}_{\varepsilon_{j_0}}})^T[M^T(Ax-y)] - \varepsilon\widehat{e}\right)^+ \\ (\widetilde{w}_1 + \widetilde{w}_2 - \widehat{e})^+ \\ A^T M\Gamma_{\mathcal{Q}_{\varepsilon_{j_0}}}\widetilde{w}_3 + \widetilde{w}_1 - \widetilde{w}_2 \\ \widehat{e}^T t + \left(\varepsilon\widehat{e} + (M\Gamma_{\mathcal{Q}_{\varepsilon_{j_0}}})^T y\right)^T \widetilde{w}_3 \\ (V)^+ \end{bmatrix}\right\|_1 ,
$$

$$
\tag{6.82}
$$

where $(V)^+ = ((-\widetilde{w}_1)^+, (-\widetilde{w}_2)^+, (-\widetilde{w}_3)^+)$, and $\overline{\gamma} = \sigma_{\infty,2}(\overline{M}^1, \overline{M}^2)$ is the Robinson's constant determined by $(\overline{M}^1, \overline{M}^2)$ in (6.76) and (6.77). By the nonnegativity of $(t, \widetilde{w}_1, \widetilde{w}_2, \widetilde{w}_3)$, we have that $(V)^+ = 0$. Since $t = |x|$, we have $(x-t)^+ = (-x-t)^+ = 0$. Since $(\widetilde{w}_1, \widetilde{w}_2, \widetilde{w}_3)$ satisfies the constraints of (6.74), we have

$$
(\widetilde{w}_1 + \widetilde{w}_2 - \widehat{e})^+ = 0, \quad A^T M\Gamma_{\mathcal{Q}_{\varepsilon_{j_0}}}\widetilde{w}_3 + \widetilde{w}_1 - \widetilde{w}_2 = 0.
$$

Thus the inequality (6.82) is reduced to

$$
\begin{aligned}
&\|x - \widehat{x}\|_2 \\
&\leq \overline{\gamma} \left\| \left( (\Gamma_{\mathcal{Q}_{\varepsilon_{j_0}}})^T [M^T(Ax - y)] - \varepsilon \widehat{\mathbf{e}} \right)^+ \right\|_1 + \overline{\gamma} \left| \widetilde{\mathbf{e}}^T t + \left[ \varepsilon \widehat{\mathbf{e}} + (M\Gamma_{\mathcal{Q}_{\varepsilon_{j_0}}})^T y \right]^T \widetilde{w}_3 \right|.
\end{aligned}
$$
$$(6.83)$$

Recall that $\phi^*(a^i) = 1$ for every $a^i \in \mathrm{Col}(\Gamma_{\mathcal{Q}_{\varepsilon_{j_0}}})$. Thus,

$$(a^i)^T(M^T(Ax - y)) \leq \phi^*(a^i)\phi(M^T(Ax - y)) = \phi(M^T(Ax - y)).$$

This implies

$$\left( (a^i)^T(M^T(Ax - y)) - \varepsilon \right)^+ \leq \left( \phi(M^T(Ax - y)) - \varepsilon \right)^+,$$

and hence,

$$\left( (\Gamma_{\mathcal{Q}_{\varepsilon_{j_0}}})^T(M^T(Ax - y)) - \varepsilon \widehat{\mathbf{e}} \right)^+ \leq (\phi(M^T(Ax - y)) - \varepsilon)^+ \widehat{\mathbf{e}}.$$

Therefore,

$$\left\| \left( (\Gamma_{\mathcal{Q}_{\varepsilon_{j_0}}})^T(M^T(Ax - y)) - \varepsilon \widehat{\mathbf{e}} \right)^+ \right\|_1 \leq \widehat{n}(\phi(M^T(Ax - y)) - \varepsilon)^+. \qquad (6.84)$$

Note that $x^T A^T u^* = x^T \zeta = \|x_S\|_1 + x_{\overline{S}}^T \zeta_{\overline{S}}$ and $|x_{\overline{S}}^T \zeta_{\overline{S}}| \leq \|x_{\overline{S}}\|_1 \|\zeta_{\overline{S}}\|_\infty \leq \|x_{\overline{S}}\|_1$. Thus,

$$\left| \widetilde{\mathbf{e}}^T |x| - x^T A^T u^* \right| = \left| \widetilde{\mathbf{e}}^T |x| - \|x_S\|_1 - x_{\overline{S}}^T \zeta_{\overline{S}} \right| \leq 2\|x_{\overline{S}}\|_1 = 2\sigma_k(x)_1.$$

Note that if $\vartheta = M^T(Ax - y)$ and $M\Gamma_{\mathcal{Q}_{\varepsilon_{j_0}}} \widetilde{w}_3 = -u^*$ and $\Gamma_{\mathcal{Q}_{\varepsilon_{j_0}}} \widetilde{w}_3 = -h$, we have

$$
\begin{aligned}
\left| \widetilde{\mathbf{e}}^T t + [\varepsilon \widehat{\mathbf{e}} + (M\Gamma_{\mathcal{Q}_{\varepsilon_{j_0}}})^T y]^T \widetilde{w}_3 \right| &= \left| \widetilde{\mathbf{e}}^T |x| + \varepsilon \widehat{\mathbf{e}}^T \widetilde{w}_3 + (x^T A^T M - \vartheta^T)\Gamma_{\mathcal{Q}_{\varepsilon_{j_0}}} \widetilde{w}_3 \right| \\
&= \left| \widetilde{\mathbf{e}}^T |x| - x^T A^T u^* + \vartheta^T \widetilde{h} + \varepsilon \widehat{\mathbf{e}}^T \widetilde{w}_3 \right| \\
&\leq 2\sigma_k(x)_1 + |\vartheta^T \widetilde{h}| + |\varepsilon \widehat{\mathbf{e}}^T \widetilde{w}_3| \\
&\leq 2\sigma_k(x)_1 + \phi(\vartheta)\phi^*(\widetilde{h}) + \varepsilon \|\widetilde{w}_3\|_1 \\
&\leq 2\sigma_k(x)_1 + \widehat{c}\phi(M^T(Ax - y)) + \widehat{c}\varepsilon, \qquad (6.85)
\end{aligned}
$$

where the last inequality follows from (6.80) and (6.81). Combining (6.83), (6.84) and (6.85) yields

$$\|x - \widehat{x}\|_2 \leq \overline{\gamma} \left\{ \widehat{n} \left( \phi(M^T(Ax - y)) - \varepsilon \right)^+ + 2\sigma_k(x)_1 + \widehat{c}\varepsilon + \widehat{c}\phi(M^T(Ax - y)) \right\}.$$
$$(6.86)$$

We now consider the three bounded convex sets $S^*, S^*_{\varepsilon_{j_0}}$ and $S_{\varepsilon_{j_0}}$. By their definitions, $S^* \subseteq S_{\varepsilon_{j_0}}$ and $S^*_{\varepsilon_{j_0}} \subseteq S_{\varepsilon_{j_0}}$. Let $x^* = \Pi_{S^*}(x)$ and $\bar{x} = \Pi_{S_{\varepsilon_{j_0}}}(x)$. Note that $\hat{x} \in S^*_{\varepsilon_{j_0}}$. By applying Lemma 6.2.2 (by setting $S = S^*, U = S^*_{\varepsilon_{j_0}}$ and $T = S_{\varepsilon_{j_0}}$), we can conclude that

$$\|x - x^*\|_2 \le d^{\mathcal{H}}(S^*, S_{\varepsilon_{j_0}}) + 2\|x - \hat{x}\|_2 \le \varepsilon' + 2\|x - \hat{x}\|_2.$$

Merging this inequality with (6.86) yields (6.78), i.e.,

$$\|x - x^*\|_2 \le 2\bar{\gamma}\{\hat{n}\left(\phi(M^T(Ax - y)) - \varepsilon\right)^+ + 2\sigma_k(x)_1 + \hat{c}\varepsilon + \hat{c}\phi(M^T(Ax - y))\} + \varepsilon'.$$

When $\phi(M^T(Ax - y)) \le \varepsilon$, i.e., $x$ is feasible to the problem (6.1), the inequality above is reduced to (6.79). □

Since every condition in Corollary 5.4.5 implies the weak RSP of order $k$, we immediately have the following result for the DS with a nonlinear constraint.

**Corollary 6.6.5** *Let A and M be given as in Theorem 6.6.4. Let $\varepsilon' \in (0, \varepsilon)$ be a fixed small constant and let $Q_{\varepsilon_{j_0}}$ be the fixed polytope represented as (6.31) such that (6.72) is achieved. Suppose that one of the following conditions holds:*

- *A (with $\ell_2$-normalized columns) satisfies the mutual coherence property $\mu_1(k) + \mu_1(k-1) < 1$;*

- *RIP of order 2k with constant $\delta_{2k} < 1/\sqrt{2}$;*

- *Stable NSP of order k with constant $\rho \in (0, 1)$;*

- *Robust NSP of order k with $\rho' \in (0, 1)$ and $\rho'' > 0$;*

- *NSP of order k;*

- *RSP of order k of $A^T$.*

*Then the conclusions of Theorem 6.6.4 are valid for the DS problem (6.1).*

## 6.7 The LASSO Problem

LASSO is a popular statistical regression method. It is also a useful method for sparse data recovery. In this section, we consider the stability issue of the nonlinear minimization problem (6.3) which is more general than the standard LASSO model. In this chapter, the problem (6.3) is also referred to as the LASSO problem. Let $\rho^*$ denote the optimal value of (6.3), i.e.,

$$\rho^* = \min_x \{\phi(M^T(Ax - y)) : \|x\|_1 \le \mu\}, \tag{6.87}$$

where $(M,A,y,\mu)$ is the given problem data, and $\phi(\cdot)$ is a norm satisfying $\phi(\mathbf{e}^{(i)}) = 1$ and $\phi^*(\mathbf{e}^{(i)}) = 1$ for $i = 1,\dots,q$. We consider the nonlinear norm $\phi$ in the sense that the inequality $\phi(x) \leq \rho$ with $\rho > 0$ cannot be equivalently represented as a finite number of linear inequalities or equalities, for example, when $\phi$ is the $\ell_p$-norm with $p \in (1,\infty)$. We show that (6.3) is also stable in the sense of Definition 6.1.1 under the weak RSP of order $k$ of $A^T$. The problem (6.3), i.e., (6.87), is equivalent to

$$\rho^* = \min_{(x,\rho)}\{\rho : \phi(M^T(Ax-y)) \leq \rho, \ \|x\|_1 \leq \mu\}, \qquad (6.88)$$

where the first constraint is nonlinear.

Let $\Lambda^*$ be the solution set of (6.3), which in terms of $\rho^*$ can be written as

$$\Lambda^* = \{x \in \mathbb{R}^n : \|x\|_1 \leq \mu, \ \phi(M^T(Ax-y)) \leq \rho^*\}.$$

The analytic method in Sections 6.5 and 6.6 can be extended to deal with the nonlinear problem (6.88).

Similar to Section 6.6, we approximate the unit ball $\mathcal{B}^\phi$ in $\mathbb{R}^q$ by the polytope $\mathcal{Q}_{\varepsilon_j}$, which is defined in (6.29) and is represented as

$$\mathcal{Q}_{\varepsilon_j} = \{u \in \mathbb{R}^q : (a^i)^T u \leq 1 \text{ for all } a^i \in \mathrm{Col}(\Gamma_{\mathcal{Q}_{\varepsilon_j}})\}.$$

The vectors $a^i$ in $\mathrm{Col}(\Gamma_{\mathcal{Q}_{\varepsilon_j}})$ are drawn from the surface of the dual unit ball, i.e., $a^i \in \{a \in \mathbb{R}^q : \phi^*(a) = 1\}$. In terms of $\mathcal{Q}_{\varepsilon_j}$, we immediately obtain a relaxation of $\Lambda^*$ as follows:

$$\Lambda_{\varepsilon_j} = \{x : \|x\|_1 \leq \mu, \ (a^i)^T(M^T(Ax-y)) \leq \rho^* \text{ for all } a_i \in \mathrm{Col}(\Gamma_{\mathcal{Q}_{\varepsilon_j}})\}. \quad (6.89)$$

Clearly, $\Lambda^* \subseteq \Lambda_{\varepsilon_j}$ for any $j \geq 1$. Then we have the following result similar to Lemmas 6.6.1 and 6.6.2.

**Lemma 6.7.1** *Let $\Lambda_{\varepsilon_j}$ be defined as (6.89). Then the following properties hold true:*

(i) *For every $j$, let $x_{\varepsilon_j}$ be an arbitrary point in $\Lambda_{\varepsilon_j}$. Then any accumulation point $\hat{x}$ of the sequence $\{x_{\varepsilon_j}\}$ satisfies that $\hat{x} \in \Lambda^*$, i.e., $\|\hat{x}\|_1 \leq \mu$ and $\phi(M^T(A\hat{x}-y)) \leq \rho^*$.*

(ii) $d^{\mathcal{H}}(\Lambda^*, \Lambda_{\varepsilon_j}) \to 0$ *as $j \to \infty$.*

*Proof.* The proof is similar to that of Lemmas 6.6.1 and 6.6.2. Note that $x_{\varepsilon_j} \in \Lambda_{\varepsilon_j}$ for any $j \geq 1$. Thus for every $j$, we have $\|x_{\varepsilon_j}\|_1 \leq \mu$ and

$$(a^i)^T(M^T(Ax_{\varepsilon_j}-y)) \leq \rho^* \quad \text{for all } a^i \in \mathrm{Col}(\Gamma_{\mathcal{Q}_{\varepsilon_j}}). \qquad (6.90)$$

Let $\hat{x}$ be any accumulation point of the sequence $\{x_{\varepsilon_j}\}$ which obeys $\|\hat{x}\|_1 \leq \varepsilon$.

Passing through to a subsequence if necessary, we may assume that $x_{\varepsilon_j} \to \widehat{x}$ as $j \to \infty$. We show this lemma by contradiction. Assume that $\phi(M^T(A\widehat{x} - y)) > \rho^*$. Then we define:

$$\sigma^* := \begin{cases} \frac{\phi(M^T(A\widehat{x}-y))-\rho^*}{\rho^*} & \rho^* \neq 0 \\ 1 & \rho^* = 0, \end{cases}$$

which is a positive constant. By the definition of $\varepsilon_j$, there is an integer number $j_0$ such that $\varepsilon_j < \sigma^*$ for any $j \geq j_0$. By a similar argument in the proof of Lemma 6.6.2, for any $j \geq j' \geq j_0$, it follows from (6.90) and the fact $\mathrm{Col}(\Gamma_{\mathcal{Q}_{\varepsilon_{j'}}}) \subseteq \mathrm{Col}(\Gamma_{\mathcal{Q}_{\varepsilon_j}})$ that

$$\sup_{a^i \in \mathrm{Col}(\Gamma_{\mathcal{Q}_{\varepsilon_{j'}}})} (a^i)^T(M^T(A\widehat{x} - y)) \leq \rho^*. \tag{6.91}$$

Let $\widehat{a} = M^T(A\widehat{x} - y)/\phi(M^T(A\widehat{x} - y))$, which is on the surface of $\mathcal{B}^\phi$. Applying Lemma 6.3.4 to $\mathcal{Q}_{\varepsilon_{j'}}$ for $j' \geq j_0$, we see that for $\widehat{a}$, there is a vector $a^i \in \mathrm{Col}(\Gamma_{\mathcal{Q}_{\varepsilon_{j'}}})$ such that

$$(a^i)^T \widehat{a} \geq \frac{1}{1+\varepsilon_{j'}} > \frac{1}{1+\sigma^*},$$

which implies

$$(a^i)^T[M^T(A\widehat{x} - y)] > \frac{\phi(M^T(A\widehat{x} - y))}{1+\sigma^*} \geq \rho^*,$$

where the second inequality follows from the definition of $\sigma^*$. This contradicts (6.91). Therefore, $\phi(M^T(A\widehat{x} - y)) \leq \rho^*$. This, together with $\|\widehat{x}\| \leq \mu$, implies that $\widehat{x} \in \Lambda^*$.

We now prove that $d^{\mathcal{H}}(\Lambda^*, \Lambda_{\varepsilon_j}) \to 0$ as $j \to \infty$. Since $\Lambda^* \subseteq \Lambda_{\varepsilon_j}$, by the continuity of $\Pi_{\Lambda^*}(\cdot)$ and compactness of $\Lambda_{\varepsilon_j}$, there exists for each $\varepsilon_j$ a point $\widetilde{x}_{\varepsilon_j} \in \Lambda_{\varepsilon_j}$ such that

$$d^{\mathcal{H}}(\Lambda^*, \Lambda_{\varepsilon_j}) = \sup_{x \in \Lambda_{\varepsilon_j}} \inf_{z \in \Lambda^*} \|x - z\|_2 = \sup_{x \in \Lambda_{\varepsilon_j}} \|x - \Pi_{\Lambda^*}(x)\|_2$$

$$= \left\| \widetilde{x}_{\varepsilon_j} - \Pi_{\Lambda^*}(\widetilde{x}_{\varepsilon_j}) \right\|_2. \tag{6.92}$$

Note that

$$\Lambda^* \subseteq \Lambda_{\varepsilon_{j+1}} \subseteq \Lambda_{\varepsilon_j} \text{ for any } j \geq 1,$$

which implies that $\{d^{\mathcal{H}}(\Lambda^*, \Lambda_{\varepsilon_j})\}_{j \geq 1}$ is a non-increasing non-negative sequence. Thus $\lim_{j \to \infty} d^{\mathcal{H}}(\Lambda^*, \Lambda_{\varepsilon_j})$ exists. Since the sequence $\{\widetilde{x}_{\varepsilon_j}\}_{j \geq 1}$ is bounded, passing through to subsequence of $\{\widetilde{x}_{\varepsilon_j}\}$ if necessary, we may assume that $\widetilde{x}_{\varepsilon_j} \to \widetilde{x}$

as $j \to \infty$. From Item (i), we see that $\tilde{x} \in \Lambda^*$. Therefore $\Pi_{\Lambda^*}(\tilde{x}) = \tilde{x}$. It follows from (6.92) that

$$\lim_{j \to \infty} d^{\mathcal{H}}(\Lambda^*, \Lambda_{\varepsilon_j}) = \|\tilde{x} - \Pi_{\Lambda^*}(\tilde{x})\|_2 = 0.$$

The proof is complete. □

In the remaining section, let $\varepsilon'$ be any fixed sufficiently small constant. By Lemma 6.7.1, there is an integer number $j_0$ such that

$$d^{\mathcal{H}}(\Lambda^*, \Lambda_{\varepsilon_{j_0}}) \leq \varepsilon', \tag{6.93}$$

where $\Lambda_{\varepsilon_{j_0}}$ is a fixed set defined in (6.89) which is determined by $\mathcal{Q}_{\varepsilon_{j_0}}$. Let $\widehat{n} = |\text{Col}(\Gamma_{\mathcal{Q}_{\varepsilon_{j_0}}})|$ denote the number of columns of $\Gamma_{\mathcal{Q}_{\varepsilon_{j_0}}}$ and $\widehat{e}$ the vector of ones in $\mathbb{R}^{\widehat{n}}$. Thus $\mathcal{Q}_{\varepsilon_{j_0}}$ is represented as

$$\mathcal{Q}_{\varepsilon_{j_0}} = \{u \in \mathbb{R}^q : (\Gamma_{\mathcal{Q}_{\varepsilon_{j_0}}})^T u \leq \widehat{e}\}.$$

We consider the following relaxation of (6.88):

$$\rho^*_{\varepsilon_{j_0}} := \min_{(x,\rho)} \{\rho : \|x\|_1 \leq \mu, \ (\Gamma_{\mathcal{Q}_{\varepsilon_{j_0}}})^T (M^T(Ax - y)) \leq \rho \widehat{e}\}, \tag{6.94}$$

where $\rho^*_{\varepsilon_{j_0}}$ is the optimal value of the above optimization problem. Clearly, $\rho^*_{\varepsilon_{j_0}} \leq \rho^*$ due to the fact that (6.94) is a relaxation of (6.88). Since $\Gamma_{\mathcal{Q}_{\varepsilon_{j_0}}}$ includes $\pm e^{(i)}$, $i = 1, \ldots, n$ as its columns, the variable $\rho$ in (6.94) must be non-negative. Let

$$\Lambda^*_{\varepsilon_{j_0}} = \{x \in \mathbb{R}^n : \|x\|_1 \leq \mu, \ (\Gamma_{\mathcal{Q}_{\varepsilon_{j_0}}})^T (M^T(Ax - y)) \leq \rho^*_{\varepsilon_{j_0}} \widehat{e}\}$$

be the solution set of (6.94). Note that

$$\Lambda_{\varepsilon_{j_0}} = \{x \in \mathbb{R}^n : \|x\|_1 \leq \mu, \ (\Gamma_{\mathcal{Q}_{\varepsilon_{j_0}}})^T (M^T(Ax - y)) \leq \rho^* \widehat{e}\}.$$

Clearly, $\Lambda^*_{\varepsilon_{j_0}} \subseteq \Lambda_{\varepsilon_{j_0}}$ as $\rho^*_{\varepsilon_{j_0}} \leq \rho^*$. The problem (6.94) is equivalent to

$$\begin{aligned}
\min_{(x,t,\rho)} \quad & \rho \\
\text{s.t.} \quad & x \leq t, \ -x \leq t, \ \widetilde{e}^T t \leq \mu, \\
& (\Gamma_{\mathcal{Q}_{\varepsilon_{j_0}}})^T [M^T(Ax - y)] \leq \rho \widehat{e}, \\
& (t, \rho) \geq 0,
\end{aligned} \tag{6.95}$$

where $\widetilde{e}$ is the vector of ones in $\mathbb{R}^n$. The Lagrangian dual of (6.95) is given as

$$\begin{aligned}
\max_{w_i, i=1,\ldots,4} \quad & -\mu w_3 - (y^T M \Gamma_{\mathcal{Q}_{\varepsilon_{j_0}}}) w_4 \\
\text{s.t.} \quad & A^T M \Gamma_{\mathcal{Q}_{\varepsilon_{j_0}}} w_4 + w_1 - w_2 = 0, \\
& w_1 + w_2 - w_3 \widetilde{e} \leq 0, \ \widehat{e}^T w_4 \leq 1, \\
& w_1 \in \mathbb{R}^n_+, \ w_2 \in \mathbb{R}^n_+, \ w_3 \in \mathbb{R}_+, \ w_4 \in \mathbb{R}^{\widehat{n}}_+.
\end{aligned} \tag{6.96}$$

The lemma below follows immediately from the KKT optimality condition of (6.95).

**Lemma 6.7.2** $\bar{x} \in \mathbb{R}^n$ *is a solution of (6.94) if and only if there are vectors* $\bar{t}, \bar{w}_1, \bar{w}_2 \in \mathbb{R}^n_+, \bar{\rho} \in \mathbb{R}_+, \bar{w}_3 \in \mathbb{R}_+$ *and* $\bar{w}_4 \in \mathbb{R}^{\hat{n}}_+$ *such that* $(\bar{x}, \bar{t}, \bar{\rho}, \bar{w}_1, \bar{w}_2, \bar{w}_3, \bar{w}_4) \in \mathfrak{D}^{(2)}$, *where* $\mathfrak{D}^{(2)}$ *is the set of vectors* $(x, t, \rho, w_1, w_2, w_3, w_4)$ *satisfying the system*

$$
\begin{cases}
x \leq t, \ -x \leq t, \ \tilde{e}^T t \leq \mu, \ (\Gamma_{\mathcal{Q}_{\varepsilon_{j_0}}})^T [M^T(Ax - y)] \leq \rho \hat{e}, \\
A^T M \Gamma_{\mathcal{Q}_{\varepsilon_{j_0}}} w_4 + w_1 - w_2 = 0, \ w_1 + w_2 - w_3 \tilde{e} \leq 0, \\
\rho = -\mu w_3 - (y^T M \Gamma_{\mathcal{Q}_{\varepsilon_{j_0}}}) w_4, \ \hat{e}^T w_4 \leq 1, \\
(t, \rho, w_1, w_2, w_3, w_4) \geq 0.
\end{cases}
\tag{6.97}
$$

It is easy to see that $t = |x|$ holds for any point $(x, t, \rho, w_1, w_2, w_3, w_4) \in \mathfrak{D}^{(2)}$. The system (6.97) can be rewritten as:

$$
\mathfrak{D}^{(2)} = \{z = (x, t, \rho, w_1, w_2, w_3, w_4) : \ \widehat{M}^1 z \leq \widehat{b}^1, \ \widehat{M}^2 z = \widehat{b}^2\},
$$

where $\widehat{b}^2 = 0$, $\widehat{b}^1 = (0, 0, \mu, y^T M \Gamma_{\mathcal{Q}_{\varepsilon_{j_0}}}, 0, 1, 0, 0, 0, 0, 0, 0)^T$ and

$$
\widehat{M}^1 =
\begin{bmatrix}
I & -I & 0 & 0 & 0 & 0 & 0 \\
-I & -I & 0 & 0 & 0 & 0 & 0 \\
0 & \tilde{e}^T & 0 & 0 & 0 & 0 & 0 \\
(M\Gamma_{\mathcal{Q}_{\varepsilon_{j_0}}})^T A & 0 & -\hat{e} & 0 & 0 & 0 & 0 \\
0 & 0 & 0 & I & I & -\tilde{e} & 0 \\
0 & 0 & 0 & 0 & 0 & 0 & \hat{e}^T \\
0 & -I & 0 & 0 & 0 & 0 & 0 \\
0 & 0 & -1 & 0 & 0 & 0 & 0 \\
0 & 0 & 0 & -I & 0 & 0 & 0 \\
0 & 0 & 0 & 0 & -I & 0 & 0 \\
0 & 0 & 0 & 0 & 0 & -1 & 0 \\
0 & 0 & 0 & 0 & 0 & 0 & -\widehat{I}
\end{bmatrix},
\tag{6.98}
$$

$$
\widehat{M}^2 =
\begin{bmatrix}
0 & 0 & 0 & I & -I & 0 & A^T M \Gamma_{\mathcal{Q}_{\varepsilon_{j_0}}} \\
0 & 0 & 1 & 0 & 0 & \mu & y^T M \Gamma_{\mathcal{Q}_{\varepsilon_{j_0}}}
\end{bmatrix},
\tag{6.99}
$$

where $I \in \mathbb{R}^{n \times n}$ and $\widehat{I} \in \mathbb{R}^{\hat{n} \times \hat{n}}$ are identity matrices and $0's$ are zero matrices with suitable sizes. The main result in this section is stated as follows.

**Theorem 6.7.3** *Let* $\varepsilon' > 0$ *be any fixed sufficiently small constant, and let* $\mathcal{Q}_{\varepsilon_{j_0}}$ *be the fixed polytope represented as (6.31) such that (6.93) is achieved. Let the data* $(M, A, y, \mu)$ *in (6.3) be given, where* $\mu > 0$, $A \in \mathbb{R}^{m \times n}$ $(m < n)$, *and* $M \in \mathbb{R}^{m \times q}$ $(m \leq q)$ *with* $rank(A) = rank(M) = m$. *Suppose that* $A^T$ *satisfies the weak RSP* *of order k. Then for any $x \in \mathbb{R}^n$, there is a solution $x^*$ of (6.3) approximating x with error*

$$\|x - x^*\|_2 \leq 2\widehat{\gamma} \left[ \frac{|\mu - \|x\|_1| + 2\sigma_k(x)_1}{c} + (\|x\|_1 - \mu)^+ + 2\phi(M^T(Ax - y)) \right] + \varepsilon',$$

*where c is the constant given in Theorem 5.5.2, and $\widehat{\gamma} = \sigma_{\infty,2}(\widehat{M}^1, \widehat{M}^2)$ is the Robinson's constant determined by $(\widehat{M}^1, \widehat{M}^2)$ in (6.98) and (6.99). Moreover, for any x with $\|x\|_1 \leq \mu$, there is a solution $x^*$ of (6.3) approximating x with error*

$$\|x - x^*\|_2 \leq 2\widehat{\gamma} \left[ \frac{|\mu - \|x\|_1| + 2\sigma_k(x)_1}{c} + 2\phi(M^T(Ax - y)) \right] + \varepsilon'. \qquad (6.100)$$

*Proof.* Let x be any given vector in $\mathbb{R}^n$. Set $t := |x|$ and

$$\rho := \phi(M^T(Ax - y)),$$

which implies, from $\text{Col}(\Gamma_{\mathcal{Q}_{\varepsilon_{j_0}}}) \subseteq \{a \in \mathbb{R}^q : \phi^*(a) = 1\}$, that

$$(\Gamma_{\mathcal{Q}_{\varepsilon_{j_0}}})^T (M^T(Ax - y)) \leq \rho \widehat{e}. \qquad (6.101)$$

Let S be the support of the k largest entries of $|x|$, and be decomposed into $S'$ and $S''$ where

$$S' = \{i \in S : x_i > 0\}, \ S'' = \{i \in S : x_i < 0\}.$$

Since $A^T$ satisfies the weak RSP of order k, there exists a vector $\zeta = A^T u^*$ for some $u^* \in \mathbb{R}^m$ satisfying

$$\zeta_i = 1 \text{ for } i \in S', \ \zeta_i = -1 \text{ for } i \in S'', \text{ and } |\zeta_i| \leq 1 \text{ for } i \notin S' \cup S''.$$

Let c be the constant given in Theorem 5.5.2. We now choose the vectors $(\widetilde{w}_1, \widetilde{w}_2, \widetilde{w}_3, \widetilde{w}_4)$ such that they satisfy the constraints of the problem (6.96). First, we set $\widetilde{w}_3 = 1/c$. Then, we choose

$$(\widetilde{w}_1)_i = 1/c \text{ and } (\widetilde{w}_2)_i = 0 \text{ for all } i \in S',$$

$$(\widetilde{w}_1)_i = 0 \text{ and } (\widetilde{w}_2)_i = 1/c \text{ for all } i \in S'',$$

$$(\widetilde{w}_1)_i = \frac{|\zeta_i| + \zeta_i}{2c} \text{ and } (\widetilde{w}_2)_i = \frac{|\zeta_i| - \zeta_i}{2c} \text{ for all } i \notin S' \cup S''.$$

This choice ensures that

$$(\widetilde{w}_1, \widetilde{w}_2) \geq 0, \ \widetilde{w}_1 + \widetilde{w}_2 \leq \widetilde{w}_3 \widetilde{e}, \ \widetilde{w}_1 - \widetilde{w}_2 = \zeta/c.$$

We now construct the vector $\widetilde{w}_4$. By the definition of $\mathcal{Q}_{\varepsilon_{j_0}}$, we see that

$$\{\pm e^{(i)} : i = 1, \ldots, q\} \subseteq \text{Col}(\Gamma_{\mathcal{Q}_{\varepsilon_{j_0}}}).$$

Since $M$ is a full-row-rank matrix, it has an $m \times m$ invertible square submatrix $M_{\mathfrak{J}}$, where $\mathfrak{J} \subseteq \{1,\ldots,q\}$ with $|\mathfrak{J}| = m$. Define the vector $\widetilde{g} \in \mathbb{R}^q$ as follows:

$$(\widetilde{g})_{\mathfrak{J}} = M_{\mathfrak{J}}^{-1} u^*, \ (\widetilde{g})_{\overline{\mathfrak{J}}} = 0.$$

Clearly, $M\widetilde{g} = u^*$. Then it is easy to find a vector $\widetilde{w}_4 \in \mathbb{R}_+^{\widehat{n}}$ satisfying

$$\Gamma_{\mathcal{Q}_{\varepsilon_{j_0}}} \widetilde{w}_4 = -\widetilde{g}/c, \ \|\widetilde{w}_4\|_1 \le 1. \tag{6.102}$$

In fact, without loss of generality, we assume that $\{-\mathbf{e}^{(i)} : i = 1,\ldots,q\}$ are arranged as the first $q$ columns and $\{\mathbf{e}^{(i)} : i = 1,\ldots,q\}$ as the second $q$ columns in the matrix $\Gamma_{\mathcal{Q}_{\varepsilon_{j_0}}}$. For every $i = 1,\ldots,q$, we set

$$(\widetilde{w}_4)_i = \begin{cases} (\widetilde{g})_i/c & \text{if } (\widetilde{g})_i \ge 0 \\ 0 & \text{otherwise,} \end{cases}$$

$$(\widetilde{w}_4)_{q+i} = \begin{cases} -(\widetilde{g})_i/c & \text{if } (\widetilde{g})_i < 0 \\ 0 & \text{otherwise.} \end{cases}$$

All remaining entries of $\widetilde{w}_4 \in \mathbb{R}^{\widehat{n}}$ are set to be zero. By this choice, we see that $\widetilde{w}_4 \ge 0$, $\Gamma_{\mathcal{Q}_{\varepsilon_{j_0}}} \widetilde{w}_4 = -\widetilde{g}/c$ and

$$\begin{aligned} \widehat{\mathbf{e}}^T \widetilde{w}_4 &= \|\widetilde{w}_4\|_1 = \|\widetilde{g}\|_1/c = \|\widetilde{g}_{\mathfrak{J}}\|_1/c = \|M_{\mathfrak{J}}^{-1} u^*\|_1/c \\ &= \|M_{\mathfrak{J}}^{-1}(AA^T)^{-1} A\zeta\|_1/c \\ &\le \|M_{\mathfrak{J}}^{-1}(AA^T)^{-1} A\|_{\infty\to 1} \|\zeta\|_\infty/c \\ &\le \|\zeta\|_\infty = 1. \end{aligned} \tag{6.103}$$

By an argument similar to (6.81), we have

$$\phi^*(\widetilde{g}) \le \|\widetilde{g}\|_1 \le c. \tag{6.104}$$

Note that

$$A^T M \Gamma_{\mathcal{Q}_{\varepsilon_{j_0}}} \widetilde{w}_4 = A^T M(-\widetilde{g}/c) = A^T(-u^*/c) = -\zeta/c = -(\widetilde{w}_1 - \widetilde{w}_2). \tag{6.105}$$

Thus, the vectors $(\widetilde{w}_1, \widetilde{w}_2, \widetilde{w}_3, \widetilde{w}_4)$ chosen as above satisfy the constraint of the problem (6.96). Let $\mathfrak{D}^{(2)}$ be given as in Lemma 6.7.2. Given the vector $(x,t,\rho,\widetilde{w}_1,\widetilde{w}_2,\widetilde{w}_3,\widetilde{w}_4)$, by applying Lemma 5.2.2 with $(M^1,M^2) := (\widehat{M}^1,\widehat{M}^2)$ where $\widehat{M}^1$ and $\widehat{M}^2$ are given in (6.98) and (6.99), we conclude that there is a point in $\mathfrak{D}^{(2)}$, denoted by $(\widehat{x},\widehat{t},\widehat{\rho},\widehat{w}_1,\widehat{w}_2,\widehat{w}_3,\widehat{w}_4))$, such that

$$
\left\|\begin{bmatrix} x \\ t \\ \rho \\ \widetilde{w}_1 \\ \widetilde{w}_2 \\ \widetilde{w}_3 \\ \widetilde{w}_4 \end{bmatrix} - \begin{bmatrix} \widehat{x} \\ \widehat{t} \\ \widehat{\rho} \\ \widehat{w}_1 \\ \widehat{w}_2 \\ \widehat{w}_3 \\ \widehat{w}_4 \end{bmatrix}\right\|_2 \leq \widehat{\gamma} \left\|\begin{bmatrix} (x-t)^+ \\ (-x-t)^+ \\ \left[(\Gamma_{Q_{\varepsilon_{j_0}}})^T[M^T(Ax-y)]-\rho\widehat{\mathbf{e}}\right]^+ \\ (\widetilde{\mathbf{e}}^T t - \mu)^+ \\ A^T M \Gamma_{Q_{\varepsilon_{j_0}}} \widetilde{w}_4 + \widetilde{w}_1 - \widetilde{w}_2 \\ (\mathbf{e}^T \widetilde{w}_4 - 1)^+ \\ (\widetilde{w}_1 + \widetilde{w}_2 - \widetilde{w}_3\widetilde{\mathbf{e}})^+ \\ \rho + \mu\widetilde{w}_3 + (y^T M \Gamma_{Q_{\varepsilon_{j_0}}})\widetilde{w}_4 \\ (Z)^+ \end{bmatrix}\right\|_1 , \quad (6.106)
$$

where

$$(Z)^+ = ((-t)^+,\ (-\rho)^+,\ (-\widetilde{w}_1)^+,\ (-\widetilde{w}_2)^+,\ (-\widetilde{w}_3)^+,\ (-\widetilde{w}_4)^+),$$

and $\widehat{\gamma} = \sigma_{\infty,2}(\widehat{M}^1,\widehat{M}^2)$ is the Robinson's constant determined by $(\widehat{M}^1,\widehat{M}^2)$ which are given in (6.98) and (6.99). The nonnegativity of $(t,\rho,\widetilde{w}_1,\widetilde{w}_2,\widetilde{w}_3,\widetilde{w}_4)$ implies that $(Z)^+ = 0$. The fact $t = |x|$ implies

$$(x-t)^+ = (-x-t)^+ = 0,\ \widetilde{\mathbf{e}}^T t = \|x\|_1.$$

Since $(\widetilde{w}_1,\widetilde{w}_2,\widetilde{w}_3,\widetilde{w}_4)$ is a feasible vector to the problem (6.96), we have $(\widetilde{\mathbf{e}}^T\widetilde{w}_4 - 1)^+ = 0$, and

$$(\widetilde{w}_1 + \widetilde{w}_2 - \widetilde{w}_3\widetilde{\mathbf{e}})^+ = 0,\ A^T M\Gamma_{Q_{\varepsilon_{j_0}}}\widetilde{w}_4 + \widetilde{w}_1 - \widetilde{w}_2 = 0.$$

As $\rho = \phi(M^T(Ax-y))$ implies (6.101), we have

$$\left((\Gamma_{Q_{\varepsilon_{j_0}}})^T(M^T(Ax-y)) - \rho\widehat{\mathbf{e}}\right)^+ = 0.$$

Thus it follows from (6.106) that

$$\|x-\widehat{x}\|_2 \leq \widehat{\gamma}\left\{\left|\rho + \mu\widetilde{w}_3 + y^T M\Gamma_{Q_{\varepsilon_{j_0}}}\widetilde{w}_4\right| + (\|x\|_1 - \mu)^+\right\}. \quad (6.107)$$

From the definition of $\zeta$ and $S$, we have

$$x^T\zeta = \|x_S\|_1 + x_{\overline{S}}^T\zeta_{\overline{S}},\ \|x_{\overline{S}}\|_1 = \sigma_k(x)_1.$$

Thus,

$$\left|\|x\|_1 - x^T\zeta\right| = \left|\|x_{\overline{S}}\|_1 - x_{\overline{S}}^T\zeta_{\overline{S}}\right| \leq \|x_{\overline{S}}\|_1 + \|x_{\overline{S}}\|_1\|\zeta_{\overline{S}}\|_\infty \leq 2\sigma_k(x)_1. \quad (6.108)$$

From (6.103), we see that $\|\widetilde{g}\|_1 \leq c$. By (6.102) and (6.105), we have $\Gamma_{\mathcal{Q}_{\varepsilon_{j_0}}} \widetilde{w}_4 = -\widetilde{g}/c$ and $A^T M \Gamma_{\mathcal{Q}_{\varepsilon_{j_0}}} \widetilde{w}_4 = -\zeta/c$. Defining $\psi = M^T(Ax - y)$, we have

$$
\begin{aligned}
\rho + \mu \widetilde{w}_3 + y^T M \Gamma_{\mathcal{Q}_{\varepsilon_{j_0}}} \widetilde{w}_4 &= \rho + \mu \widetilde{w}_3 + (x^T A^T M - \psi^T) \Gamma_{\mathcal{Q}_{\varepsilon_{j_0}}} \widetilde{w}_4 \\
&= \rho + \mu \widetilde{w}_3 + x^T A^T M \Gamma_{\mathcal{Q}_{\varepsilon_{j_0}}} \widetilde{w}_4 - \psi^T \Gamma_{\mathcal{Q}_{\varepsilon_{j_0}}} \widetilde{w}_4 \\
&= \rho + \frac{(\mu - x^T \zeta + \psi^T \widetilde{g}}{c}.
\end{aligned}
$$

Using (6.108), (6.104) and noting that $\rho = \phi(\psi)$ and $|\psi^T \widetilde{g}| \leq \phi(\psi)\phi^*(\widetilde{g})$, we obtain

$$
\begin{aligned}
\left| \rho + \mu \widetilde{w}_3 + y^T M \Gamma_{\mathcal{Q}_{\varepsilon_{j_0}}} \widetilde{w}_4 \right| &\leq \rho + \frac{|(\mu - \|x\|_1) + \|x\|_1 - x^T \zeta + \psi^T \widetilde{g}|}{c} \\
&\leq \rho + \frac{|\mu - \|x\|_1| + 2\sigma_k(x)_1 + |\psi^T \widetilde{g}|}{c} \\
&\leq \phi(\psi) + \frac{|\mu - \|x\|_1| + 2\sigma_k(x)_1 + \phi(\psi)\phi^*(\widetilde{g})}{c} \\
&\leq 2\phi(\psi) + \frac{|\mu - \|x\|_1| + 2\sigma_k(x)_1}{c}. \qquad (6.109)
\end{aligned}
$$

Combining (6.107) and (6.109) leads to

$$
\|x - \widehat{x}\|_2 \leq \widehat{\gamma} \left[ \frac{|\mu - \|x\|_1| + 2\sigma_k(x)_1}{c} + (\|x\|_1 - \mu)^+ + 2\phi(\psi) \right]. \qquad (6.110)
$$

Denoted by

$$
x^* = \Pi_{\Lambda^*}(x) \in \Lambda^*, \quad \overline{x} = \Pi_{\Lambda_{\varepsilon_{j_0}}}(x) \in \Lambda_{\varepsilon_{j_0}}.
$$

That is, $x^*$ and $\overline{x}$ are the projections of $x$ onto the compact convex sets $\Lambda^*$ and $\Lambda_{\varepsilon_{j_0}}$, respectively. By (6.93), we have $d^{\mathcal{H}}(\Lambda^*, \Lambda_{\varepsilon_{j_0}}) \leq \varepsilon'$. Since $\widehat{x} \in \Lambda_{\varepsilon_{j_0}}^* \subseteq \Lambda_{\varepsilon_{j_0}}$, it follows from Lemma 6.2.2 that

$$
\|x - x^*\|_2 \leq 2\|x - \widehat{x}\|_2 + \varepsilon'.
$$

Combing this inequality and (6.110) yields

$$
\|x - x^*\|_2 \leq 2\widehat{\gamma} \left[ \frac{|\mu - \|x\|_1| + 2\sigma_k(x)_1}{c} + (\|x\|_1 - \mu)^+ + 2\phi(\psi) \right] + \varepsilon'.
$$

Particularly, if $x$ satisfies $\|x\|_1 \leq \mu$, we obtain

$$
\|x - x^*\|_2 \leq 2\widehat{\gamma} \left[ \frac{|\mu - \|x\|_1| + 2\sigma_k(x)_1}{c} + 2\phi(\psi) \right] + \varepsilon',
$$

as desired. □

The above result indicates that the gap $\mu - \|x\|_1$ appears in the sparse recovery error bounds. Given a parameter $\mu > 0$, the solution $x^*$ of (6.3) might be in the interior of the feasible set, i.e., $\|x^*\|_1 < \mu$. When $\mu$ is small, the solution of (6.3) usually attains at the boundary of its feasible set, i.e., $\|x^*\|_1 = \mu$. The following result follows immediately from Theorem 6.7.3.

**Corollary 6.7.4** *Let $\varepsilon' > 0$ be any fixed small constant, and let $\mathcal{Q}_{\varepsilon_{j_0}}$ be the fixed polytope represented as (6.31) such that (6.93) is achieved. Let the data $(M, A, y, \mu)$ in (6.3) be given, where $\mu > 0$, $A \in \mathbb{R}^{m \times n}$ ($m < n$), and $M \in \mathbb{R}^{m \times q}$ ($m \leq q$) with $\text{rank}(A) = \text{rank}(M) = m$. Suppose that one of the conditions listed in Corollary 5.4.5 is satisfied. Then the following statements hold true:*

(i) *For any $x \in \mathbb{R}^n$ with $\|x\|_1 < \mu$, there is a solution $x^*$ of (6.3) approximating $x$ with error (6.100).*

(ii) *For any $x \in \mathbb{R}^n$ with $\|x\|_1 = \mu$, there is a solution $x^*$ of (6.3) approximating $x$ with error*

$$\|x - x^*\|_2 \leq 4\widehat{\gamma} \left[ \phi(M^T(Ax - y)) + \frac{\sigma_k(x)_1}{c} \right] + \varepsilon',$$

*where $c$ and $\widehat{\gamma}$ are the constants given in Theorem 6.7.3.*

The stability results for the special cases $M = I$ or $M = A$ as well as $\phi = \|\cdot\|_2$ can be obtained immediately from the above result. The statements of these results are omitted here. We only state a result for the standard LASSO problem which is a special case of (6.3), corresponding to the case $M = I$ and $\phi = \|\cdot\|_2$.

**Corollary 6.7.5** *Let $\varepsilon' > 0$ be any fixed small constant, and let $\mathcal{Q}_{\varepsilon_{j_0}}$ be the fixed polytope represented as (6.31) such that (6.93) is achieved. Consider the standard LASSO problem (6.4) with problem data $(A, y, \mu)$, where $\mu > 0$ and $A \in \mathbb{R}^{m \times n}$ ($m < n$) with $\text{rank}(A) = m$. Let $c$ and $\widehat{\gamma}$ be constants given in Theorem 6.7.3. Suppose that one of the conditions listed in Corollary 5.4.5 is satisfied. Then the following statements hold true:*

(i) *For any $x \in \mathbb{R}^n$, there is a solution $x^*$ of (6.4) approximating $x$ with error*

$$\|x - x^*\|_2 \leq 2\widehat{\gamma} \left[ \frac{|\mu - \|x\|_1| + 2\sigma_k(x)_1}{c} + (\|x\|_1 - \mu)^+ + 2\|Ax - y\|_2 \right] + \varepsilon'.$$

(ii) *For any $x$ with $\|x\|_1 \leq \mu$, there is a solution $x^*$ of (6.4) approximating $x$ with error*

$$\|x - x^*\|_2 \leq 2\widehat{\gamma} \left[ \frac{|\mu - \|x\|_1| + 2\sigma_k(x)_1}{c} + 2\|Ax - y\|_2 \right] + \varepsilon'.$$

(iii)   *For any $x \in \mathbb{R}^n$ with $\|x\|_1 = \mu$, there is a solution $x^*$ of (6.4) approximating $x$ with error*

$$\|x - x^*\|_2 \le 4\widehat{\gamma}\left[\|Ax - y\|_2 + \frac{\sigma_k(x)_1}{c}\right] + \varepsilon'.$$

## 6.8   Summary

The $\ell_1$-minimization with an $\ell_2$-norm constraint, the general DS and the LASSO problems are stable in the sense of Definition 6.1.1 under the weak RSP of $A^T$. These sparse optimization methods are general enough to encompass many important and special cases, such as the standard $\ell_1$-minimization, linear DS and the traditional LASSO. The polytope approximation techniques of the unit balls and the classic Hoffman's error bound for linear systems can be employed to develop the stability theorems for nonlinear sparse optimization methods. The error bounds discussed in Chapters 5 and 6 are measured by the so-called Robinson's constants which depend on the problem data. Many existing matrix conditions in compressed sensing imply the weak RSP of $A^T$, which is a constant-free matrix condition and naturally originated from the fundamental optimality condition of the $\ell_1$-minimization problem. This condition (i.e., the weak RSP of $A^T$) was shown to be a mild sufficient condition for the stable $k$-sparse recovery via various sparse optimization methods. It was also shown to be a necessary condition for the stable $k$-sparse recovery via the standard DS and $\ell_1$-minimization methods.

## 6.9   Notes

Candès, Romberg and Tao proved in [50] that the stable $k$-sparse recovery via $\ell_1$-minimization with an $\ell_2$-norm constraint can be guaranteed if the sensing matrix satisfies the RIP condition $\delta_{3k} + 3\delta_{4k} < 2$. This result was improved by Candès [45] who showed that if $A$ satisfies the RIP of order $2k$ with $\delta_{2k} < \sqrt{2} - 1$, then for any $x$ and $y = Ax + \eta$ with $\|\eta\|_2 \le \varepsilon$ the solution $x^*$ of the $\ell_1$-minimization with an $\ell_2$-norm constraint approximates $x$ with error

$$\|x - x^*\|_2 \le \frac{C\sigma_k(x)_1}{\sqrt{k}} + D\varepsilon,$$

where $C, D > 0$ are universal constants relying on $\delta_{2k}$. Further improvements of this result using $\delta_{2k}$ were made by many researchers. See Cai, Wang and Xu [41], Mo and Li [174], Cai and Zhang [43], Foucart and Rauhut [108], Andersson and Strömberg [7], and Cai and Zhang [44]. Combining the approaches in Cai, Wang and Xu [41] and Andersson and Strömberg [7], the stability results for $\ell_1$-minimization were improved to $\delta_{2k} < 4/\sqrt{41} \approx 0.6246$ in [108] by Foucart and Rauhut (see Theorem 6.12 in [108]). In 2014, the best-known bound $\delta_{2k} < 1/\sqrt{2} \approx 0.7071$ for stable $k$-sparse recovery with $\ell_1$-minimization was obtained by Cai and Zhang [44]. Davies and Gribonval [75] constructed matrices with $\delta_{2k}$ being arbitrarily close to $1/\sqrt{2}$ for which some $k$-sparse vectors are not recovered by $\ell_1$-minimization. So the result established by Cai and Zhang [44] is optimal for the $\ell_1$-minimization with an $\ell_2$-norm constraint. Recent stability study for the generalized $\ell_1$-minimization methods can be also found in papers, such as by Ayaz, Dirksen and Rauhut [11], Saab, Wang and Yilmaz [197] and Traonmilin and Gribonval [209]. The NSP of order $k$ is a necessary and sufficient condition for every $k$-sparse vector to be exactly reconstructed via $\ell_1$-minimization. The NSP is strictly weaker than the RIP [105, 40]. It was shown that the stable NSP or robust NSP (See Definition 3.6.3) guarantees stable $k$-sparse recovery via $\ell_1$-minimization. See Cohen et al. [65], Sun [202], Eldar and Kutyniok [97], Foucart and Rauhut [108], and Cahill et al. [40]. Theorem 6.5.4 was taken from the paper by Zhao, Jiang and Luo [244].

DS and LASSO are popular in the statistics literature [47, 46, 93, 110, 23, 39, 128]. As pointed out in [139, 23, 54, 172, 8], DS and LASSO exhibit a similar behaviour in many situations, especially in a sparsity scenario. It can be shown that DS and LASSO are stable under the sparsity assumption and some matrix conditions, including mutual coherence, restricted isometry property (RIP) and null space property (NSP). For instance, the mutual coherence introduced in [111, 210] in signal processing can ensure the LASSO being stable [171, 238]. Under the RIP assumption, Candès and Tao [47] have shown that if the true vector $\widehat{x}$ is sufficiently sparse then $\widehat{x}$ can be estimated reliably via DS based on the noise data observation $y$. Cai, Xu and Zhang [42] have shown certain improved stability results for DS and LASSO by slightly weakening the condition [47]. It is worth mentioning that the stability of LASSO can be guaranteed under the restricted eigenvalue condition (REC) introduced by Bickel, Ritov and Tsybakov [23]. This condition holds with high probability for sub-Gaussian design matrices [196]. Other stability conditions have also been examined in the literature, such as the compatibility condition [215], $H_{s,q}$ condition [141], and certain variants of RIP, NSP or REC [54, 147, 170]. A good summary of stability results of LASSO can be found in [39, 128]. The unified results discussed in this chapter, including Theorem 6.6.4 for DS and Theorem 6.7.3 and Corollaries 6.7.4 and 6.7.5 for LASSO, were shown by Zhao and Li [247].

The stability theorems in Chapters 5 and 6 were established in fairly general settings. The analysis was based on the fundamental Karush-Kuhn-Tucker (KKT) optimality conditions [149, 143] which capture the deepest properties of the optimal solutions of convex optimization problems. Thus the KKT conditions naturally lead to the so-called *weak range space property (weak RSP) of order k of $A^T$* which turns out to be a very mild assumption for the generic stability of a broad range of sparse optimization problems including $\ell_1$-minimization, DS and LASSO. For the standard $\ell_1$-minimization and DS, this assumption is tight for stable $k$-sparse recovery. Note that the weak RSP of order $k$ of $A^T$ is a constant-free matrix property in the sense that the property is defined without involving any constant. A unique feature of stability theorems presented in Chapters 5 and 6 is that the recovery error bounds are measured via the so-called Robinson's constant [192]. Many traditional assumptions, such as the RIP [51], NSP [65], mutual coherence [95], REC [23], and range space property (RSP) of $A^T$ [241, 242], imply the condition of weak RSP of $A^T$. As shown by Corollaries 5.4.5 and 6.7.5, these traditional assumptions imply the same recovery error bound measured with Robinson's constants. Lemma 5.2.2 was developed by Hoffman [133] (also by Rosenbloom [194]) and was refined later by Robinson [192] and Mangasarian [169]. Lemma 5.2.2 was first used by Zhao et al. [244] and Zhao and Li [247] as a major analytic tool to study the stability of linear sparse optimization problems. Combined with the polytope approximation of the unit balls developed by Dudley [92] and Barvinok in [21] (see also Bronshtein and Ivanov [36], and Pisier [186]), the Hoffman's Lemma can also be used to establish stability results for some nonlinear sparse optimization problems, as shown in this chapter.

Other sparsity recovery methods, such as thresholding algorithms and orthogonal matching pursuits, have not been discussed in this book. The stability analysis for these methods can be found in recent books by Foucart and Rauhut [108] and Elad [95].

# Chapter 7

# Reweighted $\ell_1$-Algorithms

In this chapter, we introduce a unified framework of the reweighted $\ell_1$-algorithms for the $\ell_0$-minimization problem

$$(P_0) \quad \min_x \{\|x\|_0 : x \in P\},$$

where $P \subseteq \mathbb{R}^n$ is a polyhedral set. There are two important and special cases which have found wide applications in signal and image processing:

- $P$ is the solution set of an underdetermined system of linear equations, namely,

$$P = \{x \in \mathbb{R}^n : Ax = b\}; \tag{7.1}$$

- $P$ is the set of non-negative solutions of an underdetermined system of linear equations, i.e.,

$$P = \{x \in \mathbb{R}^n : Ax = b, \ x \geq 0\}. \tag{7.2}$$

Throughout this chapter, we assume $b \neq 0$ in (7.1) and (7.2). Numerical experiments indicate that the reweighted $\ell_1$-algorithm is one of the most efficient algorithms for $\ell_0$-minimization problems. To derive a reweighted $\ell_1$-algorithm, we introduce the notion of merit function for sparsity. We then identify two large families of such functions, called $\mathcal{M}^{(1)}$- and $\mathcal{M}^{(2)}$-classes, which are used in both practical implementations and theoretical analysis of the reweighted $\ell_1$-algorithms. The analysis in this chapter indicates that the reweighted $\ell_1$-algorithm can be developed systematically through the linearization of the merit function for sparsity. The convergence analysis for the reweighted $\ell_1$-algorithm can be carried out under an assumption imposed on the range space of the transposed matrix and an appropriate choice of the merit function for sparsity. In particular, some convergence results for the well-known Candès-Wakin-Boyd method in [53] and the $\ell_p$-quasinorm-based reweighted $\ell_1$-method [107] can follow immediately from the generic results presented in this chapter.

## 7.1   Merit Function for Sparsity

Note that $x$ and $|x|$ admit the same $\ell_0$-norm. So an approximation function of $\|x\|_0$ can be defined only on $\mathbb{R}^n_+$ without loss of generality.

**Definition 7.1.1** *Given a set of parameters* $\theta \in \mathbb{R}^\kappa_{++}$, *let* $\Upsilon_\theta(x)$ *be a continuous function from* $\mathbb{R}^n_+$ *to* $\mathbb{R}$, *which can approximate the* $\ell_0$-norm in the sense that for any $x \in \mathbb{R}^n_+$,

$$\Upsilon_\theta(x) \to \|x\|_0 \text{ as } \theta \to 0. \tag{7.3}$$

*This function (with given* $\theta$*) and its positive scalar multiplications as well as translations (i.e.,* $\alpha \Upsilon_\theta(x) + \beta$*, where* $\alpha > 0$ *and* $\beta$ *are given constants) are called the merit functions for sparsity.*

A simple example is the quasinorm $\|x\|_p^p$ with a given 1-dimensional parameter $\theta = p \in (0,1)$. This function (defined in whole space $\mathbb{R}^n$) is a merit function for sparsity since $\|x\|_p^p \to \|x\|_0$ as $p \to 0$. Another simple example is the function

$$\||x| + \varepsilon e\|_p^p = \sum_{i=1}^n (|x_i| + \varepsilon)^p, \tag{7.4}$$

where the parameters $\theta = (\varepsilon, p)$ satisfy that $\varepsilon, p \in (0,1)$ and $\varepsilon^p \to 0$ as $(\varepsilon, p) \to 0$. Note that under (7.3), for any give constants $\alpha > 0$ and $\beta$, we have

$$\alpha \Upsilon_\theta(x) + \beta \to \alpha \|x\|_0 + \beta \text{ as } \theta \to 0.$$

Thus the $\ell_0$-minimization problem $(P_0)$ can be approximated via minimizing a merit function for sparsity with given parameters $\theta$. This transforms $\ell_0$-minimization to the following continuous minimization problem:

$$\min_x \{\Upsilon_\theta(|x|) : \ x \in P\}.$$

Harikumar and Bresler [127] pointed out that concave merit functions appear more natural than convex ones when finding the sparsest solution of linear systems, since the 'bulged' feature of the convex merit function might prohibit locating the sparsest solution. There exist many concave functions that can approximate $\|x\|_0$ to any level of accuracy. So, throughout this chapter, we focus on the concave merit functions for sparsity. Minimizing a merit function for sparsity may drive the variable $x$ to be sparse when a sparse solution exists.

For simplicity, we only consider the separable and concave merit functions with parameter $\varepsilon > 0$. The purpose by introducing this parameter is to avoid the possible zero division when calculating the gradient or the Hessian of a differentiable merit function over $\mathbb{R}^n_+$. We use the notation $F_\varepsilon(\cdot)$, instead of $\Upsilon_\theta(\cdot)$, to denote such a special merit function for sparsity. More specifically, we consider the separable function in the form

$$F_\varepsilon(|x|) = \sum_{i=1}^{n} \phi^{(i)}(|x_i| + \varepsilon), \qquad (7.5)$$

where $\phi^{(i)} : \mathbb{R}_+ \to \mathbb{R}$ is called the univariate kernel function. Besides $\varepsilon$, a merit function may include other parameters, such as $p$ in (7.4). However, we still use the same notation $F_\varepsilon(\cdot)$ to denote such a function for simplicity. Using (7.5), we obtain the following approximation of $(P_0)$ :

$$\min_x \left\{ F_\varepsilon(|x|) = \sum_{i=1}^{n} \phi^{(i)}(|x_i| + \varepsilon) : x \in P \right\}. \qquad (7.6)$$

For example, if $\phi^{(i)}(t) = t^p$ where $p \in (0,1)$ is a given parameter, we obtain the merit function (7.4), and the problem (7.6) becomes

$$\min_x \left\{ \sum_{i=1}^{n} (|x_i| + \varepsilon)^p : x \in P \right\},$$

which is an $\ell_p$-quasinorm-minimization problem (see [57, 107]). If $\phi^{(i)}(t) = \log t$, then we obtain the merit function

$$F_\varepsilon(|x|) = \sum_{i=1}^{n} \log(|x_i| + \varepsilon),$$

which was used by Gorodnitsky and Rao [117] to design their FOCUSS algorithm for sparse signal reconstruction. Other examples of merit functions are given in later sections of this chapter.

Given a separable function $F_\varepsilon(|x|)$ in (7.5) and a set $S \subseteq \{1,\ldots,n\}$, we use the notation $F_\varepsilon(|x_S|)$ to denote the reduced separable function

$$F_\varepsilon(|x_S|) := \sum_{i \in S} \phi^{(i)}(|x_i| + \varepsilon).$$

The function $F_\varepsilon(|x_S|)$ coincides with $F_\varepsilon(|x|)$ when $S = \{1,\ldots,n\}$. We also need the following notion which has been widely used in optimization and nonlinear analysis (see [132, 123]).

**Definition 7.1.2** *A function $f : \mathbb{R}^n \to \mathbb{R}$ is said to be coercive in the region $D \subseteq \mathbb{R}^n$ if $f(x) \to \infty$ as $x \in D$ and $\|x\| \to \infty$.*

For the convenience of algorithmic development and convergence analysis, we consider two major classes of merit functions for sparsity, denoted by $\mathcal{M}^{(1)}$-class and $\mathcal{M}^{(2)}$-class, respectively.

### 7.1.1 $\mathcal{M}^{(1)}$-Class Merit Functions

**Definition 7.1.3** ($\mathcal{M}^{(1)}$-class merit functions) *A merit function for sparsity $F_\varepsilon : \mathbb{R}_+^n \to \mathbb{R}$ belongs to the $\mathcal{M}^{(1)}$-class if it satisfies all the following properties:*

(i) *In $\mathbb{R}_+^n$, $F_\varepsilon(x)$ is separable and twice continuously differentiable with respect to $x \in \mathbb{R}_+^n$, and $F_\varepsilon(x)$ is strictly increasing with respect to $\varepsilon$ and every component $x_i$.*

(ii) *For any given number $\gamma > 0$ there exists a finite number $\chi(\gamma)$ such that for any $S \subseteq \{1,...,n\}$,*

$$g(x_S) := \inf_{\varepsilon \downarrow 0} F_\varepsilon(x_S) \geq \chi(\gamma)$$

*provided $x_S \geq \gamma \mathbf{e}_S$ (i.e., $x_i \geq \gamma$ for all $i \in S$). Also the above function $g(x_S)$ is coercive in the set $\{x_S : x_S \geq \gamma \mathbf{e}_S\}$.*

(iii) *In $\mathbb{R}_+^n$, the gradient $\nabla F_\varepsilon(x)$ satisfies the following conditions:*

$$\nabla F_\varepsilon(x) \in \mathbb{R}_{++}^n \text{ for any}(x,\varepsilon) \in \mathbb{R}_+^n \times \mathbb{R}_{++},$$

$$[\nabla F_\varepsilon(x)]_i \to \infty \text{ as } (x_i,\varepsilon) \to 0,$$

*and for any given $x_i > 0$ the component $[\nabla F_\varepsilon(x)]_i$ is continuous in $\varepsilon$ and tends to a finite positive number (dependent only on $x_i$) as $\varepsilon \to 0$.*

(iv) *In $\mathbb{R}_+^n$, the Hessian $\nabla^2 F_\varepsilon(\cdot)$ satisfies that*

$$u^T \nabla^2 F_\varepsilon(x)u \leq -C(\varepsilon,r)\|u\|_2^2$$

*for any $u \in \mathbb{R}^n$ and $x \in \mathbb{R}_+^n$ with $\|x\|_2 \leq r$, where $r > 0$ is a given constant, $C(\varepsilon,r) > 0$ is a constant depending on $(\varepsilon,r)$ only, and $C(\varepsilon,r)$ is continuous in $\varepsilon$ and bounded away from zero as $\varepsilon \to 0$. (So $F_\varepsilon(x)$ is strictly concave with respect to x.)*

The $\mathcal{M}^{(1)}$-class is a large family of the merit functions for sparsity, and it is very easy to construct examples in this family. Note that any non-negative combination of a finite number of the functions in $\mathcal{M}^{(1)}$-class is still in this class. So $\mathcal{M}^{(1)}$ is a convex cone of the merit functions for sparsity.

**Example 7.1.4** *Let $\varepsilon, p, q \in (0,1)$ be given parameters. All the following func-tions defined on $\mathbb{R}^n_+$ are merit functions for sparsity in $\mathcal{M}^{(1)}$-class:*

(a) $\quad F_\varepsilon(x) = \sum_{i=1}^{n} \log(x_i + \varepsilon), \quad x \in \mathbb{R}^n_+.$

(b) $\quad F_\varepsilon(x) = \sum_{i=1}^{n} \log\left[x_i + \varepsilon + (x_i + \varepsilon)^p\right], \quad x \in \mathbb{R}^n_+.$

(c) $\quad F_\varepsilon(x) = \sum_{i=1}^{n} (x_i + \varepsilon)^p, \quad x \in \mathbb{R}^n_+.$

(d) $\quad F_\varepsilon(x) = \sum_{i=1}^{n} \left[x_i + \varepsilon + (x_i + \varepsilon)^q\right]^p, \quad x \in \mathbb{R}^n_+.$

(e) $\quad F_\varepsilon(x) = \sum_{i=1}^{n} \left[x_i + \varepsilon + (x_i + \varepsilon)^2\right]^p \text{ where } p \in (0, 1/2], \quad x \in \mathbb{R}^n_+.$

(f) $\quad F_\varepsilon(x) = \sum_{i=1}^{n} \left[\log(x_i + \varepsilon) - \dfrac{1}{(x_i + \varepsilon)^p}\right], \quad x \in \mathbb{R}^n_+.$

(g) $\quad F_\varepsilon(x) = \sum_{i=1}^{n} \left[x_i - \dfrac{1}{(x_i + \varepsilon)^p}\right], \quad x \in \mathbb{R}^n_+.$

As an example, we now verify that the function (a) above is in $\mathcal{M}^{(1)}$ class. For functions (b)-(g), we list their gradients and Hessian matrices, from which it is easy to verify that these functions also belong to $\mathcal{M}^{(1)}$-class.

■ Note that for $x \in \mathbb{R}^n_+$,

$$\left(n + \frac{\sum_{i=1}^{n} \log(x_i + \varepsilon)}{-\log \varepsilon}\right) \to \|x\|_0 \text{ as } \varepsilon \to 0.$$

A suitable shift and positive scalar multiplication of this function yields the function (a) in Example 7.1.4, i.e., $F_\varepsilon(x) = \sum_{i=1}^{n} \log(x_i + \varepsilon)$. Thus, this function is a merit function for sparsity. Clearly, this function is sep-arable, twice continuously differentiable over the neighborhood of $\mathbb{R}^n_{++}$, and increasing with respect to $\varepsilon > 0$ and every component $x_i$. The gradi-ent of this function at $x \in \mathbb{R}^n_+$ is given by

$$\nabla F_\varepsilon(x) = \left[\frac{1}{x_1 + \varepsilon}, \dots, \frac{1}{x_n + \varepsilon}\right]^T \in \mathbb{R}^n_{++}, \tag{7.7}$$

and the Hessian

$$\nabla^2 F_\varepsilon(x) = -\text{diag}\left[\frac{1}{(x_1 + \varepsilon)^2}, \dots, \frac{1}{(x_n + \varepsilon)^2}\right]. \tag{7.8}$$

Let $S \subseteq \{1,\dots,n\}$. If $x_S \geq \gamma e_S$, we see that

$$g(x_S) = \inf_{\varepsilon \downarrow 0} F_\varepsilon(x_S) = \sum_{i \in S} \log(x_i) \geq \sum_{i \in S} \log \gamma = |S| \log \gamma \geq \chi(\gamma),$$

where $\chi(\gamma) = -n|\log\gamma|$. We also see that $g(x_S) \to \infty$ as $x_S \geq \gamma e_S$ and $\|x_S\| \to \infty$. Therefore, $g(x_S)$ is coercive on $\{x_S : x_S \geq \gamma e_S\}$. Hence, the conditions (i) and (ii) in Definition 7.1.3 are satisfied. From (7.7), it is evident that the condition (iii) of Definition 7.1.3 is also satisfied. From the Hessian matrix (7.8), for any $u \in \mathbb{R}^n$ and $x \in \mathbb{R}^n_+$ satisfying $\|x\|_2 \leq r$, we have

$$u^T \nabla^2 F_\varepsilon(x) u \leq -\sum_{i=1}^n \frac{u_i^2}{(x_i+\varepsilon)^2} \leq -\sum_{i=1}^n \frac{u_i^2}{(r+\varepsilon)^2} = -C(\varepsilon,r)\|u\|_2^2,$$

where $C(\varepsilon,r) = \frac{1}{(r+\varepsilon)^2}$ is continuous in $\varepsilon$, tending to $1/r > 0$ as $\varepsilon \to 0$. The condition (iv) of Definition 7.1.3 is also satisfied. Therefore, the function (a) is in $\mathcal{M}^{(1)}$-class. Similarly, we can verify that the functions (b)-(g) in Example 7.1.4 are also in $\mathcal{M}^{(1)}$-class. The details are omitted here. In what follows, we list only their gradients and Hessian matrices.

■ Let $p \in (0,1)$ be a given number. Note that on $\mathbb{R}^n_+$

$$\left[ n + \frac{\sum_{i=1}^n \log\left(x_i + \varepsilon + (x_i+\varepsilon)^p\right)}{-\log(\varepsilon+\varepsilon^p)} \right] \to \|x\|_0 \quad \text{as } \varepsilon \to 0.$$

By a shift and positive scalar multiplication of the function above, we get the merit function (b) in Example 7.1.4, to which the gradient at $x \in \mathbb{R}^n_+$ is given as

$$[\nabla F_\varepsilon(x)]_i = \frac{p + (x_i+\varepsilon)^{1-p}}{(x_i+\varepsilon)^{1-p}\left(x_i+\varepsilon+(x_i+\varepsilon)^p\right)}, \quad i = 1,\dots,n, \qquad (7.9)$$

and the Hessian $\nabla^2 F_\varepsilon(x)$ is a diagonal matrix with diagonal entries

$$-\frac{1}{(x_i+\varepsilon+(x_i+\varepsilon)^p)^2}\left[1 + \frac{p(3-p)}{(x_i+\varepsilon)^{1-p}} + \frac{p}{(x_i+\varepsilon)^{2(1-p)}}\right], \quad i = 1,\dots,n.$$

■ Given $p \in (0,1)$, the gradient of (c) in Example 7.1.4 at $x \in \mathbb{R}^n_+$ is

$$\nabla F_\varepsilon(x) = \left[ \frac{p}{(x_1+\varepsilon)^{1-p}}, \dots, \frac{p}{(x_n+\varepsilon)^{1-p}} \right]^T \in \mathbb{R}^n_{++}, \qquad (7.10)$$

and the Hessian

$$\nabla^2 F_\varepsilon(x) = -\text{diag}\left[ \frac{p}{(x_1+\varepsilon)^{2-p}}, \dots, \frac{p}{(x_n+\varepsilon)^{2-p}} \right].$$

■ Let $q \in (0,1)$ be a fixed number independent of $(\varepsilon, p)$. Note that on $\mathbb{R}^n_+$ if $\varepsilon^p \to 0$ as $(\varepsilon, p) \to 0$, we have

$$F_\varepsilon(x) = \sum_{i=1}^{n} [x_i + \varepsilon + (x_i + \varepsilon)^q]^p \to \|x\|_0 \text{ as } (\varepsilon, p) \to 0.$$

Thus the function (d) in Example 7.1.4 is a merit function which can be seen as a modification of (c). The gradient of (d) at $x \in \mathbb{R}^n_+$ is given by

$$[\nabla F_\varepsilon(x)]_i = \frac{p(q + (x_i + \varepsilon)^{1-q})}{(x_i + \varepsilon)^{1-q} [x_i + \varepsilon + (x_i + \varepsilon)^q]^{1-p}}, \quad i = 1, \ldots, n, \quad (7.11)$$

and the Hessian of (d) is a diagonal matrix with diagonal entries

$$-\frac{p}{[x_i + \varepsilon + (x_i + \varepsilon)^q]^{2-p}} \left[ 1 - p + \frac{q(3 - q - 2p)}{(x_i + \varepsilon)^{1-q}} + \frac{q(1 - pq}{(x_i + \varepsilon)^{2(1-q)}} \right].$$

■ The gradient of the function (e) in Example 7.1.4 on $\mathbb{R}^n_+$ is

$$[\nabla F_\varepsilon(x)]_i = p \left( \frac{1 + 2(x_i + \varepsilon)}{(x_i + \varepsilon + (x_i + \varepsilon)^2)^{1-p}} \right), \quad i = 1, \ldots, n. \quad (7.12)$$

The Hessian matrix of (e) is a diagonal matrix with diagonal entries

$$-\left[ \frac{p(1-p)}{(x_i + \varepsilon + (x_i + \varepsilon)^2)^{2-p}} + \frac{2p(1-2p)}{(x_i + \varepsilon + (x_i + \varepsilon)^2)^{1-p}} \right].$$

■ Note that

$$n - \sum_{i=1}^{n} \frac{\varepsilon^p}{(|x_i| + \varepsilon)^p} \to \|x\|_0 \text{ as } \varepsilon \to 0.$$

Thus $\sum_{i=1}^{n} -\frac{1}{(|x_i| + \varepsilon)^p}$ is a merit function for sparsity. The function (f) in Example 7.1.4 is the sum of this merit function and the function (a). The gradient of (f) at $x \in \mathbb{R}^n_+$ is given by

$$\nabla F_\varepsilon(x) = \left[ \frac{1 + (x_1 + \varepsilon)^p}{(x_1 + \varepsilon)^{p+1}}, \ldots, \frac{1 + (x_n + \varepsilon)^p}{(x_n + \varepsilon)^{p+1}} \right], \quad (7.13)$$

and the Hessian

$$\nabla^2 F_\varepsilon(x) = -\text{diag} \left[ \frac{p + 1 + (x_1 + \varepsilon)^p}{(x_1 + \varepsilon)^{p+2}}, \ldots, \frac{p + 1 + (x_n + \varepsilon)^p}{(x_n + \varepsilon)^{p+2}} \right].$$

■ Note that

$$n + \sum_{i=1}^{n} \left[ |x_i| - \frac{1}{(|x_i| + \varepsilon)^p} \right] \varepsilon^p \to \|x\|_0 \text{ as } \varepsilon \to 0.$$

Thus the function (g) is also a merit function. The gradient of (g) on $\mathbb{R}^n_+$ is given as

$$[\nabla F_\varepsilon(x)]_i = \frac{1 + (x_i + \varepsilon)^{p+1}}{(x_i + \varepsilon)^{p+1}}, \ i = 1, \ldots, n, \tag{7.14}$$

and the Hessian is given as

$$\nabla^2 F_\varepsilon(x) = -\mathrm{diag}\left[\frac{p+1}{(x_1 + \varepsilon)^{p+2}}, \ldots, \frac{p+1}{(x_n + \varepsilon)^{p+2}}\right].$$

## 7.1.2 $\mathcal{M}^{(2)}$-Class Merit Functions

We now introduce another class of merit functions for sparsity which will be used in Chapter 8. The reader may postpone reading this section until Chapter 8.

**Definition 7.1.5** ($\mathcal{M}^{(2)}$-class merit functions). *A merit function for sparsity $F_\varepsilon$ : $\mathbb{R}^n_+ \to \mathbb{R}$, where $\varepsilon > 0$ is a parameter, belongs to the $\mathcal{M}^{(2)}$-class if it satisfies the following conditions:*

(i)  *For any given $s \in \mathbb{R}^n_+$, $F_\varepsilon(s) \to \|s\|_0$ as $\varepsilon \to 0$;*

(ii)  *$F_\varepsilon(s)$ is continuously differentiable and concave with respect to $s$ over an open set containing $\mathbb{R}^n_+$;*

(iii)  *For any given constants $0 < \delta_1 < \delta_2$, there exists a small $\varepsilon^* > 0$ such that for any given $\varepsilon \in (0, \varepsilon^*]$,*

$$F_\varepsilon(s) - F_\varepsilon(s') \geq 1/2 \tag{7.15}$$

*holds for any $0 \leq s, s' \leq \delta_2 \mathbf{e}$ satisfying $\|s'\|_0 < \|s\|_0$ and $\delta_1 \leq s_i \leq \delta_2$ for all $i \in \mathrm{supp}(s)$.*

In this definition, the number "1/2" in (7.15) is not essential and can be replaced by any positive constant in $(0, 1)$. Roughly speaking, the functions in $\mathcal{M}^{(2)}$-class possess some monotonicity property in the sense that when $\|s\|_0$ decreases, so does the value of $F_\varepsilon(s)$. Thus minimizing a merit function in $\mathcal{M}^{(2)}$-class may drive $s$ to be sparse, and maximizing may drive $s$ to be dense. It is not difficult to construct a function in $\mathcal{M}^{(2)}$-class, as shown by the next lemma.

**Lemma 7.1.6** *Let $\varepsilon \in (0, 1)$ be given. All functions below belong to the $\mathcal{M}^{(2)}$-class:*

$$F_\varepsilon(s) = \sum_{i=1}^{n} \left(1 - e^{-\frac{s_i}{\varepsilon}}\right), \tag{7.16}$$

*where $s \in \mathbb{R}^n$;*

$$F_\varepsilon(s) = \sum_{i=1}^{n} \frac{s_i}{s_i + \varepsilon}, \tag{7.17}$$

*where $s_i > -\varepsilon$ for all $i = 1, \ldots, n$;*

$$F_\varepsilon(s) = n - \left( \sum_{i=1}^{n} \log(s_i + \varepsilon) \right) / \log \varepsilon, \qquad (7.18)$$

*where $s_i > -\varepsilon$ for all $i = 1, \ldots, n$;*

$$F_\varepsilon(s) = \sum_{i=1}^{n} (s_i + \varepsilon^{1/\varepsilon})^\varepsilon = \left\| s + \varepsilon^{1/\varepsilon} e \right\|_\varepsilon^\varepsilon, \qquad (7.19)$$

*where $s_i > -\varepsilon^{1/\varepsilon}$ for all $i = 1, \ldots, n$.*

*Proof.* It is straightforward to verify that every function in (7.16)–(7.19) is a concave and continuously differentiable merit function for sparsity over the neighborhood of $\mathbb{R}^n_+$. So they satisfy the conditions (i) and (ii) of Definition 7.1.5. We now prove that these functions also satisfy the condition (iii) of Definition 7.1.5. To this purpose, let $0 < \delta_1 < \delta_2$ be two constants, and let $s \in \mathbb{R}^n_+$ be any vector satisfying the condition $\delta_1 \leq s_i \leq \delta_2$ for all $i \in \text{supp}(s)$, and let $s' \in \mathbb{R}^n_+$ be any vector satisfying $s' \leq \delta_2 e$ and $\|s'\|_0 < \|s\|_0$. We now prove that for every function in (7.16)–(7.19) there is a small $\varepsilon^* > 0$ such that (7.15) holds for any $\varepsilon \in (0, \varepsilon^*]$ and any $(s, s')$ satisfying the above conditions.

(i) We first prove that the function (7.16) is in $\mathcal{M}^{(2)}$-class. Note that there exists an $\varepsilon^* \in (0,1)$ such that $ne^{-\frac{\delta_1}{\varepsilon}} < 1/2$ for any $\varepsilon \in (0, \varepsilon^*]$. Thus by the choice of $s$, for all $\varepsilon \in (0, \varepsilon^*]$, we have

$$F_\varepsilon(s) = \sum_{s_j \neq 0} (1 - e^{-\frac{s_j}{\varepsilon}}) \geq \sum_{s_j \neq 0} (1 - e^{-\frac{\delta_1}{\varepsilon}}) = \|s\|_0 (1 - e^{-\frac{\delta_1}{\varepsilon}})$$

$$\geq \|s\|_0 - ne^{-\frac{\delta_1}{\varepsilon}} \geq \|s\|_0 - 1/2.$$

We also note that $1 - e^{-\frac{s'_j}{\varepsilon}} \leq 1$ since $s'$ is non-negative. Thus,

$$F_\varepsilon(s') = \sum_{s'_j \neq 0} (1 - e^{-\frac{s'_j}{\varepsilon}}) \leq \|s'\|_0.$$

Combining the above two relations yields

$$F_\varepsilon(s) - F_\varepsilon(s') \geq (\|s\|_0 - 1/2) - \|s'\|_0 \geq 1/2,$$

where the last inequality follows from $\|s\|_0 > \|s'\|_0$, i.e., $\|s\|_0 - \|s'\|_0 \geq 1$. So the function (7.16) satisfies the condition (iii) of Definition 7.1.5 and thus it belongs to the $\mathcal{M}^{(2)}$-class.

(ii) Consider the function (7.17). It is evident that there exists $\varepsilon^* \in (0,1)$ such that for any $\varepsilon \in (0,\varepsilon^*]$ the following inequalities hold for any $s_i \in [\delta_1,\delta_2]$ :

$$1 - \frac{1}{2n} \le \frac{\delta_1}{\delta_1 + \varepsilon} \le \frac{s_i}{s_i + \varepsilon} \le \frac{\delta_2}{\delta_2 + \varepsilon} \le 1.$$

Thus at any vector $s \in \mathbb{R}_+^n$ with $s_i \in [\delta_1,\delta_2]$ for all $i \in \text{supp}(s)$, we have

$$F_\varepsilon(s) = \sum_{i=1}^n \frac{s_i}{s_i + \varepsilon} = \sum_{s_i \in [\delta_1,\delta_2]} \frac{s_i}{s_i + \varepsilon} \ge \|s\|_0 \left(1 - \frac{1}{2n}\right).$$

On the other hand, we have

$$F_\varepsilon(s') = \sum_{s_i' > 0} \frac{s_i'}{s_i' + \varepsilon} \le \|s'\|_0.$$

Note that $\|s'\|_0 < \|s\|_0 \le n$. Merging the above two inequalities yields

$$F_\varepsilon(s) - F_\varepsilon(s') \ge (1 - \frac{1}{2n})\|s\|_0 - \|s'\|_0 = (\|s\|_0 - \|s'\|_0) - \frac{1}{2n}\|s\|_0$$

$$\ge 1 - \frac{1}{2n}\|s\|_0 \ge 1/2.$$

Thus the function (7.17) is in $\mathcal{M}^{(2)}$-class.

(iii) We now show that (7.18) is in $\mathcal{M}^{(2)}$-class. As $\log \varepsilon < 0$ for $\varepsilon \in (0,1)$, the function $\log(t + \varepsilon)/\log \varepsilon$ is decreasing with respect to $t$. Thus for any $t \in [0,\delta_1)$ and $\varepsilon \in (0,1)$, we have

$$\log(\delta_1 + \varepsilon)/\log \varepsilon \le \log(t + \varepsilon)/\log \varepsilon \le 1, \qquad (7.20)$$

and for any $t \in [\delta_1,\delta_2]$ and $\varepsilon \in (0,1)$, we have

$$\log(\delta_2 + \varepsilon)/\log \varepsilon \le \log(t + \varepsilon)/\log \varepsilon \le \log(\delta_1 + \varepsilon)/\log \varepsilon. \qquad (7.21)$$

Note that

$$\lim_{\varepsilon \downarrow 0_+} \log(\delta_1 + \varepsilon)/\log \varepsilon = \lim_{\varepsilon \downarrow 0_+} \log(\delta_2 + \varepsilon)/\log \varepsilon = 0.$$

There exists $\varepsilon^* \in (0,1)$ such that the following inequalities hold for any $\varepsilon \in (0,\varepsilon^*]$ :

$$|\log(\delta_1 + \varepsilon)/\log \varepsilon| \le 1/6n, \quad |\log(\delta_2 + \varepsilon)/\log \varepsilon| \le 1/6n. \qquad (7.22)$$

Since $s_i \in [\delta_1,\delta_2]$, it follows from (7.21) and (7.22) that

$$\left| \sum_{s_i > 0} \log(s_i + \varepsilon)/\log \varepsilon \right| \le \|s\|_0 (1/6n) \le 1/6$$

for any $\varepsilon \in (0, \varepsilon^*]$. This implies that for any given $\varepsilon \in (0, \varepsilon^*]$,

$$F_\varepsilon(s) = n - \sum_{s_i > 0} \log(s_i + \varepsilon)/\log\varepsilon - \sum_{s_i = 0} \log(s_i + \varepsilon)/\log\varepsilon$$

$$= \|s\|_0 - \sum_{s_i > 0} \log(s_i + \varepsilon)/\log\varepsilon$$

$$\geq \|s\|_0 - 1/6. \tag{7.23}$$

On the other hand,

$$F_\varepsilon(s') = n - \sum_{s'_i \neq 0} \log(s'_i + \varepsilon)/\log\varepsilon - \sum_{s'_i = 0} \log(s'_i + \varepsilon)/\log\varepsilon$$

$$= \|s'\|_0 - \sum_{s'_i \in [\delta_1, \delta_2]} \log(s'_i + \varepsilon)/\log\varepsilon - \sum_{s'_i \in (0, \delta_1)} \log(s'_i + \varepsilon)/\log\varepsilon.$$

If $s' = 0$, then $F_\varepsilon(s') = 0$. If $s' \neq 0$, then either $\{i : s'_i \in [\delta_1, \delta_2]\} \neq \emptyset$ or $\{i : s'_i \in (0, \delta_1)\} \neq \emptyset$. By (7.21), (7.20) and (7.22), for the former case above, we see that

$$\left| \sum_{s'_i \in [\delta_1, \delta_2]} \log(s'_i + \varepsilon)/\log\varepsilon \right| \leq \|s'\|_0 (1/6n) \leq 1/6,$$

and for the latter case,

$$\sum_{s'_i \in (0, \delta_1)} \log(s'_i + \varepsilon)/\log\varepsilon \geq \sum_{s'_i \in (0, \delta_1)} \log(\delta_1 + \varepsilon)/\log\varepsilon \geq \sum_{s'_i \in (0, \delta_1)} -1/6n \geq -1/6.$$

Therefore, in any case, the following inequality holds:

$$F_\varepsilon(s') \leq \|s'\|_0 + 1/6 + 1/6 = \|s'\|_0 + 1/3,$$

which, combined with (7.23), yields

$$F_\varepsilon(s) - F_\varepsilon(s') \geq (\|s\|_0 - 1/6) - (\|s'\|_0 + 1/3) \geq 1/2,$$

where the last inequality follows from that $\|s\|_0 > \|s'\|_0$, i.e., $\|s\|_0 - \|s'\|_0 \geq 1$.

(iv) Consider the function (7.19). For any fixed $t \geq 0$, $(t + \varepsilon^{1/\varepsilon})^\varepsilon \to 1$ as $\varepsilon \to 0$. Thus there exists a number $\varepsilon^* < 1/(2(2n+1))$ such that for any $\varepsilon \in (0, \varepsilon^*]$ and for any $s_i \in [\delta_1, \delta_2]$, the following relations hold:

$$1 - \frac{1}{2(2n+1)} \leq (\delta_1 + \varepsilon^{1/\varepsilon})^\varepsilon \leq (s_i + \varepsilon^{1/\varepsilon})^\varepsilon \leq (\delta_2 + \varepsilon^{1/\varepsilon})^\varepsilon \leq 1 + \frac{1}{2(2n+1)}. \tag{7.24}$$

Thus for any vector $s$ with $s_i \in [\delta_1, \delta_2]$ for all $i \in \mathrm{supp}(s)$, we have

$$F_\varepsilon(s) = \sum_{s_i > 0} (s_i + \varepsilon^{1/\varepsilon})^\varepsilon + \sum_{s_i = 0} (s_i + \varepsilon^{1/\varepsilon})^\varepsilon \geq (1 - \frac{1}{2(2n+1)}) \|s\|_0 + (n - \|s\|_0)\varepsilon.$$

For $0 \leq s' \leq \delta_2 \mathbf{e}$, it follows from (7.24) that

$$F_\varepsilon(s') = \sum_{s'_i > 0}(s'_i + \varepsilon^{1/\varepsilon})^\varepsilon + \sum_{s'_i = 0}(s'_i + \varepsilon^{1/\varepsilon})^\varepsilon \leq (1 + \frac{1}{2(2n+1)})\|s'\|_0 + (n - \|s'\|_0)\varepsilon.$$

Note that $\varepsilon^* \leq 1/(2(2n+1)) < 1/2$, $\|s\|_0 - \|s'\|_0 \geq 1$ and $\|s\|_0 + \|s'\|_0 \leq 2n$. For any $\varepsilon \in (0, \varepsilon^*]$, we have

$$F_\varepsilon(s) - F_\varepsilon(s') \geq (1 - \frac{1}{2(2n+1)})\|s\|_0 + (n - \|s\|_0)\varepsilon$$

$$- (1 + \frac{1}{2(2n+1)})\|s'\|_0 - (n - \|s'\|_0)\varepsilon$$

$$= (\|s\|_0 - \|s'\|_0)(1 - \varepsilon) - \frac{1}{2(2n+1)}(\|s\|_0 + \|s'\|_0)$$

$$\geq (1 - \frac{1}{2(2n+1)}) - \frac{1}{2(2n+1)}(2n) = 1/2 > 0,$$

So the function (7.19) also belongs to $\mathcal{M}^{(2)}$-class.


## 7.2 Reweighted $\ell_1$-Methods

Based on a merit function in $\mathcal{M}^{(1)}$-class, we may derive a family of reweighted $\ell_1$-algorithms to solve the $\ell_0$-minimization problem. Note that for any $F_\varepsilon \in \mathcal{M}^{(1)}$-class the function $F_\varepsilon(|x|)$ is increasing with respect to every component of $|x|$. Thus the problem (7.6) is equivalent to

$$\min_{(x,v)}\{F_\varepsilon(v) : x \in P, |x| \leq v\} = \min_{(x,v) \in \mathcal{F}} F_\varepsilon(v), \tag{7.25}$$

where

$$\mathcal{F} = \{(x, v) \in \mathbb{R}^n \times \mathbb{R}^n_+ : x \in P, |x| \leq v\}.$$

Since $F_\varepsilon(v)$ is a concave function on $\mathbb{R}^n_+$, the problem (7.25) is a concave programming problem which remains difficult to solve. Linearization is one of the traditional approximation methods for concave programming problems. Assume that $(x^k, v^k)$ is the current iterate. At $v^k$, we consider the following first-order approximation of the merit function, namely,

$$F_\varepsilon(v) \approx F_\varepsilon(v^k) + \nabla F_\varepsilon(v^k)^T(v - v^k).$$

The simplest tractable approximation of (7.25) is the problem of minimizing the above linear approximation of $F_\varepsilon(v)$ at the current point $v^k$ over the same feasible set $\mathcal{F}$. Thus it makes sense to solve the following problem to generate the next iterate $(x^{k+1}, v^{k+1})$ which is anticipated to be a better approximate solution of (7.25) than the current iterate:

$$
\begin{aligned}
(x^{k+1}, v^{k+1}) &= \arg\min_{(x,v)\in\mathcal{F}} \left\{ F_\varepsilon(v^k) + \nabla F_\varepsilon(v^k)^T (v - v^k) \right\} \\
&= \arg\min_{(x,v)\in\mathcal{F}} \nabla F_\varepsilon(v^k)^T v.
\end{aligned}
\tag{7.26}
$$

This is a linear programming problem, which can be efficiently solved by interior-point methods or simplex methods. Note that $v^k \in \mathbb{R}^n_+$ and $\nabla F_\varepsilon(v^k) \in \mathbb{R}^n_{++}$ (this follows from (iii) in Definition 7.1.3). It is easy to see that the solution $(x^{k+1}, v^{k+1})$ of (7.26) always satisfies that

$$
v^{k+1} = |x^{k+1}|,
\tag{7.27}
$$

which holds for every $k \geq 0$. Hence, from (7.27) and the positiveness of $\nabla F_\varepsilon(v^k)$, it immediately yields

$$
\nabla F_\varepsilon(v^k)^T v^{k+1} = \nabla F_\varepsilon(|x^k|)^T |x^{k+1}| = \left\| \mathrm{diag}\left(\nabla F_\varepsilon(|x^k|)\right) x^{k+1} \right\|_1.
$$

Thus the iterative scheme (7.26) is exactly the same as

$$
x^{k+1} = \arg\min_x \left\{ \left\| \mathrm{diag}\left(\nabla F_\varepsilon(|x^k|)\right) x \right\|_1 : x \in P \right\}.
\tag{7.28}
$$

In other words, $x^{k+1}$ is the solution to the *reweighted $\ell_1$-minimization problem*

$$
\min_x \left\{ \left\| W^k x \right\|_1 : x \in P \right\}
$$

with weight

$$
W^k = \mathrm{diag}\left(\nabla F_\varepsilon(|x^k|)\right),
$$

which is determined by the gradient of the merit function for sparsity at the current iterate $x^k$.

By the property (iii) of Definition 7.1.3, we see that $[\nabla F_\varepsilon(v^k)]_i \to \infty$ as $(v_i, \varepsilon) \to 0$, so for small components $v_i^k (= |x_i^k|)$ of the current iterate $(x^k, v^k)$ and small parameter $\varepsilon > 0$, the corresponding components of the weight $w_i^k = [\nabla F_\varepsilon(v^k)]_i$ is large. The large components of the weight will penalize the corresponding components of the variable $x$ in weighted $\ell_1$-minimization problem, so that the corresponding components of the next iterate $x^{k+1}$ would vanish or continue to be small. The iterative scheme (7.26) (equivalently, (7.28)) provides a unified approach to derive reweighted $\ell_1$-algorithms for sparse points in $P$. We now describe the algorithm as follows.

## Algorithm (A) (Reweighted $\ell_1$-Algorithm)

S1.  Choose $\tau$, $\varepsilon^0 \in (0,1)$, and let $(x^0, v^0) \in \mathbb{R}^n \times \mathbb{R}^n_+$ be an initial point.

S2.  At the current iterate $(x^k, v^k)$ with $\varepsilon^k > 0$, compute

$$(x^{k+1}, v^{k+1}) = \arg \min_{(x,v)\in \mathcal{F}} \left(\nabla F_{\varepsilon^k}(v^k)\right)^T v \tag{7.29}$$

where $\mathcal{F} = \{(x,v) \in \mathbb{R}^n \times \mathbb{R}^n_+ : x \in P, |x| \leq v\}$.

S3.  Set $\varepsilon^{k+1} = \tau \varepsilon^k$. Replace $(x^k, v^k, \varepsilon^k)$ by $(x^{k+1}, v^{k+1}, \varepsilon^{k+1})$ and repeat S2.

The solution of (7.29) satisfies the relation (7.27) for any $k \geq 0$. Thus by eliminating $v^k$, Algorithm (A) can be simplified to the following equivalent version which is referred to as Algorithm (B).

## Algorithm (B) (Reweighted $\ell_1$-Algorithm)

S1.  Choose $\tau$, $\varepsilon^0 \in (0,1)$, and let $x^0 \in \mathbb{R}^n$ be an initial point.

S2.  At the current iterate $x^k$ with $\varepsilon^k > 0$, compute

$$x^{k+1} = \arg \min_x \{\|W^k x\|_1 : x \in P\}$$

where

$$W^k = \text{diag}(\nabla F_{\varepsilon^k}(|x^k|)).$$

S3.  Set $\varepsilon^{k+1} = \tau \varepsilon^k$. Replace $(x^k, \varepsilon^k)$ by $(x^{k+1}, \varepsilon^{k+1})$ and repeat S2.

Some modifications for the above algorithm can be made. For instance, the parameter $\varepsilon$ can be fixed without any reduction in the course of iterations and certain stopping criteria can be used. Let $\varepsilon^*$ be a prescribed tolerance. Then $\|v^{k+1} - v^k\| < \varepsilon^*$ can be used as a stopping criterion, and when $\varepsilon$ is reduced after every iteration, $\varepsilon^k < \varepsilon^*$ can also be a stoping criterion. A large amount of empirical experiments indicate that the significant improvement in the sparsity level of iterates usually takes place during the first few iterations. Thus a widely used stoping rule for reweighted $\ell_1$-algorithms is allowing the algorithm to perform only a few iterations, say, 4 or 5 iterations.

When $P$ is given as (7.1), the weighted $\ell_1$-algorithm is used to locate the sparsest solution of an underdetermined system of linear equations. In the case of (7.2), the algorithm is used to find the sparsest non-negative solution of an underdetermined system of linear equations. Algorithms (A) and (B) can apply to any feasible set $P$ which may not be a polyhedral set. When $P$ is a non-polyhedral convex set, the minimization problem at Step 2 of Algorithm (A) is not an LP problem. However, it can still be efficiently solved by an interior-point method.

It is also worth noting that the concave minimization problem is a long-lasting research topic in the field of global optimization (see [135]). From a concave minimization point of view, Algorithms (A) or (B) is not new, which is essentially a linearization method for concave minimization. However, it is the objective function (i.e., the merit function for sparsity) that makes the algorithm special for solving $\ell_0$-minimization problems.

## 7.2.1 Examples of Weights

From the above-discussed general framework of reweighted $\ell_1$-algorithms, specific weights can be immediately obtained by choosing suitable merit functions for sparsity. We now demonstrate a few concrete examples of such weights by using the functions in Example 7.1.4,

**Example 7.2.1** (CWB) The gradient of (a) in Example 7.1.4 is given in (7.7). Choosing this merit function, Algorithm (B) with

$$w_i^k = \frac{1}{|x_i^k| + \varepsilon}, \quad i = 1,\ldots,n$$

is exactly the well-known reweighted $\ell_1$-method proposed by Candès, Wakin and Boyd [53]. This method has been widely studied and used in the literature (see [99, 98, 160, 53, 178]). Some convergence properties for this method can be obtained from the generic analysis for a large family of the reweighted $\ell_1$-algorithms (see [246] and Section 7.4 of this chapter for details).

**Example 7.2.2** (NW1) Let $p \in (0,1)$. Consider the function (b) in Example 7.1.4, to which the gradient is given in (7.9). This merit function can be seen as a modification of (a) in Example 7.1.4. Using the function (b), the algorithm with the following weights was termed the 'NW1' method in [246]:

$$w_i^k = \frac{p + (|x_i^k| + \varepsilon)^{1-p}}{(|x_i^k| + \varepsilon)^{1-p} \left[ |x_i^k| + \varepsilon + (|x_i^k| + \varepsilon)^p \right]}, \quad i = 1,\ldots,n.$$

**Example 7.2.3** (Wlp) Let $p \in (0,1)$. Consider the function (c) in Example 7.1.4. By this merit function with gradient (7.10), the associated algorithm with weights

$$w_i^k = \frac{1}{(|x_i^k| + \varepsilon)^{1-p}}, \quad i = 1,\ldots,n,$$

is referred to as the 'Wlp' algorithm, which was studied in [107, 150, 246, 44].

**Example 7.2.4** (NW2, NW3) Let $p,q \in (0,1)$ be given. Consider the functions (d) and (e) in Example 7.1.4, respectively. Their gradients are given in (7.11) and (7.12), respectively. Using the function (d) with gradient (7.11) yields the algorithm called 'NW2' in [246]. This method uses the weights

$$w_i^k = \frac{q + (|x^k|_i + \varepsilon)^{1-q}}{(|x^k|_i + \varepsilon)^{1-q}\left[|x^k|_i + \varepsilon + (|x^k|_i + \varepsilon)^q\right]^{1-p}}, \quad i = 1,\ldots,n.$$

By utilizing the merit function (e) with gradient (7.12), the algorithm is called the 'NW3' in [246] with weights

$$w_i^k = \frac{1 + 2(|x_i^k| + \varepsilon)}{(|x_i^k| + \varepsilon + (|x_i^k| + \varepsilon)^2)^{1-p}}, \quad i = 1,\ldots,n$$

**Example 7.2.5** (NW4) Let $p \in (0,\infty)$ be fixed. Consider the merit function (f) in Example 7.1.4, to which the gradient is given as (7.13). The associated algorithm is called the 'NW4' in [246] with the following weights:

$$w_i^k = \frac{1 + (|x_i^k| + \varepsilon)^p}{(|x_i^k| + \varepsilon)^{p+1}}, \quad i = 1,\ldots,n.$$

Similarly, the gradient of (g) in Example 7.1.4 is given by (7.14), resulting in the following algorithm with weights:

$$w_i^k = \frac{1 + (|x_i^k| + \varepsilon)^{p+1}}{(|x_i^k| + \varepsilon)^{p+1}}, \quad i = 1,\ldots,n.$$

Every function in $\mathcal{M}^{(1)}$-class yields a reweighted $\ell_1$-algorithm which can be used to locate the sparse point in $P$. The family of such algorithms is large. As shown from the above discussion, it is not difficult to construct a merit function for sparsity satisfying the desired properties. Notice that the positive combination of a finite number of the functions in $\mathcal{M}^{(1)}$-class is still in this family. The combination can also be used to generate new merit functions from known ones. For instance, a simple combination of (a) and (c) in Example 7.1.4 produces

$$F_\varepsilon(v) = \left(\sum_{i=1}^n (v_i + \varepsilon)^p\right) + \left(\sum_{i=1}^n \log(v_i + \varepsilon)\right)$$

in $\mathcal{M}^{(1)}$-class, where $p \in (0,1)$ is a given parameter. The kernel function here is $\phi^{(i)}(t) \equiv t^p + \log(t)$ for every $i = 1,\ldots,n$. From the viewpoint of sparsity-seeking ability, the concavity of a function is a desired property for locating the sparse point in $P$ [127]. The concavity of a merit function can be enhanced by choosing the value of the parameters in the function. For instance, the concavity of (c) in Example 7.1.4 can be enhanced by reducing the value of $p \in (0,1)$. Another important concavity-enhancement approach is to apply the log operation to the function at least once. For instance, if $\phi : \mathbb{R}_+ \to \mathbb{R}_+$ is a strictly concave function, then $\log(1 + \phi(t))$ is more concave than $\phi(t)$, and if we apply log twice, the level of concavity of the resulting function $\log(1 + \log(1 + \phi(t)))$ will be further improved. Even if starting with a non-negative convex kernel function, a concave merit function may still be constructed by applying the log operation to the kernel function. In fact, applying the log operation to a convex function several times may reverse the convexity to concavity (see Zhao, Fang and Li [243] for details). For instance, if $\phi : \mathbb{R}_+ \to \mathbb{R}_+$ is a twice differentiable, strictly increasing and convex function obeying

$$\phi''(t)(1 + \phi(t)) < (\phi'(t))^2,$$

then $\log(1 + \phi(t))$ is concave. Since the log operation maintains the coercivity and monotonicity of the original function $\phi(x)$, this approach can be used to construct a concave merit function for sparsity even from a convex kernel function.

## 7.3 Numerical Experiments

As shown in the previous sections, $\mathcal{M}^{(1)}$-class is a large family of merit functions for sparsity, based on which the reweighted $\ell_1$-algorithms can be developed. The weight in Algorithm (B) depends on the choice of merit functions. It is interesting to compare the behavior of these algorithms with different choices of merit functions. For simplicity, in this section, let us compare the performance of algorithms in locating the sparsest solutions of systems of linear equations, i.e., the case $P = \{x : Ax = b\}$. We consider the algorithms with the merit functions listed in Example 7.1.4. The weights generated from these functions are named in Section 7.2.1. Put simply, the iterative schemes in Algorithm (B) with these weights can be summarized as follows.

- **NW1 algorithm**

$$x^{k+1} = \arg\min_{x \in P} \sum_{i=1}^{n} \left[ \frac{p + (|x_i^k| + \varepsilon^k)^{1-p}}{(|x_i^k| + \varepsilon^k)^{1-p} \left(|x_i^k| + \varepsilon^k + (|x_i^k| + \varepsilon^k)^p\right)} \right] |x_i|,$$

where $p \in (0, 1)$.

- **NW2 algorithm**

$$x^{k+1} = \arg\min_{x \in P} \sum_{i=1}^{n} \left[ \frac{q + (|x_i^k| + \varepsilon^k)^{1-q}}{(|x_i^k| + \varepsilon^k)^{1-q} \left(|x_i^k| + \varepsilon^k + (|x_i^k| + \varepsilon^k)^q\right)^{1-p}} \right] |x_i|,$$

where $p, q \in (0, 1)$.

■ **NW3** algorithm

$$x^{k+1} = \arg\min_{x \in P} \sum_{i=1}^{n} \left[ \frac{1 + 2(|x_i^k| + \varepsilon^k)}{(|x_i^k| + \varepsilon^k + (|x_i^k| + \varepsilon^k)^2)^{1-p}} \right] |x_i|,$$

where $p \in (0, 1/2]$.

■ **NW4** algorithm

$$x^{k+1} = \arg\min_{x \in P} \sum_{i=1}^{n} \left[ \frac{1 + (|x_i^k| + \varepsilon^k)^p}{(|x_i^k| + \varepsilon^k)^{1+p}} \right] |x_i|,$$

where $p \in (0, \infty)$.

■ Candès-Wakin-Boyd (**CWB**) method

$$x^{k+1} = \arg\min_{x \in P} \sum_{i=1}^{n} \left[ \frac{1}{|x_i^k| + \varepsilon^k} \right] |x_i|.$$

■ **Wlp** method

$$x^{k+1} = \arg\min_{x \in P} \sum_{i=1}^{n} \left[ \frac{1}{(|x_i^k| + \varepsilon^k)^{1-p}} \right] |x_i|,$$

where $p \in (0, 1)$.

To compare the performance of these algorithms in finding the sparse solutions of underdetermined systems of linear equations, the matrix $A \in \mathbb{R}^{50 \times 250}$ and the $k$-sparse vector $x \in \mathbb{R}^{250}$ can be randomly generated. Assume that the entries of $A$ and non-zero components of the $k$-sparse vector $x$ are i.i.d Gaussian random variables with zero mean and unit variances, and the location of non-zero components of $x$ is also random. For every realized pair $(A, x)$, setting $b := Ax$ yields the underdetermined system of linear equations $b = Az$ with known $k$-sparse solution $x$. For every sparsity level $k = 1, 2, \ldots, 30$, 500 pairs of $(A, x)$ are randomly generated. The above-mentioned algorithms were performed on these examples, and the success frequencies of every algorithm in locating the $k$-sparse solutions were recorded. In these experiments, every reweighted $\ell_1$-algorithm was executed only four iterations, and the same parameters $\tau = 0.5, \varepsilon^0 = 0.01$ and the initial iterate $x^0 = \mathbf{e} \in \mathbb{R}^{250}$ was also used. So the first iteration of the algorithm is actually the standard $\ell_1$-minimization. Given a $k$-sparse solution $x$ of $Az = b$, the algorithm is called 'success' in finding (or recovering) $x$ if the solution $x^k$ generated by the algorithm satisfies that

$$\|x^k - x\| / \|x^k\| \leq 10^{-5}.$$

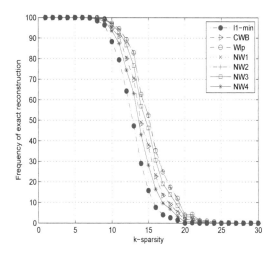

**Figure 7.1:** Success frequencies of seven algorithms in locating $k$-sparse solutions of linear systems. The size of the random matrix $A$ is $50 \times 250$. 500 attempts were made for every sparsity level $k = 1, \ldots, 30$. $p = 0.5$ and the updating scheme $\varepsilon^{k+1} = \varepsilon^k / 2$ were used in algorithms.

Clearly, the main computational cost in Algorithm (B) is for solving and resolving the weighted $\ell_1$-minimization problems. To solve these problems, we use CVX, a package for specifying and solving convex programs [118].

In the NW2 method, we set $q = p \in (0,1)$ in all experiments. Simulations indicate that for a fixed $p \in (0,1)$ ($p$ is only restricted in $(0, 1/2]$ in NW3), all reweighted $\ell_1$-algorithms described above outperform the standard $\ell_1$-minimization method in locating the sparse solutions of linear systems. Using the updating scheme $\varepsilon^{k+1} = \varepsilon^k / 2$, the numerical results for these algorithms with $p = 0.5$ are summarized in Figure 7.1, in which the success rate of standard $\ell_1$-minimization is also included. Algorithms NW2 and NW3 and Wlp perform better than other methods in this experiment. This experiment demonstrated that the family of reweighted $\ell_1$-algorithms usually outperform the standard $\ell_1$-minimization method, and in the above experiment environment NW2, NW3 and Wlp perform better than CWB, NW1 and NW4.

However, these numerical results cannot imply that the overall performance of NW2, NW3, and Wlp is always better than CWB, NW1, and NW4. The behavior of these algorithms may depend on other factors, such as the choice of the parameter $p$ or $q$ as well as the updating scheme of $\varepsilon^k$. Candès, Wakin and Boyd [53] proposed the following updating scheme for $\varepsilon$ :

$$\varepsilon^k = \max\left\{ [\mathcal{SD}(x^k)]_{i_0}, 10^{-3} \right\}, \qquad (7.30)$$

where $[\mathcal{SD}(x^k)]_{i_0}$ is the $i_0$th component of $\mathcal{SD}(x^k)$ (which sorts the components of $|x^k|$ into decreasing order) and $i_0$ is the nearest integer number to

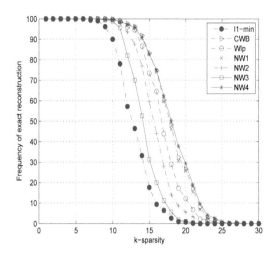

**Figure 7.2:** Success rates of seven algorithms in finding $k$-sparse solutions of linear systems. The size of the random matrix $A$ is $50 \times 250$. 500 attempts were made for each sparsity level $k = 1, \ldots, 30$. $p = 0.5$ was taken and the updating rule (7.30) was used.

$m/[4\log(n/m)]$. Let us replace the updating scheme $\varepsilon^{k+1} = \varepsilon^k/2$ by (7.30), and redo the aforementioned experiments. The results (for $p = 0.5$) were summarized in Figure 7.2, from which it can be seen that reweighted algorithms still outperform the standard $\ell_1$-minimization, but this time CWB, NW1, and NW4 are quite comparable to each other, and they perform better than NW2, NW3, and Wlp under the updating scheme (7.30).

## 7.4 Theoretical Analysis

For the convenience of discussion, we only analyze the case (7.1), namely,

$$P = \{x \in \mathbb{R}^n : Ax = b\}.$$

From the discussion in previous sections, there are many reweighted $\ell_1$-algorithms which can be used to find the sparse points in $P$. Thus it is necessary to study these algorithms in a unified manner in order to identify their common properties. The purpose of this section is to carry out such a unified convergence analysis for Algorithm (A) (which is equivalent to Algorithm (B)) based on the merit functions for sparsity in $\mathcal{M}^{(1)}$-class. Clearly, Algorithm (A) can start from any initial point $(x^0, v^0)$ with $v^0 = |x^0|$, where $x^0$ is not necessarily a solution to the linear system $Ax = b$. After the first step, the algorithm will generate an iterate $(x^1, v^1)$ satisfying $v^1 = |x^1|$ and $Ax^1 = b$. Thus all subsequent iterates $(x^k, v^k)$ will satisfy the linear equation $Ax = b$ and (7.27), i.e., $v^k = |x^k|$ for all $k \geq 1$. Before showing the convergence of Algorithm (A) under certain assumptions, let us first point out that Algorithm (A) is well defined.

## 7.4.1 Well-Definedness of Algorithms

The first lemma below shows that the value of the merit function for sparsity strictly decreases at the $k$th iteration of Algorithm (A), provided that $v^{k+1} \neq v^k$.

**Lemma 7.4.1** *Suppose that $F_\varepsilon(\cdot)$ is a merit function in $\mathcal{M}^{(1)}$-class. For a given parameter $\varepsilon^k > 0$ and a given vector $(x^k, v^k) \in \mathcal{F} = \{(x,v) : Ax = b, |x| \leq v\}$ with $v^k = |x^k|$, let*

$$(x^{k+1}, v^{k+1}) = \arg \min_{(x,v) \in \mathcal{F}} \nabla F_{\varepsilon^k}(v^k)^T v. \tag{7.31}$$

*If $v^{k+1} \neq v^k$, then*

$$F_{\varepsilon^k}(v^{k+1}) < F_{\varepsilon^k}(v^k). \tag{7.32}$$

*Proof.* Note that $(x^k, v^k) \in \mathcal{F}$. By optimality, the minimizer $v^{k+1}$ of the problem (7.31) satisfies that

$$\nabla F_{\varepsilon^k}(v^k)^T v^{k+1} \leq \nabla F_{\varepsilon^k}(v^k)^T v^k.$$

If this inequality holds strictly, i.e., $\nabla F_{\varepsilon^k}(v^k)^T (v^{k+1} - v^k) < 0$, then it must be the case $v^{k+1} \neq v^k$, and the concavity of $F_{\varepsilon^k}(v)$ implies that

$$F_{\varepsilon^k}(v^{k+1}) \leq F_{\varepsilon^k}(v^k) + \nabla F_{\varepsilon^k}(v^k)^T (v^{k+1} - v^k) < F_{\varepsilon^k}(v^k),$$

which yields (7.32). When $v^{k+1} \neq v^k$ and $\nabla F_{\varepsilon^k}(v^k)^T v^{k+1} = \nabla F_{\varepsilon^k}(v^k)^T v^k$, by letting $r > 0$ be a constant such that $\|v^k\|_2 \leq r$, we see that for any sufficiently small scalar $t > 0$,

$$\begin{aligned}
F_{\varepsilon^k}(v^k + t(v^{k+1} - v^k)) &= F_{\varepsilon^k}(v^k) + t\nabla F_{\varepsilon^k}(v^k)^T (v^{k+1} - v^k) \\
&\quad + \frac{1}{2}t^2(v^{k+1} - v^k)^T \nabla^2 F_{\varepsilon^k}(v^k)(v^{k+1} - v^k) + o(t^2) \\
&= F_{\varepsilon^k}(v^k) + \frac{1}{2}t^2(v^{k+1} - v^k)^T \nabla^2 F_{\varepsilon^k}(v^k)(v^{k+1} - v^k) + o(t^2) \\
&\leq F_{\varepsilon^k}(v^k) - \frac{t^2}{2}C(\varepsilon^k, r)\|v^{k+1} - v^k\|^2 + o(t^2) \\
&< F_{\varepsilon^k}(v^k). \tag{7.33}
\end{aligned}$$

The first inequality above follows from the condition (iv) of Definition 7.1.3. The concavity of $F_{\varepsilon^k}(\cdot)$ also implies that for any sufficiently small $t > 0$,

$$\begin{aligned}
F_{\varepsilon^k}(v^k + t(v^{k+1} - v^k)) &\geq tF_{\varepsilon^k}(v^{k+1}) + (1-t)F_{\varepsilon^k}(v^k) \\
&= t(F_{\varepsilon^k}(v^{k+1}) - F_{\varepsilon^k}(v^k)) + F_{\varepsilon^k}(v^k).
\end{aligned}$$

Combining this inequality and (7.33) leads to (7.32). □

The following corollary shows that the merit function strictly decreases after every iteration.

**Corollary 7.4.2** *Let $F_\varepsilon(\cdot)$ be a function in $\mathcal{M}^{(1)}$-class and let $\{(x^k, v^k)\}$ be generated by Algorithm (A). Then the sequence $\{F_{\varepsilon^k}(v^k)\}$ is strictly decreasing in the sense that $F_{\varepsilon^{k+1}}(v^{k+1}) < F_{\varepsilon^k}(v^k)$ for all $k \geq 1$.*

*Proof.* It is obvious that $F_{\varepsilon^k}(v^{k+1}) \leq F_{\varepsilon^k}(v^k)$. This follows directly from Lemma 7.4.1. Since $F_\varepsilon$ is strictly increasing in parameter $\varepsilon$ as well according to the property (ii) of Definition 7.1.3, we conclude from $\varepsilon^{k+1} < \varepsilon^k$ that

$$F_{\varepsilon^{k+1}}(v^{k+1}) < F_{\varepsilon^k}(v^{k+1}) \leq F_{\varepsilon^k}(v^k),$$

as desired. □

The following lemma will be used to show the convergence of Algorithm (A).

**Lemma 7.4.3** *Let $F_\varepsilon(\cdot)$ be a function in $\mathcal{M}^{(1)}$-class and $\{(x^k, v^k)\}$ be the sequence generated by Algorithm (A). If there is a subsequence, denoted by $\{(x^{k_j}, v^{k_j})\}_{j \geq 1}$, satisfying that $|x^{k_j}| \geq \gamma e$ for all $j$ where $\gamma > 0$ is a constant, then there is a finite number $\vartheta^* > 0$ such that*

$$\sum_{j=1}^{\infty} \left\| |x^{k_j+1}| - |x^{k_j}| \right\|_2^2 = \sum_{j=1}^{\infty} \left\| v^{k_j+1} - v^{k_j} \right\|_2^2 \leq \vartheta^*.$$

*In particular,*

$$\left\| |x^{k_j+1}| - |x^{k_j}| \right\|_2 = \left\| v^{k_j+1} - v^{k_j} \right\|_2 \to 0 \text{ as } j \to \infty.$$

*Proof.* We first prove that the sequence $\{F_{\varepsilon^{k_j}}(v^{k_j})\}$ is bounded. Note that the sequence $\{(x^k, v^k)\}$ generated by Algorithm (A) always satisfies that $v^k = |x^k|$ for all $k \geq 1$. From $v^{k_j} = |x^{k_j}| \geq \gamma e$ and the condition (ii) of Definition 7.1.3, it follows that

$$F_{\varepsilon^{k_j}}(v^{k_j}) \geq F_{\varepsilon^{k_j}}(\gamma e) \geq \inf_{\varepsilon \downarrow 0} F_\varepsilon(\gamma e) \geq \chi(\gamma).$$

On the other hand, by Corollary 7.4.2, the sequence $\{F_{\varepsilon^k}(v^k)\}$ is strictly decreasing, and hence,

$$F_{\varepsilon^{k_j}}(v^{k_j}) \leq F_{\varepsilon^0}(v^0) \text{ for any } j \geq 1. \tag{7.34}$$

So the sequence $\{F_{\varepsilon^{k_j}}(v^{k_j})\}$ is bounded. By (ii) of Definition 7.1.3, the function $g(v) = \inf_{\varepsilon \downarrow 0} F_\varepsilon(v)$ is coercive over the set $\{v : v \geq \gamma e\}$. This implies that the sequence $\{v^{k_j}\}$ is bounded. In fact, if $\{v^{k_j}\}$ is unbounded, there must exist a subsequence, denoted still by $\{v^{k_j}\}$, such that $\|v^{k_j}\|_2 \to \infty$ as $j \to \infty$. Since $v^{k_j} \geq \gamma e$, it follows from (ii) of Definition 7.1.3 that

$$F_{\varepsilon^{k_j}}(v^{k_j}) \geq \inf_{\varepsilon \downarrow 0} F_\varepsilon(v^{k_j}) = g(v^{k_j}) \to \infty \text{ as } \|v^{k_j}\|_2 \to \infty,$$

which contradicts (7.34). So there is a positive constant $\gamma' > \gamma$ such that

$$\gamma \mathbf{e} \leq v^{k_j} \leq \gamma' \mathbf{e} \text{ for all } j \geq 1. \tag{7.35}$$

For any $\varepsilon > 0$, since $F_\varepsilon(v)$ is separable in $v \in \mathbb{R}^n_+$ and $[\nabla^2 F_\varepsilon(v)]_{ii}$ is negative, we see that for every $i$, $[\nabla F_\varepsilon(v)]_i$ is decreasing with respect to $v_i$. This implies that

$$\nabla F_{\varepsilon^{k_j}}(\gamma' \mathbf{e}) \leq \nabla F_{\varepsilon^{k_j}}(v^{k_j}) \leq \nabla F_{\varepsilon^{k_j}}(\gamma \mathbf{e}) \text{ for all } j \geq 1. \tag{7.36}$$

The condition (iii) in Definition 7.1.3 implies that for every $i$, the components $[\nabla F_\varepsilon(\gamma' \mathbf{e})]_i$ and $[\nabla F_\varepsilon(\gamma \mathbf{e})]_i$ are both positive, and bounded from above and away from zero for $\varepsilon \in (0, \varepsilon^0]$. This, together with (7.36), implies that there are two constants $0 < \beta_1 < \beta_2$ such that

$$\beta_1 \mathbf{e} \leq \nabla F_{\varepsilon^{k_j}}(v^{k_j}) \leq \beta_2 \mathbf{e} \quad \text{for all } j \geq 1. \tag{7.37}$$

By optimality, we have

$$\nabla F_{\varepsilon^{k_j}}(v^{k_j})^T v^{k_j+1} \leq \nabla F_{\varepsilon^{k_j}}(v^{k_j})^T v^{k_j} \text{ for any } j \geq 1.$$

With (7.35) and (7.37), the above inequality implies that the sequence $\{v^{k_j+1}\}$ is bounded.

Since $\{F_{\varepsilon^{k_j}}(v^{k_j})\}$ is decreasing and bounded from below, we have $F_{\varepsilon^{k_j}}(v^{k_j}) \to F^*$ as $j \to \infty$, where $F^*$ is a constant. Let $r > 0$ be a constant such that

$$\max \left\{ \max_{j \geq 1} \|v^{k_j}\|_2, \max_{j \geq 1} \|v^{k_j+1}\|_2 \right\} \leq r,$$

which is finite since $\{v^{k_j}\}$ and $\{v^{k_j+1}\}$ are bounded. Note that

$$\varepsilon^{k_{j+1}} \leq \varepsilon^{k_{j+1}-1} \leq \cdots \leq \varepsilon^{k_j+1} < \varepsilon^{k_j}.$$

By the decreasing property of the sequence $\{F_{\varepsilon^k}(v^k)\}$ and properties (ii) and (iv) of Definition 7.1.3, we have

$$F_{\varepsilon^{k_{j+1}}}(v^{k_{j+1}}) \leq F_{\varepsilon^{k_{j+1}}}(v^{k_j+1}) < F_{\varepsilon^{k_j}}(v^{k_j+1})$$

$$= F_{\varepsilon^{k_j}}(v^{k_j}) + \nabla F_{\varepsilon^{k_j}}(v^{k_j})^T (v^{k_j+1} - v^{k_j}) + \frac{1}{2}(v^{k_j+1} - v^{k_j})^T \nabla^2 F_{\varepsilon^{k_j}}(\hat{v})(v^{k_j+1} - v^{k_j})$$

$$\leq F_{\varepsilon^{k_j}}(v^{k_j}) + \nabla F_{\varepsilon^{k_j}}(v^{k_j})^T (v^{k_j+1} - v^{k_j}) - \frac{1}{2}C(\varepsilon^{k_j}, r)\|v^{k_j+1} - v^{k_j}\|_2^2,$$

where $\hat{v}$ lies between $v^{k_j+1}$ and $v^{k_j}$, and hence $\|\hat{v}\|_2 \leq r$. The last inequality above follows from (iv) of Definition 7.1.3. Note that $\nabla F_{\varepsilon^{k_j}}(v^{k_j})^T (v^{k_j+1} - v^{k_j}) \leq 0$. The above inequality implies that

$$\frac{1}{2}C(\varepsilon^{k_j}, r)\|v^{k_j+1} - v^{k_j}\|_2^2 \leq F_{\varepsilon^{k_j}}(v^{k_j}) - F_{\varepsilon^{k_{j+1}}}(v^{k_{j+1}}).$$

By (iv) of Definition 7.1.3, there is a constant $\rho^* > 0$ such that $C(\varepsilon^{k_j}, r) \geq \rho^* > 0$ for all $j$. Thus the inequality above implies that

$$\lim_{j \to \infty} \|v^{k_j+1} - v^{k_j}\|_2 = 0,$$

$$\sum_{j=0}^{\infty} \|v^{k_j+1} - v^{k_j}\|_2^2 \leq \frac{F_{\varepsilon^0}(v^0) - F^*}{\rho^*} =: \vartheta^*.$$

as expected.  □

Algorithm (A) satisfies the properties stated in Lemmas 7.4.1 and 7.4.3 and Corollary 7.4.2, provided that the merit function is picked from $\mathcal{M}^{(1)}$-class. From (a) and (g) in Example 7.1.4, we see that a merit function in $\mathcal{M}^{(1)}$-class is not necessarily bounded from below as $|x_i| \to 0$. However, if a merit function is bounded from below (such as (c) and (e) in Example 7.1.4), the result of Lemma 7.4.3 holds for the whole sequence, instead of a subsequence.

**Corollary 7.4.4** *Let $F_{\varepsilon}(\cdot)$ be a function in $\mathcal{M}^{(1)}$-class and let $F_{\varepsilon}(x)$ be bounded from below for $(x, \varepsilon) \in \mathbb{R}_+^n \times \mathbb{R}_{++}$, and let $g(x) = \inf_{\varepsilon \downarrow 0} F_{\varepsilon}(x)$ be coercive in $\mathbb{R}_+^n$. If the sequence $\{(x^k, v^k)\}$ is generated by Algorithm (A), then $\{(x^k, v^k)\}$ is bounded and there exists a finite number $\vartheta^*$ such that*

$$\sum_{k=1}^{\infty} \||x^{k+1}| - |x^k|\|_2^2 = \sum_{k=1}^{\infty} \|v^{k+1} - v^k\|_2^2 \leq \vartheta^*.$$

*In particular,*

$$\||x^{k+1}| - |x^k|\|_2 = \|v^{k+1} - v^k\|_2 \to 0 \text{ as } k \to \infty.$$

Under the assumption of the corollary and by Corollary 7.4.2, there exists a constant $F^*$ such that

$$F^* \leq F_{\varepsilon^k}(v^k) \leq F_{\varepsilon^0}(v^0) \text{ for all } k.$$

Together with the coercivity of $g(x) = \inf_{\varepsilon \downarrow 0} F_{\varepsilon}(x)$, the inequality above implies that $\{v^k\}$ is bounded. Replacing $\{v^{k_j}\}$ by $\{v^k\}$ in the proof of Lemma 7.4.3 immediately yields Corollary 7.4.4.

## 7.4.2 Convergence to Sparse Points

As shown in the previous chapters of this book, the RSP-type matrix property is fundamental to ensure the stable recovery of sparse vectors by $\ell_1$-minimization methods. We also demonstrated that the RSP-type matrix property is also essential for the sign recovery of sparse signals in 1-bit compressed sensing settings. In this section, we investigate the convergence of reweighted $\ell_1$-algorithms under the RSP-type assumption. Throughout this section, for any subset $S \subseteq \{1, \dots, n\}$, we still use the notation $\overline{S} = \{1, \dots, n\} \backslash S$ to denote the complement of $S$.

**Assumption 7.4.5** *Let A be an* $m \times n$ *matrix with* $m < n$. *There is a constant* $\rho > 0$ *and an integer number K such that*

$$\|\xi_{\bar{S}}\|_1 \leq \rho \|\xi_S\|_1 \tag{7.38}$$

*for any set* $S \subseteq \{1,\ldots,n\}$ *with* $|S| \geq K$ *and for any* $\xi \in \mathcal{R}(A^T)$, *the range space of* $A^T$.

It is easy to see that if (7.38) holds for any $S \subseteq \{1,\ldots,n\}$ with $|S| = K$, then it must hold for all $S$ with $|S| > K$. So the inequality $|S| \geq K$ in Assumption 7.4.5 can be replaced by the equality $|S| = K$. Assumption 7.4.5 is a property of the range space of $A^T$. This property is described differently from the traditional notions of the RSP of $A^T$ used in previous chapters. The condition stated in Assumption 7.4.5 is equivalent to the following one:

■ *There exist a constant* $\rho > 0$ *and an integer number K such that*

$$\|\xi_S\|_1 \leq \rho \|\xi_{\bar{S}}\|_1$$

*for any set* $S \subseteq \{1,...,n\}$ *with* $|S| \leq n - K$ *and for all* $\xi \in \mathcal{R}(A^T)$.

It is interesting to understand the relationship between Assumption 7.4.5 and the null space property (NSP) of $A$ which has been widely used in the compressed sensing literature. Recall that $A$ has the stable NSP of order $k$ with a constant $0 < \tau < 1$ if

$$\|\eta_S\|_1 \leq \tau \|\eta_{\bar{S}}\|_1$$

for any $S \subseteq \{1,\ldots,n\}$ with $|S| \leq k$ and for any $\eta \in \mathcal{N}(A)$. The following link is easy to verify.

**Proposition 7.4.6** *Let* $A \in \mathbb{R}^{m \times n} (m < n)$ *and* $M \in \mathbb{R}^{(n-m) \times n}$ *be full-rank matrices satisfying* $AM^T = 0$. *Then M has the stable NSP of order* $k^*$ *with constant* $\tau \in (0,1)$ *if and only if* $A^T$ *satisfies Assumption 7.4.5 with* $K = (n - k^*)$ *and* $\rho = \tau < 1$.

*Proof.* Note that $A$ and $M$ are full-rank matrices and $AM^T = 0$, and hence $MA^T = 0$. This means the columns of $A^T$ provide a basis of the null space of $M$. Therefore,

$$\mathcal{R}(A^T) = \mathcal{N}(M).$$

Suppose that $M$ has the stable NSP of order $k^*$ with constant $\tau \in (0,1)$. Then $\|\eta_L\|_1 \leq \tau \|\eta_{\bar{L}}\|_1$ for any $\eta \in \mathcal{N}(M)$ and for any set $L \subseteq \{1,\ldots,n\}$ with $|L| \leq k^*$. By setting $S = \bar{L}$, this is equivalent to saying that $\|\eta_{\bar{S}}\|_1 \leq \tau \|\eta_S\|_1$ for any $\eta \in \mathcal{R}(A^T)$ and for any set $S \subseteq \{1,\ldots,n\}$ with $|S| \geq K := n - k^*$. Thus $A^T$ satisfies Assumption 7.4.5 with $K = (n - k^*)$ and $\rho = \tau$. Clearly, the converse can be shown in a similar way. $\square$

Thus if $M \in \mathbb{R}^{(n-m)\times n}$ has the stable NSP, we may construct a matrix satisfying Assumption 7.4.5 by simply choosing $A^T = [v_1, \ldots, v_m]$, where $v_1, \ldots, v_m \in \mathbb{R}^n$ are the basis of the null space of $M$. The next property is useful in the proof of convergence of Algorithm (A).

**Lemma 7.4.7** *Let $A \in \mathbb{R}^{m\times n}(m < n)$ be a given matrix. If $A^T$ satisfies Assumption 7.4.5 with order $K$ and constant $\rho > 0$, then the transpose of any submatrix $\widehat{A} \in \mathbb{R}^{m'\times n'}$ which is extracted from $A$ with $m' \leq n'$ and $n' > K$ (i.e., $\widehat{A}$ is obtained by deleting some columns or rows of $A$) will still satisfy Assumption 7.4.5 with the same order $K$ and constant $\rho > 0$.*

*Proof.* We first show that for any $S \subseteq \{1, \ldots, n\}$ with $|S| > K$, the matrix $A_S^T$ (the transpose of $A_S$) satisfies Assumption 7.4.5 with the same $(K, \rho)$ as that of $A^T$. Indeed, let $\eta \in \mathcal{R}(A_S^T)$. That is, there exists a $\lambda$ such that $\eta = A_S^T \lambda$. By setting $\eta' = A_{\overline{S}}^T \lambda$ and rearranging the components of $(\eta, \eta')$ if necessary, we have $(\eta, \eta') \in \mathcal{R}(A^T)$. For any $L \subseteq S$ with $|L| \geq K$, since $A^T$ satisfies Assumption 7.4.5, we have

$$\|\eta_{\overline{L}}\|_1 \leq \|(\eta_{\overline{L}}, \eta')\|_1 \leq \rho \|\eta_L\|_1,$$

where $\overline{L} = S \backslash L$. Thus $\|\eta_{\overline{L}}\|_1 \leq \rho \|\eta_L\|_1$ holds for any $L \subseteq S$ with $|L| \geq K$. This means $A_S^T$ satisfies Assumption 7.4.5 with the same $(K, \rho)$. Similarly, we can show that for any $J \subseteq \{1, \ldots, m\}$, the matrix $(A^T)_J$ still satisfies Assumption 7.4.5 with the same $(K, \rho)$. This is straightforward by noting that any $\eta \in \mathcal{R}((A^T)_J)$ is also in $\mathcal{R}(A^T)$. In fact,

$$\eta = (A^T)_J \lambda = (A^T)_{\overline{J}} 0 + (A^T)_J \lambda \in \mathcal{R}(A^T),$$

where $\overline{J} = \{1, \ldots, m\} \backslash J$. Since $A^T$ satisfies Assumption 7.4.5, we immediately see that $\|\eta_{\overline{L}}\|_1 \leq \rho \|\eta_L\|_1$ holds for any $L \subseteq \{1, \ldots, n\}$ with $|L| \geq K$, as desired. Note that $\widehat{A} \in \mathbb{R}^{m'\times n'}$ with $m' \leq n'$ and $n' > K$ is obtained by deleting $n - n'$ columns and $m - m'$ rows from $A$. Thus the transpose of this submatrix satisfies Assumption 7.4.5 with the same $(K, \rho)$ as that of $A^T$. $\quad\square$

We now prove some properties of the reweighted $\ell_1$-algorithms under Assumption 7.4.5. The initial result below shows that under Assumption 7.4.5, Algorithm (A) with $F_\varepsilon(\cdot)$ in $\mathcal{M}^{(1)}$-class generates a sparse solution in the sense that at least one component of $x^k$ tends to zero. Recall that $\mathcal{SD}(\cdot)$ is the sorting operation which sorts the absolute entries of a vector into descending order.

**Theorem 7.4.8** *Let $A \in \mathbb{R}^{m\times n}$ $(m < n)$ satisfy Assumption 7.4.5 with $(K, \rho)$ satisfying $(1 + \rho)K < n$. Let $F_\varepsilon(\cdot)$ be a function in $\mathcal{M}^{(1)}$-class and $\{(x^k, v^k)\}$ be generated by Algorithm (A). Then,*

$$\min_{1 \leq i \leq n} |x_i^k| \to 0 \ as \ k \to \infty. \tag{7.39}$$

*In particular, $[\mathcal{SD}(x^k)]_n \to 0$ as $k \to \infty$, where $[\mathcal{SD}(x^k)]_n$ denotes the n-th component of the vector $\mathcal{SD}(x^k)$.*

*Proof.* Assume the contrary that (7.39) does not hold. Then there exist a constant $\gamma > 0$ and a subsequence, $\{(x^{k_j}, v^{k_j})\}_{j=1}^{\infty}$, such that

$$\min_{1 \leq i \leq n} |x_i^{k_j}| \geq \gamma > 0$$

for all $j$. Thus $v^{k_j}(=|x^{k_j}|) \geq \gamma e$ for all $j$. By Lemma 7.4.3, $\|v^{k_j+1} - v^{k_j}\|_2 \to 0$ as $j \to \infty$. So there exists a $j'$ such that for all $j \geq j'$ the vector $v^{k_j+1}$ is positive, i.e., $v^{k_j+1} \in \mathbb{R}_{++}^n$. Let $j \geq j'$ and consider the $k_j$-th step of the algorithm. At $k_j$-th step, $x^{k_j}, v^{k_j}$ and $\varepsilon^{k_j}$ are given. The vector $(x^{k_j+1}, v^{k_j+1})$ is the solution to the LP problem

$$\min_x \left\{ \nabla F_{\varepsilon^{k_j}}(v^{k_j})^T v : Ax = b, \ |x| \leq v \right\},$$

which can be written as

$$\min_x \left\{ \nabla F_{\varepsilon^{k_j}}(v^{k_j})^T v : Ax = b, \ x \leq v, \ -x \leq v \right\}.$$

By the KKT optimality conditions, there are Lagrangian multipliers $\alpha^{k_j}, \beta^{k_j} \in \mathbb{R}_+^n$ and $\lambda^{k_j} \in \mathbb{R}^m$ such that

$$Ax^{k_j+1} = b,$$

$$-x_i^{k_j+1} - v_i^{k_j+1} \leq 0, \ \alpha_i^{k_j}\left[-x_i^{k_j+1} - v_i^{k_j+1}\right] = 0, \ i = 1,\dots,n, \tag{7.40}$$

$$x_i^{k_j+1} - v_i^{k_j+1} \leq 0, \ \beta_i^{k_j}\left[x_i^{k_j+1} - v_i^{k_j+1}\right] = 0, \ i = 1,\dots,n, \tag{7.41}$$

$$A^T \lambda^{k_j} = \alpha^{k_j} - \beta^{k_j}, \tag{7.42}$$

$$\nabla F_{\varepsilon^{k_j}}(v^{k_j}) = \alpha^{k_j} + \beta^{k_j}. \tag{7.43}$$

The condition $v^{k_j+1} \in \mathbb{R}_{++}^n$ implies that for every $i$, one of the inequalities $x_i^{k_j+1} - v_i^{k_j+1} \leq 0$ and $-x_i^{k_j+1} - v_i^{k_j+1} \leq 0$ must hold strictly. Thus from (7.40) and (7.41), we see that either $\alpha_i^{k_j} = 0$ or $\beta_i^{k_j} = 0$ for every $i = 1,\dots,n$. Due to the conditions $v^{k_j} \in \mathbb{R}_{++}^n$, $\varepsilon^{k_j} > 0$ and $F_{\varepsilon^{k_j}} \in \mathcal{M}^{(1)}$-class, we immediately see that $\nabla F_{\varepsilon^{k_j}}(v^{k_j}) \in \mathbb{R}_{++}^n$. Therefore, the condition (7.43) implies that $\alpha^{k_j} \in \mathbb{R}_+^n$ and $\beta^{k_j} \in \mathbb{R}_+^n$ are strictly complementary, i.e.,

$$\alpha_i^{k_j}\beta_i^{k_j} = 0, \ \alpha_i^{k_j} + \beta_i^{k_j} > 0, \ i = 1,\dots,n.$$

This implies that $\alpha_i^{k_j} + \beta_i^{k_j} = |\alpha_i^{k_j} - \beta_i^{k_j}|$. It follows from (7.42) and (7.43) that

$$\nabla F_{\varepsilon^{k_j}}(v^{k_j}) = |A^T \lambda^{k_j}| = |\xi^{k_j}|,$$

where $\xi^{k_j} = A^T \lambda^{k_j}$. This implies that $\mathcal{SD}(\nabla F_{\varepsilon^{k_j}}(v^{k_j})) = \mathcal{SD}(\xi^{k_j})$. By Assumption 7.4.5, we have,

$$\left\|\xi_{\overline{S}}^{k_j}\right\|_1 \leq \rho \left\|\xi_S^{k_j}\right\|_1, \tag{7.44}$$

for any $S \subseteq \{1,\ldots,n\}$ with $|S| \geq K$. Let $S$ denote the set of indices of the $K$ smallest components of $|\xi^{k_j}|$. Then,

$$\left\|\xi_S^{k_j}\right\|_1 = \sum_{i=n-K+1}^{n} [\mathcal{SD}(\xi^{k_j})]_i = \sum_{i=n-K+1}^{n} [\mathcal{SD}(\nabla F_{\varepsilon^{k_j}}(v^{k_j}))]_i,$$

and

$$\left\|\xi_{\overline{S}}^{k_j}\right\|_1 = \sum_{i=1}^{n-K} [\mathcal{SD}(\xi^{k_j})]_i = \sum_{i=1}^{n-K} [\mathcal{SD}(\nabla F_{\varepsilon^{k_j}}(v^{k_j}))]_i.$$

The two relations above, together with (7.44), yields

$$\sum_{i=1}^{n-K} [\mathcal{SD}(\nabla F_{\varepsilon^{k_j}}(v^{k_j}))]_i \leq \rho \sum_{i=n-K+1}^{n} [\mathcal{SD}(\nabla F_{\varepsilon^{k_j}}(v^{k_j}))]_i. \qquad (7.45)$$

On the other hand, we note that $(1+\rho)K < n$ implies $n - K > \rho K$ and that $\nabla F_{\varepsilon^{k_j}}(v^{k_j}) \in R_{++}^n$ implies $[\mathcal{SD}(\nabla F_{\varepsilon^{k_j}}(v^{k_j}))]_{n-K+1} > 0$. Therefore, we have

$$\begin{aligned}
\sum_{i=1}^{n-K} [\mathcal{SD}(\nabla F_{\varepsilon^{k_j}}(v^{k_j}))]_i &\geq (n-K) [\mathcal{SD}(\nabla F_{\varepsilon^{k_j}}(v^{k_j}))]_{n-K+1} \\
&> \rho K [\mathcal{SD}(\nabla F_{\varepsilon^{k_j}}(v^{k_j}))]_{n-K+1} \\
&\geq \rho \sum_{i=n-K+1}^{n} [\mathcal{SD}(\nabla F_{\varepsilon^{k_j}}(v^{k_j}))]_i. \qquad (7.46)
\end{aligned}$$

Clearly, (7.46) contradicts (7.45). Therefore (7.39) holds. □

The above result, established for the family of merit functions for sparsity in $\mathcal{M}^{(1)}$-class, implies that Algorithm (A) guarantees to generate a solution with at least one component being zero if Assumption 7.4.5 is satisfied. Based on this result, some stronger convergence result can be shown. The remaining of this section is devoted to this proof. The next technical result is helpful.

**Lemma 7.4.9** *Let $F_\varepsilon(\cdot)$ be a function in $\mathcal{M}^{(1)}$-class, and let $A \in \mathbb{R}^{m \times n}$ with $m < n$, and assume that $A^T$ satisfies Assumption 7.4.5 where $K$ and $\rho$ satisfy $(1+\rho)K < n$. Let $\{(x^k, v^k)\}$ be generated by Algorithm (A) such that $\|v^{k+1} - v^k\| \to 0$ as $k \to \infty$. If there is a constant $\lambda > 0$ such that $|J_\lambda(x^k)| \geq K$ for all sufficiently large k, where $J_\lambda(x^k) = \{i : |x_i^k| \geq \lambda\}$, then there exists a $k'$ such that $\|x^{k'}\|_0 < n$ and*

$$\text{supp}(x^k) \subseteq \text{supp}(x^{k'}) \text{ for all } k \geq k'.$$

*Proof.* At the $k$-th step, $(x^{k+1}, v^{k+1})$ is a solution to the LP problem

$$\min\{\nabla F_{\varepsilon^k}(v^k)^T v : Ax = b, \ x \leq v, \ -x \leq v\}.$$

By the KKT optimality conditions, there are Lagrangian multipliers $\alpha^k, \beta^k \in \mathbb{R}^n_+$ and $u^k \in \mathbb{R}^m$ such that

$$A^T u^k - \alpha^k + \beta^k = 0, \tag{7.47}$$

$$\nabla F_{\varepsilon^k}(v^k) - \alpha^k - \beta^k = 0, \tag{7.48}$$

$$-x_i^{k+1} - v_i^{k+1} \leq 0, \ \alpha_i^k \left[-x_i^{k+1} - v_i^{k+1}\right] = 0, \ i = 1, \dots, n, \tag{7.49}$$

$$x_i^{k+1} - v_i^{k+1} \leq 0, \ \beta_i^k \left[x_i^{k+1)} - v_i^{k+1}\right] = 0, \ i = 1, \dots, n, \tag{7.50}$$

$$Ax^{k+1} = b. \tag{7.51}$$

Note that $F_\varepsilon(v)$ is separable in $v$. For every $i$, $[\nabla F_{\varepsilon^k}(v^k)]_i$ depends on $v_i^k$ only. According to (iv) of Definition 7.1.3, the second order derivative $[\nabla^2 F_{\varepsilon^k}(v^k)]_{ii}$ is negative, so $[\nabla F_{\varepsilon^k}(v^k)]_i$ is decreasing with respect to $v_i^k$. Note that $J_\lambda(x^k) = J_\lambda(v^k)$ due to $v^k = |x^k|$. Thus,

$$[\nabla F_{\varepsilon^k}(v^k)]_i \leq [\nabla F_{\varepsilon^k}(\lambda e)]_i \ \text{for all } i \in J_\lambda(x^k). \tag{7.52}$$

Since $\|v^{k+1} - v^k\| \to 0$ as $k \to \infty$, we see that $v_i^{k+1} \neq 0$ for every $i \in J_\lambda(x^k)$ and all sufficiently large $k$. Thus, for every $i \in J_\lambda(x^k)$, (7.49) and (7.50) imply that either $\alpha_i^k = 0$ or $\beta_i^k = 0$. It is easy to show that $\alpha^k$ and $\beta^k$ are strictly complementary. In fact, by (iii) of Definition 7.1.3, we have $\nabla F_{\varepsilon^k}(v^k) \in \mathbb{R}^n_{++}$. This fact, together with (7.48), implies that for every $i$, either $\alpha_i^k \neq 0$ or $\beta_i^k \neq 0$. Therefore, for every $i \in J_\lambda(x^k)$, $\alpha_i^k$ and $\beta_i^k$ must be strictly complementary. That is, one and only one of them vanishes. Thus,

$$|\alpha_i^k - \beta_i^k| = \alpha_i^k + \beta_i^k = \left[\nabla F_{\varepsilon^k}(v^k)\right]_i \ \text{for every } i \in J_\lambda(x^k). \tag{7.53}$$

By (7.52) and (7.53), for all sufficiently large $k$ we have

$$\sum_{i \in J_\lambda(x^k)} |\alpha_i^k - \beta_i^k| = \sum_{i \in J_\lambda(x^k)} \left[\nabla F_{\varepsilon^k}(v^k)\right]_i \leq \sum_{i \in J_\lambda(x^k)} [\nabla F_{\varepsilon^k}(\lambda e)]_i.$$

By (iii) of Definition 7.1.3, for each $i \in \{1, \dots, n\}$, $[\nabla F_\varepsilon(\lambda e)]_i$ is continuous in $\varepsilon$ and there is a constant $\gamma_i^* > 0$ such that $[\nabla F_\varepsilon(\lambda e)]_i \to \gamma_i^*$ as $\varepsilon \to 0$. Thus there is a constant $C^*$ such that

$$\sum_{i=1}^n [\nabla F_\varepsilon(\lambda e)]_i \leq C^* \ \text{for all } \varepsilon \in (0, \varepsilon^0].$$

Note that $\varepsilon^k \in (0, \varepsilon^0]$. Combining the above two inequalities leads to

$$\sum_{i \in J_\lambda(x^k)} |\alpha_i^k - \beta_i^k| \leq \sum_{i \in J_\lambda(x^k)} [\nabla F_{\varepsilon^k}(\lambda e)]_i \leq \sum_{i=1}^n [\nabla F_{\varepsilon^k}(\lambda e)]_i \leq C^*, \tag{7.54}$$

which holds for all sufficiently large $k$. We now prove that $\|x^k\|_0 < n$ for all sufficiently large $k$. From (iii) of Definition 7.1.3, $[\nabla F_\varepsilon(v)]_i \to \infty$ as $(v_i, \varepsilon) \to 0$. Thus there exists a small constant $0 < \varepsilon^* < \lambda$ such that

$$[\nabla F_\varepsilon(v)]_i > \rho C^* \text{ for any } v_i + \varepsilon \leq \varepsilon^*. \tag{7.55}$$

By Theorem 7.4.8, we have that $[\mathcal{SD}(x^k)]_n \to 0$ as $k \to \infty$. Thus there exists a sufficiently large number $k'$ such that

$$\min_{1 \leq i \leq n} |x_i^k| + \varepsilon^k < \varepsilon^*$$

for all $k \geq k'$. Let $i_0$ be the index such that $v_{i_0}^{k'} = |x_{i_0}^{k'}| = \min_{1 \leq i \leq n} |x_i^{k'}|$. Since $\varepsilon^* < \lambda$, we see that $i_0 \notin J_\lambda(x^{k'})$. Consider the next point $(x^{k'+1}, v^{k'+1})$, which satisfies the optimality condition (7.47)-(7.51) where $(u^k, v^k, x^{k+1}, v^{k+1}, \alpha^k, \beta^k, \varepsilon^k)$ is replaced by $(u^{k'}, v^{k'}, x^{k'+1}, v^{k'+1}, \alpha^{k'}, \beta^{k'}, \varepsilon^{k'})$. We now prove that $x_{i_0}^{k'+1} = 0$. In fact, if it is not, by (7.48)-(7.50), one and only one of $\alpha_{i_0}^{k'}$ and $\beta_{i_0}^{k'}$ is zero. This, together with (7.48) and (7.55), implies that

$$|\alpha_{i_0}^{k'} - \beta_{i_0}^{k'}| = \alpha_{i_0}^{k'} + \beta_{i_0}^{k'} = \left[\nabla F_{\varepsilon^{k'}}(v^{k'})\right]_{i_0} > \rho C^*,$$

and thus

$$\sum_{i \notin J_\lambda(x^{k'})} |\alpha_i^{k'} - \beta_i^{k'}| \geq |\alpha_{i_0}^{k'} - \beta_{i_0}^{k'}| > \rho C^*. \tag{7.56}$$

However, by assumption, we have $|J_\lambda(x^{k'})| \geq K$. By (7.47) and (7.54) and Assumption 7.4.5, we have

$$\sum_{i \notin J_\lambda(x^{k'})} |\alpha_i^{k'} - \beta_i^{k'}| = \sum_{i \notin J_\lambda(x^{k'})} |A^T u^{k'}|_i$$

$$\leq \rho \sum_{i \in J_\lambda(x^{k'})} |A^T u^{k'}|_i = \rho \sum_{i \in J_\lambda(x^{k'})} |\alpha_i^{k'} - \beta_i^{k'}|$$

$$\leq \rho C^*.$$

This contradicts (7.56). So we conclude that $x_{i_0}^{k'+1} = 0$ and thus $\|x^{k'+1}\|_0 < n$. This also indicates that $\min_{1 \leq i \leq n} |x_i^{k'+1}| = v_{i_0}^{k'+1} = 0$. Replacing $x^{k'}$ by $x^{k'+1}$, considering the point $(x^{k'+2}, v^{k'+2})$ and repeating the same proof above, we can show that $x_{i_0}^{k'+2} = 0$. By induction, we conclude that $x_{i_0}^k = 0$ for all $k > k'$. This proof can be applied to any other component $x_i^{k'} = 0$ from which we can show that $x_i^k = 0$ for all sufficiently large $k > k'$. Thus there exists a $k'$ such that $\text{supp}(x^k) \subseteq \text{supp}(x^{k'})$ for all $k \geq k'$. □

The requirement '$\|v^{k+1} - v^k\| \to 0$ as $k \to \infty$' in Lemma 7.4.9 is mild, and can be met trivially when the merit function is suitably chosen. For instance, by Corollary 7.4.4, the functions (c) and (d) in Example 7.1.4 can ensure this requirement being met. In what follows, we prove the main convergence result for Algorithm (A). Let $J_\lambda(x)$ be defined as in Lemma 7.4.9. Since $b \neq 0$, there exists a small number $\lambda_0 > 0$ such that for any given $\lambda \in (0, \lambda_0)$ the set $J_\lambda(x) \neq \emptyset$ for any solution of the system $Ax = b$. Clearly, we have $J_\lambda(x) \subseteq \operatorname{supp}(x)$ (and thus $|J_\lambda(x)| \leq |\operatorname{supp}(x)|$) for any $x \in \mathbb{R}^n$. The following result is stronger than Theorem 7.4.8.

**Theorem 7.4.10** *Let $A \in \mathbb{R}^{m \times n}$ with $m < n$. Assume that $A^T$ satisfies Assumption 7.4.5 where $K$ and $\rho$ satisfy $(1+\rho)K < n$. Let $F_\varepsilon(\cdot)$ be a function in $\mathcal{M}^{(1)}$-class and the sequence $\{(x^k, v^k)\}$ be generated by Algorithm (A). If $\|v^{k+1} - v^k\|_2 \to 0$ as $k \to \infty$, then there is a subsequence $\{x^{k_j}\}$ such that*

$$[\mathcal{SD}(x^{k_j})]_{\lfloor(1+\rho)K\rfloor+1} \to 0 \text{ as } j \to \infty,$$

*where $[\mathcal{SD}(x^{k_j})]_{\lfloor(1+\rho)K\rfloor+1}$ denotes the $(\lfloor(1+\rho)K\rfloor + 1)$-th component of the vector $\mathcal{SD}(x^{k_j})$. That is, $\{x^{k_j}\}$ converges to a $\lfloor(1+\rho)K\rfloor$-sparse solution of the linear system $Ax = b$.*

*Proof.* We prove this theorem by contradiction. Assume that there is no subsequence of $\{x^k\}$ convergent to a $\lfloor(1+\rho)K\rfloor$-sparse solution. Then there exists a number $\lambda^* > 0$ such that

$$[\mathcal{SD}(x^k)]_{\lfloor(1+\rho)K\rfloor+1} \geq \lambda^*$$

for all sufficiently large $k$. In other words,

$$|J_{\lambda^*}(x^k)| \geq \lfloor(1+\rho)K\rfloor + 1 > (1+\rho)K$$

for all sufficiently large $k$. By Lemma 7.4.9, there exists a $k'$ such that $\|x^{k'}\|_0 < n$ and

$$\operatorname{supp}(x^k) \subseteq \operatorname{supp}(x^{k'}) \text{ for all } k \geq k'. \tag{7.57}$$

Note that $J_{\lambda^*}(x^k) \subseteq \operatorname{supp}(x^k)$. For any $k \geq k'$, we have

$$n > \|x^{k'}\|_0 = |\operatorname{supp}(x^{k'})| \geq |\operatorname{supp}(x^k)| \geq |J_{\lambda^*}(x^k)| > (1+\rho)K > K. \tag{7.58}$$

If $|\operatorname{supp}(x^k)| > |J_{\lambda^*}(x^k)|$ at the $k$-step $(k \geq k')$, we now show that the algorithm will continue to reduce the value of $|\operatorname{supp}(x^k)|$ until for some $k'' > k'$ we have $|\operatorname{supp}(x^k)| = |J_{\lambda^*}(x^k)|$ for all $k \geq k''$. Since $F_\varepsilon(v)$ is separable in $v$, it can be represented as

$$F_\varepsilon(v) = \sum_{i=1}^{n} \phi^{(i)}(\varepsilon, v_i) \tag{7.59}$$

where $\phi^{(i)}$'s are kernel functions. From (7.57), we see that if $x_i^{k'} = 0$ then $x_i^k = 0$ for all $k \geq k'$. Thus for all $k \geq k'$ the problem (7.29), i.e.,

$$\min\{\nabla F_{\varepsilon^k}(v^k)^T v : Ax = b, |x| \leq v\}$$

is exactly equivalent to the reduced problem

$$\min\left\{[\nabla F_{\varepsilon^k}(v^k)]_S^T v_S : A_S x_S = b, \ |x_S| \le v_S\right\}, \tag{7.60}$$

where $S = \text{supp}(x^{k'})$. In other words, for all $k \ge k'$ the solution $(x^{k+1}, v^{k+1})$ of the problem (7.29) can be partitioned into $x^{k+1} = (x_S^{k+1}, 0), v^{k+1} = (v_S^{k+1}, 0)$ where $(x_S^{k+1}, v_S^{k+1})$ is the solution of the reduced problem (7.60). The merit function for sparsity associated with the problem (7.60) is given by

$$F_{\varepsilon}(v_S) := \sum_{i \in S} \phi^{(i)}(\varepsilon, v_i), \tag{7.61}$$

which still satisfies the conditions (i)-(iv) of Definition 7.1.3 in space $\mathbb{R}_+^{|S|}$, where $|S| = |\text{supp}(x^{k'})| > K$ by (7.58). The function (7.61) is obtained from (7.59) by removing the components $\phi^{(i)}(\varepsilon, v_i)$ with $i \notin S$.

Note that $A_S \in \mathbb{R}^{m \times |S|}$. If $m > |S|$, some equations in the system $A_S x_S = b$ must be redundant, and can be eliminated from this system without any change of the solutions to the system $A_S x_S = b$. Let $\widehat{A}_S x_S = \widehat{b}$ denote the resulting system after eliminating the redundant equations. Thus the problem (7.60) is reduced to

$$\min\left\{[\nabla F_{\varepsilon^k}(v^k)]_S^T v_S : \widehat{A}_S x_S = \widehat{b}, \ |x_S| \le v_S\right\}, \tag{7.62}$$

where the size of the matrix $\widehat{A}_S$ is $m' \times |S|$ with $m' \le |S|$. Note that $|S| > K$. This submatrix of $A$ satisfies the condition of Lemma 7.4.7, by which we see that $(\widehat{A}_S)^T$ satisfies Assumption 7.4.5 with the same constant as that of $A^T$. Therefore, applying Lemma 7.4.9 to the problem (7.62) with the reduced merit function (7.61) where $v_S \in \mathbb{R}^{|S|}$, we conclude that there exists a $k'' > k'$ such that $|\text{supp}(x_S^{k''})| < |S|$ and $\text{supp}(x_S^k) \subseteq \text{supp}(x_S^{k''})$ for all $k \ge k''$. Note that $x^{k''}$ and $x^k$ are partitioned, respectively, into $(x_S^{k''}, 0)$ and $(x_S^k, 0)$ for all $k \ge k''$. This is equivalent to

$$|\text{supp}(x^{k''})| < |S| = |\text{supp}(x^{k'})|,$$

and

$$\text{supp}(x^k) \subseteq \text{supp}(x^{k''}) \ \text{for all} \ k \ge k''.$$

If $|\text{supp}(x^{k''})|$ remains larger than $|J_{\lambda^*}(x^{k''})|$, which is larger than $\lfloor(1+\rho)K\rfloor$ by (7.58), then replace $x^{k'}$ by $x^{k''}$ and repeat the same proof above, we can conclude that there exists $k''' > k''$ such that $|\text{supp}(x^{k'''})|$ is strictly smaller than $|\text{supp}(x^{k''})|$. Therefore, by induction, there must exist an integer number, denoted still by $k'''$, such that

$$\text{supp}(x^k) = J_{\lambda^*}(x^k), \ \text{supp}(x^k) \subseteq \text{supp}(x^{k'''}) \ \text{for all} \ k \ge k'''.$$

Let $S = J_{\lambda^*}(x^k)$, which is larger than $(1+\rho)K$ by (7.58). The above relation implies that for all $k \ge k'''$ the vector $x^k$ is a $|S|$-sparse vector where $|S| = |J_{\lambda^*}(x^k)| >$

$(1+\rho)K$, and hence all non-zero components of $x^k$ are bounded below by $\lambda^* > 0$. All the rest iterations are equivalent to solving the reduced minimization problem (7.60) with $S = J_{\lambda^*}(x^k) = \text{supp}(x^k)$. Note that $\widehat{A}_S$ is a submatrix of $A$, so $\widehat{A}_S$ satisfies Assumption 7.4.5 with the same $(K, \rho)$ as that of $A^T$. Thus applying to the reduced merit function $F_\varepsilon(x_S)$, Theorem 7.4.8 implies that the smallest component of $|x_S^k|$ tends to zero, which contradicts the fact $|x_S^k| \geq \lambda^* > 0$ for all $i \in S$. This contradiction shows that there must exist a subsequence $\{x^{k_j}\}$ convergent to a $\lfloor (1+\rho)K \rfloor$-sparse solution in the sense that $[\mathcal{SD}(x^{k_j})]_{\lfloor (1+\rho)K \rfloor + 1} \to 0$ as $j \to \infty$. □

An immediate result is given as follows.

**Corollary 7.4.11** *Under the same condition of Theorem 7.4.8. Let $\{(x^k, v^k)\}$ be the sequence generated by Algorithm (A), and let $\{(x^{k_j}, v^{k_j})\}$ be the subsequence such that $[\mathcal{SD}(x^{k_j})]_{\lfloor (1+\rho)K \rfloor + 1} \to 0$ as $j \to \infty$. Then the following statements hold true:*

(i) *For any given integer number $t \geq 1$, the subsequence $\{x^{k_j+t}\}$ converges also to $\lfloor (1+\rho)K \rfloor$-sparse solution in the sense that*

$$[\mathcal{SD}(x^{k_j+t})]_{\lfloor (1+\rho)K \rfloor + 1} \to 0 \text{ as } j \to \infty.$$

(ii) *If $v^k \to v^*$, then any accumulation point of $\{x^k\}$ is a $\lfloor (1+\rho)K \rfloor$-sparse solution of $Ax = b$.*

(iii) *If the $\lfloor (1+\rho)K \rfloor$-sparse solution of $Ax = b$ is unique, then the subsequence $\{x^{k_j}\}$ converges to the sparsest solution of $Ax = b$. In particular, if $x^k \to x^*$ or $v^k \to v^*$, then $x^k$ converges to the sparsest solution of the system $Ax = b$.*

*Proof.* The results (ii) and (iii) are obvious. It is also easy to show (i). It follows from $\|v^{k+1} - v^k\|_2 \to 0$ that

$$\left\| v^{k_j+t} - v^{k_j} \right\| \leq \sum_{i=1}^{t} \left\| v^{k_j+i} - v^{k_j+(i-1)} \right\|_2 \to 0 \text{ as } j \to \infty.$$

On the other hand,

$$\left| [\mathcal{SD}(x^{k_j+t})]_{\lfloor (1+\rho)K \rfloor + 1} - [\mathcal{SD}(x^{k_j})]_{\lfloor (1+\rho)K \rfloor + 1} \right|$$
$$\leq \left\| \mathcal{SD}(x^{k_j+t}) - \mathcal{SD}(x^{k_j}) \right\|_2 = \left\| \mathcal{SD}(v^{k_j+t}) - \mathcal{SD}(v^{k_j}) \right\|_2 \leq \left\| v^{k_j+t} - v^{k_j} \right\|_2.$$

Combining the two relations above leads to the result (i). □

The requirement $\|v^{k+1} - v^k\|_2 \to 0$ used in Theorem 7.4.10 and Corollary 7.4.11 can be removed when the merit functions are suitably chosen. As shown by Corollary 7.4.4, some functions in $\mathcal{M}^{(1)}$-class can ensure that the sequence $\{v^k\}$ is bounded and $\|v^{k+1} - v^k\|_2 \to 0$ (e.g., (c) and (d) in Example 7.1.4). We summarize this result as follows.

**Theorem 7.4.12** *Assume that $A^T$ satisfies Assumption 7.4.5 where $K$ and $\rho$ satisfying $(1+\rho)K < n$. Let $F_\varepsilon(\cdot)$ be a function in $\mathcal{M}^{(1)}$-class and let $F_\varepsilon(v)$ be bounded below in $(x,v) \in \mathbb{R}^n_+ \times \mathbb{R}_+$, and $g(x) = \inf_{\varepsilon \downarrow 0} F_\varepsilon(x)$ be coercive in $\mathbb{R}^n_+$. Let $\{(x^k, v^k)\}$ be generated by Algorithm (A). Then there is a subsequence $\{x^{k_j}\}$ convergent to the $\lfloor (1+\rho)K \rfloor$-sparse solution of the system $Ax = b$ in the sense that*

$$[\mathcal{SD}(x^{k_j})]_{\lfloor (1+\rho)K \rfloor + 1} \to 0 \text{ as } j \to \infty.$$

## 7.5 Summary

Minimizing $\|x\|_0$ can be approximated by minimizing a concave merit function for sparsity (which can be twice continuously differentiable in the first orthant). The linearization of a merit function for sparsity provides a unified approach for the development of reweighted $\ell_1$-algorithms. This unified approach not only makes it easy to construct specific reweighted $\ell_1$-algorithms for the sparse solutions of linear systems, but also enables us to carry out a unified convergence analysis for a large family of such algorithms. Except for Corollary 7.4.4 and Theorem 7.4.12, the results shown in this section can be viewed as the common properties of the reweighted $\ell_1$-algorithms based on the merit function in $\mathcal{M}^{(1)}$-class. Theorem 7.4.8 claims that under Assumption 7.4.5, many reweighted $\ell_1$-minimization algorithms associated with the merit functions in $\mathcal{M}^{(1)}$-class can locate the sparse solutions of underdetermined systems of linear equations. If the sequence generated by the algorithm satisfies $\|v^{k+1} - v^k\|_2 \to 0$, then Theorem 7.4.10 claims that, under Assumption 7.4.5 with $(1+\rho)K < n$, the algorithm can find a $\lfloor (1+\rho)K \rfloor$-sparse solution of the linear system. Since the CWB method falls into the framework of Algorithm (A) and it is based on a merit function in $\mathcal{M}^{(1)}$-class (see (a) in Example 7.1.4), a convergence result for CWB can be implied immediately from Theorems 7.4.8 and 7.4.10 and their corollaries. From the discussion in this chapter, it can be seen that the Wlp, NW2, and NW3 methods can ensure that the generated sequence is bounded and satisfies the property $\|v^{k+1} - v^k\|_2 \to 0$. Thus, under Assumption 7.4.5, the convergence results for Wlp, NW2, and NW3 methods can be also obtained immediately from Theorem 7.4.12 which is stronger than Theorem 7.4.10.

## 7.6 Notes

The $\ell_1$-minimization method was introduced to deal with the sparse signal recovery by Chen, Donoho and Saunders [62]. It has been exploited also in learning theory and statistics (see Mangasarian [167], and Tibshirani [207]). The efficiency of $\ell_1$-minimization has been analyzed in the context of compressed sensing and under various assumptions, such as the mutual coherence [83, 95], restricted isometry property (RIP) [51], null space property (NSP) [65], exact recovery condition (ERC) [210, 111], and the range space property of $A^T$ [241, 242]. Encouraged by the success of $\ell_1$-minimization, it is expected to develop certain methods that might be more efficient than $\ell_1$-minimization. Numerical experiments indicate that the reweighted $\ell_1$-algorithm does outperform the unweighted $\ell_1$-minimization in many situations [53, 107, 150, 71, 246, 44].

The reweighted $\ell_1$-method was proposed by Candès, Wakin and Boyd in [53], and the numerical efficiency of this method for sparse signal reconstruction was demonstrated in [53]. Needell [178] showed that the error bound for noisy signal recoveries via the reweighted $\ell_1$-method might be tighter than that of standard $\ell_1$-minimization under the RIP assumption. Asif and Romberg [9] showed that the homotopy method can solve the reweighted $\ell_1$-minimization problem inexpensively as the weight changes, and they also utilized the reweighted $\ell_1$-method to cope with the sparse recovery of streaming signals from streaming measurements (see Asif and Romberg [10]). Foucart and Lai [107] proved that their reweighted $\ell_1$-method is also efficient for sparse signal recoveries under a RIP-type condition. Lai and Wang [150] and Chen and Zhou [44] further proved that under RIP or NSP-type conditions, the accumulation point of the sequence generated by the reweighted $\ell_1$-algorithm proposed by Foucart and Lai [107] can converge to a stationary point of certain '$\ell_2 - \ell_p$' minimization problem that can be viewed as a certain approximation of the $\ell_0$-minimization problem.

In [246], Zhao and Li provided a unified derivation and theoretical analysis for a large family of reweighted $\ell_1$-algorithms and proved that the sequences of iterates generated by such a family of algorithms may converge to the truly sparse solutions of underdetermined linear systems if the transpose of the matrix satisfies certain range space conditions. This family includes many reweighted $\ell_1$-algorithms as special cases, such as the ones in [53, 107, 150, 224, 43]. Moreover, the reweighted $\ell_1$-method is also used for partial-support-information-based signal recovery (see Khajehnejad et al. [145], and Needell, Saab and Woolf [179]). Other studies for weighted $\ell_1$-algorithms as well as their applications can be found in such references as [9, 200, 251].

Although the merit functions for sparsity discussed in this book are separable in $x$, it is worth mentioning that some nonseparable iterative reweighted methods were also studied by some authors, such as Wipf and Nagarajan [224]. Extensions and applications of reweighted $\ell_1$-algorithms were also made to other problems, for instance, the problem arising from computer vision (Ochs et al. [183]), sparse composite regularization problems (Ahmad and Schniter [3]), principal component analysis (Park and Klabjan [184]), and sparse recovery with prior information (Needell at al. [179]). Extensions from vector forms to matrix versions, often referred to as the reweighted nuclear (atomic) norm minimization, have also been widely investigated (see Mohan and Fazel [175], Fornasier, Rauhut and Ward [102], Yang and Xie [229], and Jiang and Cheng [203]). However, the understanding of reweighted $\ell_1$-algorithms and their extensions remain incomplete. For instance, the majority of existing studies for reweighted $\ell_1$-algorithms has only shown that the iterates generated by the algorithm may converge to the stationary points of certain continuous optimization problems under suitable conditions. The deterministic analysis for the convergence of reweighted $\ell_1$-methods to a sparse solution of the linear system was carried out by Zhao and Li in [246] under a range space property of the transposed matrix (see also Zhao and Kocvara [245] and Zhao and Luo [248] for a different derivation and analysis of reweighted $\ell_1$-algorithms). This chapter follows the general idea of the paper [246].

While the majority study of reweighted $\ell_1$-methods has been carried out since 2008, the reweighted least squares (RLS) method has a relatively long history (see [134, 116, 101, 58, 224, 71, 13, 162]). As pointed out by Wipf and Nagarajan [224], both reweighted $\ell_1$- and $\ell_2$-methods can be derived by estimating the upper bound of certain sparsity merit functions. RLS was proposed by Lawson [155] in 1960s, and was extended to $\ell_p$-minimization later. The idea of RLS methods was also used in the algorithm for robust statistical estimation [134], and in FOCUSS methods [117] for the sparse solution of linear systems. The interplay of null space property (NSP) and RLS method was clarified in [71].

The reweighted $\ell_1$-method discussed in this chapter can be derived through the first-order approximation of a concave merit function for sparsity. This approximation method has been explored for many years in the field of global optimization and nonlinear optimization. Under certain mild conditions, Mangasarian [167, 165] has shown that the sequence of iterates generated via the linearization method generally converges to a stationary point of the original concave optimization problem. It is also worth mentioning that the reweighted $\ell_1$-method can be also viewed as a special case of the well-known Majorization-Minimization (MM) method which is widely used in statistics and sparsity recover problems (see Lange [151], Ahmad and Schniter [3], and Sun, Babu and Palomar [204]).

# Chapter 8

# Sparsity via Dual Density

## 8.1   Introduction

In this chapter, we propose a distinct sparsity-seeking principle for linear systems. The key idea behind this principle is to locate the sparse solution of a linear system via seeking the corresponding dense slack variables of the dual problem of the weighted $\ell_1$-minimization problem. Based on this principle, we develop an algorithm for the $\ell_0$-minimization problem with non-negative constraints, namely,

$$\min_{x \in P} \|x\|_0, \tag{8.1}$$

where $P$ is the set of non-negative solutions of a system of linear equations, i.e.,

$$P = \{x \in \mathbb{R}^n : Ax = b, \ x \geq 0\}, \tag{8.2}$$

where $A \in \mathbb{R}^{m \times n}$ and $b \in \mathbb{R}^m$ are given. *We assume that $m < n$, $b \neq 0$ and $P \neq \emptyset$ throughout this chapter.* Under this assumption we see that $0 \notin P$. We also generalize the algorithm for the above problem to an underdetermined system of linear equations without non-negative constraints. The algorithms discussed in this chapter can be called the *reweighted $\ell_1$-algorithms via dual density*. These algorithms are remarkably different from the traditional reweighted $\ell_1$-algorithms presented in Chapter 7.

As shown in Chapter 7, the weighted $\ell_1$-algorithm is one of the most plausible methods for solving the NP-hard $\ell_0$-minimization problems. However, the central question concerning how the weight should be explicitly chosen so that the solution of weighted $\ell_1$-minimization coincides with that of the $\ell_0$-minimization problem remains open. By using the classic strict complementarity theory of linear programs, we first prove that finding the sparsest point in $P$ amounts to searching for the corresponding densest slack variable of the dual problem of weighted $\ell_1$-minimization with all possible choices of non-negative weights. As a result, $\ell_0$-minimization in the original (primal) space can be converted, in theory, to $\ell_0$-maximization in dual space subject to certain nonlinear constraints, which can be cast as a bilevel programming problem with a special structure (see Theorem 8.2.3 for details). This observation provides a theoretical basis and an incentive for the development of reweighted $\ell_1$-algorithms going beyond the traditional algorithmic framework. The weight used in this algorithm is computed via a certain convex optimization instead of being defined directly and locally at an iterate generated in the course of the algorithm. The theoretical efficiency of this algorithm is shown under certain conditions, and the performance of the algorithm has also been demonstrated by empirical simulations. These experiments indicate that in many situations this algorithm outperforms the standard $\ell_1$-minimization when locating the sparse solutions of linear systems. Finally, we end this chapter by discussing how to enhance the sparsity level of the solution of a weighted $\ell_1$-minimization problem when the solution found by an algorithm is not sparse enough.

## 8.2   $\ell_0$-Minimization with Non-negative Constraints

Throughout this section, let $P$ be given as (8.2). It is well known that the $\ell_1$-minimization problem

$$\min_{x \in P} \|x\|_1$$

is one of the most efficient methods for solving $\ell_0$-minimization problems in many situations. However, it may fail to solve an $\ell_0$-minimization problem since the sparsest point in $P$ may not necessarily admit the least $\ell_1$-norm among the points in $P$. So a typical situation where $\ell_1$-minimization fails is when $S^0 \cap S^* = \emptyset$, where $S^0$ denotes the solution set of (8.1) and $S^*$ the solution set of the above $\ell_1$-minimization problem. This motivates one to consider the weighted $\ell_1$-minimization problem since a suitable change of the weight may increase the chance for the sparsest point in $P$ to be located by weighted $\ell_1$-minimization. More specifically, let $S(W)$ be the solution set of the following problem:

$$\min_{x \in P} \|Wx\|_1.$$

Changing from $W = I$ (standard $\ell_1$-minimization) to $W \neq I$ may yield a different solution set $S(W)$, and may lead to $S^0 \cap S(W) \neq \emptyset$ for some $W$. In fact, as shown in Chapter 3, there exists a weight $W^*$, called the optimal weight such that $S(W^*) \subseteq S^0$, and hence the weighted $\ell_1$-minimization method solves the $\ell_0$-minimization problem exactly in such cases. Thus *a fundamental question is how an optimal weight (or nearly optimal weight) can be computed.* The traditional reweighted $\ell_1$-algorithm presented in Chapter 7 was not developed along this direction, and they were not designed directly to compute an optimal weight or its approximation as well.

## 8.2.1 Optimal Weight via Dual Density

Given $W = \text{diag}(w)$, where $w \in \mathbb{R}_+^n$, we consider the problem

$$\gamma^* = \min_{x \in P} \|Wx\|_1,$$

where $\gamma^*$ denotes the optimal value of the problem. Note that replacing $w$ by $\lambda w$ for any scalar $\lambda \neq 0$ does not affect the solution of the weighted $\ell_1$-minimization problem. Thus the solution set of weighted $\ell_1$-minimization problem is invariant under a non-zero scaling of the weight. Thus when $\gamma^* \neq 0$, replacing $W$ by $W/\gamma^*$ yields

$$1 = \min_{x \in P} \|(W/\gamma^*)x\|_1.$$

Thus without loss of generality we consider the following problem with optimal value 1:

$$1 = \min_{x \in P} \|Wx\|_1. \tag{8.3}$$

We use $\mathcal{W}$ to denote the set of such weights, i.e.,

$$\mathcal{W} := \left\{ w \in \mathbb{R}_+^n : 1 = \min_{x \in P} \|Wx\|_1 \right\}, \tag{8.4}$$

which may not be bounded. We define the optimal weight as follows.

**Definition 8.2.1** *A weight $w \in \mathcal{W}$, given as (8.4), is called an optimal weight if the solution to the weighted $\ell_1$-minimization problem (8.3) with this weight is a sparsest point in P.*

From Theorems 3.5, we immediately have the following fact.

**Corollary 8.2.2** *For any sparsest point $x$ in P, there is an optimal weight in $\mathcal{W}$ such that $x$ is the unique solution to the weighted $\ell_1$-minimization problem (8.3).*

Although Corollary 8.2.2 seems intuitive and some informal discussions can be found in the literature, such as [117], this property with a rigorous analysis was given in Zhao and Luo [248] (also in Zhao and Kocvara [245]). Corollary 8.2.2 indicates that an optimal weight $w \in \mathcal{W}$ always exists and thus locating the sparsest point of a polyhedral set can be achieved, in theory, by solving a weighted $\ell_1$-minimization problem (a linear program) via an optimal weight. In other words, solving an $\ell_0$-minimization problem amounts to computing an optimal weight for the weighted $\ell_1$-minimization problem. Depending on the sparsest point $x$, however, the optimal weight satisfying (3.21) is not given explicitly.

The existence analysis carried out in Chapter 3 does not imply a practical computational approach for finding an optimal weight. Clearly, how to efficiently compute an optimal weight is a fundamentally important question in this area. The aim of this section is to develop certain optimization problem so that the optimal weight is a solution to such an optimization problem. As a result, finding an optimal weight can be achieved, in theory, by solving a certain optimization problem.

Given a weight $w \in \mathbb{R}_+^n$, recall that the dual problem of (8.3) is given by

$$\max_{(y,s)}\{b^T y : A^T y + s = w, \ s \geq 0\}, \tag{8.5}$$

where $s$ is called the dual slack variable. It is well known that any feasible LP problem with a finite optimal objective value must have a strictly complementary solution (see Lemma 2.1.2 in Chapter 2) in the sense that there exists a pair $(x, (y,s))$, where $x$ is a solution to (8.3) and $(y,s)$ is a solution to (8.5), such that

$$(x,s) \geq 0, \ x^T s = 0, \ x + s > 0.$$

Using this property, we first prove that solving an $\ell_0$-minimization problem is equivalent to finding a weight $w \in \mathcal{W}$ such that the problem (8.5) has the densest non-negative vector $s = w - A^T y$ among all possible choices of $w \in \mathcal{W}$. The weight that satisfies this criterion turns out to be the optimal weight.

**Theorem 8.2.3** *Let $P = \{x : Ax = b, x \geq 0\}$. Let $(w^*, y^*, s^*)$ be a solution to the following problem:*

$$\max_{(w,y,s)} \ \|s\|_0$$
$$\text{s.t.} \quad b^T y = 1, \ s = w - A^T y \geq 0, \ w \geq 0, \tag{8.6}$$
$$1 = \min_{x \in P} \|Wx\|_1,$$

*where $W = diag(w)$. Then any solution $x^*$ of the problem*

$$\min_{x \in P} \|W^* x\|_1, \tag{8.7}$$

*where $W^* = diag(w^*)$, is the sparsest point of P. Moreover, $\|x^*\|_0 + \|s^*\|_0 = n$. Conversely, let $w^* \in \mathcal{W}$, given in (8.4), satisfy that any solution to the weighted $\ell_1$-minimization problem (8.7) is the sparsest point of P. Then there is a vector $(y^*, s^*)$ such that $(w^*, y^*, s^*)$ is a solution to the problem (8.6).*

*Proof.* Let $(w^*, y^*, s^*)$ be a solution to the problem (8.6). We now prove that any solution of (8.7) is the sparsest point in P. Let $\tilde{x}$ be a sparsest point of P. By Corollary 8.2.2, there exists a weight $\tilde{w} \in \mathcal{W}$ such that $\tilde{x}$ is the unique solution to the weighted $\ell_1$-minimization problem

$$\min_{x \in P} \|\tilde{W} x\|_1,$$

where $\widetilde{W} = \text{diag}(\widetilde{w})$. The dual of this problem is given as

$$\max_{(y,s)}\{b^T y: \ s = \widetilde{w} - A^T y, \ s \geq 0\}.$$

By Lemma 2.1.2, there is a solution $(\widetilde{y}, \widetilde{s})$ to this problem such that $\widetilde{x}$ and $\widetilde{s}$ are strictly complementary in the sense that $\widetilde{x} \geq 0, \widetilde{s} \geq 0, \widetilde{x}^T \widetilde{s} = 0$ and $\widetilde{x} + \widetilde{s} > 0$. Thus,

$$\|\widetilde{x}\|_0 + \|\widetilde{s}\|_0 = n. \tag{8.8}$$

By the optimality conditions and noting that $\widetilde{w} \in \mathcal{W}$, we have

$$b^T \widetilde{y} = \|\widetilde{W}\widetilde{x}\|_1 = \min_{x \in P} \|\widetilde{W}x\|_1 = 1,$$

which implies that the vector $(\widetilde{w}, \widetilde{y}, \widetilde{s})$ satisfies the constraints of the problem (8.6). Note that $(w^*, y^*, s^*)$ is a solution of (8.6). Therefore, $\|s^*\|_0$ is the maximal value of (8.6), and hence

$$\|\widetilde{s}\|_0 \leq \|s^*\|_0. \tag{8.9}$$

Let $x^*$ be an arbitrary solution of (8.7), to which the dual problem is given as

$$\max_{(y,s)}\{b^T y: \ s = w^* - A^T y, \ s \geq 0\}. \tag{8.10}$$

By the optimality conditions again, the constraints of (8.6) imply that $(y^*, s^*)$ is a solution to the problem (8.10). Thus $x^*$ and $s^*$ are complementary in the sense that $x^* \geq 0, \ s^* \geq 0$ and $(x^*)^T s^* = 0$. Therefore,

$$\|x^*\|_0 + \|s^*\|_0 \leq n. \tag{8.11}$$

Merging (8.8), (8.9) and (8.11) yields

$$\|x^*\|_0 \leq n - \|s^*\|_0 \leq n - \|\widetilde{s}\|_0 = \|\widetilde{x}\|_0$$

which implies that $x^*$ must be the sparsest point in $P$. Therefore, $\|x^*\|_0 = \|\widetilde{x}\|_0$. This in turn implies from the above inequalities that $\|x^*\|_0 = n - \|s^*\|_0$.

Conversely, for a given weight $w^* \in \mathcal{W}$, assume that any solution of the problem (8.7) is the sparsest point of $P$. We now prove that there exists a vector $(y^*, s^*)$ such that $(w^*, y^*, s^*)$ is a solution to the problem (8.6). Let $(w, y, s)$ be an arbitrary point satisfying the constraints of (8.6). For this $w$, let $x$ be a solution to the weighted $\ell_1$-minimization problem

$$\min_{z \in P} \|Wz\|_1$$

with $W = \text{diag}(w)$. By the LP duality theory, the constraints of (8.6) imply that $(y, s)$ is a solution to the dual problem of this weighted $\ell_1$-minimization problem. Hence, $x$ and $s$ are complementary, and thus

$$\|s\|_0 \leq n - \|x\|_0 \leq n - z^*, \tag{8.12}$$

where $z^* = \min_{x \in P} \|x\|_0$. So $n - z^*$ is the upper bound for the optimal value of the problem (8.6).

Consider the problem (8.7) with weight $w^*$ and its dual problem. Let $(x^*, (y^*, s^*))$ be a pair of strictly complementary solutions of (8.7) and its dual problem. Then,

$$\|s^*\|_0 = n - \|x^*\|_0 = n - z^*, \qquad (8.13)$$

where the last equality follows from the assumption that any solution of (8.7) is the sparsest point in $P$. Since $(w^*, y^*, s^*)$ is a solution of (8.6), it follows from (8.12) and (8.13) that $\|s\|_0 \leq \|s^*\|_0$ for any feasible point $(w, y, s)$ of (8.6). This means $\|s^*\|_0$ is the maximal value of (8.6). So $(w^*, y^*, s^*)$ is a solution to the problem (8.6). □

For any given weight $w \in \mathcal{W}$, let $x(w)$ denote a solution of the problem (8.3), and let $(y(w), s(w))$ be a solution of the problem (8.5). Since $x(w)$ and $s(w)$ are complementary, that is,

$$x(w) \geq 0, \ s(w) \geq 0, \ x(w)^T s(w) = 0,$$

We conclude that

$$\|x(w)\|_0 + \|s(w)\|_0 \leq n \ \text{ for any } w \in \mathcal{W}. \qquad (8.14)$$

The equality can be achieved in (8.14) by picking $x(w)$ and $s(w)$ as a strictly complementary solution pair, which always exists for every given $w \in \mathcal{W}$. From (8.14), an increase in $\|s(w)\|_0$ may lead to a decrease of $\|x(w)\|_0$. Thus the dense possible vector in $\{s(w) : w \in \mathcal{W}\}$, denoted by $s(w^*)$, yields the sparsest vector $x(w^*)$ which must be the sparsest point in $P$. The vector $(w^*, y(w^*), s(w^*))$ is a solution to the optimization problem (8.6). By Definition 8.2.1, any weight satisfying

$$w^* \in \arg\max_w \{\|s(w)\|_0 : w \in \mathcal{W}\}$$

is an optimal weight by which the sparsest point of $P$ can be immediately obtained via (8.7). Let us summarize this observation as follows.

**Corollary 8.2.4** *If $s(w^*)$ is the densest vector among $s(w)$ for all possible choices of $w \in \mathcal{W}$, i.e.,*

$$s(w^*) = \max_w \{\|s(w)\|_0 : w \in \mathcal{W}\}, \qquad (8.15)$$

*then $w^*$ must be the optimal weight and the corresponding vector $x(w^*)$ must be the sparsest point in $P = \{x : Ax = b, \ x \geq 0\}$.*

Note that $s(w)$ in the objective of the problem (8.15) stands as the solution of the dual problem (8.5) for the given weight $w \in \mathcal{W}$. Thus $s(w)$ must satisfy the constraints of the dual problem and satisfy the strong duality property. Specifically, $s(w)$ is characterized by the following set of conditions:

$$s = w - A^T y \geq 0, \ w \geq 0, \ b^T y = 1, \ w \in \mathcal{W}.$$

Thus the $\ell_0$-maximization problem (8.15) is exactly the same as (8.6). The former can be seen as the concise version of the latter. Problems (8.6) and (8.15) can be referred to as the *dense optimization problem*, which seek for the densest variable $s \in \mathbb{R}_+^n$ of the dual problem (8.5) by taking into account all possible choices of $w \in \mathcal{W}$. As shown by Theorem 8.2.3, any solution $w^*$ to the optimization problem (8.6), or equally (8.15), must be an optimal weight for weighted $\ell_1$-minimization. In other words, seeking the sparsest solution of a linear system can be achieved by finding the densest slack variable $s \in \mathbb{R}_+^n$ of the dual problem of the weighted $\ell_1$-minimization problem with all possible choices of $w \in \mathcal{W}$. The ground base of this sparsity-seeking principle is the fundamental complementary theory of linear optimization.

In this chapter, we introduce a reweighted $\ell_1$-algorithm based on Theorem 8.2.3. Such an algorithm, solving the sparse optimization problem in primal space via approximately solving a dense optimization problem in dual space, is referred to as the *dual-density-based reweighted $\ell_1$-algorithm* (DDRW for short).

## 8.2.2 Dual-Density-Based Reweighted $\ell_1$-Algorithm

As shown below, the problem (8.6) can be viewed as a bilevel optimization problem which is generally difficult to solve (see [163]). However, it is possible to find some approximation or relaxation of the problem (8.6). Let $F_\varepsilon(s)$ be a merit function for sparsity as defined in Chapter 7. Replacing the objective of (8.6) by $F_\varepsilon(s)$ leads to the following continuous approximation of (8.6):

$$\begin{aligned} \max_{(w,y,s)} \ & F_\varepsilon(s) \\ \text{s.t.} \ & b^T y = 1, \ s = w - A^T y \geq 0, \ w \geq 0, \\ & 1 = \min_{x \in P} \|Wx\|_1. \end{aligned} \qquad (8.16)$$

By the duality theory, the constraints of (8.16) imply that for any given $w \in \mathcal{W}$, the vector $(y, s)$ satisfying these constraints is a solution to the problem (8.5) which maximizes $b^T y$ subject to the constraint $s = w - A^T y \geq 0$. Namely, the problem (8.16) can be written as follows:

$$\begin{aligned} \max_{(w,s)} \ & F_\varepsilon(s) \\ \text{s.t.} \ & s = w - A^T y, \ w \in \mathcal{W}, \ w \geq 0, \\ & \text{where } y \text{ is a solution to} \\ & \max_y \{b^T y : \ w - A^T y \geq 0\}. \end{aligned} \qquad (8.17)$$

In this bilevel optimization model, both the objectives in upper and inner levels, $F_\varepsilon(s)$ and $b^T y$, need to be maximized, subject to the constraint $s = w - A^T y \geq 0$ with all possible choices of $w \in \mathcal{W}$. Thus we consider the following relaxation of (8.6) in order to possibly maximize both objectives:

$$\max_{(w,y,s)} \{b^T y + \alpha F_\varepsilon(s) : s = w - A^T y \geq 0, \ w \geq 0, \ w \in \mathcal{W}\}, \qquad (8.18)$$

where $\alpha > 0$ is a given parameter. In (8.17), the upper level objective $F_\varepsilon(s)$ is maximized based on the condition that the inner level objective $b^T y$ is maximized over the feasible set of (8.18). This suggests that the parameter $\alpha$ should be chosen small in (8.18) in order to meet this condition as possible.

Note that the objective of (8.18) is convex. Obviously, the major difficulty of the problem (8.18) lies in the constraint $w \in \mathcal{W}$, i.e., $w$ satisfies that

$$1 = \min_{x \in P} \|Wx\|_1,$$

which by the strong duality property is equivalent to

$$1 = \max_{(x,y)} \{b^T y : s = w - A^T y \geq 0\}.$$

Thus the condition $b^T y \leq 1$ is a relaxation of the constraint $w \in \mathcal{W}$. In fact, this condition follows from the LP weak duality property as well. This suggests the following relaxation of (8.18):

$$\max_{(w,y,s)} \{b^T y + \alpha F_\varepsilon(s) : s = w - A^T y \geq 0, \ b^T y \leq 1, \ w \geq 0\}.$$

We note that when $\|w\|_\infty$ is large, the optimal value $\gamma^*$ of the weighted $\ell_1$-minimization problem may be also large, in which case $w$ can be scaled down to $\widetilde{w} = w/\gamma^*$ so that $\widetilde{w} \in \mathcal{W}$. Any such non-zero scaling does not change the solution of the weighted $\ell_1$-minimization problem. Therefore, we may introduce an upper bound on the weight by confining the weight $w$ to a bounded convex set $\Omega$ in $\mathbb{R}^n_+$ so that the magnitude of the weight is not too large. Based on the above motivation, we propose the following convex relaxation of (8.18):

$$\max_{(w,y,s)} \{b^T y + \alpha F_\varepsilon(s) : s = w - A^T y \geq 0, \ b^T y \leq 1, \ w \geq 0, \ w \in \Omega\}, \qquad (8.19)$$

where $\Omega \subseteq \mathbb{R}^n_+$ is a bounded convex set. From the above discussion, we see that small values should be chosen for $(\alpha, \varepsilon)$ in order to ensure that (8.19) is a certain approximation of (8.6), and thus the vector $w$ resulting from (8.19) can be seen as an approximation of the optimal weight.

Clearly, the solution of (8.19) relies on the choice of $\Omega$. For the convenience of computation and efficiency analysis, $\Omega$ can be chosen as follows:

$$\Omega = \{w \in \mathbb{R}^n_+ : (x^0)^T w \leq \Theta, \ w \leq \Theta^* \mathbf{e}\}, \qquad (8.20)$$

where $\Theta$ and $\Theta^*$ are two given positive numbers, and $x^0$ is the solution to the initial weighted $\ell_1$-problem such as the standard $\ell_1$-minimization. The solution of the initial weighted $\ell_1$-minimization problem, $x^0$, possesses a certain level of sparsity and the sparsity pattern of $x^0$ might carry some information that might be useful for the selection of a weight. In traditional framework of reweighted $\ell_1$-algorithms (in Chapter 7), the weight selection often relies on the magnitude of the components of the current iterate. Taking $x^0$ as an example, if $x^0$ is not the sparsest one, the traditional idea for the selection of weights is to assign large weights corresponding to small components of $x^0$, typically, $w_i = \Theta/(x_i^0 + \varepsilon)$ for $i = 1, \ldots, n$, where $\Theta$ is a given constant and $\varepsilon > 0$ is a small number. This idea for the weight selection is roughly reflected by the inequality $(x^0)^T w \leq \Theta$. So we may incorporate this condition into the set (8.20).

From the above discussion, we are now in a position to describe a framework of the so-called dual-density-based reweighted $\ell_1$-algorithm (DDRW) for solving $\ell_0$-minimization problems.

**Algorithm (I) (General Framework for DDRW).** Let $\varepsilon^0$, $\alpha^0 \in (0,1)$ be the given initial parameters, $w^0 \in \mathbb{R}_+^n$ be the initial weight, and $\Omega^0 \subseteq \mathbb{R}_+^n$ be the initial bounded convex set.

■ Step 1. At $(\varepsilon^k, \alpha^k, w^k, \Omega^k)$ (if certain stopping criterion is satisfied, stop; otherwise), solve the convex optimization

$$\max_{(w,y,s)} \left\{ b^T y + \alpha^k F_{\varepsilon^k}(s) : s = w^k - A^T y \geq 0, \ b^T y \leq 1, \ w \geq 0, \ w \in \Omega^k \right\}$$

to obtain a solution $(w^{k+1}, y^{k+1}, s^{k+1})$.

■ Step 2. Solve the problem

$$\min_x \{\|W^{k+1} x\|_1 : Ax = b, \ x \geq 0\}$$

with $W^{k+1} = \text{diag}(w^k)$ to get a solution $x^{k+1}$.

■ Step 3. Update the parameters $(\varepsilon^k, \alpha^k, \Omega^k) \to (\varepsilon^{k+1}, \alpha^{k+1}, \Omega^{k+1})$, replace $k$ by $k+1$, and return to Step 1.

Some modifications can be made to Algorithm (I) in terms of the choice of $\Omega^k$ and more importantly the relaxation method of (8.6). Clearly, a key difference between Algorithm (I) and the ones introduced in Chapter 7 lies in the principle for tackling $\ell_0$-minimization. The traditional reweighted $\ell_1$-algorithms working in primal space were derived via minimizing the first-order approximation of non-linear merit functions for sparsity, and thus the weight is given by the gradient of the merit function at the current iterate. Algorithm (I) can be seen as an initial development pursuing the sparsity-seeking principle promoted by Theorem 8.2.3, which indicates that locating the sparse solution in primal space can be achieved through finding the corresponding dense slack variables of the dual problems, and a good weight can be computed by solving a relaxation of the bilevel optimization problem (8.6). The weights in Step 2 of Algorithm (I) can be viewed as an approximate optimal weight generated by the convex optimization in Step 1. So, remarkably different from existing reweighted $\ell_1$-methods, $w^k$ in Algorithm (I) is globally computed in dual space through a convex optimization, instead of being defined in terms of the current iterate $x^k$. Therefore, a relaxation of (8.6) leads to the reweighted $\ell_1$-algorithm going beyond the traditional framework of the algorithm discussed in Chapter 7.

In particular, performing only one iteration of the above algorithm and using the set $\Omega$ defined in (8.20) leads to a concrete heuristic algorithm as follows.

**Algorithm (II) (One Step DDRW)** Let $\alpha$, $\varepsilon \in (0,1)$ be given parameters and let $w^0 \in \mathbb{R}^n_{++}$ be a given vector.

- Initialization: Solve $\min\{\|W^0 x\|_1 : x \in P\}$, where $W^0 = \mathrm{diag}(w^0)$, to obtain a minimizer $x^0$. Set $\gamma^0 = \|W^0 x^0\|_1$ and choose constants $\Theta$ and $\Theta^*$ such that
$$1 \leq \Theta \leq \Theta^* \text{ and } \Theta\|w^0\|_\infty/\gamma^0 \leq \Theta^*.$$

- Step 1. Solve the convex optimization problem
$$\max_{(w,y,s)} \quad b^T y + \alpha F_\varepsilon(s)$$
$$\text{s.t.} \quad s = w - A^T y \geq 0, \ b^T y \leq 1, \ (x^0)^T w \leq \Theta, \qquad (8.21)$$
$$0 \leq w \leq \Theta^* \mathbf{e}.$$

Let $(\widetilde{w},\widetilde{y},\widetilde{s})$ be a solution to this problem.

- Step 2. Set $\widetilde{W} = \mathrm{diag}(\widetilde{w})$ and solve
$$\min_{x \in P} \|\widetilde{W} x\|_1 \qquad (8.22)$$

to obtain a point $\widetilde{x}$.

### 8.2.3 Numerical Experiments

To demonstrate the numerical performance of Algorithm (II) and to compare its performance to some reweighted $\ell_1$-algorithms presented in Chapter 7, we generate the polyhedral sets randomly based on the following assumption: The entries of $A$ and components of the non-negative vector $x^*$ on its support are i.i.d Gaussian random variables with zero mean and unit variances. For each sparsity level $k$, we generate a large number of pairs $(A, x^*)$ to which Algorithm (II) is applied and the success rates of the algorithm are recorded.

Let us first clarify what it means by 'success' of the algorithm when applied to a polyhedral set. When $x^*$ is the unique sparsest point in $P$ and when the algorithm does find this point, we say that $x^*$ is exactly recovered (or re-constructed) by the algorithm. In general, $x^*$ may not be the sparsest point in $P$, and even if $x^*$ is the sparsest point, it may not be the unique sparsest point in $P$. In such situations, even if the algorithm successfully finds a sparsest point which may not necessarily coincide with $x^*$. Thus the criterion *'exact recovery'* used in signal recovery scenarios is not appropriate to measure the success of the algorithm concerning solving $\ell_0$–minimization problems. Clearly, when solving an $\ell_0$-minimization problem, the algorithm succeeds no matter which sparsest points are found. Thus for a given sparsity level $k$, we say that an algorithm succeeds if it does generate a $k$-sparse point in $P$.

The theoretical analysis in the next section indicates that when $P$ satisfies certain properties, there exists a threshold $(\alpha^*, \varepsilon^*)$ such that Algorithm (II) with fixed parameters $(\alpha, \varepsilon)$, where $\alpha \leq \alpha^*$ and $\varepsilon \leq \varepsilon^*$, can find the sparsest point in $P$. Thus we implement Algorithm (II) as follows: Choose $w^0 = \mathbf{e}$ as an initial weight and set the constants $(\Theta, \Theta^*)$ as

$$\Theta = 100, \ \Theta^* = \Theta(1 + \max(1, 1/\gamma^0)) > \Theta/\gamma^0 \ (= \Theta(\|w^0\|_\infty/\gamma^0)), \qquad (8.23)$$

and choose (7.18) as a default merit function for sparsity unless otherwise stated. Algorithm (II) with the above choices is termed 'NRW' method in this section.

Our first experiment confirms that the performance of NRW is not sensitive to the choice of the small parameters $(\alpha, \varepsilon)$. For each sparsity level $k = 1, 2, \ldots, 25$, we generated 400 pairs of $(A, x^*)$, where $A \in \mathbb{R}^{40 \times 200}$ and $\|x^*\|_0 \leq k$, and apply the NRW method to these examples.

The success frequencies of the NRW method with $\alpha = 10^{-8}$ and four different values of $\varepsilon$ were given in Figure 8.1(i), from which it can be seen that the performance of NRW is insensitive to the change of $\varepsilon$. Similarly, by fixing $\varepsilon = 10^{-10}$ and setting of $\alpha = 10^{-5}$, $10^{-10}$, $10^{-15}$ and $10^{-20}$, respectively, the experiments show that the performance of the NRW is also insensitive to the change of small $\alpha$. (The numerical result, similar to Figure 8.1(i), was omitted here.) Thus we set

$$\alpha = 10^{-8}, \ \varepsilon = 10^{-10} \qquad (8.24)$$

as default values in Algorithm (II).

Note that any positive combination of merit functions for sparsity is still a merit function for sparsity. So, combination can be used to generate new merit functions from known ones. The performance of the NRW algorithm with three different merit functions has been summarized in Figure 8.1(ii). These functions include (7.18) (termed as 'log-merit'), (7.17) (termed as 'nonlog-merit'), and the sum of (7.18) and (7.17) (termed as 'combination'). It can be seen from Figure 8.1(ii) that the success rates of the NRW is generally not sensitive to the choice of merit functions.

Using (8.23), (8.24) and (7.18) in the NRW method, we compare its perfor-mance with the reweighted $\ell_1$-algorithms proposed in [53] by Candès, Wakin and

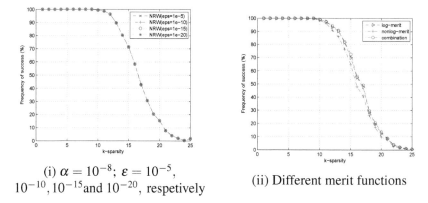

(i) $\alpha = 10^{-8}$; $\varepsilon = 10^{-5}$, $10^{-10}, 10^{-15}$ and $10^{-20}$, respetively

(ii) Different merit functions

**Figure 8.1:** Performance of the NRW algorithm with different values of $(\alpha, \varepsilon)$ and different merit functions for sparsity. The experiments were carried out on randomly generated pairs $(A, x^*)$, where $x^* \in \mathbb{R}_+^{200}$ and $A \in \mathbb{R}^{40 \times 200}$, and 400 attempts were made for each sparsity level $k = 1, 2, \ldots, 25$.

Boyd (termed as 'CWB'), quasi-$\ell_p$-norm-based algorithms in [107] (termed as 'Wlp'), and the 'NW2' method in [246]. Given parameters $p, q, \widehat{\varepsilon} \in (0,1)$, the weight

$$w^k = \frac{1}{|x^k| + \widehat{\varepsilon}}$$

is used in CWB, and

$$w^k = \frac{1}{(|x^k| + \widehat{\varepsilon})^{1-p}}$$

is used in Wlp, and the weight

$$w^k = \frac{q + (|x_i^k| + \widehat{\varepsilon})^{1-q}}{(|x_i^k| + \widehat{\varepsilon})^{1-q} \left[ |x_i^k| + \widehat{\varepsilon} + (|x_i^k| + \widehat{\varepsilon})^q \right]^{1-p}}$$

is used in the NW2, respectively. Experiments show that the performance of the above algorithms are sensitive to the choice of $\widehat{\varepsilon} > 0$. When $\widehat{\varepsilon}$ is very small, their performances are very similar to that of standard $\ell_1$-minimization. Numerical simulations indicate that $\widehat{\varepsilon} = 10^{-2}$ is one of the good choices for these algorithms to outperform $\ell_1$-minimization. The parameter $p$ in Wlp and NW2 algorithms should be chosen small in order to achieve a better performance. So we set $p = 0.05$ for Wlp and $p = q = 0.05$ for NW2. Also, CWB, Wlp and NW2 were executed only four iterations in the experiments since there was no clear improvement on the sparsity level of iterates after a few iterations.

The success rates of the above-mentioned algorithms for locating $k$-sparse points of polyhedral sets were given in Figure 8.2, showing that the NRW outperforms the standard $\ell_1$-minimization method, and the NRW also performs bet-

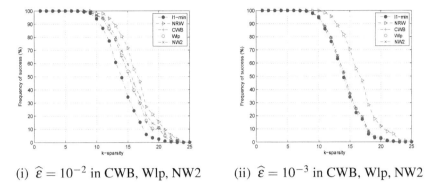

(i) $\widehat{\varepsilon} = 10^{-2}$ in CWB, Wlp, NW2      (ii) $\widehat{\varepsilon} = 10^{-3}$ in CWB, Wlp, NW2

**Figure 8.2:** Comparison of the frequency of success of the NRW, $\ell_1$-minimization, CBW, Wlp, and NW2 algorithms. For every sparsity level $k = 1, 2, ..., 25$, 400 pairs of $(A, x^*)$ were realized, where $A \in \mathbb{R}^{40 \times 200}$ and $\|x^*\|_0 \leq k$.

ter than the CWB, Wlp and NW2 with a fixed parameter $\widehat{\varepsilon}$. For instance, Figure 8.2(i) demonstrates that when locating 15-sparse points (i.e., $\|x^*\|_0 \leq 15$) in polyhedral sets, the success rate of the NRW method is about 72%, while the success rate of $\ell_1$-minimization is only 37%, NW2 is about 60%, Wlp is about 54%, and CBW is about 54%. Such a gap between the performance of NRW method and other methods becomes wider when a smaller $\widehat{\varepsilon}$ is used, as shown by Figure 8.2(ii) in which $\widehat{\varepsilon} = 10^{-3}$ was used in CWB, Wlp and NW2. Simulations indicate that when $\widehat{\varepsilon}$ is small enough, for instance, $\widehat{\varepsilon} \leq 10^{-3}$, there is no clear difference between the numerical behaviors of CWB, Wlp and NW2 and that of $\ell_1$-minimization. In fact, the weight $w_i^k$ that corresponds to the small component $x_i^k \approx 0$ would be huge when $\widehat{\varepsilon}$ is very small. As a result, the weighted $\ell_1$-minimization will force the component $x_i^{k+1}$ to take a small value. This implies that when $\widehat{\varepsilon}$ is very small the sparsity pattern of $x^{k+1}$ would be very close to that of $x^k$. Thus when $\ell_1$-minimization fails to locate the sparsest point, the traditional reweighted $\ell_1$-algorithms might also fail when $\widehat{\varepsilon}$ is very small. In summary, the preliminary experiments demonstrate that the dual-density-based algorithms (DDRW) discussed in this chapter is a promising approach worth investigating further.

## 8.2.4 Theoretical Performance

Algorithm (II) is efficient for locating the sparsest point in $P$ under some conditions. To show such a result, we make use of a merit function for sparsity in $\mathcal{M}^{(2)}$-class (see Definition 7.1.5). Recall that the functions in $\mathcal{M}^{(2)}$-class satisfy the following three major properties:

■ For any given $s \in \mathbb{R}_+^n$, $F_\varepsilon(s) \to \|s\|_0$ as $\varepsilon \to 0$;

- $F_\varepsilon(s)$ is continuously differentiable, and concave with respect to $s$ over an open set containing $\mathbb{R}^n_+$;

- For any given constants $0 < \delta_1 < \delta_2$, there exists a small $\varepsilon^* > 0$ such that for any given $\varepsilon \in (0, \varepsilon^*]$,

$$F_\varepsilon(s) - F_\varepsilon(s') \geq 1/2$$

holds for any $0 \leq s, s' \leq \delta_2 \mathbf{e}$ satisfying $\|s'\|_0 < \|s\|_0$ and $\delta_1 \leq s_i \leq \delta_2$ for all $i \in \text{supp}(s)$.

As shown in Lemma 7.1.6, $\mathcal{M}^{(2)}$-class is a large family of the merit functions for sparsity. For instance, (7.18) and (7.17) are popular ones in this class, i.e.,

$$F_\varepsilon(x) = n - \left( \sum_{i=1}^n \log(x_i + \varepsilon) \right) / \log \varepsilon,$$

and

$$F_\varepsilon(x) = \sum_{i=1}^n \frac{x_i}{x_i + \varepsilon},$$

where $x_i > -\varepsilon$ for all $i = 1, \dots, n$,

To show the efficiency of Algorithm (II), i.e., the one-step DDRW algorithm, the following condition is imposed on the matrix $A$.

**Assumption 8.2.5** *Let $A \in \mathbb{R}^{m \times n}$, where $m < n$, be a matrix satisfying that the set $\{y \in \mathbb{R}^m : A^T y \leq w\}$ is bounded for some $w \in \mathbb{R}^n_+$.*

This mild condition is equivalent to saying that the set $\{d \in \mathbb{R}^m : A^T d \leq 0\} = \{0\}$ (see Theorem 8.4 in [193]). The following constant will also be used in the later proof:

$$\sigma^* = \min_{x \in Z^*} \left\| A^T_{\overline{\text{supp}(x)}} A_{\text{supp}(x)} (A^T_{\text{supp}(x)} A_{\text{supp}(x)})^{-1} \right\|_\infty, \tag{8.25}$$

where $\overline{\text{supp}(x)} = \{1, \dots, n\} \backslash \text{supp}(x)$, and $Z^*$ is the set of the sparsest points of $P$, given by (8.2). By Lemma 3.3.1, for every $x \in Z^*$, the matrix $A_{\text{supp}(x)}$ has full column rank. Therefore, no two distinct sparsest points share the same support set. This means that $Z^*$ is a finite set and the minimum value $\sigma^*$ in (8.25) is attained.

We first establish two technical results. The first one below claims that $\Omega$, defined as (8.20), contains an optimal weight for the weighted $\ell_1$-minimization problem provided that $\Theta$ and $\Theta^*$ are suitably chosen.

**Lemma 8.2.6** *Let $P$ be given by (8.2), $\sigma^*$ be given in (8.25), and $x^* \in Z^*$ be the sparsest point achieving the minimum in (8.25), i.e.,*

$$\left\| A^T_{\overline{\text{supp}(x^*)}} A_{\text{supp}(x^*)} (A^T_{\text{supp}(x^*)} A_{\text{supp}(x^*)})^{-1} \right\|_\infty = \sigma^*. \tag{8.26}$$

*Let $w^0 \in \mathbb{R}_{++}^n$ be any given vector and $(\gamma^0, x^0)$ be generated at the initial step of Algorithm (II). Then there exist a number $\widehat{\Theta} \geq 1$ and an optimal weight $w^* \in \mathcal{W}$ such that the following properties hold:*

- *For any $\Theta \geq \widehat{\Theta}$ and any $\Theta^* \geq \Theta \max\{1, \|w^0\|_\infty/\gamma^0\}$,*

$$w^* \in \Omega = \{w \in \mathbb{R}_+^n : (x^0)^T w \leq \Theta, \ w \leq \Theta^* \mathbf{e}\}. \tag{8.27}$$

- *$x^*$ is the unique solution to the problem*

$$\gamma^* = \min_x \{\|W^* x\|_1 : Ax = b, \ x \geq 0\}, \tag{8.28}$$

*where $W^* = diag(w^*)$ and $\gamma^* = 1$.*

*Proof.* Let $P$ be given as (8.2). Note that $\gamma^0$ is the optimal value and $x^0$ is a solution to the problem

$$\min_{x \in P} \|W^0 x\|_1.$$

Since $w^0 \in \mathbb{R}_{++}^n$ and $b \neq 0$, we see that $x^0 \neq 0$ and $\gamma^0 > 0$. Let $\widehat{w} = w^0/\gamma^0$ and $\widehat{W} = diag(\widehat{w})$. Then $x^0$ is still a solution to the problem

$$\widehat{\gamma} = \min_{x \in P} \|\widehat{W} x\|_1 \tag{8.29}$$

with the optimal value $\widehat{\gamma} = 1$. Let $x^*$ be the sparsest point achieving the minimum of (8.25), i.e., $x^* \in Z^*$ satisfies (8.26). For simplicity, we denote the support of $x^*$ by $J$, i.e., $J = \text{supp}(x^*)$. Define

$$\widehat{\rho} = \|\widehat{W} x^*\|_1 = (\widehat{w}_J)^T x_J^*.$$

From (8.29), we see that $\widehat{\rho} \geq \widehat{\gamma} = 1$. Note that $\sigma^*$ is a finite constant. Let $\widehat{\sigma}$ be a number such that $\widehat{\sigma} > \sigma^*$. By using $(\widehat{w}, \widehat{\rho}, \widehat{\sigma})$, we set the vector $w^*$ as

$$w_J^* = \widehat{w}_J/\widehat{\rho}, \ w_{\overline{J}}^* = \widehat{\sigma}(\|\widehat{w}_J\|_\infty)\mathbf{e}_{\overline{J}}, \tag{8.30}$$

where $\overline{J} = \{1, \ldots, n\} \backslash J$, and we define the constant $\widehat{\Theta} := \max\{1, \widehat{\sigma}\beta\}$, and

$$\beta := \|w^0\|_\infty/(\min_{1 \leq i \leq n} w_i^0) \geq 1.$$

We now show that (8.27) holds for any $\Theta \geq \widehat{\Theta}$ and $\Theta^* \geq \Theta \max\{1, \|w^0\|_\infty/\gamma^0\}$. By the definition of $\widehat{w}$ and $\beta$, we have

$$\|\widehat{w}_J\|_\infty = \|w_J^0\|_\infty/\gamma^0 \leq \beta(\min_{1 \leq i \leq n} w_i^0)/\gamma^0.$$

Therefore,

$$(x_{\overline{J}}^0)^T(\|\widehat{w}_J\|_\infty \mathbf{e}_{\overline{J}}) \leq \beta(x_{\overline{J}}^0)^T \left[ (\min_{1 \leq i \leq n} w_i^0)\mathbf{e}_{\overline{J}}/\gamma^0 \right] \leq \beta(x_{\overline{J}}^0)^T w_{\overline{J}}^0/\gamma^0 = \beta(x_{\overline{J}}^0)^T \widehat{w}_{\overline{J}}.$$

Since $\widehat{\rho} \geq 1$ and $(x^0)^T \widehat{w} = \widehat{\gamma} = 1$, by (8.30), we have

$$(x^0)^T w^* = (x_J^0)^T \widehat{w}_J/\widehat{\rho} + (x_{\overline{J}}^0)^T (\widehat{\sigma}\|\widehat{w}_J\|_\infty e_{\overline{J}}) \leq (x_J^0)^T \widehat{w}_J/\widehat{\rho} + (\widehat{\sigma}\beta)(x_{\overline{J}}^0)^T \widehat{w}_{\overline{J}}$$
$$\leq \max\{1/\widehat{\rho}, \widehat{\sigma}\beta\}[(x_J^0)^T \widehat{w}_J + (x_{\overline{J}}^0)^T \widehat{w}_{\overline{J}}]$$
$$\leq \widehat{\Theta} \leq \Theta$$

and

$$\|w^*\|_\infty = \max\{\|w_J^*\|_\infty, \|w_{\overline{J}}^*\|_\infty\} \leq \max\{1/\widehat{\rho}, \widehat{\sigma}\}\|\widehat{w}_J\|_\infty$$
$$\leq \max\{1, \widehat{\sigma}\beta\}\|\widehat{w}\|_\infty \leq \Theta\|w^0\|_\infty/\gamma^0 \leq \Theta^*.$$

Therefore, (8.27) holds. We now show that $w^*$ is the optimal weight and $x^*$ is the unique solution to the problem (8.28). In fact, it follows from (8.26), (8.30) and $\widehat{\rho} \geq 1$ that

$$\left\|A_{\overline{J}}^T A_J (A_J^T A_J)^{-1} w_J^*\right\|_\infty \leq \left\|A_{\overline{J}}^T A_J (A_J^T A_J)^{-1}\right\|_\infty \|w_J^*\|_\infty$$
$$< \widehat{\sigma}\|\widehat{w}_J\|_\infty/\widehat{\rho} \leq \widehat{\sigma}\|\widehat{w}_J\|_\infty.$$

This, combined with (8.30), implies that

$$A_{\overline{J}}^T A_J (A_J^T A_J)^{-1} w_J^* < \widehat{\sigma}(\|\widehat{w}_J\|_\infty)e_{\overline{J}} = w_{\overline{J}}^*.$$

Thus, by Theorem 3.5.6, $x^*$ is the unique solution to the problem (8.28). Moreover,

$$\gamma^* = \|W^* x^*\|_1 = (w_J^*)^T x_J^* = (\widehat{w}_J)^T x_J^*/\widehat{\rho} = 1.$$

Therefore, $w^* \in \mathcal{W}$ is an optimal weight. □

We now prove the next technical result.

**Lemma 8.2.7** *Let $F_\varepsilon(\cdot)$ be a function in $\mathcal{M}^{(2)}$-class, and let $A \in \mathbb{R}^{m \times n}$ $(m < n)$ satisfy Assumption 8.2.5. Let $x^*$ be the sparsest point satisfying (8.26), $w^*$ be the optimal weight satisfying (8.27) and $\Theta^*$ be the constant given in Lemma 8.2.6. Let $(y^*, s^*)$ be the solution to the dual problem of (8.28), i.e.,*

$$(y^*, s^*) \in \arg\max_{(y,s)}\{b^T y: s = w^* - A^T y, s \geq 0\},$$

*such that $s^*$ and $x^*$ are strictly complementary. Then there exists $\varepsilon^* \in (0,1)$ such that*

$$F_\varepsilon(s^*) - F_\varepsilon(s') \geq 1/2 \tag{8.31}$$

*holds for any $\varepsilon \in (0, \varepsilon^*]$ and any vector $s' \in \Upsilon(\Theta^*)$ with $\|s'\|_0 < \|s^*\|_0$, where*

$$\Upsilon(\Theta^*) = \{s \in \mathbb{R}_+^n: s = w - A^T y \geq 0, 0 \leq w \leq \Theta^* e\}. \tag{8.32}$$

*Proof.* Firstly, we consider the dual problem of (8.28), i.e.,

$$\max_{(y,s)}\{b^T y:\ s = w^* - A^T y,\ s \geq 0\}. \tag{8.33}$$

By the choice of $w^*$, $x^*$ is the unique solution to the problem (8.28). Thus by Lemma 2.1.2, there is a solution $(y^*, s^*)$ to the problem (8.33) such that $x^*, s^* \in \mathbb{R}_+^n$ are strictly complementary. We now show that $\mathrm{supp}(s^*) \neq \emptyset$. The uniqueness of $x^*$ also implies that $A_{\mathrm{supp}(x^*)} \in \mathbb{R}^{m \times |\mathrm{supp}(x^*)|}$ has full column rank. Therefore,

$$\|x^*\|_0 = |\mathrm{supp}(x^*)| = \mathrm{rank}(A_{\mathrm{supp}(x^*)}) \leq m.$$

Since $m < n$, the strict complementarity of $s^*$ and $x^*$ implies that

$$|\mathrm{supp}(s^*)| = n - |\mathrm{supp}(x^*)| \geq n - m > 0.$$

So the following number is positive:

$$\delta_1 = \min_{i \in \mathrm{supp}(s^*)} s_i^*. \tag{8.34}$$

Secondly, we show that the set $\Upsilon(\Theta^*)$, given in (8.32), is bounded. By Theorem 8.4 in [193], a convex set is bounded if and only if its recession cone consists of the zero vector alone. Note that $\{d \in \mathbb{R}^m :\ A^T d \leq 0\}$ is the recession cone of $\{y \in \mathbb{R}^m : A^T y \leq \Theta^* \mathbf{e}\}$. So Assumption 8.2.5 ensures that

$$\{d \in \mathbb{R}^m :\ A^T d \leq 0\} = \{0\},$$

which implies that the set $\{y \in \mathbb{R}^m :\ A^T y \leq \Theta^* \mathbf{e}\}$ is bounded. Note that

$$\{y \in \mathbb{R}^m :\ A^T y \leq w,\ 0 \leq w \leq \Theta^* \mathbf{e}\} \subseteq \{y \in \mathbb{R}^m :\ A^T y \leq \Theta^* \mathbf{e}\}.$$

The set $\Upsilon(\Theta^*)$, given in (8.32), is bounded. As a result, there exists a number $\delta_2 > 0$ such that $0 \leq s \leq \delta_2 \mathbf{e}$ for all $s \in \Upsilon(\Theta^*)$. By the choice of $w^*$ which satisfies (8.27) and by the definition of $(y^*, s^*)$, we see that $s^* = w^* - A^T y^* \geq 0$ and $w^* \leq \Theta^* \mathbf{e}$, so $s^* \in \Upsilon(\Theta^*)$. By the definition of $\delta_1$ in (8.34), we see that $s^* \in \Upsilon(\Theta^*)$ implies that $0 < \delta_1 \leq s_i^* \leq \delta_2$ for all $i \in \mathrm{supp}(s^*)$. Since $F_\varepsilon(s)$ is a function in $\mathcal{M}^{(2)}$-class, there is a number $\varepsilon^* \in (0, 1)$ such that (8.31) holds for any $\varepsilon \in (0, \varepsilon^*]$ and any $s'$ satisfying $\|s'\|_0 < \|s^*\|_0$ and $0 \leq s' \leq \delta_2 \mathbf{e}$. In particular, the inequality (8.31) holds for any $s' \in \Upsilon(\Theta^*)$ with $\|s'\|_0 < \|s^*\|_0$. $\quad\square$

The following result due to Mangasarian and Meyer [168] will also be used in the proof of the efficiency of Algorithm (II).

**Lemma 8.2.8** [168] *Let $\psi$ be a continuously differentiable convex function on some open set containing the feasible set $\Lambda$ of the LP problem $\min\{c^T x:\ x \in \Lambda\}$. If the solution set $\widehat{S}$ of the LP problem is nonempty and bounded, and $c^T x + \widetilde{\alpha}\psi(x)$ is bounded from below on the set $\Lambda$ for some number $\widetilde{\alpha} > 0$, then the solution set of the problem $\min\{c^T x + \alpha \psi(x):\ x \in \Lambda\}$ is contained in $\widehat{S}$ for sufficiently small number $\alpha > 0$.*

Note that (8.21) is solved for given parameters $\alpha, \varepsilon \in (0,1)$. In the following proof, the vector $(\widetilde{w}, \widetilde{y}, \widetilde{s})$ generated at Step 1 of Algorithm (II) is written as $(\widetilde{w}_{(\alpha,\varepsilon)}, \widetilde{y}_{(\alpha,\varepsilon)}, \widetilde{s}_{(\alpha,\varepsilon)})$, and the optimal solution $\widetilde{x}$ of (8.22) as $\widetilde{x}_{(\alpha,\varepsilon)}$. We can now prove the next Theorem. This theorem indicates that when $(\alpha, \varepsilon)$ are small enough and $(\Theta, \Theta^*)$ are large enough, a sparsest point in $P$ can be located via Algorithm (II) if the solution $\widetilde{x}$ of (8.22) satisfies $\widetilde{w}^T \widetilde{x} = 1$.

**Theorem 8.2.9** *Let $F_\varepsilon(\cdot)$ be a merit function for sparsity in $\mathcal{M}^{(2)}$-class and let*

$$P = \{x \in \mathbb{R}_+^n : Ax = b, x \geq 0\}.$$

*Suppose that Assumption 8.2.5 is satisfied. Let $w^0 \in \mathbb{R}_{++}^n$ be given and $\gamma^0 = \min_{x \in P} \|W^0 x\|_1$. Then there exists a number $\widehat{\Theta} \geq 1$ such that the following statement holds: For any given numbers $\Theta \geq \widehat{\Theta}$ and $\Theta^* \geq \Theta \max\{1, \|w^0\|_\infty / \gamma^0\}$, there is a number $\varepsilon^* \in (0,1)$ such that for any $\varepsilon \in (0, \varepsilon^*]$, there is $\alpha^* \in (0,1)$ such that for any $\alpha \in (0, \alpha^*]$, the vector $\widetilde{x}$ generated by Algorithm (II) with such given parameters $(\Theta, \Theta^*, \alpha, \varepsilon)$ is the sparsest point in $P$ provided that*

$$(\widetilde{w})^T \widetilde{x} = 1,$$

*where $\widetilde{w}$ is the weight generated at Step 1 of Algorithm (II).*

*Proof.* Let $(w^0, \gamma^0, x^0)$ be given as the initial step of Algorithm (II). Consider the sparsest point $x^* \in P$ satisfying (8.26). By Lemma 8.2.6, there exist a number $\Theta \geq 1$ and an optimal weight $w^*$ satisfy the following properties: For any constants $(\Theta, \Theta^*)$ satisfying $\Theta \geq \widehat{\Theta}$ and $\Theta^* \geq \Theta \max\{1, \|w^0\|_\infty / \gamma^0\}$, we have that

(i)  $w^* \in \mathcal{W} \cap \Omega$, where $\Omega = \{w \in \mathbb{R}_+^n : (x^0)^T w \leq \Theta, w \leq \Theta^* e\}$, and

(ii)  $x^*$ is the unique solution to the problem (8.28) with $W = \text{diag}(w^*)$.

Under Assumption 8.2.5, it follows from Lemma 8.2.7 that there exists a small number $\varepsilon^* \in (0,1)$ such that (8.31) holds for any $\varepsilon \in (0, \varepsilon^*]$ and any $s' \in \Upsilon(\Theta^*)$ with $\|s'\|_0 < \|s^*\|_0$, where $\Upsilon(\Theta^*)$ is defined by (8.32).

Let $\varepsilon \in (0, \varepsilon^*]$ be any fixed number. We now prove that there is a number $\alpha^* \in (0,1)$ satisfying the desired property as described in Theorem 8.2.9. Consider the problem (8.21) and the LP below:

$$\max_{(w,y,s)} \quad b^T y$$

$$\text{s.t.} \quad s = w - A^T y \geq 0, \ b^T y \leq 1, \ (x^0)^T w \leq \Theta, \tag{8.35}$$

$$0 \leq w \leq \Theta^* e.$$

Let $\mathcal{T}^*$ be the set of optimal solutions of (8.35). Note that attaching the term $\alpha F_\varepsilon(s)$ to the objective of (8.35) will yield the problem (8.21). As shown in the proof of Lemma 8.2.7, under Assumption 8.2.5, the set $\{y \in \mathbb{R}^m : A^T y \leq \Theta^* e\}$ is bounded. This implies that the solution set $\mathcal{T}^*$ of the problem (8.35) is bounded since the feasible set of this problem is bounded. As $F_\varepsilon(\cdot)$ is in $\mathcal{M}^{(2)}$-class, $F_\varepsilon(s)$ is a continuously differentiable concave function over an open neighborhood of $\mathbb{R}^n_+$. This is equivalent to saying that the function

$$\widehat{F}_\varepsilon(w, y, s) := F_\varepsilon(s) + 0^T w + 0^T y = F_\varepsilon(s)$$

is a continuously differentiable concave function over an open neighborhood of the feasible set of (8.35). Since the feasible set of (8.35) is a compact set, for any given $\alpha > 0$, the concave function

$$b^T y + \alpha F_\varepsilon(s) = b^T y + \alpha \widehat{F}_\varepsilon(w, y, s)$$

is bounded over the feasible set of (8.35). Note that maximizing a concave function is equivalent to minimizing the negative of this function. The negative of a concave function is convex. By Lemma 8.2.8, it implies that there exists $\alpha^* \in (0, 1)$ such that for any given $\alpha \in (0, \alpha^*]$, the solution set of (8.21) is a subset of $\mathcal{T}^*$. Thus the solution $(\widetilde{w}_{(\alpha, \varepsilon)}, \widetilde{y}_{(\alpha, \varepsilon)}, \widetilde{s}_{(\alpha, \varepsilon)})$ of (8.21) is also a solution of the problem (8.35) for any given $\alpha \in (0, \alpha^*]$.

With the constraint $b^T y \leq 1$, the optimal value of (8.35) is at most 1. We now further prove that the optimal value of this problem is actually equal to 1. Let $\widehat{w} = w^0/\gamma^0$. As shown at the beginning of the proof of Lemma 8.2.6, the optimal value $\widehat{\gamma}$ of (8.29) is equal to 1. By the duality theory, there is a solution $(y^{(1)}, s^{(1)})$ to the problem

$$\max_{(y, s)} \{ b^T y : s = \widehat{w} - A^T y \geq 0 \}$$

such that $b^T y^{(1)} = \widehat{\gamma} = 1$. By the definition of $\widehat{w}$, it is straightforward to verify that $\widehat{w} \in \Omega$, where $\Omega$ is given in (8.27). In fact, as $x^0$ is a solution to the problem (8.29), we have

$$(x^0)^T \widehat{w} = \widehat{\gamma} = 1 \leq \widehat{\Theta} \leq \Theta$$

and by the definition of $\widehat{w}$,

$$\| \widehat{w} \|_\infty = \| w^0 \|_\infty / \gamma^0 \leq \Theta \| w^0 \|_\infty / \gamma^0 \leq \Theta^*,$$

which implies that $\widehat{w} \leq \Theta^* \mathbf{e}$. Thus $(\widehat{w}, y^{(1)}, s^{(1)})$ satisfies the following conditions:

$$b^T y^{(1)} = 1, \ s^{(1)} = \widehat{w} - A^T y^{(1)}, \ (x^0)^T \widehat{w} \leq \Theta, \ 0 \leq \widehat{w} \leq \Theta^* \mathbf{e}.$$

These conditions imply that $(w, y, s) = (\widehat{w}, y^{(1)}, s^{(1)})$ is a solution to the problem (8.35) and the optimal value of the problem (8.35) is equal to 1. Note that $(\widetilde{w}_{(\alpha, \varepsilon)}, \widetilde{y}_{(\alpha, \varepsilon)}, \widetilde{s}_{(\alpha, \varepsilon)})$ is a solution to (8.35) for any given $\alpha \in (0, \alpha^*]$. We can conclude that

$$b^T \widetilde{y}_{(\alpha, \varepsilon)} = 1 \ \text{ for any } \alpha \in (0, \alpha^*]. \tag{8.36}$$

Given the vector $\widetilde{w}_{(\alpha,\varepsilon)}$, let us consider the LP problem

$$\widetilde{\gamma}_{(\alpha,\varepsilon)} := \max_{(y,s)} \{b^T y : \ b^T y \leq 1, \ s = \widetilde{w}_{(\alpha,\varepsilon)} - A^T y \geq 0\} \tag{8.37}$$

with its dual problem

$$\min_{(x,t)} \{(\widetilde{w}_{(\alpha,\varepsilon)})^T x + t : \ Ax + tb = b, \ (x,t) \geq 0\}. \tag{8.38}$$

From (8.37), we see that $\widetilde{\gamma}_{(\alpha,\varepsilon)} \leq 1$. Note that for any given $\alpha \in (0, \alpha^*]$, $(\widetilde{y}_{(\alpha,\varepsilon)}, \widetilde{s}_{(\alpha,\varepsilon)})$ satisfies the constraints of (8.37) and $\widetilde{y}_{(\alpha,\varepsilon)}$ satisfies (8.36). Thus $(\widetilde{y}_{(\alpha,\varepsilon)}, \widetilde{s}_{(\alpha,\varepsilon)})$ is a solution to (8.37) and $\widetilde{\gamma}_{(\alpha,\varepsilon)}$ is actually equal to 1. By the duality theory, the optimal value of (8.38) is also equal to 1. Thus the solution set of (8.38) is given as

$$U_{(\alpha,\varepsilon)} = \{(x,t) : \ Ax + bt = b, \ (\widetilde{w}_{(\alpha,\varepsilon)})^T x + t = 1, \ (x,t) \geq 0\}.$$

We now show that the condition $(\widetilde{w}_{(\alpha,\varepsilon)})^T \widetilde{x}_{(\alpha,\varepsilon)} = 1$ implies that $\widetilde{x}_{(\alpha,\varepsilon)}$ must be the sparsest point in $P$. In fact, for this case, we see that $(\widetilde{x}_{(\alpha,\varepsilon)}, 0)$ is a solution to the problem (8.38) since $(x,t) = (\widetilde{x}_{(\alpha,\varepsilon)}, 0) \in U_{(\alpha,\varepsilon)}$. At the solution $(\widetilde{y}_{(\alpha,\varepsilon)}, \widetilde{s}_{(\alpha,\varepsilon)})$ of (8.37), the variable $\widetilde{x}_{(\alpha,\varepsilon)}$ in (8.37) corresponds to the dual slack variable $\widetilde{s}_{(\alpha,\varepsilon)}$. By the complementary slackness property, $\widetilde{x}_{(\alpha,\varepsilon)}$ and $\widetilde{s}_{(\alpha,\varepsilon)}$ are complementary, i.e.,

$$(\widetilde{s}_{(\alpha,\varepsilon)})^T \widetilde{x}_{(\alpha,\varepsilon)} = 0.$$

As $\widetilde{x}_{(\alpha,\varepsilon)}$ and $\widetilde{s}_{(\alpha,\varepsilon)}$ are non-negative, the above equality implies that

$$\|\widetilde{x}_{(\alpha,\varepsilon)}\|_0 + \|\widetilde{s}_{(\alpha,\varepsilon)}\|_0 \leq n. \tag{8.39}$$

We now prove that the point $\widetilde{x}_{(\alpha,\varepsilon)}$ must be the sparsest point in $P$. We prove this fact by contradiction. Suppose that $\widetilde{x}_{(\alpha,\varepsilon)}$ is not the sparsest point of $P$. Then,

$$\|x^*\|_0 < \|\widetilde{x}_{(\alpha,\varepsilon)}\|_0, \tag{8.40}$$

where $x^*$ is the sparsest point of $P$ satisfying (8.26). There exists a solution $(y^*, s^*)$ to the dual problem of (8.28) such that $x^*$ and $s^*$ are strictly complementary. Thus $\|x^*\|_0 + \|s^*\|_0 = n$. Thus it follows from (8.39) and (8.40) that

$$\|s^*\|_0 - \|\widetilde{s}_{(\alpha,\varepsilon)}\|_0 \geq n - \|x^*\|_0 - (n - \|\widetilde{x}_{(\alpha,\varepsilon)}\|_0) = \|\widetilde{x}_{(\alpha,\varepsilon)}\|_0 - \|x^*\|_0 > 0.$$

Thus $\|\widetilde{s}_{(\alpha,\varepsilon)}\|_0 < \|s^*\|_0$. It is easy to see that $\widetilde{s}_{(\alpha,\varepsilon)} \in \Upsilon(\Theta^*)$, where $\Upsilon(\Theta^*)$ is given in (8.32). From Lemma 8.2.7, we conclude that (8.31) is satisfied, and hence

$$F_{\varepsilon}(s^*) - F_{\varepsilon}(\widetilde{s}_{(\alpha,\varepsilon)}) > 1/2. \tag{8.41}$$

On the other hand, the vector $(w^*, y^*, s^*)$ is a feasible point to the problem (8.21). Since $(\widetilde{w}_{(\alpha,\varepsilon)}, \widetilde{y}_{(\alpha,\varepsilon)}, \widetilde{s}_{(\alpha,\varepsilon)})$ is a solution of (8.21), we must have

$$b^T \widetilde{y}_{(\alpha,\varepsilon)} + \alpha F_{\varepsilon}(\widetilde{s}_{(\alpha,\varepsilon)}) \geq b^T y^* + \alpha F_{\varepsilon}(s^*).$$

By the strong duality, Lemma 8.2.6 (ii) implies that $b^T y^* = 1$. Thus by (8.36), the inequality above is equivalent to $F_\varepsilon(\tilde{s}_{(\alpha,\varepsilon)}) \geq F_\varepsilon(s^*)$, which contradicts (8.41). So we conclude that the vector $\tilde{x} = \tilde{x}_{(\alpha,\varepsilon)}$, generated by Algorithm (II), is the sparsest point in $P$. □

From the above proof, we see that $(\tilde{w}, \tilde{y}, \tilde{s}) = (\tilde{w}_{(\alpha,\varepsilon)}, \tilde{y}_{(\alpha,\varepsilon)}, \tilde{s}_{(\alpha,\varepsilon)})$ generated by Algorithm (II) satisfies (8.36) for any given small $(\alpha, \varepsilon)$. As $b^T(\tilde{y}_{(\alpha,\varepsilon)}) = 1$ and $(\tilde{y}_{(\alpha,\varepsilon)}, \tilde{s}_{(\alpha,\varepsilon)})$ is a feasible point to the problem

$$\max_{(y,s)}\{b^T y : \ s = \tilde{w}_{(\alpha,\varepsilon)} - A^T y \geq 0\},$$

the optimal value of this problem is greater or equal to 1. By the weak duality theory, the optimal value of (8.22) is also greater than or equal to 1. Therefore,

$$(\tilde{w}_{(\alpha,\varepsilon)})^T \tilde{x}_{(\alpha,\varepsilon)} \geq 1$$

for any given small parameters $(\alpha, \varepsilon)$. The above analysis was not carried out under the traditional assumptions, such as the mutual coherence, RIP, NSP, RSP or ERC. Assumption 8.2.5 is a mild condition imposed on polyhedral sets. Such a mild assumption is generally not enough to guarantee Algorithm (II) to solve the $\ell_0$-minimization problem, unless some further conditions are also imposed. This is reflected by the condition $\hat{w}^T \hat{x} = 1$ (i.e., $(\tilde{w}_{(\alpha,\varepsilon)})^T \tilde{x}_{(\alpha,\varepsilon)} = 1$) in Theorem 8.2.9.

## 8.3   DDRW for Standard $\ell_0$-Minimization

Consider the following $\ell_0$-minimization without non-negative constraints:

$$\min_x\{\|x\|_0 : \ Ax = b\},$$

which is to locate the sparsest solution of an underdetermined system of linear equations. Following a similar idea in Section 8.2, we briefly introduce how a dual-density-based reweighted $\ell_1$-algorithm can be developed for this $\ell_0$-minimization problem, which is often called the standard $\ell_0$-minimization problem. Given a weight $w \in \mathbb{R}^n_+$, the weighted $\ell_1$-minimization problem

$$\min_x\{\|Wx\|_1 : \ Ax = b\} \tag{8.42}$$

is equivalent to

$$\min_{(x,t)}\{w^T t : \ Ax = b, \ |x| \leq t\} \tag{8.43}$$

It is evident that $x^*$ is a solution to (8.42) if and only if $(x^*, t^*)$, where $t^* = |x^*|$, is a solution to (8.43). Introducing the slack variables $\zeta, \beta \in \mathbb{R}^n_+$ into the problem (8.43) leads to the following LP problems:

$$\min_{(t,x,\zeta,\beta)} \{w^T t : \ t - x - \zeta = 0, \ -t - x + \beta = 0, \ Ax = b, \ (t, \ \zeta, \ \beta) \geq 0\}. \tag{8.44}$$

Let $(x^*, t^*, \zeta^*, \beta^*)$ be the solution of this problem, which must satisfy the following relations:

$$t^* = |x^*|, \ \zeta^* = t^* - x^* = |x^*| - x^*, \ \beta^* = t^* + x^* = |x^*| + x^*.$$

It is very easy to verify that the dual problem of (8.44) is given as

$$\max_{(u,z,y)} \{b^T y : \ u - z - w \leq 0, \ u + z - A^T y = 0, \ -u \leq 0, \ z \leq 0\}.$$

Setting $v = -z$ and $s = w - (u - z) = w - u - v$ in the above problem leads to

$$\max_{(s,y,u,v)} \{b^T y : \ A^T y - u + v = 0, \ s = w - u - v, \ (s,u,v) \geq 0\}. \tag{8.45}$$

Let $(s^*, y^*, u^*, v^*)$ be the solution to this problem. By the complementary slackness property, the solutions of (8.44) and (8.45) satisfy the following conditions:

$$(t^*)^T s^* = 0, \ (\zeta^*)^T u^* = 0, \ (\beta^*)^T v^* = 0, \ (t^*, \zeta^*, \beta^*, s^*, u^*, v^*) \geq 0. \tag{8.46}$$

Note that $t^* = |x^*|$. The first condition $(t^*)^T s^* = 0$ implies that

$$\|x^*\|_0 + \|s\|_0 = \|t\|_0 + \|s\|_0 \leq n.$$

So the sparsity of $t$ in the primal problem (8.44) is related to the density of the variable $s$ in the dual problem (8.45). Moreover, there exists a pair of solutions to (8.44) and (8.45) which are strictly complementary in the sense that they satisfy (8.46) as well as the following relations: $t^* + s^* > 0$, $\zeta^* + u^* > 0$ and $\beta^* + v^* > 0$. These properties are summarized in the Lemma below.

**Lemma 8.3.1** *Let $w \in \mathbb{R}^n_+$ be given. Then $x^*$ is a solution to the weighted $\ell_1$-minimization problem (8.42) if and only if $(t^*, x^*, \zeta^*, \beta^*)$ is a solution to the problem (8.44). Any solution $(t^*, x^*, \zeta^*, \beta^*)$ of (8.44) satisfies the relations*

$$t^* = |x^*|, \ \zeta^* = |x^*| - x^*, \ \beta^* = |x^*| + x^*.$$

*Moreover, there always exists a solution $(t^*, x^*, \zeta^*, \beta^*)$ to the problem (8.44) and a solution $(s^*, y^*, u^*, v^*)$ to (8.45) such that $(t^*, s^*) \geq 0$, $(t^*)^T s^* = 0$ and $t^* + s^* > 0$.*

The strict complementarity of $s^*$ and $t^*$ implies that

$$\|x^*\|_0 + \|s^*\|_0 = \|t^*\|_0 + \|s^*\|_0 = n.$$

Similar to Theorem 8.2.3, we can prove the following result which claims that the solution of some bilevel optimization problem provides an optimal weight $w^*$ for the $\ell_1$-minimization problem. Certain practical dual-density-based reweighted $\ell_1$-algorithms can be developed to locate the sparsest solution of the underdetermined system of linear equations.

**Theorem 8.3.2** *Let $(s^*, y^*, w^*, u^*, v^*, \gamma^*)$ be the solution to the bilevel optimiza-tion problem*

$$\max_{(s,y,w,u,v,\gamma)} \quad \|s\|_0$$

$$\text{s.t.} \quad b^T y = \gamma, \ A^T y - u + v = 0, \ s = w - u - v, \ (s, u, v, w) \geq 0, \quad (8.47)$$
$$\gamma = \min_x \{\|Wx\|_1 : Ax = b\},$$

*where $W = \mathrm{diag}(w)$. Then $w = w^*$ is an optimal weight for the weighted $\ell_1$-problem (8.42) so that the solution to this problem is the sparsest solution of the system $Ax = b$.*

*Proof.* Suppose that $\hat{x}$ is the sparsest solution to the system $Ax = b$. By Corollary 3.5.4 , there exists a weight $\widehat{W} = \mathrm{diag}(\hat{w})$, where $\hat{w} \in \mathbb{R}^n_+$, such that $\hat{x}$ is the unique solution to the weighted $\ell_1$-minimization problem

$$\min_x \{\|\widehat{W}x\|_1 : Ax = b\},$$

Then by Lemma 8.3.1, $(\hat{t}, \hat{x}, \hat{\zeta}, \hat{\beta})$ is the unique solution to the problem (8.44) with $w = \hat{w}$, and this solution satisfies that

$$\hat{t} = |\hat{x}|, \ \hat{\zeta} = |\hat{x}| - \hat{x}, \ \hat{\beta} = |\hat{x}| + \hat{x}.$$

The dual problem of (8.44) with $w = \hat{w}$ is given as follows:

$$\max_{(s,y,u,v)} \{b^T y : A^T y - u + v = 0, \ s = \hat{w} - u - v, \ (s, u, v) \geq 0\}.$$

By Lemma 8.3.1, there exists a solution, denoted by $(\hat{s}, \hat{y}, \hat{u}, \hat{v})$, to this problem such that $\hat{t}$ and $\hat{s}$ are strictly complementary. Thus $\|\hat{t}\|_0 + \|\hat{s}\|_0 = n$, and hence

$$\|\hat{x}\|_0 = \|\hat{t}\|_0 = n - \|\hat{s}\|_0. \quad (8.48)$$

The optimality (or strong duality) implies that

$$b^T \hat{y} = \hat{\gamma} := \min_x \{\|\widehat{W}x\|_1 : Ax = b\}.$$

Thus $(\hat{s}, \hat{y}, \hat{w}, \hat{u}, \hat{v}, \hat{\gamma})$ satisfies the constraints of (8.47). Since $(s^*, y^*, w^*, u^*, v^*, \gamma^*)$ is a solution to (8.47), we have

$$\|\hat{s}\|_0 \leq \|s^*\|_0. \quad (8.49)$$

Let $x^*$ be a solution to the problem $\min_x \{\|W^*x\|_1 : Ax = b\}$ where $W^* = \mathrm{diag}(w^*)$. We now prove that $x^*$ must be the sparsest solution to the system.

By Lemma 8.3.1 again, $(t^*, x^*, \zeta^*, \beta^*)$ with $t^* = |x^*|, \zeta^* = |x^*| - x^*$ and $\beta^* = |x^*| + x^*$ is a solution to the problem (8.44) with $w = w^*$. By the assumption,

$(s^*, y^*, w^*, u^*, v^*, \gamma^*)$ is a solution to the problem (8.47), so these vectors satisfy the constraints of (8.47), which imply that

$$b^T y^* = \gamma^* = \min_x \{\|W^* x\|_1 : Ax = b\},$$

and thus by LP duality $(s^*, y^*, u^*, v^*)$ is a solution to the dual problem (8.45) with $w = w^*$. Notice that the vectors $s^*$ and $t^* = |x^*|$ are complementary, i.e., $(t^*)^T s^* = 0$. This implies that $\|t^*\|_0 + \|s^*\|_0 \leq n$. Combining this fact with (8.48) and (8.49) yields

$$\|x^*\|_0 = \|t^*\|_0 \leq n - \|s^*\|_0 \leq n - \|\hat{s}\|_0 = \|\hat{x}\|_0.$$

Since $\hat{x}$ is the sparsest solution, the inequality above implies that $x^*$ must also be the sparsest solution to the linear system. □

The above result implies that seeking the sparsest solution of a linear system can be achieved by finding the corresponding densest slack variable $s \in \mathbb{R}_+^n$ of the dual problem of the weighted $\ell_1$-minimization problem for all possible choices of $w \in \mathbb{R}_+^n$. This observation provides an alternative perspective to tackle $\ell_0$-minimization problems. In fact, let $x(w)$ be a solution to the weighted $\ell_1$-minimization problem (8.42), and let $(t(w), x(w), \zeta(w), \beta(w))$ be a solution to the problem (8.44), and let $(s(w), y(w), u(w), v(w))$ be a solution to the dual problem (8.45). Since $s(w)$ and $t(w)$ are complementary, the inequality $\|s(w)\|_0 + \|t(w)\|_0 \leq n$ holds for any given $w \in \mathbb{R}_+^n$. Note that $t(w) = |x(w)|$. We must have

$$\|s(w)\|_0 + \|x(w)\|_0 \leq n \text{ for any } w \in \mathbb{R}_+^n. \tag{8.50}$$

By Corollary 3.5.4, for any sparsest solution $x^*$, there exists a weight $w^*$ such that $x^* = x(w^*)$ is the unique solution to the weighted $\ell_1$-minimization problem (8.42) with weight $w^*$. By picking a strictly complementary solution $(s(w^*), y(w^*), u(w^*), v(w^*))$ of its dual problem (8.45), the equality can be achieved in (8.50), i.e., $\|s(w^*)\|_0 + \|x^*\|_0 = n$. As a result, $s(w^*) = n - \|x^*\|_0$ is the densest vector among all possible choices of $w \in \mathbb{R}_+^n$, i.e.,

$$s(w^*) = \arg\max_w \{\|s(w)\|_0 : w \in \mathbb{R}_+^n\}.$$

We summarize these facts as follows.

**Corollary 8.3.3** *Let $x^*$ be the sparsest solution to the underdetermined linear system $Ax = b$. Then there exists a weight $w^* \in \mathbb{R}_+^n$ such that the dual problem (8.45), where $w = w^*$, possesses a solution $(s^*, y^*, u^*, v^*)$ satisfying $\|x^*\|_0 = n - \|s^*\|_0$.*

The above discussion indicates that the optimal weight $w^*$ can be found, in theory, by searching for the densest dual variable $s(w)$ among all possible choices of $w \in \mathbb{R}^n_+$. It is the strict complementarity theory of linear programs that provides such a perspective to understand the $\ell_0$-minimization problem. Solving the bilevel optimization problem (8.47) yields an optimal weight by which the sparsest solution of a system of linear equations can be found. However, a bilevel optimization problem is often very difficult to solve. It is more realistic to consider certain relaxation or approximation of the problem (8.47). Let $\gamma(w)$ denote the optimal value of (8.42), i.e.,

$$\gamma(w) := \min_x \{ \|Wx\|_1 : Ax = b \},$$

where $W = \mathrm{diag}(w)$. For any feasible point $(y, s, w, u, v, \gamma)$ of (8.47), the constraints of (8.47) imply that $(y, s, u, v)$ must be the solution of the LP problem (8.45). Thus the bilevel optimization problem (8.47) is actually to achieve two levels of maximization. At the lower level, $b^T y$ is maximized subject to the constraints of (8.45) for every given $w \geq 0$. This yields the feasible point $(y(w), s(w), w, u(w), v(w), \gamma(w))$ to the bilevel problem (8.47). Then at the higher level, $\|s(w)\|_0$ is maximized among all possible choices of $w \geq 0$. By the structure of (8.47), the maximization of $\|s\|_0$ should be carried out under the constraint that $(y, s, u, v)$ is a solution to the LP problem (8.45). Following a similar relaxation in last section, we use the following model as an approximation of (8.47):

$$\begin{aligned} \max_{(y,s,u,v,w)} \quad & \alpha \|s\|_0 + b^T y \\ \text{s.t.} \quad & A^T y - u + v = 0, \ s = w - u - v, \ (s, u, v, w) \geq 0, \\ & b^T y = \min_x \{ \|Wx\|_1 : Ax = b \}, \end{aligned}$$

where $\alpha > 0$ is a given small parameter. Replacing $\|s\|_0$ by $F_\varepsilon(s)$, a merit function for sparsity, yields the following model:

$$\begin{aligned} \max_{(y,s,u,v,w)} \quad & \alpha F_\varepsilon(s) + b^T y \\ \text{s.t.} \quad & A^T y - u + v = 0, \ s = w - u - v, \ (s, u, v, w) \geq 0, \qquad (8.51) \\ & b^T y = \min_x \{ \|Wx\|_1 : Ax = b \}. \end{aligned}$$

This model remains hard to solve due to the difficult constraint

$$b^T y = \gamma := \min_x \{ \|Wx\|_1 : Ax = b \}. \qquad (8.52)$$

The following observation is useful for a further relaxation of (8.51).

**Proposition 8.3.4** (i) *The solution to the weighted $\ell_1$-minimization problem (8.42) is invariant when $w$ is replaced by $\lambda w$ for any positive number $\lambda > 0$.* (ii) *If $(y, s, w, u, v, \gamma)$ is a solution to the problem (8.47), then $\lambda(y, s, w, u, v, \gamma)$ is also a solution to (8.47) for any positive number $\lambda > 0$, due to the fact $\|\lambda s\|_0 = \|s\|_0$.*

This means any weight that is large in magnitude can be scaled down to a smaller one without affecting the solution of (8.42) and the optimal objective value of (8.47). So $w$ can be restricted to a bounded convex set $\Omega \subseteq \mathbb{R}^n_+$. The value of $\gamma$ is not essential in (8.47) since by a suitable scaling of $w$ the constraint (8.52) can be replaced by

$$b^T y = 1 = \min_x \{\|Wx\|_1 : Ax = b\} \qquad (8.53)$$

without any damage of the conclusion in Theorem 8.3.2. This has been seen in Theorem 8.2.3. Hence, it is sufficient to consider the restricted choice $w \in \mathcal{W}$, instead of $w \in \mathbb{R}^n_+$. By the weak duality property, the constraint $b^T y \leq 1$ can be used as a relaxation of the condition (8.53). This relaxation, together with the restriction $w \in \Omega$, can be incorporated into (8.51), leading to the following convex optimization model:

$$\max_{(y,s,u,v,w)} \quad \alpha F_\varepsilon(s) + b^T y$$
$$\text{s.t.} \quad A^T y - u + v = 0, \ s = w - u - v, \ b^T y \leq 1, \ w \in \Omega, \ (s,u,v,w) \geq 0.$$

Either $v$ or $u$ can be eliminated in order to slightly simplify the model. For instance, eliminating $v$ yields

$$\max_{(y,s,u,w)} \quad \alpha F_\varepsilon(s) + b^T y$$
$$\text{s.t.} \quad A^T y + w - s - 2u = 0, \ w - u - s \geq 0, \ b^T y \leq 1, \qquad (8.54)$$
$$w \in \Omega, \ (s,u,w) \geq 0.$$

Based on the model (8.54), an algorithm can be developed for finding the sparsest solution of an underdetermined system of linear equations. Such an algorithm is also referred to as the dual-density-based reweighted $\ell_1$-algorithm (DDRW).

**Algorithm (III) (General Framework of DDRW)**
Let $\varepsilon^0, \alpha^0 \in (0,1)$ be a given constant. Let $0 < \alpha^* \ll \alpha^0$ be a prescribed tolerance. Choose a bounded and closed convex set $\Omega^0 \subseteq \mathbb{R}^n_+$.

*S1.* If $\alpha^k \leq \alpha^*$, stop; otherwise, solve the convex optimization

$$\max \quad \alpha^k F_{\varepsilon^k}(s) + b^T y$$
$$\text{s.t.} \quad A^T y + w - s - 2u = 0, \ w - u - s \geq 0, \ b^T y \leq 1, \qquad (8.55)$$
$$w \in \Omega^k, \ (w,s,u) \geq 0.$$

Let $(w^{k+1}, y^{k+1}, s^{k+1}, u^{k+1})$ be the solution to this problem.

*S2.* Set $W^{k+1} = \text{diag}(w^{k+1})$, and solve the weighted $\ell_1$-minimization problem

$$\gamma^{k+1} = \min_x \{\|W^{k+1}x\|_1 : Ax = b\} \qquad (8.56)$$

to obtain a solution $x^{k+1}$.

*S3.* Update $(\alpha^k, \varepsilon^k, \Omega^k)$ to obtain $(\alpha^{k+1}, \varepsilon^{k+1}, \Omega^{k+1})$. Replace $k$ by $k+1$ and return to *S1*.

The above algorithm may have a number of variants in terms of the updating schemes for $\varepsilon^k, \alpha^k$ and $\Omega^k$ and the stoping criteria. From a computational point of view, $\Omega^0$ and $\Omega^k$ should be chosen as simple as possible. For instance, we may simply choose $\Omega^0 = \{w \in \mathbb{R}_+^n : \|w\|_1 \leq \vartheta\}$, where $\vartheta$ is a given constant. We may also pick an initial point $x^0 \in \mathbb{R}^n$ and set

$$\Omega^0 = \{w \in \mathbb{R}_+^n : |x^0|^T w \leq \vartheta,\ w \leq \Gamma \mathbf{e}\},$$

where $\vartheta > 0$ and $\Gamma > 0$ are two given constants. We may fix $\Omega^k \equiv \Omega^0$ for all iterations or change $\Omega^k$ iteratively in the course of algorithm. Also, we have a large freedom to choose concave merit functions. The problem (8.55) is convex and can be solved efficiently by various optimization methods, such as interior-point-type methods.

To see a concrete example of Algorithm (III), we consider a specific version of the algorithm as follows, in which $\varepsilon$ is a fixed parameter and $(\alpha, \Omega)$ are changed iteratively.

## Algorithm (IV) (Iterative DDRW)

Given $\alpha^0 \in (0,1)$, $\tau \in (0,1)$, $\varepsilon \in (0,1)$, $0 < \alpha^* \ll \alpha^0$ and $\vartheta \geq 1$; perform the following steps:

*S0* (Initialization) Let $x^0$ and $\gamma^0$ be the solution and optimal value of the problem $\min_x\{\|x\|_1 : Ax = b\}$, respectively. Set $\Gamma^0 \geq \vartheta \max\{1, 1/\gamma^0\}$ and let

$$\Omega^0 = \{w \in \mathbb{R}_+^n : |x^0|^T w \leq \vartheta,\ w \leq \Gamma^0 \mathbf{e}\}.$$

*S1* If $\alpha^k \leq \alpha^*$, stop; otherwise, solve the convex optimization problem (8.55) to obtain the vector $(w^{k+1},\ y^{k+1},\ s^{k+1},\ u^{k+1})$.

*S2* Set $W^{k+1} = \mathrm{diag}(w^{k+1})$ and solve the weighted $\ell_1$-minimization problem (8.56) to obtain $(x^{k+1},\ \gamma^{k+1})$.

*S3* Set $\alpha^{k+1} = \tau \alpha^k$ and

$$\Gamma^{k+1} \geq \vartheta \max\{1, \|w^{k+1}\|_\infty / \gamma^{k+1}\},$$

and let
$$\Omega^{k+1} = \{w \in \mathbb{R}_+^n : |x^{k+1}|^T w \leq \vartheta,\ w \leq \Gamma^{k+1}\mathbf{e}\}.$$

Replace $k$ by $k+1$ and return to *S1*.

A preliminary convergence analysis and numerical experiments for this algorithm were carried out by Zhao and Kocvara in [245].

## 8.4 Sparsity Enhancement for Weighted $\ell_1$-Minimizers

The solution of the weighted $\ell_1$-minimization, called weighted $\ell_1$-minimizer, can be obtained by any LP solvers. Given a weight $w \in \mathbb{R}^n_+$, the solution to the weighted $\ell_1$-minimization problem

$$\min_x \{\|Wx\|_1 : Ax = b, \ x \geq 0\} \tag{8.57}$$

may not be the solution to the $\ell_0$-minimization problem for two reasons:

■ The intersection of the solution sets of $\ell_0$-minimization and weighted $\ell_1$-minimization are empty.

■ The intersection of the solution sets of $\ell_0$-minimization and weighted $\ell_1$-minimization are nonempty, but the solution of weighted $\ell_1$-minimization is not unique.

For the former case, (8.57) completely fails to solve the $\ell_0$-minimization problem, while for the latter case, (8.57) may or may not fail, depending on the mechanism of the algorithm for $\ell_1$-minimization. In both cases, we would like to enhance the sparsity of the solution of weighted $\ell_1$-minimization if it is not sparse enough. In other words, we may develop a certain procedure to further improve the sparsity of the solution so that a solution sparser than the underlying one can be obtained.

Although we have shown the existence of an optimal weight and it can be obtained, in theory, by solving the optimization problem (8.6), the question of how to efficiently compute such an optimal weight remains open. Any weight obtained by certain practical approaches (such as the ones introduced in Chapter 7 and this chapter) might not guarantee the success of the weighted $\ell_1$-algorithm in solving $\ell_0$-minimization due to the NP-hardness of the problem. When the algorithm fails to solve $\ell_0$-minimization, the solution found by the algorithm is not sparse enough. So it is worth developing a certain procedure to enhance the sparsity of the found solution.

At the solution $x$ of (8.57), if the columns of $A_{\mathrm{supp}(x)}$ are linearly dependent, the solution of (8.57) is not unique. The following result shows that in this case, a solution sparser than $x$ is available.

**Theorem 8.4.1** *Let $w \in \mathbb{R}^n_{++}$ and let $x$ be a solution to the problem (8.57).*

(i) *If $A_{\mathrm{supp}(x)}$ has full column rank, then there is no other solution $z \neq x$ with $\mathrm{supp}(z) \subseteq \mathrm{supp}(z)$.*

(ii) *If $A_{\mathrm{supp}(x)}$ does not have full column rank, then there exists a sparser solution than $x$, denoted by $z$, satisfying that $\|Wz\|_1 = \|Wx\|_1$ and $\mathrm{supp}(z) \subset \mathrm{supp}(x)$.*

*Proof.* (i) Let $A_{\text{supp}(x)}$ have full column rank. Assume that there is a solution $z \neq x$ such that $\text{supp}(z) \subseteq \text{supp}(x)$. Thus, we have

$$A_{\text{supp}(x)} x_{\text{supp}(x)} = b, \ x_{\text{supp}(x)} \geq 0,$$

$$A_{\text{supp}(z)} z_{\text{supp}(z)} = b, \ z_{\text{supp}(z)} \geq 0.$$

Denote by $J = \text{supp}(x) \setminus \text{supp}(z)$. Then $\text{supp}(x) = \text{supp}(z) \cup J$. Combining the two relations above leads to

$$0 = A_{\text{supp}(x)} x_{\text{supp}(x)} - A_{\text{supp}(z)} z_{\text{supp}(z)} = A_{\text{supp}(z)} \left( x_{\text{supp}(z)} - z_{\text{supp}(z)} \right) + A_J x_J. \quad (8.58)$$

Since $\text{supp}(z) \subseteq \text{supp}(x)$ and $z \neq x$, we have either $x_{\text{supp}(z)} \neq z_{\text{supp}(z)}$ or $x_J \neq 0$. Thus (8.58) implies that the columns of $A_{\text{supp}(x)}$ are linearly dependent. This is a contradiction.

(ii) Let $x$ be a solution to the problem (8.57). We now assume $A_{\text{supp}(x)}$ does not have full column rank. Then there exists a vector $v$ such that

$$A_{\text{supp}(x)} v = 0, \ v \neq 0, \ v \in \mathbb{R}^{|\text{supp}(x)|}. \quad (8.59)$$

Note that $x$ is a solution to (8.57). Let $y$ be an optimal solution to the dual problem of (8.57), i.e., $\max_y \{ b^T y : A^T y \leq w \}$. Let

$$s = w - A^T y \in \mathbb{R}^n_+.$$

By the optimality theory, $x \geq 0$ and $s \geq 0$ are complementary in the sense that $x^T s = 0$. This implies that

$$s_i = 0 \ \text{ for all } i \in \text{supp}(x),$$

i.e.,

$$(A^T y - w)_i = 0 \ \text{ for all } i \in \text{supp}(x).$$

Therefore,

$$w_{\text{supp}(x)} = (A^T y)_{\text{supp}(x)} = (A_{\text{supp}(x)})^T y.$$

Thus $w_{\text{supp}(x)}$ is in the range space (column space) of $(A_{\text{supp}(x)})^T$. By (8.59), $v$ is in the null space of $A_{\text{supp}(x)}$. Thus,

$$(w_{\text{supp}(x)})^T v = 0. \quad (8.60)$$

Note that $w \in \mathbb{R}^n_{++}$ and $v \neq 0$. The above relation implies that $v$ must have at least two non-zero components with different signs, i.e., $v_i v_j < 0$ for some $i \neq j$. We define the vector $\tilde{v} \in \mathbb{R}^n$ as follows: $\tilde{v}_{\text{supp}(x)} = v$ and $\tilde{v}_i = 0$ for all $i \notin \text{supp}(x)$. Consider the vector

$$x(\lambda) = x + \lambda \tilde{v}, \ \lambda \geq 0.$$

Note that $x(\lambda)_i = 0$ for all $i \notin \mathrm{supp}(x)$. Since $x_i > 0$ for all $i \in \mathrm{supp}(x)$, when $\lambda > 0$ is small, we have $x(\lambda) \geq 0$. We also note that

$$Ax(\lambda) = Ax + A(\lambda \widetilde{v}) = b + \lambda A_{\mathrm{supp}(x)} v = b.$$

Thus $x(\lambda)$ is also a solution to the system $Ax = b$. By the definition, the vector $\widetilde{v}$ has at least one negative component. Thus, let

$$\lambda^* = \frac{x_{i_0}}{-\widetilde{v}_{i_0}} = \min\{\frac{x_i}{-\widetilde{v}_i} : \widetilde{v}_i < 0\},$$

where $\lambda^*$ must be a positive number and $i_0 \in \mathrm{supp}(x)$. By such a choice of $\lambda^*$ and the definition of $x(\lambda^*)$, we conclude that $x(\lambda^*) \geq 0$, and $x(\lambda^*)_i = 0$ for $i \notin \mathrm{supp}(x)$, and $x(\lambda^*)_{i_0} = 0$ with $i_0 \in \mathrm{supp}(x)$. Thus, $x(\lambda^*)$ is a non-negative solution to the linear system $Ax = b$, which is sparser than $x$, i.e., $\|x(\lambda^*)\|_0 < \|x\|_0$. We now prove that $\|Wx(\lambda^*)\|_1 = \|Wx\|_1$. So $x(\lambda^*)$ remains the least weighted $\ell_1$-norm solution of the linear system. In fact,

$$\|Wx(\lambda^*)\|_1 = w^T x(\lambda^*) = w^T(x + \lambda^* \widetilde{v}) = w^T x + \lambda^* (w_{\mathrm{supp}(x)})^T v = \|Wx\|_1,$$

where the last equality follows from (8.60). Replace $x$ by $x(\lambda^*)$, and repeat the above analysis, if $A_{\mathrm{supp}(x(\lambda^*))}$ does not have full column rank. Then we can continue to find a sparser solution than $x(\lambda^*)$, with the same weighted $\ell_1$-norm. Thus after a few such reductions, we obtain a solution $z$ satisfying that $\|z\|_0 < \|x\|_0$ and the associated columns of $A_{\mathrm{supp}(z)}$ are linearly independent. ☐

The above theorem shows that if the columns of $A$ corresponding to the support of the solution $x$ of (8.57) are linearly independent, then $x$ must be the sparsest one among the solution $z$ satisfying $\mathrm{supp}(z) \subseteq \mathrm{supp}(x)$, i.e., there is no other solution $z \neq x$ satisfying $\mathrm{supp}(z) \subseteq \mathrm{supp}(x)$. However, such a solution may still not be the globally sparsest solution of the $\ell_0$-minimization problem. A global solution $x$ of the $\ell_0$-minimization problem satisfies that $\|x\|_0 \leq \|z\|_0$ for any $z \in P$. The proof of the above theorem yields the following procedure.

**Sparsity enhancement procedure.** Let $x$ be a solution to the weighted $\ell_1$-minimization problem (8.57). Denoted by $S_+ = \mathrm{supp}(x) = \{i_1, i_2, \ldots, i_K\}$ where $K = \|x\|_0 = |S_+|$ and $i_1 < i_2 < \cdots < i_K$.

- ◼ *Step 1.* Find a vector $v \neq 0$ such that $\begin{pmatrix} A_{S_+} \\ W_{S_+} \end{pmatrix} v = 0$. If $v = 0$ is the only solution to this homogenous system, stop. Otherwise, go to step 2

- ◼ *Step 2.* Let

$$\lambda^* = \min_{1 \leq k \leq K} \left\{ \frac{x_{i_k}}{-v_k} : v_k < 0 \right\}.$$

  Define $x^+$ as

$$x_{S_+}^+ = x_{S_+} + \lambda^* v, \quad \text{and } x_i^+ = 0 \text{ for all } i \notin S_+.$$

  Then set $S_+ = \mathrm{supp}(x^+)$, $K = |S_+|$, and return to *Step 1*.

This procedure may find a solution $x^+$ which is sparser than the underlying solution $x$ when the associated columns of $A$, i.e., $A_{supp(x)}$ are linearly dependent. In fact, when $x$ is a weighted $\ell_1$-minimizer, the above procedure will find the sparsest one among the weighted $\ell_1$-minimizers $z$ satisfying

$$supp(z) \subseteq supp(x).$$

However, this procedure still cannot ensure that the generated vector is the global solution of the $\ell_0$-minimization problem.

## 8.5 Notes

The reweighted $\ell_1$-algorithm introduced in Chapter 7 is one of the most plausible convex optimization methods for solving $\ell_0$-minimization problems. The dual-density-based theory and reweighted $\ell_1$-algorithms presented in this chapter were first proposed by Zhao and Kocvara [245], and Zhao and Luo [248]. The $\ell_0$-minimization problem is a special case of the matrix rank minimization problems and low-rank-matrix recovery problems (see Recht, Fazel and Parrilo [191], Hiriart-Urruty [131], Chandrasekaran et al. [55], Zhao [239], and Darvenpot and Romberg [73]). These problems arise from a wide range of practical applications. So extending the algorithms introduced in Chapters 7 and 8 to rank minimization and low-rank-matrix recovery is clearly a worthwhile topic for the future research.

Some important algorithms are not discussed in this book, such as the orthogonal matching pursuits [166, 78, 76, 68, 210, 212, 181], thresholding-type algorithms [70, 25, 180, 22, 95, 27, 164], and their variants. Nonconvex optimization and Bayesian framework [57, 225] are not discussed in this book as well. A good introduction and survey of these methods can be found in Bruckstein, Donoho and Elad [37], Elad [95], and Tropp and Wright [214]. The theoretical efficiency of these algorithms has been shown under various conditions in literature. For instance, the efficiency of orthogonal matching pursuits was proved under various conditions including the mutual coherence (see Elad [95]), RIP (see Foucart and Rauhut [108]), and the ERC assumption (see Fuchs [111], Tropp [210], and Tropp and Gilbert [212]). The mutual coherence and the RIP-type assumptions can also ensure the success of thresholding methods for $\ell_0$-minimization problems (see Elad [95], Blumensath, Davies and Rilling [27], and Foucart and Rauhut [108]).

The efficiency of reweighted $\ell_1$-methods introduced in Chapter 7 was analyzed by Needell [178] and Foucard and Lai [107] under the RIP-type assumptions, and by Zhao and Li [246] under a range space property of the transposed matrix. Assumption 7.4.5 was first used by Zhao and Luo [248] to analyze the theoretical efficiency of the dual-density-based reweighted $\ell_1$-method. However, the study of this method is still at its infant stage. Whether the method can be shown efficient for solving $\ell_0$-minimization problems under a traditional assumption, such as the RIP or NSP is not clear at the moment. How to efficiently compute an optimal or a nearly optimal weight for weighted $\ell_1$-minimization remains a challenging question.

# References

[1] V. Abolghasemi, S. Ferdowsi, and S. Sanei. A gradient-based alternating minimization approach for optimization of the measurement matrix in compressive sensing. *Signal Process.*, 92:999–1009, 2012.

[2] J. Acharya, A. Bhattacharyya, and P. Kamath. Improved bounds for universal one-bit compressive sensing. In *Proc. of 2017 IEEE International Symposium on Information Theory (ISIT)*, pages 2353–2357. IEEE, 2017.

[3] R. Ahmad and P. Schniter. Iteratively reweighted $\ell_1$ approaches to sparse composite regularization. *IEEE Trans. Comput. Imaging*, 1:220–235, 2015.

[4] A. Ai, A. Lapanowski, Y. Plan, and R. Vershynin. One-bit compressed sensing with non-gaussian measurements. *Linear Algebra Appl.*, 441:222–239, 2014.

[5] G. Alberti, G. Franceschetti, V. Pascazio, and G. Schirinzi. Time-domain convolution of one-bit coded radar signals. *IEE Proceedings-F*, 138:438–444, 1991.

[6] E. Amaldi and V. Kann. On the approximability of minimizing nonzero variables or unsatisfied relations in linear systems. *Theoret. Comput. Sci.*, 209:237–260, 1998.

[7] J. Andersson and J. O. Strömberg. On the theorem of uniform recovery of structured random matrices. *IEEE Trans. Inform. Theory*, 60:1700–1710, 2014.

[8] M. Asif and J. Romberg. On the LASSO and Dantzig selector equivalence. In *IEEE 44th Annual Conference on Information Sciences and Systems*, pages 1–6. IEEE, 2010.

[9] M.S. Asif and J. Romberg. Fast and accurate algorithms for reweighted $\ell_1$-norm minimization. *IEEE Trans. Signal Process.*, 61:5905–5916, 2013.

[10] M.S. Asif and J. Romberg. Sparse recovery of streaming signals using $\ell_1$-homotopy. *IEEE Trans. Signal Process.*, 62:4209 – 4223, 2014.

[11] U. Ayaz, S. Dirksen, and H. Rauhut. Uniform recovery of fusion frame structured sparse signals. *Appl. Comput. Harmon. Anal.*, 41:341–361, 2016.

[12] U. Ayaz and H. Rauhut. Nonuniform sparse recovery with subgaussian matrices. *Electronic Trans. Numer. Anal.*, 41:167–178, 2014.

[13] D. Ba, B. Babadi, P. Purdon, and E. Brown. Convergence and stability of iteratively reweighted least squares algorithms. *IEEE Trans. Signal Process.*, 62:183–195, 2014.

[14] H. Bai, G. Li, S. Li, Q. Li, Q. Jiang, and L. Chang. Alternating optimization of sensing matrix and sparsifying dictionary for compressed sensing. *IEEE Trans. Signal Process.*, 63:1581–1594, 2015.

[15] H. Bai, S. Li, and X. He. Sensing matrix optimization based on equiangular tight frames with consideration of sparse representation error. *IEEE Trans. Multimedia*, 18:2040–2053, 2016.

[16] A. Bandeira, E. Dobriban, D. Mixon, and W. Sawin. Certifying the restricted isometry property is hard. *IEEE Trans. Inform. Theory*, 59:3448–3450, 2013.

[17] R. Baraniuk, M. Davenport, R. DeVore, and M. Wakin. A simple proof of the restricted isometry property for random matrices. *Constr. Approx.*, 28:253–263, 2008.

[18] R. Baraniuk, S. Foucart, D. Needell, Y. Plan, and M. Wootters. Exponential decay of reconstruction error from binary measurements of sparse signals. *IEEE Trans. Inform. Theory*, 63:3368–3385, 2017.

[19] J. Bardsley and J. Nagy. Covariance-preconditioned iterative methods for nonnegativity constrained astronomical imaging. *SIAM J. Matrix Anal. Appl.*, 27:1184–1198, 2006.

[20] R. Bartels, A. Conn, and J. Sinclair. Minimization techniques for piecewise differentiable functions: The $\ell_1$ solution to an overdetermined linear system. *SIAM J. Numer. Anal.*, 15:224–241, 1978.

[21] A. Barvinok. Thrifty approximations of convex bodies by polytopes. *Int. Math. Res. Notices*, 16:4341–4356, 2014.

[22] A. Beck and M. Teboulle. A fast iterative shrinkage-thresholding algorithm for linear inverse problems. *SIAM J. Imaging Sci.*, 2:183–202, 2009.

[23] P. Bickel, Y. Ritov, and A. Tsybakov. Simultaneous analysis of lasso and Dantzig selector. *Ann. Statist.*, 37:1705–1732, 2009.

[24] T. Blumensath. Compressed sensing with nonlinear measurements and related nonlinear optimization problems. *IEEE Trans. Inform. Theory*, 59:3466–3474, 2013.

[25] T. Blumensath and M. Davies. Iterative thresholding for sparse approximations. *J. Fourier Anal. Appl.*, 14:629–654, 2008.

[26] T. Blumensath and M. Davies. Iterative hard thresholding for compressed sensing. *Appl. Comput. Harmon. Anal.*, 27:265–274, 2009.

[27] T. Blumensath, M. Davies, and G. Rilling. Greedy algorithms for compressed sensing. In *Compressed Sensing: Theory and Applications*, pages 348–393. (Y. Eldar and G. Kutyniok Eds.) Cambridge University Press, 2012.

[28] P. Boufounos. Greedy sparse signal reconstruction from sign measurements. In *Proc. 43rd Asilomar Conf. Signals Syst. Comput.*, pages 1305–1309. Pacific Grove, CA, 2009.

[29] P. Boufounos. Reconstruction of sparse signals from distorted randomized measurements. In *IEEE Int. Conf. Acoustics, Speech, and Signal Process.*, pages 3998–4001. Dallas, TX, 2010.

[30] P. Boufounos and R. Baraniuk. 1-bit compressive sensing. In *Proc. 42nd Ann. Conf. Inf. Sci. Syst*, pages 16–21. Princeton, NJ, 2008.

[31] A. Bourquard, F. Aguet, and M. Unser. Optical imaging using binary sensors. *Opt. Express.*, 18:4876–4888, 2010.

[32] A. Bourquard and M. Unser. Binary compressed imaging. *IEEE Trans. Image Process.*, 22:1042–1055, 2013.

[33] P. Bradley, U. Fayyad, and O. L. Mangasarian. Mathematical programming for data mining: formulations and challenges. *INFORMS J. Comput.*, 11:217–238, 1999.

[34] P. Bradley, O. L. Mangasarian, and J. Rosen. Parsimonious least norm approximation. *Comput. Optim. Appl.*, 11:5–21, 1998.

[35] A. Brauer. Limits for the characteristic roots of a matrix. *Duke Math. J.*, 13:387–395, 1946.

[36] E. M. Bronshtein and L. D. Ivanov. The approximation of convex sets by polyhedra. *Siberian Math. J.*, 16:852–853, 1975.

[37] A. Bruckstein, D. Donoho, and M. Elad. From sparse solutions of systems of equations to sparse modeling of signals and images. *SIAM Rev.*, 51:34–81, 2009.

[38] A. Bruckstein, M. Elad, and M. Zibulevsky. On the uniqueness of non-negative sparse solutions to underdetermined systems of equations. *IEEE Trans. Inform. Theory*, 54:4813–4820, 2008.

[39] P. Bühlmann and S. van de Geer. *Statistics for High-Dimensional Data: Methods, Theory and Applications*. Springer, Berlin, 2011.

[40] J. Cahill, X. Chen, and R. Wang. The gap between the null space property and the restricted isometry property. *Linear Algebra Appl.*, 501:363–375, 2016.

[41] T. Cai, L. Wang, and G. Xu. New bounds for restricted isometry constants. *IEEE Trans. Inform. Theory*, 56:4388–4394, 2010.

[42] T. Cai, G. Xu, and J. Zhang. On recovery of sparse signals via $\ell_1$ minimization. *IEEE Trans. Inform. Theory*, 55:3388–3397, 2009.

[43] T. Cai and A. Zhang. Sharp RIP bound for sparse signal and low-rank matrix recovery. *Appl. Comput. Harmon. Anal.*, 35:74–93, 2013.

[44] T. Cai and A. Zhang. Sparse representation of a polytope and recovery of sparse signals and low-rank matrices. *IEEE Trans. Inform Theory*, 60:122–132, 2014.

[45] E. Candès. The restricted isometry property and its implications for compressed sensing. *C.R. Math. Acad. Sci. Paris*, 346:589–592, 2008.

[46] E. Candes and T. Tao. Rejoinder: The Dantzig selector: statistical estimation when $p$ is much larger than $n$. *Ann. Statist.*, 35:2392–2404, 2007.

[47] E. Candes and T. Tao. The Dantzig selector: statistical estimation when $p$ is much larger than $n$. *Ann. Statist.*, 35:2313–2351, 2007.

[48] E. Candès. Compressive sampling. In *Proceedings of the International Congress of Mathematicians*. Madrid, Spain, 2006.

[49] E. Candès, J. Romberg, and T. Tao. Robust uncertainty principles: Exact signal reconstruction from highly incomplete frequency information. *IEEE Trans. Inform. Theory*, 52:489–509, 2006.

[50] E. Candès, J. Romberg, and T. Tao. Stable signal recovery from incomplete and inaccurate measurements. *Comm. Pure Appl. Math.*, 59:1207–1223, 2006.

[51] E. Candès and T. Tao. Decoding by linear programming. *IEEE Trans. Inform. Theory*, 51:4203–4215, 2005.

[52] E. Candès and T. Tao. Near optimal signal recovery from random projections: Universal encoding strategies? *IEEE Trans. Inform. Theory*, 52:5406–5425, 2006.

[53] E. Candès, M. Wakin, and S. Boyd. Enhancing sparsity by reweighted $\ell_1$ minimization. *J. Fourier Anal. Appl.*, 14:877–905, 2008.

[54] Y. De Castro. A remark on the LASSO and the Dantzig selector. *Stat. Prob. Lett.*, 83:304–314, 2013.

[55] V. Chandrasekaran, B. Recht, P. Parrilo, and A. Willsky. The convex geometry of linear inverse problems. *Found. Comput. Math.*, 12:805–849, 2012.

[56] L. Chang and J. Wu. An improved RIP-based performance guarantee for sparse signal recovery via orthogonal matching pursuit. *IEEE Trans. Inform. Theory*, 60:707–710, 2014.

[57] R. Chartrand. Exact reconstruction of sparse signals via nonconvex minimization. *IEEE Signal Process. Lett.*, 14:707–710, 2007.

[58] R. Chartrand and W. Yin. Iteratively reweighted algorithms for compressive sensing. In *IEEE International conference on Acoustics, Speech and Signal Processing (ICASSP)*, pages 3869–3872, 2008.

[59] G. Cheang and A. Barron. A better approximation for balls. *J. Approx. Theory*, 104:183–203, 2000.

[60] C. Chen and J. Wu. Amplitude-aided 1-bit compressive sensing over noisy wireless sensor networks. *IEEE Wir. Commun. Lett.*, 4:473–476, 2015.

[61] D. Chen and R. Plemmons. Nonnegativity constraints in numerical analysis. In *Symposium on the Birth of Numerical Analysis*, 2007.

[62] S. Chen, D. Donoho, and M. Saunders. Atomic decomposition by basis pursuit. *SIAM J. Sci. Comput.*, 20:33–61, 1998.

[63] M. Cheraghchi, V. Guruswami, and A. Velingker. Restricted isometry of fourier matrices and list decodability of random linear codes. In *Proceedings of the 24th annual ACM-SIAM symposium on discrete algorithms*, pages 432–442. SIAM, Philadelphia, PA, 2013.

[64] J. Cho, Y. Chen, and Y. Ding. On the (co)girth of a connected matroid. *Discrete Appl. Math.*, 155:2456–2470, 2007.

[65] A. Cohen, W. Dahmen, and R. DeVore. Compressed sensing and best $k$-term approximation. *J. Amer. Math. Soc.*, 22:211–231, 2009.

[66] A. Cohen, W. Dahmen, and R. DeVore. Orthogonal matching pursuit under the restricted isometry property. *Constr. Approx.*, 45:113–127, 2015.

[67] D. Dai, L. Shen, Y. Xu, and N. Zhang. Noisy 1-bit compressive sensing: models and algorithms. *Appl. Comput. Harmon. Anal.*, 40:1–32, 2016.

[68] W. Dai and O. Milenkovic. Subspace pursuit for compressive sensing signal reconstruction. *IEEE Trans. Inform. Theory*, 55:2230–2249, 2009.

[69] G. Dantzig. *Linear Programming and Extensions*. Princeton University Press, Princeton, NJ, 1963.

[70] I. Daubechies, M. Defrise, and C. D. Mol. An iterative thresholding algorithm for linear inverse problems with a sparsity constraint. *Comm. Pure Appl. Math.*, 57:1413–1457, 2004.

[71] I. Daubechies, R. DeVore, M. Fornasier, and C.S. Güntürk. Iteratively reweighted squares minimization for sparse recovery. *Commun. Pure. Appl. Math.*, 63:1–38, 2010.

[72] M. Davenport, Y. Plan, E. van den Berg, and M. Wootters. 1-bit matrix completion. *Inform. Infer.*, 3:189–223, 2014.

[73] M. Davenport and J. Romberg. An overview of low-rank matrix recovery from incomplete observations. *IEEE Sel. Topic Signal Process.*, 10:608–622, 2016.

[74] M. Davenport and M. Wakin. Analysis of orthogonal matching pursuit using the restricted isometry property. *IEEE Trans. Inform. Theory*, 56:4395–4401, 2010.

[75] M. Davies and R. Gribonval. Restricted isometry constants where $\ell_p$ sparse recovery can fail for $0 < q \leq 1$. *IEEE Trans. Inform. Theory*, 55:2203–2214, 2009.

[76] G. Davis, S. Mallat, and Z. Zhang. Adaptive time-frequency decompositions. *Opt. Eng.*, 33:2183–2191, 1994.

[77] J. Determe, J. Louveaux, L. Jacques, and F. Horlin. On the exact recovery condition of simultaneous orthogonal matching pursuit. *IEEE Signal Process. Lett.*, 23:164–168, 2016.

[78] R. DeVore and V. Templyakov. Some remarks on greedy algorithms. *Adv. Comput. Math.*, 5:173–187, 1996.

[79] R. Diestel. *Graph Theory*. p.8. 3rd Edition, Springer-Verlag, 2005.

[80] X. Dong and Y. Zhang. A MAP approach for 1-bit compressive sensing in synthetic aperture radar imaging. *IEEE Geo. Rem. Sensing Lett.*, 12:1237–1241, 2015.

[81] D. Donoho. *Neighborly polytopes and sparse solutions of underdetermined linear equations.* Technical report, Stanford Univ., 2005.

[82] D. Donoho. Compressed sensing. *IEEE Trans. Inform. Theory*, 52:1289–1306, 2006.

[83] D. Donoho and M. Elad. Optimally sparse representation in general (nonorthogonal) dictionaries via $\ell_1$ minimization. *Proc. Natl. Acad. Sci.*, 100:2197–2202, 2003.

[84] D. Donoho, M. Elad, and V. Temlyakov. Stable recovery of sparse overcomplete representation in the presence of noise. *IEEE Trans. Inform. Theory*, 52:6–18, 2006.

[85] D. Donoho and X. Huo. Uncertainty principles and ideal atomic decomposition. *IEEE Trans. Inform. Theory*, 47:2845–2862, 2001.

[86] D. Donoho and B. Logan. Signal recovery and the large sieve. *SIAM J. Appl. Math.*, 52:577–591, 1992.

[87] D. Donoho and J. Tanner. Sparse nonnegative solutions of underdetermined linear equations by linear programming. *Proc. Natl. Acad. Sci.*, 102:9446–9451, 2005.

[88] D. Donoho and J. Tanner. Counting the faces of randomly-projected hypercubes and orthants with applications. *Discrete Comput. Geom.*, 43:522–541, 2010.

[89] D. Donoho, Y. Tsaig, I. Drori, and J.-L. Starck. Sparse solution of underdetermined systems of linear equations by stagewise orthogonal matching pursuit. *IEEE Trans. Inform. Theory*, 58:1094–1121, 2012.

[90] C. Dossal. A necessary and sufficient condition for exact sparse recovery by $\ell_1$ minimization. *C. R. Acad. Sci. Paris, Ser. I*, 350:117–120, 2012.

[91] J. M. Duarte-Carvajalino and G. Sapiro. Learning to sense sparse signals: Simultaneous sensing matrix and sparsifying dictionary optimization. *IEEE Trans. Image Process.*, 18:1395–1408, 2009.

[92] R. Dudley. Matric entropy of some classes of sets with differentiable boundaries (Correction, *J. Approx. Theory*, 26 (1979), pp. 192–193). *J. Approx. Theory*, 10:227–236, 1974.

[93] B. Efron, T. Hastie, and R. Tibshirani. Discussion: the Dantzig selector: statistical estimation when p is much larger than n. *Ann. Statist.*, 35:2358–2364, 2007.

[94] M. Elad. Optimized projections for compressed sensing. *IEEE Trans. Signal Process.*, 55:5695–5702, 2007.

[95] M. Elad. *Sparse and Redundant Representations: From Theory to Applications in Signal and Image Processing*. Springer, New York, 2010.

[96] M. Elad and A. Bruckstein. A generalized uncertainty principle and sparse representation in pairs of bases. *IEEE Trans. Inform. Theory*, 48:2558–2567, 2002.

[97] Y. Eldar and G. Kutyniok. *Compressed Sensing: Theory and Applications*. Cambridge University Press, 2012.

[98] M. Fazel, H. Hindi, and S. Boyd. Log-det heuristic for matrix rank minimization with applications to Hankel and Euclidean distance matrices. In *Proc. Am. Control Conf.*, pages 2156–2162. IEEE, 2003.

[99] M. Fazel, H. Hindi, and S. Boyd. Rank minimization and applications in system theory. In *Proc. Am. Control Conf.*, pages 3273–3278. IEEE, 2004.

[100] A. Feuer and A. Nemirovski. On sparse representation in pairs of bases. *IEEE Trans. Inform. Theory*, 49:1579–1581, 2003.

[101] M. Figueiredo, J. Bioucas-Dias, and R. Nowak. Majorization-minimization algorithms for wavelet-based image restoration. *IEEE Trans. Image Process.*, 16:2980–2991, 2007.

[102] M. Fornasier, H. Rauhut, and R. Ward. Low-rank matrix recovery via iteratively reweighted least squares minimization. *SIAM J. Optim.*, 21:1614–1640, 2011.

[103] S. Foucart. A note on guaranteed sparse recovery via $\ell_1$-minimization. *Appl. Comput. Harmon. Anal.*, 29:97–103, 2010.

[104] S. Foucart. Hard thresholding pursuit: An algorithm for compressed sensing. *SIAM J. Numer. Anal.*, 49:2543–2563, 2011.

[105] S. Foucart. Stability and robustness of $\ell_1$-minimizations with weibull matrices and redundant dictionaries. *Linear Algebra Appl.*, 441:4–21, 2014.

[106] S. Foucart and D. Koslicki. Sparse recovery by means of nonnegative least squares. *IEEE Sig. Process. Lett.*, 21:498–502, 2014.

[107] S. Foucart and M. Lai. Sparsest solutions of underdetermined linear systems via $\ell_p$-minimization for $0 < q \leq 1$. *Appl. Comput. Harmon. Anal.*, 26:395–407, 2009.

[108] S. Foucart and H. Rauhut. *A Mathematical Introduction to Compressive Sensing*. Springer, NY, 2013.

[109] G. Franceschetti, V. Pascazio, and G. Schirinzi. Processing of signum coded SAR signal: Theory and experiments. *IEE Proceedings-F,*, 138:192–198, 1991.

[110] M. Friedlander and M. Saunders. Discussion: the dantzig selector: statistical estimation when p is much larger than n. *Ann. Statist.*, 35:2385–2391, 2007.

[111] J. J. Fuchs. On sparse representations in arbitrary redundant bases. *IEEE Trans. Inform. Theory*, 50:1341–1344, 2004.

[112] S. Geršchgorin. Über die abgrenzung der eigenwerte einer matrix. *Bulletin de l'Académie des Sciences de l'URSS*, 6:749–754, 1931.

[113] J. C. Gilbert. On the solution uniqueness characterization in the l1 norm and polyhedral gauge recovery. *J. Optim. Theory Appl.*, 172:70–101, 2017.

[114] A. Goldman and A. Tucker. *Theory of Linear Programming (pp. 53-98), in Linear Inequalities and Related Systems.* (AM-38), Edited by A. W. Tucker et al., Princeton University Press, 1956.

[115] S. Gopi, P. Netrapalli, P. Jain, and A. Nori. One-bit compressed sensing: Provable support and vector recovery. In *Proc. 30th Int. Conf. Machine Learning*, pages 154–162. Atlanta Georgia, 2013.

[116] I. Gorodnitsky, J. George, and B. Rao. Neuromagnetic source imaging with focuss: A recursive weighted minimum norm algorithm. *Electroen. Clin. Neuro.*, 95:231–251, 1995.

[117] I. Gorodnitsky and B. Rao. Sparse signal reconstruction from limited data using FOCUSS: A reweighted minimum norm algorithm. *IEEE Trans. Signal Proc.*, 45:600–616, 1997.

[118] M. Grant and S. Boyd. CVX: Matlab software for disciplined convex programming, Version 1.21, Arpil 2011.

[119] M. Grasmair, O. Sherzer, and M. Haltmeier. Necessary and sufficient conditions for linear convergence of l1-regularization. *Comm. Pure Appl. Math.*, 64:161–182, 2011.

[120] H. Greenberg. An analysis of degeneracy. *Naval Res. Logist. Quart.*, 33:635–655, 1986.

[121] H. Greenberg. The use of the optimal partition in a linear programming solution for postoptimal analysis. *Oper. Res. Lett.*, 15:179–185, 1994.

[122] R. Gribonval and M. Nielsen. Sparse decompositions in unions of bases. *IEEE Trans. Inform. Theory*, 49:3320–3325, 2003.

[123] O. Güler. *Foundations of Optimization*. Springer, New York, 2010.

[124] O. Güler, A. J. Hoffman, and U. Rothblum. Approximations to solutions to systems of linear inequalities. *SIAM J. Matrix Anal. Appl.*, 16:688–696, 1995.

[125] A. Gupta, R. Nowak, and B. Recht. Sample complexity for 1-bit compressed sensing and sparse classification. In *IEEE Int. Symp. Inf. Theory*, pages 1553–1557. IEEE, 2010.

[126] E. Hale, W. Yin, and Y. Zhang. Fixed-point continuation for $\ell_1$-minimization: Methodology and convergence. *SIAM J. Optim.*, 19:1107–1130, 2008.

[127] G. Harikumar and Y. Bresler. A new algorithm for computing sparse solutions to linear inverse problems. In *Proc. Int. Conf. Acoustics, Speech, Signal Processing (ICASSP)*, pages 1331–1334, 1996.

[128] T. Hastie, R. Tibshirani, and M. Wainwright. *Statistical Learning with Sparsity: The Lasso and Generalizations*. Chapman & Hall/CRC Press, 2015.

[129] R. He, W. Zheng, B. Hu, and X. Kong. Nonnegative sparse coding for discriminative semi-supervised learning. In *Proc. IEEE conf. Comput. Vision & Pattern Recog. (CVPR)*, pages 2849–2856, 2001.

[130] C. Herzet, A. Dremeau, and C. Soussen. Relaxed recovery conditions for OMP/OLS by exploiting both coherence and decay. *IEEE Trans. Inform. Theory*, 62:459–470, 2016.

[131] J. B. Hiriart-Urruty and H. Y. Le. A variational approach of the rank function. *TOP*, 21:207–240, 2013.

[132] J. B. Hiriart-Urruty and C. Lemaréchal. *Fundamentals of Convex Analysis*. Springer-Verlag, New York, 2001.

[133] A. J. Hoffman. On the approximation solution of systems of linear inequalities. *J. Res. Nat. Bur. Standards*, 49:263–265, 1952.

[134] P. Holland and R. Welsch. Robust regression using iteratively reweighted least-squares. *Comm. Statist. Theory Methods*, 6:813–827, 1977.

[135] R. Horst, P. Pardalos, and N. Thoai. *Introduction to Global Optimization, 2rd Edition*. Kluwer Academic Publishers, 2000.

[136] X. Huang, Y. Xia, L. Shi, Y. Huang, M. Yan, J. Hornegger, and A. Maier. Mixed one-bit compressive sensing with application to overexposure correction for CT reconstruction. *arXiv*, 2017.

[137] Y. Itoh, M. Duarte, and M. Parente. Perfect recovery conditions for nonnegative sparse modeling. *IEEE Trans. Signal Process.*, 65:69–80, 2017.

[138] L. Jacques, J. Laska, P. Boufounos, and R. Baraniuk. Robust 1-bit compressive sensing via binary stable embeddings of sparse vectors. *IEEE Trans. Inform. Theory*, 59:2082–2102, 2013.

[139] G. James, P. Radchenko, and J. Lv. Dasso: connections between the dantzig selector and lasso. *J. Roy. Statist. Soc. Ser. B*, 71:127–142, 2009.

[140] A. Juditsky, F. Karzan, and A. Nemirovski. Verifiable conditions of $\ell_1$-recovery for sparse signals with sign restrictions. *Math. Program. Ser. B*, 127:89–122, 2011.

[141] A. Juditsky and A. Nemirovski. On verifiable sufficient conditions for sparse signal recovery via $\ell_1$ minimization. *Math. Program., Ser. B*, 127:57–88, 2011.

[142] U. Kamilov, A. Bourquard, A. Amini, and M. Unser. One-bit measurements with adaptive thresholds. *IEEE Signal Process. Lett.*, 19:607–610, 2012.

[143] W. Karush. *Minima of functions of several variables with inequalities as side constraints, MSc Dissertation*. Univ. of Chicago, Chicago, 1939.

[144] M. Khajehnejad, A. Dimakis, W. Xu, and B. Hassibi. Sparse recovery of nonnegative signals with minima expansion. *IEEE Trans. Signal Proc.*, 59:196–208, 2011.

[145] M. Khajehnejad, W. Xu, A. Avestimehr, and B. Hassibi. Weighted $\ell_1$ minimization for sparse recovery with prior information. In *Proceedings of the 2009 IEEE international conference on Symposium on Information Theory*, pages 483–487, 2009.

[146] K. Knudson, R. Saab, and R. Ward. One-bit compressive sensing with norm estimation. *IEEE Trans. Inform. Theory*, 62:2748–2758, 2016.

[147] Y. Kong, Z. Zheng, and J. Lv. The constrained dantzig selector with enhanced consistency. *J. Machine Learning Res.*, 17:1–22, 2016.

[148] J. B. Kruskal. Three-way arrays: rank and uniqueness of trilinear decompositions, with application to arithmetic complexity and statistics. *Linear Algebra Appl.*, 18:95–138, 1997.

[149] H. W. Kuhn and A. W. Tucker. Nonlinear programming. In *Proceedings of 2nd Berkeley Symposium*, pages 481–492. University of California Press, Berkeley, 1951.

[150] M. Lai and J. Wang. An unconstrained $\ell_q$ minimization with $0 < q \leq 1$ for sparse solution of underdetermined linear systems. *SIAM J. Optim.*, 21:82–101, 2010.

[151] K. Lange. *MM Optimization Algorithms*. SIAM, 2016.

[152] J. Laska. *Regime change: Sampling rate vs bit-depth in compressive sensing*. PhD thesis, Rice university, 2011.

[153] J. Laska and R. Baraniuk. Regime change: bit-depth versus measurement-rate in compressive sensing. *IEEE Trans. Signal Process.*, 60:3496–3505, 2012.

[154] J. Laska, Z. Wen, W. Yin, and R. Baraniuk. Trust but verify: Fast and accurate signal recovery from 1-bit compressive measurements. *IEEE Trans. Signal Process.*, 59:5289–5301, 2011.

[155] C. Lawson. *Contributions to the theory of linear least maximum approximation*. PhD thesis, University of California, Los Angeles, 1961.

[156] B. Le, T. Rondeau, J. Reed, and C. Bostian. Analog-to-digital converters. *IEEE Signal Process Mag.*, 22:69–77, 2005.

[157] S. Levy and P. Fullagar. Reconstruction of a sparse spike train from a portion of its spectrum and application to high-resolution deconvolution. *Geophysics*, 46:1235–1243, 1981.

[158] F. Li, J. Fang, H. Li, and L. Huang. Robust one-bit bayesian compressed sensing with sign-flip errors. *IEEE Signal Process. Lett.*, 22:857–861, 2015.

[159] W. Li, D. Gong, and Z. Q. Xu. One-bit compressed sensing by greedy algorithms. *Numer. Math.: Theory, Methods Appl.*, 9:169–184, 2016.

[160] M. Lobo, M. Fazel, and S. Boyd. Portfolio optimization with linear and fixed transaction costs. *Ann. Oper. Res.*, 152:341–365, 2007.

[161] B. Logan. *Properties of high-pass signals*. PhD thesis, Columbia University, 1965.

[162] Z. Lu. Iterative reweighted minimization methods for $\ell_p$ regularized unconstrained nonlinear programming. *Math. Program. Ser. A*, 147:277–307, 2014.

[163] Z. Q. Luo, J. S. Pang, and D. Ralph. *Mathematical Programming with Equilibrium Constraints*. Cambridge University Press, Cambridge, 1996.

[164] D. Malioutov and A. Aravkin. Iterative log thresholding. In *2014 IEEE International Conference on Acoustic, Speech and Signal Processing (ICASSP)*, pages 7198–7202. IEEE, 2014.

[165] S. Mallat. *A Wavelet Tour of Signal Processing*. Academic Press, San Diego, CA, 1999.

[166] S. Mallat and Z. Zhang. Matching pursuits with time-frequency dictionaries. *IEEE Trans. Signal Process.*, 41:3397–3415, 1993.

[167] O. L. Mangasarian. Machine learning via polyhedral concave minimization. In *Applied Mathematics and Parallel Computing-Festschrift for Klaus Ritter (H. Fischer, B. Riedmueller and S. Schaeffler eds.)*, pages 175–188. Springer, Heidelberg, 1996.

[168] O. L. Mangasarian and R. R. Meyer. Nonlinear perturbation of linear programs. *SIAM J. Control & Optim.*, 17:745–752, 1979.

[169] O. L. Mangasarian and T. Shiau. Lipschitz continuity of solutions of linear inequalities, programs and complementarity problems. *SIAM J. Control & Optim.*, 25:583–595, 1987.

[170] R. Mazumder and P. Radchenko. The discrete Dantzig selector: Estimating sparse linear models via mixed integer linear optimization. *IEEE Trans. Inform. Theory*, 63:3053–3075, 2017.

[171] N. Meinshausen and P. Bühlmann. Stability selection. *J. Royal Stat. Soc. Ser. B*, 72:417–473, 2010.

[172] N. Meinshausen, G. Rocha, and B. Yu. Discussion: a tale of three cousins: lasso, L2 boosting and Dantzig. *Ann. Statist.*, 35:2373–2384, 2007.

[173] S. Mendelson, A. Pajor, and N. Tomczak-Jaegermann. Uniform uncertainty principle for Bernoulli and subgaussian ensembles. *Constr. Approx.*, 28:277–289, 2008.

[174] Q. Mo and S. Li. New bounds on the restricted isometry constant $\delta_{2k}$. *Appl. Comput. Harmon. Anal.*, 31:460–468, 2011.

[175] K. Mohan and M. Fazel. Reweighted nuclear norm minimization with application to system identification. In *2010 American Control Conference, Baltimore*, pages 2953–2959, 2010.

[176] A. Movahed, A. Panahi, and G. Durisi. A robust RFPI-based 1-bit compressive sensing reconstruction algorithm. In *IEEE Inf. Theory Workshop*, pages 567–571. Laussane, Switzerland, 2012.

[177] B. Natarajan. Sparse approximate solutions to linear systems. *SIAM J. Comput.*, 24:227–234, 1995.

[178] D. Needell. Noisy signal recovery via iterative reweighted $\ell_1$-minimization. In *Proceedings of the 43rd Asilomar conference on Signals, Systems and Computers*, pages 113–117. IEEE, 2009.

[179] D. Needell, A. Saab, and T. Woolf. Weighted $\ell_1$-minimization for sparse recovery under arbitrary prior information. *Inform. Infer.*, 6:284–309, 2017.

[180] D. Needell and J.A. Tropp. CoSaMP: Iterative signal recovery from incomplete and inaccurate samples. *Appl. Comput. Harmon. Anal.*, 26:301–321, 2009.

[181] D. Needell and R. Vershynin. Uniform uncertainty principle and signal recovery via regularized orthogonal matching pursuit. *Found. Comput. Math.*, 9:317–334, 2009.

[182] R. Obermeier and J. A. Martinez-Lorenzo. Sensing matrix design via mutual coherence minimization for electromagnetic compressive imaging applications. *IEEE Trans. Comput. Imaging*, 3:217–229, 2017.

[183] P. Ochs, A. Dosovitskiy, T. Brox, and T. Pock. On iteratively reweighted algorithms for nonsmooth and nonconvex optimization in computer vision. *SIAM J. Imaging Sci.*, 8:331–372, 2015.

[184] Y. Park and D. Klabjan. Iteratively reweighted $\ell_1$ least squares algorithms for L1-norm principal component analysis. In *Proceedings of the 16rd IEEE Inter. Conf. on Data Mining*, pages 430–438. IEEE, 2016.

[185] V. Pascazio and G. Schirinzi. Synthetic aperture radar imaging by one bit coded signals. *Electron. Commun. Eng. J.*, 10:17–28, 1998.

[186] G. Pisier. *The volume of convex bodies and Banach space geometry*. Cambridge Tracts in Mathematics 94, Cambridge University Press, 1989.

[187] Y. Plan and R. Vershynin. One-bit compressed sensing by linear programming. *Comm. Pure Appl. Math.*, 66:1275–1297, 2013.

[188] Y. Plan and R. Vershynin. Robust 1-bit compressed sensing and sparse logistic regression: A convex programming approach. *IEEE Trans. Inform. Theory*, 59:482–494, 2013.

[189] M. Plumbley. On polar polytopes and the recovery of sparse representations. *IEEE Trans. Inform. Theory*, 53:3188–3195, 2007.

[190] H. Rauhut. Compressive sensing and structured random matrices. In *Theoretical Foundations and Numerical Methods for Sparse Recovery*, pages 1–92. (Ed. by M. Fornasier.) Radon Series on Computational and Applied Mathematics, Berlin, 2010.

[191] B. Recht, M. Fazel, and P.A. Parrilo. Guaranteed minimum-rank solutions of linear matrix equations via nuclear norm minimization. *SIAM Rev.*, 52:471–501, 2010.

[192] S. M. Robinson. Bounds for error in the solution set of a perturbed linear program. *Linear Algebra Appl.*, 6:69–81, 1973.

[193] R. T. Rockafellar. *Convex Analysis*. Princeton University Press, Princeton, New Jersey, 1970.

[194] P. Rosenbloom. Quelques classes de problèmes extrémaux. *Bull. Soc. Math. France*, 79:1–58, 1951.

[195] M. Rudelson and R. Vershynin. On sparse reconstruction from fourier and gaussian measurements. *Comm. Pure Appl. Math.*, 61:1025–1045, 2008.

[196] M. Rudelson and S. Zhou. Reconstruction from anisotropic random measurements. *IEEE Trans. Inform. Theory*, 59:3434–3447, 2013.

[197] R. Saab, R. Wang, and O. Yilmaz. Quantization of compressive samples with stable and robust recovery. *Appl. Comput. Harmon. Anal.*, 44:123–143, 2018.

[198] M. Sadeghi and M. Babaie-Zadeh. Incoherent unit-norm frame design via an alternating minimization penalty method. *IEEE Signal Process. Lett.*, 24:32–36, 2017.

[199] T. Sakdejayont, D. Lee, Y. Peng, Y. Yamashita, and H. Morikawa. Evaluation of memory-efficient 1-bit compressed sensing in wireless sensor networks. In *Proc. IEEE Region 10 Human. Tech. Conf., Sendai, Japan*, pages 326–329. Springer, 2013.

[200] L. Shen and B. Suter. Blind one-bit compressive sampling. *arXiv*, 2013.

[201] Y. Shen, J. Fang, and H. Li. One-bit compressive sensing and source location is wireless sensor networks. In *Proc. Chin. Summit Int. Conf. Signal Inf. Process.*, pages 379–383. Springer, 2013.

[202] Q. Sun. Recovery of sparsest signals via $\ell_q$-minimization. *Appl. Comput. Harmon. Anal.*, 32:329–341, 2012.

[203] T. Sun, H. Jiang, and L. Cheng. Convergence of proximal iteratively reweighted nuclear norm algorithm for image processing. *IEEE Trans. Image Process.*, 26:5632–5643, 2017.

[204] Y. Sun, P. Babu, and D. Palomar. Majorization-minimization algorithms in signal processing, communications, and machine learning. *IEEE Trans. Signal Process.*, 65:794–816, 2017.

[205] A. Szlam, Z. Guo, and S. Osher. A split Bregman method for nonnegative sparsity penalized least squares with applications to hyperspectral demixing. In *IEEE Inter. Conf. Imag. Process.*, pages 1917–1920, 2010.

[206] H. Taylor, S. Banks, and J. McCoy. Deconvolution with the $\ell_1$ norm. *Geophysics*, 44:39–52, 1979.

[207] R. Tibshirani. Regression shringkage and selection via the lasso. *J. Royal Statist. Soc. B*, 58:267–288, 1996.

[208] A. Tillmann and M. Pfetsch. The computational complexity of the restricted isometry property, the nullspace property, and related concepts in compressed sensing. *IEEE Trans. Inform. Theory*, 60:1248–1259, 2014.

[209] Y. Traonmilin and R. Gribonval. Stable recovery of low-dimensional cones in hilbert spaces: One rip to rule them all. *Appl. Comput. Harmon. Anal.*, 44:(to appear), 2018.

[210] J. A. Tropp. Greed is good: Algorithmic results for sparse approximation. *IEEE Trans. Inform. Theory*, 50:2231–2242, 2004.

[211] J. A. Tropp. Just relax: Convex programming methods for identifying sparse signals in noise. *IEEE Trans. Inform. Theory*, 52:1030–1051, 2006.

[212] J. A. Tropp and A. Gilbert. Signal recovery from random measurements via orthogonal matching pursuit. *IEEE Trans. Inform. Theory*, 53:4655–4666, 2007.

[213] J. A. Tropp, A. Gilbert, and M. Strauss. Algorithms for simultaneous sparse approximation. Part I: Greedy pursuit. *Sig. Process.*, 86:572–588, 2006.

[214] J. A. Tropp and S. Wright. Computational methods for sparse solution of linear inverse problems. *Proc. of the IEEE,*, 98:948–958, 2010.

[215] S.A. van de Geer and P. Bühlmann. On the condition used to prove oracle results for the lasso. *Electron. J. Stat.*, 3:1360–1392, 2009.

[216] A. Vardy. The intractability of computing the minimum distance of a code. *IEEE Trans. Inform. Theory*, 43:1757–1766, 1997.

[217] R. S. Varga. *Matrix Iterative Analysis*. Second Edition, Springer-Verlag, Berlin, Heidelberg, 2000.

[218] N. Vo, B. Moran, and S. Challa. Nonnegative-least-square classifier for face recognition. In *Proc. of the 6th Inter. Symposium on Neural Networks: Advances in Neural Networks*, pages 449–456. Springer, 2009.

[219] R. Walden. Analog-to-digital converter survey and analysis. *IEEE J. Sel. Areas Commun.*, 17:539–550, 1999.

[220] M. Wang and B. Shim. On the recovery limit of sparse signals using orthogonal matching pursuit. *IEEE Trans. Signal Process.*, 60:4973–4976, 2012.

[221] M. Wang, W. Xu, and A.Tang. A unique nonnegative solution to an underdetermined system: from vectors to matrices. *IEEE Trans. Signal Process.*, 59:1107–1016, 2011.

[222] L. Welch. Lower bounds on the maximum cross-correlation of signals. *IEEE Trans. Inform. Theory*, 20:397–399, 1974.

[223] J. Wen, Z. Zhou, J. Wang, X. Tang, and Q. Mo. A sharp condition for exact support recovery with orthogonal matching pursuit. *IEEE Trans. Signal Process.*, 65:1370–1382, 2017.

[224] D. Wipf and S. Nagarajan. Iterative reweighted $\ell_1$ and $\ell_2$ methods for finding sparse solutions. *IEEE J. Sel. Topics Signal Process.*, 4:317–329, 2010.

[225] D. Wipf and B. Rao. Sparse bayesian learning for basis selection. *IEEE Trans. Signal Process.*, 52:2153–2164, 2004.

[226] C. Xu. *Sparsity Optimization and RRSP-based Theory for 1-bit Compressive Sensing*. PhD Dissertation, University of Birmingham, 2015.

[227] M. Yan, Y. Yang, and S. Osher. Robust 1-bit compressive sensing using adaptive outlier pursuit. *IEEE Trans. Signal Process.*, 60:3868–3875, 2012.

[228] M. Yang and F. de Hoog. Orthogonal matching pursuits with thresholding and its application in compressed sensing. *IEEE Trans. Signal Process.*, 63:5479–5486, 2015.

[229] Z. Yang and L. Xie. Enhancing sparsity and resolution via reweighted atomic norm minimization. *IEEE Trans. Signal Process.*, 64:995–1006, 2016.

[230] W. Yin, S. Osher, D. Goldfarb, and J. Darbon. Bregman iterative algorithms for $\ell_1$ minimization with applications to compressed sensing. *SIAM J. Imaging Sci.*, 1:43–168, 2008.

[231] H Zayyani, F. Haddadi, and M. Korki. Double detector for sparse signal detection from 1-bit compressed sensing measurements. *IEEE Signal Process. Lett.*, 23:1637–1641, 2016.

[232] L. Zelnik-Manor, K. Rosenblum, and Y. Eldar. Sensing matrix optimization for block-sparse decoding. *IEEE Trans. Signal Process.*, 59:4300–4312, 2011.

[233] H. Zhang, M. Yan, and W. Yin. One condition for solution uniqueness and robustness of both l1-synthesis and l1-analysis minimization. *Adv. Comput. Math*, 42:1381–1399, 2016.

[234] H. Zhang, W. Yin, and L. Cheng. Necessary and sufficient conditions of solution uniqueness in 1-norm minimization. *J. Optim. Theory Appl.*, 164:109–122, 2015.

[235] Y. Zhang. *A simple proof for recoverability of $\ell_1$-minimization (II): the nonnegative case*. Technical Report, Rice University, 2005.

[236] Y. Zhang. *On theory of compressive sensing via $L_1$-minimization: Simple derivations and extensions*. Technical Report, Rice University, 2005.

[237] Y. Zhang. Theory of compressive sensing via $\ell_1$-minimization: A non-RIP analysis and extensions. *J. Oper. Res. Soc. China*, 1:79–105, 2013.

[238] P. Zhao and B. Yu. On model selection consistency of lasso. *J. Machine Learning Res.*, 7:2541–2567, 2006.

[239] Y. B. Zhao. An approximation theory of matrix rank minimization and its application to quadratic equations. *Linear Algebra Appl.*, 437:77–93, 2012.

[240] Y. B. Zhao. New and improved conditions for uniqueness of sparsest solutions of underdetermined linear systems. *Appl. Math. Comput.*, 224:58–73, 2013.

[241] Y. B. Zhao. RSP-based analysis for sparsest and least $\ell_1$-norm solutions to underdetermined linear systems. *IEEE Trans. Signal Process.*, 61:5777–5788, 2013.

[242] Y. B. Zhao. Equivalence and strong equivalence between the sparsest and least $\ell_1$-norm nonnegative solutions of linear systems and their applications. *J. Oper. Res. Soc. China*, 2:171–193, 2014.

[243] Y. B. Zhao, F. C. Fang, and D. Li. Constructing generalized mean functions using convex functions with regularity conditions. *SIAM J. Optim.*, 17:37–51, 2006.

[244] Y. B. Zhao, H. Jiang, and Z. Q. Luo. Weak stability of $\ell_1$-minimization methods in sparse data reconstruction. *Math. Oper. Res.*, 43 (to appear), 2018.

[245] Y. B. Zhao and M. Kočvara. A new computational method for the sparsest solution to systems of linear equations. *SIAM J. Optim.*, 25:1110–1134, 2015.

[246] Y. B. Zhao and D. Li. Reweighted $\ell_1$-minimization for sparse solutions to underdetermined linear systems. *SIAM J. Optim.*, 22:1065–1088, 2012.

[247] Y. B. Zhao and D. Li. Theoretical analysis of sparse recovery stability of Dantzig selector and Lasso. *arXiv:1711.03783*, 2017.

[248] Y. B. Zhao and Z. Q. Luo. Constructing new reweighted $\ell_1$-algorithms for the sparsest points of polyhedral sets. *Math. Oper. Res.*, 42:57–76, 2017.

[249] Y. B. Zhao and C. Xu. 1-bit compressive sensing: Reformulation and RRSP-based sign recovery theory. *Sci. China Math.*, 59:2049–2074, 2016.

[250] S. Zhou, L. Kong, and N. Xiu. New bounds for RIC in compressed sensing. *J. Oper. Res. Soc. China*, 1:227–237, 2013.

[251] S. Zhou, N. Xiu, Y. Wang, L. Kong, and H. Qi. Exact recovery for sparse signal via weighted $\ell_1$-minimization. *Inform. Infer.*, 5:76–102, 2016.

# Index

For Product Safety Concerns and Information please contact
our EU representative GPSR@taylorandfrancis.com Taylor & Francis
Verlag GmbH, Kaufingerstraße 24, 80331 München, Germany

T - #0156 - 230425 - C296 - 234/156/13 - PB - 9780367781101 - Gloss Lamination